Grammar and Syntax

Developing School-Age Children's Oral and Written Language Skills

Grammar and Syntax

Developing School-Age Children's Oral and Written Language Skills

Monica Gordon-Pershey, EdD, CCC-SLP

PLURAL PUBLISHING INC.

5521 Ruffin Road
San Diego, CA 92123

e-mail: information@pluralpublishing.com
Web site: https://www.pluralpublishing.com

Typeset in 10.5/13 Palatino by Achorn International Inc.
Printed in the United States of America by Integrated Books International

Library of Congress Cataloging-in-Publication Data

Names: Gordon-Pershey, Monica, author.
Title: Grammar and syntax : developing school-age children's oral and written
    language skills / Monica Gordon-Pershey.
Description: San Diego, CA : Plural Publishing, Inc., [2022] |
    Includes bibliographical references and index.
Identifiers: LCCN 2021055628 (print) | LCCN 2021055629 (ebook) |
    ISBN 9781944883553 (paperback) | ISBN 194488355X (paperback) |
    ISBN 9781944883560 (ebook)
Subjects: MESH: Language Development Disorders—diagnosis | Language
    Development Disorders—therapy | Language Development | Infant | Child |
    Adolescent
Classification: LCC RJ496.L35 (print) | LCC RJ496.L35 (ebook) | NLM WL 340.2 |
    DDC 618.92/855—dc23/eng/20220106
LC record available at https://lccn.loc.gov/2021055628
LC ebook record available at https://lccn.loc.gov/2021055629

Contents

Preface

*G*rammar and Syntax: Developing School-Age Children's Oral and Written Language Skills is a professional reference book that emphasizes that speech-language pathologists' (SLPs') practical decision-making is guided by a synthesis of expert knowledge and skills. This book is intended to enhance four main components of professional expertise. First, this book offers extensive information that can advance SLPs' *academic and theoretical knowledge* of language as a faculty of the human mind and an attribute of human performance. Specifically, this book offers a compendium of information on English grammar and syntax that can be applied to speech-language diagnostic and therapy practices. Effectively diagnosing and treating language impairments chiefly depends upon how thoroughly an SLP understands the principal components of language as they are employed by capable users.

Second, this text reinforces that SLPs need to cultivate a range of *strategies for gathering diagnostic evidence*, so that SLPs supplement their formal testing of grammar and syntax with multiple forms of observational, real-life, and experiential diagnostic evidence. Third, this book promotes that SLPs seek, understand, and apply *the evolving scientific evidence* that describes the factors that influence children's and adolescents' language and literacy development and growth and, specifically, that they address how grammar and syntax are essential for successful school learning and performance. To achieve this aim, this book is amply sourced with published *research across disciplines*, including the fields of speech-language pathology, linguistics, education, and psychology. Fourth,

this book is designed to encourage *creative approaches to curriculum-based speech-language therapy practices* that can help children and adolescents improve their language and literacy capabilities and achieve academic success. To this end, grammar and syntax are situated among the range of language and literacy skills that older school-age learners need for success and that SLPs can support.

Although this book presents more extensive detail about the expressive grammar and syntax of oral language, syntactic comprehension is of great importance, too. The focus on expression stems partly from the fact that there is somewhat more available theoretical and empirical information about expressive grammar and syntax development and impairment. Chapter 5, which addresses the role of grammar and syntax in reading, examines receptive processing of sentence syntax as an aspect of reading comprehension. Chapter 6 considers how grammar and syntax are expressed in writing.

Preschool children's refinement of the systems of grammar and syntax is an important aspect of acquiring language as a means for interpersonal communication. During the school years, using grammar and syntax to read, write, and learn academic material become simultaneous demands. This book discusses at length how grammatical and syntactic difficulties can manifest in younger children's oral language but also explains how grammatical and syntactic difficulties may not appear until learners are faced with advanced oral language and literacy demands in school. Some children may learn oral language adequately, then show a breakdown in learning to read and write. Other children may struggle with learning academic concepts, comprehending stories, and acquiring a fund of higher-level verbal information drawn from the texts they read. Some children may have both of these kinds of difficulties. The grammatical and syntactic language bases that underlie literacy and learning difficulties are described in detail throughout this book, as are methods of identifying and diagnosing these needs.

Speech-language interventions can focus on strategies for helping children learn the grammatical and syntactic competencies needed for oral language, reading, and writing. SLPs can provide services that meaningfully enhance classroom learning for students of any age. Emphasis is placed throughout this text on how to provide academically relevant speech-language services to school-age children and adolescents who struggle with classroom oral language and with learning to read and write owing to difficulties with grammar and syntax. Topics include multipurpose intervention strategies to help students whose grammar and syntax deficits have a negative effect on their academic learning, completion of classroom assignments, and performance on achievement testing. Suggestions for adapting mainstream curriculum and assignments, differentiating instruction to accommodate learners of varying levels of ability, and designing classroom accommodations and modifications are given.

This book emphasizes how an SLP's clinical decision-making is guided by a synthesis of (1) knowledge of the theories of language, (2) scientific evidence regarding ascertaining language performance, and (3) clinical, observational evidence of how children and teens learn grammar and syntax and how impairment in grammar and syntax is manifest.

One of my goals as an author and educator is to reference primary sources and original authors of information. I refer to a topic's "classic" texts and authors whenever possible. Included, too, are citations for work by the preeminent authors in the fields of speech-language pathology and literacy studies. Even so, this book is more than a compendium of information that can be found in other books, articles, and online sources. I extensively offer my own conceptualizations about language and language impairments and provide my own strategies for diagnosis and treatment. I infuse this book with my extensive academic background and with the lessons I have learned during my research and clinical experiences with culturally, linguistically, and economically diverse learners in three regions of the United States.

My purpose is to prepare SLPs to understand the complexities of language impairment and to develop multiple perspectives for understanding the ramifications of language impairment. I bring to this book nearly four decades of experience as a clinical SLP and over 25 years as a language scholar, professor, and provider of professional development for SLPs and teachers. My doctoral studies in language arts and literacy instruction and my continued involvement in organizations that promote literacy research and education have influenced me to author a book that prepares SLPs to address students' literacy needs and academic success. I aspire that readers of this book will develop the expertise to enact the American Speech-Language-Hearing Association (ASHA, 1991, 2001, 2004, 2010, 2016, 2018b, n.d.-a, n.d.-b, n.d.-c, n.d.-d) recommendations that SLPs diagnose how language deficits contribute to students' literacy needs and enhance students' participation in literacy activities.

The chapters of this book include special features to enhance the reader's learning. Each chapter begins with an Anticipation Guide (Head & Readence, 1992; Wood et al., 2008), which is a list of questions to stimulate readers to prepare for reading by thinking about the material that will be covered in the chapter. Headers in each chapter allow for ready reference to sections of the text. Accompanying the chapters is a glossary of key terms. The terms that appear in bold italic print are found in the glossary.

Acknowledgments

I owe a debt of thanks to many individuals who contributed to the creation of this book. First, sincere thanks to the many children and adults who I have had the privilege to provide speech-language services for and to teach, and who have taught me so much about language, literacy, and learning. Many Cleveland State University speech-language pathology graduate assistants spent long hours helping me assemble reference materials, by diligently scanning documents, searching online for resources that I used in this book, and creating resource lists and databases, and I appreciate their hard work. To my many professional mentors and colleagues from the various universities, schools, and professional organizations with whom I have been associated and who have influenced my career over these many years, I offer thanks for their brilliance, thoughtfulness, kindness, friendship, and guidance. I cannot overstate how much I have valued their expressions of their knowledge over these many years. My fellow members of the Board of Directors and the Advisory Council of International Dyslexia Association Northern Ohio were just an email away to answer questions and help me clarify my thinking. Fellow members of the Editorial Board of *Perspectives on Language and Literacy*, published by the International Dyslexia Association, have been an intellectual inspiration. They have taught me so much about what really matters in literacy education and about how to transmit quality research and information to readers. Being part of this editorial board, as well as a manuscript reviewer for many other academic journals, has taught me how to carefully examine my own writing and editing. I am honored to have provided service to a number of ASHA committees, boards, and programs, where I worked alongside dedicated, insightful, intelligent, caring, and progressive colleagues. Many thanks to the people who post on the virtual networks that keep me connected to the larger community of practice. I am often cheered and inspired by professionals' and consumers' posts on social media, which I look forward to reading every day. And, recalling the earliest point in my career as a scholar, I am grateful for the valued learning experiences that I shared with my professors and fellow students during my doctoral studies in literacy at the University of Massachusetts at Lowell.

While I was authoring this book, so many thoughtful friends and relatives and valued professional colleagues allowed me to solicit their ideas and opinions—and their encouragement and good humor—as I may have complained just a little too much about the rigors of book writing. I thank them especially for their stories that I have reimagined and fictionalized as some of the anecdotes and examples used in this book.

And, of course, I offer my heartfelt appreciation for Ed Pershey, my husband and cherished partner in life.

Reviewers

Plural Publishing and the author thank the following reviewers for taking the time to provide their valuable feedback during the manuscript development process. Additional anonymous feedback was provided by other expert reviewers.

Kathy Evangelista, MS, CCC-SLP
Adjunct Professor
Department of Communication Sciences and Disorders
Elmhurst University
Elmhurst, Illinois

Michelle L. Ivey, PhD, CCC-SLP
Instructional Associate Professor
University of Houston
Houston, Texas

Judith O. Roman, SLPD, CCC-SLP
Clinical Faculty
Northwestern University
Evanston, Illinois

Shannon W. Salley, SLPD, CCC-SLP
Department Chair
Social Work/Communication Sciences and Disorders
Associate Professor
Longwood University
Farmville, Virginia

Reviewers

In memory of my mother and father.

CHAPTER 1

Introduction: Educational Contexts for Improving School-Age Learners' Grammar and Syntax

This chapter describes background information on the language and learning expectations of K–12 educational contexts. Language arts and literacy curricula require learners to attain competence in grammar and syntax. This chapter discusses the overall educational purposes that SLPs' language interventions address and offers reasons why SLPs would focus on learners' grammatical and syntactic skills.

Anticipation Guide

After reading this chapter, readers will be able to answer the following questions:

- Why is it important for speech-language pathologists to be able to describe, diagnose, and intervene to help school-age children and adolescents who struggle with grammar and syntax?
- What is the rationale for, and what are the benefits of, describing school-age children and adolescents who struggle with grammar and syntax as having a "language impairment?"
- Why are speakers from communities with language that varies from General American English, such as speakers of dialects of American English, not considered to have a language impairment?

- What kinds of grammatical and syntactic skills have been achieved by typically developing children by the time they reach 5 years of age?
- What are some general considerations for assessing the grammar and syntax of school-age children and adolescents?
- What are some of the curricular language and literacy demands that may be difficult to achieve for school-age children and adolescents who have difficulties with grammar and syntax?
- What do the data collected on a national level report on populations of students with language impairments?
- What is the rationale, and what is the importance, for collaborative, curriculum-based, inclusive approaches to improving the grammar and syntax of school-age children and adolescents?
- How can speech-language services for grammar and syntax become a meaningful component of students' school learning?

A Professional Reference Book

This book is designed to be a professional reference for practitioners, researchers, university faculty, and students in the field of speech-language pathology. Practitioners and students in fields allied with speech-language pathology also may benefit from its content. Teachers of regular education and special education students in preschool through Grade 12, teachers of English language arts, learning disabilities teachers and intervention specialists, reading teachers and literacy specialists, teachers of English language learners (ELLs), and the university faculty who prepare preprofessionals for their careers in these fields may find that this text provides information on grammar and syntax that supplements their current knowledge and practices. Students enrolled in courses in special education, reading and literacy education, child development, and linguistics may find this text's content is relevant to their studies. This text is intended to be a useful resource in higher education courses offered by any academic departments with coursework in language development, language disorders, literacy education, learning disabilities, and developmental disorders. Some content may be of use in speech-language pathology clinical methods courses and practicum settings, and in K–12 educational practica and student teaching settings. Tutoring centers and speech-language clinics might acquire this book as a professional reference.

Children and adolescents with language impairments may have difficulties in learning language and acquiring literacy capabilities. Traditionally, speech-language pathologists (SLPs) understand the nature of impaired language development, but they may not have detailed professional knowledge of how impaired language adversely affects school learning and academic success. The purpose of this book is to prepare SLPs to have a broad base of knowledge that will inform their interventions with children and teens and enhance their collaborations with regular education teachers, special educators, tutors, and parents (Gordon Pershey, 1998). Clinical identification of language impairment requires a thorough understanding of typical language development. SLPs use typical development as the guidepost against which language deficiencies are measured. Although the nature of language deficits is carefully described throughout this book, the intent is to provide a developmental focus, not a deficit focus. The aim is to moderate the pathologization of learners' differences.

Most importantly, this book is meant to be inclusive and accessible for all its readers. Grammar and syntax can be confusing and intimidating subject matter even for SLPs and education professionals (Justice & Ezell, 1999). One reason for this apprehension may be because, as Rowley (2011) suggested, there is some evidence that SLPs may not have sufficient knowledge of syntax, morphology, and grammar. SLFs' self-reports of their own grammar instruction prior to entering graduate school have varied from no instruction to minimal instruction (Long, 1996; Rowley, 2011). Clinicians may not be prepared to diagnose and treat deficits in advanced syntax in school-age children and adolescents and may actually ignore these areas of language impairment (Justice & Ezell, 1999, 2008). SLPs may feel comfortable providing interventions for language as a mode of communication but may not feel prepared to focus learners' attention on the structure of language. Teachers may feel similarly underprepared to focus on the linguistic elements of literacy instruction (Joshi et al., 2009; Moats & Foorman, 2003). It is only by acquiring an in-depth knowledge of the grammatical and syntactic properties of language that an SLP can diagnose developmental difficulties and appropriately intervene to improve language learning. Explicit and direct teaching of the structure of language is necessary when SLPs and educators assist students in gaining skills in reading decoding and comprehension, and in the written language skills of spelling, word study, sentence structure, and learning and applying the conventions of grammar (International Dyslexia Association, 2010; Moats & Foorman, 2003).

Grammar and Syntax: Professional Skills for Descriptions, Diagnosis, and Interventions

The intention of this text is to help professionals improve their working knowledge of grammar and syntax, with a focus on three necessary skill sets: describing grammar and syntax as aspects of the structure of language and describing the skills of competent users of grammar and syntax, diagnosing deficits in grammar and syntax, and providing interventions to improve grammar and syntax. These skill sets entail:

(1) Readers of this text may acquire the conceptual knowledge and nomenclature for *describing* elements of grammar and syntax; to this end, the intention is to help readers develop the professional vocabulary to better describe the important

components of grammar and syntax. To facilitate readers' knowledge of linguistic terminology, the descriptive language used in this text to explain grammatical and syntactic concepts is meant to be basic, straightforward, direct, and user-friendly. These descriptions may spark readers' interest in learning more about linguistics. Readers can seek out linguistics texts and websites if they desire more complex explanations. Throughout this book, many references to original linguistics sources are provided when linguistic concepts are explained. The reference list for this book provides resources for learning more about the grammatical and syntactic concerns in school-age and adolescent students.

(2) Readers of this text may learn about methods for *diagnosing* learners' difficulties with grammar and syntax; to this end, this text provides diagnostic approaches to help identify when learners have grammatical and syntactic difficulties. Standardized diagnostic tests of grammar and syntax yield numerical results that provide accountability for diagnostic decision-making and that SLPs are familiar with interpreting. This text focuses more on informal assessment via language sampling and analyses. Classroom observations and assessment of students' classroom work samples are two other approaches for informal assessment. This text offers suggestions for applying the findings of informal assessments of grammar and syntax to diagnose language deficits and to explain why students may be struggling with school curricular demands.

(3) Readers of this text may find recommendations and suggestions for *interventions and teaching*; to this end, instructional ideas are described in general terms that can be of use to SLPs and teachers. Practitioners can adapt these informal, multipurpose suggestions to the more formal wording of goals, objectives, and methods that is needed for clinical reports and intervention plans. These informal examples are meant to be nonprescriptive and might offer better inspiration for professionals' creative thought than a step-by-step series of instructions would afford. Readers of this book may feel validated and may become motivated and encouraged to apply this book's suggestions to their own innovative approaches to interventions and instruction. Many of the suggestions given relate to the academic expectations put forth in the *Common Core State Standards* (CCSS; National Governors Association Center for Best Practices, Council of Chief State School Officers, 2010), to be useful in contexts where a standards-based intervention is applicable.

Terminology Used in This Book: "Language Impairment"

To describe children and adolescents with language difficulties, a few terms are used rather generally and interchangeably throughout this book, but most frequently, *"language impairment"* is used in this text, along with expressions like "language difficulties," "struggling learners" (as in struggling with language, reading, and/or writing), "language needs," and similar nonclinical wording. The profession of speech-language pathology uses the terms "language impairment," *"language disorder,"* and *"language delay"* (American Psychiatric Association, 2013; Individuals With Disabilities Education Act [IDEA], 2004; Leonard, 2020; Murza & Ehren, 2020;

Paul, 2020; Rice, 2020; Volkers, 2018). Practitioners tend to use the terms "language impairment," "language disorder," or "communication disorder" interchangeably. "Language disability" is used to convey that impaired language has a negative effect on daily living and an adverse impact on academic achievement (Justice, 2010; Paul, 2002). There has been a trend among some researchers and practitioners toward the use of *"developmental language disorder,"* or DLD (Green, 2020; McGregor et al., 2020; Owen Van Horne et al., 2018). There are conceptual distinctions and practical realities attendant to the use of each of these terms, some of which deal with symptomatology or measurement variables, for instance, IQ verbal and performance discrepancy scores or determining cut scores for applying certain diagnostic labels. In some children, progress in language development follows a generally typical pattern but is delayed. In other children, progress is disordered and takes on an atypical trajectory. Language delays and language disorders have some similar traits and some distinct dissimilarities. Because it is not possible to maintain these numerous conceptual distinctions when discussing children's and teens' difficulties with the language subsystems of grammar and syntax alone, the following explanation is a rationale for employing the more general term "language impairment" throughout this text.

The World Health Organization WHO (2001, 2014) described an *impairment* as an abnormality in the structure or function of a bodily entity or system. "Language impairment" is a term that conveys that *language, as a structured system, is not intact.* Moreover, "language impairment" suggests that *language, as a functional system, is compromised.* The structure and/or the

function of language are not optimal. The structure of language involves its properties as a code and a system. The functions of language are to represent ideas, accommodate the conventions of shared meanings, and communicate.

In the WHO (2001, 2014) model, *disorder* is the **functional** consequence of an impairment. If a bodily entity or system is impaired, then the function that is supposed to be carried out by the entity or system is not readily achieved. To be disordered means to not operate properly for functional use. A "language disorder" would be the extent to which *language, as a functional system, is not operating properly for functional use.* The system's impairment limits its functionality. *A language disorder is the functional consequence of a language impairment.*

These definitions of the terms "impairment" and "disorder" bring about many considerations, implications, and questions. Discussion is necessary in order to forge a deeper understanding of what goes wrong when language does not develop as expected. While an academic understanding of the distinctions between language impairment and language disorder is important, attempting to maintain this distinction is probably not practical for SLPs in clinical practice. Even in policy and legislative documents, it appears that the words "impairment" and "disorder" might be used interchangeably or somewhat synonymously. The American Speech-Language-Hearing Association's (ASHA, 1993) definition of language disorder is that language is impaired: "A **language disorder** is impaired comprehension and/or use of spoken, written and/or other symbol systems. The disorder may involve (1) the form of language (phonology, morphology, syntax), (2) the content

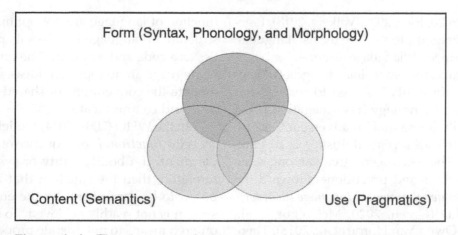

Figure 1–1. The domains of language. Adapted from Bloom, L., & Lahey, M. (1978). *Language development and language disorders.* John Wiley & Sons.

of language (semantics), and/or (3) the function of language in communication (pragmatics) in any combination." Figure 1–1 depicts how the language domains of content (semantics), form (syntax), and use (pragmatics) (Bloom & Lahey, 1978) interrelate to form the basis for competent language comprehension and production. When there is a deficit in any of the domains, overall language competence can be compromised. Chapter 2 describes content and form development. Chapter 3 relates pragmatic development to the development of syntactic form.

Throughout this book, the term "language impairment" is used rather generally (cf. Owens, 2004) to describe the condition that occurs when an impairment in the structure and/or function of language is the result of developmental factors or acquired conditions. *Within this book, the point of any discussion of language impairment is to describe the impairment along with its functional consequences.* Use of the term "language impairment" acknowledges the reality that "language disorder" oc-

curs concomitantly when any aspects of functional language are affected. Reciprocally, when the term "language disorder" is used, it brings to bear the underlying impairment of the structured system of language.

Language Deficits Versus Language Differences

An additional caveat applies to the delimitations to the content of this book, which is a discussion of developmental language difficulties and not a discussion of the nonclinical language differences that arise from cultural, linguistic, and/or environmental variables. Cultural and linguistic diversity are important considerations for the practice of speech-language pathology. ASHA (2017) mandated that SLPs provide culturally and linguistically relevant interventions that adapt to clients' experiences, values, identities, and needs. However, the information provided in this text is entirely about the linguistic forms of *General American English* (GAE) grammar and syntax, with the exception of one section of Chapter 2, titled "African American English Features of Morphology and Syntax," which describes some features of morphology, grammar, and syntax used by some speakers of African American English. Although practitioners' knowledge of cultural and linguistic diversity (as described by ASHA, 2017) is paramount for culturally competent professional practice, for purposes of this reference book, only GAE forms of grammar and syntax are examined. It is beyond the scope of this text to compile the numerous linguistic descriptions that would be needed to explain the language variations found in the numerous *dialects* of American English, or to describe the variations in grammar and syntax that might be used by newer speakers of English as they transition from their native languages, or to document the grammar and syntactic systems of languages other than English that may influence speakers of English who live in diverse multilingual communities.

There is no intention in this text to suggest that ELLs or dialect users have any impairment in grammar or syntax. American English dialects are rule-governed linguistic systems that show the grammatical competence of the speakers who use these systems (Reaser et al., 2017). SLPs need an appropriate understanding of the linguistic features found in the dialects of the students they serve so that dialect features can be differentiated from language deficits. SLPs are obligated to identify when diagnostic instrumentation may be subject to test bias and need be able to use procedures for nondiscriminatory testing (ASHA, 2003). SLPs need to evaluate dialect speakers' and ELLs' performance on standardized language tests and the contents of the language samples they pro-

duce in relation to the grammatical and syntactic forms present in their dialects and first languages (ASHA, 2003, 2017).[1]

Chapters 2 Through 6: The Developmental Trajectory for Grammar and Syntax

Chapter 2 offers a summary of typical grammar and syntax development, with detailed descriptions of the normative grammatical and syntactic forms that young children learn to produce. Portions of the content of Chapter 2 may be familiar to SLPs who have completed language development and language disorders coursework, particularly the beginning sections of Chapter 2 that discuss linguistic theory as relevant to syntactic development. Then, extensive developmental linguistic information pertaining to English morphology, grammar, and syntax is given, to catalog the basic requirements for English language form that most children master by the end of the 4-year-old age range and have in place for entry into kindergarten.

Chapters 3, 4, 5, and 6 focus on later language development, from age 4 through adolescence. Syntax is well documented as an area of language impairment in school-age children and adolescents (Nippold, 2007; Nippold et al., 2009). "By 5 years of age, most children have acquired the ability to produce grammatically well-formed sentences containing all types of subordinate clauses . . . the ability to express increasingly abstract ideas in longer sentences containing multiple and embedded subordinate clauses continues to develop

---

[1]Suggested readings pertinent to grammar and syntax in linguistically diverse populations are provided at the end of Chapter 2.

throughout the school-age years, adolescence, and into adulthood" (Nippold et al., 2009, p. 242). Deficits in these abilities would be considered a delay or disorder of syntactic language.

The information on older learners' grammar and syntax given in these chapters may diverge from the early language knowledge base that SLPs may have as most familiar and may provide an expansion of that knowledge base. The available developmental information on older learners' grammar and syntax includes a lesser degree of emphasis on age-based normative expectations (cf. Loban, 1963, 1970, 1976). This is due in part to the fact that many grammatical forms typically would have been acquired at an earlier age. Normative information for performance of syntactic targets may be derived from the scoring criteria for standardized tests and would have been generated by the cross-sectional data obtained based on the performance of the tests' standardization samples of children and teens of various ages. These scoring norms show age-related performance on test items, rather than a developmental sequence of grammatical and syntactic development.

This text presents information on the grammatical and syntactic constructions that SLPs would look for when analyzing language samples produced by older children and teens. Language sample analysis systems tend to rely on whether the speaker has demonstrated the use of a wide array of mature grammatical and syntactic forms. These systems allow the presence, absence, accuracy, and/or error patterns to be described, rather like taking an inventory of the language forms that a speaker produced. The combined use of multiple grammatical elements within utterances is observed, as is the speaker's production of novel and spontaneous con-structions in a way that shows facility with language. This type of performance assessment differs from analyses of younger children's syntax, where the attainment of a more specific set of developmental syntactic constructions is assessed and where there is extensive longitudinal developmental data on the acquisition of normative targets.

The assessment of older children's grammar and syntax in the context of academic achievement is quite different from the assessment of younger children's use of language form in daily communication. The purpose of an older student's language assessment is often to determine whether the student's language is strong enough to support academic learning (ASHA, n.d.-a; Ehren & Whitmire, 2009). SLPs' use of diagnostic tests of language competence might not be the most effective tools for assessing academic language competence and performance, in part because the tasks used for diagnostic testing do not closely resemble academic language tasks. Academic language performance is not specifically measured by tests that are intended to yield diagnostic norms; these are two different assessment considerations. Many diagnostic tests have strong concurrent and predictive validity and can identify that students' academic difficulties are related to the underlying psychometric construct of language aptitudes and abilities. Diagnostic test scores may substantiate that a language weakness is an underlying reason why students are struggling in school. However, establishing the basis for academic struggles serves a different purpose than administering a curriculum-based assessment that will uncover the actual language skills that students are struggling with in academic settings. *Functional, performance-based assessment of academic language skills would be needed to accurately describe a student's deficiencies.* Students' performance on standardized tests of language development and the standardized scores obtained may or may not be similar to how a student is performing academically. For each student, these different sources of data would be compared, and the data may reconcile or may not. The age norms that standardized tests afford would be supplanted by data on how well students meet grade-level curriculum requirements as the standard for measuring students' competence and growth over time.

School learning necessitates going beyond the use of language for daily communication to a metalinguistic awareness of how to use language to read with comprehension and express ideas in writing. Chapters 3, 4, 5, and 6 focus on assessment of the *metalinguistic skills* needed for the conscious use of grammar and syntax in academic language tasks. In addition to oral language sampling and testing, assessment of competence would include evaluating written work samples and observing students' classroom performance. Chapters 5 and 6 discuss how to connect weaknesses in oral grammar and syntax to deficits in reading comprehension and written language, along with strategies for interventions for reading comprehension and written language form and expression.

Learners Who Will Benefit When Professionals Apply the Content of This Text

In all, this book is a resource for professionals who work with students whose goals are to develop competence in the language skills needed for academic tasks. Often, these would be learners with mild-to-moderate levels of language and learning needs. The purpose of this text is to offer information, insights, and inspiration for SLPs who work with school-age children and adolescents whose language needs make it difficult for them to participate in mainstream curriculum and instruction without supplemental instruction and interventions. Developmental language deficits may persist into adolescence and hamper students' academic progress (Aram et al., 1984; Beitchman et al., 1996; Conti-Ramsden & Durkin, 2008; Johnson et al., 1999; King et al., 1982; Snowling et al., 2000; Stothard et al., 1998), so for that reason, Chapter 2 explains the developmental origins of these later difficulties. Chapters 3, 4, 5, and 6 describe teaching and learning strategies that are common to both SLPs and teachers. The intention is to help SLPs become more aware of the complexity of language that is required for older students to succeed in school and then design curriculum-based interventions that may help students to meet national and state academic standards (cf. Schuele, 2017).

Language Arts and Literacy Instruction in the Schools

Language arts, with its focus on reading, writing, speaking, and listening, and its emphasis on the narrative and expository genres of language, is apt to be a curricular area that is challenging for school-age children and adolescents with language needs. Other areas of academic study, such as science and social studies, each with an emphasis on expository language, may require intensive amounts of classroom listening and assigned reading. Students are often graded on how well their oral and written responses show comprehension of the material they read. A language impairment can encumber students' success in all areas of the school curriculum. As summarized by Soifer (2018), lesser syntactic capabilities can contribute to reduced comprehension of complex sentences, immature expressive grammar and sentence production, and difficulties manipulating verbs and conjunctions in multipart sentences. Weaker syntax can also hinder the cognitive abilities needed for information processing. Students may have difficulty remembering, processing, and repeating information that they have heard during classroom instruction. Some students may have difficulty following spoken directions or keeping a sequence of steps in mind. When syntactic processing is not strong, it can contribute to difficulty organizing thoughts and remembering a series of points within an informational context. Students may not be able to effectively abstract details from the verbal messages they have heard spoken or read. Comprehension of syntax can be a factor in being able to evaluate the content of information and make inferences. Expressively, students' language may seem disorganized. They may be unable to speak their thoughts succinctly. Their messages may lack detail or they may not express concepts effectively.

Ehren and Whitmire (2009) discussed the essential roles of SLPs in literacy instruction for students of all ages, with special emphasis on the importance of SLPs remaining involved in middle school and secondary education, where educational teams may not regard SLP services as necessary and SLPs' roles may be reduced to minimal involvement. Developmental language disorders can have a lasting negative affect on academic language and literacy growth (Bishop & Adams, 1990;

Catts, 1993; Catts et al., 1999; Catts & Kamhi, 2005; Nation et al., 2004; Scarborough & Dobrich, 1990; Stothard et al., 1998; Tallal et al., 1989; Torgesen, 2002). Aging out of primary education does not automatically signal the end of students' needs for SLP services. Language deficits can be at the root of learners' academic problems throughout their school careers. SLPs can add value to students' secondary education experiences because their services emphasize the advanced cognitive-linguistic development necessary for school success and are instituted from a diagnostic-prescriptive approach (Ehren & Whitmire, 2009).

Populations of Students Who Have Language Needs That May Impede Their Success in Language Arts and Literacy Instructional Contexts

The National Center for Education Statistics (NCES, 2020) reported that 14% of the students enrolled in U.S. schools in 2018 received special education services under the Individuals with Disabilities Education Act (IDEA). Within the special education population, 33% had specific learning disabilities and 19% had speech or language impairments. As stated by the NCES, closely paraphrasing IDEA (2004), "Specific learning disability is a disorder in one or more of the basic psychological processes involved in understanding or using language, spoken or written, that may manifest itself in an imperfect ability to listen, think, speak, read, write, spell, or do mathematical calculations." Taking into consideration the overlapping academic needs of students with specific learning disabilities and language impairments, the NCES reported that a significant proportion of students are clustered together to provide data on those who are counted as having learning disabilities and language impairments as their primary concerns: "Among Hispanic, American Indian/Alaska Native, Pacific Islander, and White students ages 3–21, the percentage of students who received special education services in 2018–19 for specific learning disabilities combined with the percentage who received services for speech or language impairments accounted for 50 percent or more of students served under IDEA. Among their peers who were Black, of two or more races, and Asian, the percentage accounted for between 40 and 50 percent of students served under IDEA." The NCES data accounted for other populations with language disability secondary to a primary developmental disorder or as related to a sensory disorder, such as hearing loss. "Students with autism, developmental delays, intellectual disabilities, and emotional disturbances each accounted for between 5 and 11 percent of students served under IDEA" (NCES, 2020).

Regarding the 2018 school year data that the NCES data reported in 2020, over 60% of special education students spent at least 80% of their school time in regular education classes and another 30% spent 40% to 79% of their school time in regular education classes. Students with learning disabilities and language impairments are likely to spend significant proportions of their time attempting to meet the expectations for classroom language and literacy performance.

A Closer Look at Diagnostic Designations

The diagnostic populations most likely to have difficulties with syntax and that might benefit from the types of interventions described in this text are students with specific learning disabilities, spoken language disorder, specific language impairment, and language-based learning disabilities (LBLD). Gordon-Pershey (2018a) differentiated between these diagnostic labels: The IDEA (2004) defined *specific learning disability* (SLD) as a disorder in one or more of the basic processes involved in understanding or producing spoken or written language, as manifested in the ability to listen, think, speak, read, write, spell, or perform mathematical calculations. ASHA (n.d.-c) explained that a *spoken language disorder*, also known as an oral language disorder, involves a deficit in auditory comprehension and/or spoken production of any of the five domains of language (i.e., phonology, morphology, syntax, semantics, and pragmatics). A spoken language disorder may occur in the presence of other conditions, such as intellectual disabilities (IDs), autism spectrum disorders, or attention-deficit/hyperactivity disorder (ADD). When a spoken language disorder is not accompanied by any other disorder, disability, or medical condition, it is considered a *specific language impairment* (SLI).

Nippold et al. (2008, 2009) differentiated SLI from nonspecific language impairment (NLI). Children with SLI perform within normal limits on tests of nonverbal intelligence, but children with NLI perform below average on nonverbal measures and may exhibit more severe language deficits (Nippold et al., 2008). Additional diagnostic measures of language and other domains of development may be necessary for accurate diagnosis of NLI.

Pennington et al. (2019) described all of these diagnostic labels as neurodevelopmental disorders. Within a comprehensive description of learning disabilities, these neurodevelopmental conditions have in common some genetic factors, brain mechanisms, and neuropsychological manifestations. Although careful discussion of the nuances of the different types of developmental problems present behind these labels is necessary in any clinical report on a specific child, when looking at populations of children, inherent problems with the neural processes that control language and learning are predominant. Comorbidity of speech-language disorders and learning disabilities is common (Pennington & Bishop, 2009; Pennington et al., 2019). Pennington et al. (2005), as reported by Pennington et al. (2019), found that the cognitive profiles of learning disabilities, language disorders, and attention disorders have more factors in common than factors that differ. Comorbidity can be explained by the interactions of shared etiological, neural, and cognitive risk factors. Pennington et al. (2005) posited a multifactorial model of the etiology of behaviorally defined developmental disorders, as would occur in deficits in learning, language, and attentional behaviors. Multiple genetic and environmental risk factors combine to produce the symptoms of a disorder. Some of these risk factors are shared by multiple disorders. This multifactorial model accounts for the comorbidity of developmental disorders.

As such, some students may have co-existing diagnoses of language disorders and specific learning disabilities (ASHA, n.d.-b; Pennington & Bishop, 2009). They may be described as having a *language-based learning disability* (LBLD) or *language learning disability* (LLD). Both are perhaps redundant terms in that SLD entails a disorder of understanding or producing spoken or written language (ASHA, n.d.-b; Gordon-Pershey, 2018a; IDEA, 2004).

Other primary conditions and etiologies that might cause learners to present with difficulties learning mainstream school curriculum and who would have similar language learning concerns as the learning disabilities populations would include students with attention-deficit/hyperactivity disorder, autism spectrum disorder, intellectual disability, traumatic brain injury, and other conditions that cause impairments in learning, executive function, and memory. Language concerns would be secondary to these primary impairments.

Professional Considerations for SLPs

The main topic of this text is to explore how SLPs can help students develop their capabilities in syntax and grammar. It is important to note that in some ways, this text is not founded upon on traditional speech-language therapy models. The content of this text goes beyond a traditional diagnosis and treatment model and considers the language needs of learners as members of their schools and communities (Peterson & Stoddard, 2018). The emphasis of this text is on how children and teens function in their academic settings and in their daily lives, not on how they function in the settings where speech-language therapy takes place. Carryover of learners' accomplishments in speech-language therapy to academic progress is the ultimate goal (cf. ASHA, 1991, 2001, 2016, n.d.-a; Schuele & Larrivee, 2004).

The diagnostic components of this text are provided to help SLPs identify when difficulties with syntax and grammar may impede students' progress in oral language reception and expression, reading, and written language. Although formal and informal diagnostic procedures can identify these difficulties, in this text, a main emphasis is on how SLPs observe and document how students with language needs perform on classroom language tasks by using curriculum-based assessments (Deno, 1993, 2003). Diagnostic techniques provided in this text resemble assessment of the language performance needed for successfully learning curriculum-based content and completing grade-level assignments. In most cases in this text, diagnostic performance examples related to the general education K–12 curriculum are based on the *Common Core State Standards* (National Governors Association Center for Best Practices, Council of Chief State School Officers, 2010).

SLPs who are readers of this text will find that the focus of this text's intervention content is on how SLPs can learn to think about syntax and grammar as being embedded in the language capabilities that school-age children and teens use all day long, every day. The focus is on inclusion of students in mainstream learning contexts. SLPs would work on targets established by interdisciplinary teams, such that the team members focus on similar strategies for student success (ASHA, 1991, 2001, 2004, 2010, 2016, 2018a, n.d.-a; Feeney, 2008; Gordon Pershey, 1998; Gordon Pershey & Rapking, 2003). Speech-language therapy in school settings should not be a secluded, mysterious process, nor should it be regarded as a quasi-medical service or as a "fix" or a "cure" for learning needs. School SLPs instruct children by using specialized and therapeutic means, which may include alterations in the typical amount of time spent on certain skills, or in the teaching materials used, the physical location for learning, and the methods

of assessment and progress monitoring. But the ultimate commonality between therapy settings and classroom settings is that adults are helping youngsters learn, and the final decisions come down to three simple considerations (Hunter, 1982): what the person who is teaching must do, what the person who is learning must do, and the materials and conditions used to bring about learning. The intention of this text is to highlight SLPs' teaching and intervention decisions, offer ideas for establishing SLPs' learning expectations for their students, and discuss materials and other conditions that SLPs would employ when working with learners in school settings.

These intentions reawaken professional beliefs in a decades-old expression, whose attribution has been lost to the ages: "Special education is not a place; it's a service." Schwartz (2007) outdid the original expression, saying, "Special education is a service, not a sentence." Both slogans may have been coined to reinforce that the Education of All Handicapped Children Act of 1975 (P.L. 94-142), the precursor to the IDEA (2004), legislated that special education services are mandated to take place in the least restrictive environment (LRE) for the learner. Educational personnel ideally would connect the LRE with *the most functional environments* for learning and skills to be acquired and applied. Schwartz (2007) stated that access to the regular education curriculum is the right of all students. SLP services can be designed to facilitate inclusion and educational access.

Mainstream Education: An Emphasis on Metalanguage

To teach any learners about syntax and grammar is to teach about ways to consciously explore how language structures are used in oral and written language contexts. *Metalanguage* is the language used to talk about language. Throughout this text, notably in Chapters 3, 4, 5, and 6, school-age learners' *metalinguistic* skills are a main consideration. Syntactic and grammatical knowledge cannot be matured by drill alone, although repeated opportunities for practice are important. Syntax and grammar are improved when the practices that learners engage in increase their metalinguistic *insights* into the syntax and grammar of their language. The emphasis in this text is not on syntax and grammar interventions that utilize stimulus-response therapy techniques. *Metalinguistic awareness* is a language user's ability to explore language itself—to consider language as an object for exploration and manipulation (Britton, 1984). Metalinguistic awareness is foundational to literacy because printed symbols must be consciously manipulated.

The intervention techniques provided in this text resemble curriculum-based content, mostly as K–12 curriculum is described by the *Common Core State Standards* (National Governors Association Center for Best Practices, Council of Chief State School Officers, 2010) and are meant to provide access to mainstream content for struggling learners. The recommendations within this text resemble classroom instructional modifications and *Response to Intervention* (RTI) techniques (National Center on Response to Intervention, 2010). RTI is an instructional model where assessment data and progress monitoring identify the students who need learning supports and inform educators' judgments about the types of instructional supports and their intensity (Ehren & Whitmire, 2009; Hall-Mills, 2018; Jimerson et al., 2007).

Educational Systems: The Contexts That Surround School-Based Speech-Language Therapy

Federal, state, and local educational mandates govern how students receive speech-language therapy services. At the federal level, school-based services are governed by the Every Student Succeeds Act (ESSA) of 2015 and by IDEA (2004). State and local agencies develop their procedures for student assessment and for delivery of special education services, which include speech-language services, in accordance with these federal mandates. IDEA requires that students with disabilities are included in regular education instructional settings to the extent that is possible for each student and that students are given the supports they need to participate in and make progress in regular education initiatives. IDEA requires that students who receive speech-language therapy have an Individualized Education Program (IEP) that identifies the specific components of their special education services, including speech-language therapy services. IEPs establish students' measurable "academic and functional" annual learning and performance goals and objectives (IDEA, 2004). Here, the term "functional" learning and performance means nonacademic learning and performance. *Functional* learning and performance goals can be predominant for students who are better served by working on activities of daily living to a greater extent than on academic subject matter (Gordon-Pershey, 2019a, 2019b). Functional learning and performance goals can supplement academic learning and performance goals for students who need to make progress in both instructional areas. The IEP teams' decisions about whether academic and/or functional language goals are addressed are governed by IDEA's requirement that schools provide a free and appropriate public education (FAPE) to students with disabilities. An appropriate education can be determined by whether a student is "receiving a meaningful educational benefit from services" (Hall-Mills, 2018, p. 171). Meaningfulness can be determined in part by whether speech-language services are given in the optimal environments (e.g., in a "pullout" setting, such as in a speech-language therapy room, or in a classroom "push-in" setting, or as a consultative or monitoring service where the student is not seen directly by the SLP—or not seen often— and the SLP advises other staff as to how to enhance the student's language learning) and whether services and settings address the optimal language skills needed for academic success (Cirrin et al., 2010; McGinty & Justice, 2006). Syntax and grammar have been repeatedly documented as essential language skills for learning spoken and written information and for academic success (Nippold, 1993, 1998; Scott, 1995a; Scott & Windsor, 2000).

Secord (2014) identified numerous aspects of the local, state, and national systems of education that have bearing on how speech-language therapy services are delivered. Paraphrased and expanded, Secord's considerations would include how local, state, and national education agencies (as managed by individual school administrations, district and state boards of education, and the U.S. Department of Education, and by the entities that conduct the operations of private schools) act in relation to the following:

- The quality of educational leaders, and the principles and influences that affect their leadership;

- The degree of focus on literacy within a school, district, state, or nation, and the extent to which literacy is viewed as integral to school success;
- Efforts to provide access to all of the benefits of schooling to all learners;
- Cultural and linguistic diversity of learners, and preparing learners for their futures in global societies and marketplaces;
- Poverty and the educational inequities experienced by underserved communities;
- Digital learning, and how underserved populations may have unequal access to digital learning;
- The negative consequences of regarding regular education and special education as two different educational systems.

The present text takes account of these larger educational considerations, in that the suggestions given in this text for speech-language practices consider how speech-language services are subsumed under the educational agencies' broader aims for their students' successes. School speech-language therapy would be one means by which education agencies would address their goals for equal access to funding, benefits, and opportunities. Valuing diversity, promoting literacy, parity for special education students, and inclusivity would also be addressed by successful speech-language services. For students who are capable of meeting academic language goals, progress in therapy would be subsumed under their progress in academics and would be regarded as an aspect of their overall enhancement as a learner, as is recommended by ASHA

(2004, 2018a, 2018b, n.d.-a). As Peterson and Stoddard (2018) observed regarding academic language, "complexity of language closely matches what school-based SLPs are most interested in measuring—language that is aligned with national and state standards" (p. 188).

Collaborative Goals and Service Delivery

When success in school endeavors that take place outside of the speech-language therapy setting is the ultimate goal of speech-language therapy services, then speech-language therapy sessions would be designed to include the mainstream curriculum information and the instructional approaches that are commonly used in classrooms, as that would be the logical way to reach this goal (Feeney, 2008; Nippold, 2007; Schuele, 2009b). Speech-language therapy would use fewer methods and materials that are dissimilar to classroom methods and materials. Collaborative academic goal setting and instructional designs across school service providers would be prized (cf. Ehren & Ehren, 2007). Ehren and Whitmire (2009) stated, "(1) SLPs have to be oriented toward curriculum and literacy. (2) Educators have to understand the role of language in curriculum and instruction and perceive SLPs as front and center resources in literacy, curriculum, and behavior. (3) Service delivery models have to expand" (p. 96). Service delivery models need to creatively

address the realities of how difficult it is for SLPs to schedule sessions to accommodate the busy school schedules of older students. Pull-out speech-language sessions might cause older students to miss valuable class time. Students may resist leaving their classroom peers to attend speech-language services in pull-out settings. Telepractice may open new opportunities to work with students during the school day or after school. A student might find a telepractice session to be a fairly private option, carried out using the student's mobile device and earphones, with no one else able to see or hear who the student is talking with or know why the student is using his or her device. As another option, SLPs may be able to include indirect services provided through a consultative model where SLPs offer their perspectives and strategies to teachers and tutors, who then implement these techniques with students.

To these ends, the approaches to intervention described in this text more closely resemble classroom instructional techniques than traditional therapy's short-answer drills and atomistic tasks. This text offers considerations for holistic language processing and production approaches and for addressing the disciplinary literacy skills needed for success in academic content areas (Ehren & Whitmire, 2009). As Peterson and Stoddard (2018) averred, "Ultimately, what students are expected to understand and produce in school is oral and written academic language in a communicative, meaningful way" (p. 188).

The Development of Grammar and Syntax: Foundations From First Words Through the Preschool Years

This chapter describes the typical grammatical and syntactic forms that children learn to understand and produce. Figure 2–1 guides this chapter's description of the components of form. Form is realized as a language's grammar, that is, the rules for constructing phrases, clauses, and sentences. A speaker's grammatical competence involves following the grammatical rules for effectively employing the elements of form to construct complex words and sentences that convey deep structures and surface structures. Speakers enact the properties of the seven grammatical categories of English in order to encode meaning through the manipulation of syntax. These grammatical categories are explained. Table 2–3 guides the explanation of the syntactic growth that occurs during this developmental period. Development of form can be measured, in part, by length of utterance. Language impairment may be characterized by insufficient development and generalization of the regularities of syntactic patterns or by insufficient use of productive variations in syntactic constructions. As form development matures, speakers develop interpropositional devices, including the phrase elaborations that are integral to forming clauses and complex sentences. Clauses are combined by the processes of coordination, complementation, embedding, and relativization. More sophisticated use of free and bound morphemes is acquired. Deficits in form may be involve impaired syntactic comprehension and use of the grammar and syntax needed for academic achievement.

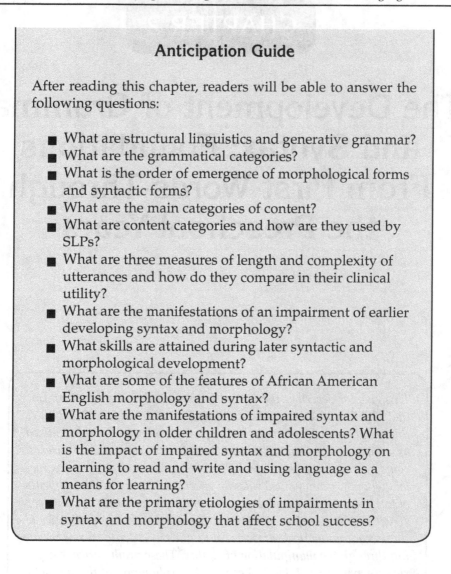

Anticipation Guide

After reading this chapter, readers will be able to answer the following questions:

- What are structural linguistics and generative grammar?
- What are the grammatical categories?
- What is the order of emergence of morphological forms and syntactic forms?
- What are the main categories of content?
- What are content categories and how are they used by SLPs?
- What are three measures of length and complexity of utterances and how do they compare in their clinical utility?
- What are the manifestations of an impairment of earlier developing syntax and morphology?
- What skills are attained during later syntactic and morphological development?
- What are some of the features of African American English morphology and syntax?
- What are the manifestations of impaired syntax and morphology in older children and adolescents? What is the impact of impaired syntax and morphology on learning to read and write and using language as a means for learning?
- What are the primary etiologies of impairments in syntax and morphology that affect school success?

This chapter provides a summary of the elements of language form and structure. SLPs possess foundational knowledge of the complexities of language form (ASHA, 2004, 2016), which guides their accurate determination of the nature of a child's language impairment and their recommendations for attainable objectives. Clinical knowledge involves a fairly detailed background in how linguists characterize morphology and syntax, including the terminology used in the study of the linguistic structure of English. Included in this chapter is a summary of structural linguistics and generative grammar, two of the theories that underlie how form and syntax are acquired. The beginning of this chapter discusses relevant theory and detailed information on English morphology and syntax. Then, extensive developmental information is given, pertaining to preschool, school-age, and adolescent expectations for language form.

Language Form

Every language has form, referred to as its *grammar*. A grammar encompasses the totality of the language's phonological, semantic, morphological, and syntactic patterns. Within the study of form, words are classified as parts of speech: nouns, verbs, adjectives, and so on. Grammatical competence is predicated upon using a finite number of elements—primarily parts of speech, affixes, and sentence patterns—to construct an infinite number of sentences. Figure 2–1 depicts the components of form: phonology, morphology, and syntax.

The phonological structure of language contributes to grammatical form. As Figure 2–1 indicates, phonemes and syllables provide language with segmental form. Spoken phonology provides suprasegmental form, which is characterized by prosody, intonation, syllable stress, word stress, pauses between words, and the phrasing patterns of utterances.

The semantic language system interacts with the grammatical system to yield use of language form. Inspection of Figure 2–1 reveals that lexicon is listed as an aspect of form, although a lexicon is commonly considered to be a semantic storehouse of words. The reason for this apparent contradiction is that when form is the focus of study, lexical elements (words) are regarded as a component of form, not as semantic content. The lexicon is embedded within the component of form that includes morphology, because a lexicon consists of *free morphemes* (true words that have no affixation) and free morphemes that have *bound morphemes*

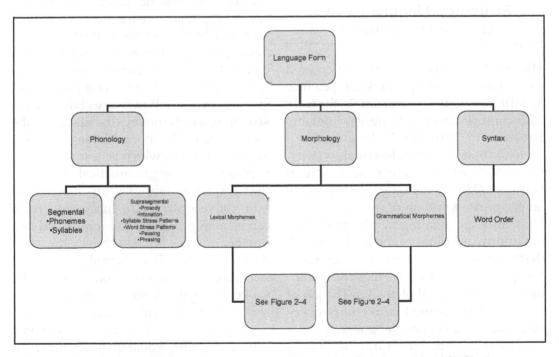

Figure 2–1. Language form. Adapted from Bloom, L., & Lahey, M. (1978). *Language development and language disorders*. John Wiley & Sons.

(affixes) attached. *Lexical morphology* is concerned with word formation rules (Kiparsky, 1982). It is not a contradiction to say that, when semantic content is the focus of study, a lexicon serves the semantic purpose of imparting linguistic meaning and that, when form is the focus, lexical items are elements of the form and structure of utterances. It is merely a matter of which perspective is adopted. Grammatical morphology is concerned with how language users manipulate words and parts of words to produce phrases and sentences. The focus is on how these manipulations reveal a speaker's knowledge of the rules of language form. In the study of language form, there is little regard for how words are used to impart meaning, other than to *focus on how the ordered arrangement of words in phrases and sentences conveys meaning.*

Structural Linguistics and Generative Grammar

Historically, *structural linguistics* attempted to account for how speakers can produce an infinite variety of sentences. To the early 20th-century structural linguists, notably Saussure in 1916 (1983), language is a "self-contained, non-referential system" with "necessary and universal structural features" (Hicks, 2004, pp. 43–44). Every language has a system of rules for inflecting words, conjugating words, and building multiword phrases and sentences. All that is necessary for learning language is for speakers to learn the rules for manipulating grammatical elements. The job of the structural linguist is to codify every rule that exists in every language.

To that end, structural linguistics attempted to account for the entirety of languages' *syntactic universals*: the principles of

the world's languages' phonological, morphological, and syntactic systems. Chomsky (1965, 1968; see also Searle, 1972) considered the structural linguists' analyses of corpora of phonemes and morphemes to be efficient systems for codifying any language's finite number of phonemes and morphemes. However, Chomsky was not satisfied that structural linguistic codifications of word order could sufficiently explain human acquisition and use of syntax. Given that each language is governed by a set of fairly convergent and invariant patterns involving word order and morphological manipulation of words, Chomsky attempted to describe how speakers can construct an unlimited variety of unique sentences. Chomsky accounted for this linguistic creativity by theorizing that formal grammar is an unconscious and innate rule-governed language system that allows language users to generate and comprehend an unlimited number of language constructions. Chomsky searched for sets of rules that allow speakers to generate all possible sentences but concluded that sentences' rules actually represent two syntactic levels that speakers manipulate. All messages have a *deep structure*, which conveys the ideas that the message is really about. Messages have a *surface structure*, which is how a message is phrased by the grammatical structures that a speaker employs. In many communicative instances, a surface structure can be manipulated and paraphrased in a number of ways but still convey the same deep structure. For example, the deep structure "I want some coffee" could be spoken using that sentence form or as "coffee," "can I have some coffee," "can I get a cup of coffee," "please may I have some coffee," "a coffee would do nicely now," "if it's not too much trouble, could we break for coffee now," and any number of other surface structure constructions. Sometimes a surface structure has more than one deep structure meaning, as an old cartoon humorously portrayed. The sentence *The duck is ready for dinner* is illustrated in one panel as an eager bird nibbling grain but in another panel as a sumptuous platter for human consumption featuring roasted fowl. The caption can be applied to both pictures by using the same surface structure, but the deep structure of the caption as applied to each picture conveys an entirely different meaning. In short, syntax is not an isolated linguistic skill. The surface structure of a message manipulates syntactic form and semantic content to achieve the semantic and pragmatic meaning of its deep structure.

Chomsky's work (1965, 1968) discussed at length how the use of deep structures and surface structures entails additional innate cognitive properties that go beyond knowledge of a set of syntactic rules. *Children hear numerous surface structures, but they come to grasp the meaning of the deep structure behind these various statements.* Children can understand the underlying meanings of differently constructed grammatical messages at an early age. Chomsky posited the principle of *learnability*: Children all over the world learn the syntactic structures of their languages and speak in sentences in just a few years. Intact human minds have a mental representation of syntax—humans are "hardwired" to use sentences. Chomsky maintained that human beings can innately and intuitively use patterns of words in rule-governed ways to generate syntactic constructions. *The patterns and rules are the **generative grammar** of a given language—the components that speakers use to generate syntactic constructions.* A speaker's grammatical competence involves following the grammatical rules

for effectively employing the elements of form to construct complex words and sentences that convey deep structures and surface structures.

Grammaticality

Basing their views on Chomsky's theories, generative linguists (e.g., Pinker, 2007) support the "mentalist" notion that native speakers of a language have an innate, intuitive sense that guides the acquisition of grammatical elements and the formation of sentences. Speakers unconsciously or covertly judge whether the sentences they hear and say are well formed or not. These judgments allow young children to acquire form by matching their linguistic constructions to the patterns and rules used by the speakers around them. *Grammaticality means that speakers can acquire the patterns and rules of their linguistic community.*

To some people, the term "grammar" implies correctness of form—"grammar" brings to mind sixth-grade worksheets for practicing how to use parts of speech and diagram sentences. Grammaticality, however, means that speakers have the "language instinct" (Pinker, 2007) to internalize the rules governing the syntactic and morphological constructions that they hear. Patterns and rules vary across linguistic communities, and not all young children are exposed to the same usages of the lexicon, syntax, and morphology. *The linguistic community's patterns become the speaker's innate language.* Language communities vary the surface structure forms to convey the same deep structure meanings. For instance, the deep structure is the same for "Scott don't got no children" as "Scott doesn't have any children," although the surface features vary. If a child can learn the patterns of form that are in use in his or her linguistic community, the child evidences a sense of grammaticality.

To linguists, "grammar" is a neutral term. The form of language that speakers use reflects the rules and patterns that have evolved in communities over time. *Descriptive grammar* refers to the patterns and rules that speakers use, without judging their correctness or appropriateness (Angell, 2009). *Dialect* is also a neutral term. A dialect is a speech or language variation that arises from the regional and/or social backgrounds of speakers (ASHA, 2003; Reaser et al., 2017). In contrast, *prescriptive grammar* entails teaching and using the phonological, semantic, morphological, and syntactic patterns that conform to a language's standard rules and patterns. In the United States, prescriptive grammar is generally referred to as *General American English* (GAE), *Standard American English* (SAE), or *Mainstream American English* (MAE). Speakers whose linguistic communities use linguistic patterns that differ from GAE/SAE/MAE are said to have a *language difference. Code-switching* is a means for a speaker to consciously change linguistic patterns to adopt the elements of standard form that are in use in certain communities, including schools, universities, the political arena, the mainstream media, and in commerce and industry. Code-switching between dialects or languages to conform to a communicative context can be complex and challenging, both cognitively and linguistically, and may provoke emotions and feelings pertaining to a speaker's cultural self-identity. Kent (2004) summarized the importance of reducing language bias and allowing for various options. Choices include: (1) helping a child acquire GAE/SAE/MAE forms, (2) working on form development within the patterns used by the child's dialect, or (3) helping a child learn to code-switch.

ASHA (2003, 2014, 2017) provided and has continually updated an official statement on the knowledge and skills that SLPs need to have in order to provide culturally and linguistically appropriate services. In short, SLPs are expected to gather resources to learn as much as possible about typical speech-language development in a child's linguistic community, culture, and communication environment.[1] Differential diagnosis of language impairment versus language difference includes determining how a child's language differs from the language patterns that he hears spoken around him. The central diagnostic question is whether the child's language demonstrates an insufficient representation of the community's language system. The children's difficulties would emerge as difficulties learning the forms common to their communities' dialects, rather than as difficulties learning the GAE forms that they may or may not hear spoken around them.

Language learning issues are differentiated from any linguistic, dialect, or cultural differences and from issues related to bilingualism, English language learning (ELL), or *bidialectal* confusions. To provide a full speech-language report, a child's attainments in language and learning are carefully reported as being associated with or unrelated to the characteristics of other diagnoses, for example, specific learning disability, specific language impairment, and so on.

SLPs determine the appropriate languages or dialects to use in the treatment and management of a child's language impairment. The linguistic standards of

---

[1]Suggested readings pertinent to grammar and syntax in linguistically diverse populations are provided at the end of this chapter.

the child's community or communication environment are considered when determining goals, objectives, interventions, and criteria for dismissal from speech-language therapy.

Syntactic Competence and Performance

Chomskian theories of syntactic competence accounted for how speakers acquire knowledge of the patterns and rules of language form. Language, as an intellectual faculty of the human mind, is predicated upon grammaticality. In this view, *form precedes function*: When a child develops single words and then multiword constructions, the child's linguistic purposes will be enacted, and communication may ensue. Grammatic competence (which is intellectual) leads to grammatic performance, which is demonstrated by speaking in sentences that follow linguistic rules (Slobin, 1966).

Syntactic analysis of language is not essentially concerned with how speakers use words to convey semantic meaning or to enact pragmatic intent. Syntactic theory stands in contrast to the *functional linguistics* view of pragmatics (Halliday, 1973, 1975) (see Chapter 3). The functional linguistic view is that communicative competence precedes linguistic competence (Hymes, 1971). Children first begin to communicate preverbally by enacting pragmatic intent, such as reaching, pointing, or grabbing objects. *Function precedes form*, in that children can request, greet, share, show feelings, and enact other intents nonverbally or by using sounds, babbling, jargon, or just a few true words. Performance can precede competence, in that the child who experiences functional communication in a social field will attend to language and develop the cognitive-linguistic aptitude to acquire the linguistic

structures in use around him or her. Linguists who proposed a functional explanation for grammar explored how discourse shapes linguistic structure (Halliday, 1973, 1975; Skarakis-Doyle & Mentis, 1991). Within interactional settings, there are semantic and pragmatic motivations for grammar; speakers arrange the elements of form in order to make a point. Figure 2–2 depicts the two contrasting views on the emergence of syntax. In the "structural" column on this figure, form precedes function. In the "functional" column, function precedes form.

Gleitman (1990) and later Finch and Chater (1992) and Fisher et al. (2010) speculated that children acquire syntax in part through a cognitive process known as *bootstrapping*, a phenomenon of learning that applies when a learner has to learn new categories of meaning, organization, or form when he or she has no prior learning to build upon—a kind of learning from scratch. The learner must infer the relevant categories, concepts, and rules. To learn syntax, children manipulate concepts about language form and structural rules so that syntactic elements stay in category. For example, a child may learn to say "I saw a bear. He was brown" but must learn not to say, "I saw a he." In theory, the child is bootstrapped into using "he" to fill some categorical slots but not others because the child identifies not only words but the positions of words in a sentence. Bootstrapping suggests that the process of combining words into phrases and sentences is inherently meaningful to children and that bootstrapping is a process of generalizing the "combinatorial behavior" of words (Fisher et al., 2010, p. 143). Children learn plausible words to place into the categorical slots in sentences. Intuitively learned *distributional rules* help guide sentence formation. Fisher et al. (1994, p. 337) proposed that

Structural	Functional
A speaker calls upon the elements of form → syntax orders words into acceptable patterns that form sentences → that serve pragmatic purposes in communication	A speaker has a pragmatic impetus to communicate → then calls upon the elements of form → syntax orders words into acceptable patterns that form sentences

Figure 2–2. Structural and functional views of syntax.

children use "structural and situational evidence" and observe "contingencies for word use." Children are "armed with sophisticated perceptual, conceptual, and pragmatic knowledge" that is used to establish "word-to-world pairings." This would suggest that children are bootstrapped into syntax via their awareness of the contextual pragmatic purpose of a message and the array of semantic elements that can be linked together to impart an intended meaning (because form provides meaning; also, meaning determines form). Perceptual elements needed would include intonation, word stress, and prosody, and conceptual knowledge would include logic, reasoning, and perhaps contextual, categorical, and/or temporal relationships that affect the meaning of the message. These elements inform the deep structure and the surface structure of the message. Employing these perceptual, conceptual, semantic, and structural elements within a linguistic context, it is possible for a speaker to differentiate when to say, "Who lives in the white house?" from when to say, "Who lives in the White House?"

Defining and Describing Morphology

Morphology involves the structure of word forms. Morphological competence is an important part of a speaker's sense of grammaticality. Patterns for morpheme usage allow speakers to form plurals, mark verb tenses, conjugate verbs, derive words by applying affixes (prefixes and suffixes), mark the possessive case, use contractions, understand the construction of two-word verbs (e.g., hang on, hang out, hang up, hang in, hang around), and form compound words (hangover).

Free Morphemes and Bound Morphemes

A *lexeme* is a single word, for instance, "look." Any form a word can take is itself a lexeme—"looks," "looked," and so on. "Look" is the *lemma* or the canonical form of the lexeme—the unconjugated, uninflected form of the word. The lemma is sometimes referred to as the citation form of the word—the word form that appears in a dictionary. A free morpheme (also called a root morpheme) is a lexeme or a lemma that cannot be reduced to any smaller constituents because it has no affixation. Bound morphemes are affixes that have no word meaning by themselves (such as "-ed" and "pre-"). *Inflectional rules* allow lexemes to take on ***inflectional morphemes*** to form grammatical variants, such as changing present tense to past tense, but the resulting lexemes retain the same part of speech—"look" and "looked" are both verbs. *Derivational rules* allow a lexeme to take on affixes and may or may not change its part of speech: Adding the bound morpheme "-er" to "teach" to form 'teacher" changes a verb to a noun but adding "un" to "tie" to create "untie" does not change the part of speech (both are verbs). "Un-" is a bound morpheme but it is not an inflection because it does not result in a grammatical variant (such as a change in tense). In this example, "-er" and "un-" are ***derivational morphemes*** or *derivational affixes*. Words such as "walk," which can be used distinctly as one part of speech or another (a "walk" is a noun, as in a paved walk; to "walk" is a verb) without any change in the form of the word, are referred to as having zero derivation. Words that cannot be inflected are called *"invariable."* For example, "is" cannot take on any inflection. In compounding, two free morphemes are joined together to form a compound word ("snow" + "ball" forms "snowball").

In English, bound morphemes are generally affixed and pronounced in spoken language. There are a few words that have *null morphemes*, where the affix is implied, for example, the plural of "sheep" is "sheep," (the plural "-s" is not added). This is an unusual word form because *count nouns* tend to take on plural

"-s" or "-es" ("toys," "boxes"). "Sheep" is a count noun, not a *mass noun* or *noncount noun*, which is a noun that does not have any plural form (such as "mud," "information," "equipment," "happiness," or "radar"). A noncount noun cannot be put in the sentence "There are some _____."

Defining and Describing Syntax

Syntax has been defined as "the architecture of phrases, clauses, and sentences" (Shapiro, 1997, p. 254). Each language has rules for constructing phrases, clauses, and sentences (referred to in this chapter as the grammar of the language). Syntax is the result of the grammatical manipulation of free and bound morphemes in order to produce syntactic constructions. Elements of syntactic form have both morphological and syntactic properties (Comrie, 1989). ***Morphosyntax*** accounts for how linguistic elements are definable by both morphological and syntactic criteria. For example, "snowball" is defined syntactically as a noun and morphologically as a compound word. Morphosyntactic rules govern how linguistic elements have both morphological and syntactic properties (morphosyntax, 2021).

As Justice and Ezell (2008) summarized, "[a] consideration of syntax must take into account two distinct levels of syntax: syntactic form and syntactic function" (p. 2). *Syntactic form refers to parts of speech*: noun, verb, adjective, and so on. Every word is designated by at least one part of speech. *Syntactic function* "refers to the role of a word or a group of words in relation to the rest of the elements in a phrase, clause, or sentence" (Justice & Ezell, 2008, p. 2). *Syntactic function refers to the syntactic elements of phrases, clauses, and sentences. Syntactic constructions are analyzed as to the presence of a subject, predicate, object, and other elements.*

The study of child language generally uses syntactic function to gauge syntactic development. Assessments of child language may document whether children use parts of speech, generally to represent their use of syntactic form. But assessment routinely documents syntactic function, that is, the use of the patterns of word order that allow speakers to construct phrases, clauses, and sentences. For example, the subject + predicate pattern can be documented by a child's use of agent + action + object ("Mandy throws a ball"). "Ball," a noun, is used as an object in the predicate of the sentence (the part of the sentence that follows the main verb). Speech-language intervention would then encourage a child to use the noun "ball" in the subject of a sentence ("The ball went into the street") and use the agent + action + object syntactic pattern in other contexts, for example, "Mommy drives a car," so that syntactic form and syntactic function can both be developed. Interventions of this nature help children develop syntactic *propositions*, which are constructions that involve a *predicate* (the event or state indicated by the verb) and where *referents* (subjects and/or objects) are associated with the verb (Nelson, 2010).

Grammatical Categories

The *parameters* of the syntax of a language are the finer points of the syntactic code. The parameters of English syntactic form and syntactic function can be explained by examination of **grammatical categories**. Production of the syntactic constructions within each of the grammatical categories necessitates that a speaker manipulate morphemes to attain syntactic word ordering. The grammatical categories of English provide sets of rules for combining words to form phrases, clauses, and sentences. Grammatical categories account for morphosyntax, because there is explanation of the bound morphemes that are inherent to the construction of words, and hence to the construction of phrases, clauses, and sentences.

Speakers enact the properties of the grammatical categories in order to encode meaning through the manipulation of syntax. In English, the seven grammatical categories are:

Grammatical person

Grammatical number

Grammatical tense

Grammatical aspect

Grammatical mood

Grammatical voice

Grammatical gender

Grammatical Person: Pronoun Usage

Grammatical person refers to grammatical distinctions that correspond to pronoun forms. Grammatical person includes first person singular, second person singular, third person singular, first person plural, second person plural, and third person plural. Table 2–1 shows grammatical person in relation to pronoun forms.

Personal pronouns substitute for *proper nouns* (proper names that are capitalized, such as Michael, Idaho, and Starbucks) and *common nouns* (such as man, state, and coffee). A list of personal pronouns appears in Table 2–1. *Personal pronouns are either within the subjective case (appearing*

Table 2–1. Grammatical Person: Pronoun Usage

Grammatical Person	Personal Subjective Pronouns	Personal Objective Pronouns	Personal Possessive Pronouns	Personal Reflexive Pronouns (Objective)
First person singular	I	me	my (subjective) mine (objective)	myself
Second person singular	You	you	your (subjective) yours (objective)	yourself
Third person singular	he, she (animate) it (inanimate)	him, her (animate) it (inanimate)	his, her (animate) (subjective) his, hers (objective) its (inanimate)	himself, herself (animate) itself (inanimate)
First person plural	We	us	ours	ourselves
Second person plural	You	you	yours	yourselves
Third person plural	They	them	their (subjective) theirs (objective)	themselves

within the subject part of a sentence) or within the objective case (appearing as the object or recipient of an action). Subjective pronouns are sometimes referred to as *nominative pronouns.* In the sentence "He brought his mother to see me," "he" is the *subjective pronoun* and "me" is the *objective pronoun.*

Notice some of the morphological intricacies involved in the use of possessive and reflexive pronouns. Sometimes the possessive pronoun case is expressed by the use of unique free morphemes (my, mine, his, their, theirs). Sometimes an inflection (a bound morpheme) is affixed to produce the grammatical variant of changing objective pronouns to possessive pronouns. Three objective pronouns are inflected to show possession: hers, its, yours. Reflexive pronouns are produced by compounding the word "self" or "selves" to objective pronouns (him, her, it, them) or possessive pronouns (my, your, our). Reflexive pronouns are sometimes called compound personal pronouns. (Note that "their selves" is a two-word construction of a pronoun plus a noun.)

Because the reflexive pronoun "myself" is compounded from an objective pronoun, "myself" should never be used in the subject of a sentence ("William and myself welcome you to Westwood" should be "William and I welcome you to Westwood"). When a sentence needs an objective pronoun, a reflexive pronoun should not be substituted ("The panel will be moderated by Martin and myself" is incorrect; "Martin and me" is appropriate—and "by myself" might confusingly connote accomplishing the task alone). Perhaps a sense of modesty motivates speakers to hesitate to use "I" or "me," but substitution of a reflexive pronoun does nothing to add humility or propriety.

Grammatical Number

Grammatical number has to do with usage of plural nouns, demonstratives, possessive forms, articles, and conjugation of verbs. Nouns and pronouns are singular or plural. Verbs agree with singular or plural nouns and pronouns ("Sasha wants"; "Sasha and Terrell want"). Noncount nouns tend to be used as singular ("Information is transmitted electronically," "Happiness is a warm puppy"). *Demonstratives* (which, in this case, are also known as determiners or limiting adjectives), such as "this," "that," "these," and "those," agree in number with the nouns they identify or modify ("this house"; "these shirts"). Demonstrative pronouns that take the place of nouns must also agree in number with the nouns

they substitute for ("I did not order a blue carpet. I don't want this." "Children can easily spread colds. Those who are sick should stay at home."). *Articles* agree in number with the nouns they identify ("a car," not "a cars"). Possessive forms are structured to account for number, and number governs where an apostrophe is placed in written English: "Dad bought a dresser larger enough to hold his teenage boy's clothing" (singular) versus "The department store stocks boys' fall clothing beginning in July" (plural).

Nouns and pronouns agree in number. A singular noun is referred to by a singular pronoun: "The patient said she can't sleep." Speakers sometimes use the animate third person plural pronoun ("they") to replace animate singular nouns ("the patient"): "The patient said they can't sleep." This replacement is less likely to be used when the gender of the person in question is known and the singular "he" or "she" can be used. However, when the gender of the person is not known, saying both of the singular pronouns "his or her" in noun reference or to explain possession may be awkward: "The burglar left his or her glove near the broken window." "The burglar left their glove" is easier to say. In sum, third person singular subject pronoun or possessive pronoun substitution using "they" or "their" may be common because there is not a gender-neutral third person singular subject pronoun or possessive pronoun that refers to animate objects whose gender is unknown. However, if the gender of the noun referent is known, the third person singular pronoun for animate objects is likely to be used grammatically to refer to the noun or to indicate possession. It is a separate consideration when an individual prefers not to be referred to by a gender-binary pronoun and would like to be pronominalized as "they, them, their, theirs, or themselves." For more information on the considerate use of persons' pronoun preferences, in compliance with individuals' gender identity and civil rights (Clark, 2019), see the Diversity Center of Northeast Ohio's (2016) *Pronouns: A How-To*, or other online sources that are regularly updated to pursue the evolving societal issue of gendered pronoun forms.

Noun-verb agreement can be particularly difficult when word order is inverted. "There are three cats living in the church basement" is correct—the plural noun "cats" agrees with the verb "are," but contemporary American English, even broadcast English, is commonly using the colloquial (but incorrect) form "There's three cats living in the church basement." "There" as a pronoun that is used to introduce a condition can be followed by "is" or "are," depending upon whether the nouns in the sentence are singular, plural, or noncount. It has become common to default to "is" without regard for the plural noun in the sentence. This phrasing may have something to do with economy of form, for example, it's becoming standard to say, "There's pizza, salad, and peaches for dinner," to let "is" be the main verb in a sentence where noncount nouns predominate and not create a separate phrase or sentence to say, "there are peaches." But it is not standard to say, "There's peaches for dinner," although this is common.

Inflecting nouns and adjectives is known as *declension*. Rules for the *genitive case* govern the grammar used to inflect nouns to mark possession ("Tim's bicycle), composition ("a pack of dogs" but "a bowl of soup"; "grains of sand" but "piles of shoes") and some descriptions ("the head of the table") or classifications ("women's hairstyles," "a day's work"). Inflection of adjectives in English is limited to the singular and plural usages of "this," "that," "these," and "those" and to comparative and superlative endings "-er" and "-est" ("smaller," "smallest").

Verb use, sometimes called *verbing*, is one of the more complicated aspects of language form. *Conjugation* rules apply to how verbs take on inflectional morphemes to form grammatical variants, such as changing present tense to past tense or being used in the first, second, or third person. Each inflected form of the verb is a lexeme. Verbs that are in a conjugated form are called *finite forms*. Verbs that are not conjugated or that remain unchanged during conjugation are called *nonfinite forms* of the verb. An *infinitive* is a verb form with no conjugation that is proceeded by "to," as in "to look."

In English, *regular verbs* follow the conventions of conjugation. Grammatical person and grammatical number regulate how verbs are conjugated. Conjugation by grammatical person and grammatical number follows the subjective pronouns (in this case, in the present tense):

I look	we look
you look	you look
he/she/it looks	they look

The above conjugation is an example of a *conjugation table* or a *verb paradigm*. SLPs' interventions may focus on helping children improve their verbing.

An *irregular verb* is a verb whose conjugation in any tense deviates from regular conjugation. Irregular present tense verbs may show their irregularity in the third person: "Have" is irregular because the third person form is "he has" instead of "he haves." Irregular past tense verbs are common in English and include "go," "see," "have," "say," and "get." These irregular past tense verbs do not follow standard rules for using the bound morpheme "-ed" to mark the past tense. Instead, a past tense free morpheme is used: "went," "saw," "had," "said," and "got."

Grammatical Tense

Tense is a grammatical category that refers to present, past, or future time. In order to produce tense, English speakers must use *verbals*—the derived forms of verbs, where bound morphemes are attached (for example, "-ed" "-en," and "-ing") or where verb forms are altered ("see" and "saw"; "get" and "got"). A past tense verb that has "-ed" (or its spelling variation) attached is a *past participle* verb; a present tense verb that has "-ing" attached is a *present participle* verb. Regular verbs that add "-ed" have the same word as their simple past and past participle forms. But a simple past tense verb that is irregular ("saw," "went") is not a participle. Some irregular verbs have both simple past forms and past participle forms ("seen" and "gone").

In English, the three dimensions of time—present, past, and future—are expressed by approximately 30 tense and aspect forms for using verbs and auxiliaries (Purdue Online Writing Lab [OWL], n.d.-b). The basic tenses in English are the *simple*, *progressive* (sometimes called the *continuous tense*), and *perfect* (Justice & Ezell, 2008). Some sources consider a fourth tense, the *perfect continuous*, sometimes known as the *perfect progressive*, to be a basic tense (The English Club, 1997–2021a). Therefore, the English tense structure involves the following tenses:

Present: simple present, present progressive, present perfect, present perfect continuous

Past: simple past, past progressive, past perfect, past perfect continuous

Future: simple future, future progressive, future perfect, future perfect continuous

Table 2–2 shows two examples of each tense (one regular verb, "walk," and one irregular verb, "go") and indicates the verbs, verbals, and auxiliaries needed for the tense.

The simple tense conjugates the verb and requires past tense verbals (generally "-ed") to be added to regular verbs to form the past participle. However, the use of the simple tense can be anything but simple when verbs are irregular. For irregular verbs, the past participle is a unique lexeme. The complexities of the irregular past tense can result in nonstandard syntactic usage. A commonly heard simple past tense variation involves the word "see." "Saw" is the lexeme used in the simple past tense of "see"; "seen" is the lexeme used as the past participle that is employed to construct the perfect tense (present—"I have seen," past—"I had seen," future—"I will have seen"). Some speakers substitute the past participle for the simple past, as in "I seen him."

The progressive tense may be called the continuous tense because this tense connotes ongoing actions. The progressive tense employs the present participle form of a verb, adding "-ing." The present progressive requires the auxiliaries "am," "is," or "are"; the past requires "was" or "were"; and the future requires "will be" or "shall be."

The perfect tense encompasses the past, up to and including the present time. The perfect tense adds the *perfective auxiliaries* "have" or "had" to the past participle form of a verb. In the present perfect, the condition being described could

Table 2–2. Verb Tenses

	Present	Past	Future
Simple	Takes place now	Took place at one point in time	Will take place at one point in time
	Regular: "I walk"	Regular: "I walked"	Regular: "I will walk"
	Irregular: "I go"	Irregular: "I went"	Irregular: "I will go"
		Requires affixation of "-ed" or use of an irregular past tense form	Requires auxiliary verb "will" or "shall"
Progressive (-ing)	Takes place now and is ongoing, continuous	Was ongoing or continuous in the past	Will be ongoing or continuous in the future
	Regular: "I am walking"	Regular: "I was walking"	Regular: "I will be walking"
	Irregular: "I am going"	Irregular: "I was going"	Irregular: "I will be going"
	Requires auxiliary verb "am," "are," or "is"	Requires auxiliary verb "was" or "were"	Requires auxiliary verbs "will be" or "shall be"
Perfect	Began in the past, continues up to and includes the present	Began in the past, before another event	Will be completed by or before a time in the future
	Regular: "I have walked"	Regular: "I had walked"	Regular: "I will have walked"
	Irregular: "I have gone"	Irregular: "I had gone"	Irregular: "I will have gone"
	Requires auxiliary verb "have" or "has" linked to the past participle	Requires auxiliary verb "have" or "has" linked to the past participle	Requires auxiliary verbs "will have" or "shall have" linked to the past participle
Perfect continuous	Began in the past and remains ongoing	Began in the past, before another event	Will be completed by or before a time in the future; remains ongoing
	Regular: "I have been walking"	Regular: "I had been walking"	Regular: "I will have been walking"
	Irregular: "I have been going"	Irregular: "I had been going"	Irregular: "I will have been going"
	Requires auxiliary verbs "have been" or "has been" + progressive "-ing" linked to the present participle	Requires auxiliary verbs "have been" or "has been" + progressive "-ing" linked to the present participle	Requires auxiliary verbs "have been" or "has been" + progressive "-ing" linked to the present participle

have been completed ("The baby has slept through the night") or the condition could still be the case ("I have seen *Avatar*"). The past perfect describes a past event or condition that occurred before another event in the past (OWL, n.d.-a) ("When the baby woke up, Dad had gone to work already"). The future perfect describes events that will be completed by or before a time in the future ("Dad will have gone to work by the time the baby wakes up").

Speaker variations in the production of the perfect tense more commonly occur in conditions where the past participle is an irregular verb. For regular verbs, the simple past and the past participle are identical forms, as in, respectively, "walked" and "have walked," "said" and "have said." For other perfective tense verbs, "-en" is added to the present tense verb, as in "eat" and "have eaten" or "take" and "have taken." Nonstandard constructions such as "I have ate" employ the simple irregular past, rather than the derived past participle needed for the perfect tense, "eaten." The word "go," used as an example of an irregular verb in Table 2–2, is similar to "eat," in that it has a unique lexeme, "went," as the simple past tense form, and the simple past of "eat" is the unique lexeme "ate." But "gone" is the unique lexeme that is the past participle used to construct the perfect tense of "go." Speakers may substitute "'went" for "gone" in the present perfect ("I have went"), the past perfect ("I had went"), and the future perfect ("I will have went"). So, part of the confusion may be that some irregular verbs have a unique lexeme as the simple past form and a derived lexeme as the past participle ("ate" and "eaten," respectively) and some verbs have two unique lexemes as their simple past and past participle forms ("went" and "gone," respectively).

The English language has many grammatical rules, nearly all of which are meant to be broken. But a tense-aspect rule that is generally upheld is "be + ing" and "have + en" (Partee, 1973). When a form of "to be" is the auxiliary in a construction, the progressive "-ing" is employed: "I am walking." When a form of "to have" is the auxiliary, if a verb has a past participle "-en" form, it is used, as in "I have taken" and the irregular past participle variants that phonologically mimic the "-en" suffix, as in "I have seen" and "I have gone."

The *perfect continuous tense*, also known as the *perfect progressive tense*, requires the use of the auxiliaries "have been" or "has been" plus the progressive "-ing." This tense describes conditions that have gone on for a long time (Future Perfect Continuous Tense, 1997–2001).

Another case of bending a grammatical rule is the *gerund*. Gerunds use the present participle "-ing" form of a verb as a noun: "Singing is my hobby." A participle is a gerund if it can be replaced with a subject pronoun ("It is my hobby") or a demonstrative pronoun ("That is my hobby"). "Walking with Grandma" is not a gerund because "It with Grandma" is nonsensical. Gerunds are within a category of words called *verbals*. Verbals are words derived from verbs. Recall that derived forms involve affixation or combining words together. Gerunds are verbals because the "-ing" is added. Infinitives and participles are also verbals—the infinitive adds "to" to a verb and the participles add "-ing," "-ed," or irregular derivational forms.

Grammatical Aspect

Grammatical aspect employs grammatical tense and verb conjugation. Linguists consider English as having a tense-aspect system (Comrie, 1976, 1985, 1989). Aspect has to do with time concepts and the temporal point of view of the speaker. A condition's frequency, duration, continuation, or completion is described by variations in grammatical aspect. A speaker may refer to a unitary event that is bounded by time ("I went home"), known as the *perfect aspect*. An event that is not unitary or pertains to a time range is expressed by using the *imperfect aspect*: Some conditions are *habitual* ("I used to go home at 5 p.m."), and some conditions are continuous within a particular time frame ("I was going home early during the week that my sister was hospitalized"); other conditions are continuous with relevance to more than one time frame ("I have gone home through several winter storms").

English speakers manipulate the neutral, progressive, perfect, progressive perfect, and habitual aspects to convey experience, uncertainty, possibility, permission, and evidentiality (evidentiality as shown by an utterance like "I was going to go home but I *heard* a storm might be on the way"). Manipulation of grammatical aspect interfaces with pragmatic language skill to allow speakers to convey their messages indirectly or tentatively or in order to achieve politeness or diplomacy (Olsen, 1997).

In addition to grammatical aspect, verbs and verb phrases have *lexical aspect*. Dahl (1985) noted how temporal concepts are conveyed by lexical aspect. Lexical aspect allows verbs to convey states ("I have a summer cottage at the shore"), activities ("I swam and fished on vacation"), accomplishments (Smith, 1997) ("I caught a fish"), achievements (Smith, 1997) ("I got a suntan"), and the semelfactive lexical aspect (Comrie, 1976) that conveys momentary events ("On Labor Day, I shook the congressman's hand"). A verb with a telic aspect, or telicity, conveys a goal or an end-state ("My son grew an inch and gained four pounds on vacation"). Some of the verbs in these example sentences are actions (swam, fished, caught, shook), but lexical aspect accounts for verbs that are not action words or that may be idiomatic—for example, expressing understanding with "I got it," an idiomatic statement of accomplishment and telicity. Consider constructions that are built upon a speaker's knowledge of lexical aspect, such as "I tend to _____," "I seem to _____," "It appears to _____," "It is beginning to _____." It is necessary to use these constructions to achieve mature pragmatic competence.

In sum, use of grammatical tense, grammatical aspect, and lexical aspect is integral to constructing lengthier and more complex phrases, clauses, and sentences. Children's verb use involves considerably more than just expressing action in conversation or learning how to conjugate verbs in school. To some linguists, communicative discourse abilities are grammar-driven (Smith, 2003), with discourse made possible or constrained by a speaker's grammatical capabilities.

Grammatical Mood

Mood allows speakers to express meanings related to attitudes, specifications, provisions, requirements, restrictions, desires, requests, states of mind, intentions, conditions, and the like. Mood, also referred to as *modality*, involves morphological choices and syntactic arrangements of words. *Modal auxiliary verbs* include "may," "can," "must," "ought," "will," "shall," "need," "dare," "might," "could," "would," and "should." Modals precede an unconjugated form of a verb ("might be," "may have," "can deliver," etc.) Mood is distinct from tense and aspect, but some modal auxiliaries are used within constructions of tense ("I will have been going"—the perfect continuous tense) and grammatical aspect ("I could have always gone home"—the habitual aspect) and lexical aspect ("I might have won the lottery"—accomplishment, or "You could have sneezed without spreading germs"—semelfactive).

English has three moods, the *indicative*, *subjunctive*, and *imperative*. Mood may be determined by morphological and syntactic criteria or by semantic criteria. That is, a mood construction exists either because the construction uses the syntax and morphology of modality or because its semantic meaning expresses mood.

Mood is the grammatical category perhaps most closely linked to pragmatic competence. Using language form to create meaning is a hallmark of skillful linguistic pragmatics and social pragmatics. The choice of grammatical mood can be responsible for the pragmatic function of a message. Mood constructions can affect how messages *cohere*, meaning, how messages meaningfully and logically follow from one to the next, both within a speaker's conversational turn and across speakers' turns.

The indicative mood (sometimes called the declarative mood or the evidential or evidentiary mood) is a *realis* mood, used in statements of objectivity, fact, reality, or probability, as well as for opinions and questions (Hacker, 2003). Most English utterances are indicatives, although all indicatives do not use modal auxiliary verbs. For example, the future indicative employs the overt syntax and morphology of mood: "Your teacher next year *will* be Ms. Waterman," but the past indicative is "Your teacher last year was Ms. Waterman" and the present indicative is "Your teacher this year is Ms. Waterman." These examples of the past and present indicative do not use the syntax and morphology of mood, but they are modals in the semantic sense—they convey realistic conditions that have specifications, restrictions, or conditions.

Some indicative constructions assert a premise that has no alternatives. "Your teacher next year will be Ms. Waterman" may or may not leave room for argument. This is why the indicative mood is also called the declarative mood—indicatives can announce an unalterable condition.

Generic indicatives may leave room for speculation: A listener must decide if the generic indicative "Raw clams are safe to eat" carries the implied meaning "Raw clams might be safe to eat." As such, grammatical mood may force speakers and listeners to consider whether the illocutionary act is equal in meaning to the perlocutionary act (SIL International, 2020). The problem here might be that the indicative does not appear to be an *irrealis* mood, which conveys statements of subjectivity, unreality, or counterfactuality. However, the indicative conveys what is in fact, as well as what might be—a promise, threat, wish, hope, fear, or possibility; or what could be or what should be—an inference, judgment, opinion, necessity, or logical premise; or what ought to be—a command, request, or requirement. If the seaside vacationer has not yet eaten the clams, the irrealis "Raw clams might be safe to eat" seems to be the more apt interpretation, and the *conditional* modal "might" is the key word in that sentence. Presenting opinions or possibilities as statements of fact by using modal constructions is the stock-in-trade of advertisers and politicians, from "The lowest prices you *will* find at any dealership in the county" to "I *will* not raise taxes."

Therefore, the indicative mood expresses conditions of certainty and uncertainty. Indicatives convey evidentiality—that which is *epistemic* (Aikhenvald, 2004). Epistemic refers to what a speaker knows, is sure of, or has confidence in, or, by diminishing degrees of certainty, believes, infers, guesses, estimates, doubts, disbelieves, or discredits. The modal construction "This *may be* legal" is epistemic.

Within the indicative mood, the *deontic* modality uses "can" and "may" to express possibility, ability, and permission, and to convey obligation (using "should" or "must"). As an example, "Can I help you?" is a different morphological choice than "May I help you?" Until recent years, it was a standard expression for a store sales employee to say, "May I help you?" to a customer. "Can I help you?" was considered incorrect in form as well as in meaning, as it would have meant "Am I able to help you?" or "Am I permitted to help you" not "What can I do for you?" However, contemporary American English allows "may" and "can" to be used almost interchangeably to connote the possibility that the clerk could help the customer. (And perhaps a "clerk" is now a "sales associate" or a "brand representative" or a "customer experience team member.") In other contexts, "may" and "can" remain conceptually distinct.

Question forms, which deal with uncertainty, are within the indicative mood, as questions seek to determine fact, reality or probability ("Who is your teacher this year?" "Who was your teacher last year?" and "Who will be your teacher next year?") Questions pertinent to the future indicative use modal syntax and morphology.

Indicatives can be energetic ("Samantha certainly *would* accept your invitation!"). These written constructions are often punctuated by exclamation points. Or the emphatic use of the auxiliary verb "do," "does," or "did" makes the indicative stronger ("I do want to go home at 5 p.m.").

The *subjunctive mood* is used when an action or a condition has not occurred yet. The subjunctive mood is an irrelais mood. A subjunctive is a grammatical construction used in a dependent clause (also called a subordinate clause: a clause that has a subject and a predicate but must be combined with an independent clause to form a full sentence). A subjunctive clause (a type of dependent clause) is usually introduced by the subordinating conjunction "if" ("*if* he were to go") or the relative pronoun "that" ("it is critical *that* he go"). Notice some of the changes in verb conjugation that the subjunctive requires. The future subjunctive (as in "if he *were* to go") uses the plural form of the past tense "to be" even for singular nouns and pronouns, plus an infinitive form of a verb ("if he were *to go*," "if Gary were *to take* a new job"). There is no use of "was" in a subjunctive (Hacker, 2003). "It is critical that I *go*" is the present subjunctive, which uses an uninflected (unconjugated) form of any verb for all singular and plural nouns and pronouns ("If Gary were to take a new job, it is important that he *take* his wife's career into account," "The police officers demanded that the man *leave*," "The requirement is that everyone *be* quiet") (Englishpage.com, 1997–2021; English Plus, 1997–2001).

Hacker (2003) allowed that informal English uses the indicative form "was" to replace the subjunctive form "were" in counterfactual clauses that express a wish: "Christopher wishes it *was* Christmas all year."

The imperative mood is used to express orders, commands, requests, directions, and prohibitions: "go to bed," "stop talking," "do your homework" "give me that towel." Imperatives can sound curt, blunt, rude, or harsh. Granted, if a person is about to hurt himself, it is appropriate to shout "Stop!" or "Don't!" to hastily prevent an accident. Otherwise, most speakers tend to avoid construction of direct imperatives and instead use pragmatic constructions that are more courteous. Sentences like "I would like to use that towel" or even "I need that towel" impart imperative meaning but may sound more like the use of the indicative mood. Speakers who use **semantic mitigators** (also called *semantic softeners*) deliver the imperative by selecting words that are more pragmatically appropriate. Examples of semantic softeners are "please," "how about, "would you mind," and other words and phrases with similar semantic meanings and pragmatic intents. Caregivers instruct children by using softened imperatives like "we don't jump on the sofa" or "you need to stop screaming now."

Imperatives that are produced without a subject in the sentence have the second person subject pronoun implied. "Sit down" is a sentence with the *null subject* "you" implied—"you sit down." Although English is a language that requires sentences to have subjects, English allows for omission (actually, the nonuse) of the subject in order to construct the imperative. The lack of use of "you" could actually be less harsh than using the subject "you." Pragmatically, in an imperative where the pronominal subject is included, the demanding tone is magnified, as in "you go to bed," "you stop talking," "you do your homework." Use of a listener's name as the subject of an imperative construction can suggest a softening or a sharpening of the tone: "Jasper! Sit down!" (welcoming) or "Jasper! Sit down!" (censoring). The null subject imperative is not considered rude when giving directions ("go to the next stoplight and turn right") or in certain expressions that are inherently nondirective ("let me see").

Imperatives are not necessarily brief commands. Lengthy sets of instructions, rulebooks, or codes of conduct can be written in the imperative.

Modal constructions are an important milestone in children's development of language form (and of earlier semantic relations). Brown (1973) described mood as changing the basic meaning of a message by "tuning" or "modulating" its meanings (as cited by Bloom & Lahey, 1978, p. 177). Time and interevent and intraevent relationships are produced by using modals. It is by using modals that children show a sense of time orientation, particularly knowledge of sequence and of planning future actions.

Children first use modals as wish or intention (Lyons, 1968) by using the **catenatives** "wanna" and "gonna" (Bloom & Lahey, 1978). A catenative verb is similar to an auxiliary verb, as both are referred to as helping verbs or linking verbs, but a catenative is called a chain verb, because it can link with other verbs to form a chain or series of events. Verbs such as "keep," "promise," "want," and "seem" can be used as catenatives (Nordquist, 2018); example constructions would be "keep working," "promise you will go," "I want to work on it," and "I seem to have the wrong answer." In children's language and in adults' informal language, the assimilated constructions "wanna" and "gonna" plus a verb convey intent or wish: A child says "wanna play," and an adult says "I wanna take tomorrow off"; a child says "gonna have juice," and an adult says "I'm gonna have a nice vacation when this project is done." Early modals that children use are "can't," to convey rejection or denial (Bloom & Lahey, 1978), and "can," which conveys certainty and possibility (Lyons, 1968), followed by modals that convey necessity and obligation, such as "hafta" (have to) and "gotta" (for "got to," "must," or "should").

Grammatical Voice

Grammatical voice is concerned with the arrangement of the words that represent the subject, action, and object in a phrase, clause, or sentence. Typical constructions involving subjects plus verbs are:

subject – verb + direct object (the direct object is the recipient of an action): "George fixed the computer" (the computer is the recipient of the action). (Note: "Fixed" is a *transitive verb*—a verb that requires an object. "He fixed" is incomplete without an object.)

subject + verb + indirect object (the indirect object is the beneficiary of an action): "George showed Anthony how to fix the computer" (Anthony is the beneficiary of the action). ("Showed" is a transitive verb.)

Some verbs are not followed by objects. *Copulas* and *intransitive verbs* are followed by *complements* or *predicate nominatives*:

subject + verb + complement (complements follow a *copular verb* [any form of "to be"] and provide description of the subject: "George is highly skilled."

subject + verb + predicate nominative (predicate nominatives follow a copular verb to tell what the subject is): "George is a technician."

subject + verb + complement (complements follow an intransitive verb [a verb that does not require an object]): "George succeeds" has no complement; "George succeeds *when he tries*" includes a complement.

Voice conveys whether the subject is committing an action or is receiving or benefiting from an action (Justice & Ezell, 2008). "George fixed the computer" shows that "George" is the subject and "fixed" is the action. This sentence is in the *active voice* because the subject of the sentence is given first in a subject + verb + object pattern. In the *passive voice* construction, "The computer was fixed by George," the subject is "computer." The subject was acted upon by George (i.e., the subject is the recipient of the action). In the active voice to passive voice transformation, the word that was the direct object ("computer") becomes the subject, and the original subject ("George") appears in a prepositional phrase beginning with "by" (Hacker, 2003).

In some passive constructions, the actor is omitted or not stated: "The computer was fixed." There is no phrase beginning with "by."

The active construction emphasizes the actor. The passive construction emphasizes the receiver or beneficiary of the action. When the receiver is of importance, a passive construction provides this emphasis (Hacker, 2003). In the example "The computer was fixed by George," the computer is of enough importance that a passive construction may be appropriate.

Some stylistic guidelines suggest that clinical reports and scientific research be written in the third person (Roth & Worthington, 2005) and that the passive voice be used to place emphasis on the process, not on the actor (i.e., the clinician) (Hacker, 2003): "The *Expressive One-Word*

Picture Vocabulary Test-4 was administered to establish a vocabulary baseline score."

Grammatical Gender

English grammar uses little grammatical gender. Third person pronouns must agree in gender to their noun referents, as in "Alice loves her baby brother." Third person gender-neutral pronouns are "it," "they," and "them." An animal whose gender is not known is referred to as "it" although it is animate. Contemporary GAE has reduced the usage of many words that have gender-defining suffixes, such as "-ess," "-ette," and "-rix," as in "waitress," "usherette," and "executrix." "She" is occasionally used to refer to a country, a vessel, a vehicle, or a machine in a poetic or archaic way.

The Development of Morphology and Syntax

Children hear numerous surface structures but, from the beginning of their development of receptive language, they come to grasp the meanings of the deep structures behind these various surface structures. Children comprehend the underlying meaning of grammatically constructed messages of great variety at an early age. Contextual meaning is important, with children developing the cognitive-linguistic insight that language form illuminates the deeper meanings and functional purposes of adult utterances. "Functional" here means useful, practical, necessary, or meaningful. Children acquire receptive and expressive syntax and morphology in the context of purposeful interactions with adults and other children.

Children exhibit the earliest expression of morphology and syntax in their inflected jargoning. Babies imitate adult prosody in their jargoning, which may or may not include the insertion of true words. As early as 16 months of age, or once children have a vocabulary inventory of about 50 words (Rescorla, 1989), children begin to adhere bound morphemes to free morphemes and use two-word utterances. *Semantic relations* (Brown, 1973) is attained when children can use combinations of morphemes. Children are able to join morphemes together to produce multiword combinations. Acquiring this skill bridges basic word morphology into syntactic arrangements when short phrases and sentences are formed. Children use patterns for putting together words that are more efficient, expressive, and effective than using one word at a time. Children experiment by using the constructions that they hear used in the language around them, but the principle of *productivity*, often considered in relation to semantic development, is operative in syntactic development (i.e., children can produce utterances that they have not heard said by others). The principle of *productivity* implies that a language user can produce and understand an infinite number of linguistic constructions that they have never said and/or heard before (this principle is also known as recombination, recursion, or generativity; see Berko Gleason & Bernstein Ratner, 2009).[2]

---

[2]Note that productivity does not imply that a child cannot also productively use the language patterns that she hears around her—the point is that a child is generating purposeful language, not just repeating or echoing what she hears. Using the same meaningful utterances that adults use is productive language, especially when the adult utterances are carried over to a new context. Delayed imitation of a modeled utterance can be considered productive as well, if the utterance is used purposefully.

Children *productively* innovate their own unique linguistic constructions. Children's grammar may evidence their experimentation with form; during this developmental period, children produce unique grammatical constructions. In time, *a sense of grammaticality allows children to unconsciously internalize the linguistic rules that create grammatical and meaningful utterances.* Syntactic and morphological complexity is developed as preschool children continue to learn the features of the grammatical categories and the syntactic parameters unconsciously or consciously. Children acquire the numerous patterns for putting words together to form phrases and sentences and for affixing morphological markers. Some caregivers actively correct children's grammar in an attempt to impart to the children a conscious awareness of conventional syntax, but adult-driven syntactic instruction is likely to be provided in the service of pragmatic growth, as in "Don't say 'can I have the crayons.' Say 'may I have the crayons, please, Mommy.'" Therefore, parents may successfully correct children's grammar and lengthen their utterances because of the emergence of *syntactic synonymy* (Nelson, 2010): Mature users of syntax can paraphrase a message by using an array of varied surface structures but retain a similar deep structure.

The next several sections of this chapter discuss at length how children acquire morphology and syntax. First, the development of morphology from the onset of language through the preschool period is presented, followed by an explanation of the syntactic growth that co-occurs during this developmental period. Developmental information is encapsulated in Table 2–3, which provides a side-by-side comparison of the various developmental data that are described in this

chapter. To provide a complete comparative reference for content and form development, Table 2–3 includes the Bloom and Lahey (1978) phases of content and form development.

After that, the next section of this chapter describes techniques for measuring length of utterance and syntactic complexity of utterances. Following that, a description of syntactic difficulties in the preschool years is presented. Next, later syntactic development is addressed, with a focus on noun phrase and verb phrase elaborations and developmental expectations for syntactic expansions in school-age children and adolescents. Then, a list of common syntactic difficulties in older children is given. The discussion of syntax concludes with a description of how syntactic difficulties in school-age children and adolescents are manifest as difficulties in literacy development and school success.

Order of Emergence of Morphological Forms

Children's development of English morphology has been widely researched. There is evidence of a fairly predictable pattern of emergence of the earliest morphological forms. For four decades, SLPs and linguistics researchers have relied upon Brown's (1973) sequence of morphological development. Brown established the overarching stages of language development during which morphemes emerge (see Table 2–3). Stage I through Stage V+ delineate the sequential periods of language growth. Within these stages, various language milestones occur, two of which are (1) morpheme acquisition and (2) an increase in mean length of utterance (MLU) that arises from the acquisition

Table 2–3. Composite Sequence of Morphology and Syntax Development

Age Range in Months	Bloom-Lahey Content/Form Development Phase, Brown's Stages, and MLU (Brown, 1973)	The First 14 Morphemes (Brown, 1973)	Modal Verbs (Includes Contractions) (Tyack & Gottsleben, 1974)	Progressive Tense (Includes Contractions)	Pronouns	Negation (Includes Contractions)	Question Formation (Interrogative)	Noun Phrase and Verb Phrase Elaborations, Clausal Formation, Embedding, Conjoining	Affixes (Bound Morphemes)	Language Content: What Do Young Children Talk About? (See Table 2–4)	Bloom & Lahey (1978) Terminology for Content Categories
12–21	1 Early I 1–1.5		want wanna			no gone all gone	rising intonation on a single word to ask yes/no question	jargon; single words; two-word phrases; serial naming without "and"		Objects "No" "More"	Existence Nonexistence Rejection Denial Recurrence
21–26	1 Late I 1.5–2.0				I mine	no not (sometimes used interchangeably)	what + noun where + noun that + noun	serial naming with "and"; imperatives with subject noun omitted ("push truck")		Describing words Possession Location Movement	Attribution Possession Locative Action Action
19–28	2, Early II, 1.5–2.0–2.25	Present progressive –ing ("walking")	hafta gonna	–ing	my me	no + noun no + verb not + noun not + verb	what + noun phrase	gonna + verb			
27–30	2, Early II, 1.5–2.0–2.25	Preposition "in"				don't can't		in ("put in box")			
27–30	2, Early II, 1.5–2.0–2.25	Preposition "on"						on ("put on table")			

Age (mo.)	Stage / MLU	Morphology / Syntax	Auxiliary / Copula / Modal	Pronouns / Contractions	Negation	Questions	Complex sentences	Derivational morphology		
24–33	2, Late II, 2.25–2.5	Plural -s ("toys")			don't can't (sometimes used interchange-ably with "no" and "not")	wh + noun + verb + predicate; wh + copula + noun				
25–46	2, Early III, 2.5–2.75	Irregular past tense ("broke," "fell")	is (aux.)	he she we you your	no + noun phrase; no + verb phrase; not + noun phrase; not + verb phrase	wh + be + noun	infinitives in phrases; but so if or			
26–40	2, Early III, 2.5–2.75	Possessive 's ("Mommy's")			negative placed between subject and verb ("the boy not going")					
25–46	2, Late III, 2.75–3.0				won't					
27–39	3, Early IV, 3.0–3.5	Uncontractible copula ("this is hot")	will could can do did does be shall (future tense)	are 're am 'm / me you him her it us them his hers they	present tense modal + negation ("can't")		object noun phrase complements ("I wear my hat with flowers"); clausal conjoining with "and"; because	-er as derivational suffix ("farmer"); -er suffix as comparative ("bigger") (affixed to nouns, adjectives, and verbs)	Secure states Quantity	Locative State State Quantity

continues

Table 2-3. *continued*

Age Range in Months	Bloom-Lahey Content/Form Development Phase, Brown's Stages, and MLU (Brown, 1973)	The First 14 Morphemes (Brown, 1973)	Modal Verbs (Includes Contractions) (Tyack & Gottsleben, 1974)	Progressive Tense (Includes Contractions)	Pronouns	Negation (Includes Contractions)	Question Formation (Interrogative)	Noun Phrase and Verb Phrase Elaborations, Clausal Formation, Embedding, Conjoining	Affixes (Bound Morphemes)	Language Content: What Do Young Children Talk About? (See Table 2–4)	Bloom & Lahey (1978) Terminology for Content Categories
28–46	3, Late IV, 3.5–3.75	Articles a, the				isn't aren't doesn't don't	wh-question and non-wh-question formed by inverting auxiliary verb and subject noun or pronoun				
26–48	3, Late IV, 3.5–3.75	Regular past tense -ed ("played")			subjective pronouns: it	negative placed between auxiliary and verb ("the girl is not going")	who when how why	conjunction "and" combines two phrases or sentences			
26–46	3, Late IV, 3.5–3.75	Third person present tense -s, regular ("he works")				"there" and "it" as expletives ("there is a man"; "it is raining")		relative clauses (usually in object of sentence: "I see what it is")			
28–50–56	4, V, 3.75–4.5						wh-question formed by inverting modal verb and subject noun or pronoun	clausal conjoining with "if"			

										Notice	Notice
28-50-50-56	4, V–V+, 4.5+	Third person present tense, irregular ("she has")	won't can't don't gotta	was		was not wasn't (past tense modal + negation); aux + negative + verb ("he is not going")	word-order inversion for non-wh- questions	embedded clauses; separate verb from adverb ("take it off"); conjunction in the subject of a sentence ("Mommy and Daddy")		Time	Time
42–56	4, V–V+, 4.5+		would may might must		their our ours theirs	couldn't shouldn't					
29-48-56	4, V–V+, 4.5+	Uncontractible auxiliary ("she was winning")	should better doesn't		noun-pronoun reference ("Mommy said she would")	forms of "do" + negative (doesn't); noun phrase + aux + negative + verb phrase	forms of "do" in wh- and non wh- questions	double past tense ("she said she did")			
								multiple embeddings and/or conjoinings in a sentence, infinitive phrase follows main verb ("I said to go home")	-est suffix as superlative ("biggest") (affixed to nouns, adjectives, and verbs)	Sequences ("and") Causes ("and") "To" "For" (to give something to someone) Placeholder words (pronouns, especially "this," "that")	Coordinate Causality Dative Specifier

continues

Table 2-3. continued

Age Range in Months	Bloom-Lahey Content/Form Development Phase, and Brown's Stages, MLU (Brown, 1973)	The First 14 Morphemes (Brown, 1973)	Modal Verbs (Includes Contractions) (Tyack & Gottsleben, 1974)	Progressive Tense (Includes Contractions)	Pronouns	Negation (Includes Contractions)	Question Formation (Interrogative)	Noun Phrase and Verb Phrase Elaborations, Clausal Formation, Embedding, Conjoining	Affixes (Bound Morphemes)	Language Content: What Do Young Children Talk About? (See Table 2–4)	Bloom & Lahey (1978) Terminology for Content Categories
								multiple conjoinings in a sentence using so, if, because, but, when; passive voice; relative clauses in the subject of a sentence ("The girl who went to the party got a prize")		"I know" "Can" (for possibility and permission) Opposing conditions (something that is and also is not the case)	Epistemic Mood Antithesis

Note: The cell boundaries in Table 2–3 delineate developmental continua. Closed boundary lines show that development is expected within a specific time frame. Open boundary lines indicate that development may commence at an expected age and then continue to be refined with age. The open spaces suggest that there is continuation of earlier developmental expectations within successive age ranges. Sources for this table include Bernstein and Levey (2009), Bloom and Lahey (1978), Brown (1973), Owens (2004), and Tyack and Gottsleben (1974). Age ranges marked * should be compared to age ranges supplied by Owens (2004), which extend the age ranges given by Brown (1973).

of a greater number and variety of morphemes. (The importance of MLU and the other language milestones that occur during these stages are described later in this chapter.) In Table 2–3, morpheme acquisition is juxtaposed against length of utterance, to show the syntactic skill that is generally needed to make use of these morphemes. Children acquire morphemes and link them together to produce lengthier and more complex utterances.

Brown maintained that the order of development of morphemes is not directly dependent upon how frequently children are exposed to morphemes in caregivers' speech. Instead, Brown concluded that new words and word formation rules (and hence the use of morphemes) are acquired in order of syntactic and semantic complexity. Some observations about how the first 14 morphemes advance in complexity include the following:

- Earlier morphemes can be used in single words and in very short utterances; later morphemes tend to be used in utterances that are at least three morphemes in length.
- Earlier morphemes have fewer meanings and fewer variations in use; later morphemes have many meanings and variations in uses: For example, the contracted copula "I'm" conveys "I'm happy" (state) and "I'm tall" (attribute).
- Earlier morphemes require fewer intraword manipulations than later morphemes.
- The irregular past develops before the inflected regular past, perhaps because it is less complex to produce the uninflected free morphemes used to convey the irregular past tense than it is to affix a bound

morpheme to produce an inflected regular past tense form; however, the third person present tense -s inflection is used before the third person present tense irregular forms.

The development of morphology extends well beyond the acquisition of the first 14 morphemes. Morpheme acquisition is a component of young children's (1) knowledge of word meanings, (2) their development of semantic relations, and (3) the development of *lexical morphology* (i.e., the rules and patterns for the formation of words). *As Figure 2–1 depicts, children develop semantics and syntax by adding more free morphemes to their lexicon.* Envision Figure 2–3 branching down from the lowest level of Figure 2–1. Following through to Figure 2–3, *a variety of substantive and relational words are needed to fill grammatical slots and to convey semantic meaning pertaining to objects, actions, states, locations, possession, attributes of nouns, and other meanings. Bound morpheme acquisition is a component of how children learn the patterns of word formation.* Bound morphemes are affixed to signal possession, quantity, states, time (via the use of verb tense), comparative and superlative relationships, and other meanings. *Generative grammar allows speakers to use free and bound morphemes to produce complex syntactic constructions that more fully enact the grammatical categories.* Other morphological milestones in the preschool period, typically in Brown's Stage V or Stage V+, include:

- Derivational endings for nouns: adding -er (or -or) to a noun or verb to indicate a person who completes a task, for example, adding -er to "farm" to create "farmer" (Note this amusing anecdote: A mom

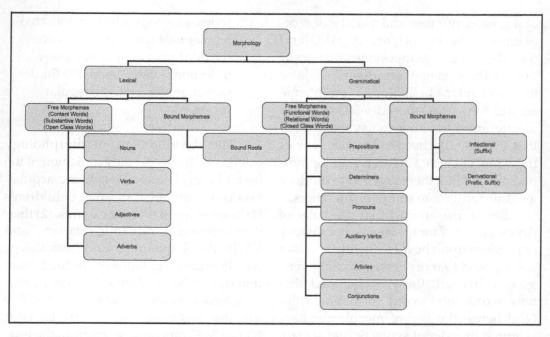

Figure 2–3. Morphology: lexical and grammatical branches. Adapted from Bloom, L., & Lahey, M. (1978). *Language development and language disorders*. John Wiley & Sons.

told her young daughter that a plumber was coming to their house. Not knowing what a plumber does, the child used her derivational skills to ask, "Is he going to come over and plumb?" In fact, he was, but certainly "plumb" was not in the child's vocabulary, but she had the metalinguistic notion that when -er is removed from a job title, we can find out what a person does.)

- Comparative endings for adjectives: -er is added to show the property of being more or greater than, as in "big" and "bigger."
- Both nouns and verbs take the -s ending (nouns for pluralization and verbs for third person singular), but in GAE/SAE/MAE, noun-

verb agreement adds the -s to one word or the other ("boy goes" or "boys go"); morphological skill is integral to mastery of noun-verb agreement.

- Superlative endings for adjectives: -est is added to show the property of being the most or the greatest, as in "biggest."
- Derivational endings to show various descriptive properties, for example, -y ("sticky," "sleepy"), -ness ("happiness"), -ly ("slowly").
- Compounding words ("snowman").

A fuller understanding of how children acquire advanced morphological forms is embedded within the more detailed investigation of syntactic development that follows in this chapter.

Order of Emergence of Syntactic Forms

Within the literature on syntactic development in English, there is evidence of a fairly predictable pattern of emergence of syntax. Bloom and Lahey (1978) stated that the structure of language is at once semantic and syntactic. As Figure 2–1 depicts, speaking in sentences involves knowledge of the relations between words. Substantive and relational words are used to enact knowledge of objects, actions, states, locations, possession, attributes, and other meaningful linguistic content. The development of syntactic structure progresses from a child's use of single words to the use of *successive single word utterances,* then to *linear syntactic relationships,* then to *hierarchical syntactic structures.*

Successive Single-Word Utterances

The syntactic development process begins with the use of the *holophrastic phrase*— the use of a single word to convey the meaning that a phrase or sentence might hold. As early as approximately 16 months of age, children produce successive single-word utterances. For example, a child may utter "truck—truck—more." Words are said in succession without a true attempt to slot the words into a syntactic pattern. *Substantive content words* (see Figure 2–1) are uttered most frequently. As in the example "truck—truck—more," the substantive content words are likely to be repeated as the first words in an utterance.

Linear Syntactic Relationships

Next, and in many children's cases within a short time of just weeks or months

children combine words into phrases that evidence linear syntactic relationships, as in "truck go" or "my truck go." *Linear syntactic relationships string together the meanings of the words in an utterance to create meaningful phrases and short sentences.* When the meanings of the words are added together, the result is the cumulative meaning of the words strung together (Bloom & Lahey, 1978). Children may imitate or echo stereotyped constructions ("all gone," "no more," "bye-bye," "want up") as they learn to combine words into linear syntax. These phrases may be imitated immediately following a model or may be carried over for spontaneous use at a later time. In typical development of form, by about 20 months of age, children use *routinized* short phrases that are common to daily living ("bye-bye, Daddy") as well as spontaneous productive (self-initiated) short phrases.

Brown (1973) identified nine structures that children use in their earliest linear phrases.[3] These are:

- Agent: Agent nouns are used in the subject of a phrase or sentence to indicate who or what commits an action.
- Action: An observable movement or activity (not state verbs, such as "be" or "want").
- Object: Object nouns are the recipient of actions.
- Demonstrative: Used to point out a noun referent ("this" or "that").
- Entity: A label (a noun used without any action).
- Locative: A location or place.

---

[3]Notice the reciprocity of ideas between Brown's (1973) typology and the Bloom and Lahey's (1978) content codings. The two systems complement one another.

- Possessor: Someone or something that is in possession of someone or something.
- Possession: Something that is possessed by someone or something or associated with someone or something.
- Attribute: A descriptive word.

Brown determined that children's earliest linear relations often are comprised of these nine structures, arranged to form predictable are two-word phrases. Eight two-term patterns, known as *Brown's Prevalent Semantic Relations*, are:

- Agent-Action ("Mommy push")
- Action-Object (Push truck")
- Agent-Object ("Mommy truck")
- Demonstrative-Entity ("That truck")
- Entity-Locative ("Truck in")
- Action-Locative ("Push in")
- Possessor-Possession ("Mommy truck" or "Mommy's truck")
- Attribute-Entity ("Big truck")

Although two-word noun phrases are early to emerge, as in "Daddy car," a two-word verb phrase, as in "Daddy go," introduces the use of an "agent." Agent nouns are used in the subject of a phrase or sentence to indicate who or what commits an action.

Brown found that it is typical that when about 50% of a child's utterances are two-word phrases, then three-word phrases begin to emerge. This generally occurs at about 24 months of age. "Mommy push truck" adds together agent + action + object. Linear syntactic relationships are evidenced in some incomplete sentences, such as "my car in box," however, linear syntactic relationships promote children's gradual development of the fixed word

order of conventional syntactic propositions, for example, using agent + action + object in a linear syntactic relationship. The prevalent three-term semantic relations are:

- Agent-Action-Locative ("Mommy put in")
- Action-Object-Locative ("Put car in")
- Agent-Object-Locative ("Mommy car in")

Children learn that the *relational meaning* of a phrase is determined by the placement of the words in one linear structure (agent + action) or another (action+ object, or agent + action + object). Meaning and form are interdependent. For instance, the different meanings of the phrases "Mommy push" and "push Mommy" depend upon how the words are arranged. "Mommy" can be an agent or an object. Bloom and Lahey (1978, p. 157) propose the criteria that when children spontaneously and consistently utter two-word agent + action ("Mommy push"), action + object ("push truck"), and agent + object ("Mommy truck") constructions, semantics and syntax have become "inseparable."

Linear syntactic relations allow children to add function words to their utterances. For example, the function words "no," "this," "that," "there," "gone," and "more" are used in relation to other words in order to produce a cumulative meaning. "No bath" is quite different in meaning and communicative intent than "more bath." If a function word is used in a single-word utterance (e.g., "No"), there is an understood referent and context for the use of this word, because function words may have little meaning unless they are spoken in relation to other words. Types of words that are used in relation to other words in an utterance include describing words (adjectives) ("big car"), pronouns that denote possession ("me car" or "my car"), and determiners (articles "a" and "the").

Hierarchical Syntactic Relationships

In hierarchical syntactic relationships, children move beyond simple additive linear word order and progress in their productive use of the subject + predicate pattern. Children's grammar advances from restricted use of particular multi-word constructions to generalized use of many sentence forms of increasing variety and sophistication. Children appear to be managing the slot-filling aspect of syntactic development: Many object names, action words, location words, attributes, and so on are manipulated to fill the slots in a variety of subject + predicate patterns. Underlying deep structures take on different surface structures as children begin to show skill in grammatical transformations. *Semantic relations* gives way to *word order relations* (Bloom & Lahey, 1978). Meaning making is dependent upon where words are used in a sentence. The verb in a sentence guides how words are used: before the verb (within the subject) and after the verb (within the predicate). Words are used in certain ways to form the subject of a sentence and in certain other ways to form the predicate. Importantly, meaning might not be represented by any of the individual or specific lexical terms in a sentence. The relations between words take sentence meaning beyond the additive meaning of the single words used. Word meanings are formed by word order; by extension, then, fuller ideas, or new ideas, are formed by word order. Children's development of content and form is inseparable. Recall that linguistic productivity is dependent upon spontaneous use of novel, meaningful constructions.

Bloom and Lahey's (1978) research suggests that the development of hierarchical syntactic relationships is evidenced by consistent use of transitive verbs (verbs that take an object, such as "hit"— an action that requires an object, such as "the ball"), verbs and verb phrases that denote location ("get in," "go on," "put under"), and verbs that relate action to place ("move over there," "fall down on the floor"). Children who use copular structures that show states of existence ("Fluffy is a cat"), states of location ("Fluffy is at home"), states of possession ("Fluffy is Troy's pet"), and states of attribution (i.e., the descriptive attributes of a noun) ("Fluffy is white") are using hierarchical structures, as are children who express possessive states using forms of "to have," as in "Fluffy has whiskers." Children produce hierarchical structures by using demonstrative pronouns to represent states of existence, location, possession, and attributes of a noun (as in, respectively, "*This* is a cat," "*That* is where Fluffy sleeps," "*It* is Fluffy's toy," "*These* are pet toys"). In these examples of hierarchical syntactic relationships, the subject + predicate form is used. Hierarchical syntax allows children to describe conditions within events and between events, which may involve temporal sequencing. Using negation, contractions, relative clauses, embedded clauses, conjunctions, and question forms all evidence hierarchical syntactic relationships.

In accord with the functional categories hypothesis (Eyer & Leonard, 1995; Leonard 1995; Miller, 1993), lengthier utterances are built when words from one lexical category (i.e., one part of speech) complement or enhance words from another lexical category within an utterance. Adjectives enhance the meaning of nouns, and adverbs enhance the meaning of verbs. Children learn to place adjectives before nouns ("strong boy") and adverbs before a verb ("quickly running"), but use of adjectives and adverbs following the nouns and verbs in an utterance is a more complex skill. Noun phrases and verb phrases (which are discussed in detail later in this chapter) emerge as the nouns and verbs are modified and complementized. Earlier modifications include the use of inflections that modify verbs (e.g., "-ing") and determiners that modify nouns and verbs ("this," "that," "these," etc.). Later syntactic development involves use of noun postmodifiers, as in "a child with a cold," or descriptions that follow intransitive verbs ("I win when I try hard") or copulas ("I am a strong boy").

Defining and Describing Language Content and Its Relationship to Form

Bloom and Lahey (1978) described the semantic domain of language as "content." *Content refers to the verbal information that a person's semantic language system has stored.* Simply put, this is the system of concepts and information that a person's language "contains."

When a person has any sensory perception, any experience, or any thought, it is processed in the brain as information. As part of the brain's information processing system, the semantic system symbolizes sensory, experiential, and cognitive information as words and then stores these relevant words in *semantic memory*. Speakers have a fund of semantic information—concepts, ideas, experiences, names

of objects, and so on—that they refer to by using words. The words are the referents that symbolize the information that has been accumulated and stored. Hence, the semantic system stores a fund of "content."

Content: A Fund of Information

A child's semantic system is the repository of all of the verbal information that a child has acquired. Content is stored as a *fund of information*. The semantic terms that a child can understand and use reveal a good portion of the child's overall knowledge base (with other forms of knowledge evidenced by behaviors driven by the nonverbal domains of motor and perception, as well as demonstrations of instinctual and emotional responses). If a child has transformed experiential information into semantic information, it is stored by semantic memory. This semantic information is retrieved from semantic memory when a child needs to use it for functional linguistic purposes.

In summary, semantic output shows the verbal and experiential information that a child has "contained" in his or her fund of information. An immediate context calls for the recollection of past experiences and semantic symbols, and results in an immediate judgment by the child as to whether any general concepts or specific instances can be brought to mind. The child organizes the properties of the new context into his or her fund of information and *semanticizes* accordingly, affixing words to the concepts and potentially verbalizing these words aloud.

Content Categories

Bloom and Lahey (1978) stated that language content consists of "a taxonomy of categories, with rules for the assimilation of new topics as well as rules for relating categories to one another" (p. 13). These content categories are shown in Table 2–4 and further explained throughout this chapter.

The content categories represent the acquisition of distinct conceptual meanings: objects, actions, quantities, and many other properties of meaning, and, when children speak these words in phrases, they document their use of semantic relations. Bloom and Lahey (1978) proposed that the content categories emerge in a fairly predictable hierarchical order, from the content categories that emerge with first words to those that are mastered in the 3- to 4-year-age range. The content categories guide SLPs' assessment of children whose language skills are in the 1- to 4-year age range. Children who are not gradually acquiring the content categories during this period or children who have passed the age of 4 who do not spontaneously produce of all of the content categories may have a semantic and/or syntactic language impairment.

Bloom and Lahey (1978) formulated 21 distinct content categories. *A content analysis is not strictly a vocabulary analysis; it is a meaning analysis, and children make meaning by using words in combination. The content categories actually represent the intersection of content and form* (see Figure 1–1). An SLP gathers a sample of a child's language and sees how words are used meaningfully in early constructions of utterances with one or more morphemes. *The content categories are a typology of how children acquire distinct word meanings while simultaneously acquiring the semantic relations for linking words to one another. Children are concurrently becoming able to enact greater meaning and to produce elaborated constructions of form.* The main distinction between an analysis of these content categories and a syntactic analysis is that a syntactic anal-

ysis looks at syntactic structures, but a content analysis looks at semantic relations—how children put semantic elements together to make meaning.

Bloom and Lahey's (1978) research on content analysis was influenced by Fillmore's case structure grammar (sometimes known as *case grammar*). Case grammar is a semantic grammar that looks at a speaker's selection and ordering of semantic elements (Fillmore, 1968). Case grammar is not a grammar of syntactic (and morphological) usage of elements. *Young speakers fill an intuitive semantic frame—a frame used for expressing meaning—where semantic elements take on flexibility* (Cook, 1989). Learning a word involves learning its semantic frame for how each word is used in phrases and sentences to convey its meaning. *An experienced language user can place a word into its multiple grammatical positions in a phrase or sentence.*

Although it has been over four decades since the Bloom and Lahey (1978) content categories were first published, and while hundreds of researchers have produced copious information about language development and language disorders since then, there is no suggestion in the professional literature that the codings are flawed, insufficient, or outdated, and no scheme of early semantic analysis supersedes this system. These categories are the "gold standard" for the analysis of child language—although other methods of analysis exist, none appear to be more sensitive to the nuances of content development and semantic relations, and none have greater specificity for identifying the presence or absence of productive semantics. This system of analysis cannot be replaced. An SLP needs this content development typology as part of his or her knowledge base.

Table 2–4 shows the Bloom and Lahey (1978) content categories within an

Table 2–4. Language Content: What Do Young Children Talk About?

Age of Onset of Category Use	Content Categories of Children's Language
Approximately 12 months	EXISTENCE: Children talk about objects. • Labels for objects in the here-and-now • Particular people or pets' names • Later, "+s" plural allows for category names ("Those are animals.") (Unless "+s" plural is not used by the child's dialect) • Vocatives (To call for someone by name: As in "to evoke," to cause something to appear) ("Mommy!" "Rover!") • Later, labels for objects out of the here-and-now (out of sight or from the past or future)
Approximately 12 to 16 months	NONEXISTENCE, DENIAL, REJECTION: Children say "No." • "No" means disappearance (Peek-a-boo games: "No baby," "No ball") NONEXISTENCE • "No" is used to deny a feeling or perception ("No tired," "No in box") DENIAL • "No" is used to discuss what is and what is not (Adult shows a child a dog, says, "Is this a cat?" Child says, "No") DENIAL • "No" is used to negate ("No" means "Can't" or "Didn't": "I no get ball") DENIAL • "No" is used to signal an action ("No" means "Get away," "Don't") REJECTION • "No" is used to refuse (Adult: "Come here"; Child: "No") REJECTION
Approximately 12 to 16 months	RECURRENCE: Children ask for "More." • More of an object ("More water") or of an action ("More playing")
Approximately 18 to 24 months	ATTRIBUTION: Children use describing words. • Red—red shoe, red car—The property of "red" is easy to perceive, so this is an easier attribution • Big—big boy, big store—The property of "big" is not as easy to perceive, has many different meanings, may be abstract to a child, so this is a more difficult attribution • "Be good"—The property of "good" is abstract and variable across situations that have different expectations for behavior • Later: Comparatives ("+er"—bigger) and superlatives ("+est"—biggest)

Table 2–4. *continued*

Approximately 18 to 24 months	POSSESSION: Children use words that explain ownership. • "Mine." • Possessive *'s* (Develops by the child progressing through a series of utterances until finally saying "Daddy's shoe": First, "Shoe," then "Daddy," then "Shoe Daddy," then "Daddy shoe," then "Daddy's shoe") (Some dialects do not use the possessive *'s*, in which case "Daddy shoe" is the final adult form)
Approximately 16 to 18 months	LOCATIVE ACTION AND ACTION: Children talk about things that move. • LOCATIVE ACTION shows that objects or people change their locations or move into different positions • Commands to tell people to move or move an object ("Open door," "Go") LOCATIVE ACTION • Words that signal changing the place where an object or person is ("Car go in tunnel," "Pick me up," "Bear outta bed") LOCATIVE ACTION • Instruments that cause things to move (Playing with a wind-up key, a child says, "Go"; with a power switch, "Go"; with a doorknob, "Open"; with a bat and ball, "Run") LOCATIVE ACTION • Later—Intention is added—Moving will take place at a future time ("Gonna hit the ball," "Wanna ride in the car") LOCATIVE ACTION • ACTIONS are movements but locations of objects or people do not change ("Smile," "Sneeze," "Paint," "Hug")
Approximately 24 months	LOCATIVE STATE AND STATE: Children talk about "secure states." • LOCATIVE STATE talks about objects and people in the locations where they belong or where they remain for a while • Where something is located—Moving is not implied ("Baby in bed," "Mommy at work," "Jay gone bye-bye") LOCATIVE STATE • Container states ("All toys in box") LOCATIVE STATE • STATE is often a form of "to be," "want," "have," "like," or another internal or external state • State of being ("Baby sleep," "I'm thirsty") STATE • State of need ("I want book") STATE • Former states (Child points to photo of himself and Santa at the mall at Christmas, says "Me and Santa") STATE

continues

Table 2–4. *continued*

Age of Onset of Category Use	Content Categories of Children's Language
Approximately 28 months	QUANTITY: Children talk about quantity. • Plural +s (If used by the child's dialect) • Developmental constructs ("Two cow"—regardless of dialect, the child may not use the +s when pluralizing) • Number words ("Three," "Many," "Some," "All")
Approximately 30 months	NOTICE: Children issue "Notice." • Signal words ("Look," "Listen," "Hey," "Watch") (Their meaning is, "Notice this, please.")
Approximately 38 months	TIME: Children talk about time as measured in events, rather than by telling time. • Time orientation—"Dinner time" (Not six o'clock) • Interevent—"Play after dinner" • Intraevent—At dinner: "Veggies then cookies" • Later: Time concepts: Hours, minutes, days of the week, seasons
Approximately 42 months	CAUSALITY: Children talk about causes for events and sequences of events. • Causality ("I run and get tired" "Dirty hands, gotta wash 'em") • Sequencing ("Hit the ball then run") • Problem solving (Explains how a toy got broken: "It fell down")
Approximately 38 to 42 months	COORDINATE: Children use the word "and." • Use "and" to talk about parallel objects ("Your toys and my toys") • Use "and" to coordinate parallel actions ("You paint and I paint") • Use "and" to coordinate events + time ("Night and sleeping") • Use "and" with different objects ("Your Legos and my paint") • Use "and" with different actions ("I color it and you cut it.") • Later: Other coordinating conjunctions: "But," "So," "Because"
Approximately 38 to 42 months	DATIVE: Children grant favors. (Early prepositions) • "Give some *to* Kallie." • "Open the door *for* Jill."

Table 2–4. *continued*

Approximately 38 to 42 months	SPECIFIER: Children use placeholder words. (Early pronouns) • Early placeholders, "this," "that," can appear at 16 to 18 months (The "Whazzit" or "Was dat?" phase) • Objects ("Those [toys] are mine.") • Placeholders replace object names: "Gimme that marker!" reiterated as "Gimme that!" or "Gimme it!" (Ellipsis)
Approximately 38 to 48 months	EPISTEMIC: Children say, "I know. . . ." • Also say: "I know how. . . ." "I don't know. . . ." "I don't know how. . . ." • Knowledge involves memories, procedures, and social expectations *Memory* • "I know that story"—Knowing the story in a book *Procedures* • "I know" means "I know how to do something this time" • "I know" means "I know how to do something all the time" *Social expectations for behavior and self-control* • "I know how to be good"—Reading social expectations— Aware of consistencies for behavior
Approximately 38 to 48 months	MOOD: Children use the word "can." (Modal constructions) • "Can" means possibility ("Can fish fly?") • "Can" means permission ("Can I go?") • "Can" means to profess knowing ("I can do it" means "I know how") • Later: Other modals, such as "Could," "Should"
Approximately 42 to 48 months	ANTITHESIS: Children describe opposing conditions. • One visible condition, event, or object is stated, then an opposite or an objection is given (At the zoo, seeing the primates across a cliff and moat: "The gorilla is here but he's not coming out.") • An abstract condition, event, or object is stated, then an opposite or an objection is given ("You're not my friend anymore!")

Source: Adapted from Bloom, L., & Lahey, M. (1978). *Language development and language disorders.* John Wiley & Sons.

explanatory frame. The content categories answer the question posed in the title of the table, "What do young children talk about?" The explanatory frame offers an informal explanation of the content categories, with some of the categories grouped to show similar meanings and intentions, along with the actual names of the content categories as posited by Bloom and Lahey (1978). Examples are of each category given in Table 2–4, but note that each category could have numerous words used to convey the category's content. The content categories, in order of developmental emergence, are Existence, Nonexistence, Recurrence, Rejection, Denial, Attribution, Possession, Action, Locative Action, Locative State, State, Quantity, Notice, Time, Coordinate, Causality, Dative, Specifier, Epistemic, Mood, and Antithesis.

Interventions for young children with language impairments stimulate children to develop the content categories and use combinations of these categories within longer utterances. Interventions stimulate use in roughly the established order of emergence. Growth is seen when children acquire more words in each of the categories and can join words together in more meaningful ways to construct a greater number and variety of grammatical and syntactic forms and enact a greater number of functional message intents. With the growth of form comes pragmatic language growth.

Verb Phrase Constituents

To develop linear syntactic relationships and hierarchical syntactic relationships, children acquire the use of **verb phrase constituents**. Tyack and Gottsleben (1974) proposed an order of development of verb phrase constituents, which is shown in Table 2–5.

This sequence of development of verb phrase constituents corresponds to Brown's (1973) stages to a fair extent. Tyack and Gottsleben's (1974) developmental timeline varies somewhat from Brown's, particularly for the copular and auxiliary forms of "to be" and for past tense "-ed." Table 2–3 includes all of the Tyack and Gottsleben data except the Stage V "-ed," which is listed as emerging in Brown's Stage Late IV, 26 to 48 months of age.

Use of the Brown (1973) first 14 morphemes and the Tyack and Gottsleben (1974) early verb phrase constituents allows children to produce *contractions*, *negation*, and *question forms*. *Contractions* are morphological transformations that allow sentence syntax to differ slightly. Some copular forms and some auxiliaries can be contracted. Estimates of age of emergence of contracted forms vary. Table 2–3 shows some of the variation in developmental data. (The information on contractions in Table 2–3 is found within the columns that describe the emergence of modal verbs, copula, present progressive tense, and negation.) The varying estimates of age of emergence (Brown, 1973; Miller, 1981; Owens, 2004; Tyack & Gottsleben, 1974) suggested that the contractible copula ("he's a puppy") most commonly emerges anywhere from 29 to 48 months. The contractible auxiliary ("he's getting a puppy") typically emerges anywhere from 30 to 50 months. Contracted modals develop over time throughout the preschool period.

Negation

Negation requires the use of specific lexical items (words) and the manipulation of syntactic forms. Table 2–3 notes the progression by which negation is acquired.

Table 2–5. Emergence of Verb Phrase Constituents

Stage	Modal Verbs	Copula	Present Progressive Tense	Present Tense, Third Person Singular	Past Tense
I	want wanna				
II	hafta gonna		-ing		
III		is 's	is (aux.)		
IV	will could can shall	are 're am 'm	are 're am 'm	-s (/s/, /z/) -es (/ɛz/)	
V	won't can't don't gotta would may might should better doesn't	was	was		-ed (/d/, /t/) -ed (/ɛd/)

Source: Adapted from Tyack, D.. & Gottsleben, R. (1974). *Language sampling, analysis, and training: A handbook for teachers and clinicians.* Consulting Psychologists Press.

Children tend to proceed through three phases of refinement of the use of negation (Bernstein & Levey, 2009). In the first phase, a negative element is placed outside of a word or phrase ("no bed," "no sit down"). Negation begins with the use of the word "no" plus a noun in the 12- to 21-month range (Brown, 1973). From 21 to 28 months, "no" and "not" might be used interchangeably before a noun or verb. This construction relies on a choice of words and involves little syntactic manipulation. A child may continue to place the negative word before a noun phrase or verb phrase while learning to negate more complex utterances ("no hafta go take a bath") or to negate a more elaborate utterance that an adult has said. Table 2–3 shows this phase persisting through Brown's Stage III, as late as 46 months of age.

In the second phase of the development of negation, at about 28 or 29 months, the negative term "no" or "not," and sometimes "can't" or "don't," is placed between a subject and a verb ("I no want a bath," "he not sleeping," "I can't see it"). At about 33 to 34 months, "won't" emerges, adding to the number of negative terms used. It is at this stage children begin experimenting with the changes in sentence form that are needed to create negative sentences. The syntactic manipulation of placing the negative word before a verb has occurred.

The third phase in the development of negation involves adding the auxiliary or modal. At about 35 to 39 months, in Stage III or IV, the subject + auxiliary + negative+ verb construction appears, as in "He cannot go" or "He doesn't go." This construction allows for a child to advance to using subject + contracted copula + negative + verb + predicate ("I'm not playing catch"). The ability to use constructions of at least four morphemes is needed to create full negative sentences.

Regarding Table 2–3, advancement in negation is observed as a child's use of modals and auxiliaries and is refined in Stages IV and V, from about 27 to 46 months, during which time children acquire additional negation words and increase their repertoires of negation forms. As children's competent use of verb tenses is refined, they can apply negation to past, present, and future tense constructions.

Constructions such as "would not," "could not," "should not," "may not," "better not," and "might not" are among the latest to develop, along with the indefinite negative words that involve compounding: "nobody," "no one," "nowhere," and "nothing." It may take the entire preschool period for children to master negation words and forms.

Question Formation

Question formation (shown in Table 2–3) involves learning the vocabulary of question words as well as learning the syntactic transformations necessary to produce three forms of *interrogatives*: *yes/no questions, wh-questions (sometimes called constituent questions), and tag questions*. Children who are using linear syntactic relationships begin to form questions, and question formation skill advances as children develop hierarchical syntactic relationships. Yes/no questions emerge at about 21 to 26 months, in Stage I, (Brown, 1973), with children coding questions prosodically, by using rising vocal intonation at the end of a simple indicative statement of a noun, a verb, or a noun + verb ("Mommy sleep?"). By about 28 months, children place "what" or "where" before a noun to form a question that is an incomplete sentence ("Where Mommy?"). At about 30 to 32 months, in Stage II, "what" or "where" are uttered before a simple indicative statement of noun + verb ("Where Mommy go?") and in basic constructions of *word-order inversion* (wh-Q + be + noun: "Where is Mommy?"). For some children, question formation heralds the "What dat?" "What's this?" or "Whatsis?" phase that accompanies a vocabulary explosion (a rapid acquisition of many new words) (Hahne et al., 2004; Mills et al., 2005; Rivera-Gaxiola et al., 2005; Silva-Pereyra et al., 2005) (see Chapter 3). It makes sense that the first wh-question words would emerge at this stage: "What" serves as a pronoun when there is no noun in an utterance ("What dat?"), and other early pronouns are emerging at this time. Adult speakers tend to respond to the child's question by replacing the all-purpose pronoun ("that" in the content category of specifier) with a noun: "It's a robin."

Regarding the vocabulary of question formation and the concepts represented by this vocabulary, the order of emergence of the question forms that follow "what" and "where" is "who," "when," "why," and "how" (Ervin-Tripp, 1970). "What," "where," and "who" refer to simpler concepts; the answers to these questions are likely to involve noun concepts, action words, and adjectival concepts that can be experienced by the senses. "Who" might be the subject of a short sentence, such as "Who is there?" (Angell, 2009). "When," "why," and "how" questions refer to events that may be out of the here and now, or to processes, or, as Bernstein and Levey (2009) noted, are meant to uncover contextual variables or people's intentions and plans. Even so, there is some concurrence and recursiveness in the emergence of question forms. "Who," "why," and "how" questions emerge between about 24 and 41 months, in Brown's Stage III. "When" questions emerge in the approximately 28- to 45-month range, in Stage IV, as children acquire the concepts of time and sequence of events. During this developmental period, children may use these question words in constructions where no auxiliary is present, by uttering a wh-word + a statement: "Where Mommy go?" or "Why you color that?"

The vocabulary of question formation is further supported by advances in the use of auxiliaries and modals, beginning in Stages III and IV, occurring from approximately 28 to 48 months of age.

In Stages IV, V, and V+, syntactic manipulation advances considerably.

Word order inversion is necessary not only for wh-questions but for non-wh-question forms ("Is Mommy going?" "Can Mommy go?"). The syntactic manipulation of word order to produce interrogatives follows a few main rules (Angell, 2009). This skill emerges in Stage IV, often at about 35 to 39 months:

- For non-wh-questions, an auxiliary verb is inverted to precede a subject: "Jerry is walking home" becomes "Is Jerry walking home?"
- For non-wh-questions, a copula is inverted to precede a subject: "Ivan is sad" becomes "Is Ivan sad?"
- For wh-questions, begin the utterance with a question word and invert the auxiliary verb and the subject: "Mommy is going" becomes "Where is Mommy going?"
- For non-wh-questions, begin the utterance with a question word and invert the copula and the subject: "They are home" becomes "Are they home?"
- Insertion of a form of "do" before a subject if there is no copula or auxiliary verb in a sentence: Use of the auxiliary verb "do" is integral to question formation, for both wh-question and non-wh-question forms (as in, respectively, "Where do you want to go?" and "Do you like the park?"). "Do" is considered a placeholder word that is serves as the copula or auxiliary verb would. For example:
  "I smell smoke." "*Do* I smell smoke?" (In the negative form: "Don't I smell smoke?")
  "I felt relieved." "What *did* I feel?" (Negative: "What didn't I feel?")

"Gina likes wintertime." "What *does* she like?" (Negative: "What doesn't she like?" Or "What does she not like?")

Children who omit "do" from question formation have not "slot filled" to replace a copula or auxiliary with a form of "does."

In sentences where "do" is the main verb, double usage of forms of "do" might be needed to form a question ("Why did you do that?"). This complex construction emerges later, as late as Stages V and V+, as late as 56 months of age. Children may developmentally simplify the construction by not inverting and not inserting a form of "do" before the subject, producing "Why you did that?"

Tag questions, which generally do not emerge until Stage V and V+, as late as 56 months of age or later, are discussed along with later syntactic development below in this chapter.

Pronouns

The sequence of emergence of *pronouns* is shown in Table 2–3 (cf. Bernstein & Levey, 2009). Conceptually, pronoun usage involves *anaphora*, or anaphoric reference, which is the use of words to refer to something that has been said, established, or indicated previously. Pronouns refer to noun concepts that have been labeled verbally or have been somehow indicated to exist in the present environment or have been established as occurring in the past or future. In "Janis found her missing locket right where she had left it," "it" makes anaphoric reference to the antecedent noun "locket." *Cataphora*, or cataphoric reference, develops somewhat later. Here, pronouns are used to signal referents that will be established later

on in an utterance, as in "Because he was sick, Pedro stayed home from school."

Pronouns are *deictic terms*, which are words that change their contextual meanings depending upon who is speaking. Pronoun *deixis* for concepts relating to people and living beings (I/you, mine/yours) develops before spatial contrasts deixis (here/there, this/that, these/those).

Measuring Length and Complexity of Utterances

Measures for determining the length and complexity of utterances tend to compute the morpheme constituents or the clausal constructions that speakers use within utterances.

Mean Length of Utterance (MLU)

SLPs most commonly measure the length and complexity of young children's syntactic constructions by looking at the number of morphemes used per utterance. Using a language sample of at least 50 to 100 spontaneous utterances, an SLP can tally the total number of morphemes that a speaker used in each sentence, divide by the number of utterances spoken, and compute the child's *mean length of utterance* (MLU) (Brown, 1973) (see also Miller's 1981 developmental norms). The result is the arithmetic average of the lengths of utterance that the child produced during sampling. The MLU can be more accurately called the MLUm, with "m" signifying an average number of morphemes, not an average number of words (which is noted as MLUw). (Since mean averages may be misleading, accurate measurement is enhanced by reporting additional descriptive statistics. The range of lengths of utterance [from the shortest utterance to the longest], with a tally of the number of utterances of each length that were the basis for the computed average, shows the distribution of utterance lengths. This frequency distribution for the length of utterance data allows for determining the mode [i.e., the most frequently occurring length of utterance]. In this way, the mean and the mode can be compared. A median for the frequency distribution can also be located.)

The mean is compared to a table of norms for young children throughout the early school years. *Age and MLU covary*, with MLU increasing at a steady rate until about age 5 (see Table 2–3). The MLU is commonly used to assess children from age 1 through about age 8, but this measure can be used with a speaker of any age whose syntactic production is characteristic of the developmental period, so that a comparison to an age equivalence can be suggested. Several studies indicated that MLU can reliably distinguish between children with language impairment and children who are developing language typically (Leonard, 2000; Rice et al., 2006; Rice et al., 2012). The MLU is particularly useful for pointing out a child's use of bound morphemes, which is a critical skill for very young speakers.

MLU as Corresponding to Syntactic Forms

MLU alone is a measure of quantity of morphemes per utterance and does not indicate the quality or complexity of grammatical development beyond the child's application of bound morphemes (see a fuller description in Eisenberg et al., 2001). As such, MLU does little to describe grammatical development (Klee & Fitzgerald, 1985) and syntactic development (Scott & Stokes,

1995). Paul (1981) and Tyack and Gottsleben (1986) sought to *correspond MLU to frequency of use of syntactic forms*. Paul's and Tyack and Gottsleben's data are abridged in Table 2–6. The findings of these two studies showed a fair degree of similarity, although it is important to keep in mind that the participants, tasks, and other variables and procedures differed across studies, so any reasons or justifications for the similarity in performance are not discernable. While these data are not standardized for clinical use, an SLP might informally compare these figures to the percentage of complex syntactic forms produced in a child's language sample and the child's MLU. The forms that were produced by Paul's (1981) sample of children included infinitives and infinitive clauses (as in "he wants *to go outside*"); prepositional phrases following a verb ("he climbs *under the bed*"); conjunctions "and," "if," "because," "when," "so" (in their order of emergence); question forms; and gerunds. The forms produced by the Tyack and Gottsleben sample were infinitives, coordinated constructions (using "and," "but," "or," "so"), phrases containing adverbs, questions, relative clauses, and multiple embeddings. More information on the specific order of acquisition of forms is available in Paul (1981) and Tyack and Gottsleben (1986).

Bloom and Lahey (1978) used MLU as somewhat of an index of semantic and syntactic attainment. *MLU does not stand alone as a measure of quantity of language produced; MLU points to expectations for quality of content and form*. Bloom and Lahey aligned the development of form with the development of content by proposing eight successive *phases of content-form interaction* that are determined by MLU (see Table 2–3). The MLU a child has attained places him or her within a specific phase of development, Phase 1 through Phase 8.

Table 2–6. MLU as Corresponding to Syntactic Forms in Two Studies

Age in Months	MLU (in Morphemes)	Paul (1981) Percentage of Complex Sentences in Language Samples	Tyack & Gottsleben (1986) Percentage of Complex Sentences in Language Samples
Mean 21.9	2.0–2.49		.6
Mean 25.1	2.50–2.99		1.9
Mean 28.4	3.00–3.99		8.8
34–37	3.00–3.50	1–10	
38–42	3.51–4.00	1–10	
Mean 36	4.0–4.99		17.5
43–46	4.01–4.50	10–20	
47+	4.50–5.00	10–20	
47+	5.01+	≥21	
Mean 40.9	5.0–5.99		25.9

Source: Adapted from Paul, R. (1981). Analyzing complex sentence development. In J. F. Miller (Ed.), *Assessing language production in children: Experimental procedures* (pp. 36–40). University Park Press, and Tyack, D., & Gottsleben, R. (1974). *Language sampling, analysis, and training: A handbook for teachers and clinicians.* Consulting Psychologists Press.

Certain features of content, grammatical morphology, inflectional and derivational morphology, and phrase and sentence syntax are expected within each phase. The expectations for each phase provide a way to show that MLU accounts for a certain quality or complexity of semantic and form development.

Bloom and Lahey (1978, pp. 381 and 437) indicated that only nine content categories are needed to represent the typical content of Phases 1 and 2; 14 categories are needed to represent Phase 4, but all 21 content categories are needed to represent Phases 7 and 8. Bloom and Lahey used MLU as an index only through an MLU of 3.0. However, their descriptions of content-form interactions confirmed that in Phases 4, 5, 6, 7, and 8, children use utterances that are longer and more complex than simple subject + verb + object constructions. Syntax in the later phases shows use of a variety of connective elements that produce lengthier and more complex sentences.

Accuracy and Representativeness of MLU

For children who are age 4 or older and/or who have an MLU of 4.0 or greater (Owens, 2004), other formal or informal tools that provide an analysis of the form and complexity of utterances are generally more relevant than the MLU. Even if an SLP's purpose is solely to measure quantity of morphemes produced, one particular drawback of the MLU is that one-shot sampling cannot reveal what a child would produce in other contexts and with other communication partners. Sometimes the MLU is only as good as the sampling situation and the sampling skills of the examiner. A child's MLU can be inaccurate if his or her language sample includes shorter utterances that were produced as part of the dialogue with the examiner (for instance, "yes" and "no" responses to forced-choice yes-or-no questions). In reality, there can be any number of other reasons why a child might have produced a proportion of shorter utterances that would cause an MLU to be an inaccurate estimation of length of utterance. (Examples: A child who habitually says "OK," "right," or another brief interjection, which arithmetically reduces the mean length of utterance; a child who frequently addresses the examiner by name, resulting in many similar one- or two-word utterances; a sampling situation where the child asks brief questions ["Why?"]; or a sample that involves some one-word naming or labeling of objects, colors, or other items.) If an SLP is concerned that the sampling situation may have artificially reduced the length of utterances and that the MLU might not reflect the length of utterance that a child might produce in other contexts, Johnston (2001) suggested calculating the MLU without including any elliptical utterances, imitative utterances, and single-word yes/no responses. Another procedure is the calculation of MLUw, rather than MLUm. Parker and Brorson (2005), in a study of 3-year-olds, found a near-perfect correlation of MLUm with MLUw. Similarly, the *mean syntactic length* (MSL), proposed by Klee and Fitzgerald (1985) and Klee (1992), does not count

morphemes but counts only utterances of two words or more. According to Owens (2004), based on Klee (1992), MSL norms for ages 21 to 51 months generally reveal a mean utterance length that is about one word longer for all ages reported. For example, at 24 months, the MLU is 1.9 and the MSL is 2–9, but bear in mind that all of the utterances used to compute the MSL have at least two true words. A child would have to produce successive single-word utterances, linear syntactic relationships, or hierarchical syntactic relationships. Thus, the stringency of the MSL is worthy of consideration. The MSL offers more of a window into word order relations and grammatical complexity. All of the utterances that are included in the MSL reveal some form of grammar. The drawback is that a child's earliest single-word lexicon and simple semantic relations (i.e., affixing bound morphemes) are discounted. It may be more difficult for a 24-month-old child to obtain a MSL of 2–9 than an MLU of 1.9 and the MSL might be potentially less revealing of the semantic relations expected for 2-year-olds. But it may be more revealing if the expectation for 48 months is an MSL of 4–9 rather than an MLU of 3.9, because the use of bound morphemes to compute the MLU could obscure a child's lesser use of word order relations. Because MSL does not count bound morphemes, its calculation of words per utterance may have more face value to parents and teachers. Note, however, that when the MSL or MLUw is used, another tool for assessing the child's morphology would have to be applied.

T-Units

Analysis of the length and complexity of older children's syntactic constructions takes into account their use of more elaborate constructions. A method for analysis of the syntactic language of children aged 5 or older is to tally the production of *T-units* (Hunt, 1965). T-units measure each main clause (independent clause) and all of its subordinate and embedded clauses (dependent clauses). "T-unit" is an abbreviation for "minimal terminable unit," which means that the unit is complete and terminated (as opposed to run-on and interminable).

A T-unit analysis of a language sample involves counting the number of words in each T-unit. Some analyses provide additional information by counting the clauses per T-unit and the number of words per clause. Owens (2004) collapsed studies of school-age children to report an increase in words per T-unit from an average of about 7 in Grades 3 to 4 to about 11 in Grades 10 to 11 and recommended that language sampling take place during an information-giving task in order to achieve optimal performance. Examples of T-units within sentence types are:

- Simple sentence (*one independent clause* = 1 T-unit)
  "*My sister braids her hair.*"
- Complex sentence (one independent clause + *one dependent clause* = 1 T-unit)
  "*My sister braids her hair because it looks awesome.*"[4]
- Compound sentence (joins two independent clauses = 2 T-units)
  "*My sister braids her hair and she wears big earrings.*"

- Compound sentence (joins three independent clauses = 3 T-units)
  "*My sister braids her hair and she wears big earrings but Mom won't let me do that.*"

Longer T-units may show that speakers are using more elaborate phrasing involving interpropositional devices. Shorter T-units may show that speakers are using basic, shorter sentence patterns, although, as with MLUs, quantity of words is not always a true indicator of syntactic competence. Nippold (1993) and Scott (1998) noted that some shorter phrases involving participles, gerunds, and infinitives show syntactic sophistication. (For example, the participle [gerund] "Singing is my hobby" is shorter but more sophisticated than a compound of two T-units such as "I like to sing and it is my hobby.") SLPs can use a sample of 50 to 100 utterances to calculate a mean length of T-unit (MLTU) to represent a speaker's average performance. The *Systematic Analysis of Language Transcripts* (SALT) software (Miller & Chapman, 2003; Miller et al., 2011; Miller et al., 2016) is a tool for analyzing samples by T-unit and provides an MLU so that the two forms of analysis can be compared.

Various published studies of T-unit samples are useful for showing how to use T-units to analyze language. Studies offer comparative data that may illustrate a child's standing relative to age peers (Hunt, 1965; Justice et al., 2006; Nippold et al., 2008; Smith et al., 2001), but SLPs should exercise caution in applying these comparisons to children who are undergoing assessment. These research data were obtained using tasks that may not be comparable to each other or to tasks that an SLP can present during an assessment and, with the exception of the Justice et al.

---

[4]The increased length of utterance that results from the addition of the dependent clause is not accounted for in a T-unit analysis. Perhaps supplementing a T-unit analysis with an MLU or MSL would reveal additional information about a speaker's syntax.

index, these data were obtained for illustrative purposes, not for the specific purpose of providing a replicable, reliable, or valid criterion for comparison. T-unit assessments are perhaps most useful for observing changes in a child's own performance over time, which is accomplished by comparing a child's past performance to current performance on similar tasks, such as description of the same picture.

Scott and Stokes (1995) commented that T-unit analyses of utterance boundaries use structural criteria that clinicians and researchers can consistently apply. T-unit counts are more replicable and reliable than calculating spoken utterance boundaries by pause and intonation criteria, which clinicians and researchers might find to be subjective and inconsistent. T-units are useful for analyzing older children's and adolescents' written language, as is described in Chapter 6.

C-Units

Another measure of syntactic analysis is the *C-unit* (Loban, 1963), which is the abbreviation for a "communication unit" or a "minimal communication unit." The C-unit is useful for analysis of informal spoken language because incomplete utterances are common in casual speech. C-unit analysis gives credit for independent clauses plus their modifiers (Craig et al., 1998). Single-word constructions ("yes") and other shorter or incomplete utterances are scored if they are interactional responses. Exclamations or interjections ("Hey!") are scored. Elliptic constructions that are common in conversation are credited. For example, a transitive verb ("she *finished* braiding her hair") that is used as its intransitive variant ("she finished") is scored, because the reference to what was "finished" is understood. Owens (2004) collapsed data from different studies to show that words per C-unit may increase from roughly 3 at age 4 to roughly 11 in Grades 10 to 12. The SALT software (Miller & Chapman, 2003; Miller et al., 2011; Miller et al., 2016) analyzes C-units and allows for calculation of the mean length of C-unit (MLUC). (For more detailed discussion of C-units, see Foster et al., 2000. For an illustration of T-units and C-units as analysis methodologies, see Scott & Stokes, 1995.) C-unit calculations are also presented in Chapter 4.

Manifestations of Impairment of Morphology and Syntax in Preschool Children

Initially, younger children who are having difficulty acquiring morphology and syntax may show delays in acquiring the earlier developing morphemes and in producing combinations of words. Because content and form are inseparable, it is important for an SLP to assess whether and how a child is representing any specific linguistic meanings by forming relationships between words. The relations between words take sentence meaning beyond the additive meaning of the single words used. Saying "my doll" provides a meaning that the single words "doll" and "my" alone do not convey. Fuller ideas are formed and conveyed by manipulating word order.

Why might language learners have difficulty forming multiword constructions? Some difficulties may relate to the use of syntactic regularities, syntactic variations, and the overuse or lack of resolution of use of developmental constructs, discussed in the following sections. Some common characteristics of form difficulties in earlier developing language are itemized later in this chapter.

Syntactic Regularities and Syntactic Variation

Bloom and Lahey (1978) stressed that the acquisition of sentence forms reveals the synergistic interplay of content, form, use, cognition, and environmental context. Children must simultaneously master the *regularities* of syntax and the *variations* inherent in sentence formation. Language impairment may be characterized by insufficient development of the regularities of syntactic patterns or by insufficient use of productive variations in syntactic constructions. Children who have not mastered the regularities of syntax lack an inventory of patterns, and they may not have achieved a level of syntax that includes, first, linear syntactic relationships and, later, hierarchical syntactic relationships. Some children who have not mastered the regularities of syntax use syntactic patterns incorrectly. In these instances, an SLP would provide opportunities for children to develop their use of patterns. Other children, who have not mastered the variety inherent in syntactic development, use a limited, restricted repertoire of overlearned syntactic patterns, without syntactic innovation. These children would need to enhance their syntactic synonymy, so speech-language therapy would provide the opportunity to rephrase deep structures by using a variety of surface structures. Many children show some degree of weakness in both syntactic regularity and syntactic variety, such that intervention addresses gaining skill using regular patterns and productive variations.

Developmental Constructs

It is important to keep in mind that there are known *developmental constructs*, which are simplified forms that children use for a period of time while they are on the way to acquiring more mature syntax. Form simplification is especially noted for pluralization, verbing, pronouns, possession, negation, and question formation. In the typical course of language development these developmental constructs are abandoned and replaced by conventional constructions (either standard forms or the forms that are used in the child's dialect community). Note that the examples given in this section do not account for dialect differences. These forms may be typical of some dialects rather than revealing children's simplified forms of adult GAE.

It is common to hear a child produce developmental *overregularization* errors, such as "feets," "he gots," or "I goed." Overregularization means to use a morphological or syntactic pattern in more ways or in more contexts than an adult would use this pattern. In the examples given here, children apply the morphology for pluralization or past tense in contexts where it is not needed. Adults would not add -s to "feet" or -ed to "go," because adults know that these words have been marked for plural and past tense, respectively. Overregularization occurs in part because children are developing linguistic productivity. They strive to spontaneously create novel language constructions. The strategy of overregularization is used when children have difficulty acquiring irregular forms, such that a child produces a word like "maked," which would be the past tense of "make" if it were a regular verb.

Underregularization means to use a morphological or syntactic pattern in fewer ways or in fewer contexts than an adult would use it. A common developmental construction might be to omit the plural -s marker after a number word. An example of this would be "two cow," which is an underregularization error. Adults would add the -s to pluralize "cow." Reduction in the use of the copula, as in "I not," or of the auxiliary, as in "I going" (in both cases, "am" is omitted), are underregularization errors.

Children who produce developmental constructs but who are essentially typical language learners master regular morphological and syntactic patterns readily during the preschool years. Their transition to appropriate form appears seamless or is highly responsive to adult cuing. However, a lack of resolution of use of developmental constructs may indicate a delay or disorder of form.

Characteristics of Form Difficulties

Consulting Table 2–3 allows for review of the milestones that typically occur; documentation of difficulty can be established by comparing child language samples to the known milestones. To cull a summary description of difficulties from the large amount of information presented in this chapter and in Table 2–3, the following list of difficulties may suggest syntactic impairment. This description of difficulties relates to children who utter single uninflected words but whose development beyond this point is at issue. Speakers may show some or all of these deficits and, in cases of more severe impairment, these behaviors may remain unresolved through the school years, adolescence, and adulthood. This list of difficulties in the production of language form moves from lack of attainment of earlier expectations

to difficulties meeting later preschool expectations. Children who are not attaining syntactic milestones may show particular difficulties in the following areas.

Morpheme Use

- In single-word utterances, limited adherence of bound morphemes to words (reveals a lack of use of semantic relations at the word level).
- Limited development of the earlier morphemes that are typical of linear syntactic relations (-ing, "in," "on," irregular past, -s plural [in GAE], -s possessive [in GAE]).
- Sporadic and/or nonchronological acquisition of bound morphemes and function words (differs from the order of emergence proposed by Brown [1973] and Owens [2004]).
- Underregularization of inflected forms of nouns (usually plural -s), resulting in developmental constructions ("two cow").
- A child may use adequate inflection in single words but not embed inflected forms into lengthier multiple word constructions.

Phrase Construction and Linguistic Productivity

- Limited production of successive single-word utterances (this reveals a lack of use of semantic relations).
- Limited production of linear constructions (word-order relations), such as:
  doggie go/ (noun + verb [existence + locative action])
  go Mommy/ (verb + noun [locative action + existence]).
- Use of linear constructions is simple; use of a smaller array

of types of linear constructions; utterances are formed of mostly *content words* with fewer of the basic *form words* (e.g., articles) needed for specifiers and locatives (this reveals diminished productivity):

> doggie get toy/ (noun + verb + noun [existence + locative action + existence])
> big doggie/ (adjective + noun [attribute + existence])
> see doggie run/ (verb + noun + verb [action + object + locative action]).

■ Reliance on the subject-omitted imperative to satisfy wants and needs ("push truck," "want up").

■ Early utterances are not unique and novel; child merely imitates adult speech (either immediate or delayed imitation) (reveals diminished productivity).

■ Hierarchical constructions do not emerge or are produced with errors (reveals difficulty attaining syntactic regularity and syntactic variations).

■ Few *function words* that are necessary for hierarchical syntactic relations: few prepositions (of, by, for, to) (notably, the child may be limited to location words [in, on, under, down]); few conjunctions, auxiliaries, articles.

■ Pronouns are not used, rarely used, or misused (commonly, objective case pronouns are substituted for subjective case pronouns, as in "her going" instead of "she is going"); limited use of reflexive pronouns (i.e., acquiring words such as "myself").

■ Pronoun reference to antecedent nouns within an utterance is limited (the child may not form a construction like "Danny says he wants a kitten").

■ At the phrase and sentence levels, limited use of inflections (bound morphemes) to modify verbs (e.g., "-ing," "-ed"); lesser use of grammatical morphemes (Leonard et al., 1997; Oetting & Horohov, 1997; Rice et al., 1995; Rice et al., 1998) results in a lack of use of more complex verb tenses.

■ Later (Hadley & Rice, 1996) or atypical (Beverly & Williams, 2004) use of forms of "be."

■ Limited use of determiners that modify nouns and verbs ("this," "that," "these," etc.).

■ Delay in emergence of relative clauses beyond age 4 (Paul, 1981; Tyack & Gottsleben, 1986).

■ Errors in producing relative clauses (Schuele & Nicholls, 2000) (or omitted or incorrect use of relative clause markers "that," "what," and "where": "I know that you have something," "I see what you have," "I know where it is").

■ Limited use of complementizers (noun postmodifiers, as in "a child with a cold," or descriptions that follow intransitive verbs ["I win when I try hard"] or copulas ["I am a strong boy"]).

■ Unclear use of complementizers ("Trudi gave the pennies to the children from the kitchen counter"; the modifier "from the kitchen counter" should modify "pennies," not "children").

■ Unclear anaphoric reference (i.e., the ability to make clear reference to something stated earlier in an utterance ["Doug took his dog outside then he had a chewy treat"—who had the treat, Doug or the dog?]).

- Limited use of compound constructions using "and" to link words and/or phrases; conversely, overuse of "and" rather than use of more sophisticated clausal formations (a run-on construction like "Grandma took me home and Grandma gave me a bath" rather than the subordinated clausal construction "When we got home, Grandma gave me a bath" or some other similarly constructed utterance).

Negation

- Limited use of negation and/ or reliance on developmentally earlier negation forms (the negation word is used to begin an utterance, not embedded within an utterance).
- Limited use of contractions ("can't," "don't," "won't").

Question Formation

- Question formation errors, particularly involving forming a wh-question that involves an auxiliary: errors using wh+ an indicative statement (without inverted word order) (e.g., "Where Mommy is going?" instead of "Where is Mommy going?"); for copular constructions ("She is here"), the child might not invert subject and copula ("Where she is?"), or might omit the copula ("Where she?"), or revert to rising intonation ("She here?" or "She is here?").

Qualitatively, children with limited syntax may appear to be nonautomatic or nonfluent in their production of form, such that lengthier utterances are produced "choppily." It may appear that linguistic disfluency is evident. This may appear as hesitations between words, repetitions of parts of an utterance or a full utterance (which might seem to appear as if a child is rehearsing the intended production), revisions of an utterance, rephrasing or restating a point, and immediate or delayed self-correction of form. This linguistic disfluency should not be confused with speech disfluency (i.e., stuttering).

Syntactic and Morphological Development in the Early School Years

Later syntactic development, at the end of the preschool period and into the school years, involves use of the various syntactic forms that exemplify the grammatical categories. Speakers produce a greater array of syntactic functions involving more complex phrases, clauses, and sentences. The syntactic constructions produced by school-age children (and on into adolescence) are more sophisticated than the propositions that have a subject, predicate, object, and other basic elements. Speakers develop *interpropositional devices*. Regarding the semantic meaning of interpropositional devices, some examples include attributive phrases, which describe or characterize a noun ("My older sister *has curlier hair than me* and is *good at braiding cornrows*"), temporal clauses ("*Before we went back to school*, my sister braided her two friends' hair"), causal phrases ("*Because I wanted to learn how to braid*, I watched my sister doing the braiding"), and disjunctive phrases ("I would ask her to braid my friend's hair, *but my sister does not have time herself*") (cf. Nelson, 2010). Regarding the syntax of interpropositional devices, these constructions entail the use of elaborated noun phrases and verb phrases, clausal formation, passive voice, and more complex pronouns, conjunctions, and prepositions. Morphological manipulations that produce compound words, affixation, derivation, and inflection contribute to the development of elaborated syntax.

All of these syntactic elements warrant detailed explanation. Phrase elaborations, clausal formation, passive voice, pronouns, conjunctions, prepositions, and advanced morphology are discussed in this chapter. Note, throughout, how development of a larger lexicon (vocabulary) is needed for speakers to acquire elaborated form. Particularly, school-age children have the need to use a variety of different verbs. Thordardottir and Weismer (2001) reported that school-age children with language impairment use fewer different verbs and rely on simpler "all-purpose" verbs.

Phrase Elaborations

Elaborated syntax includes intersentential phrases. Phrase elaborations allow speakers to convey meaning about the nouns and verbs they use the in phrases that are contained within their independent clauses and dependent clauses. For the most part, these are attributive phrases that add descriptive meanings to nouns and verbs.

Noun Phrase Elaboration

Noun phrase elaboration consists of words and phrases used before or after a noun that modify the noun's attributes. *Premodifiers* appear before nouns and *postmodifiers* appear after nouns. Noun phrases are used in the subjects and predicates of sentences. Rudimentary noun phrases emerge in Brown's Stage II, when attributes are used to modify nouns ("big cat"), but fuller usage occurs in Brown's Stage IV, when lengthier utterances are spoken (Bernstein & Levey, 2009). As children approach 4 years of age (Menyuk, 1969; Paul, 1981), their vocabulary and syntactic skills allow them to begin to elaborate on the nouns they use in phrases. Children generally begin to modify nouns by using one modifier, often a color word or a vivid descriptor, such as "a scary pumpkin." Noun phrase elaboration grows in sophistication throughout adolescence, allowing speakers to communicate explicitly about objects, events, and ideas, and contributing to the ability to narrate (Greenhalgh & Strong, 2001; Eisenberg et al., 2008; Loban, 1976; Nippold, 1998). SLPs can document the quantity of elaborated noun phrases that a child produces and the variety of the elaborations produced.

The premodifiers used in noun phrases include initiators, determiners (which include articles, demonstratives, numerals, possessives, quantifiers), adjectivals, and nouns or pronouns that modify nouns. Table 2–7 provides description of these phrasal elements and some examples (adapted from Owens, 2004). Note that not all noun phrases contain all of these components. Sentences may contain more than one instance of any of these components.

Some noun phrases use descriptive nouns to modify other nouns or pronouns. *Appositives* describe a noun or pronoun by placing the description immediately adjacent to the noun or pronoun, as in "my car, a Honda," or "I, John

Table 2–7. Noun Phrase Elaboration

(Pre–Noun Modifier) Initiator	(Pre–Noun Modifier) Determiner	(Pre–Noun Modifier) Adjectival	Nouns or Pronouns That Modify Nouns	Post–Noun Modifier
Limits the information to follow Similar to quantifiers, often adverbs (at least, nearly, partially, even, merely, almost)	Articles (a, an, the), demonstratives (this, that, these, those), Numerals, possessives (pronouns my, your, his, her, its, our, their), quantifiers (all, both, half, no, some, either, any, twice, double)	Possessives, nouns (Billy's) ordinals (first, last, final, next to last, second favorite), adjectives	Descriptive nouns (*football game*, *leather glove*), appositives	Prepositional phrases, relative clauses, adverbs, adjectivals May be complements (essential to sentence meaning)

Smith." Postmodifiers (also called post-noun modifiers) provide modification or description of the noun. Postmodifiers are prepositional phrases, such as "a piece *of cloth*," "lunch *from home*," "a child *with a cold*." More elaborated postmodifiers can also be appositives, as in "the space station, a spectacle of aerospace engineering." Postmodifiers can be relative clauses, as in "the cloth *that I tore*," or "the room *where I sew*"; adverbs ("that cloth *there*"); or adjectival ("the man *next door*," "a film *loved by all*," "an apron *sewn by Grandma*"). Complements are postmodifiers that are necessary to imparting meaning: "A child" is different from "a child with a cold." If a postmodifier is not necessary for specific meaning but is just a general descriptor, it is not a complement. (All complements are postmodifiers, but not all postmodifiers are complements.)

Noun phrase modifiers are used in an expected sequential order in English. Consider this example of an elaborated noun phrase:

"Nearly every time his old girlfriend from high school. . . ."

"Nearly" is an initiator: It limits or quantifies the information to follow. "Every time" is a determiner: It quantifies or specifies the information the information further. "His old" are adjectival elements: They serve to modify the noun or mark possession. "Girlfriend" is the noun in the phrase. "From high school" is the postmodifier (in the form of a prepositional phrase). The Eisenberg et al. (2008) review of developmental research suggested that postmodification occurs more regularly in school-age children's language. For example, it is more likely for a child to say, "my lunch from home" rather than "my homemade lunch."

Verb Phrase Elaboration

Verb phrase elaboration involves use of the grammatical categories of person, number, aspect, tense, voice, and mood. Throughout the preschool years and into the early school years, children's verb phrase constructions advance to include using modal constructions, auxiliaries, transitive and intransitive verbs, the copula, conjugated verb forms, and post-verb elements such as prepositional phrases and adverbial phrases that modify the verb. The information in this section expands on the developmental information on verb phrase constituents provided throughout this chapter.

Kamhi and Nelson (1988) reported that children begin using verbs when they attain an MLU of about 1.5. Children use verbs in single-word utterances, but regular use of verbs after an MLU of 1.0, at the point where bound morphemes, successive single-word utterances, or other short phrases (e.g., "more cookie") are used, would suggest that children may begin their use of verbs in an effort to construct phrases, as in "car go" or "push truck." It is interesting to consider whether the syntactic bootstrapping hypothesis described earlier in this chapter is at work. Recall that the hypothesis proposes that young language learners identify not only words but the positions of words in a sentence. Combining words into phrases and sentences is inherently meaningful to children, and intuitive distributional rules influence how children learn plausible words to place into the syntactic slots in sentences. Verbs may be acquired in relation to the other words that are said along with verbs, suggesting that the developmental course for learning verbs is to learn to use them in phrases.

Verbs in children's early language are initially unmarked for person, number, aspect, or tense, and the copula is omitted (Owens, 2004). Recalling Brown's (1973) stages (see Table 2–3), the present progressive "-ing" and the copula are used by about 27 to 28 months of age, when a child's MLU is about 2.0. Verb phrasing emerges shortly thereafter, at about 28 to 29 months, when the MLU is approaching 2.5, and is often characterized by the use of *catenatives* ("gonna go") and negation inserted between a noun and a verb ("doggy no go" or "doggy not go"). Verb phrase development continues as auxiliaries are added and word order is inverted to form questions (typically at about 30–32 months). Then, more advanced negation (including the use of contractions) and interrogative syntax develops continuously through the completion of the developmental stages, at approximately 56 months. Verb phrasing is enhanced by the clausal conjoining of two verbs using the conjunction "and," which typically begins at about 35 to 39 months, and by clausal embedding of more than one verb related to a single subject ("I think I see Jackson"). Infinitive phrases are used at 39 to 42 months, most commonly at the end of a sentence ("I want *to go*"). Between 42 and 56 months, infinitive phrases advance to include infinitives that have the same subject as the main verb in a sentence ("I go *to see* Jackson"; the subject is "I" in "I go" and "I see") and embedded infinitives ("I want *to go to see* Jackson"). Reviewing the information in this paragraph, children's initial skill in verb phrasing is noted to emerge during a period of only about 8 months, roughly from 27 to 35 months of age. The next 21 months, from 35 months through Brown's (1973) 56+ month age range, is a period of gradual development of the intricate use of verb phrases. Movement from linear syntactic relationships to hierarchical syntactic relationships occurs as word order relations become more sophisticated. Movement between Brown's Stage II and Stage V allows for development of the syntactic and morphological forms that are needed to construct verb phrases (Bernstein & Levey, 2009). Forms of note are auxiliaries, present progressive -ing, and modals. The perfect tense (e.g., "has gone"), which emerges in Stages V to V+, is a key element in the development of verb phrase elaboration.

Table 2–8 provides a summary of the possible components of verb phrases (adapted from Owens, 2004). Not all verb phrases contain all of these components. Sentences may contain more than one instance of any of these components. Taken together, these elements form the predicate of a sentence, because each element tells something about what happened to the subject of the sentence or conveys information that is true of the subject. Independent clauses, which, by definition, could stand alone as sentences, each have their own subjects and predicates.

Verb phrase elaboration occurs in an expected sequential order within sentences in English. Consider this example of an elaborated verb phrase:

"Lisa could have played in the final soccer game; except she was sick."

"Lisa" is the subject of the sentence. "Could" is a modal auxiliary that begins the verb phrase elaboration. "Have" is a perfective auxiliary. "Played" is the main verb in the sentence ("play" is intransitive in this case). "In the final soccer game" is a prepositional phrase that completes the verb phrase elaboration ("the final soccer game" is a noun phrase consisting of an article, an ordinal adjective, and a noun).[5] Taken together, this utterance so far is an independent clause (one T-unit) and is a verb phrase elaboration of the verb "play." "Except" is the conjunction that conjoins the second independent clause in the sentence. "She" is the subject pronoun. "Was" is the copula. "Sick" is predicate adjective that modifies "she" and renders this clause a verb phrase elaboration. The entire utterance is two T-units (two independent clauses = 2 T-units). This level of syntactic skill is generally in place by the early years of elementary school.

Forming and Combining Clauses

Clausal formation emerges in a fairly predictable order. The formation of clauses is dependent upon a child's production of lengthier utterances that have a subject and predicate. *Intransitive clauses* appear earliest (i.e., clauses involving verbs that do not take an object, such as "he sneezed"), followed by *transitive clauses* (clauses with verbs that take an object, as in "he took the bus"), then *equative clauses* (clauses that contain a copula and a complement, as in "he is my friend") (Bernstein & Levey, 2009). In older children, clauses are combined by the processes of *coordination, complementation, embedding,* and *relativization.*

---

[5] "Played in" could be considered a two-word verb, in which case "the final soccer game" is a noun phrase that follows the main verb "played in."

Table 2–8. Verb Phrase Elaboration

(Pre-Verb) Modal Auxiliary	(Pre-Verb) Perfective Auxiliary	(Pre-Verb) Auxiliary	(Pre-Verb) Negation	Verbs	(Pre- and Post-Verb) Passive Voice Form	(Post-Verb) Predicate Components
Modals Catenatives	Have, has, had	Do, does Forms of "to be" as auxiliary	Not (contracted or uncontracted)	All verbs, transitive or intransitive Copula	was/were + verb + by	Direct object of the verb Indirect object of the verb Complement Predicate nominative Noun Pronoun Prepositional phrase Noun phrase Predicate adjective Adverbial phrase

Coordination

Coordination (also called compounding or conjoining) involves using "and" to link two related propositions. Coordination has its emergence in the stereotypical phrases that young children use ("up and down"). Children master the process of clausal coordination throughout Brown's Stage IV (about 26–48 months) and beyond (Bernstein & Levey, 2009).

Coordination involves linking together both kinds of clauses: independent clauses (clauses that could stand alone as sentences) and dependent clauses (clauses that cannot stand alone as complete sentences; also called subordinate clauses). *Sentential coordination* links two independent clauses to form one sentence. Verb phrases are linked to produce compound sentences that connect the two main clauses with the word "and" (e.g., "I'll color the leaves and you color the trunk"). *Phrasal coordination* links two independent clauses by using "and" but reduces any redundant elements to a phrase. It would be awkward to state "Jonah went to the doctor and Jonah got a prescription." A second independent clause is not necessary. Instead, phrasal coordination produces "Jonah went to the doctor and got a prescription." "Got a prescription" is a dependent clause because it is not a complete sentence. Speakers manipulate clausal elements to achieve economy of form.

Coordinated sentences develop in the following order (Bernstein & Levey, 2009; Bloom, 1991):

- Additive: Combining two statements that go together ("I'll color the leaves and you color the trunk").
- Temporal: Combining two statements to show a sequence of events ("He opened the door and went outside").
- Causal: Combining two statements to show that one event led to another ("She fell down and scraped her knee").
- Adversative: Combining two statements to show a contrast ("You like chocolate and I like vanilla").

Later, speakers produce coordinated sentences to convey conditional statements ("You can stay *if* you be quiet") and disjunctive relationships ("I like that shirt *although* it is not my favorite color"), and to narrate any series of events (Angell, 2009).

Complementation

Complementation is essential to sentence meaning. Recall that noun phrases and verb phrases are formed when a sentence's nouns and verbs are modified and/or complemented. Complements are clauses that follow nouns or verbs. There is some developmental information on the order of emergence of complementation (Bernstein & Levey, 2009; Bloom et al., 1980). Complements are first used with verbs that pertain to states of being, particularly states of need, feeling states, and intentions. Children's first complements are clauses that follow the state of being words "want," "like," and "need." Complementation of these verbs requires the infinitive "to + verb" to follow the state verb, as in "I want to play." (Note that "want" is a transitive verb; "I want water" would be a subject + verb + object construction.) Next, children complement verbs that signal notice, as in "see," "look," and "watch." Complementation of these verbs requires the pronoun "what" to follow the verb, as in "See what I did?" Children then typically complement verbs related to knowledge (the epistemic content category), such as "know" and "think." These verbs are followed by the pronouns "what" or "that," as in, "I think that I saw it." Then, children complement verbs related to speaking, including "ask," "tell," and "promise." Complementation of these verbs requires the infinitive "to + verb" to follow the speaking verb, as in "I promise to be quiet."

Embedding

Embedding joins subordinate clauses with main clauses. (Note that the subordinate clause is also a dependent clause, because it cannot stand alone as an independent clause.) This skill emerges in late Stage V and is refined throughout the school years. The embedded subordinate clause may be (Angell, 2009):

- A prepositional phrase (preposition + noun): "I saw her *after school.*"
- A participle phrase (a phrase that begins with a verb ending in -ing, -ed, -t, or -en: "The song *playing on the radio* is #1 this week."
- A gerund phrase (a phrase that begins with a verb ending in -ing that functions as a subject or an object): "*Singing* carols is fun," (subject); "I like *singing* carols" (object). Gerunds tend to emerge first in the object position.
- An infinitive phrase ("to" + verb): "*To sing carols* is fun" (functions as a subject); "I like *to sing carols*" (functions as a direct object); "I invited Meg *to sing carols*" (functions as an adverb modifier).

Relativization is a form of embedding. *Relative clauses* can modify the subject nouns or the object nouns of a sentence.

The clauses are introduced by the relative pronouns "who," "which," "that," "what," "whom," or "whose." Relativization produces, at minimum, complex sentences that have one main clause and one embedded relative clause (an example being, "The book *that the teacher read at school* was funny"; in this case, the subject noun is modified). Children generally produce objective relative clauses ("My mom got me the doll *that I wanted*") before they produce subjective relative clauses (Bernstein & Levey, 2009). More sophisticated child speakers can produce relative clauses that contain embedded clauses: "My mom got me the doll that I wanted to take (infinitive, direct object) *camping* (gerund) *with us* (prepositional phrase) *on the weekend* (prepositional phrase)."

Other aspects of form that allow children to learn to construct clauses are the passive voice, pronouns, conjunctions, and prepositions.

Passive Voice

In a passive sentence, the agent or actor is not the subject of the sentence. In many cases, the agent (also called the actor) is the direct object ("The winning run was hit by Brian"). Speakers may need to be as old as 11 to 13 years to completely master three forms of passive constructions (Angell, 2009):

- Reversible: "Luke was helped by Pat": If the nouns were reversed, the action of the sentence could still make sense (both could be agents).
- Agentive Nonreversible: "The book was written by Pat": The object noun is the agent, and the actions cannot be reversed.
- Instrumental Nonreversible: "Luke was helped by the medicine" or

"The book was ruined by the rain": The object noun is the agent, but it is an inanimate object and the actions cannot be reversed.

Pronouns

By school age, children typically have mastered the semantic and syntactic use of singular and plural subjective and objective personal pronouns ("I," "you," "they," "them," etc.), singular and plural possessive pronouns (including the subjective and objective variants of my [subjective]/mine [objective], our [subjective]/ours [objective], their [subjective]/theirs [objective], etc.), and singular and plural reflexive pronouns (pronouns ending in -self or -selves, as in "myself"). School-age and adolescent speakers use reflexive pronouns in the intensive pronoun form (that is, using a pronoun to add emphasis to a noun or pronoun used in a sentence [Angell, 2009]): "I would ask her to braid my friend's hair, but my sister does not have time *herself*." By school age, children use demonstrative pronouns ("this," "that," "these," "those") as specifiers and use relative pronouns ("who," "which," "that," "what," "whom," "whose") to produce relative clauses. Some wh-question words are interrogative pronouns ("who," "which," "what," "whom," "whose"). School-age speakers use many indefinite pronouns, such as "everybody," "either," "each," "much," "neither," "few," "several," "most." Some of these terms reflect conceptual knowledge of quantity, comparison, and grouping.

Conjunctions

School-age children and adolescents use a variety of advanced conjunction forms to produce coordinated sentences, complements, and clausal constructions. Conjunctions provide yet another example of how content and form are intertwined. Conjunctions are important for sentence meaning as well as for sentence construction. Three types of conjunctions (Angell, 2009) link phrases and/or clauses within sentences and provide linkages from sentence to sentence:

- Coordinating conjunctions connect ideas of equal importance; examples include "and," "or," "but," "so," "for," "yet," "nor."
- Correlative conjunctions are word pairs whose meanings are taken together; examples include "either . . . or," "neither . . . nor," "whether . . . or."
- Subordinating conjunctions introduce subordinate clauses (i.e., dependent clauses); examples include "although," "because," "as," "since," "unless."

Conjunctive adverbs have a grammatical function that is similar to conjunctions, in that they link phrases, clauses, and sentences. Examples include "therefore," "besides," "finally," "hence," "however," "thus," "otherwise," "nevertheless," "also."

Prepositions

School-age children and adolescents use a variety of advanced prepositions to describe location, direction, time (Angell, 2009), and condition. Again, content and form are interrelated, in that prepositions denote meaning but also provide form to sentences and phrases. More sophisticated prepositions that signify location include "above," "beneath," and "beyond." Direction is expressed with "through," "toward," and "about." Time prepositions include "during," "as," and "until." Some prepositions express condition. These concepts sometimes require compound prepositions (Angell, 2009), such as "according to," "in spite of," "by means of," "aside from," "instead of," and "prior to."

Later-Developing Morphology

Figure 2–3 illustrates the branches of morphology. Lexical morphology entails the free morphemes that are known as *content words, substantive words,* or *open class words.* These are the nouns, verbs, adjectives, and adverbs that form the meaning—the substantive content—of utterances. Lexical morphology includes some root words that are not independent morphemes, for example, the bound root "vert," which means "turn," and produces words like convert, subvert, avert, invert, and vertigo. Bound roots are included as lexical morphemes because their meaning is essentially that of nouns, verbs, adjectives, or adverbs.

Grammatical morphology entails the free morphemes that are known as the *function words, relational words,* or *closed class words* that contribute to the grammatical structure of utterances. These are true words, such as "of" (preposition), "for" (preposition), "an" (article), "could" (auxiliary verb or modal verb), but they occur meaningfully in sentence contexts where *they provide relational meaning between content words.* These words are sometimes referred to as the "glue" words that make sentences stick together.

School learning may emphasize working with *bound morphemes* to form words that are morphologically complex. Bound morphemes are meaningful only when combined with free morphemes and/or other bound morphemes. By themselves, bound morphemes can seem rather abstract, unless the meaning of the morpheme is known. Academic subjects like science, mathematics, and history introduce students to specific vocabulary, much of which is derived from Greek and Latin words. Learners must analyze how to form whole words using unfamiliar bound morphemes. Syntactically, learners explore how to use these constructed words in sentences and phrases. As Figure 2–3 shows, the types of bound morphemes that school-age and adolescent learners encounter include (Angell, 2009):

- *Bound roots:* (Known also as base morphemes) Bound roots are similar to root words (also called free roots or base words), except bound roots are roots that are bound morphemes, not free morphemes (true words). Bound roots form the base for the construction of words when they are attached to other free or bound morphemes. Examples of bound roots are micro-, tele-, phon-, dict-.
- *Affixes:* Bound morphemes that are attached to the beginning or ends of free or bound morphemes are affixes.
- *Prefixes* are attached to the beginnings of words or to other bound morphemes. Prefixes add additional meaning or change the meaning of the words to which they are affixed. Consider some of the many prefixes that cause a word to take on an opposite or negated meaning: a-, dis-, con-, un-, in-, ir-, im-, il-, non-, ex-, mis-. English prefixes are *derivational morphemes*: These are bound morphemes that, when attached, cause a bound

morpheme or word to change to a different part of speech and/or to change meaning (Derivational Morphemes in English, 2010).

- *Suffixes* are attached to the endings of nouns, adjectives, verbs, and adverbs or to bound morphemes. Suffixes change, enhance, or extend the meanings of words. Suffixes serve to either change or maintain the part of speech of the original word. Some English suffixes are derivational morphemes and may cause a change in part of speech. Some examples of derivational morphemes are -er (applied to a verb, such as "drive," to form a noun, "driver"), -cian (applied to the noun "music" to form the noun "musician"), -tion, -ment, -ity, -ous, -ly, -ful, -ize (Angell, 2009). Affixes may be inflectional morphemes, which do not change the part of speech of the original word. Inflectional endings can be applied to show possession (as in the pronoun "hers," or -'s added to nouns), number (plural -s and -es), gender (host*ess*), verb tense (-ed, -ing, -en), and comparison (-er, -ier, -est). Inflectional endings are usually acquired before derivational morphemes, generally by about age 7 (Angell, 2009; Owens, 2005).

When a root is combined with an affix, it forms a *stem morpheme* to which other bound morphemes can be added. For example, "believable" is a stem: It has a root (believe) plus one affix (-able). Other bound morphemes could be added, such as -ly or un- (Analysis of the English Word and Sentence Structure, 2009). Multiple affixations require complex morphological skill, and this linguistic process is essential for school learning ((Nagy et al., 2006).

School-age and adolescent learners use a variety of *compound words*, which are two free morphemes united to form a new word. Semantic considerations for compounding are apparent: The compound word may be close in meaning to its word parts ("snowball"), or the compound may offer a new meaning beyond the words from which it is formed ("passport," "butterfly," "spearmint," "hotdog," "honeymoon," "honeysuckle," "ponytail," and "blackjack" all have meanings that are not literally the compounding of their parts). Most compounds are formed as one word, but some are hyphenated ("best-seller") and some remain as two words ("tennis shoes") (Angell, 2009).

Summary: Later Developmental Expectations

In terms of an SLP's documentation of speakers' syntax in the later preschool years and into the school-age years and adolescence, it would appear that a quantitative analysis of length of utterance would not provide sufficient detail to portray whether a speaker has competent use of syntax. Moreover, as indicated earlier in this chapter, it is difficult to compare clinical MLU and T-unit analyses to published data. Rather, a qualitative examination of the syntactic forms that a speaker uses is needed to provide sufficient evidence of whether a speaker is mastering use of clausal constructions and intrasentential elements. A school-age child should not rely on the basic subject + verb + object sentence pattern but rather should use a range of elaborated constructions. An

SLP can document a speaker's frequency of use of these forms, correctness of form, and range or variability of usage, along with a description of the types of errors a speaker produces, be that omission, or nonuse, of forms or of elements within forms, substitution of forms or of elements within forms, overuse of forms or of elements within forms, or lack of generalization of forms or of elements within forms. Language samples can provide evidence of a speaker's use of the following structures that emerge in the later developmental period (cf. Owens, 2004).

Negation

- Negation that agrees with singular and plural subjects ("isn't" and "aren't"; "don't" and "doesn't") (with dialect variations noted).
- Past tense negation ("didn't").
- Negation of modals ("shouldn't").
- Indefinite negatives ("nobody," "nothing").
- Negative interrogatives ("wouldn't you like to know?").
- Negative imperatives ("be careful not to fall").
- Bound morphemes that negate ("un-," "non-," etc.).

Contractions

- Contractions of auxiliaries used in perfect verb tenses ("I'll have been walking").

Question Formation

- Question formation using "what," "where," "who," "why," "when," "how," "how come."
- Tag questions (a statement followed by a question—"he won, *didn't*

he?") (tag questions add a clause to a sentence).

Sentence Formation and Clausal Constructions (Sometimes Appearing as Noun Phrase Elaborations and Verb Phrase Elaborations)

- Intransitive verbs ("she finished").
- Imperatives ("be quiet").
- Sentence predicates following transitive verbs ("George *fixed* the computer").
- Sentence predicates following an uncontracted or contracted copula that provide the required adjective, noun, or adverb complement to the copula (uncontracted—"Karen is taller than Pam"; contracted—"She's taller than Pam" ["taller" is a predicate adjective]; or the complement to the copula could be a noun, as in "Karen is a singer," or an adverb, as in "Karen is first").
- Sentence predicates with adverbial phrases ("He walked *slowly home*") (recall that adverbs modify verbs, adjectives, or other adverbs to describe manner ["slowly," "very"], time ["recently," "before"], recurrence ["again"], and other properties).
- Sentence predicates that indicate an instrument used to complete an action ("He cut it *with a knife*").
- Using sentential coordination to combine two independent clauses into one sentence.
- Using phrasal coordination to eliminate redundant words and achieve economy of sentence form.
- Using a variety of conjunctions besides "and" to conjoin independent clauses or an

independent and a dependent clause, for example, "either," "because."

■ Using correlative conjunctions: for example, neither . . . nor, not only . . . but also, either . . . or.

■ Prepositional phrases of manner ("He read his comics at night *in secret*," "He is *in love*"), place ("We are *at home*"), and time ("I'll show you *in a minute*").

■ Relative clauses used first at the end of sentences ("This is the toy *that I want*"), then in the middle ("This is the toy *that I want* to buy Anna for her birthday"), then a relative clause as the subject of a sentence ("*Whatever* happened to your hair?" "*Whose* is this?").

■ Complement clauses that follow verbs and nouns ("George succeeds *when he tries*").

■ Multiple embedded and/or conjoined phrases in one sentence (complex clausal constructions).

Tense, Aspect, Mood, Voice

■ Participles ("walking with Grandma"), gerunds ("singing is my hobby"), infinitives ("to walk").

■ Subjunctive mood used in a dependent clause introduced by the subordinating conjunction "if" ("Is it OK if he goes") or the relative pronouns "that" ("This is the toy that I want") or "what" ("This is what I want"). The subordinating conjunction introduces a relative clause (the clause "that I want" is a post–noun modifier—an object noun complement that follows the object noun "toy"); using irregular past tense verbs that are derived from morphophonemic ("ride"

and "rode") and lexical ("go" and "went") variations.

■ Tense-aspect relations (such that time concepts of frequency, duration, continuation, or completion are described by verb usage) ("I am going home early today").

■ Modal auxiliary verbs preceding an unconjugated verb ("I might be") or within constructions of tense ("I will have been going") and aspect ("I might have won").

■ Emergence of the perfect and perfect continuous tenses for past and present, then for future (with the present and past perfect "have + verb + -en" being among the earlier forms used—"the dog has taken a bath").

■ Passive voice (used in some simple constructions, e.g., "the dog was given a bath"[6]).

Manifestations of Syntactic Impairment in the School-Age Years

The language and learning capabilities needed for early syntactic development provide the foundation for the advanced syntax used by school-age youth. Impairment of syntactic skills can negatively

---

[6]Note the similarity in form of the passive voice construction "the dog was given a bath" to the perfect tense construction in the active voice "the dog has taken a bath." This is perhaps another example of syntactic bootstrapping. Children employ generative grammar and distributional rules to formulate similar patterns of word order. In so doing, grammatical tense and grammatical voice are obtained. In this case, it might be that skill in tense has supported skill in voice.

affect successful academic learning and mastery of school curricular and instructional demands.

Language and Communication

Syntactic difficulties may persist from preschool through adolescence (Stothard et al., 1998). Less advanced development of morphology (Windsor et al., 2000) may be evidenced. Lower MLU scores and use of fewer word roots may occur (Hewitt et al., 2005). School-age children and adolescents who have difficulty constructing sentences may experience difficulty imparting complex meaning (Donahue, 1987; Leonard & Fey, 1991). Syntactic limitations can cause their pragmatic skills to appear inferior, and they can experience social penalties when speaking with children and adults because they struggle to express their ideas using effectively constructed messages. They may not be able to utilize language form sufficiently well enough to convey their pragmatic intents. The form used to construct the message may be taken for the intent of the message: Their shorter utterances and simpler, more direct messages may make them appear bold, impolite, or ill tempered. Topic management may suffer when speakers are less able to create elaborated sentences to produce extended discourse (Mentis, 1984).

Children with difficulties in language form and content (vocabulary development and/or word usage), with or without impaired discourse (pragmatic language) and/or phonology, not attributable to other primary cognitive or developmental impairments, may be diagnosed with *specific language impairment* (SLI) (Bishop & Snowling, 2004; Catts et al., 2005; Fraser et al., 2010; Leonard, 1987, 2000; Rice, 2007), as described in Chapter 1.

Impairment in Receptive Syntax

School-age children or adolescents with expressive syntax difficulties may or may not have receptive syntactic difficulty as well. Students with expressive syntactic deficits may be lacking in the foundational receptive syntactic language skills needed to derive meaning from the syntactic patterns used by the speakers in their environments. Receptive syntactic limitations may inhibit a school-age child's or adolescent's ability to process and comprehend lengthy and complex messages. As such, language and communication, both in and out of school, may suffer when the syntax of language is not readily processed, comprehended, and retained for later expressive use. It would be essentially not possible to stimulate learners to productively use syntactic patterns that are not a meaningful part of their receptive language storehouse.

Receptive language testing may reveal difficulties pertaining to processing and comprehending syntax. Students with syntactic deficits may perform less well on *tasks of sentence repetition* because they have difficulty repeating the sentence forms that they do not have in their syntactic repertoire. Receptive language testing may reveal that listeners may err when asked to *identify the meaning of sentences by pointing to a picture that is described by a sentence* (for example, to identify the meaning of "She was going to open the door," the learner should point to a picture that shows a woman who is standing in front of a closed door with her hand outstretched toward the doorknob, not to a picture of a woman walking through an open doorway, or a picture of a woman walking away from her house, or a picture of a woman sitting in a chair watching TV in a room with an open door).

As such, careful assessment of receptive syntax is warranted during formal language testing. Chapter 4 addresses these assessment considerations in greater detail.

Impairment in Syntactic Regularities and Syntactic Variation

As with early syntactic development, mature syntactic development entails simultaneously mastering the *regularities* of syntax and the *variation* inherent in sentence formation. Speakers may vary in their use of more mature and less mature forms, sometimes producing both (Eisenberg, 2006; Owens, 2004). With respect to learning syntactic regularities, school-age and adolescent speakers with language impairments may have acquired some additional patterns beyond the basic subject + verb + object patterns, but they may not have developed a full range of syntactic forms. Language may be characterized by insufficient development of the regularities of the more advanced syntactic patterns. These learners may struggle to learn regular patterns; they may seem to be haphazard in the construction of more complex utterances and their messages may be poorly constructed, agrammatical, and sometimes hard for listeners to understand. An example of a moderate level of syntactic difficulty that evidences instability in syntactic regularity and that affected message construction was evidenced by a 9-year-old child: "Brittany coming with me before I have recess Mr. Goldman get something." An example of a milder level of syntactic error produced by a fifth grader that evidences instability in syntactic regularity is "He is all the time lately" (instead of "He is late all of the time"). A minimal error of syntactic

regularity produced by a fifth grader is "I went to the bank for I could get money" (Josephson & Gordon Pershey, 2007).

To help learners acquire *syntactic regularities,* speech-language interventions can address gaining skill using regular patterns, such as conventional construction of clauses and noun phrase and verb phrase elaborations. Direct modeling and teaching of the structures that emerge in the later developmental period can be useful. Nonschool speech-language interventions can stimulate the use of syntactic forms that are useful in daily living and social situations. School-based interventions can offer the chance to learn the syntactic forms that are used in the context of class work, classroom routines, and other school activities, both curricular and extracurricular. Although learning syntax often necessitates a slot-filling, drill-and-practice approach to sentence patterning, curriculum content can provide the context from which the practice words and forms are drawn. In this way, language growth is embedded within learning the language used in the classroom. Working on receptive comprehension of the syntax used in classroom materials might doubly serve to reinforce the student's learning of classroom material. The use of class work during expressive syntactic practice can help establish the language skills that can enhance classroom participation.

In addition to class work, SLPs can arrange for opportunities for peer-to-peer conversational practice that can build syntax skills. Noncurricular functional language that allows students to share their out-of-school experiences with their schoolmates and that allows students to connect life experiences to school learning is beneficial to school success. The fairly repetitive content of peer-to-peer conversations can reinforce syntactic regularities.

Many learners with syntactic impairments show some degree of weakness in generating *syntactic variety*. As such, these speakers would be less adept at using productive variations in syntactic constructions but would rely on known syntactic regularities. Syntax is not an isolated skill: Pragmatic competence is in part dependent upon use of variable syntactic patterns. Syntactic variation is important for success in interpersonal communications. The pragmatic expectations of different social registers require speakers to vary the surface structures of their productions. Grice's (1975) rule of "quantity" (i.e., don't say too much or too little) might be violated, in that shorter, regularized utterance patterns might be viewed as production of an insufficient quantity of language for a given situation. Elaborated and varied syntax is needed for developing language beyond conversational abilities to production of narration and, later on in the school years and teen years, for exposition (e.g., linguistic contexts such as responding in class, public speaking, formal reporting, and providing information in work settings). SLPs would encourage speakers to develop their use of syntactic patterns, moving speakers from a limited, restricted repertoire of overlearned syntactic patterns to the ability to innovate new syntactic forms. Speech-language therapy would provide the opportunity to *rephrase deep structures by using a variety of surface structures*. Noun phrase and verb phrase elaborations are essential structures for learning syntactic variety. Opportunities to increase syntactic variation include *practice with syntactic synonymy, sentence combining (arranging two short sentences into one longer, more complex sentence), and clausal embedding*. Role-play can simulate the pragmatic settings where different structures are appropriate, or contextualized language interventions can offer supported opportunities for using syntactic variety. Similarly, Fey et al. (2003) recommended that grammar interventions should take place in the context of meaningful conversation or classroom routines and that oral language and written language facilitation should be complementary.

African American English Features of Morphology and Syntax

African American English (AAE) is a rule-governed system. While some language researchers considered AAE to be a distinct language, involving its own form, content, and use (e.g., Van Keulen et al., 1998), others (Battle, 2009, 2011; Campbell, 1993; Craig et al., 1998; Roseberry-McKibbin, 2007, 2008) suggested that AAE is a dialect of GAE. A dialect is a rule-governed variation of a language. A number of factors contribute to whether children use AAE, including exposure to dialect, children's gender (Craig et al., 1998), age (Craig et al., 2003a; Isaacs, 1996; Ivy & Masterson, 2011), socioeconomic status (Craig et al., 1998; Roseberry-McKibbin, 2008), and home environment and daily experiences (Jackson & Roberts, 2001; Roseberry-McKibbin, 2007, 2008). Use of AAE is a language difference, not a language impairment. Some observations about use of AAE are:

- Not all speakers who are African American use AAE syntax and morphology.
- Some speakers who are not African American use AAE syntax and

morphology (generally because of exposure to dialect); some forms used in AAE are used by speakers of other dialects, in slang, in casual English, and in art forms such as rap music.

- Not all speakers use all of the dialect features.
- Not all speakers use the syntactic and morphological features of AAE to the same degree.
- Not all speakers of AAE use this dialect on all occasions or with the same regularity; speakers may code-switch.
- Speakers may use the dialect features in some words, sentences, or phrasing contexts, but not in others (for example, this sentence spoken by a store security guard, a speaker of AAE: "Leave all bag and packages at the counter"; the speaker used a form variation for plural nouns on "bag" but not on "packages," perhaps with the nonuse of the pluralizing morpheme being differentially influenced for the -s versus the -es morpheme) (note that this is known as "zero use" or "zero marking" of the plural -s, rather than as a morphophonological omission).

- Use of variations in syntax and morphology may vary across oral and written language, with features used inconsistently across the two modalities.
- Speakers' use of features and patterns vary by geographical regions of the United States, with each regional dialect adding its own characteristics to AAE (e.g., AAE in New York City is not the same as AAE in Montgomery, Alabama, in syntax, morphology, phonology, semantics, or pragmatics).

Table 2–9 shows some of the semantic and morphological features of AAE (cf. Craig et al., 2003b; Fogel & Ehri, 2006; Roseberry-McKibbin, 2007, 2008).

The following sources are useful for learning about language form in culturally and linguistically diverse speakers: Battle (2009, 2011), Bedore and Peña (2008), Craig and Washington (2004a, 2004b), Craig et al. (1998), Crowley (2003), Cruz-Ferreira (2010), Garrity and Oetting (2010), Goldstein (2000, 2006, 2011), Gutiérrez-Clellen and Peña (2001), Jackson and Pearson (2010), Jackson and Roberts (2001), Johnson (2005), Paradis et al. (2011), Pearson (2009), and Roseberry-McKibbin (2007, 2008).

Table 2–9. African American English as Related to Syntax and Morphology

Syntax
Grammatical Tense and Grammatical Aspect
Forms of "to be"
Nonuse of forms of "to be," copular and auxiliary (present, past, future tenses) (zero use or zero marking of the copula) She sick (She is sick) (copula) (present) I not saying you can't go (I'm not saying you can't go) (auxiliary) (present) You not having a good day (You are not having a good day) (auxiliary) (present) She at home last night (She was at home last night) (copula) (past) He going home tomorrow (He is going home tomorrow) (auxiliary) (future)
Forms of "have"
Nonuse of the auxiliary "have" in past perfect and perfect continuous tenses (zero use or zero marking of the auxiliary) I done my work (I have done my work) Yous had yours (You have had yours)
Nonuse of the auxiliary "have" (zero marking) in past perfect and past perfect continuous tenses; perfective "been" insertion to indicate past tense (connotes distant past or final completion) ("been" may substitute for another auxiliary or content-form construction) I been had that teacher's class last year (I had that teacher's class last year) I been done with that (I am done with that) I been known that; I been done known that (I have known that; I have always known that; I already know that)
Forms of "do"
"Done" used for "did" You done it (You did it) It was not something I done (It was not something I did)
Past tense "done" inserted to connote completion (completive "done") (double marks the past) He done did that (He did that) He done sold it (He sold it) I been done known that (I have known that; I have always known that; I already know that)

Table 2–9. *continued*

"Do" used for "does" (third person singular); "don't" used for "doesn't" (third person singular) It do snow a lot in January (It does snow a lot in January) Where do she have her hair done at? (Where does she have her hair done?) He don't have a pet (He doesn't have pet)
Nonuse or zero marking of the auxiliary "do" Where she have the party at? (Where did she have the party?) Where she have her hair done at? (Where does she have her hair done?)
Nonuse or zero marking of the progressive -ing Where she have the party at? (Where is she having the party?) (present tense) Where she have the party at? (Where was she having the party?) (past tense) Where she have the party at? (or, Where she gonna have the party at?) (Where will she be having the party?) (future tense) What she run for? (What is she running for) (present tense) Why she say that? (Why is she saying that? also, Why did she say that?) (present tense, past tense) When she play that? (When is she playing that? also, When did she play that? When will she play that?) (present tense, past tense, future tense) (Note there is not necessarily an inversion of subject and verb in question formation)
Nonuse (zero marking) of past tense -ed, -d (affects some pronunciations of irregular verbs) He play baseball in high school (He played baseball in high school) He say I can't go (He said I can't go) I ask her did she like it (I asked her if she liked it)
Grammatical Person and Grammatical Number
Forms of "to be"
"Be" used in place of conjugated forms of "to be" as a copula or auxiliary to describe a current state of being She be sick (She is sick) We be in the same class (We are in the same class) We be sitting in the same row (We are sitting in the same row) Sometimes it be that way (Sometimes it is that way)

continues

Table 2–9. *continued*

"Be" used in place of conjugated forms of "to be" (Known as the *invariant be* or *distributive be*, to connote the distant past, events over time, or a condition that is not changing) That be an old story (That's an old story) (Distant past) She be my mom's teacher and mine (She was my mom's teacher and mine) (State of events over time) He be having a rough time (He has been having a rough time) (State of events over time) That be my watch (That is my watch) (A condition that is not changing)
Person and number agreement in forms of "to be" Present tense "is" used for "are" (first, second, and third person, singular and plural) Tim, you is not going (Tim, you are not going) We is going (We are going) Is they going? (Are they going?) Past tense "was" used for "were" (first, second, and third person, singular and plural) We was going (We were going) Sophia, you was right (Sophia, you were right) Was they going? (Were they going?)
Person and number agreement in conjugated forms She see him (She sees him) (third person singular -s is nonused or zero marked) She have a cold (She has a cold) (irregular third person variant)
Grammatical Mood
Future tense "gonna" used for "is going to" and "are going to"; "will" and "won't" She gonna take that home (She is going to take that home; She will take that home) They gonna buy some (They are going to buy some; They will buy some) Where she gonna have the party at? (or, Where she have the party at?) (Where will she have the party?) She not gonna let them win (She won't let them win)
Multiple modal auxiliaries I might could have won (I might have won; I could have won)

Table 2–9. *continued*

Modal intention
"I'mma," "bouta," "fixin' to," or "fitna" (He fitna get ready to go) (He bouta get ready to go)

Negation

"Not" used without auxiliary forms of "to be" (Nonuse of auxiliary)

I not saying you can't go (I am not saying you can't go)

"Ain't" used for "not," "do/did/does not," "have/has not" (past, present, future tense)

I ain't saying you can't go (I am not saying you can't go") (present)

I ain't said you can't go (I did not say you can't go") (past)

They ain't gone there (They have not gone there) (past)

I ain't had dinner yet (I have not had dinner yet) (future)

You ain't have to go (You don't have to go) (future)

Multiple negatives ("no" or "none" used for "any")

I ain't got none (I don't have any)

Ain't nobody got none? (Doesn't anybody have any?)

Can't nobody win (Nobody can win)

Question Formation

Question formation without subject-predicate inversion

Why you not got your light on? (Why don't you have your light on?)

Where she have the party at? (Where did she have the party?)

Add "at" to "where" questions—double marks place

Where your friend at? (Where is your friend?)

Where you at now? (Where are you now?)

Where she have the party at? (Where is she having the party?)

Embedded questions use "did" instead of "if"

I ask her did she like it (I asked her if she liked it)

Noun and Pronoun Use

Subject expression (also called appositive pronoun) (subject noun restated by a pronoun)

My mother, she at work (My mother is at work)

My father, he say I can't go (My father said I can't go)

continues

Table 2–9. *continued*

"Them" used for "those"
Them boys in my class (Those boys are in my class)
She took them puppies home (She took those puppies home)

Pronoun determiners are double marked
That there man need help (That man needs help)

Lexical Usage

"Got" used for "had"
I got three weeks' vacation (I had three weeks' vacation)

Indefinite article "a" used for "an" (before words beginning with a vowel)
A apple (An apple)

Morphophonological Features

Possessive -'s is nonused or zero marked
He went to Hillary house (He went to Hillary's house)

Plural -s is nonused or zero marked
He got two bag (He got two bags)

Reduplicated or reinterpreted -s (some words, e.g., girlses, mens, womens, yous)
Those shoes are for girlses (Those shoes are for girls)
They give the better jobs to the mens (They give the better jobs to the men)

CHAPTER 3

Cognitive-Linguistic, Psycholinguistic, and Pragmatic Language Factors That Influence the Competent Use of Grammar and Syntax Throughout Childhood and Adolescence

This chapter describes the cognitive-linguistic, psycholinguistic, and pragmatic language factors that influence how, by about age 4, typically developing children would have acquired the foundations for competent use of English grammar and syntax. The theoretical and empirical perspectives described in this chapter inform why SLPs would consider learners' cognitive and pragmatic language abilities as a basis for their development of grammatical and syntactic skills. The relationship of pragmatic language competence to syntactic skills is addressed.

Anticipation Guide

After reading this chapter, readers will be able to answer the following questions:

- What are the cognitive-linguistic factors that contribute to grammatical and syntactic competence?
- How do theories of information processing contribute to a professional knowledge base about grammatical and syntactic competence?

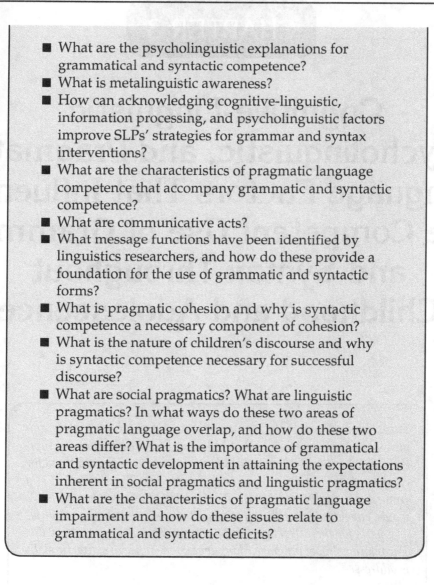

- What are the psycholinguistic explanations for grammatical and syntactic competence?
- What is metalinguistic awareness?
- How can acknowledging cognitive-linguistic, information processing, and psycholinguistic factors improve SLPs' strategies for grammar and syntax interventions?
- What are the characteristics of pragmatic language competence that accompany grammatic and syntactic competence?
- What are communicative acts?
- What message functions have been identified by linguistics researchers, and how do these provide a foundation for the use of grammatic and syntactic forms?
- What is pragmatic cohesion and why is syntactic competence a necessary component of cohesion?
- What is the nature of children's discourse and why is syntactic competence necessary for successful discourse?
- What are social pragmatics? What are linguistic pragmatics? In what ways do these two areas of pragmatic language overlap, and how do these two areas differ? What is the importance of grammatical and syntactic development in attaining the expectations inherent in social pragmatics and linguistic pragmatics?
- What are the characteristics of pragmatic language impairment and how do these issues relate to grammatical and syntactic deficits?

The Magic of Turning 4

Based on the extensive information on the development of grammar and syntax reported in Chapter 2, it is reasonable to conclude that children within the 4-year to 5-year age range typically reach a fair degree of syntactic competence. It seems that when children reach the age of 4 or so and continue to advance in their language skills, they can efficiently use language and become fully participating conversational partners with adults. Their semantic skills advance beyond the Bloom and Lahey (1978) content categories outlined in Chapter 2. Their vocabularies have grown, and they express their knowledge and experiences using semantically and conceptually appropriate wording that is arranged within a fairly complete grammatical and syntactic repertoire. They have vocabulary words for ideas ("e.g., "important," "by accident," "making choices"), concepts (e.g., "it's like . . ." or "it's not like . . .," "better than," "favorite," "sometimes"), feelings (e.g., "scared," "excited," "left out," "proud"), and complex states of being (e.g., being "not sure," "in charge," or "helpful"). Much of their conversation is mentally reflective and may be evaluative of themselves and their surroundings. They discuss their memories of the past and their plans for the future. They are aware of what they know and can do, and of what they do not know and cannot do.

No wonder it all seems magical. Such complicated thought and language is being accomplished by a person who has been on this earth for only about 4 or 5 years!

So, what are the sources of this magic? As described by Dick et al. (2004), several biological and psychological origins contribute to how language learners typically acquire the ability to use the linguistic rules and regularities that are needed for competent performance in grammar and syntax. For a developing language user, if these rules and regularities are inconsistently used or are absent, syntactic performance is considered to be impaired. Dick et al. (2004, p. 361) stated that disparities in how well children use the rules and regularities can be attributed to its being the product of some "language performance factor." The variables that underlie this language performance factor are the subject of linguists' and psychologists' theoretical discourses, primarily related to cognitive-linguistic or psycholinguistic explanations for language competence, which situate language not as a self-developing faculty, as Chomsky (1965, 1968) proposed, but rather hold that language is a faculty that

is dependent upon cognitive operations for its growth. Cognitive-linguistic and psycholinguistic explanations for grammatical and syntactic abilities are the topic of later sections of this chapter.

Another school of thought, somewhat different in its approach to identifying the origins of the ability to use linguistic rules and regularities, is *systemic functional linguistics* (SFL; Halliday, 1973, 1975) (see Chapter 2 and Figure 2–2). Here, the theoretical basis that explains syntactic competence is built upon a performance factor within the domains of language themselves, that being the foundational premise of pragmatic language competence. The pragmatic foundations for grammatical and syntactic maturity are described later in this chapter.

Cognitive-Linguistic Competence as Foundational to Grammatical and Syntactic Skills

Cognitive-linguistic competence appears to be a precondition that children need so that they can talk about the ideas, concepts, feelings, and states of being described above, among many other cognitive-linguistic concepts that emerge as children learn. Grammar and syntax flourish when children are thinking complex thoughts and represent these thoughts semantically in the words they speak. As Figure 1–1 in Chapter 1 depicts, content and form interface. But Figure 1–1 doesn't show what this linguistic interface allows speakers to do, which is to speak their thoughts and express their mental reasoning. Cognition is notably absent from this model of the components of language. Thought is presumed to be the impetus for language, but it is not explicitly depicted in this model.

Because sematic language is the storehouse of words, and words represent concepts, cognition might be thought of as integral to the semantic domain. Even so, cognition, as a precondition to semantic and syntactic competence, deserves consideration.

Cognition is a term that describes *thinking—the various mental processes that include perception, awareness, attention, memory, comprehension, reasoning, organization, problem-solving, judgment, planning, self-regulation, imagination, and intuition.* Both cognition and language are innate properties of the brain and mind, and these faculties are evidenced by children's performance of developmentally appropriate cognitive and linguistic behaviors. For over a century scientists, linguists, and philosophers have debated whether and how language and cognition are related mental faculties. There are some cognitive tasks that can be accomplished without language (for example, thinking about motor planning, or thinking in visual images instead of words), but, arguably, there are no language tasks that are accomplished without elements of cognition infused. Or, reductively, it would be difficult to identify how cognition is absent from language use. At minimum, semantic memory needs to be engaged for language to be used. Because the field of speech-language pathology tends to focus on language to a greater extent than on cognition, but because the intellect that contributes to grammatical and syntactic competence is dependent upon cognitive operations, it is important to address the cognitive considerations that can contribute to effective diagnostic and therapeutic practices. Two fundamental questions would be: How do language and thought interface? Is language a part of thinking or is language a separate skill?

Cognitive Connectionism

Nelson (2010) summarized the contributions of theorists who promoted the theory of *cognitive connectionism,* including Bates and MacWhinney (1987), Tomasello (2003), Tomasello and Bates (2001), and Tomasello and Slobin (2005). Cognitive connectionism suggested that language arises from cognitive processes, including attention, perception, memory, information processing, and pattern recognition. Rather than proposing an innate language instinct, where language is thought to be a separate mental operation (cf. Chomsky, 1965, 1968), the cognitive connectionists maintained that the brain has the ability to form the neural connections that correspond to learning the patterns of language. *Syntax would expand from a foundation of neural patterns. Moreover, the neural patterns responsible for syntax flourish when children are engaged in complex thinking.*

Simply put, to view syntactic development from a cognitivist perspective suggests that language is enhanced because a thinking child is immersed in an intellectually stimulating environment. Language is a means to represent thought and externalizes what a child is thinking about internally. The brain and mind externalize their cognitions by choosing and using linguistic symbols (i.e., speech sounds, words, and sentence forms). *Cognition is the impetus for language, cognition subserves language,* and *cognition promotes language.*

Cognitivists are scientific investigators who rely on empirical observations of behaviors to determine the presence of cognitive or linguistic skills (Kuhl, 2010). Children's language reveals their underlying cognitive development. Reciprocally, children's cognitive development reveals their preparedness to use applicable lexical and grammatical elements. In the cognitivist view, cognition and language skills should be commensurate, given their unimpaired attainment of developmental regularities. At all age levels, children's cognitive and linguistic skills would be proportionate, reciprocal, and interdependent. Piaget, a cognitivist (Ginsburg & Opper, 1979; Piaget, 1952, 1954), proposed that children's intellectual mastery of progressively more complicated logical reasoning and problem-solving tasks underlies children's advances in language development. As cognitive development advances, so does language. The cognitive maturation that precedes or co-occurs with early language emergence is characteristic of the first of four stages of cognitive development, the sensorimotor period, which lasts from birth through about age 2, when children's early reflexes give way to motor learning. The subsequent three stages of cognitive development are, in brief, the preoperational period, from 2 through 7 years, when children learn problem-solving skills and develop competent use of the semantic content categories and syntactic forms described in Chapter 2, when grammar and syntax burgeon. Concrete operations, from 7 to 11 years, is when children acquire logical thinking and conceptual development, and when syntax matures to include most adult constructions. The fourth stage, formal operations, from 11 to 15 years, is when abstract thinking develops more fully and when syntax can reflect hypothetical reasoning and combine multiple linguistic propositions. Examples of the grammar and syntax used in the stages of concrete operations and formal operations are provided in Chapters 4, 5, and 6, when more advanced language and literacy skills are described.

The accomplishments of each of the cognitive stages of development would suggest the need for children to acquire co-occurring words. For example, children would acquire locative action words to represent the physical movements that are integral to their sensorimotor experiences, such as "move," "push," and "throw"; logical thinking during the preoperational, concrete operations, and formal operations stages would require mental state words, such as "suppose" and "predict." To develop a child's language, the first step is to develop a child's thought. A cognitivist, such as Piaget (Ginsburg & Opper, 1979; Piaget, 1952, 1954), might envision that the mind of the young child would say, "What I can think about, I can talk about. If I can think about it, I can talk about it."

Information Processing and Syntactic Abilities

Some descriptions of cognitive processes compare the operations of the human brain to how a computer processes information. This analogy yields descriptions of how the brain processes, stores, and recalls information. The physical brain, likened to the computer hardware, uses its processing operations (the software, as it were) to enact the workings of the mind, the emotions, and all other capabilities of human performance (cf. Owens, 2004). *Grammar and syntax are made possible by the brain's myriad patterns of activation, connectivity, and processing.*

Information processing theory explores the workings of the brain's "storage units," those being the brain centers that neurobiological research has identified as being responsible for human capabilities. Not only does the brain store information, but it also activates, or reactivates, information that it has stored. The interconnections among brain regions result in a multitude of activation patterns (Kuhl, 2010). If this is the case, information processing theory could describe how grammatical and syntactic patterns come to be used repeatedly. More frequent usage of these patterns would result in continuous strengthening of these connections. Syntactic *productivity* might be a consequence of innumerate activation patterns along with the unlimited novel, creative variations that the brain allows within these patterns. This is because, unlike a computer, a brain is capable of original thought. A brain searches for patterns of occurrence, but a brain also originates its own occurrences. A brain can originate thought that has minimal relationship to any patterns or occurrences it has witnessed. Human behavior is unpredictable; ingenuity and creativity are unbounded; new connections are all predicated on having enriching learning experiences as a basis for cognitive growth.

Furthermore, computers are programmed for resource allocation. A computer system has a finite capacity of resources to draw upon, and the computer's performance is affected by how the computer manages and allocates resources during tasks. The brain has its resource limitations as well, and human performance is dependent upon how well the brain allocates resources to tasks. It could be maintained that SLPs' and teachers' emphasis on grammatical and syntactic skills teaches the learner's brain to allocate resources to these operations. The brain may come to expect to allocate resources to syntax. A learner might mentally perceive this resource allocation as a cognitive or psychological need or desire to learn more about grammar and syntax.

Familiarity with grammar and syntax skills might make learners feel motivated and comfortable when they are learning more skills in this domain. In some ways, it can be said that practice might not make perfect, but practice can make for the brain's regular allocation of resources. Resource allocation can make for an expectation that a concept or skill will be experienced more often and to a greater extent. In this way, the brain is primed *repeatedly* for learning about grammar and syntax.

Resource allocation also relates to efficiency, speed, and competency when learning. Learners improve their functioning when given practice and repeated experiences. Psychologists have differentiated between the learning and performance behaviors of "novices" and "experts" (Dreyfus & Dreyfus, 1980, 1986). Language users begin as novices and need time and practice to become experts. Novices allocate attention and energy more consciously and deliberately than experts do; novices have not yet developed an "auto pilot" for cruising through tasks with little effort. Experts have strong connections and associations for the familiar tasks they perform. *Language learners need repetition, review, and practice to move from novice to expert skill.*

The brain, like a computer, performs *serial processing* (which means doing one thing and then another, in succession) and *parallel processing* (doing more than one thing at a time, or multitasking). Although parallel processing taxes the brain's resources, being able to coordinate multiple physiological and cognitive tasks is essential. A notable example of parallel processing is that children learn language as they learn how to play (Lenneberg, 1967; Westby, 2000). Thus, the ability to parallel process is foundational to language growth. Moreover, language itself is a parallel processing task because the domains of language are used simultaneously.

This line of reasoning would suggest that *the brain is primed to learn grammar and syntax in the context of engaging in other cognitive and physical activities.* Syntactic learning would be embedded, for example, in the enjoyment of poems, stories, and songs, and in creating messages to share with other people, perhaps through audio or video recordings of spoken language or in written communication formats. Grammar and syntax drills would represent serial processing tasks, where elements of form are learned one at a time, which is a necessary step to call a learner's attention to these elements and introduce new information at a manageable pace. But drill would be deemphasized as soon as it is reasonable to do so, to allow the brain to engage in the parallel processing of language along with other activities, in recognition of what the brain is designed to do naturally. *Parallel processing provides a credible rationale for contextualizing the learning of grammar and syntax within authentic, meaningful, and enjoyable language activities.*[1]

There is evidence that the brain is an information processing system that can change how it functions because of its experiences. Hebb's (1949) theory, which has been sloganized as "neurons that fire together wire together," suggested that brain cells change when they stimulate the activation of other cells. These "cell assemblies" benefit the efficiency of the activator and activated cells. *The brain benefits from its own experiences.* Notably, the brain is endowed with *neural plasticity* (or some-

times referred to as "neuroplasticity"): The brain's experiences can change the brain's activation patterns and cellular structure (Michelon, 2008). In computer terminology, the term "configuration" applies to how the components of hardware and software are arranged and interconnected. When life experiences cause the brain to activate differently and arrange new activation patterns and interconnections, it can be said that experiences change the configuration of the brain and result in reconfiguration.

As one example, studies using neuroimaging technologies provided evidence of how learning experiences can result in *neuroplastic reconfiguration* of the language areas of the brain in persons with dyslexia. Brain activation patterns of individuals who had been taught specific reading strategies showed different patterns of activation at pre- and postintervention (Shaywitz, 2003). Some medical practitioners suggested that changes in brain activation and configuration can be seen in various brain regions after therapeutic application of certain learned behaviors intended to alleviate conditions that have a biochemical, brain-and-mind interface, such as fatigue, anger, anxiety, depression, and difficulties in attention and concentration (Amen, 1998). Even if some of this intervention evidence would be discounted owing to the difficulty of replicating identical teaching treatment conditions across numerous cases of matched participants, it is undeniable that daily learning changes the brain. From moment to moment, the plastic brain, as a processing system, is not a static entity, and hence its capabilities are always in flux. The "hardware" changes its physical composition and the "software" changes its functionality because of their exposure to learning and experiences, which take place in the context of expression of the

---

[1]See Owens (2004) for a discussion of simultaneous coding (the higher-level thought processes that allow the meaning of language to be synthesized) and successive coding (the linear processing that allows for using the components of language content and form).

individual's genetic propensities, over-all state of health, ingested nutrients and chemicals, maturation, and/or aging and degeneration, which themselves also instigate neural changes.

The configuration of the brain can change simply because of the passage of time. In children, neural maturation is apparent (Kuhl, 2010; Lenneberg, 1967) and has been seen to coincide with emergence of behavioral and learning capabilities, including the "vocabulary explosion" and onset of syntax that occur at about age 2 (Hahne et al., 2004; Mills et al., 2005; Rivera-Gaxiola et al., 2005; Silva-Pereyra et al., 2005). In older individuals' brains, reduced brain activity and/or degeneration of the composition of brain structures are readily apparent via neuroimaging techniques (Amen, 1998).

The cognitivist perspectives and the analogies to information processing have several implications for speech-language diagnostic and therapy practices, which include:

- There is a relationship between brain development and language development. As a child's brain matures, its structures and its processing activity change over time. Brain development leads to language development, and language development changes the brain; this growth is "bidirectional" (Clancy & Finlay, 2001). Repeated exposure to grammatical and syntactic structures is crucial to enhance the activation patterns that are necessary for cognitive-linguistic facility and resourcefulness.

- Brain areas work together. Speech-language interventions can capitalize on how the brain is

designed to allocate its resources to simultaneously attend, process, store, and retrieve. The brain is designed to transfer information across the sensory, language, affective, cognitive, and language processing areas. Therefore, children respond to lively, multisensory experiences that provoke an affective response, which may be thought of as "making learning fun." (For example, singing an amusing song, with bodily movements, can teach syntactic concepts to younger children. A "me, myself, and I" song might teach pronouns. School-age learners might draw clever cartoons to illustrate syntactic relationships anthropomorphized by parts of speech "characters.") Children, when pleasantly engaged, are using parallel processing and are not consciously aware that they are completing repeated practice tasks.

- Because the brain is a processing system with dedicated areas for receptive language, expressive language, memory, affect, cognition, reading, and the motor control needed to accomplish speech, handwriting, or keyboarding, persons can have differential strengths and weaknesses in their language abilities. Grammatical and syntactic abilities inform listening and reading comprehension and oral and written expression, and individuals may exhibit variable skill levels across these modalities.

- Literacy development entails learning how to perform conscious inspection of the grammar and syntax of text, along with the activation of individual processors for phonemes, alphabetic symbols, word meaning, and text meaning (as popularized by Adams, 1990) (see Chapters 4, 5, and 6). The processing analogy contributes to designing teaching and therapy techniques to help learners identify the specific elements of language they are attending to during reading and writing tasks (Moats, 2000).

In conclusion, taken together, the connectionist and information processing theories, which explain how cognition subserves language, serve as a reminder that language does not exist as a unitary human faculty (Kuhl, 2010) and that grammar and syntax are not isolated skills. Even though the brain has language centers, language is not a unitary faculty of the mind. These connectionist theories reinforce the position that an SLP is responsible for treating a "whole" individual, not just stimulating isolated performances of language. Clinical skills for diagnosing a syntactic language deficit and then planning and executing therapy depend upon the clinician's observations of the connections between cognition and language, with related consideration of perceptual and motor skills, social development, cultural factors, and environmental conditions. Assessments and interventions address how the child's language development manifests these various factors.

Psycholinguistic Explanations for Grammatical and Syntactic Abilities

Psycholinguistics, a domain of study within two fields, psychology and linguis-

tics, investigates *the interface of thought and language*. Psycholinguistic research delves into the numerous ways that *thought, cognition, and language are reciprocal processes*.

As a domain of psychology, *psycholinguistics explores how the human mind is organized to generate and process language. Theoretical and empirical research is concerned with how the mind works when language is being used. The purpose is to discover what the mind of a language user is doing. It appears that when language is in use the mind is engaging certain conscious ideas and intellectual faculties, along with activating unconscious processes, memories, and reflexive or instinctual behaviors.* Language users thus experience unconscious and conscious use of their stored systems of grammar and syntax. Speech-language interventions might be a means for enhancing the unconscious, productive use of grammar and syntax, or may offer learners strategies for developing their conscious examination of grammatical and syntactic structures. Chapters 5 and 6 consider these intervention options in the context of enhancing reading, writing, and academic success.

As a domain of linguistics, psycholinguistic investigations are both theoretical and empirical. *Psycholinguistics explores how speakers acquire and use a set of internal rules for the production of grammar and syntax and how speakers process the meanings of words.*

Psycholinguistics is also concerned with how the mind works when language is being thought about consciously, that is, what the mind is doing when language users are self-aware of their language use. *Metalinguistic awareness* is a language user's ability to explore language itself. Language users are able to consider language as an object for exploration and manipulation (Britton, 1984). Metalinguistic awareness is foundational to literacy because printed symbols must be consciously manipulated. Psycholinguists study the mental processes involved during the use of print, and the similarities and differences in brain activity during oral language and written language. Children develop the complex ability to use language to learn to read and to manipulate the components and structures of written language. Metalinguistic ability contributes to developing sophisticated vocabulary and syntax skills and to comprehending higher-level oral language and written text. In addition, empirical psycholinguistic research explores how the brain organizes motor control for speech. Speech is examined as a rule-governed intellectual process that interfaces with motor skill. It would seem that the daily practices of SLPs are continual demonstrations of applied psycholinguistics.

From a psycholinguistic perspective, language is a complex mechanism that involves five main properties (Bloom & Lahey, 1978): (1) language is a code, (2) language represents ideas about the world, (3) language is a system, (4) language is a convention, and (5) language is used for communication. Language emerges as a child's brain develops the psycholinguistic capacity to generate the rule-governed systems that constitute language. In this competence-based model, children with language difficulties may struggle to conceptualize language as a code, to represent ideas by using language, to learn the systems of language, to learn the conventions of language, and/or to communicate. These difficulties may inhibit a child's communicative competence (Hymes, 1971).

Dick et al. (2004) recounted an alternative psycholinguistic model that differs from a competence-based model. The Competition Model (Bates et al., 2001;

Bates & MacWhinney, 1987; MacWhinney, 1987; MacWhinney & Bates, 1989) is a connectionist model that characterizes linguistic knowledge not as a set of rules but as a complex network of "form-meaning mappings" (p. 361) that grow stronger over time. Learners acquire lexical, syntactic, morphological, and prosodic "cues" for universal meanings (e.g., language universals such as word order, the agent role in an utterance, or subject-verb agreement). The receptive language system is exposed to these constructions repeatedly. To produce language, the expressive language system then considers and weighs "probabilistic values . . . until the system settles into the best available fit between meaning and form" (Dick et al., 2004, p. 361). Language development involves "a gradual process of the tuning of these mappings" (Dick et al., 2004, p. 361). In this model, a well-formed language system is predicated upon how well the system acquires and stores its cues and calculates probability. When an individual is mentally constructing an utterance, within a span just a fraction of a second, the psycholinguistic system maps the syntactic form needed onto the meaning of the words. This is done by using probability of fit to yield accuracy. Meaning, form, and function are weighted and assembled. The system determines the probability that groups of words joined together will function to convey the appropriate meanings when the words are used together. This includes applying the right grammatical structures. This activity occurs second by second, moment by moment, whenever verbal thought—that is, thinking in sentences—and spoken language are needed. Written language would be considered to require the extra steps of writing down these verbal assemblies.

This model may account for why semantic and syntactic deficits may co-occur. Syntactic immaturity would mean that the form-meaning mapping is somehow faulty, and the cue and probability systems are not subserving the construction of grammatical utterances. For comparatively competent language users, such as older children and teens with mild to moderate language impairments or specific learning disabilities, it's sometimes difficult to extricate semantic difficulties from syntactic difficulties. A differential diagnosis is elusive because the parts of the system are not meant to be disassociated. The system is meant to be the sum of its parts, not the workings of the parts themselves.

Therefore, in summary, the psycholinguistic examination of thought and language attempts to uncover the activity of the brain, the nature of the mind, and the human capacity for generating the rule-governed systems that constitute language and speech. More information on psycholinguistic explanations of grammar and syntax is available from Bergmann et al. (2007), Berko Gleason and Bernstein Ratner (1997), Field (2003), Harley (2008), and Pinker (2007).

Pragmatic Language Competence as Foundational to Grammatical and Syntactic Skills

This section describes the linguistic study of pragmatics and the pragmatic properties of message function, *cohesion*, and discourse, and then considers the relationship of pragmatic competence to grammatic and syntactic abilities.

Pragmatics is the branch of linguistics that explores the use, purpose, and intention of spoken and written messages. Pragmatic language skill involves using language at length, in a coordinated fashion, with elaboration and complexity, in order to engage in interpersonal communication, to narrate experiences or events, and to speak publicly to a group or an audience. Interaction takes place during face-to-face verbal or signed communication but also when an individual is reading or writing any form of printed text. Inherent to pragmatic language skills are sentence-level meaning making and processing abilities. Messages are shaped in part by their grammatical and syntactic components. Sentence-level skills for effective reading comprehension and written expression are discussed in Chapters 5 and 6, respectively.

The pragmatic-syntactic relationship is not only an expressive language achievement. Pragmatic competence involves both receptive and expressive language capabilities. Each communicative interchange involves a *locutionary act*, an *illocutionary act*, and a *perlocutionary act* (Searle, 1971; Strawson, 1971). The locutionary act is the words and sentences that are spoken or written (in print, this includes punctuation and other print devices, as well as symbols and graphics). The illocutionary act (sometimes called the illocutionary force) is the speaker or writer's intended meaning, and the perlocutionary act is what the listener or reader interprets the message to mean. (A fourth component, the perlocutionary effect [sometimes called the perlocutionary force] is the effect of the message on the receiver. The speaker's intended meaning of a message may or may not be what the listener perceives the message to mean, and beyond that intention, the message may have some kind of additional effect on the listener.)

This three-part (or four-part) characterization emphasizes that pragmatic skill has an expressive and a receptive component. Pragmatic intention is not only an aspect of expressive language. Pragmatic skill pertains to receptive language, in that receivers process messages' intentions to understand their meanings while simultaneously making intellectual, social, and emotional judgments about the communicators who send the messages. *Pragmatic competence entails being able to understand each individual message within a lengthier communication, as well as the ability to distill the overall gist of the entire discourse.* Receptively, pragmatic language skill allows people to understand spontaneous face-to-face communication as well as preformulated language, such as lectures, presentations, and dialogue in movies, TV shows, or plays, and to comprehend any form of written text and symbols. *Receptive pragmatic competence has to do with whether a language user perceives and interprets another individual's message in the way that the sender intended it.* A reader's pragmatic competence allows for comprehension of an author's intended meaning and purpose. Adapting to the interactional environment established by the author is a pragmatic skill and a vital part of reading for meaning (Gordon Pershey, 2000).

Syntactic abilities have an impact on the pragmatics of language comprehension. Receptive pragmatic language processing is dependent upon understanding the purposes and intents of other speakers. Pragmatic language ability influences how well listeners follow along when they need to process an extended series of verbal messages, which means that they are processing syntax at length, sentence by sentence. Older children and teens need to be able to understand speakers' lengthy messages that contain multiple syntactic forms per utterance. The length and complexity of these messages require simultaneous syntactic and pragmatic interpretations.

Pragmatic meaning and intention are generally driven by the circumstances under which a message, often called "a text," is shared. Pragmatic intention underlies all contexts where language is used and where a "text," meaning a listener's or reader's interpretation, is created (cf. Rosenblatt, 1978). Pragmatic skill involves the use of communicative symbols in context in order to convey beliefs, knowledge, and intents and to meet the needs of the communicative situation. *Semiotics*, which is the study of how people use and interpret signs and symbols as cultural phenomena, considers how meaning is conveyed by users' choices in semantics, syntax, and pragmatics ("Semiotics," 2021). These pragmatic symbols can be conveyed by paralinguistics of speech and intonations of voice, by manually produced signs and gestures, facial expressions, body postures, body language, and even by apparel and other consumer goods, hairstyles, and anything else that sends a message about a speaker. Text is processed when a person is listening to the lyrics of a song, viewing visual symbols and pictures (still or moving), and interpreting punctuation or graphic notations.

Sometimes SLPs focus their interpretation of pragmatics solely upon how well a person demonstrates social skills. Social behavior is just a small subset of pragmatic language. Pragmatic language entails far more than just conversational participation, politeness routines, and social courtesies. Pragmatic development is a social-cognitive-linguistic phenomenon (Hymes, 1971; Prutting, 1982). Pragmatic language competence brings together numerous interrelated cognitive-linguistic and social processes. Sometimes pragmatics is regarded as the domain of language that is taught by adults in order to cultivate a "well-socialized child" (as stated by Jean Berko Gleason in the WGBH television program *Baby Talk*, 1985). This is true, but this cannot be accomplished by teaching rote phrasing of "please" and "thank you." It is the child's cognitive-linguistic skills, along with social insights, that allow pragmatic behaviors to develop and to be generalized across communicative contexts. Children commonly experience both success and failure navigating the social field. Smith (1977) and Halliday (1973) agreed that children experiment with the ability to express their intentions, refining what they say and how they say it over time. With this refinement, children come to know that they should select the words and sentence structures that best serve their purposes and meet the expectations of their listeners (described by Vinson, 2012, as "linguistic selection"). Having a bank of words, sentence structures, and paralinguistic behaviors allows children to convey messages by nuances of word choice, phrasing, expressivity, and tone that will lead to social success.

In the model depicted in Chapter 1, Figure 1–1, pragmatic language is referred to as "use" (Bloom & Lahey, 1978). Language use interfaces with semantic and syntactic skills, such that speakers need to craft every message's syntactic structure to impart the message's purposes and intents. The purpose of the following discussion of pragmatics is to describe the syntactic-pragmatic interface that makes this conversational competence possible and to explain the origins of this competence.

Pragmatic language competence is related to complex *social cognitions* that enable speakers to perceive the situational determinants that allow them to craft a purposeful message in a communicative context (Fiske & Taylor, 1991; Kunda, 1999) and then to selectively use (1) the essential *message functions* (i.e., communicative purposes); (2) *pragmatic cohesion* strategies, so that the topics of their successive messages flow together logically during a conversation or other form of communicative interaction; and (3) participation in a range of different forms of *discourse*, such as conversations, storytelling, or classroom instruction (Roth & Spekman, 1984). Children are bombarded with discourse for hours each day during their preschool and school years, and discourse comprehension and production are fundamental for school success in all grades. For messages to be transmitted in a way that promotes understanding, a speaker or writer must use appropriate message function and cohesion, in order that that a comprehensible, contextually appropriate discourse might be formed (Prutting, 1982).

Linguistic skill for *message formulation* underlies the communicative success of any spoken or written messages. Expressive and receptive language competence involves facility with messages that have explicit or implied meanings and that are literal or not. Speakers must master conventional and unconventional language usages within an interchange. Words and phrases may have alternative meanings, depending on their context. *A good part of these nuances of expression is derived from the syntactic arrangement of words into phrases and sentences. Self-monitoring of the use of the syntax necessary for message formulation is an essential component of pragmatic competence.* **Metalinguistic** skill provides the ability that speakers need to examine the syntactic characteristics of their messages and refine their pragmatic and syntactic quality. Pragmatic development and pragmatic self-monitoring are both innate and socially conditioned competencies (Kates, 1980).

Regarding pragmatic language development, with its attendant syntactic and metalinguistic capabilities, why is 4 years old a magic age? It seems that when typically developing children reach the age of 4 that they efficiently use language and become fully participating conversational partners. They are pragmatically adept and can carry out a number of linguistic intents and purposes, going well beyond simply talking about the people, objects, and places in their immediate circumstances (Halliday, 1973, 1975; Walden & Gordon-Pershey, 2014). They can competently convey what occurred during events and the experiences they have had; can explain what common household machines, appliances, tools, and gadgets do; can argue their points of view and persuade others; can create and discuss imaginative concepts; and can recite nursery rhymes and chants and sing numerous songs from memory. They display a range of feelings and emotions and they can comment on their feelings and the feelings of others, and then they can act verbally to attempt to manipulate others' feelings by consoling, bribing, or other interpersonal tactics. They have a sense of humor that might be a bit silly for adults to appreciate, but children who are 4 are known to playfully tease, joke, and attempt to create riddles. Many children love the element of surprise and use surprise as a meaning-making device—they might say "Guess what? or "You want to know something?" They are particularly pragmatically adept at *heuristic* language, meaning they use language to find out what other people

know and to learn from others. Four-year-olds notoriously ask a lot of questions and seek the reasons behind the circumstances that they are experiencing or that others tell them about. Rounding out this pragmatic development, their communicative acts advance beyond conversational exchanges, and they not only converse but also *narrate* to describe events they have experienced and use *expository* language to discuss information and facts (Westerveld & Vidler, 2016). They build up longer communicative exchanges with others, sometimes exchanging several utterances to discuss a topic. To accomplish all of these communicative behaviors, they produce declarative, imperative, and interrogative utterances (see Chapter 2). Adults may be amazed by just how much 4-year-olds understand about pragmatics. It's ironic that adults may need to find ways to keep children from hearing and understanding adult-to-adult messages that the children would be better off not hearing, and these adult evasions seem to make the children instantly interested in the conversation. For example, 4-year-olds may not know how to spell, but their pragmatic knowledge is such that they may know when adults are spelling the words that they'd rather have children not hear. Considering pragmatic capabilities alone, 4-year-olds have become magically skillful communicators!

Because mature speakers are adept at so many different communicative purposes, they require an array of more advanced syntactic forms to convey their messages (Leonard & Fey, 1991; Skarakis-Doyle & Mentis, 1991). The influential nature of pragmatics in this relationship between the pragmatic and syntactic domains of language warrants a visual representation. Recall that Figure 1–1 in

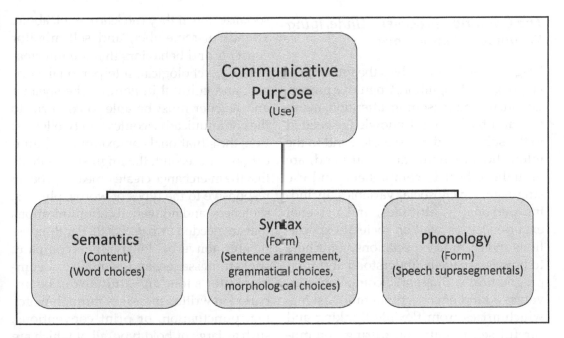

Figure 3–1. A functional linguistics perspective on syntax.

Chapter 1 depicts syntax, semantics, and pragmatics as three coequal domains of language that interface. However, if, as posited by SFL, it can be argued that function drives the refinement of form (see Halliday 1973, 1975), Figure 1–1 would not show how pragmatics propels the development and use of syntax. To illustrate pragmatic intention as the driving purpose behind the use of syntactic form, Figure 3–1 offers a reconfiguration of Figure 1–1. In Figure 3–1, conceived from a functional linguistics perspective, the intention of this illustration, when read from the top down to the bottom, is to show that the relationship between pragmatics and the other language domains arises due to somewhat of a provocation by the pragmatic domain, rather than as an interface of the three domains. Reading the figure from the bottom to the top, syntax and semantics are diagrammed as

being employed to contribute to achieving overarching pragmatic purposes, but the relationship is not entirely directional and remains reciprocal. However, while the form and content domains are considered individually, each is ultimately considered in relationship to pragmatic language. It might be a bit of an exaggeration to say that syntax and semantics subsist in the service of pragmatics, since the operations of the three domains are reciprocal, and having knowledge of certain words or sentences might inspire or allow speakers to enact certain intents that they could not enact if they did not have the necessary vocabulary or syntactic forms. In recognition of the preeminence of pragmatic competence and its connection with the development and growth of syntax (Skarakis-Doyle & Mentis, 1991), the following sections of this chapter offer detailed descriptions of the pragmatic language domain.

The Cognitive Processes Underlying Pragmatic Competence

Pragmatic ability involves the interface of language and cognition. Cognitive properties, including reasoning, attention, memory, and background knowledge related to the subject under discussion and to the interactional circumstances at hand, are brought to bear to comprehend and use language. Psychosocial variables, including personality, attitudes, and personal experiences, as well as societal expectations and cultural expectations, contribute to how language is understood and used pragmatically. Pragmatic competence involves a kind of conceptual multitasking, which arises from flexible thinking and careful self-monitoring during communicative interactions. Receptive language processing is an example of this cognitive-linguistic multitasking. A listener attends to what a speaker says and then, to comprehend the message, instantly applies what the listener already knows about the topic and how the listener feels about the topic, while also determining the speaker's purpose and intentions. What the listener knows and feels have been derived from previous learning experiences and were psychologically, socially, and/or culturally conditioned. The listener's reply conveys his or her own purposes and intents, which are mediated by his or her knowledge, psychological makeup, and perceptions of the social and cultural expectations that need to be brought to bear during the interchange. All of that linguistic processing will require careful syntactic selections. (The importance of prior knowledge in reading comprehension is discussed in Chapter 5.)

While pragmatic language is often described as the social use of language (Vinson, 2012), speakers or listeners can socialize only if they can learn, think about, attend to, remember, and self-monitor concepts and behaviors that are informational, psychological, interpersonal, societal, and cultural in nature. The speaker and listener must be able to conform to the communicative context on two levels: first, the situational context for communication and, second, the linguistic contexts that the interchange creates, meaning, being responsive to the types of words, phrases, sentences, and nonverbal communications that are needed (Moats, 2000). Paralinguistic and nonverbal behaviors accompany spoken messages, and, similarly, a communicator's tone and attitude can be imparted in written messages through wording, punctuation, or print conventions, such as large or bold type, all of which are interpreted cognitively and semiotically.

Pragmatic Language Purposes: Ideational, Interpersonal, and Textual

Pragmatic purposes can be found in all contexts where language is used. Within the study of pragmatics, three purposes for language are explored: the *ideational purpose* (i.e., the mental functions that process experience and govern logic), the *interpersonal purpose* of language (for communication with other persons [and, arguably, with animals]), and the *textual purpose* (the internal organization and communicative nature of a verbal text—a conversation, a monologue, a script, or a written passages) (Teich, 1999). The textual purpose is to produce a text, along with considerations for the structural properties of the text. The structure is part of the meaning of a text, as is described in Chapter 6.

To further describe each of these three purposes, the ideational purpose governs individuals' access to their cognitive storehouses of concepts and ideas. An individual's receptive language processing of the pragmatic intents inherent in the messages produced by other people is dependent upon the capacity to mentally generate ideational purposes and then ascribe these purposes to others, even when the speakers do not explicitly state them. Part of cognitive development in the preschool years is to develop *presuppositional* skills. Children develop the ability to be able to think about what another person might be thinking. Listeners can presuppose what speakers' pragmatic purposes might be. In this way, a listener is thinking about what a speaker might be intending to communicate, perhaps even before the communication occurs, and certainly during the communicative interchange. Presuppositional ability is related to how children develop a *theory of mind* (Baron-Cohen et al., 1985), meaning, the developmental awareness that other people have different thoughts, perspectives, and frames of reference than the child has himself or herself. Ideational purposes tend to be rather general and consistent across communication settings, and many ideational purposes become predictable and routine. Listeners replicate common ideational purposes on demand, for instance, knowing that others are offering greetings, expressing their wants and needs, or issuing directives. Expressively, ideational purposes allow speakers to behave consistently and logically. Speakers do not have to generate new ideational purposes for each communication interchange. This would suggest that a repertoire of syntactic constructions would be maintained and reused during routine communicative exchanges.

As Bloom and Lahey (1978) outlined, the ideational purpose includes using language as an intrapersonal processing mechanism, where language is used in the mind to think and to problem solve. Inner language, sometimes called "private speech," has a *mathetic* purpose, with "mathetic" meaning "learning" (in contrast with "didactic": having the purpose of teaching). Language can function to support perception, as when seeing something unfamiliar prompts the thought or the utterance "What is that?" and subsequent verbal speculation as to what it is. Thinking is verbally mediated; individuals have a fund of verbal information, which is purposefully and intentionally accessed. Pragmatic intent is discernable even within one's own thoughts. Mathetic competence allows speakers and listeners to communicate not only about events being experienced in the here-and-now. Using language to discuss events out of the here-and-now (be that past or future, or conceptual information that has little or no relationship to lived-through experiences, also known a decontextualized or displaced information) is a mathetic act.

The interpersonal purpose pertains to the use of language in interactive contexts. Here, too, a repertoire of syntactic constructions would serve frequent interpersonal patterns well. The textual purpose allows speakers to create a monologue or conversation and allows writers to fabricate texts. The syntactic arrangement of the elements of grammatical form within every message serves as part of the effort to create a text that conveys an intended meaning. The interpersonal and textual purposes of language rest upon the assumption that a message derives its meaning from how it exists in the context of a spoken or written communicative interchange. Pragmatic meaning and intention are generally driven by the circumstances under which the message is shared.

Communicative Acts and Their Syntactic Properties

Communicative acts, meaning messages' purposes, intents, or functions, are enacted by speakers' use of words, sentences, and other communicative symbols. Speakers' intents are characterized so that their functions and forms can be analyzed. Some typologize for characterizing communicative acts are described in this section. Careful understanding of the breadth of communicative acts can help SLPs design functional grammatic and syntactic interventions that will provide the language forms needed to express these communicative acts.

Skinner (1957, 1986) proposed that children develop propositional units of language in response to three sets of stimuli: (1) internal, generally physiological, stimuli; (2) external or environmental stimuli; and (3) one's own prior verbal behaviors, where the stimulus is a previous utterance and the subsequent verbal response is enacted in order to expand upon one's own prior utterance. Skinner limited the impetus for the development of verbal behaviors to these three main causes, and, in this model, all language output is produced in response to these stimuli (see a more complete explanation in Hegde & Maul, 2006).

Skinner's framework for analysis of early language proposed that there are six observable propositional language behaviors that arise in cause-and-effect cycles. These categories of behaviors are called "functional units," which in behaviorist terminology means a cause-and-effect relationship. While Skinner's categories of message types are not a pragmatic typology per se, children's development of these propositional language behaviors is relevant to the discussion of pragmatic

skill. Skinner's functional units of verbal behaviors are a typology for describing language in use.

Hegde and Maul (2006) summarized Skinner's functional units of verbal behaviors as including *mands, tacts, echoics, intraverbals, autoclitics,* and *textuals.* Mands are demands, whether they are phrased as direct commands or indirect requests. Mands are driven by internal and external needs. Skinner stated that the action the utterance demands supplies the reinforcement the speaker is seeking. The child who says, "Cookie, please," is reinforced by receiving a cookie. The adult who says, "Don't step on that broken glass!" is reinforced by averting an injury to another person.

Tacts are descriptions and comments about the environment. Tacts are not produced in order to meet an immediate need. To tact is to share an observation or experience with another person in a somewhat disinterested way, but generally a speaker is seeking social reinforcement as revealed by positive listener reactions, such as approval, praise, sympathy, companionship, or agreement with the speaker's own opinions. An example of a tact is, "What a heat wave we're having!" and the tact response is, "A great day for the beach!" A tact ends when the reinforcing comment is offered by the conversational partner. The speaker needs no further reinforcement.

Social media posts are often tacts. Posts that show off a picture and a message about a new haircut, a cute kitten, or successfully cooking a special recipe for dinner have become the tacts of millions of people's social media personalities. Creating posts is an enjoyable communicative act and is therefore intrinsically reinforcing, and the recognition from other people that the post garners is an extrinsic reinforcer, with these both being the reinforcers that elicit subsequently more posting. Posting to social media can be an important practical communication skill for SLPs to help students acquire. The syntax of social media posts is a written language skill that is based on the pragmatic demands of this context. Crafting writing to achieve these types of contemporary, everyday message functions is discussed in Chapter 6.

Echoics are responses that echo, partially echo, or paraphrase the initial verbal stimulus. When an adult models an utterance for a child, the intent is to stimulate an imitation or an approximate imitation. The adult hopes to be able to fade out the modeling so that the child can use the words or phrases independently on another occasion in another context. For competent language users, echoics help listeners process information (e.g., a listener repeats exactly when a speaker says, "Turn left onto Lee Road then right on Fairmount Boulevard" or clarifies with a partial echo, "Left on Lee, right on Fairmount") A mand is followed by an echoic. To show agreement, a tact is followed by an echoic (e.g., "That's the best show on TV!" provokes, "It's the best show.").

Intraverbals are messages caused by a speaker's own prior messages. What the speaker has said serves to stimulate the speaker's next message. In pragmatic language terms, this is referred to as adding elaboration or complexity to a message. The category of intraverbals accounts for the use of familiar language units and is therefore composed of pragmatic, semantic, and syntactic elements. There are several types of utterances that are intraverbals and several types of contexts that warrant intraverbals. Recitations (e.g., automatic language, such as reciting the alphabet, or overlearned

familiar text, such as the Pledge of Allegiance), common word pairs ("black and white," "back and forth"), and proverbs and figures of speech are all intraverbals. The initial part of the language unit serves as the stimulus, and the continuation of the unit is the speaker's response. An SLP may ask a child to count by modeling, "1, 2, ..." The child's production of "1, 2," is an echo and then the child's "3, 4," and the continuation of the counting is an intraverbal. For competent language users, a fund of information that is spoken about at length is categorized as intraverbal language. It is more than echoing what has been memorized or reciting overlearned information. Intraverbals account for "thinking on one's feet." Once the message has begun, it serves as a stimulus so that the speaker can produce the rest of the communication.

Autoclitics use linguistic elements to refine messages and provide additional information. Autoclitics allow speakers to use morphemes and syntactic and grammatical constructions to make a point. For example, inflectional morphemes, such as plural -s, allow a speaker to change meaning. The autoclitic morpheme modifies the tact "My dog" to "My dogs." In behaviorist terms, the autoclitics use grammatical elements to refer to the aspects of the environment that are the stimuli for the speaker's verbal behavior. If the environment features two dogs, the autoclitic plural -s morpheme needs to be used in response. Autoclitics signify quantity (e.g., dogs), time ("He was seen earlier"), and degree, strength, or magnitude ("very much"). Autoclitics may signal that a tact is false or questionable ("I did not see it, but Jessie said she kissed Mike last night.") or may signal that a speaker's tact is evasive ("You wouldn't catch me saying that the boss is a liar."). The autoclitic forms serve a speaker's intended communicative functions and semantic meanings.

Textuals are responses that are provoked by the characteristics of written language. The print stimulus controls the reader's verbal responses. Whether a text is read aloud or silently, the print stimulates the reader to say the words that are written, stop at the periods, and intone the questions that are marked. Textual responses follow from the conventions of print that a reader has learned, meaning that textuals occur when readers have learned the meaning of the printed stimuli and know the expected responses. In recent years, within the study of textuals as cognitive phenomena, attention has turned to how textual responses may change depending upon the format in which the print is presented. Computer technologies have made it possible for whole new classifications of textual responses to emerge. Electronic print on the screens of computers, tablets, and smartphones has caused readers to touch print, using their fingertips or mouse pointers, to respond to print in ways that were never called for when print was simply ink on paper. Today's readers are increasingly being expected to provide physical or verbal textual responses because sources of electronic print are designed to be interactive. Graphical user interfaces (GUIs) are the graphical icons that readers have to understand and use to retrieve and activate text. Being able to use print means being able to selectively point and click, which is a far more complicated set of skills than just being able to open a paper book. Some electronic print and GUIs are designed to control the electronic devices themselves, such as the icons that users tap to open software applications ("apps"). The electronic print and graphical stimuli can control the readers' textual responses in new and increasing ways that include verbal, visual, and tactile responses. Reading comprehension has expanded to include the ability to respond to the interactive properties of the text formats being read.

In conclusion, behaviorism as an approach to speech-language interventions is sometimes difficult to reconcile with an emphasis on the development of communicative competence, as these can be contrasting positions. Skinner's propositional units have had an influence on how some SLPs stimulate semantic and syntactic development. When an SLP stimulates a child to echo the model "doll" while naming a picture of a doll, presumably the ultimate purpose would be for the child to later independently mand "doll" as a request for the toy, or to tact "doll" as a comment about a present or absent doll. Behavioristic techniques have heavily influenced how SLPs provide speech-language services, but behaviorism *discounts the notion of pragmatic insight*. Behaviorism doesn't account for how children would spontaneously transition the use of a linguistic symbol across message functions, in this case from echo to request or comment. The behaviorist view is that if a child internalizes the label during a drill and response naming paradigm, the child will use the label to seek reinforcement of a need that provokes a mand (the child wants the doll) or a tact (the child wants to receive verbal praise for talking about the doll).

It seems to be behaviorism's conceptual and procedural oversight to expect that an SLP can train a child to use the word "doll" in the context of labeling when the desired outcome is actually that the child would spontaneously use "doll" to request or comment. Decontextualized drill misses the important consideration that children need to learn words and forms within the contexts where it would be reinforcing to use the words and forms. If pragmatic competence in requesting and commenting is desired, it would be beneficial to provide these communicative opportunities as intrinsic reinforcements, rather than to expect that a sticker or some other extrinsic reinforcer that is awarded following a naming drill would inspire the child to transition to the desired functional pragmatic outcomes, without any direct teaching, on another occasion. Language practice needs to occur in situations that can enact the desired pragmatic outcomes. Interventions would help the child develop the cognitive-linguistic insight, albeit most likely an unconscious insight, into the occasions when saying "doll" will result in a functionally reinforcing outcome. To evoke Figure 3–1, semantics would be developed in the service of pragmatics.

Typologies of Message Function and Their Syntactic Properties

Other pragmatic typologies that focus on the applied study of pragmatic intent have arisen from speech act theory (Austin, 1962). Austin was interested in discovering how speakers select and use words to fashion utterances that carry a speaker's intended aims, impact, or effect. Austin set out to label as many speech acts as possible. Speech act theory established a base of over 10,000 pragmatic intents in English. However, a theoretical understanding of 10,000 speech acts would not be likely have a workable application to practical contexts. Austin, as well as Searle (1975), devised alternate methods of classifying speech acts into manageable taxonomies that could be usable in the fields of child language development

second language instruction, anthropology, ethnography, or literary criticism (Flowerdew, 1990).

Following this lead, many researchers proposed taxonomies of *message function* that collapsed the many speech acts into categories of meaningful purpose and intent (as described by Ninio et al., 1994; Ogilvie, 1984). Message functions label intent but also reflect the various cognitive, linguistic, and social competencies necessary for communication. Ninio and Snow (1996), for example, provided a comprehensive description of codification schemes that serve either to isolate or to synthesize the social, cognitive, linguistic, procedural, cultural, and developmental properties of messages.

Researchers have explored the developmental sequence of the emergence of speech acts (Dore, 1974, 1975, 1977a, 1977b; Dore et al., 1978; Jose, 1988). SLPs use this developmental information to determine whether children have attained the use of the message functions that are needed for communication (see Duchan et al., 1994; Gallagher & Prutting, 1983, 1991; McTear & Conti-Ramsden, 1992). Dore (1974) and Halliday (1975) offered two of the most common codification schemes for determining whether children are developing the use of message functions. Notice how both of these categorization schemes for message function bear some resemblance to Skinner's functional units of verbal behavior.

Dore proposed two levels of complexity within the development of message function. Children begin their use of pragmatic intent by using *primitive speech acts* (see Table 3–1) in their babbling and jargoning, when they appear to be calling for someone, protesting, or repeating adults but they are not yet using true words. Then, early use of words and phrases conveys these pragmatic intents. For example, first intents may be to call out for "mama." The use of "no" is an answer to an adult question or a protest. Children then progress to using *conversational speech acts* (see Table 3–1). However, it is important to know that use of primitive speech acts and conversational speech acts overlaps and co-occurs. Acquisition of a greater variety of intents is a gradual process and may extend through the preschool period. It is not as if children master all of the primitive acts, then master all of the conversational acts in a discrete order. Since the conversational acts carry more interactional complexity, the sum and substance of the primitive acts emerge first. As children become more adept at using more words and longer phrases, the conversational acts can be conveyed. But the primitive acts continue to be used while the conversational acts are being integrated and even after the conversational acts have been attained. Notably, some children with impaired language do not progress beyond use of the primitive speech acts or have limited use of the conversational acts. For

Table 3–1. Dore's Primitive Speech Acts and Conversational Speech Acts

Primitive Speech Acts
Labeling: Children say the names of objects, people, animals, places, etc.
Example: (Pointing to a toy car) "Car."
Repeating: Children repeat all or part of what others say.
Example: (Mother says, "Time for a bath.") "Bath."
Answers to adult questions or bids
Example: (Father asks, "Would you like to go outside?") "Go on the swing."
Requesting action
Example: (Outside on a swing) "Push me."
Requesting answer
Example: "What's that?"
Calling
Example: (Running toward the room where Mother is) "Mommy!"
Protesting
Example: (Mother says, "Time for a bath.") "No!"
Practicing
Example: Child talks rotely (counting, saying the alphabet, reciting a rhyme; may be repetitive or unrelated to the situation; may be when talking to himself or herself while playing; could be for humor or self-amusement)

Table 3–1. *continued*

Conversational Speech Acts
Request information, clarification, permission
Example: "Can I go outside?"
Request for the conversational floor
Example: "Can I have a turn?" "I wanna tell the story."
Respond with information, clarification, or to agree to a request or deny a request
Example: "No, he's not Spot, he's Rover."
Description
Example: "The water is cold."
Statement of rules, procedures, definitions, emotions, beliefs, mental states, internal events
Example: "No, this car goes first." "No, I think it goes here."
Acknowledgment of a request by approving or disapproving
Example: "Yeah, you can have a turn."
Organizational device (to open or close a conversation; introduce or change a topic; seek attention; politeness markers; backchannel feedback[a] *within an interchange)*
Example: "You know what I got?"
Performative (protest, complain, humor/playfulness, warning)
Example: "I bet you can't find me!"

[a]*Backchannel feedback* (Garvey, 1984) refers to remarks that are made to keep the flow of a conversation going. "Uh-huh," "Right," "Yeah," "Mmmm," are commonly used. These messages have intent, but they are also *cohesive devices.*

the development of these speech acts to proceed, children need to employ the syntactic capabilities described throughout Chapter 2.

The Dore typology is useful for the study of children's language but is not applicable after the preschool period. Importantly, Halliday (1973, 1975), as founder of the school of thought known as systemic functional linguistics (SFL, or systemic functional grammar), detailed seven discrete categories of message function that are evident in the language of children and that can continue to be applicable to examining the message intents of mature speakers throughout the life span.

Halliday (1975, p. 7) described language development as a process by which children gradually "learn how to mean." A child's interactions with others have meaning, and experiential meaning provokes language. Children's initial language

Table 3–2. Halliday's Functions of Language

Instrumental: Children use language to satisfy a personal need and to get things done.
Example: "I want a toy."
Regulatory: Children use language to control the behavior of others.
Example: "Buy me a toy now, Mommy."
Interactional: Children use language to get along with others.
Example: "You want to play?"
Personal: Children use language to tell about themselves.
Example: "I'm running fast. I'm gonna win."
Heuristic: Children use language to find out about things, to learn things.
Example: "What are those cats doing?"
Imaginative: Children use language to pretend, to make believe.
Example: "Let's play spaceman."
Informative: Children use language to communicate something for the information of others. (Sometimes referred to as the *Representational* function)
Example: "I'll tell you how this game works."

development is based on experience: What can be said reflects what can be done. Language is learned when it is functionally related to experience. Table 3–2 lists Halliday's message functions and provides examples of child utterances that express each function. The functions progress in developmental complexity in the order they are listed (Ogilvie, 1984), with simple Instrumental language first used to satisfy wants and needs, moving on to social courtesies, greetings, and farewells coded as Interactional language, culminating in the Imaginative and Informative functions that require children to have the cognitive capacity to take on perspectives outside of their own frames of reference. Imaginative language requires

thinking about an alternate reality. Informative language requires providing information that the child presupposes that another person needs to know and entails communicating expository information. Speakers and writers need advanced grammatical and syntactic forms to enact Halliday's advanced functions of language. Halliday's message functions are applied in Chapter 6 where writing for communicative purposes is discussed.

Smith (1994) added three message functions to Halliday's list. These are more complex functions that occur in mature oral language and often in written language. The functions are *divertive* (e.g., puns, jokes, riddles, etc.; potentially, this could be considered an extension of Dore's performatives and/or Halliday's imaginative function), *authoritative* (also called *contractual;* describing how some conditions must be, with statutes, laws, regulations, rules, contracts, agreements, and schedules, etc., which is primarily both regulatory and informative), and *perpetuating* (recording the past with diaries, notes, records, histories, scores, notes, meeting minutes, and inscriptions, etc., which is largely informative and personal).

Stewart (1987) described how SLPs can integrate **metalinguistic awareness** of message functions within literacy interventions. Message function and metapragmatic awareness of message functions, as related to reading comprehension and written language enhancement, are discussed in Chapters 5 and 6.

Pragmatic Cohesion

Pragmatic cohesion refers to how speakers or writers manage the transitions between utterances or messages (Roth & Spekman, 1984). Cohesion describes how communication partners sequence and connect utterances to build meaning over the duration of an entire **discourse**. A discourse is the entirety of any communicative interaction, such as a conversation or an exchange of text messages or emails. A discourse also may be a lengthier message constructed by a sole communicator, as in the case of a written report, a novel, an advertisement, a poem, or song lyrics. Table 3–3 summarizes the elements of pragmatic cohesion.

Pragmatic cohesion, also known as *pragmatic coherence* or *pragmatic contingency,* means that the individual utterances or messages within a discourse build logically upon one another to make a coherent point that is shared by the communicative participants, be that between conversation partners, or a lecturer and an audience, or a writer and a reader. Communicative interchanges *cohere* when the verbal and/ or nonverbal signals that are exchanged join together to support meaning making. The utterances or parts of a message link together in a coherent fashion to maintain or to shift topics and to allow the discourse to progress. In conversation, lapses in cohesion, where communication partners digress from topic or have illogical leaps from idea to idea, need to be repaired so that a focused interaction can resume. Contingent communication utilizes appropriate message intents. Questions, comments, requests, self-disclosures (personal language), humor, and other message functions are used at the right junctures of the conversation. Some studies have attempted to determine whether use of pragmatic contingency behaviors could identify differences between children with typical language development and children with language impairment (Prutting, 1982; Prutting & Kirchner, 1987).

One way to explain the concept of pragmatic coherence is to offer a nonexample of when messages do not cohere. A simple example of a lapse in pragmatic coherence is where one conversational partner asks, "What time is it?" and the other conversational partner answers, "My birthday is November 10th." This obvious non sequitur shows two messages that do not logically cohere. Roth and Spekman (1984) proposed that cohesion means that a speaker is obliged to try to structure a message that is in relation to the needs of the listener. This goes beyond simply answering the question that is asked. Three central verbal behaviors that demonstrate pragmatic coherence are presuppositional skills, contributing to a conversation, and topic skills.

Table 3–3. Pragmatic Cohesion

Messages build logically upon one another

- The speaker can hold the conversational floor
- The speaker's successive utterances build message elaboration and message complexity
- The speaker can take conversational turns with conversational participants
- The speaker can supply backchannel feedback

Memory for communication

- The speaker recalls what all conversational participants have said (including the speaker himself or herself)

Presupposition

- The conversational partners have shared background knowledge and experiences
- The conversational partners share perceptions of the current interactional context
- Theory of Mind (the conversational partners are aware that their own presuppositions may differ from others' presuppositions)

Topic skills

- Topic choice
- Topic introduction
- Topic development
- Topic maintenance
- Topic shift
- Topic closure

Roth and Spekman (1984) proposed that cohesion is integrally related to *presupposition*. *To presuppose is to make an assumption about what another person knows, believes, feels, or has experienced.* People may try to make an informed presupposition by attempting to determine something about the characteristics and experiences of another person—to identify what is mutual between themselves and others. The shared presuppositions between conversational partners will vary depending upon the amount of knowledge and experience they have in common. They may have a shared recent past or a shared long history together; they may have frequent or infrequent contact with one another; they may have a shared family, community, or culture; or they may have no connections beyond sharing the present moment. People often hope that any shared context would increase the likelihood that presupposition between speakers would be multiplied. The proverbial "strangers on a train" may strike up an intricate conversation about train travel because their mutual presuppositions about past experiences riding trains allow for common ground.

The pragmatic ability to craft messages so that a speaker may communicate with others with whom they either do or do not share presuppositions is a language skill that is based on *social cognitions* regarding situational determinants. Communicators use overt or covert strategies to determine the existence of other persons' shared presuppositional knowledge. There might be a fine pragmatic line between establishing mutual presuppositions and prying or asking personal questions. Sometimes it may be more situationally appropriate and logical to presume that another person has presuppositional knowledge, because asking questions about people's background knowledge may be considered rude or condescending.

Children with impaired language may have difficulty formulating presuppositional judgments. As with the examples just given, their presuppositional errors may appear to be non sequiturs, or they may seem evasive, or they may look like they are stating the obvious, being redundant, or talking down to others. Language intervention sometimes targets helping children navigate the differing contexts where presuppositional judgments need to be made so that communicative interchanges can cohere and so that they can meet the needs of their listeners. Applicable grammatical and syntactic skills are needed for formulating presuppositional judgments.

Cohesion skill makes it possible for speakers to contribute to a conversation and to hold and share the conversational floor. Concurrently, as speakers judge how to produce an adequate length of utterance and gauge the length their conversational turns, they are judging how to build upon what has been said by everyone in the conversation and may be leading the way to what will be said later in the conversation. Pragmatically competent speakers produce messages that are contingent to the messages of other participants in the conversation, so that a topic is developed by the participants as they share ideas in a logical fashion. Successful speakers have adequate attention and memory to store and retrieve the content of the conversation, both the messages that have been said by the speakers themselves and by the conversation partners. Competent cohesion means that speakers are contingent to what others have said and to their own prior contributions to the conversation. Their messages logically build upon what they have said earlier in the conversation. They proceed with elaboration or can rephrase or summarize their earlier points; they speak without too much self-repetition and without self-contradiction. Speakers can reintroduce topics that have been covered before when clarification or elaboration are necessary. Cohesion skill is therefore dependent upon *memory for communication*, that is, the ability to retain and recall the substance of a discourse.

Along with contributing to a conversation, speakers must be able to surrender the conversational floor. This may involve comprehending verbal or nonverbal signals that another person would like to speak. On the other hand, sometimes speakers have to use strategies to bring another person into a conversation, often by asking them a question. These skills contribute to adequate conversational turn-taking.

Topic-related pragmatic skills are the sum and substance of cohesion. Cohesion skill is integral to starting a communicative interchange, which involves *topic choice* and *topic introduction*. A speaker who introduces a topic at the right time and in the right place is producing messages that are appropriate to the conversational setting. It could be said that the messages cohere to the setting, as opposed to being out of place and not cohering to the expectations for the setting. The topic choice should cohere to what has already occurred or what could reasonably occur in the conversational setting. Topic introduction occurs at the beginning of a conversation or in mid-conversation when a prior topic has reached closure. Continuing a conversation is a primary function of cohesion skill. To carry on a conversation involves *topic development*, *topic maintenance*, and *topic shifting*, as well as conversational turn-taking and contributing **backchannel feedback**. Ending an interchange, which requires appropriate *topic closure*, ties up the conversational threads so that the discussion is complete, or signals that the topic will be continued at a later time.

The implications of pragmatic cohesion within and across messages are applied in Chapter 4 in reference to the assessment of children's oral grammar and syntax skills as obtained by language sampling of conversational, narrative, and expository discourses, as well as in Chapter 6, where writing for communicative purposes is discussed.

The Pragmatics of Discourse

A *discourse* represents the entirety of any communication or text. In theory, a stop sign or a "no entry" sign may constitute a discourse (Hinkel & Fotos, 2002). Typically, however, a discourse is a lengthy and continuous oral or written verbalization by a sole communicator or an exchange of verbalizations among participants. Discourse refers to the linguistic mechanisms by which human beings interact and to the product of human language output. In linguistic analyses, a discourse can be parsed in terms of its speech acts, sentences, conversational turns, or any other structures of the text—lines, paragraphs, chapters, passages, and so on.

Sachs (2009) reported several studies that concluded that young children benefit from continuous daily exposure to ambient adult discourse during caregiving and play. Immersion in caregivers' connected speech promotes the development of communication and language, regardless of the caregivers' interactional styles (Bruner, 1978). In other words, while high-quality **child-directed speech** is of great value, the quantity of environmental exposure to connected discourse is also important. It appears that tuning in to ambient discourse is a universal early language skill (Kuhl, 2010). Kuhl posited that there is a "social brain" that actively apprehends discourse at a very early age. It may be that the developing brain needs discourse as a priming agent for learning the interrelated systems of language, notably, grammar and syntax in relation to word choices, as described in the discussion of the expansion of semantic relations in Chapter 2. Tuning in to discourse may prepare the brain for the end goal it needs to achieve, that being the production of full sentences in connected discourse. Kuhl stated that "brain and behavioral studies indicate a very complex set of interacting brain systems in the initial acquisition of language, many of which appear to reflect adult language processing, even early in infancy. . . . In adulthood, language is highly modularized. . . .

Infants, however, must begin life with brain systems that allow them to acquire any and all languages. . . . The infant brain is exquisitely poised to 'crack the speech code' . . . the speech code requires infants to combine a powerful set of domain-general computational and cognitive skills with their equally extraordinary social skills. Thus, the underlying brain systems must mutually influence one another during development" (p. 715). The infant's brain appears to need exposure to discourse to develop the specialized but interrelated domains of language that will later contribute to discourse.

Although Kuhl's scientific studies showed that humans are cognitively and linguistically predisposed to process and use discourse, comprehending and formulating discourse can be a significant challenge for children with language impairments. The demands for participation in discourse begin early in life. Initially adults communicate with infants, toddlers, and younger preschoolers by using *child-directed speech* (Sachs, 2009), where adult input is brief, precise, and immediately referential to items and events within the present environment, and where the child's response can be uncomplicated. But by the time children attend preschool, it is beneficial for educators, caregivers, and parents to present children with rich, stimulating, age-appropriate continuous discourse spoken in full sentences of varied types (see, for example, the position statement of the National Association for the Education of Young Children [NAEYC], 2009, promoting language-rich preschool environments). The demands for participation in discourse increase during the preschool years, and it is here that many children begin to reveal difficulties learning pragmatic language. There is a breakdown in their use of message functions and cohesion strategies and they do not progress well into participating in interactional play, conversations, and enjoying lengthier discourses, such as storybooks.

Table 3–4 presents the elements of children's development of discourse. The left column describes the early pragmatic discourse foundations explained in the above descriptions of children's adult interactions and play with people and toys. The center column describes the many discourse demands of the preschool period previously mentioned in this chapter, culminating with skills in conversation and narration that are acquired by about age 4. The right column explains the discourse demands for school-age learners. Spoken language demands include participating in multipart narratives shared with other communicators, along with a greater need for awareness of social roles and *social registers* (i.e., standards for formality and politeness), *proxemics* (i.e., conventions for physical distance between communicators), and *code-switching* (i.e., when a speaker consciously changes linguistic patterns to adopt the usage or standards of a context, group, or community, as when a speaker moves back and forth between using a regional dialect and GAE). School-age learners need to master interactional skills such as slang, humor, and ways to repair a conversation after misunderstandings or other gaffes. Written discourse involves using print technologies and online applications of print, such as social media, and writing about abstract information. Reading involves text comprehension and text analysis (such as finding a main idea or using charts and graphs). Chapter 4 provides information on assessment of discourse skills in school-age learners and adolescents relative to the complexity of

Table 3–4. Pragmatics and Discourse

Early Pragmatics	Preschool Pragmatics and Discourse	School-Age Pragmatics and Discourse
Eye contact	Gestures and verbal messages have function, purpose, and intent	Daily communication involves complex, multipart narratives
Joint attention	Language describes events in the here-and-now and out of the here-and-now	Social register, proxemics, code-switching, social behaviors such as diplomacy and equivocation
	Follow directions in context, follow examples	Slang, humor, indirect meanings
Reciprocal play	Respond to topics Initiate topics Cohere to topics	Awareness of the perspectives of others, complex conversational repair (clarification)
Imitation of movements and sounds	Repair communication (misunderstandings, misstatements)	Text comprehension
Initiation of movements and sounds	Early story comprehension	Text analysis (e.g., author's purpose, main idea, interpreting text features like charts and headings)
	Songs, rhymes	Technology (texting, social media)
	Simple narratives	Written language describes factual and fictitious events out of the here-and-now and reveals abstract thinking
	Discourse is constrained by child's attention span and interest in a task	

grammar and syntax that is involved in mature discourse. Chapter 5 presents information on discourse comprehension as a factor in reading comprehension, which is in part predicated on comprehending the grammar and syntax of written passages. Chapter 6 provides information on helping students craft written discourse at the sentence and passage levels. These three chapters emphasize how syntax is

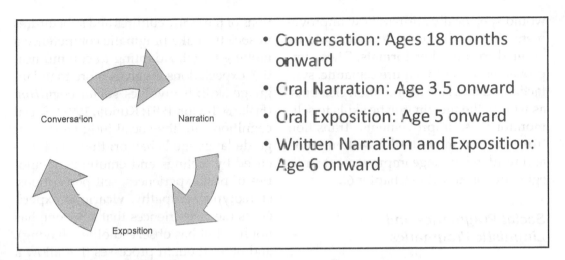

- Conversation: Ages 18 months onward
- Oral Narration: Age 3.5 onward
- Oral Exposition: Age 5 onward
- Written Narration and Exposition: Age 6 onward

Figure 3–2. Progression from conversation to narration to exposition.

an integral part of communicative and academic success.

For messages to be transmitted in a way that promotes understanding, a speaker or writer must use appropriate message function and cohesion, in order that that a comprehensible, contextually appropriate discourse might be formed (Prutting, 1982).

Figure 3–2 illustrates progress in children's use of three discourse genres or formats: conversations, narrations, and expository language. Researchers have established that there is a general developmental progression across these three competencies (cf. Nippold, 1998; Nippold et al., 2005; Westerveld, 2001; Westerveld & Vidler, 2016). Conversation emerges at about 18 months and continues onward through the developmental period and throughout the life span. People can continue to develop conversational competence throughout their lives. The popular media, in print and online, regularly run articles and commentaries on how to improve adults' conversational skills Oral narration begins at about ages 3 to 5, when children relate their daily expe-

riences in narrative fashion and begin to discuss stories they have read and tell stories of their own (Applebee, 1978; Gee, 1985; Greenhalgh & Strong, 2001; Michaels, 1981, 1986, 1991). Like conversational skill, narrative abilities are continually refined throughout the life span. Oral exposition is a skill that is brought about by the demands of classroom recitation and participation (Hadley, 1998; Van Dongen, 1986), which begins at about age 5 and continues throughout the life span, to allow adults to discuss information during their daily lives at home, at work, and in their communities. When children learn to write, beginning at about age 6, speakers learn that their oral discourses can be written down, and then written narration and written exposition mature and support print-based interactional skills throughout the life span. The circular motif in Figure 3–2 signifies that these three genres of discourse skills influence one another and are ongoing in their refinement. If an individual improves in one genre of discourse, it could conceivably improve one or both of the other forms. SLPs who address these discourse genres would specifically address how improvements in one discourse format could be applied to the other formats. These improvements would feature semantic, syntactic, and message formulation elements, as well as the metalinguistic skills to self-monitor these improvements. Transition from the oral mode to the written mode and written language improvement strategies are discussed in Chapter 6.

Social Pragmatics and Linguistic Pragmatics

A distinction needs to be made between *social pragmatics* and *linguistic pragmatics* (Turkstra, 2000), although, in actual communicative interactions, they are inextricably woven together. While both types of pragmatic skills work together, it is important to know their related but unique properties. Table 3–5 summarizes the attributes of social pragmatics and linguistic pragmatics.

Social pragmatics implies that a speaker or listener is meeting situational expectations for appropriate communicative behavior. Expectations can be consistent across contexts or can vary according to circumstances. Communicative expectations within a setting may change due to many factors, even as simple as the time of day. For example, it is commonly expected that coworkers greet one another with "good morning," but few greet one another later in the day with "good afternoon." Part of being pragmatically adept is being aware of the nuances of communicative acceptability. Often there are expectations related to the formality of the communicative setting and to the ages, genders, social rankings, and familiarity of the communication partners. These attributes, coupled with the varying expecta-

tions of the many cultures and subcultures in society, make pragmatic competence a moving target. Adapting to communicative expectations involves more than language skill; it involves *social cognition* (Fiske & Taylor, 1991; Kunda, 1999). Social cognitions are the social judgments that guide language behavior; they are influenced by feelings and emotions, memories of past experiences, self-perceptions, stereotypes, empathy, vicarious experiences (i.e., experiences that someone has not had but has observed others having), and other thought processes that allow a speaker to meet the needs of a communication partner.

Appropriate pragmatic behavior, on the one hand, is unique to the individual communicator and changes moment-by-moment with situational expectations and, on the other hand, is bound by widely held rules and routines for conduct that, if not followed, can result in social penalties. A pragmatically competent communicator has a large repertoire of pragmatic behaviors and is flexible in employing these behaviors. "Reading" the social field allows the speaker to recognize when to use the appropriate *social register*, that being the needed level of formality and politeness that is based on perceptions of a conversational partner's status, power, and familiarity. The adept communicator notices situational conventions and can predict the social costs of breaking with convention. Sometimes the motivation for personable pragmatic behavior is the desire to be liked, well thought of, or somehow rewarded. There are developmental differences in how well learners can interpret the situational variables that call for shifts in pragmatic style.

SLPs often emphasize helping children develop the kinds of social prag-

Table 3–5. Attributes of Social Pragmatics and Linguistic Pragmatics

Social Pragmatics	Linguistic Pragmatics
Social cognitions	Message formulation
Social conventions	Grice's maxims
Social register (social status and social roles)	Clarity
Social courtesies	Expressivity (figures of speech)
Conversational turn-taking	Economy (ellipsis)
Politeness routines	Implication
Self-monitoring	Self-monitoring

matics that are characterized by overt interactional behaviors and social courtesies, such as cooperation, conversational participation, conversational turn-taking, politeness routines, use of negotiation strategies, acknowledgment of the status and roles of communication partners, nonverbal communication behaviors, and self-monitoring. (For an example of a social pragmatics intervention study using case examples, see Beilinson & Olswang, 2003.)

Social pragmatics entails verbal flexibility that is dependent upon skills that, strictly considered, are inherent to linguistic pragmatics. *Linguistic pragmatics* accounts for the verbal flexibility that allows subtle gradations of meaning to be achieved. Linguistic pragmatics is concerned with how a communicator structures the linguistic content of a spoken or written message, including its grammar and syntax. Myers and Gray (1983) suggested that linguistic context dictates which words a speaker (or writer) will choose and how the speaker (or writer) will structure or phrase a message. *Message formulation* reveals the confluence

of semantic and syntactic skill with linguistic pragmatics. The key features of linguistic pragmatics that a speaker (or writer) must consider are *clarity*, *expressivity*, and *economy* (Turkstra, 2000).

Clarity means that ideas are expressed logically or sequentially, that ambiguity is at a minimum, and that the right words, phrases, and sentences are chosen to convey ideas. The speaker or writer is responsible for crafting a message with good "processability," meaning, a message that is readily processed by a receiver. This involves providing a message that meets the linguistic needs of listeners or readers. This need can vary, depending upon contextual factors such as the familiarity of the communication partners, the formality of the verbal exchange, the amount of time there is to converse, or the type of document being written. Clarity involves the syntactic skill of rephrasing messages; a speaker is able to repair a message if it is not clear to the listener.

Expressivity affects message clarity. The affect displayed along with a message should enhance (or merely not diminish) the processability of the message. Another linguistic pragmatic variable is brevity or economy. A message should be neither too long nor too short to convey adequate meaning. Economy should not sacrifice message detail. As with social pragmatics, a communicator's self-monitoring contributes to crafting messages with clarity, expressivity, and economy.

Grice's (1975) four maxims of message formulation and conversational logic are one doctrine of linguistic pragmatics that defines clarity, expressivity, and economy in practical terms. Summarized by Davis (2010), these are the *Maxim of Quality—messages should be truthful, not false or unjustified*; the *Maxim of Quantity—messages should be as informative as required, neither too long nor too short to provide sufficient information*; the *Maxim of Relation—messages should be relevant to the context and situation; and the Maxim of Manner—messages should be orderly, not ambiguous, not obscure, and not hard to process.*

Grice (as reported by Davis, 2010) accounted for how stylized messages are conveyed and processed. Efficient, logical communication may not be a speaker's only goal. Grice encouraged speakers to speak in ways that are stylish, beautiful, distinctive, entertaining, and interesting. No speaker is expected to be direct, literal, and explicit all of the time, because that would be tedious and dull. Figures of speech, irony, wit, and sarcasm contribute to expressivity. Implication and ellipsis are necessary to avoid redundancy. (An ellipsis is the omission of an implied word or words, for example, Joe says, "Are you ready for the exam?" and Jeff says, "Not quite"; the words Jeff omitted can be understood in context and from mutual knowledge.) Implication and ellipsis are not a violation of the maxim of quantity. But notice how potential violations of quality, quantity, manner, and relation can all be observed in Davis's (2010) example: "Alan asks, 'Did you talk to your friends at the party?' and Barb answers 'Some of them,' implying that she did not talk to all." Barb is either literal-minded or being evasive or sarcastic. Did she mean that not all of her friends were at the party? Or that some of the people she talked to were not her friends? It is necessary to use social cognitions to simultaneously make intellectual, social, and emotional judgments about Barb and the message she uttered. Social pragmatics and linguistic pragmatics intersect when communicative analyses of messages' social purposes and linguistic construction really cannot be separated.

The syntactic constructions used by speakers contribute to clarity, expressivity, economy, and the actualization of Grice's maxims. When SLPs' interventions target improvement of linguistic pragmatics, attention to sentence formulation is inherent in this process. Conversely, when interventions target sentence formulation, the effect on linguistic pragmatics is inherent. For instance, it would be of little use to have students create sentences that are so long that clarity and economy are violated. SLPs need to undertake improving sentence construction in meaningful contexts where the sentences achieve the necessary linguistic pragmatic considerations. Moreover, starting with meaningful intents as the basis for working on sentence formation skills allows for form to follow from function.

Social Validity

The communicative success of the social pragmatic and linguistic pragmatic characteristics of messages is judged by the criteria of *social validity* (Turkstra, 2000). The success of the oral message is a matter of the appraisals made by listeners.

Evaluation of the pragmatic success of a message may differ across listeners. Listeners may equate use of conventional grammatical structures with interpersonal communicative competence and may judge speakers' grammatical variations quite harshly. A speaker whose message meets Grice's maxims and is clear, expressive, and economical may be poorly judged due to social pragmatic variables, such as limited use of politeness markers, seeming too familiar by calling a listener by a first name, or some other social pragmatic gaffe. In addition, listener presuppositions may influence their judgments of pragmatic success; these evaluations may be dependent upon culturally conditioned values that dictate credibility that are entirely extraneous to the content of the message, such as a speaker's reputation, wealth, appearance, or physical fitness. In this regard, given the weight of these listener variables, a speaker's linguistic competence might not predict her social competence. Conversely, social competence can sometimes mask cognitive or linguistic deficits. A very charming speaker may be illogical, factually incorrect, or agrammatical but still perform well in a social field.

Manifestations of Pragmatic Language Impairments

Learners with pragmatic language impairments may experience a variety of difficulties involving language purposes, communicative acts, use of nonverbal behaviors, message function, cohesion, discourse, social pragmatics, and linguistic pragmatics. The impact of pragmatic deficits on reading comprehension and written language is presented more fully in Chapters 5 and 6, respectively. Pragmatic language issues include:

Language Purposes
- Difficulty using inner language to think and reason.
- Delayed, limited, and/or impaired social interaction skills.
- Impaired understanding and/or use of language texts: songs, stories, nursery rhymes, and so on.
- Lesser understanding and/or use of communicative symbols (e.g., for young children, a stop sign; hats or costumes used to dress up and pretend and that send communicative signals; for school-age learners, logos, flags, uniforms, emojis [ideograms] and animated gifs [graphics interchange format], memes, and graffiti).
- A speaker's communication might only pertain to events in the here-and-now; difficulty using language to discuss events out of the here-and-now (past or future, or conceptual information that has little or no relationship to lived-through experiences; lesser ability to discuss abstract concepts).

Communicative Acts
- Late onset, limited use, and/or impaired use of infants' preverbal illocutionary and locutionary acts, including joint attention, nonverbal social reciprocity, and preverbal vocalizations; potential late onset of babbling and true words.
- Late onset, limited use, and/or impaired use of initiation and/or reciprocation for verbal and/or nonverbal interactions with caregivers and other children (limitations using the

illocutionary and locutionary acts of expressive pragmatics).
- Impaired perlocution: Difficulty comprehending the meaning of the verbal and/or nonverbal interactions offered by caregivers and other children (receptive pragmatics).
- May not be able to formulate self-perceptions of what other speakers' utterances mean (insufficient perlocutionary force) (for older children, this may lead to a lack of understanding of indirect language, humor, sarcasm, slang, figures of speech, etc.).
- Late onset, limited use, and/ or impaired use and/or interpretation of gestures, body language, and facial expressions; poorer proxemics and understanding the boundaries of personal space.

Message Function
- Late onset, limited use, and/or impaired use and/or interpretation of message functions.
- Struggle to understand and use some or all of Dore's (1974, 1975, 1977a, 1977b; Dore et al., 1978) and Halliday's (1973, 1975) categories of message intent.
- Limitations may result in a stilted social demeanor and/or impaired ability to access social participation from others.

Cohesion and Discourse
- Difficulties with message cohesion, such that the flow of conversation is disturbed.
- Difficulties with topic skills.
- Dependence upon a conversational partner to carry the burden of interaction.

- Lesser "theory of mind" and presuppositional skills.
- Difficulty engaging in lengthier discourse, such that conversational interaction and/ or participation in social routines and school routines is limited.
- Difficulty learning larger language texts—learning songs, nursery rhymes, and so on in the preschool years and, during the school years, difficulty comprehending multisentence passages, book chapters, assignment sheets.
- Lesser engagement with story books, movies, plays, and other imaginative scenarios.
- Lesser knowledge of typical social scripts for common social interactions.
- Difficulty clearly conveying lengthier or more complex meanings (to share information or demonstrate knowledge).

Social Pragmatics
- Lesser social cognitions, awareness of social determinants for interactional behaviors.
- Late onset, limited use, and/or impaired use of social courtesies, taking turns.
- Misreading social cues during verbal interactions.
- Difficulty adapting to social roles and social registers; use of inappropriate social register (e.g., a child speaking to other children as if he is their teacher, rather than as peer to peer).
- Difficulty anticipating and judging listeners' reactions.
- Performance of social faux pas, such as bluntness, curtness,

lack of politeness, lack of consideration or empathy, or social awkwardness.
- Imitation of interactive behaviors without judging their appropriateness.

Linguistic Pragmatics
- Lesser awareness that word meanings are often ascertained by considering contextual factors.
- Inappropriate message length or turn length (too long or too short).
- Message clarity is at issue.
- Lesser expressivity (e.g., figures of speech are not understood or used).
- Confused by ellipsis and implication.

How Language Is Impaired: Structural and Functional Deficits

Recall the properties of language accounted for by psycholinguistic principles: Language is a code, represents ideas about the world, is a system, is a convention, and is used for communication. A fundamental language impairment, then, would potentially interfere with language's code function. The impairment would break down a child's ability to refer to objects, actions, and concepts and to understand the references made by others. A child with a language impairment would be less able to represent ideas about the world and to learn by talking about concepts. Events outside of the children's immediate experience and abstract ideas and concepts would be beyond their mental grasp. Language would be an obscure system. Its rules and patterns would remain unfamiliar, even after repeated attempts at practice and memorization. If some progress

is made, parts of the system may become known, so that a child could use some words, morphemes, and sentence patterns, but a child's inventory of linguistic elements would remain sparse and the patterns and combinations of elements the child uses would be quite rote, routine, and predictable. The system would have little range of variation. Relatedly, the conventions of language would not be meaningful. A child would struggle with nuance and would communicate in basic, invariant, concrete, and literal terms. Social graces would be limited. Language would not be fun—joking, double meanings, figures of speech, poetic language, riddles, and rhymes would all be difficult. Finally, children with a language impairment would struggle to communicate and meet little success making a point and obtaining what they need. The end result would be frustration and negative behaviors. The examples and descriptions given in this paragraph are stark and represent frank, fundamental problems, which do occur in many children's cases. There are, however, a myriad of more subtle language problems that SLPs detect and treat. The potential range of language impairment varies from nearly imperceptible to a profound lack of communication ability.

Children with difficulties in conceptualizing the code, representing ideas, learning the system, learning conventions, and/or communicating may be limited as to achieving a hierarchy of three necessary life skills (cf. Hymes, 1971):

- Language performance
- Communicative competence
- Communicative independence

Without performance of language behaviors, a child would struggle to become a competent communicator. Without communicative competence, a child would be held back from becoming an independent communicator. It is therefore essential to regard language impairment as a hierarchical deficit in performance, and/or competence, and/or independence, and to determine how interventions can help a child achieve performance of specific language behaviors, and/or use language behaviors to communicate competently, and/or use language behaviors to become more independent of the assistance of caregivers, peers, and communication partners. Independent communica-

tion reduces barriers to social access and participation.

In all, a multifaceted receptive and expressive pragmatic base underlies any speaker's syntactic language productions. When a person speaks or writes with pragmatic intent, it means that on a conscious or unconscious level, he or she has processed and internalized the linguistic, cognitive, interpersonal, situational, and cultural variables that make this expression possible. The pragmatic and syntactic language systems interface to make sentence-level processing and production possible.

CHAPTER 4

Grammar and Syntax in School-Age Children and Adolescents: Conceptualizations and Measurements

This chapter describes the components of mature grammar and syntax. Cognitivist and social constructivist perspectives contribute a rationale for how learners achieve mature grammar and syntax. This chapter considers how receptive language and speakers' metalinguistic awareness influence successful learning of grammar and syntax. Practical considerations addressed in this chapter include how SLPs can conceptualize and document learners' competent use of the elements of sentence construction. Grammatical and syntactic terminology is defined and described. Techniques are offered to elicit school-age and adolescent students' language samples. Manual and computerized language sample analysis tools are explained in detail. How standardized diagnostic testing can reveal school-age learners' competent use of grammar, syntax, and metalinguistic awareness is discussed, as is how instruction and interventions can target attaining mature spoken grammar and syntax.

Anticipation Guide

After reading this chapter, readers will be able to answer the following questions:

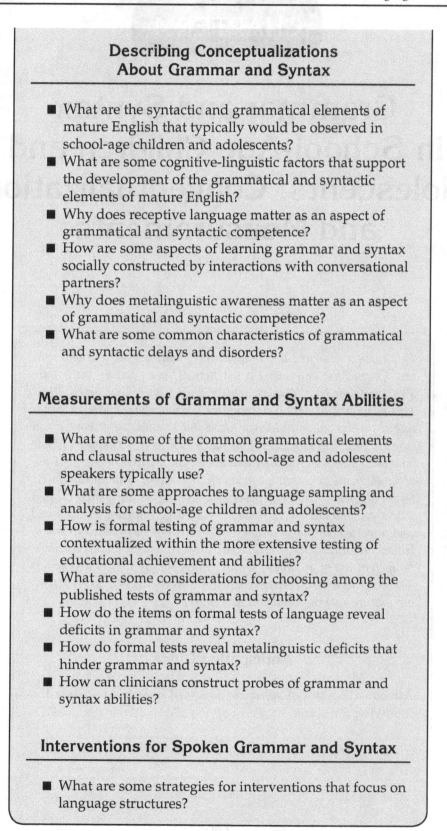

Describing Conceptualizations About Grammar and Syntax

- What are the syntactic and grammatical elements of mature English that typically would be observed in school-age children and adolescents?
- What are some cognitive-linguistic factors that support the development of the grammatical and syntactic elements of mature English?
- Why does receptive language matter as an aspect of grammatical and syntactic competence?
- How are some aspects of learning grammar and syntax socially constructed by interactions with conversational partners?
- Why does metalinguistic awareness matter as an aspect of grammatical and syntactic competence?
- What are some common characteristics of grammatical and syntactic delays and disorders?

Measurements of Grammar and Syntax Abilities

- What are some of the common grammatical elements and clausal structures that school-age and adolescent speakers typically use?
- What are some approaches to language sampling and analysis for school-age children and adolescents?
- How is formal testing of grammar and syntax contextualized within the more extensive testing of educational achievement and abilities?
- What are some considerations for choosing among the published tests of grammar and syntax?
- How do the items on formal tests of language reveal deficits in grammar and syntax?
- How do formal tests reveal metalinguistic deficits that hinder grammar and syntax?
- How can clinicians construct probes of grammar and syntax abilities?

Interventions for Spoken Grammar and Syntax

- What are some strategies for interventions that focus on language structures?

Effectively diagnosing and treating any type of language impairment chiefly depends upon how thoroughly an SLP understands the structural components of language. This chapter describes the linguistic properties of mature grammar and syntax and provides the necessary foundational information for SLPs who aspire to conduct full and accurate assessments of the grammatical and syntactic performance of school-age and adolescent learners (Balthazar & Scott, 2015). Of primary importance is the considerable information on the clausal structures that typify mature English included in this chapter. Knowledge of clausal structure serves as a basis for the procedures and considerations that SLPs apply to assess grammar and syntax abilities and impairments. Measuring the syntax and grammar of more mature speakers is in part related to some of the available data on developmental trajectories, but assessment might be more specifically guided by knowledge of how speakers arrange multiple grammatical forms to build more grammatically complex utterances (Diessel, 2004).

SLPs would have a need for strategies that are useful when conducting a manual computational assessment of the syntax and grammar of older children and adolescents. Manual computational assessment would entail that an SLP examines a language sample or observes language performance in context and scores the sample for the occurrence of certain grammatical and syntactic forms. SLPs and researchers may prefer to use computer software programs to analyze grammar and syntax rather than compute manual analyses. This chapter presents a brief overview of one widely used program, the Systematic Analysis of Language Transcripts (SALT, originally developed by Leadholm & Miller, 1994, and Miller & Chapman, 2003, that is

currently available as SALT 20), as well as descriptions of other online tools.

It is useful for SLPs to compare the measurement information that can be obtained via language sampling to the results of formal language testing. Some commonly used published tests can be compared to sampling results to offer a battery of assessment information. This chapter details the grammatical and syntactic abilities that standardized and informal tests can reveal. Finally, this chapter explores some potential interventions for spoken grammar and syntax in school-age and adolescent learners. Considerations for interventions address how syntactic form is developed in part by metalinguistic awareness of language form.

Describing the Form of Language: The Grammatical and Syntactic Elements of Mature English

It is important to explore the trajectory of syntactic and grammatical growth that is typical for school-age children and adolescents. Information on normative development of language beyond the early developmental period has been empirically derived in applied research settings (e.g., Gleitman et al., 2005). However, within the literature on later developing syntactic and grammatical constructions, the exact age milestones for the use of specific linguistic structures are not documented with the same chronological precision that milestones are recorded for young children's production of earlier constructions (Dick et al., 2004; Nippold, 1993, 1998). Nevertheless, there is a substantial body of evidence that describes the grammatical and syntactic performance of school-age and adolescent learners that has been obtained by researchers in the fields of linguistics, psychology, English language arts education, and speech-language pathology.

The effort to establish grammatical and syntactic normative data was initially pursued by linguistics researchers who gathered ethnographic samples of student performance within school English language arts instructional contexts, notably by observing spoken language use in classrooms and collecting written language samples (e.g., Hunt, 1965, 1970; Loban, 1963, 1970, 1976; Moffat, 1968; O'Donnell et al., 1967). Their cross-modal efforts were predominantly an attempt to determine whether students' overt language capabilities and curriculum expectations corresponded and, conversely, whether students' observable language could be substantively related to the curriculum and instruction they had experienced. Field investigators documented students' language in use in academic settings, then inductively constructed grade-level language performance reports based on their extensive ethnographic data. Within these lengthy and detailed reports can be found lists of the grammatical and syntactic constructions that students were observed to utter and to write. This research was prominent for many years, as it was disseminated by the U.S. government and the National Council of Teachers of English, a professional association for language arts educators that is influential in educational policy development. The findings were utilized in an effort to improve schools' curriculum content and teachers' instructional techniques and to provide an empirical basis for future research.

Relatedly, over much of the 20th century, normative expectations for grammar and syntax were associated with the influence of English language arts textbook authors and publishers, whose textbooks, basal readers, workbooks, curriculum materials, teachers' guides, and tests set the standards for language competence and performance among students in Grades K–12 (Goodman & Shannon, 1994; Goodman et al., 1988; Shannon, 1989, 1990, 1992, 1995). Presumably, the grammatical and syntactic skills that students demonstrated were influenced to some extent by their teachers' widespread use of the instructional materials produced by the major educational publishing companies (cf. Holloway, 1986). Although these teaching materials were widely used throughout the nation, language performance expectations were mostly established by school districts or other local or state education agencies, who set the criteria for advancement from grade to grade and high school graduation. In the 1980s and 1990s, the growing awareness of the magnitude of the nationwide illiteracy crisis took on great importance (e.g., Kozol, 1985), and for some educators and policymakers, the nation's decentralized and nonuniform educational requirements and expectations became a focus of concern. The U.S. Department of Education's publication of *A Nation at Risk: The Imperative for Educational Reform* (1983) and the subsequent No Child Left Behind legislation of 2001 (NCLB, 2002) had significant effects on the movements toward statewide mandated testing and teacher accountability. From the 1990s onward into the 21st century, there has been a reduction in local school district control of curriculum and assessment (cf. Gordon Pershey, 2003). States instituted statewide curricula and mandated achievement tests, which were followed by the nationwide *Common Core State Standards* (CCSS; National Governors Association Center for Best Practices,

Council of Chief State School Officers, 2010) for curriculum and instruction and, in turn, then, each state's interpretations of the CCSS. Academic achievement testing remains a function of state departments of education, with most accountability measures being in the form of criterion-referenced academic achievement tests rather than standardized tests that establish age-level or grade-level norms. Students who do not meet the achievement standards for the states in which they reside may be suspected of having nonnormative abilities and might be referred for psychometric testing by school diagnostic team personnel or outside psychoeducational practitioners. Some diagnostic tests, often those used to diagnose language disorders or learning disabilities, have norms for specific language behaviors that are allied with grammatical and syntactic competence or that can be associated with sentence processing in listening and reading and sentence production skills in speaking and writing. It is important to note that students with cultural and linguistic differences may be at a disadvantage relative to the normative competencies that these instruments established, with test bias being a threat to the reliability of testing.

Within the field of speech-language pathology, normative data, or, in place of norms, reliable evidence of age-level performance demonstrations for older children's grammatical elements and syntax, have been ascertained by numerous studies (e.g., Eisenberg & Guo, 2016; Guo et al., 2018; Guo et al., 2019, 2020; Guo & Schneider, 2016; Miller & Paul, 1995; Miller et al., 2016, 2019; Nippold, Frantz-Kaspar, et al., 2017; Nippold & Sun, 2008; Nippold, Vigeland, et al., 2017; Owens et al., 2018; Pavelko & Owens, 2017, 2018, 2019; Pavelko et al., 2016; Reed et al., 2009; Rice

et al., 1998; Rice et al., 2006; Rice et al., 2010; Scott & Stokes, 1995; Scott & Windsor, 2000). Some studies observed learners' performance during conversational sampling and/or on elicited language production tasks. Specifically, some studies obtained samples via elicited narrative production techniques where examinees were expected to converge upon a plausible narrative to match pictorial stimuli, and where the stimuli might reasonably have elicited a narrative that would be likely to contain the grammatical and syntactic forms under investigation. The researchers derived normative information or performance expectations based on these convergent samples. The widely used language sample analysis software program, the Systematic Analysis of Language Transcripts (SALT; Leadholm & Miller, 1994; Miller & Chapman, 2003; SALT, 2020b), embeds an array of norms or developmental standards within its analytic tools and offers diagnostic materials for contrasting SLPs' obtained clinical samples with the developmentally representative samples found on the SALT 20 (2020b) product website. Further, some studies resulted in tools for professional practice, such as the banks of norms or performance expectations available on the project website for Sampling Utterances and Grammatical Analysis Revised (SUGAR; Owens & Pavelko, 2020).

Learners' Ability to Develop Syntactic Language Complexity

Leonard (1998) proposed that language impairment may arise from general processing limitations. Affected children develop mental representations of mature morphosyntactic forms more slowly because they are generally slower in processing language, information, sensory, and motor operations (Leonard, 1998; Miller et al., 2001). Language learning may pose more difficulties than other developmental areas because language requires rapid sensory, perceptual, and computational processing (Fey et al., 2003). Learning grammar and syntax would require that adults teach children that language forms are meaningful and salient, and adults would give children frequent opportunities to imitate and spontaneously produce target grammatical constructions in pragmatically relevant contexts (Fey et al., 2003).

Mason et al. (2013) explained that "syntax and semantics develop concurrently and independently through early- to middle-childhood" (p. 1136). Productive, spontaneous, and independent use of syntactically complex sentences that contain a main clause and dependent clauses develops gradually (Diessel, 2004; Nippold, 2004; Scott & Stokes, 1995; Weiler & Schuele, 2014; Windsor et al., 2000) and is dependent upon the growth of semantic abilities (i.e., vocabulary enhancement, concept development [such as the temporal concepts associated with tense and aspect, as noted by Wagner, 1998], and the higher-level thinking that requires more complex terminology for thoughts to be expressed). As described in Chapter 3, syntactic growth is dependent upon better pragmatic abilities (i.e., communicating about abstract events out of the here-and-now and describing more wholistic concepts, rather than just discussing simple, immediate events in the present environment; also, taking the perspectives of other people and discussing those perspectives) as described by Nippold (1993, 1998), and upon more complex narrative abilities, where multiple experiences are recounted and longer, more extensive dis-

course is used to explain occurrences (e.g., Hadley, 1998; Nippold, Vigeland, et al., 2017). In order to speak about concepts and events at length, a speaker's language needs to include more elaborate syntactic structures (MacLachlan & Chapman, 1988; Scott & Stokes, 1995).

Receptive Language Influences on Expressive Syntactic Maturity

To some extent, when assessing later grammatical and syntactic competence, the distinction between receptive and expressive language necessarily needs to be blurred. Communication is simultaneously receptive and expressive (Denes & Pinson, 2007). In a spoken interchange, a speaker is not just speaking; he or she is moving back and forth between speaking and listening to other speakers. While a speaker is speaking, he or she is self-monitoring, which means that he or she is listening to himself or herself. Listening itself simultaneously involves the acoustic processing of auditory input, the symbolic processing of language input, the cognitive processing of information input, and, at times, processing visual input (such as gestures, body language, facial expressions, etc.). While listening, participants in spoken communication tend to be anticipatorily engaged in the expressive response tasks of message planning, message formulation, and message production that they will need to respond. They may also be engaged nonverbally, so as not to verbally interrupt, by nodding, smiling, frowning, and so on, while listening. With all of these operations ongoing, syntactic processing is occurring during language reception (Blank et al., 2020; Johnston, 1994; Ninio, 2006).

For expressive grammar and syntax to mature, a well-developed receptive grammatical and syntactic repertoire is of importance (Ferreira & Patson, 2007; Hsu et al., 1985). Receptive language underlies expressive language and is generally a stronger skill set than expressive language (Pan & Uccelli, 2009). By and large, expressive language reveals the storehouse of language that a speaker can understand, which may be more extensive and complex than what a speaker can express. Any assessment of an individual's expressive grammar and syntax is by extension an assessment of their underlying receptive grammatic and syntactic system. Experimental research (Bock, 1986) on linguistic representation, that is, the mental representation of language in the brain and mind, showed the influence of syntactic input on syntactic expression. When participants heard certain sentence forms in the context of one task, this had the effect of priming their use of those forms expressively during a subsequent task that differed in content and purpose. The structural priming effects were specific to the carryover of sentence forms but were independent of the sentence content or meaning. This syntactic repetition effect suggested that speakers' sentence formulation processes are somewhat influenced by the frequency or recency of their exposure to particular structural forms. Speakers tend to reuse their own and others' syntactic structures (Branigan & Pickering, 2017). Moreover, the combinatorial behavior that is needed for the arrangement of syntactic elements is responsive to the influence of structural priming (Pinker, 1984, 1989). In all, the receptive capabilities for unconsciously parsing the structure of sentences, being sensitive to a language's grammatical constraints, and being attuned to frequently used linguistic constructions are among the cognitive-linguistic operations that inform receptive language processes (Clahsen & Felser, 2006; Johnston, 1994).

Specific to language form, listeners process a number of elements. Receptive syntactic processing and comprehension entail several interrelated cognitive-linguistic processes:

- Perceiving syntactic forms within the context of a flow of auditory input of words and pauses, nuanced by the speaker's prosody and intonation, which entails listening for stress patterns, changes in vocal volume and pitch, and other auditory cues to the syntactic contours and the phrasing of messages.
- Processing and comprehending language input:
  - Identifying the meanings of free and bound morphemes as grammatical elements.
  - Organizing word order and syntactic patterns to process phrases and sentences; grouping related ideas and meanings.
  - Interfacing language input with stored memories of syntactic forms and patterns, for example, agent + action + object, or adjective + noun.
  - Determining the syntactic meanings of messages, such as present or past tense as denoted by verb choices.
  - Ascertaining meaningful cognitive-linguistic information from the syntactic constructions heard.
  - Comparing new grammatical and syntactic input to a storehouse of known grammatical and syntactic concepts to interpret the meaning of the new, unfamiliar, or different input.

- Applying grammatical and syntactic input to personal affective traits and states, such as attitudes, feelings, predispositions, beliefs, and so on, in order to process the affective communicative content of messages.
- Transferring grammatical and syntactic input to long-term memory, in order to retain the language that is heard.
- Retrieving grammatical and syntactic language from long-term memory for subsequent use, either within the present interchange or at a later time.
- Planning a response; using receptive language to underlie expressive language (i.e., a speaker can express the language that he or she can understand).
- Using growth in receptive language as the basis for future growth in expressive language.

In summary, syntactic expression is built upon syntactic comprehension. The task of grammatical and syntactic comprehension is varied and complex and subserves expressive grammar and syntax. An individual can generally only express the elements of language form that he or she can comprehend (Hsu et al., 1985; Ninio, 2006; Pan & Uccelli, 2009).

Learning and Memory

Regardless of the types of syntactic difficulties that speakers manifest, when language deficits persist beyond the preschool developmental period, the problem is protracted and chronic. Pennington et al. (2019, p. 6) explained that developmental language disorders, as with all learning disabilities, have the hallmark of "heterotypic continuity." An underlying learning difficulty remains present throughout the course of development, but its manifestations or symptoms change as children grow older (see also McGregor, 2020). When children with developmental learning difficulties encounter new task demands, different symptoms emerge. For example, when a child is too young to be expected to read and write, the various symptoms of reading and writing difficulties remain hidden. When these learning expectations arise, the symptoms that are interfering with literacy learning become apparent. It may be that the level of syntactic processing and production that is needed for literate language is subject to this trajectory of emerging symptomatology. As such, difficulties with grammar and syntax might not become apparent until children are required to use oral and written academic language, meaning, they cross from the oral mode to the written mode of language (cf. Nippold & Schwarts, 1996).

Pennington et al. (2019) pointed out that language is always dependent upon *implicit memory*, which is largely unconscious and aids in the learning of new skills and patterns and which is dependent upon subcortical structures, mainly within the basal ganglia and the cerebellum. Implicit memory and the learning it supports requires diffuse areas of the brain to be functional and coordinated. Implicit memory arises from locations in the brain that are outside of the language centers of the left hemisphere of the brain and illustrates that learning language relies on coordinated neurodevelopmental processes. Early language is highly dependent upon implicit memory, and language learning seems unconscious. Older language learners continue to use implicit memory but also face the need to accomplish *metalinguistic* demands, and *explicit memory*, meaning the declarative knowledge that is stored in long-term memory, is used to learn how to analyze sentence grammar, recognize text structures, and perform other linguistic analyses. There is a continuity of the cognitive risk factors but a discontinuity in the cognitive demands that learners encounter. The underlying risk for learning difficulty remains regardless of the conditions, tasks, or expectations that environments present. This may explain why it is possible that some children's language and literacy difficulties are not discovered until they are past the period of early literacy development. These children were not challenged to engage in more advanced literacy tasks, so their low levels of literacy competence were sufficient to meet these basic demands. The environment provided a set of protective factors that ultimately proved false, when protection from these demands was no longer possible.

Therefore, two lessons that can be learned from the continuity of cognitive risk might be: (1) If SLPs do not challenge learners to use literate language that goes beyond the basics of the oral syntax of daily language, learners' higher-level syntactic difficulties may not be revealed, and (2) if school curriculum does not afford students with the opportunity to read challenging texts and engage in authentic writing opportunities, syntactic problems might not be revealed. All members of the educational teams that serve children with language learning needs should focus on providing children with learning experiences that will build higher-level oracy and literacy skills.

Pennington et al. (2019, p. 7) cautioned that their continuity model is "probabilistic not deterministic." Cognitive risk interacts with environmental risks and protective factors in ways that are unique to each learner. Even so, the presence of heterotypic continuity should serve as a signal to professionals who serve younger children. Service delivery planning should consider not only young learners' current developmental concerns but should also think ahead to project how the present difficulties could continue to be manifest when the learners are older. Pennington et al. (2019) characterized this as considering how cognitive risk factors could manifest in the presence of advancing developmental demands.

Social Interactionism, Social Constructivism, and Dynamic Assessment of Grammar and Syntax

Social interactionist theory, also called social interactionism, proposes that children acquire language and refine its use in order to navigate the social field. Like cognitivism, social interactionism maintains that language requires a cognitive basis, but cognitive development is a product of interactions with people in the context of social relations. Social development is the foundation for language development. Children construct their own knowledge about the world based upon their interactional experiences. All learning, including learning language form, is a product of interaction with the social world. The structure of language is important in the sense that language learners create the linguistic structures they need to use in their social fields (Scott & Stokes, 1995; Skarakis-Doyle & Mentis, 1991). Language structure arises from association learning (i.e., learners pair interactional contexts with the language structures that need to be functionally used there). Knowledge of language structure emerges from exposure to how language structures are used in meaningful experiential contexts. Therefore, syntactic skills are socially constructed, meaning they are co-constructed during interactions with others. A child's repertoire of grammatical and syntactic form is the product of the forms that other speakers have shared with the child and that the child has shared with others in his or her linguistic communities.

The social interactionist model is frequently described in relation to the work of Vygotsky, a Russian sociocultural theorist who died in 1934 (Wertsch, 1985). Vygotsky's theories remained relatively unnoticed for decades (see Winsler, 2003) until various scholars of psychology, linguistics, education, Russian and Soviet history, and culture studies popularized these notions in the late 1970s through the 1990s. Vygotsky maintained that cognitive development is socially mediated. Learners construct knowledge about language form by experiencing how other speakers use language form and by following the lead of capable language models. Talking with others helps learners learn, whether the objective is to learn information or to learn about how to use language itself. It might be facile to sloganize Vygotskian thought as "What I can talk about, I can think about," but this short axiom describes the essential premise that interactional communication is foundational to any learning and development, especially to language learning and development.

Vygotsky's sociocultural theory promotes the notion that all social interactions take place within a cultural milieu. Therefore, all language takes place within a cultural context. "Culture" refers to ethnic, geographic, religious, linguistic, or racial groups, but also to groups based on gender, sexual orientation, age, family composition, and socioeconomic status, and to other affiliated groups such as schools, teams, occupations, neighborhoods, clubs, and interest-based groups, as well as to any other social grouping that forms an identity and has its codes for conduct and mores. Therefore, learning language structures entails learning the cultural customs that provide the framework for any interactional settings. Language learners are influenced by a culture's use of grammar and syntax. Many speakers develop the capacity to adapt to more than one set of cultural expectations, for example, adapting to the differing expectations for how to use grammar and syntax at home, in school, and in social settings. These speakers would *code-switch*, consciously or unconsciously, across the different sets of grammatical and syntactic forms that are employed in various cultural or social contexts.

While the educational philosophy of constructivism suggests that individuals construct knowledge, *social constructivism* suggests that groups construct knowledge. Group members invest in learning how to be members of the group. Members share meanings and participate in the creation of group culture and group knowledge. Children learn language as part of a group, then use language to contribute to the knowledge of the group. The proliferation of online communities has actualized the principles of social constructivism to a greater extent than ever before. Children are becoming members of online group cultures and are being introduced to the *co-construction of knowledge* at a very young age.

SLPs who are guided by social interactionist principles assess how children use grammar and syntax in interactions with other people. Assessment includes evidence of how children use grammar and syntax in social contexts with familiar and/or unfamiliar interactional partners. Because learning is socially mediated, language testing and sampling procedures might include an opportunity to show how well a child performs when another person gives the child help, guidance, feedback, or cues, or simplifies or modifies the task. Independent, unassisted performance of grammar and syntax behaviors would certainly be assessed, but if a child does not perform well, the next step would be to assess how the child responds to social interactions that are designed to aid grammatical and syntactic performance. Vygotsky proposed the *zone of proximal development* (ZPD), which is the array of behaviors that a child can perform when given some minimal assistance, that is, when co-constructing knowledge with another individual. *Scaffolding* refers to the adult supports that are offered; scaffolded behaviors are those that a child can perform with help. *Mediation* guides a learner to self-examine how to perform a behavior. Mediation entails a level of self-reflective learning that scaffolding does not necessarily include. For instance, a learner might be scaffolded to break a task into separate actions and then, as mediation, be asked to explain how to do each action. Mediation is a technique to help learners develop *metalinguistic awareness*.

The belief that assessment of the competencies within a child's ZPD is as important as documentation of independent behaviors has led some SLPs to adopt *dynamic assessment*. When an examinee does not respond correctly to test stimuli but there is reason to believe that the tasks are within the child's ZPD, dynamic assessment involves scaffolding subsequent opportunities to respond. After a test is administered (either immediately after or at a later time), the SLP coaches

the child on the competencies that the child did not demonstrate and perhaps has the child practice the competencies, and then presents the assessment stimuli again, to see whether the child can succeed after being given some help. The child's readiness to learn is assessed, as well as his or her ability to co-construct knowledge. SLPs may refer to the opportunity to perform a task after being given some form of help or a demonstration of the target performance as an assessment of *stimulability*. With guidance, the learner produces the target behavior.[1]

Metalinguistic Awareness of Syntax

Syntactic language development entails far more than just rotely acquiring language form. Syntactic integrity is related to complex cognitive-linguistic processes that allow speakers to perceive the situational determinants for the use of applicable elements of grammar and syntax. Linguistic skill for message formulation underlies the success of any oral communication or any creation of written text. Metalinguistic skill provides the ability to examine the grammar and syntax of a message and refine its quality (cf. Britton, 1984).

---

[1]Dynamic assessment invalidates the administration of most formal assessments. Most test instructions require that tests scores be based upon independent behaviors and initial, unaided competencies. Dynamic assessment occurs only at a point in the testing sequence when an initial score has been obtained and when scaffolding to obtain an aided score does not invalidate the initial test administration. The results of dynamic assessment are not reported as test scores but are included in the section of a test report that describes the SLP's observations. Dynamic assessment of culturally and/or linguistically diverse children has the potential to yield functionally relevant results that reflect their cultural understandings of the test items (Gutiérrez-Clellen & Peña, 2001).

Of paramount importance is that SLPs are cognizant of the fact that any interventions that employ language learning strategies that necessitate a slot-filling, drill-and-practice approach to sentence patterning are *asking learners to move from simply using language to communicate to a metalinguistic examination of how to use language to complete the drill.* This is true whether the purpose of the practice is to help learners make gains in their use of *syntactic regularities* or to enhance *syntactic variety. Conscious, overt examination of sentence patterning in order to fill linguistic slots* entails **metalinguistic awareness**, that is, a conscious awareness of language as an object that can be scrutinized and manipulated (Britton, 1984). The speaker is no longer an unconscious language user but becomes a conscious metalinguistic analyst. To learn sentence patterns and the **metalanguage** that labels the elements of sentence patterns (words such as "subject" or "noun," or even simpler terms like "who is doing something" and "action"), learners must be able to understand at least a little bit about the abstract nature of the language that they use. Learners must generalize patterns from an example construction to other examples that use different words—although the syntax may be patterned, the constructions may have different semantic meanings and/or different pragmatic purposes. The SLP is attempting to stimulate the examinee to *attend to the sentence form in addition to its meaning*; however, a learner who has deficits in unconsciously producing language form will no doubt have trouble engaging in the conscious and more difficult **metasyntactic awareness** skills that are needed to analyze form. This is a compounded problem: *The learner has a weakness in the form skills needed to analyze form.* Slot-filling tasks may not be effective with learners who cannot conceive of the need for syntactic slots. Without metasyntactic awareness, improving language form can be challenging. Speech-language therapy progress may be slower and difficult to attain. Contextual use of better syntax in frequently occurring daily situations might be achievable first, before a child attains a generalized use of syntactic structures.

Relatedly, a learner develops the **metalinguistic awareness** or **metalinguistic insight** to understand that speakers must plan the linguistic form of their messages that will be appropriate for an audience and a situation. Children learn through insight and social conditioning how to fine-tune messages to meet the communicative needs of a situation (Bruner, 1978) and therefore become syntactically and pragmatically competent, interfacing these two language systems (Bates et al., 1991).

Although syntactic language develops unconsciously in a preverbal child, syntax might be the domain of language that ultimately requires greater introspection for practical application than the other domains (Balthazar & Scott, 2015). While phonology, semantics, and pragmatics require the speaker to sometimes use conscious self-regulation of language behavior, syntactic competence requires assiduous and recursive self-monitoring, especially in the written mode. It takes a degree of **metalinguistic awareness** to analyze the grammatical forms needed to assemble messages, especially when writing. Children may be initially exposed to self-analysis of their syntax when a parent says, "Say that again with correct English," or some similar cautionary or corrective remark. Syntactic skill is refined throughout the development of language and on into adulthood, as cognitive-linguistic skills mature and the variety of oral and written communicative fields that people need to navigate become numerous and more complex. This chapter discusses how formal and informal testing can assess metalinguistic awareness and offers suggestions for metalinguistic awareness interventions. Chapters 5 and 6 address metalanguage in greater detail in the contexts of reading comprehension and written expression, respectively.

It may be developmentally advantageous for children to gain an emerging metalinguistic awareness by first being taught to be conscious of the *paralinguistic* behaviors that convey meaning and intent and that accompany the forms of sentences. Interpreting *paralanguage* is likely to be a simpler metalinguistic learning task than becoming consciously aware of message form. The physical, visual, and sensory aspects of paralinguistic behaviors allow them to be concrete and experiential, while sentence grammar and syntax can be laden with abstract concepts that require advanced interpretations. Schoolchildren receive and produce a range of paralinguistic behaviors, such as gestures, body language, and facial expressions, and they may be readily able to engage in metalinguistic discussion of the meaning of these nonverbal messages (cf. Crais, 2006; Goldin-Meadow, 2009) and how they accompany sentence forms, such as statements and questions. It may be easier for children to discern and metalinguistically describe the meanings of these overt physical behaviors than to examine the structures behind complicated linguistic features such as verb tense, question formation, adjectives, and so on. Young learners may easily identify how a person behaves physically when asking a question versus stating a fact.

Nelson (2010) mentioned two main classifications of nonverbal behaviors: *proxemics* (how spatially close communication partners can comfortably be, from barely an inch to many feet apart) and *kinesics* (physical movements that convey meaning by accompanying or replacing verbalizations). Kinesic mechanisms include *emblems* (gestures that translate to verbalizations, such as nodding the head to say "yes," shaking the head to say "no," shrugging, or waving), *illustrators* (e.g., hand gestures to illustrate a point, such as showing the size of an object), *affective displays* (e.g., putting a hand over one's heart to show love, honesty, or devotion), *regulators* (such as using eye contact to exert authority or dominance), and *adaptors* (gestures produced with low awareness, such as yawning). Gibson and Gordon Pershey (2011) summarized the literature that refers to gestures as *deictic, beat, metaphoric, or iconic*. Deictic gestures indicate physical points of reference (as in pointing to a chair that someone should sit upon). Beat gestures are baton-like movements that accompany speech repairs or are used for emphasis. Metaphoric gestures concretize an abstract concept, for example, moving the hands like flapping wings to illustrate freedom. Iconic gestures pantomime an action. Metalinguistic awareness of syntactic language is a gradual developmental process but given that gestures can be so conceptually close to the physical movements that are observed in daily life, commencing children's metalinguistic awareness with gestural awareness may be advantageous.

Deficits in Grammar and Syntax

Difficulties with language form may manifest in many different ways. The deficits common to younger children, notably a paucity of grammatical and syntactic forms and a use of simpler sentence constructions, continue to be among the primary manifestations of deficits in school-age and adolescent students. However, the grammatical and syntactic forms that the older speakers use are more complex than the younger children use, but these forms show reductions in complexity as compared to age-appropriate and grade-appropriate syntactic maturity. Grammatical and syntactic accuracy, variety, and meaningfulness may be compromised.

Eisenberg (2006) noted that some children whose syntax is not maturing may *speak in simple sentences, using basic wording*. Some speakers with grammatical and syntactic difficulties might use a repertoire of grammatical and syntactic forms fairly regularly but have *lapses in the consistent and efficient use of forms in daily language*. They might not always be able to use the forms that they know in on-demand circumstances, resulting in uneven language performance. Variations in performance may or may not be context dependent. Lapses in performance might be an artifact of an inherent weakness in the syntactic domain of language, which might be exacerbated in challenging language contexts (Bishop et al., 2000). Moreover, speakers with difficulties *may not be able to "fine-tune" their usage of syntactic forms*, so their spoken language can appear *less mature and less accurate* (Dick et al., 2004). Scott (1988) and Scott and Stokes (1995, p. 309) characterized the need to measure older children's grammar and syntax difficulties along these dimensions:

■ Language development involves diversifying the use of the forms in their repertoires and functionally using these diverse forms; SLPs can observe spoken and written language modes to ascertain grammar and syntax skills, and can explore speakers' skills during the genres of conversation, narration, and exposition; this means that there are contextual differences for how students use grammar and syntax, and they may have distinct repertoires in these different contexts.

■ School-age children and adolescents typically add syntactic structures to their repertoires, but they may not use their more complex structures in daily language, so establishing conditions where SLPs can observe their optimal language performances may be difficult.

■ It is difficult to judge older grammar and syntax development against an adult standard because a well-defined adult standard doesn't actually exist; the variability of adult language in terms of geographic, ethnic, cultural, economic, and educational variables makes it difficult to establish the adult standard that adolescents should achieve.

Based on these and many other considerations, several authors recommended that SLPs obtain naturalistic language samples in addition to standardized diagnostic test results (Hewitt et al., 2005; Larson & McKinley, 2003; Nelson, 1998; Nippold et al., 2009; Paul, 2007; Scott & Stokes, 1995). Sampling can allow SLPs to gain many insights into a speaker's language productions that testing alone may not reveal (Costanza-Smith, 2010).

Syntax Delay Versus Syntax Disorder

When grammar and syntax do not develop as expected, the structural system of language form is impaired. "Language impairment," as described in Chapter 1, is a term that conveys that language, as a structured system, is not intact. Moreover, "language impairment" suggests that language, as a functional system, is compromised. The structure and/or the function of language are not optimal (Scott & Stokes, 1995; Skarakis-Doyle & Mentis, 1991). A practical and necessary clinical distinction must be made between impairment that is characterized as a grammar and syntax delay versus an impairment that is characterized as a grammar and syntax disorder. In some learners, progress in grammar and syntax follows a generally typical pattern but is delayed, meaning, progress occurs at a slower rate and takes more time to be achieved. In other learners, progress is disordered, meaning, progress takes on an atypical trajectory or features other irregularities. The distinction between grammar and syntax delay versus a grammar and syntax disorder warrants discussion.

Syntax Delay

At an early age, children with a grammar and syntax delay exhibit language form skills that are developing slowly. The grammatical and syntactic forms that the child produces are not much different from the behaviors that are expected as form typically develops (see Chapter 2), but these forms emerge at a later age than would be expected and/or at a slower rate of growth. Grammar and syntax are at an earlier level of development than would be expected for age. The grammar and syntax behaviors are essentially typical and the sequence of development is essentially normative, but the rate of growth is delayed (Liles & Watt, 1984; Vinson, 2012). Syntax lags at an earlier level of development and complexity than would

be expected, given a child's supportive cognitive or intellectual functioning. As cognition and intellect grow, syntax may grow commensurately, to express newly learned ideas, concepts, and skills. Experiential learning in and out of school, literacy acquisition, and academic learning can influence growth in language form. It is important that learners with form delays have supported literacy instruction, as is discussed in Chapters 5 and 6.

For some children, a syntax delay occurs in the presence of other delays across the language systems of content and use (see Chapter 1, Figure 1–1). Syntax may be developing at a similar rate as content and use or could be developing comparatively more slowly. It is unlikely that syntax would be developing more rapidly than semantic content and vocabulary because a repertoire of words is needed to create grammatical and syntactic arrangements of words, but it is possible that forms can emerge from a basic vocabulary (cf. Braginsky et al., 2015, on the interplay of the lexical and grammatical systems as they develop). A grammatical system is built around frequently used words even in cases where a child's or teen's vocabulary is not well varied.

Possible characteristics of syntax delay (cf. Bedore & Leonard, 1998; Kaderavek, 2011; Vinson, 2012) include:

- Grammar and syntax onset may be late, or some aspects of grammar and syntax may first emerge at the expected ages but then subsequent emergence of additional forms is delayed.
- Language may be commensurate with other developmental progress, such as in cognition or motor skills, or could be the child's highest or lowest area of skill; language may

be more delayed or less delayed than other areas of development. Grammar and syntax are within the overall level of delay in the language domain as compared to developmental delays in other domains.

- Acquisition of grammar and syntactic competencies is at a slower rate than expected; the progression of development is at a slower pace; this pace continues throughout the school years.

- Grammar and syntax skills are said to be "behind" for age-level or for grade-level expectations.

- The sequence of development of grammar and syntax is slower or protracted, such that there is a delay between milestones; the time between milestones is lengthier than expected; similarly, it is difficult for school-age learners to accomplish the gains that are expected during a school year, so that the student does not make a year's progress in a year's time.

- Delays may be more pronounced in grammar and syntax than in pragmatics and/or semantics.

- Grammar and syntax development may plateau at times, meaning progress may reach a certain level and remain there for a period of time. (Vinson [2012] speculated upon reasons for a plateau: Sometimes, when there is more active growth in other domains of development, such as growth in motor skills, language growth stagnates and is "on hold"; other times, a plateau is caused by a temporary setback, such as an illness.)

- Grammar and syntax errors may be persistent and embedded, such that:

- Grammar and syntax errors that many children commonly produce, but easily resolve, persist beyond the typical age of resolution in children with form delays.

- Grammar and syntax errors that children commonly produce are produced with greater frequency in children with form delays (for example, bound morphemes, such as suffixes, are omitted from many words, not just a few, occasional words, or word order is often incorrect).

- Grammar and syntax errors are resistant to interventions for extended periods of time; growth is slow or spotty.

- The beneficial effects of interventions take a long time to be attained.

- Oral grammatical and syntactic deficits may be minimal and not consistently observed by adults until these weaknesses have an impact on reading comprehension, reading fluency, academic learning, and/or written expression.

Regarding the persistence of grammar and syntax delays, an important consideration is the discrepancy between a child's chronological age and language age as obtained by normative testing. A child who is 4 years old whose grammar and syntax are at the 2-year level can reasonably be said to have a grammar and syntax delay, but a child of 11 whose grammar and syntax are at the 2-year level may better fit the description of a child with a grammar and syntax disorder. There does not appear to be any published criteria for determining when a grammar and syntax delay persists for so long that the appropriate designation would be a grammar and syntax disorder. Vinson (2012) mentioned that a delay that extends into a child's early elementary school years appears to be a disorder. LaParo et al. (2004) explored factors that contribute to persistence of language deficits in preschoolers. Rather than simply slower growth, other characteristic grammatical and syntactic deficits that constitute a grammar and syntax disorder would have to be applicable. For instance, Rice and Wexler (1996) established the importance of difficulties with verb tensing. Perhaps guidelines that pertain to multidimensional developmental impairments might suggest criteria for determining when a grammar and syntax delay persists for so long that the appropriate designation would be a grammar and syntax disorder. Within the IDEA (2004) guidelines regarding developmental delay (Center for Parent Information Resources, 2017), age 3 to 9 constitutes the developmental period, and the developmental deficits of children within this age range can be characterized as developmental delays. The Developmental Disabilities Assistance and Bill of Rights Act Section 102(8) (2000) stated that deficits that persist during and beyond childhood are described as developmental disabilities because of their onset prior to age 22 and their failure to resolve. Following both of these lines of reasoning, a grammar and syntax delay would most like not be diagnosed in a child older than about age 9, and a child who had been diagnosed with a grammar and syntax delay prior to age 9 would be reassessed at or about age 9 so that a more appropriate designation could be determined.

Syntax Disorder

When a delay in grammar and syntax delay persists for many years and is not resolved by maturation and/or intervention, then the appropriate designation might be that of a grammar and syntax disorder. A learner of any age with a grammar and syntax disorder has experienced a *disruption* in learning grammar and syntax. There is a problem in the acquisition of skills, and/or in achieving an appropriate developmental sequence, and/or in the pace of development (cf. Vinson, 2012). The grammar and syntax skills that a learner has may show some of the properties of an earlier level of development, but other considerations beyond delayed learning are apparent. The grammar and syntax behaviors are notably, perhaps considerably, different from the behaviors that are expected. Grammar and syntax are limited or aberrant. These irregularities characterize the grammar and syntax disorder, meaning, the deficits plus the differences from typical development are the characteristics of the disorder. The deficits occur because the learner does not have the linguistic, cognitive-linguistic, and/or social-linguistic resources to develop grammar and syntax appropriately. Despite adequate exposure to learning environments and input from language models, the learner's grammar and syntax are not progressing to include the forms used by his or her linguistic community. In the worst case, a grammatical system may not develop at all, resulting in one-word or short utterances without grammatical structure. Leonard's (2000) data showed that the gap in language skills between children with typical language and disordered language tends to widen over time; that is, as they age, children with language disorders have a progressively smaller chance of catching up with their typical peers.

In some cases, the language form repertoire of a learner with a grammar and syntax disorder may contain instances of appropriate grammar and syntax. However, there are generally gaps in the behaviors and skills that would constitute a full grammar and syntax repertoire. For example, a learner with a grammar and syntax disorder may have some, or just a few, of the grammar and syntax skills that children need (for example, being able to speak in simple sentences but not in sentences with multiple clauses leaves the speaker without a needed skill for imparting complex meanings) (cf. Barako Arndt & Schuele, 2013; Scott & Stokes, 1995; Weiler & Schuele, 2014). This notable irregularity in the number and extent of grammatical and syntactic skills is a main characteristic of a grammar and syntax disorder.

Potentially, it may be because of the presence of a number of language irregularities that a lesser amount of growth in grammar and syntax is attained. In some cases, growth in grammar and syntax may be impeded because of the more profound nature of the learner's language problems. The unusual or complex characteristics of the problem may preclude growth of appropriate language. For instance, a child with a very limited vocabulary might scream for several lengthy periods each day in an attempt to communicate or to express frustration at the inability to communicate. The presence of screaming impedes the play and social interactions that would build language. Or, in another example, a very restricted phonological repertoire may impede the acquisition of new words. Both of these conditions would impede the onset of grammar and syntax and underlie a disorder of the development of the structure of language.

Possible characteristics of a disorder of grammar and syntax (cf. Kaderavek, 2011; Vinson, 2012) include:

■ The ability to learn grammar and syntax is disrupted.

■ The trajectory of grammar and syntax development deviates from expected patterns of growth.

■ Possible irregularities in the expected sequence of grammar and syntax development, which sometimes appear as gaps in skills, spotty skills, or splinter skills; plateauing is possible.

■ A learner has some or just a few of the grammar and syntax skills that persons their age need.

■ Deficits may be more pronounced in some area(s) of grammar and syntax development than in others.

■ Difficulty integrating language form, content, and use (Bloom & Lahey, 1978), such that there is not a functional basis for intentional communication and/or there is not the needed vocabulary for developing grammar and syntax.

■ Less use of natural or conventional gestures in place of speaking or to accompany speaking; the gestural system is not being used as a scaffold for developing verbal language.

■ Less gestural use when speaking (Thal & Tobias, 1992), leading to lesser expressivity overall and fewer grammatical and syntactic constructions used.

■ Vocabulary may not be strong for age level, leading to not having the wording for grammatical and syntactic constructions.

■ Syntax may be unusual or haphazard.

■ Possible poorer meaning making (e.g., dependence upon others to presuppose the speaker's meaning), leading to lack of origination of grammatical and syntactic constructions.

- Concrete use of language for daily living, with less abstract use of language for reasoning; concepts that are both concrete and abstract, such as temporal and spatial concepts, are difficult to acquire; therefore, the grammatical and syntactic constructions used to express these concepts are not acquired.
- Possible poorer message formulation (e.g., slow and/or effortful construction of messages), leading to lesser use of grammatical and syntactic constructions.
- Poor metalinguistic skills (i.e., poorer insight into the grammar and syntax of language, such that drill, contrast, and slot-filling exercises are not meaningful to the learner).
- Irregular behaviors may impede language growth.
  - Sensory behaviors (refusal to touch toys).
  - Interactional behaviors (screaming, silence) that replace use of language.
  - Stereotypic speech (i.e., unintentional use of real or invented words or phrases that have little meaning) (Vinson, 2012).
- Atypical, idiosyncratic errors (as in idiosyncratic syntax or idiolect).

Commonalities Between Syntax Delay and Syntax Disorder

Grammatical and syntactic delays and disorders may have some overlapping characteristics. Children whose language is delayed may resemble children whose language is disordered, and vice versa, to the extent that a differential diagnosis is difficult, but the commonality would be the presence of the hypothesized neuro-developmental bases that underlie difficulties anywhere along the continuum of severity (McGregor, 2020). Some of the traits that are common to both grammatical and syntactic delay and disorder are:

- Grammar and syntax do not meet expectations for chronological age.
- Late attainment of grammatical and syntactic milestones (i.e., problems that are "developmental").
- Longer sentence length, sentence expansions, and clausal density are areas of difficulty, being achieved at a slower rate and/or with less competence (Scott & Stokes, 1995).
- Periodic plateaus in grammatical and syntactic development are possible (Vinson, 2012).
- Grammatical and syntactic skills may be demonstrated in some contexts and/or may improve when given supports, but the child does not integrate these same skills for spontaneous use (therefore, skills remain within the ZPD for a longer period of time than is typical and are not consolidated into the child's repertoire of spontaneous grammar and syntax).
- Grammatical and syntactic weaknesses may disrupt the cognitive and/or social (interpersonal) demands that are placed on a child.
- Grammatical and syntactic functioning may be better than or worse than social functioning.
  - In some cases, it may appear that if social development were to improve, then grammar and syntax would improve.
  - In other cases, it may appear that if grammar and syntax

were to improve, then social development would improve.

- Language functioning, overall, may be better than or worse than cognitive functioning.
  - In some cases, it may appear that if cognitive development were to improve, then grammar and syntax would improve.
  - In other cases, it may appear that if grammar and syntax were to improve, then cognitive development would improve.
- Grammar and syntax are discrepant from norm-referenced expectations (Justice, 2010).
- Grammar and syntax may or may not meet cultural expectations (Justice, 2010), as noted when the diagnostic process takes into consideration how a child's skills allow for communication within the expectations of home, school, and community cultures.
- Oral grammatical and syntactic deficits have an impact on reading comprehension, reading fluency, and written expression.

Linguistic Considerations for Measurement of Older Learners' Syntactic Abilities

Numerous linguistic considerations inform a computational assessment of the grammar and syntax of older children and adolescents (e.g., Biber, 1992). SLPs' assessments of syntax and grammar in older learners in schools and clinical settings may differ from the strategies that SLPs use when assessing children in the early stages of language development.

The process becomes more complicated than identifying which unique grammatical and syntactic forms are likely to be used by a certain age, as is the basic strategy for assessing young children. In the assessment of older speakers, *it's more important to assess how a speaker uses multiple forms together within an utterance and across successive utterances. The outcome of an assessment needs to show a generative command of a variety of forms*, as described in Chapter 2 (Chomsky 1965, 1968).

To examine advanced syntax, assessment would document a speakers' use of patterns of words in rule-governed ways to generate syntactic constructions. The patterns and rules are the evidence of a speaker's command of **generative grammar**, that is, the components needed to generate syntactic constructions and *transform* sentence constructions in numerous ways. It's not just a matter of a speaker using a single syntactic form correctly, one form at a time, as younger children would; it's a matter of the speaker correctly linking forms that need to co-occur to build a longer, more mature grammatical configuration and to reveal a command of the syntactic patterns of a language (cf. Guo et al., 2021; Scott & Stokes, 1995; Weiler & Schuele, 2014). *Syntax represents the building blocks of language, so an assessment of syntax needs to show how these blocks are fitted together to construct utterances with functional communicative relevance.* It follows that it's important that interventions for learners whose syntax has advanced beyond the basic forms but still needs support would establish the use of multiple syntactic forms per utterance, so that utterances can be longer and more elaborate and can convey greater meaning than short utterances are able to deliver. While an intervention plan might focus on establishing the learner's use of one grammatical form or one syntactic pattern at a time, it could well be the case that learning how to use that form means that the speaker is using the target form in utterances that also contain other forms (Balthazar & Scott, 2015, 2017, 2018).

Observing, documenting, and measuring syntax and grammar are in part related to knowledge of developmental trajectories in the acquisition of grammatical and syntactic forms, but the process might be more specifically guided by a knowledge of how grammatical forms are used to build more grammatically complex utterances. *The goals of measuring the syntax and grammar of children and teens who have a more advanced syntactic repertoire are often related to obtaining an accurate and reliable way of assessing a speaker's production of the elements of* **clauses** *along with the arrangement of multiple clauses within utterances* (cf. Scott & Stokes, 1995; Weiler & Schuele, 2014) *and to build a series of utterances.* Of importance are the *grammatical and syntactic elements that are found within clauses* and that contribute to the production of clauses. With that, also relevant are the *grammatical and syntactic transformations that allow speakers to link clauses together* to form longer utterances. Both kinds of grammatical transformations would contribute to the linguistic skills that an SLP would observe and document to perform a computational assessment of a mature speaker's grammar and syntax. Intervention targets would then include learning how to use clausal elaborations and connect clauses.

Grammatical Elements

Measuring the syntax and grammar of speakers who have a fairly complete syntactic repertoires is a complex process.

Ideally, language samples obtained would be compared to published information on grammatical and syntactic development. There exists a range of checklists of grammatical and syntactic forms that can be used for informal assessments and for planning interventions. Syntactic analysis can be an arduous process but, as Schuele (2010) pointed out, SLPs can devote themselves to becoming proficient and efficient at this undertaking.

For analyzing the syntax of younger children or for older learners with limited syntactic abilities, the analysis is focused on accounting for the speaker's use of grammatical elements within sentences (cf. Hewitt et al., 2005). One well-known system is the *Developmental Sentence Scoring* (DSS; Lee, 1970, 1974; Lee & Canter, 1971). The DSS is applicable to children from about ages 3 to 6, so more complex analysis systems will be needed for older speakers, although Reed et al. (2009) used the DSS to score samples produced by speakers as old as 8, 11, 14, and 17. The DSS provides information about children's use of foundational grammatical elements. Lee and Canter (1971) stated, "A clinician can estimate to what extent the child has generalized the grammatical rules sufficiently to use them in verbal performance. With such a guide the clinician can plan lessons which present these structures in a presumably developmental sequence, thereby introducing grammatical complexity in systematically graded steps" (p. 315). Chamberlain (2016) compared the DSS and MLU calculations and found a significant correlation. Chamberlain (2016) and Jalilevand and Ebrahimipour (2014) noted that the DSS yielded more information than the MLU alone.

DSS scoring guidelines are available in publications by Lee (1970, 1974), Lee and Canter (1971), Finestack et al. (2020),

Hughes et al. (1992), Hughes et al. (1994), and McCluskey (1984) and will be briefly recounted here. Sentence elements are scored as 1 to 8 points each. Higher scores account for the grammatical constituents that carry a greater grammatical "load" in sentences. Within each grammatical classification, specific words or structures are presented in a general developmental order. The grammatical classifications that the DSS assesses are:

(1) Personal pronouns: With regard to developmental complexity, scores increase as children advance from using singular first and second person pronouns to third person to plurals of all persons. The plurals *those* and *these* are used as personal or indefinite pronouns. The reflexive pronouns emerge next, followed by wh-pronouns that expand simple sentence kernels with second sentence kernels or sentence complements (e.g., "*I know who came* and *That's what I said*. . . . In the sentence *I know who came, who* is the subject of the second kernel; in the sentence *That's what I said, what* is the object of the second kernel" [Lee & Canter, 1971, p. 320]).

(2) Indefinite pronouns and/or noun modifiers: Indefinite pronouns and noun modifiers include *it, this, that, those,* and *these* (see Chapter 2 for the Bloom & Lahey [1978] scoring of these words as *specifiers*). Included here are pronouns, for example, *I want this; I want both,* and/or noun modifiers, for example, *I want this cookie; I want both cookies.* Quantifiers, as in "some," are scored, including words for other indefinite pronouns, as in *something, nothing, anything,* and *everything* (Lee & Canter, 1971).

(3) Main verbs: These include uninflected verbs, copulas, past tense irregular verbs, and auxiliary + verb and modal + verb combinations.

(4) Secondary verbs: These verb phrases involve the early infinitival complements *wanna, gonna, gotta, lemme,* and *let's.* (See Chapter 2 for discussion of the development of these words as *verb phrase constituents.*) Infinitival complements can link differing subjects in kernels, as in *Let him see, I had to go, I told him to go, I asked you to go.* Secondary verbs include noncomplementing infinitives (*I stopped to play; I'm afraid to look*), present or past participles (*I see a boy running; I found the toy broken*), obligatory deletions (*I'd better [to] go*), infinitive + wh-word (*I know what to get, I know how to do it*), and passive infinitival complements (*I have to get dressed. I want to be pulled*). Gerunds are included here (*Swinging is fun. I like fishing. He started laughing.*). Deletions of secondary verbs are scored, as in *I can run faster than you [can run].* (Examples drawn from Lee & Canter, 1971, pp. 327, 339–340.)

(5) Negatives: Forms of *not* in contracted or uncontracted form are scored here that negate the copula, auxiliary, or forms of *do.* Pronoun-auxiliary contractions, as in *I've not seen her,* are scored.

(6) Conjunctions: In addition to the common conjunctions of *and, but, so,* and so on, wh-conjunctions, as in *where, how,* and *when,* are scored here. In the sentence *I know where he is going* (Lee & Canter, 1971, p. 321), *where* conjoins two sentence kernels, *I know* and *he is going.* Wh-words, whether pronouns or conjunctions, are scored. A wh-word + infinitive construction has the wh-word as the object of the infinitive: *I know what to do* and *I know which to choose* (Lee & Canter, 1971, p. 321).

(7) Interrogative reversals: Reversals invert subject and verb order, as in *Was she there?* and also manipulate forms of *do* (*Does it hurt?*), modals (*Can I play?*), the auxiliary *have* (*Has he seen you?*), and form tag questions (*It is fun, isn't it?*). Sentences can have reversal of any two auxiliaries (*Has he been eating? Couldn't he have gone?*) or three auxiliaries (*Wouldn't he have been sleeping?*) (Lee & Canter, 1971, p. 340).

(8) Wh-questions: All usages of *what, who, where, when, why,* and *how* are scored.

Lee and Canter (1971) explained that many important grammatical features were "omitted from the DSS system: the use of articles, plurals, possessive markers, prepositional phrases, adverbs, word order, word selection, and so on. To account, at least in part, for these unscored items, an additional sentence point is added to the total sentence score if the entire sentence is correct in all respects" (p. 320). For example, the adverbs *somewhere, nowhere, anywhere,* and *everywhere* are more advanced than simpler quantifiers and receive an extra point. As such, the DSS scores for the occurrence of grammatical elements and for the use of grammatically and syntactically correct whole sentences, awarding 1 point regardless of the length of the sentences.

DSS scoring is designed to be relatively flexible. For example, if an examiner confuses wh-pronouns versus wh-conjunctions, the overall score will not be affected since both score 6 points. However, this would credit the wrong classification, so SLPs should be as accurate as possible in reporting the speaker's strengths and weaknesses and in planning intervention targets.

The chronology of manual scoring systems included the Language Assessment, Remediation and Screening Procedure (LARSP; Crystal et al., 1976), Assigning Structural Stage (Miller, 1981), and the Index of Productive Syntax (IPSyn; Scarborough, 1990). Scarborough (1990) catalogued 56 grammatical and syntactic structures observed in children aged 24, 30, 36, 42, and 48 months. Altenberg et al. (2018) summarized the IPSyn as developmentally sequencing these 56 syntactic structures (plus four "other" forms) within four subscales: noun phrases, verb phrases, questions/negations, and sentence structures. Scores of 0, 1, or 2 points are obtained for each structure, depending on whether the child produced the structure zero, one, or at least two times during the sampling session. The result is a compilation of the forms the child uttered or did not utter during the language sampling session. Repeated language sampling sessions can reveal a child's acquisition of new forms over time during what is typically the preschool period of language development (see Oetting et al., 2010, on the sensitivity of the IPSyn for preschool language analyses). Altenberg et al. (2018) revised the IPSyn scoring to streamline the process. Finestack et al. (2020) provided a tutorial on the IPSyn procedures and interpreting the results.

Owens and Pavelko's (2020) SUGAR system is a clinical tool that organizes grammatical elements to reflect children's normative progress in grammatical and syntactic productions. The SUGAR system allows users to compare clinical language samples to language analysis criteria established for ages 3 to 11 for the occurrence of the following grammatical elements:

- Noun phrase constituents: Quantifier, article, possessive pronoun, demonstrative, numeric, adjective, descriptor, noun

- Verb phrase constituents: BE copula, BE auxiliary, do/does + verb, regular past, irregular past, modules, infinitives
- Prepositional phrases
- Morphemes: Plural -s; progressive -ing; third person -s, past tense -ed

In summary, the SUGAR system documents the grammatical elements that speakers use to build moderately complex utterances during the mid-developmental period of about ages 3 through 8 to the later developmental period up through about age 11.

Grammatical Elements Computational Analysis: Mean Length of Utterance in Morphemes

Mean length of utterance in morphemes (MLU-morph) is a measure of syntactic productivity that is useful for measuring the complexity of language in the early or mid-developmental period (Blake et al., 1993; Eisenberg et al., 2001; Fristoe, 1979; Mason, 2013; Paul, 2007). However, as discussed in Chapter 2, counting morphemes may be of limited use for assessing the syntactic complexity of children over the age of 4 (cf. Balason & Dollaghan, 2002; Scott & Stokes, 1995; Weiler & Schuele, 2014), because the speaker's use of morphemes, which is essentially a word-building skill, is not necessarily a representation of the use of a complex arrangement of syntactic elements to convey meaning at the sentence level. The MLU-morph measurement may not reveal the range of the grammatical elements used or the complexity of a speaker's

syntactic structure (cf. DeThorne, 2005; Jalilevand & Ebrahimipour, 2014; Klee & Fitzgerald, 1985; Scarborough et al., 1986; Scarborough et al., 1991; Scott & Stokes, 1995). Mason (2013) mentioned that there is "ongoing debate over the value of MLU measures in the school-age years; however, the results of both Scott and Windsor (2000) and Nelson and Van Meter (2007) suggest that MLU is a valid measure when assessing atypical learners" (p. 1145) who, potentially, produce more limited syntax than their typically developing peers. Measures that more accurately evaluate elaborated forms of syntactic usage are necessary to evaluate school-age children and adolescents with milder presentations of language difficulties, such as students with specific learning disabilities (Nippold, 1993). As a general occurrence, more advanced speakers use longer utterances (Scott & Stokes, 1995), so sentence length is one of several valid measures of syntactic development.

Clausal Structures

Considerable detail on school-age and adolescent learners' acquisition of grammatical and syntactic complexity can be gleaned from Loban's (1976) models of clausal structures, which is described throughout this chapter. The work of Loban (1963, 1970, 1976) and other syntactic analysis pioneers is evident in the analysis codes used for programming of the SALT software (Miller et al., 2011; SALT, 2020b), which yield analyses of grammatical elements, clausal structures, and several other linguistic features. The SALT software (SALT, 2020b) is described in more detail later in this chapter, within the description of computer-based language analyses. SLPs can refer to the SALT's lists of grammatical elements and clausal structures to manually analyze language samples.

The following definitions and guidelines (based in part on SALT, 2019a, 2019b) provide a general sense of English clausal structures and, in turn, reveal how the SALT software and other software analyzes the syntax of language samples. SLPs or researchers who analyze language samples manually, particularly when observing colloquial language use, could utilize these definitions and guidelines to account for a speaker's use of clausal structures. SLPs would consider the speaker's abilities in language form, content, and use when exploring how the speaker constructs grammatical relationships between words and phrases. It is not solely the grammatical forms that a speaker can construct that are under examination; the speaker's lexical choices that contribute to the grammatical elements and functional use of the grammatical constructions to communicate are of importance as well.

(1) Sentences are composed of at least one *independent clause* or *main clause*. The independent clause's meaning stands alone. When the independent clause is the entirety of the sentence, it is one C-unit (as in, "I went out."). (See Chapter 2 for a discussion of C-units and T-units.)

(2) *Subordinate clauses*, also called *dependent clauses* or *clause modifiers*, depend on the main clause to make sense. Subordinate clauses cannot stand alone to make meaning. A subordinate clause is not a C-unit; it joins with a main clause to form a C-unit (as in, "I went out *while Dad napped*"; this dependent condition cannot stand alone to make meaning).

(3) The C-unit is "an independent clause with its modifiers. Each C-unit includes one main clause with all subordinate clauses attached to it. It cannot be further divided without the disappearance of its essential meaning" (SALT, 2019a). The clause itself, "whether it is the main clause or a subordinate clause, is a statement containing both a subject and a predicate. Grammatically, a subject is a noun phrase and a predicate is a verb phrase" (SALT, 2019a). Therefore, a C-unit *always* has an independent clause and *may* have one or more dependent clauses.

(4) Independent clauses and subordinate clauses are structured around a main verb, so *the analysis of clausal structure always accounts for the capable use of verbs.* The following examples illustrate an independent clause, a subordinate clause, a C-unit, a subject (a noun or noun phrase), and a predicate (a verb or verb phrase). This example parses the sentence "My dog is fluffy so, he is not scruffy."

An independent clause: My dog is fluffy

A subordinate clause (also known as a dependent clause or a clause modifier): so, he is not scruffy

A C-unit: My dog is fluffy (a clause that stands alone)

A C-unit: My dog is fluffy so, he is not scruffy (a clause that stands alone and with its modifiers attached to it)

A subject (a noun phrase): My dog

A predicate (a verb phrase): is fluffy, is not scruffy

If a speaker can produce an array of well-formed C-units during a language sampling session and evidences the conjoined use of independent clauses with subordinate clauses that function as clause modifiers, then that speaker's syntax is comparatively complex (Weiler & Schuele, 2014). However, a speaker who produces independent clausal constructions that do not have subordinating segments, even if these are well-constructed independent clauses, would have less elaborate syntax and could be said to be producing utterances that are shorter, less complex, and lacking in syntactic modifiers.

(5) The three types of subordinate clauses are nominal, relative, and adverbial (Crews, 1984; Nippold et al., 2009; Quirk & Greenbaum, 1973). The *nominal clause* expresses feelings, attitudes, and beliefs subordinate to an action in the main clause (as in, *"He decided* the car is too expensive."). Nippold et al. (2009, p. 242) gave examples of the common metacognitive "(e.g., decide, believe, infer, or concur)" or "metalinguistic (e.g., argue, report, agree, or defend) verbs" that are in nominal clauses. *The nominal clause shows the speaker's skill in verb use.* The *relative clause* describes the subject or object of a sentence (as in the subject modifier, "The student *who won the prize* worked hard for this honor" and the object modifier, "Blane is a hard-working student *who won an academic prize*"). The relative clause postmodifies the subject or object noun phrase and begins with a wh-pronoun (who, whom, whose, which) or the relativizer "that" (Oetting & Newkirk, 2008; Schuele & Tolbert, 2001). The *adverbial clause* expresses conditionality, time, and purpose (Nippold et al., 2009) (as in, *"Before you go out,* tell Dad where you are going," and "I went out *while Dad napped."*).

Adverbial clauses are of two types. The *restrictive adverbial clause,* also known as an *essential clause,* provides information that the sentence requires to impart

its meaning, as in, "Runners win *who are consistently the fastest."* Restrictive adverbial clauses begin with *that, who, whom,* or *which.* When *which* is used in writing, the restrictive adverbial clause needs to be set off by commas and is sometimes a more wordy, nonpreferred form for restrictive clauses (Nash, 2021), as in, "The loser of the race, *which was precisely timed,* complained about the judging"; a preferred form might be the more standard way of writing a restrictive adverbial clause: "The loser of the race *that was precisely timed* complained about the judging."

The *nonrestrictive adverbial clause,* also known as a *nonessential clause,* conveys additional meaning that is not essential to the sentence meaning, as in, "The windstorm, *which I told you about before,* blew down several trees on our property." The word *which* is used to begin a nonrestrictive adverbial clause. In writing, nonrestrictive adverbial clauses are set off by commas.

(6) *Conjunctions* are used to link clauses and are of two types, coordinating and subordinating. Sometimes clauses that begin with *coordinating conjunctions* (*and, but, so, then*) can stand alone in grammar and meaning (as in "My dog is fluffy so, he is not scruffy," "he is not scruffy" could stand alone in meaning). *Subordinating conjunctions* include earlier developmental forms (*because, that, when, who*) and later developmental forms (*after, before, what, which, although, if, unless, while, as, how, until, like, where, since, although, how, while*) (cf. Schleppegrell, 1992; Weiler & Schuele, 2014); the clauses that follow these conjunctions might not stand alone (as in, "I went out *while Dad napped,"* or could stand alone as a sentence, as in "I went out, *as I was too warm inside the house."*).

[Many of the following examples provide justifiable reasons for why counting morphemes per utterance is not an accurate or reliable strategy for analyzing the syntax of mature speakers. Valuing length of utterance is not always necessary. Producing short utterances doesn't necessarily signify an inability to produce longer utterances, as it might for younger children, and the short utterance might actually reveal a more sophisticated level of syntactic competence. The consideration is whether the clausal structure is sufficient to convey meaning and is produced correctly for the communicative context. Speakers show their presuppositional skills and their ability to express implied meanings when they construct shorter utterances. These sentence transformations are not a hindrance to being able to produce explicit meanings in longer utterances on other occasions.]

(7) *An elliptical response* or *ellipsis* allows for words to be omitted. Saying these words would add unnecessary words to a sentence whose meaning is presupposed or understood. Ellipsis reduces the redundant use of words. A full independent clause is not needed to make meaning when ellipsis is used for efficiency (for example, in response to "Call me later," the speaker says, "Will do"; in response to "Why do you want to go?" the speaker says, "Because."). The missing parts of the full utterance are not needed because meaning is derived from context and is implied (Loban, 1963).

(8) *Omission of an auxiliary.* This is a type of ellipsis that is produced as a colloquial or informal utterance (as in, "You ready to go yet?" the speaker omits "are"). The auxiliary is implied.

(9) A *null subject* or an *implied subject* is another type of ellipsis. The subject of the utterance is not stated (as in, "See that?"

"Wanna play a game?" "There, see what you've done?" In these examples, "you" is the subject of the inquiry; this colloquial or casual remark is of a shorter length than a more formal utterance. The implied subject might also entail a missing auxiliary verbing, as when "do you" or "did you" is omitted).

(10) *Successions of verbs without subjects* allow for economy of form. A subject doesn't need to be stated before each verb in an utterance, as in "Jessie made the bed, washed the floor, and straightened up the clothes in her closets."

(11) *Nonobligatory subordinating* conjunctions can be omitted. The omitted word [shown in brackets] is optional, as in "I heard [that] you want to get a new job."

(12) *Reduced infinitive constructions* occur when the use of the "to" infinitive is not obligatory, as in "I told you [to] be quiet."

(13) *Affirmations or negations* are often single-word utterances. A single-word utterance may be sufficient, as in "yes," "no," or similar terms used as a one-word utterance.

(14) *Tags* are interjections or performatives appended to utterances and may be said just for the sake of being said, as in "well," "you know," "I guess," "I mean," "like," "right" (as in, "Like, right, he was the first person to wear this brand of sneakers.").

(15) *Question tags*: The interrogative portion of an utterance appears as a tag, as in "You said you'd be on time, didn't you?"

(16) *Complements* are sentence components that convey information that expands a phrase, as in "Patty realized *she didn't have*

her wallet." A complement may follow a comma in written language, as in, "She decided, 'Oh, it doesn't matter.'"

[Overuse of the following constructions could signal a difficulty with producing mature syntax.]

(17) *Omissions of required constituents* of an utterance. Omission of the words in brackets could be considered syntactic errors rather than general colloquial language use, although some of these productions might be typical constructions for some speakers of dialects of English, where there is nonuse or zero marking of certain forms.

> Omitted auxiliary: "The power went off when they [were] watching TV."
>
> Omitted bound morpheme: "She like[s] warm weather."
>
> Omitted article: "Go sit at [the] table."
>
> Omitted direct object: "We went into [the room]."
>
> Omitted obligatory subordinating conjunction: "She was the student [who] got the prize last month."

(18) An *incorrect subordinating conjunction* is used to subordinate, as in instead of saying, "He stood up *so* he could see over other people's heads," the speaker says, "He stood up *what* he could see over other people's heads." (cf. Weiler & Schuele, 2014).

(19) *Lack of parallel form* occurs when verb forms within an utterance vary, as opposed to having consistency in form, as in, "She *swam* and *playing* in the sand."

(20) *A sentence fragment* is the use of a partial sentence, as in, "I saw the." Loban (1976, pp. 131–132) used the expression "speaking in nonsentences" to describe where errors in word order, deletions of sentence parts, or other sentence construction flaws result in a grouping of words that is limited in the properties that form true sentences.

(21) *Mazes* include hesitations, false starts, misstatements, revisions, self-corrections, or unfinished or abandoned utterances. Hesitation phenomena generally take on two forms, and most of the time these are a speaker's internal pauses for decision-making about ideas, wording, or how to make the appropriate social maneuver. A complete break-off of a word, phrase, or clause is called *aposiopesis. Anacoluthon* is a revision of an unfinished message, as in "There was a—I had my wallet sitting right here." The interruption might introduce some confusion or discontinuity in the expression of ideas. Loban (1976, p. 131) termed these occurrences "sequence interrupters." Some of these interruptions interject "inter-sentence parenthetical structures," which are supporting or contradictory ideas, as in *It was the best, well, not the very best, but it was among the best movies I've seen.* Other parentheticals are common interjections, such as *you know, I would think, as a matter of fact, in a manner of speaking.* In Table 4–2, these formulaic expressions are called "frozen language," quoting Loban (1976, p. 17). The syntactic structure of mazes results in part from the ideational, pragmatic, emotional, or social difficulties that the speaker is having with progressing though the discourse and might have little to do with syntactic competence. Or, abandoned syntax may be a result of a speaker being unable to complete the syntactic plan that he or she began. The syntactically difficult part of the message is deleted.

Clausal Elements Used in Grammatical Transformations of Sentences

Historically, language development researchers evaluated older speakers' language usage according to its syntactic properties, particularly its clausal structure (Hunt, 1965, 1970; LaBrant, 1933; Loban, 1963, 1970, 1976; Moffat, 1968; Nippold et al., 2009; Templin, 1957). Loban (1976) presented an extensive taxonomy of the syntactic structures documented during observational studies of hundreds of school-age and adolescent speakers that remains of value today for SLPs and researchers who require *a compilation of the possible syntactic forms that speakers may use* to create grammatical transformations in sentences and to elaborate sentences' clausal structures. Elaboration of clausal

structure means that a speaker employs various grammatical transformations that expand a C-unit beyond a simple subject and predicate. *Sentence elaborations* include modifications of meaning and structure accomplished by using adjectives, adverbs, dependent clauses, prepositional phrases, infinitive phrases and infinitive clauses, appositives, participles, phrasal coordination, and other grammatical constructions (Loban, 1976). Often these transformations are expansions of the verbs in sentences to become verb phrases.

Loban's (1976) taxonomy is multistructural. Table 4–1 explains the multiple clausal elements needed for grammatical transformations of sentences.

Loban (1976) identified that school-age and adolescent speakers used grammatical and syntactic forms within clauses to produce

Table 4–1. Clausal Elements Used in Grammatical Transformations of Sentences

Clausal Element	Definition	Examples
Adjective	Describing words, modifiers of nouns	*Happy* thoughts
	Can be used in clusters in cumulative sentences	*Happy, positive, cheerful* thoughts
Adverb	A word or phrase that modifies an adjective, verb, or other adverb	*Happily* smiling
		Quite happy
	Qualifies place, time, circumstance, manner, cause, degree, etc.	*There* and *then*, we knew we had lost our way.
Appositive	Nouns, noun phrases, or a series of nouns placed next to each other to identify, define, or rename these terms	*My teacher, a perfectionist,* corrects all punctuation errors.

continues

Table 4–1. *continued*

Clausal Element	Definition	Examples
Auxiliary	A helping verb used with a main verb to construct tense, mood, or voice	Forms of *be, have, will, do* before a main verb Summer semester *will* begin in May.
Catenatives	Expanded verb forms that appear as complex verb phrases, such as past perfect and future perfect	By the time he *reaches* Baton Rouge, *he will have been driving* for three hours. Gail *expected to have been waiting* for hours. (Examples from Loban, 1976, p. 65)
Connecting words, coordinates, or conjunctions	Coordinates: Connectives to create simple parallel statements, often made up of independent clauses joined by conjunctions	Conjunctions *and, but, or, so, because*
	Relational words, often adverbs, that show how ideas join together, compare, or contrast	Adverbs *moreover, although, unless, however*
	Subordinating conjunctions (temporal, causal, conditional, concessive) (Quirk & Greenbaum, 1973)	Temporal *after, as, since, once, until, when, while* Causal *because, as, since* Conditional *if, so, so that* Concessive *although, though*
Dependent clause (subordinate clause) (First-order: one dependent clause per sentence; second-order: two dependent clauses per sentence; third-order, etc.)	A group of words that contains a subject and verb but that cannot stand alone as an independent clause	
	Begins with a subordinating conjunction (e.g., *because, since*) or adverbial to describe condition, concession, time, manner, place, purpose, result, and comparison	For example, adverbial clauses of condition or time: *When* I walk in the snow, I wear boots. *If* it is snowing, I wear boots. *Because* it is snowing, I am wearing boots.

Table 4–1. *continued*

Clausal Element	Definition	Examples
Determiner	Establish specific conditions of meanings: Articles (*the*), demonstrative pronouns (*that*), possessive pronouns (*my*), numerals (*one*), ordinals (*first*), quantifiers (*some*), predeterminers (*rather*), postdeterminer (follows another determiner, such as "*all the other* kids") distributives (*every*), interrogative (*which*)	Determiners are arranged in a specific order in sentences: *My three wishes* not *Three my wishes*
Finite verb	Used in independent and dependent clauses. A verb that requires a subject and that can take as a subject *I, we, you, he, she, they*	*Love* requires a subject: *He loves parsnips.*
Gerund	A noun made from a verb + ing (i.e., the present participle verb) as the object of a verb	I like *singing.*
Gerund phrase (first-order: one within a sentence; second-order: two within a sentence; third-order, etc.)	A phrase consisting of a gerund and any modifiers or objects; functions in a sentence as a noun (subject, object, or predicate nominative)	*Traveling by car* Our priority is *traveling safely* *Running with scissors* They were *dancing the night away* (Gerund Phrase, 2021)
Idioms (with a defined syntax)[a]	A phrase or expression with a figurative, nonliteral meaning; sometimes the meanings are metaphoric and not discernible from the words used; known as formulaic language	Metaphoric: *Talking a blue streak, the light at the end of the tunnel* Literal: *more or less, once upon a time, in other words*

continues

Table 4–1. *continued*

Clausal Element	Definition	Examples
Independent clause (a kernel sentence)	A clause with a subject and predicate that can serve as a complete sentence; the clause makes sense on its own	*I went to Paris.*
Infinitive (an infinitival phrase, a to-infinitive phrase) (first-order: one within a sentence; second-order: two within a sentence; third-order, etc.)	Verb construction containing the particle *to* and the base form of the verb; can be simple or expanded by modifiers, complements, or objects	Simple: *to go* Expanded: *to boldly go* First-order: Celebrations are held *to bring* families together [First-order]. Second-order: Celebrations are held *to bring* [First-order] families together *to make memories* [Second-order].
Infinitive clause (infinitival clause or to-infinitive clause) (first-order: one within a sentence; second-order: two within a sentence; third-order, etc.)	A subordinate clause with a verb in the infinitive form; contains a subject, object, complement, or modifier	It would have been foolish *to waste the opportunity* [first-order]. *To manage his headaches,* [first-order] he takes medication. You can't expect a puppy *to want* [first-order] *to stay in the yard* [second-order].
Modal participle	A modal + have + participle form of a verb	Sam *could have taken* the storm warning seriously. Sam *should have listened* to the storm warning. Sam *might have told* his customers he would reopen his store after the storm.
Nominative absolute	A free modifier consisting of a noun + an adjective, or a participle, or an appositive noun, or phrases containing these forms; a free-standing part of a sentence that has no finite verb and that describes or modifies the main subject and verb	The bride approached the altar, *eyes sparking*. Their *phones having been confiscated* by their parents, the sisters did yoga until dinner time.

Table 4–1. *continued*

Clausal Element	Definition	Examples
Nonfinite verbs	Used in independent and dependent clauses. Occur as infinitives, participles, gerunds. Occur only if there are finite verbs in independent clauses. Verbs that act as nouns, adjectives, and adverbs; do not change their form to agree with the person, number, or tense of the rest of the sentence	Infinitive: She did not want *to wake* her father. (*want* is finite) Participle: *Forgetting* the final step, she served the salad without its dressing. (*served* is finite) Gerund: *Traveling* is my passion. (*is* is finite)
Objective complement	Word or phrase that modifies a direct object. Consists of nouns, pronouns, adjectives. Answers the question "What?" after the direct object.	Mac was elected. Elected what? Mac was elected *treasurer*. You offered him. Offered what? Your offered him *your help*. I am going to paint. Paint what? I am going to paint my bedroom *white*. We named our kitten. Named her what? We named our kitten *Amber*.
Parallel independent clauses (compound sentences, compounding)	Coordinates are used to create simple parallel statements, often independent clauses joined by *and*	I went to Paris *and* I saw the Eiffel Tower.
Participle	A nonfinite verb used as an adjective or noun	A *working* Wi-Fi connection, a *stunned* expression, a *speaking* role, a *breeding* ground

continues

Table 4–1. *continued*

Clausal Element	Definition	Examples
Participle phrase (first-order, second-order, etc.)	A phrase that starts with a participle and modifies a noun or a pronoun in a sentence; functions as an adjective or an adjective phrase	The *printed document* is required for proof. The *worried parents* sent several emails to the principal. First-order present perfect participial phrase: *Having washed* her hair, she applied conditioner. Second-order and third-order present perfect participial phrases: *Having washed* her hair but *being in a hurry*, she skipped *applying conditioner.*
Possessive	Adding 's to a noun or using a possessive pronoun	*Manuel's* family *Their* backyard
Prepositional phrase	A phrase that begins with a preposition	Leaving the house *in a hurry*, Jim forgot his cell phone.
Relative pronoun	Pronouns as objects in subordinate adjectival clause	I have a cat, *which* I feed every day (example from Loban, 1976, p. 82)

[a]See Table 4–2. Loban (1976) scored idiomatic syntax using the codes *Parenthetical* or *Insertions.*

elaborated syntax. *Speakers also used specific forms to arrange multiple clauses together.* Syntactic maturity is revealed when speakers use clausal formations to communicate more complex propositions than may be possible with simple independent clauses. Speakers use their kernel sentences, which are usually independent clauses, to generate complex sentences. Grammatical transformation strategies include sentence expansions, such as adding parallel independent clauses (i.e., sentence compounding) or embedding dependent clauses. Some *grammatical transformations require that parts of sentences be deleted* and the remaining elements become participles or gerunds. Sentence elaborations include modifications of meaning and structure by using adjectives, adverbs, dependent clauses, prepositional phrases, infinitives, appositives, participles, and other grammatical elements. As such, *syntactic maturity involves grammatical transformations that require sentence expansions, clausal embedding, and deletions of words* that are no longer necessary when the grammatical transformations occur. Elaborated syntax does not always mean that sentences have increased in length. Rather, the sentences have increased in grammatical complexity.

Loban's Elaboration Index (Loban, 1970, 1976) used over 20 elements of sentence complexity, including prepositional phrases, infinitives, gerunds, and other syntactic and grammatical structures, to characterize these expansions and obtain a weighted score, with greater weight given to the more complex constructions among the elements of sentence complexity (see Table 4–2). Loban (1976, p. 17) scored participants' language samples by adding points when speakers used certain grammatical and syntactic constructions. Although the point values Loban awarded, known as Loban's Elaboration Weights Index, were devised as criterion scores that were suitable for the computations used during Loban's study, these point values reveal the increasing complexity of each of these grammatical and syntactic structures. For example, as shown

Table 4–2. Loban's Elaboration Weights Index

Language Variable	Points
Adjective	½
Adverb	½
Adverbial clauses of cause, concession, and condition	½
Compounding	½
Auxiliary	½
Possessive	1
Determiner	1
Topic[a] A subject is repeated: *That* song, *it* was my favorite.	1
Frozen language[a] Idiomatic expressions with a defined syntax: *More or less, Once upon a time, In other words*	1
Parenthetical[a] Insertions: *Well, I guess, Like, Right*	2
Nominative absolute	2
Prepositional phrase	2
Modal participle	2
Gerund	2

continues

Table 4–2. *continued*

Language Variable	Points
Infinitive	2
Objective complement	3
Appositive	3
First-order dependent clause[b]	4
First-order participial phrase[b]	5
First-order gerund phrase[b]	5
First-order infinitive phrase[b]	5
First-order infinitive clause	5

[a]Not specifically grammatical elements. These constructions are artifacts of conversational language for which Loban (1976) needed to develop scoring codes. Frozen language and parenthetical utterances might employ a predetermined syntax, for example, "Once upon a time," and would not represent a speaker's authentic and spontaneous use of clausal elaborations. Topic repetition is a scoring code that might account for the verbal redundancy that is common in natural conversation, rather than accounting for the use of clausal elaborations.

[b]Loban (1976) noted that a speaker can produce complex constructions, such as a dependent clause within a dependent clause. Loban awarded one additional point to all dependent clauses and verbal phrases beyond first-order (i.e., second-order. third-order, etc.). For example, a second-order dependent clause received 5 points, a second-order participial phrase received 6 points, a third-order infinitive clause received 7 points, and so on.

Source: Loban, 1976, p. 17.

in Table 4–2, a structure to which Loban awarded one-half point is not as grammatically complex as a structure to which he awarded 5 points. SLPs would be cautious about generalizing the use of this point system during assessments but might find some value in adapting this scoring, or a similar conceptualization, judiciously, to characterize a speaker's grammatical performance.

How the Use of Clausal Structures Matures

Loban (1976, p. 6) reported that although stages of grammatical and syntactic growth were fairly "predictable," the "stages and velocity of growth" did not show a "steady,"

linear pattern. Instead, growth occurred in "spurts" and "plateaus." Like Moffett (1968), Loban (1976) argued that the maturation of linguistic elaboration is in many ways a function of general cognitive development, with life experience factors, such as a learner acquiring more education and adults stimulating a learner's intellect, contributing to accelerating syntactic growth. Perhaps these occurrences have greater influences on the development of sentence elaborations than formal instruction in grammar can provide. This reasoning would account for the unsteady trajectory of growth. Progress would coincide with other learning experiences that provoke a concurrent expansion of the forms of language that learners use to comprehend and express these intellectual advances.

Some conclusions about developmental improvements across the stages of grammatical and syntactic growth that Loban (1976) proposed included:

(1) It is a more advanced syntactic skill to use phrases or nonfinite constructions rather than subordinate clauses. This is a matter of economy of form. When fewer words will be as effective as many words, efficient speakers used fewer words.

(2) Advanced clausal skills include adverbial clauses of cause, concession, and condition, and each increase in frequency of use with maturity.

(3) Relational words (e.g., connectors such as *moreover, although, unless,* etc.) indicate more advanced sentence transformations. Ideas expressed might be tentative, conditional, hypothetical, suppositional, or conjecture.

(4) Using many auxiliary verbs and nonfinite verbs per utterance is a more advanced skill.

(5) Subordination of clauses, a skill that is used liberally by typically developing children by age 8 (Templin, 1957), is a more mature and difficult syntactic form than parallel statements connected by *and* or *but* (i.e., sentence coordination, forming coordinated sentences, or forming compound sentences). Subordination allows for "more coherent organization of related statements" (Loban, 1976, p. 12) and is a hallmark of mature speakers. Loban (1976) observed that mature speakers produced more dependent clauses and longer dependent clauses, in terms of the number of words within the dependent clauses they formulated. Subordination compresses ideas to achieve more meaningful

syntax. Subordination can be accomplished by using nonfinite verbs (infinitives, participles, and gerunds) and subordinating prepositional phrases, nominative absolutes, and appositives. Subordinate clause types include dependent adjectival clauses, adverbial clauses, and noun clauses. The more advanced speakers used more adjective clauses. Noun clauses (such as subject, objective complement, direct object, or predicate nominative) are the earliest developing of the three kinds of subordinate clauses and adjectival are later developing. However, noun clauses used as nominals (subjects, complements, and appositives) are later developing as well. Loban (1976) noted that noun clauses tended to be an area of proficiency for learners of higher and lower levels of abilities, which might suggest that noun expansions are a reasonable initial target for interventions aimed at sentence elaboration strategies. This includes phrases using a noun as the object of a preposition. (See Chapter 2 on the semantic category of *dative* that develops in the preschool period: "This is a gift *for mother*.")

(6) Subordination is a skill that is best used judiciously. Overly complex sentences can become a hindrance to communicating clear and direct meanings. Multiple embeddings of dependent clauses can obfuscate a speaker's or writer's message. Where fewer words will be as effective as many words, efficient communicators use fewer words. Moffett (1968) stated that learners need to expand their sentences before they can learn to trim their sentences down to careful phrasing and economy of form. It could take several years of learning about sentence expansions to then become ready to

learn about sentence economy. One strategy for economy of form is to use nonfinite constructions instead of subordinate clauses. The lengthier subordinate clause would be, "I went to my friend's house *so that we could use his custom gaming equipment*." The nonfinite dependent clause would be, "I went to my friend's house *to use his custom gaming equipment*." The nonfinite embedded clause would be, "Some gaming equipment *that is called custom* really is not customized." The nonfinite dependent clause would be, "Some gaming equipment *called custom really is not customized*." The nonfinite forms are briefer but just as expressive as the full subordinate clauses.

(7) Prepositional phrases, participial phrases, infinitive phrases, and gerund phrases are syntactical strategies for illustrating relationships among ideas. Several types of phrase modification and coordination of sentence elements can result in increased grammatical complexity. Mature constructions include appositives; nominative absolutes; noun, verb, and adjective clusters in cumulative sentences; present perfect participial phrases; infinitive phrases; and semantically advanced prepositional phrases that convey abstract concepts (e.g., *under scrutiny*) or that are idiomatic expressions (e.g., *in a hurry*). Use of appositives tended to be rare among youngsters in Loban's (1976) study and among the studies in the literature he reviewed.

(8) **Verb density** is the proportion of verbs or verbals as compared to the total number of words within a language sample. This ratio may show syntactic maturity. Low density has too few verbs, and high density has many verbs. In general, a higher verb density adds clarity and meaning. There is no target proportion, since the optimal density will vary across linguistic and communicative circumstances. Speakers would use finite and nonfinite verbs within clauses.

(9) Loban (1976, p. 69) stated that nonfinite verbs comprise a sizable proportion of many people's daily language. Speakers may show an "instinctive preference" for nonfinite verbs. Infinitive verb use did not change with maturity, with typical school-age and adolescent speakers able to use infinitive constructions.

(10) Lexical choices: While not strictly a grammatical or syntactic variable, word choices reveal a skillful use of the semantic-syntactic interface. Speakers who are more competent choose vivid, precise, descriptive, and varied wording. It would be relevant to add lexical-morphological growth as evidenced by affixation of prefixes and derivational suffixes (Nagy et al., 1991; Scott & Stokes, 1995) and how these words contribute to elaborated sentence constructions.

(11) Loban (1976, p. 72) reported that many study participants demonstrated a prosodic quality that Loban referred to as "an imparting tone." It appears that this tone of voice is a pragmatic feature that emerged in many of the study participants when they provided their language samples. Perhaps talking about school subjects or talking to a researcher caused the students to take on an academic demeanor. SLPs may want to consider that the language sampling stimuli would need to be sophisticated or challenging enough to inspire students to take on the role

of "explainer." This role might bring about the use of more adult-like grammar and syntax.

(12) Loban (1976, pp. 81–82) was reluctant to propose a definitive inventory of the "sequence and stages" of grammatical and syntactic abilities because learners at any age can "vary tremendously" in their language abilities. A few general trends included:

- Ages 5 and 6: Pronouns; present and past tense verbs; verb inflections; complex sentences; conditionality; causality; constructions using *why, because, if,* with these words expressed or implied. Utterances would range from about four to nine words per C-unit.
- Ages 6 and 7: Complex sentences; adjectival clauses; conditional dependent clauses expressed by *if.* Utterances would range from about six to nine words per C-unit.
- Ages 7 and 8: Relative pronoun *which*; subordinate clauses beginning with *when, if, because*; gerund phrase as the object of a verb (I like *singing*). Utterances would range from about seven to nine words per C-unit.
- Ages 8, 9, and 10: Relate particular instances to general ideas using words such as *meanwhile, unless, even if.* Subordinating connector *although.* Present participle active: *Sitting up,* I looked around. Perfect participle: *Having finished* my homework, I went outside. Gerund as the object of a preposition: *By looking* closely, I saw the leaf's thin veins. Utterances would range from about seven to over nine words per C-unit.
- Ages 10, 11, and 12: Complex sentences with subordinate clauses of concession introduced by connectives like *provided that, nevertheless, in spite of, unless.* More use of auxiliary *might, could, should.* More *if-then* temporal constructions (*If prices of exercise bikes go up, then no one will buy them.*). Subordinate adjectival clauses: nouns modified by a participle or participle phrase (e.g., a *sleeping* beauty, a *losing* battle, a *rented* van, a *broken and battered* tennis racket). Utterances would range from about 8 to over 10 words per C-unit.

Loban (1976) reported some general learning trends that can help inform SLPs' knowledge of how school-age and adolescent learners might use language form. Some of the findings were:

(1) Students used comparable forms in their oral language and written languages samples.

(2) Students tended to speak and write in C-units of similar lengths, with the average number of words per C-unit being nearly the same length in both forms of expressive language.

(3) Expressive oral and written language performance correlated with reading comprehension and performance in learning a foreign language.

(4) More competent speakers in kindergarten through Grade 12, in general, produced more words and greater numbers of syntactic elaborations. The less sophisticated syntactic elaborations combine or conjoin phrases or sentences. The more sophisticated syntactic elaborations involve syntactic transformations achieved by embedding clausal elements within a sentence, such as subordinate clauses, appositives, and so on.

(5) Better speakers produced fewer mazes and hesitation pauses. Mazes were scored when speakers "become confused or tangled in words" (Loban, 1976, p. 10). Maze behaviors include hesitations, false starts, or abandoning an utterance. Loban continued by saying, "A maze is a series of words (or initial parts of words), or unattached fragments which do not constitute a communication unit and are not necessary to the communication unit . . . when a maze is removed from a communication unit, the remaining material . . . constitutes a straightforward, clearly recognizable unit of communication." Computations may include the number of mazes produced, average words per maze, and maze words as a percentage of total words, all of which reveal the speaker's "degree of linguistic uncertainty." Mazes can interrupt verbal fluency and may be a consequence of the instantaneous speed at which speakers are expected to accomplish their verbal planning and put their thoughts into words. Sorting out what to say or misspeaking are universal experiences but appeared to be fewer among abler speakers. The onset of a maze may be due to the speaker's personality factors, such as self-confidence, rather than syntactic difficulties. Social contexts, communicative pressures from communication partners, discussing complicated or abstract concepts that are difficult to put into words, and communicative situations that require more verbal planning can all precipitate verbal hesitations and maze behaviors. Loban (1976, p. 75) reported that hesitations were more likely to occur before a speaker uttered a "lexical word" (a word with importance in an utterance, often a noun, verb, or adjective) than before a speaker uttered a "function word" (such as a preposition or a conjunction). Hesitations most often "preceded the least redundant elements of sentence syntax," such as key words or abstract terms that might be said only once. Hesitations least often preceded easier words that speakers say "redundantly," such as articles, prepositions, or simple, often-used verbs. Of importance is not only the factors that cause mazes to occur, but how well speakers reestablish control of their message output and extricate themselves from their mazes. Message revisions may be likely to require syntactic modifications of the utterances that speakers have begun but need to abandon. Syntactic difficulties might be observed when speakers are not easily able to revise a message to terminate a maze, which may result in a speaker not completing a message. Speakers who often find themselves unable to revise their messages may lose the motivation to try to modify their syntax and may end up not having many experiences revising and improving their message construction. This can be a compounding problem. If the message is too difficult to express, or the effort to revise is too great, or if there is no motivation to try or reward for trying, speakers who most need to practice syntactic revisions may be less likely to attempt revisions and thus do not gain practice in revising. Part of improving syntax might be the motivation and endurance needed to bother to revise messages, along with the social and communicative payoff obtained by imparting an effective message.

(6) In part because measurement techniques utilized to show grammatical

and syntactic competence are not exact, students within and across grades can exhibit great variations in grammatical and syntactic performance but can still have grade-appropriate language skills. Throughout Loban's (1976) report, various data suggested that students within a given grade can show performance variations of as much as five to seven grade levels. For example, students with Grade 4 grammatical and syntactic skills might be in the same classroom with students with Grade 11 grammatical and syntactic skills, and they might all be meeting curricular and instructional expectations, but by employing different means to this end. To contextualize this phenomenon of disparity among learners, consider how present-day large-scale student assessment systems annually report wide-ranging performance disparities within grade level. A notable example is the variability in the grade-level student performance data for the years 1992 through 2019 obtained by the National Assessment of Educational Progress (NAEP; U.S. Department of Education, National Center for Education Statistics, n.d.), whose mission is to administer educational performance assessments nationwide and provide public access to student performance data. Consider also how educators are obligated to differentiate their instruction to meet students' levels of ability and preparedness and their individual learning styles. *Differentiated instruction* is a proactive response to the failings of one-size-fits-all approaches to student learning (Tomlinson, 2017). Teachers use varied approaches to deliver content and provide students with multiple and heterogenous opportunities to dem-

onstrate their learning. (See Chapter 5 and Chapter 6 for discussion of how differentiation of reading and writing instruction can enhance grammatical and syntactic skills.)

Syntactic maturity is one aspect of how students can impart meaning effectively. Loban's (1976) observational study also considered how well students were able to communicate meaningfully and with expressivity, independent of syntax. To collect this type of data, Loban instructed the participating teachers to assess the following six meaning-making criteria using a 5-point scale, which could translate in practical terms to SLPs assigning impressionistic ratings such as *excellent, good, average, below average*, and *poor*. If SLPs were to adapt Loban's informal analysis paradigm, it then would entail, along with the computations of the forms that a speaker used, a final analysis of these six qualities of communicative functioning. Or SLPs could use clinical judgment or other methods that reflect local conditions to evaluate the six criteria. Any report of student performance would include the examiner's qualitative and/or quantitative impression of the following attributes (see Loban, 1976, p. 5):

(1) *"The amount of language produced,"* meaning, the length of the sample, as measured by the total word count or total morpheme count, the number of minutes that the student spoke, or some other metric to show how much language the student produced

(2) *"Quality of vocabulary"* (potentially based on assessing whether some of the words that the student used reflect grade-level terminology or other developmental criteria; also, the variety and expressivity of the words used; morphological complexity, such

as word derivations [e.g., Nagy et al., 1991])

(3) *"Skill in communication,"* meaning whether the speaker communicated ideas effectively during the sampling

(4) *"Organization, purpose, and control of language"* (using language with grammatical and syntactic skill and having a range of ways to use words and phrases in sentences; word order in sentences and sentence order when speaking at length; may also include phonological and morphological skills, such as adding prefixes and suffixes to words)

(5) *"Wealth of ideas"* (such as accuracy, originality, creativity, expressivity, and reflectivity)

(6) *"Quality of listening"* (participating in an interchange with the examiner and other communication partners, comprehending the discourse, and cohering to the topic of the discourse)

Performance of these communicative attributes across multiple sampling sessions could be measured cumulatively.

Approaches to Language Sampling and Analysis for School-Age Children and Adolescents

Language samples afford a representation of how speakers communicate on a daily basis (Larson & McKinley, 2003). To measure a speaker's syntax, a language sample of at least 50 to 150 utterances is obtained (cf. Eisenberg et al., 2001; Heilmann et al., 2010b; Westerveld, 2011). Guidelines for conducting language sampling sessions with younger children are available in Walden et al. (2014), Nippold (2010, 2021),

and most language development or language disorders textbooks (e.g., Berko Gleason & Bernstein Ratner, 2009; Justice, 2010; Kaderavek, 2011; Owens, 2004, 2005; Paul, 2007) and on numerous websites (e.g., Owens & Pavelko, 2020).

Elicitation of a Language Sample

Eliciting spontaneous language samples from school-age and adolescent speakers differs in some ways from eliciting language samples from young children or adults. Language sampling sessions for preschool children are usually structured around play with toys and objects. The conversation that occurs during play is the basis for the sample and subsequent analyses (cf. Eisenberg et al., 2001; Southwood & Russell, 2004). Older speakers might not use their more advanced language forms when engaged in undemanding play or diversions, so more linguistically demanding tasks are needed to elicit a true picture of the complexity of their language. Adults may respond to an interview format and speak at length in response to open ended questions, but school-age learners and teens might not be open to self-expression during an interview. A middle ground between playing and interviewing needs to be found. Similarly, obtaining a hybrid of some spontaneous language output along with some elicited language is practical. In this way, specific stimuli designed for the elicitation of complex grammatical and syntactic forms would potentially reveal productions that may not occur spontaneously. Conversational probes about a defined higher-level topic, but where responses would be open-ended, could elicit spontaneous responses but show the ability to meet a developmentally appropriate level of ideational complexity (cf. Heilmann, 2010). For instance, asking school-age learners and teens to describe a process ("How do you take care of your pets at home? "In what ways do you help out around the house?") or qualities ("Who is the nicest person you know, and what makes him or her so nice?" "Who do you like to spend time with, and why?" "What is your favorite season of the year, and why?") might elicit a lengthier and more mature response.

Nippold (1998, 2021; Nippold, Vigeland, et al., 2017) offered strategies for obtaining language samples from older children and teens, where talk is often centered on discussion of age-appropriate subject matter, such as the speakers' activities and interests, academic concepts, school extracurricular events, or reflections on a text read during the sampling session or for a school subject. Sometimes an age-appropriate game or activity would provide the stimuli for gathering a language sample from an older child or a teen, especially if this informal approach is necessary for putting the youngster at ease and establishing rapport with the SLP.

The sampling stimuli have to have the potential to yield different syntactic constructions and sentence types (Heilmann, 2010; Miles et al., 2006). SLPs need to administer sampling conditions that are pragmatically challenging enough to reveal syntactic and grammatical deficits. Tasks and activities that elicit linguistic responses that are too simple will not reveal difficulties with advanced syntax. Loban (1976) observed that "every child's language is adequate for his communicative needs at the moment the language is sampled" (p. 87). Whether the examinee and the SLP are familiar or unfamiliar interlocutors can be a factor in the quality of the interchange and the length and complexity of the examinee's utterances

(Scott & Stokes, 1995), with the relationships among these variables being difficult to predict. Sampling has its limits as a method of assessment of human performance. The data collected, including the grammatical transformations, are determined by what the communicator experiences the need to do at the moment.

One consideration is whether the utterances are produced in the context of three communicative genres: within conversation, or within a narration of events, or within the exposition of factual information (Gordon Pershey, 2016a; Hadley, 1998; Lundine, 2020; Scott & Stokes, 1995). Studies have shown that students who have capable narrative language have the probability of meeting teachers' expectations and attaining academic success (Greenhalgh & Strong, 2001; Snow, 1991; Spaulding et al., 2006), so an examination of narrative skills might help identify students at risk for academic difficulties.

Westerveld (2011) identified developmental norms for eliciting conversation, narration, and exposition. Conversation is typically stimulable during free play at age 3 and via an interview format at age 4.6. Typically, by age 3.6, children embed personal narratives into their conversations. By age 4.6, picture prompts can stimulate children to produce personal narratives. Children at age 4.4 can typically retell a fictional story, and as young as age 3.11, children will generate their own fictional story, which is the most complex narration skill. Wordless picture books can stimulate story generation (Abbeduto et al., 1995). By age 6, children can produce an expository discourse, such as explaining how to play a game. Pezold et al. (2020, p. 104) provided developmental suggestions for language sampling scenarios:

- Toy play: Early childhood and preschool (cf. Eisenberg et al., 2018)

- Conversation with adult: Preschool, early elementary, and elementary
- Story retell or story generation: Preschool, early elementary, and elementary, adolescent
- Expository: Elementary, adolescent
- Persuasive language: Adolescent

(See Chapter 3, Figure 3–2, for a visual of the recursive development of the genres of conversation, narration, and exposition.)

SLPs would need to be cautious in their administration of language elicitation protocols. Developmental expectations or speaker competence (Masterson & Kamhi, 1991) are not the only factors that influence the quality of language samples that SLPs can obtain. Conversational interchanges may stimulate shorter, informal, casual utterance structures. Narration of events might stimulate longer utterances (MacLachlan & Chapman, 1988), especially if the speaker is relating a personal anecdote that is rich in detail, or inserts dialogue into the narration, or is relating a series of events by using linking words such as "and then." Leadholm and Miller (1992) reported that average sentence length was longer in narrative discourse than in conversational for speakers 3 to 13 years of age. Talking about expository information may promote a more formal structure, which could lead to longer utterances with verbal detail, or which could lead to stilted utterances when a speaker is describing an abstract or unfamiliar topic (with the latter observed by Scott & Windsor, 2000). Again, the examiner must maintain awareness that form follows function: Communicative purpose shapes how a speaker uses syntax. For students older than age 6, a sample gathered from elicitation of a narrative and from expository language tasks would offer a more com-

plete representation of age-level grammatic and syntactic skills (Lundine, 2020; Nippold et al., 2005; Nippold et al., 2007; Nippold et al., 2008; Reed et al., 2009; Scott & Stokes, 1995; Scott & Windsor, 2000).

Another consideration is that it might be difficult to establish reliable, consistent measurements across samples, either within or across speakers, because the topic of conversation during the sampling conditions might lead to different kinds of forms being used, and there might not be equal opportunities across sampling sessions to stimulate the same kinds of language structures. It would increase reliability to select some regularly occurring syntactic variables that would be topic neutral, meaning that they are likely to occur regardless of topics of discussion (Nippold, 1993). Scott and Windsor (2000, p. 325) noted that spontaneously generated language can be characterized by "general language performance measures" (GLPMs): overall productivity and lexical diversity, fluency, grammatical complexity, and grammaticality. SLPs can report measures or impressions on a more general level, including, for example, MLU, number of words per minute, number of mazes, number of grammatical errors, and number of different words. "Fine-grained analyses" would include, for example, classification of types of verb errors. Eisenberg (2020, as summarized by Scott, 2020) characterized GLPMs as analyses that determine whether a speaker used appropriate word combinations, included required and optional sentence constituents (e.g., subject-verb-object sentences), and used complex sentences with two or more clauses. GLPMs are useful in progress monitoring and are flexible indicators of the functional effects of intervention. These general measures contrast with, for example, repeated measures of MLU or morphosyntactic accuracy. Speakers might vary their sentence lengths or morphosyntax in ways that are situation specific; as such, functional language improvements might not be demonstrated in all language sampling contexts, but general impressions could be gleaned.

Nippold et al. (2008) established that adolescents with language disorders may produce shorter, simpler utterances with fewer subordinate clauses. Diagnostic tasks need to evaluate production of longer, more complex, age-appropriate utterances. Language sampling stimuli would be constructed to include items that will stimulate an examinee to use subordinate clauses to expand upon the content of main clauses, generally to convey explanations, comparisons, descriptions, and other forms of verbal reasoning. The intentions and functions of these types of utterances would require more elaborated form. In one study, Nippold et al. (2008) asked participants to explain a favorite game or sport to a person who is unfamiliar with the game or sport and would not know how to play it or win The cognitive demands of talking about procedures for playing and strategies for winning proved to be demanding enough to reveal syntactic weaknesses. In another study, Nippold et al. (2009) employed a series of tasks designed to examine adolescents' syntax. Participants in this study provided a sample of spoken discourse elicited by a peer conflict resolution task. This is a cognitively, socially, and linguistically appropriate pragmatic task for adolescents and prompted a sufficiently complex response that Nippold et al. analyzed for mean length of T-unit, clausal density, and subordinate clauses. Responses may have contained multiple clauses per sentence. Moreover, this task is supported by research evidence regarding the need to

elicit spoken language in conversational, narrative, and expository genres (Bishop & Donlan, 2005; Lundine, 2020; MacLachlan & Chapman, 1988; Marinellie, 2004; Nippold et al., 2008; Scott & Windsor, 2000; Ward-Lonergan et al., 1999). Prompts that SLPs would use during sampling interchanges can vary as to the extent of the topic restrictions they stipulate. Examiners need to choose whether the examinee is restricted to a topic, such as when given a specific peer conflict scenario, or is less restricted to a topic, as in choosing any game or sport to discuss.

Manual and Computer-Based Computational Analyses of Language Samples

Manual computational assessments would entail that an SLP obtains a language sample or observes language performance in context and scores the sample for the occurrence of certain forms. Examples of available checklists for practical analysis of advanced linguistic forms include those used in studies by Golub and Frederick (1971), Schuele (2009a), Arndt and Schuele (2013), and Werfel et al. (2021). Alternatively, SLPs and researchers may prefer to use computer software programs to analyze syntax and grammar. A number of manual and computerized analysis systems are detailed in this section.

Manual Computational Analysis: Clausal Structures Measured by the Subordination Index

For students whose language has matured beyond the norms for the grammatical elements scored by the DSS and the SUGAR, by about age 8 or 9, SLPs can score language samples for evidence of the linguistic structures that Loban (1976) included in his taxonomy. But having such a large taxonomy would require that language analyses document how speakers' use multiple syntactic structures, which can be a difficult and time-consuming task. It would be more practical to reduce the complexity of these multistructural systems to obtain manageable tools for practical use (Mason, 2013). The following information is intended to reduce Loban's (1976) extensive data on grammatical categories down to a manageable tool for SLPs' practical application.

The *subordination index* (SI) (originally proposed by LaBrant, 1933) is a method of syntactic analysis that meets the need for relative simplicity of use and reliability across measurement sessions. The SI is an index of syntactic complexity that is based on the measurement of a speaker's use of *clauses* but is more abbreviated than the multistructure measurements used by in Loban's (1963, 1970, 1976) work. The SI is applicable for analyzing language samples produced by children whose language has matured well enough to use an arrangement of clauses, which is noted to be a typical skill for children beyond the 4-year range (Mason, 2013). The SI unit of analysis measures linguistic form well beyond the morpheme level and can be used regardless of the topics discussed during sampling. The measures account for phrases that are composed of at least two words.

The SI is determined by counting the total number of clauses found in a language sample. Clauses can be independent, meaning they have a main verb and have the syntactic structure to stand alone as a sentence, or subordinate, which are also known as dependent clauses or clause

modifiers, meaning that as a syntactic structure, they do not stand alone as a complete sentence. To calculate the SI, the total number of clauses is divided by the number of communication units ("C-units"; also described in Chapter 2) (Mason, 2013; Nippold, 2010; Nippold et al., 2005; Miller et al., 2011; Scott, 1995a; SALT, 2019a). As such, the SI metric explores the production of the total number of independent clauses plus the total number of subordinate clauses, with these segments compared to the number of units that are formed when clauses are combined in a way that conjoins their meanings. Therefore, the SI is the proportion of clauses, both independent and subordinate, compared to the number of C-units (composed of independent clauses) (Hunt, 1965). This calculation reveals *clausal density*, that is, the extent to which the utterances contain subordinate clauses (Loban, 1963; Scott & Stokes, 1995). (In Chapter 2, T-units are proposed as another similar method for the analysis of clausal segments, and C-units and T-units are compared.)

The purpose of a calculation of clausal density is to ascertain whether the number of independent clauses exceeds or is less than the number of C-units. Proportionately, in the course of a language sampling session, a mature speaker would have a greater number of C-units, meaning that the utterances contained both independent and dependent clauses. Say that a speaker produced 20 independent clauses and 10 C-units during a sampling session. That proportion is 2:1 in favor of short, independent clauses, and the quotient of 20/10 is 2. Twenty utterances were not expanded. Ten of the instances were elaborated C-units. Conversely, say that a speaker produced 10 independent clauses and 20 C-units. That proportion is 2:1 in favor of C-units, and the quotient of

10/20 is .5. Twice the number of instances, 20, contained elaborated C-units. The larger denominator (the divisor) and *the smaller quotient indicate greater complexity of utterances, meaning, the elaborated C-units outnumber simple independent clause utterances.* SLPs who are counting utterances manually can tally the proportion of utterances that have elaborated C-units, as opposed to the proportion of utterances that feature short, independent clauses. This could yield a general impression of the sentence complexity obtained during a language sampling session. These calculations do not take into account the total number of utterances produced during the sampling session.

Scott and Stokes (1995, p. 310) provided another method of calculation that takes into account the total number of utterances produced during the sampling session. Here, similarly, clausal density is regarded as the extent to which utterances contain subordinate clauses. The proportion is calculated by totaling the number of clauses (main and subordinate) per utterance and then creating a grand total across utterances. Then, this grand total is divided by the number of utterances in a sample. *The purpose is to ascertain whether the number of clauses exceeds the number of utterances.* For example, if an examinee produced a grand total of 100 clauses in a 50-utterance sample, the calculation would be 100 divided by 50, yielding the quotient of 2.0. If the examinee produced 25 clauses in a 50-utterance sample, the calculation would be 25 divided by 50, yielding the quotient of 0.5. The larger numerator (the dividend) and *larger quotient indicate greater complexity of utterances. There would be more clauses than utterances.* A quotient of 2.0 would mean that utterances contain two clauses on average, a main clause and a subordinate clause. A

quotient of 1.50 would indicate that a number of utterances in the sample contained one or more subordinate clauses. A quotient of 1.10 would mean that most of the utterances were single-clause constructions.

Realistically, the above computations might be unwieldy in daily practice settings. It would be more practical to reduce the complexity of these multistructural systems to obtain manageable analysis tools (Mason, 2013). Loban (1976) noted that a few simpler computations might suffice. SLPs' practical applications could include:

(1) Count the number of words in the dependent clauses within the sentences uttered during the sampling session. Compare this number to the number of words in the independent clauses. For example, using the sentence *My dog is fluffy so, he is not scruffy,* the independent clause *My dog is fluffy* has four words. The dependent clause *so, he is not scruffy* has five words. Consider whether the longer dependent clause lengths within the sample are appropriate and beneficial as elements of meaning-making and communication. Tally the number of sentences where the dependent clause is longer than or shorter than the independent clause. Examine several sentences in the language sample to see if there are any trends.

(2) Similarly, count the number of words in the dependent clauses of the sentences in the sample. Count the number of words in the C-units. For example, *so, he is not scruffy* has five words and *My dog is fluffy so, he is not scruffy* has nine words. Greater than half of the sentence is in the dependent clause, so the dependent clause is the greater proportion of the C-unit. Tally the number of sentences where the dependent

clause is the longer proportion of the C-unit and then determine what proportion of the total sample follows this pattern. For example, one-third, two-thirds, or some other proportion of a sample might have sentences where the dependent clause is the longer proportion of the words in the C-unit, or where the longer dependent clauses yield some observable trend, such as being longer than 50% of the length of the utterance. Consider whether the longer dependent clause lengths within the language sample are appropriate and beneficial to communication. *Loban (1976) observed that mature speakers produced longer dependent clauses that accounted for the greater proportions of the words in C-units.*

(3) Compute a simple calculation of verb density. If a speaker says, "I *ran*," count one verb. If a speaker says, "I *would have gone*," count three verbs (Loban, 1976, p. 67). Count the total number of verbs as a proportion of the total number of words in the sample. Intervention might address increasing the number of verbs per C-unit to achieve greater verb density if the number of verbs is limited, such as a pattern of one verb per utterance.

In summary, SLPs may want to report *the range of the length of C-units produced in a language sample*, along with calculating the mean length of C-unit, and count the number of nominal, relative, and adverbial clauses produced when calculating the SI (as subtypes of subordinate clauses, to show the relative representation of each subtype) (cf. Lundine, 2020). *Clausal density*, which is measured by reporting the average number of clauses produced per C-unit, would also allow for reporting the range of the number of clauses per C-unit.

Another manual calculation that is sensitive to clausal density is the Golub Syntactic Density Score (SDS; Golub, 1969, 1973; Golub & Frederick, 1971; Golub & Kidder, 1974; Kidder & Golub, 1974). Golub (1973) proposed a manual analysis that can be used to compute *readability* statistics or to measure the syntactic density of a language sample. First, the examiner counts the total number of words in the sample and the total number of T-units. Then, the SDS is based on the weighted scores given to the number of occurrences of the following elements. The number of occurrences is entered into the blanks in the right-hand column of the worksheet shown in Table 4–3. The number of occurrences is then multiplied by the weight given, such as .95, .40, and so on. For example, two occurrences of the "be auxiliary" at .40 per each would earn a score of .80. Next, add the numbers in the right-hand column and divide the total by the number of T-units to obtain the SDS quotient. Then, the SDS quotient is compared using Table 4–3 to arrive at a final readability score. The grade-level score could provide an estimate of the complexity of the speaker's or writer's language.

SLPs would be aware that attendant to any informal assessments are threats to reliability (i.e., replicability) and validity (i.e., that a test actually measures what it intends to measure). For example, Belanger (1978) cautioned that the reliability of the SDS can be affected by the total number of T-units, which might skew the results. The total obtained might be an artifact of the total length of the sample or of the speaker's syntactic complexity, which are different variables to consider, the former possibly being simply that the amount of time available for assessment was brief. O'Donnell et al. (1967) objected to the arbitrary weights used in the SDS. Andolina

Table 4-3. The Golub Syntactic Density Score (SDS) Worksheet and Conversion Table

SDS Worksheet

Variable	Loading	Frequency	Score
Total number of words		—	
Total number of T-units		—	
1) Mean words per T-unit	.95 ×	—	= —
2) Mean subordinate clauses per T-unit	.90 ×	—	= —
3) Main clause word length (mean)	.20 ×	—	= —
4) Subordinate clause length (mean)	.50 ×	—	= —
5) Number of modals (e.g., will, can, may, must, would)	.65 ×	—	= —
6) Number of *be* and *have* forms in the auxiliary	.40 ×	—	= —
7) Number of prepositional phrases	.75 ×	—	= —
8) Number of possessive nouns and pronouns	.70 ×	—	= —
9) Number of adverbs of time (e.g., when, then, once, while)	.60 ×	—	= —
10) Number of gerunds, participles, and absolutes phrases	.85 ×	—	= —

Score Total _____

Syntactic Density Score (Total divided by No. of T-units) _____

Grade-Level Conversion _____

Conversion Table

SDS Quotient	0.5	1.3	2.1	2.9	3.7	4.5	5.3	6.1	6.9	7.7	8.5	9.3	10.1	10.9
Grade-Level Readability	1	2	3	4	5	6	7	8	9	10	11	12	13	14

Source: From Golub, L. S. (1973). *Syntactic Density Score (SDS) with some aids for tabulating.*

(1980, as reported by Scott & Stokes, 1995) observed that the SDS calculates syntax alone without recognizing elements of vocabulary usage, age of the speaker, or other general language abilities. O'Neal et al. (1983) presented caveats to the SDS that would generalize to users thinking meticulously about the limitations of any syntactic scoring mechanisms.

Weiler and Schuele (2014) observed that analyzing spoken utterances differs from analyzing written sentences in that not all utterances contain a main clause. In casual communications, people often speak in *nonsentential utterances* that, in writing, would be incomplete sentences. The nonsentential utterance may be one or more dependent clause but may have complex syntax. For example, a speaker might say, "When it should have," or "After a while." These may be the preceding clauses for what would have been the main clause of an utterance. Weiler and Schuele (2014) proposed that the complexity of nonsentential utterances be taken into account during calculations of speakers' clausal usage. Restricting clausal analyses to the utterances where the speaker used a main clause and one or more dependent clauses may be an insufficient sample of the dependent clauses that a speaker is able to produce.

In all, the DSS (Lee, 1974), the IPSyn (Scarborough, 1990), the SDS (Golub, 1973), and Loban's (1976) Elaboration Index can be grouped as the available indices of syntactic growth. The SDS and the Elaboration Index provide quantitative measurements of several later developing syntactic structures and afford a more comprehensive account of how older learners advance in their linguistic complexity (Scott & Stokes, 1995, pp. 310–311). While manual analyses yield valuable descriptive data, *SLPs would use careful clinical judgment when they report any of the numerical scores, or any implica-* *tions of grade-level scores, obtained by any manual analyses.*

Computer-Based Analyses

The field of speech-language pathology has benefited from the efforts of experts in experimental linguistics who have designed an array of analysis tools. These software systems have generated corpora of language samples in many languages. An early computerized system was the Language Assessment, Remediation and Screening Procedure (LARSP; Crystal et al., 1989) that used an adult grammatical framework to provide a developmental description of child language. Since then, thousands of samples of child language have been accumulated and are used to program contemporary child language analysis software (Meakins, 2007).

Lu (2008) explained that the automated analysis systems differ as to the levels of natural language processing capabilities the programs incorporate. Most systems have in common that they use part-of-speech and morphological analyses, and the child language analysis systems often use automated computations of the DSS and the IPSyn.

CHAT (Codes for the Human Analysis of Transcripts) and CLAN are a part of CHILDES (the Child Language Data Exchange System; see MacWhinney, 1996), which provides computerized tools for studying conversational interactions and is a repository for language corpora from around the world (Bernstein Ratner & MacWhinney, 2016; MacWhinney, 2000, 2021a). CHILDES has evolved into the TalkBank Project (MacWhinney, 2021a), found at https://talkbank.org (MacWhinney, n.d.). The TalkBank Project achieved the aims that MacWhinney (2021a) outlined, including automating language sample data analyses, obtaining better and more consistent language sampling data, and providing language sample data for a range of ages and languages.

The TalkBank Project consists of three components (MacWhinney, 2021a). CHAT is the name of the transcription and coding format. Users input their transcripts according to the CHAT annotation software for formatting linguistic conventions (Bernstein Ratner et al., 2020). CLAN (Computerized Language Analysis) is the language analysis program (MacWhinney, 2021b), which functions as a tool for statistical analyses (Meakins, 2007). CHILDES (the Child Language Data Exchange System) is the original online database, the predecessor to and now one of the many databases available through the TalkBank Project.

The transcripts in the TalkBank database are in the CHAT format to facilitate a wide variety of searches and analyses. Meakins (2007) observed that "CHAT can be used without CLAN; however, CLAN is dependent on well-formatted CHAT transcripts" (p. 108). CLAN provides data accuracy so the growing TalkBank databases are integrated and comparable (MacWhinney, 2021a). CLAN automatically converts CHAT transcripts into the compatible formats used for PRAAT (phonetics software; Boersma & Weenink, n.d.), SALT (n.d.), LENA (2021; the Language Environment Analysis software), and other speech and language analysis programs (see Bernstein Ratner et al., 2020). CLAN performs data annotations and automated morphosyntactic and acoustic analyses (Bernstein Ratner et al., 2020). SLPs and researchers can compare their clinical samples' statistics to those of the TalkBank samples. CLAN and the other speech and language analysis programs made possible the compilation of the media-rich TalkBank databases and programs, which warehouse homogeneously formatted tran-

scripts (Meakins, 2007) of not only child language data but corpora for basic and applied research and clinical practice in phonology, speech fluency, aphasia, conversational interactions, and other areas of speech-language learning and disorders, all in a variety of languages (Mac-Whinney, 2021a).

Bernstein Ratner et al. (2020), Finestack et al. (2020), and Meakins (2007) provided tutorials for using CHAT and CLAN. CLAN is designed to analyze grammar and syntax from a functional perspective (Bates & MacWhinney, 1982) and to provide morphosyntactic analysis. Bernstein Ratner et al. (2020) explained that the CLAN's KIDEVAL analyses of child language samples include:

- Total number of utterances.
- Counts for Brown's (1973) 14 grammatical morphemes.
- MLU in words and MLU in morphemes with norms for ages 2–6 through 8–11.
- The number of different words in the sample (word tokens) and the number of different words (word types), separating the different word roots and inflections, to compute the *type-token ratio* (TTR), a measure of *lexical diversity*. The TTR of .001 would mean that every word in a 100-word sample is the same. A ratio of 1.0 would mean that every word in a 100-word sample is different. The TTR should not be too close to 1.0, because grammar and syntax require repeated use of basic forms (Bernstein Ratner et al., 2020). TTR developmental norms show that lexical diversity grows for the first few years of life, then stabilizes in the mid-preschool period.
- Number of clauses per utterance, and the mean number of clauses

per utterance, showing *clausal density*.

- Developmental Sentence Scoring (DSS; Lee, 1974).
- Index of Productive Syntax (IPSyn; Scarborough, 1990).
- Vocabulary diversity (VocD), similar to the TTR.

Wordbank (Frank et al., n.d., at word bank.stanford.edu) is an online tool that has amassed child language data from around the world. SLPs can compare samples to the developmental word usage trajectories and to the semantic network plots to see how utterances produced during a language sampling session compare to data for these words and phrases. Scoring tools show the analyses of archived samples, and SLPs can upload samples for scoring. Although the emphasis is on vocabulary acquisition, the software analyzes the use of words and phrases in sentences. Concurrent development of vocabulary, morphology, and syntax in younger speakers can be analyzed.

Computerized tools designed for clinical use offer rapid automated calculations of language samples' linguistic elements. The widely used computer software program, the Systematic Analysis of Language Transcripts (SALT, originally developed by Leadholm & Miller, 1994, and Miller & Chapman, 2003, currently available as SALT 20) offers a multistructural linguistic analysis of morphemes, grammar, and syntax, along with analyses of some lexical and pragmatic elements of communication. Loban's (1963, 1970, 1976) clausal expansion codes bear some similarities to the codes used for programming of the SALT software (Miller et al., 2011). SALT was designed to be a clinical tool for speech-language pathologists.

The SALT software package, as reviewed by Gordon Pershey (2018b), is "designed to assess the linguistic characteristics of samples of spoken or written language. Computational analyses of the language samples that are transcribed into the software provide examiners with the information needed to analyze the complexity of the language sample." The software's research and development have been ongoing since the 1980s. The SALT developers gathered language samples that would reflect a normative array of language behaviors in children and adolescents. Heilmann et al. (2010a) reported that the SALT language sample databases contain transcripts from over 6,000 speakers. A reference database allows software users to compare the language samples they obtain to language samples from several thousand speakers ages 2.8 through 18.9.

The *SALT 20 Selection of Sample Reports* (n.d.) and the *Guide to SALT 20 Variables* (2020a) posted on the SALT software website assist users with reliable inputting, coding, scoring, analysis, and interpretations practices. Among the scores that can be obtained is the Syntax/Morphology summary that is based on the analysis of C-units and an SI. The Errors summary reports the number and percentage of utterances with errors or omissions. These measures offer raw scores and percentages for the examinee's performance, without comparisons to other individuals, as well as comparisons to the database means.

The SALT results furnish an indicator of expressive language strengths and weaknesses and may be used to characterize the nature of an examinee's language deficits as involving semantic, syntactic, and/or pragmatic elements. As such, syntax is analyzed in the context of the speaker's use of the other language systems of content and use. The usefulness of the SALT software is that it can reduce the labor intensiveness of manual forms of language sample analyses. The software provides consistent calculations of language features. However, the examiner still needs to determine the diagnostic goals that the language assessment needs to accomplish and decide whether the SALT can fulfill each specific assessment need. The examiner would have to determine whether the program evaluates all of the language features that are needed for a particular assessment and then conduct further manual analyses if some features are missing.

SALT training is available from self-paced tutorials at https://www.saltsoftware.com/training/self-paced-online-training and on YouTube videos at https://www.saltsoftware.com/training/youtube videos.

In summary, it is apparent that these well-utilized analysis tools bear some correspondence to one another and are compatible. Pezold et al. (2020) compared the options for analyses and interpretations provided by the SALT, SUGAR, and CLAN systems. Garbarino et al. (2020) reported that the SUGAR analysis can be performed automatically in CLAN.

Another option is to consider whether text readability calculators can perform some of the functions of language sample analysis software at a fraction of the effort and cost. Online calculators of texts' linguistic elements are readily available. These are often used as text readability tools, meaning that writers can analyze the properties of their texts, including the text's developmental complexity. Scoring is often reported as equivalent to the grade-level reading competencies that would be required to read the text. Many online calculators are open access and free of charge. The utility of these tools is also mentioned in Chapters 6 in the context of the assessment of students' writing skills.

The process of moving from obtaining language sampling to conducting linguistic analyses can move expeditiously using online calculators. It is based on Golub's (1973) observation that language sampling and text readability calculations can be used reciprocally that text readability tools are included within this chapter on oral language performance. SLPs can transform recordings of oral language using speech-to-text software and then insert the written text into an online language analysis calculator. SLPs can then review *the calculators' descriptions of the linguistic elements* that these systems analyze and, if necessary or desired, use the results to create their own checklists or reference lists to be used as part of other supplemental manual analyses of speakers' linguistic elements. In effect, these online tools yield informal inventories of a speaker's use of morphology and syntax, whether for an initial assessment and/or as progress monitoring tools. Once the reference list is created, it can be used as a clinician-constructed tool to informally assess other speakers, for example, students in the same grade level or in the same district. A reference list can contribute to creating a compendium of local "norms" for performance on particular tasks, for example, story retelling, expository descriptions of pictures, and so on.

However, SLPs need to use extreme caution in reporting any of the numerical or grade-level scores obtained by text readability analyses located online. Unlike the CLAN, SUGAR, or SALT, these readibility analysis programs were not designed to be clinical diagnostic tools. *These online tools can be used to catalog the presence or absence of specific words, forms, or linguistic features in a sample of language, and they offer useful linguistic inventories to which to compare the content of language samples.* Scores can provide useful tallies of the linguistic elements that a speaker has demonstrated or not. *However, examiners would be remiss to attribute diagnostic significance to the results of these calculations.* None of these measures are standardized to show normative development, nor are they based on developmental performance criteria. The software programs may be sensitive to oral language features or not. Oral and written language features have been conflated in many of the computer-based tools' programs, or written text alone was used to program the tools, so these tools may not be specifically designed to assess oral language performance. *Extrapolations from the analysis reports to clinical descriptions of oral language performance might be tenuous.* Oral language is characterized by self-corrections and revisions, repetitions and redundancies, and ambiguities of meaning that are supplemented by paralinguistic behaviors. Spoken language may not be as carefully crafted as written text, so if oral language samples are scored according to written language criteria, they might be scored as a rather inferior performance when in fact they are not deficient oral language performances at all, but they could be a rather poorly written text (cf. Biber, 1988; Biber et al., 1999). However, since it is arduous to manually calculate linguistic forms, it is worthwhile for SLPs to consider how computerized text analysis tools can contribute to less effortful, labor-saving scoring procedures for language samples. *Ultimately, the SLPs, not the computers, will judge if speakers demonstrate the presence or absence of linguistic elements.*

Calculation of **lexical density** is an indicator of syntactic maturity (e.g., see Loban, 1976, on the indicative value of **verb density**). Many calculators compute various aspects of lexical density for the proportion of words that are the main parts of speech (nouns, verbs, adjectives, etc.), to show how frequently the high-content words are used in any text. Note that these calculators might use programs created from samples of adult oral and written grammatical structures, so they are not designed to provide a developmental description of children's language (cf. Crystal et al., 1989). Rather, they can be useful to instantaneously perform the time-consuming and detailed analyses of grammar and syntax that *can provide SLPs with an inventory of the forms used by speakers* and writers who have the developmental linguistic competency that might be typical of school-age and adolescent language learners. Some online calculators include:

(1) *Coh-Metrix* (Graesser & McNamara, 2011; Graesser et al., 2004)

Coh-Metrix is designed to analyze samples of written text, but aspects of oral language can be examined if users transcribe spoken samples into the software and then selectively analyze just the aspects of language that are relevant to the oral mode (and disregard the written language data, such as paragraph length; however, the importance of these written language calculations is discussed in Chapter 6, regarding written language proficiency, and in Chapter 5, regarding readability of texts and students' comprehension of written syntax). Coh-Metrix is designed to probe for the psycholinguistic properties of messages that allow the person who is hearing or reading a text to derive its meaning, so its analyses can show how well the originator of the text conveyed meaning via the linguistic form of the message. Coh-Metrix is comprehensive in its assessment of syntactic forms, word usage, and discourse cohesion. Lu (2008) summarized that the Coh-Metrix employs "three indexes of syntactic complexity: mean number of modifiers per noun phrase; mean number of higher-level constituents per sentence, controlling for number of words; and the number of words that appear before the main verb of the main clause in the sentences" (p. 153). Some of the linguistic elements that the *Coh-Metrix Version 3.0 Indices* (n.d.) tabulate include:

Sentence count, number of sentences

Word count, number of words

Paragraph length, number of sentences, mean, standard deviation

Sentence length, number of words, mean, standard deviation

Word length, number of syllables, mean, standard deviation

Word length, number of letters, mean, standard deviation

Narrativity, z score, percentile

Syntactic simplicity, z score, percentile

Word concreteness, z score, percentile

Referential cohesion, z score, percentile

Deep cohesion, z score, percentile

Verb cohesion, z score, percentile

Connectivity, z score, percentile

Temporality, z score, percentile

Noun overlap, adjacent sentences, binary, mean

Argument overlap, adjacent sentences, binary, mean

Stem overlap, adjacent sentences, binary, mean

Noun overlap, all sentences, binary, mean

Argument overlap, all sentences, binary, mean

Stem overlap, all sentences, binary, mean

Content word overlap, adjacent sentences, proportional, mean, standard deviation

Content word overlap, all sentences, proportional, mean, standard deviation

Anaphor overlap, adjacent sentences

Anaphor overlap, all sentences

Latent Semantic Analysis (LSA)[2] overlap, adjacent sentences, mean, standard deviation

LSA overlap, all sentences in paragraph, mean, standard deviation

LSA overlap, adjacent paragraphs, mean, standard deviation

LSA given/new, sentences, mean, standard deviation

Lexical diversity, type-token ratio,[3] content word lemmas

Lexical diversity, type-token ratio,[3] all words

Lexical diversity, all words

All connectives incidence

---

[2]LSA is a statistical technique for representing the conceptual similarity between any two text excerpts (e.g., word, clause, sentence, text) (Graesser & McNamara, 2011).

[3]*Type-token ratio* (TTR) is a measure of semantic diversity. This ratio shows the number of different words (the "types") within a total number of words in a language sample (the "tokens") and thus reveals the breadth of words that a speaker used. For example, in a sample of 87 words, if there were 62 different words, the ratio is 62/87 × 100, yielding 71.3% variability (Williamson, 2009). As with lexical density, the TTR shows the frequency of use of the linguistic elements under analysis.

Causal connectives incidence

Logical connectives incidence

Adversative and contrastive connectives incidence

Temporal connectives incidence

Expanded temporal connectives incidence

Additive connectives incidence

Positive connectives incidence

Negative connectives incidence

Causal verb incidence

Causal verbs and causal particles incidence

Intentional verbs incidence

Ratio of casual particles to causal verbs

Ratio of intentional particles to intentional verbs

LSA verb overlap

Temporal cohesion, tense and aspect repetition, mean

Left embeddedness, words before main verb, mean

Number of modifiers per noun phrase, mean

Sentence syntax similarity, adjacent sentences, mean

Sentence syntax similarity, all combinations, across paragraphs, mean

Noun phrase density, incidence

Verb phrase density, incidence

Adverbial phrase density, incidence

Preposition phrase density, incidence

Agentless passive voice density, incidence

Negation density, incidence

Gerund density, incidence

Infinitive density, incidence

Noun incidence

Verb incidence

Adjective incidence

Adverb incidence

Pronoun incidence

First person singular pronoun incidence

First person plural pronoun incidence

Second person pronoun incidence

Third person singular pronoun incidence

Third person plural pronoun incidence

Word frequency for content words, mean

Age of acquisition for content words, mean

Familiarity for content words, mean

Concreteness for content words, mean

Imageability for content words, mean

Meaningfulness, content words, mean

Polysemy for content words, mean

Hypernymy for nouns, mean

Hypernymy for verbs, mean

Hypernymy for nouns and verbs, mean

Flesch Reading Ease

Flesch-Kincaid Grade Level

Readability

Coh-Metrix is available at cohmetrix.mem phis.edu/cohmetrixhome/documentation _indices.html and at csal.gsu.edu/content /coh-metrix-quick-reference-guide.

(2) *Analyze My Writing* (n.d.) calculates the lexical density of nouns, adjectives, verbs, adverbs, prepositions, pronouns, and auxiliary verbs. Other statistics include word and sentence counts and lengths, common words and phrases used within the sample, and the readability of written samples. Again, if this calculator is used to analyze spoken language, the written text analyses would not be pertinent.

Analyze My Writing is available at https://www.analyzemywriting.com /index.html.

(3) *Text Analyzer* (Online-utility.org, n.d.) is a text analysis tool that locates the most frequently used words and phrases in a sample of language. This software counts the number of words, sentences, and syllables, and computes lexical density.

Text Analyzer is available at https:// www.online-utility.org/text/analyzer.jsp.

(4) *The Multidimensional Analysis Tagger* (MAT; Nini, 2019) analyzes narrative text for its narrative features, for example, characteristics of the language that is typical of various genres, such as the language of exposition, reportage, or persuasion. Grammatically, the MAT analyzes nouns, adjectives, verbs and tenses, pronoun usage, negation, subordination and use of clauses, wh-questions, modals, and phrasal coordination. The MAT computations include average word length, type/token ratio, adverbials, and other

grammatical and syntactic elements that speakers or writers use for informational elaboration.

The Multidimensional Analysis Tagger is available at https://sites.google.com /site/multidimensionaltagger/about?auth user=0.

(5) An array of text analysis tools is available at *Readability Formulas* (n.d.). Readability calculators are designed to show the complexity of a text so that writers can adjust their texts to be suitable for their audiences, but these computations can be used to show the characteristics of a speaker's or writer's language. From among the choices on the *Readability Formulas* list, the Spache Readability Calculator, based on the Spache Readability Formula (Spache, 1953), is designed to analyze the components of texts at or below the third-grade level, which may be more applicable for analyzing inputs of younger children's language. The New Dale-Chall Formula (Chall & Dale, 1995) analyzes language samples at or above fourth-grade complexity. The Dale-Chall Formula accounts for 3,000 words of varying levels of difficulty representing fourth-grade through college-level reading abilities. These words are all listed on the *Readability Formulas* site (Scott, n.d.) and in Table 4–4. The Dale-Chall Formula scores the percentage of "difficult words" that appear in a text and computes the sentence lengths within the text. Chall and Dale (1995) reported that 80% of the fourth graders in their studies demonstrated knowledge of the meanings of these words. This word list can be used as a comparative reference bank for SLPs' manual analyses of language samples. This list can help examiners account for the occurrence of words representing various parts of speech and with a variety of morphological features, although there is

Table 4-4. The Dale-Chall 3,000 Word List

A

a able aboard	afraid after	alarm alike alive	angel anger angry	apron are aren't	asleep at ate
about above	afternoon	all alley alligator	animal another	arise arithmetic arm	attack attend
absent accept	afterward	allow almost	answer ant any	armful army arose	attention August
accident account	afterwards again	alone along	anybody anyhow	around arrange	aunt author
ache aching acorn	against age aged	aloud already	anyone anything	arrive arrived arrow	auto automobile
acre across act	ago agree ah	also always am	anyway anywhere	art artist as ash	autumn avenue
acts add address	ahead aid aim air	America American	apart apartment	ashes aside ask	awake awaken
admire adventure	airfield airplane	among amount	ape apiece appear		away awful awfully
afar	airport airship airy	an and	apple April		awhile ax axe

B

baa babe babies	battle battleship	believe bell belong	blast blaze bleed	bought bounce	bud buffalo bug
back background	bay be beach	below belt bench	bless blessing blew	bow bowl bow-wow	buggy build
backward	bead beam bean	bend beneath	blind blindfold	box boxcar boxer	building built
backwards bacon	bear beard beast	bent berries berry	blinds block blood	boxes boy boyhood	bulb bull bullet
bad badge badly	beat beating	beside besides	bloom blossom	bracelet brain brake	bum bumblebee
bag bake baker	beautiful beautify	best bet better	blot blow blue	bran branch brass	bump bun bunch
bakery baking ball	beauty became	between bib	blueberry bluebird	brave bread break	bundle bunny
balloon banana	because become	bible bicycle bid	blush board boast	breakfast breast	burn burst bury
band bandage	becoming bed	big bigger bill	boat bob bobwhite	breath breathe	bus bush bushel
bang banjo bank	bedbug bedroom	billboard bin bind	bodies body	breeze brick bride	business busy but
banker bar barber	bedspread bedtime	bird birth birthday	boil boiler bold	bridge bright	butcher butt butter
bare barefoot	bee beech beef	biscuit bit bite	bone bonnet boo	brightness bring	buttercup butterfly
barely bark	beefsteak beehive	biting bitter	book bookcase	broad broadcast	buttermilk
barn barrel base	been beer beet	black blackberry	bookkeeper boom	broke broken brook	butterscotch
baseball basement	before beg began	blackbird	boot born borrow	broom brother	button buttonhole
basket bat batch	beggar begged	blackboard	boss both bother	brought brown	buy buzz by bye
bath bathe bathing	begin beginning	blackness	bottle bottom	brush bubble	
bathroom bathtub	begun behave	blacksmith blame		bucket buckle	
	behind being	blank blanket			

cab cabbage
cabin cabinet
cackle cage cake
calendar calf
call caller calling
came camel
camp campfire
can canal canary
candle candlestick
candy cane
cannon cannot
canoe can't
canyon cap
cape capital
captain car card
cardboard care
careful careless
carelessness
carload carpenter
carpet carriage
carrot carry cart

carve case cash
cashier castle
cat catbird catch
catcher caterpillar
catfish catsup
cattle caught
cause cave ceiling
cell cellar cent
center cereal
certain certainly
chain chair chalk
champion chance
change chap
charge charm
chart chase
chatter cheap
cheat check
checkers cheek
cheer cheese
cherry chest chew

chick chicken
chief child
childhood
children chill
chilly chimney
chin china
chip chipmunk
chocolate choice
choose chop
chorus chose
chosen christen
Christmas church
churn cigarette
circle circus citizen
city clang clap
class classmate
classroom claw
clay clean cleaner
clear clerk clever
click cliff climb
clip cloak

clock close closet
cloth clothes
clothing cloud
cloudy clover
clown club cluck
clump coach coal
coast coat cob
cobbler cocoa
coconut cocoon
cod codfish coffee
coffeepot coin
cold collar college
color colored colt
column comb
come comfort
comic coming
company compare
conductor cone
connect coo cook

cooked cooking
cookie cookies cool
cooler coop copper
copy cord cork
corn corner correct
cost cot cottage
cotton couch cough
could couldn't
count counter
country county
course court cousin
cover cow coward
cowardly cowboy
cozy crab crack
cracker cradle
cramps cranberry
crank cranky crash
crawl crazy

cream creamy
creek creep crept
cried croak crook
crooked crop
cross crossing
cross-eyed crow
crowd crowded
crown cruel crumb
crumble crush
crust cry cries
cub cuff cup cuff
cup cupboard
cupful cure curl
curly curtain curve
cushion custard
customer cut cute
cutting

continues

187

Table 4–4. *continued*

D					
dab dad daddy daily dairy daisy dam damage dame damp dance dancer dancing dandy danger dangerous dare dark darkness darling darn dart dash date daughter	dawn day daybreak daytime dead deaf deal dear death December decide deck deed deep deer defeat defend defense delight den dentist depend deposit describe desert	deserve desire desk destroy devil dew diamond did didn't die died dies difference different dig dim dime dine ding-dong dinner dip direct direction dirt dirty	discover dish dislike dismiss ditch dive diver divide do dock doctor does doesn't dog doll dollar dolly done donkey don't door doorbell doorknob doorstep dope	dot double dough dove down downstairs downtown dozen drag drain drank draw drawer draw drawing dream dress dresser dressmaker drew dried drift drill drink drip	drive driven driver drop drove drown drowsy drub drum drunk dry duck due dug dull dumb dump during dust dusty duty dwarf dwell dwelt dying
E					
each eager eagle ear early earn earth east eastern easy eat eaten	edge egg eh eight. eighteen eighth eighty either elbow elder eldest electric	electricity elephant eleven elf elm else elsewhere empty end ending enemy engine	engineer English enjoy enough enter envelope equal erase eraser errand escape eve	even evening ever every everybody everyday everyone everything everywhere evil exact except	exchange excited exciting excuse exit expect explain extra eye eyebrow

F

fable face facing
fact factory fail
faint fair fairy
faith fake fall
false family fan
fancy far faraway
fare farmer farm
farming far-off
farther fashion fast
fasten fat father

fault favor favorite
fear feast feather
February fed feed
feel feet fell fellow
felt fence fever few
fib fiddle field fife
fifteen fifth fifty fig
fight figure file fill

film finally find fine
finger finish fire
firearm firecracker
fireplace fireworks
firing first fish
fisherman fist fit
fits five fix flag
flake flame flap
flash flashlight flat
flea flesh

flew flies flight flip
flip-flop float flock
flood floor flop
flour flow flower
flowery flutter fly
foam fog foggy
fold folks follow
following fond food
fool foolish foot
football

footprint for
forehead forest
forget forgive forgot
forgotten fork form
fort forth fortune
forty forward fought
found fountain four
fourteen fourth fox
frame free freedom
freeze freight
French fresh

fret Friday fried
friend friendly
friendship frighten
frog from front
frost frown froze
fruit fry fudge
fuel full fully fun
funny fur furniture
further fuzzy

G

gain gallon gallop
game gang garage
garbage garden
gas gasoline gate
gather gave gay
gear geese general
gentle gentleman
gentlemen

geography get
getting giant gift
gingerbread girl
give given giving
glad gladly glance
glass glasses
gleam glide glory
glove glow

glue go going
goes goal goat
gobble God god
godmother gold
golden goldfish
golf gone good
goods goodbye
good-by goodbye

good-bye good-
looking goodness
goody goose
gooseberry
got govern
government gown
grab gracious
grade grain
grand grandchild
grandchildren
granddaughter
grandfather
grandma

grandmother
grandpa grandson
grandstand grape
grapes grapefruit
grass grasshopper
grateful grave
gravel graveyard
gravy gray graze
grease great green
greet

grew grind groan
grocery ground
group grove grow
guard guess guest
guide gulf gum
gun gunpowder
guy

continues

Table 4-4. *continued*

H

ha habit had hadn't hail hair haircut hairpin half hall halt ham hammer hand handful handkerchief handle handwriting hang happen happily happiness happy harbor hard hardly hardship hardware hare hark	harm harness harp harvest has hasn't haste hasten hasty hat hatch hatchet hate haul have haven't having hawk hay hayfield haystack he head headache heal health healthy heap hear hearing	heard heart heat heater heaven heavy he'd heel height held hell he'll hello helmet help helper helpful hem hen henhouse her hers herd here here's hero herself he's hey hickory	hid hidden hide high highway hill hillside hilltop hilly him himself hind hint hip hire his hiss history hit hitch hive ho hoe hog hold holder hole holiday hollow holy	home homely homesick honest honey honeybee honeymoon honk honor hood hoof hook hoop hop hope hopeful hopeless horn horse horseback horseshoe hose hospital host hot hotel hound hour house housetop	housewife housework how however howl hug huge hum humble hump hundred hung hunger hungry hunk hunt hunter hurrah hurried hurry hurt husband hush hut hymn

I

I ice icy I'd idea ideal if ill	I'll I'm important impossible improve in inch inches	income indeed Indian indoors ink inn insect inside	instant instead insult intend interested interesting into invite	iron is island isn't it its it's itself	I've ivory ivy

J

jacket jacks jail jam January jar	jaw jay jelly jellyfish jerk jig	job jockey join joke joking jolly	journey joy joyful joyous judge jug	juice juicy July jump June junior	junk just

K

keen keep kept kettle key	kick kid kill killed kind	kindly kindness king kingdom kiss	kitchen kite kitten kitty knee	kneel knew knife knit knives	knob knock knot know known

lace lad ladder	late laugh laundry	led left leg lemon	lie life lift light	little live lives	loop loose lord
ladies lady laid	law lawn lawyer	lemonade lend	lightness lightning	lively liver living	lose loser loss lost
lake lamb lame	lay lazy lead	length less lesson	like likely liking	lizard load loaf	lot loud love lovely
lamp land lane	leader leaf leak	let let's letter	lily limb lime limp	loan loaves lock	lover low luck
language lantern	lean leap learn	letting lettuce level	line linen lion lip	locomotive log lone	lucky lumber lump
lap lard large lash	learned least	liberty library lice	list listen lit	lonely lonesome	lunch lying
lass last	leather leave	lick lid		long look lookout	
	leaving				

ma machine	maple marble	meadow meal	midnight might	mix moment	move movie
machinery mad	march March	mean means	mighty mile milk	Monday money	movies moving
made magazine	mare mark market	meant measure	milkman mill miler	monkey month	mow Mr. Mrs.
magic maid mail	marriage married	meat medicine	million mind mine	moo moon	much mud muddy
mailbox mailman	marry mask mast	meet meeting	miner mint minute	moonlight moose	mug mule multiply
major make	master mat match	melt member men	mirror mischief	mop more morning	murder music
making male	matter mattress	mend meow merry	miss Miss misspell	morrow moss most	must my myself
mama mamma	may May maybe	mess message	mistake misty mitt	mostly mother	
man manager	mayor maypole	met metal mew	mitten	motor mount	
mane manger	me	mice middle		mountain mouse	
many map				mouth	

nail name nap	nearly neat neck	neither nerve	nibble nice nickel	nod noise noisy	note nothing
napkin narrow	necktie need	nest net never	night nightgown	none noon nor	notice November
nasty naughty	needle needn't	nevermore new	nine nineteen	north northern nose	now nowhere
navy near nearby	Negro neighbor	news newspaper	ninety no nobody	not	number nurse nut
	neighborhood	next			

continues

Table 4–4. *continued*

O					
oak oar oatmeal oats obey ocean o'clock October odd of off	offer office officer often oh oil old old-fashioned on once one	onion only onward open or orange orchard order ore organ other	otherwise ouch ought our ours ourselves out outdoors outfit outlaw outline	outside outward oven over overalls overcoat overeat overhead overhear overnight overturn	owe owing owl own owner ox
P					
pa pace pack package pad page paid pail pain painful paint painter painting pair pal palace pale pan pancake pane pansy pants papa paper parade pardon parent park part partly partner party	pass passenger past paste pasture pat patch path patter pave pavement paw pay payment pea peas peace peaceful peach peaches peak peanut pear pearl peck peek peel peep peg pen pencil penny	people pepper peppermint perfume perhaps person pet phone piano pick pickle picnic picture pie piece pig pigeon piggy pile pill pillow pin pine pineapple pink pint pipe pistol pit pitch pitcher pity	place plain plan plane plant plate platform platter play player playground playhouse playmate plaything pleasant please pleasure plenty plow plug plum pocket pocketbook poem point poison poke pole police policeman polish polite	pond ponies pony pool poor pop popcorn popped porch pork possible post postage postman pot potato potatoes pound pour powder power powerful praise pray prayer prepare present pretty price prick prince princess	print prison prize promise proper protect proud prove prune public puddle puff pull pump pumpkin punch punish pup pupil puppy pure purple purse push puss pussy pussycat put putting puzzle
Q					
quack quart	quarter queen	queer question	quick quickly	quiet quilt	quit quite

192

rabbit race rack	rat rate rather	redbird redbreast	rich rid riddle ride	robin rock rocky	royal rub rubbed
radio radish	rattle raw ray	refuse reindeer	rider riding right	rocket rode roll	rubber rubbish rug
rag rail railroad	reach read reader	rejoice remain	rim ring rip ripe	roller roof room	rule ruler rumble
railway rain rainy	reading ready real	remember remind	rise rising river	rooster root rope	run rung runner
rainbow raise	really reap rear	remove rent repair	road roadside roar	rose rosebud rot	running rush rust
raisin rake ram	reason rebuild	repay repeat	roast rob robber	rotten rough round	rusty rye
ran ranch rang rap	receive recess	report rest return	robe	route row rowboat	
rapidly	record red	review reward rib			
		ribbon rice			

sack sad saddle	sell send sense	shut shy sick	smile smoke	splash spoil spoke	strange stranger
sadness safe	sent sentence	sickness side	smooth snail	spook spoon sport	strap straw
safety said sail	separate	sidewalk sideways	snake snap	spot spread spring	strawberry stream
sailboat sailor	September servant	sigh sight sign	snapping	springtime sprinkle	street stretch
saint salad sale	serve service	silence silent silk	sneeze snow	square squash	string strip stripes
salt same sand	set setting settle	sill silly silver	snowy snowball	squeak squeeze	strong stuck
sandy sandwich	settlement seven	simple sin since	snowflake snuff	squirrel stable	study stuff stump
sang sank sap	seventeen seventh	sing singer single	snug so soak soap	stack stage stair	stung subject
sash sat satin	seventy several	sink sip sir sis	sob socks sod	stall stamp stand	such suck sudden
satisfactory	sew shade shadow	sissy sister sit	soda sofa soft soil	star stare start	suffer sugar suit
Saturday sausage	shady shake	sitting six sixteen	sold soldier sole	starve state station	sum summer sun
savage save	shaker shaking	sixth sixty size	some somebody	stay steak steal	Sunday sunflower
savings saw	shall shame shan't	skate skater ski	somehow	steam steamboat	sung sunk sunlight
say scab scales	shape share sharp	skin skip skirt sky	someone	steamer steel steep	sunny sunrise
scare scarf	shave she she'd	slam slap slate	something	steeple steer stem	sunset sunshine
school schoolboy	she'll she's shear	slave sled sleep	sometime	step stepping stick	supper suppose
schoolhouse	shears shed sheep	sleepy sleeve	sometimes	sticky stiff still	sure surely surface
schoolmaster	sheet shelf shell	sleigh slept slice	somewhere son	stillness sting stir	surprise swallow

continues

Table 4-4. *continued*

schoolroom scorch score scrap scrape scratch scream screen screw scrub sea seal seam search season seat second secret see seeing seed seek seem seen seesaw select self selfish	shepherd shine shining shiny ship shirt shock shoe shoemaker shone shook shoot shop shopping shore short shot should shoulder shouldn't shout shovel show shower	slid slide sling slip slipped slipper slippery slit slow slowly sly smack small smart smell	song soon sore sorrow sorry sort soul sound soup sour south southern space spade spank sparrow speak speaker spear speech speed spell spelling spend spent spider spike spill spin spinach spirit spit	stitch stock stocking stole stone stood stool stoop stop stopped stopping store stork stories storm stormy story stove straight	swam swamp swan swat swear sweat sweater sweep sweet sweetness sweetheart swell swept swift swim swimming swing switch sword swore

T

table tablecloth tablespoon tablet tack tag tail tailor take taken taking tale talk talker tall tame tan tank tap tape tar tardy task taste taught tax tea teach teacher team tear	tease teaspoon teeth telephone tell temper ten tennis tent term terrible test than thank thanks thankful Thanksgiving that that's the theater thee their them then there these they they'd they'll they're	they've thick thief thimble thin thing think third thirsty thirteen thirty this thorn those though thought thousand thread three threw throat throne through throw thrown thumb thunder Thursday thy tick ticket	tickle tie tiger tight till time tin tinkle tiny tip tiptoe tire tired title to toad toadstool toast tobacco today toe together toilet told tomato tomorrow ton tone tongue tonight too	took tool toot tooth toothbrush toothpick top tore torn toss touch tow toward towards towel tower town toy trace track trade train tramp trap tray treasure treat tree trick tricycle tried	trim trip trolley trouble truck true truly trunk trust truth try tub Tuesday tug tulip tumble tune tunnel turkey turn turtle twelve twenty twice twig twin two

U					
ugly umbrella uncle under understand underwear	undress unfair unfinished unfold unfriendly unhappy	unhurt uniform United States unkind unknown	unless unpleasant until unwilling up upon	upper upset upside upstairs uptown upward	us use used useful

V					
valentine valley valuable	value vase vegetable	velvet very vessel	victory view village	vine violet visit	visitor voice vote

W					
wag wagon waist wait wake waken walk wall walnut want war warm warn was wash washer washtub wasn't waste watch watchman water watermelon waterproof wave wax	way wayside we weak weakness weaken wealth weapon wear weary weather weave web we'd wedding Wednesday wee weed week we'll weep weigh welcome well went were	we're west western wet we've whale what what's wheat wheel when whenever where which while whip whipped whirl whisky whiskey whisper whistle white who who'd whole	who'll whom who's whose why wicked wide wife wiggle wild wildcat will willing willow win wind windy windmill window wine wing wink winner winter wipe wire	wise wish wit witch with without woke wolf woman women won wonder wonderful won't wood wooden woodpecker woods wool woolen word wore work worker workman world	worm worn worry worse worst worth would wouldn't wound wove wrap wrapped wreck wren wing write writing written wrong wrote wrung

X–Y					
yard yarn year yell	yellow yes yesterday yet	yolk yonder you you'd	you'll young youngster your	yours you're yourself yourselves	youth you've

Z (no words)

no comparative analysis of how the words are used syntactically.

The *Readability Formulas* site is available at https://readabilityformulas.com/free-readability-calculators.php.

(6) The *Tool for the Automatic Analysis of Lexical Sophistication* (TAALES; Kyle & Crossley, 2015; Kyle et al., 2018) is a tool that measures over 400 indices of lexical sophistication in spoken and written language. Among its many analyses are grammatical and syntactic elements such as adverb usage and hypernymy of nouns and verbs.

The *Tool for the Automatic Analysis of Lexical Sophistication* is available at https://www.linguisticanalysistools.org/taales.html.

(7) The *Advantage-TASA Open Standard Readability Formula for Books* (ATOS; Renaissance Learning, 2021) is an online text analyzer. Renaissance Learning, publisher of the *Accelerated Reader* (AR) reading software, partnered with Touchstone Applied Science Associates, Inc. (TASA) to create software designed to guide students to select books appropriate for their reading levels. *ATOS for Text* is an online text analyzer based on a formula that used 474 million words from 28,000 books for school-age students. The ATOS scores reflect word difficulty and sentence length, among other variables. A sample of text can be computed for its grade-level equivalence. This result should not be interpreted as meaning that a student speaks or communicates at a certain grade-level equivalence. ATOS provides a score for only the passage of text inputted and other extrapolations are unwarranted.

ATOS for Text is available at www1.renaissance.com/Products/Accelerated-Reader/ATOS/ATOS-Analyzer-for-Text.

Testing to Reveal Grammatical and Syntactic Capabilities and Performance

Examining the relationship of language sampling to formal tests of grammar and syntax reveals that language sampling and analysis have the advantage of having *ecological validity* (Hewitt et al., 2005, i.e., representing real-life circumstances) and of being thorough but have the disadvantage of being time and labor intensive. The open-ended, divergent linguistic performances that can be obtained by language sampling may differ from the results obtained by convergent testing where students have to answer specific questions to demonstrate their capabilities in grammar and syntax (cf. Ebert & Scott, 2014). One performance condition or the other might offer individuals an advantage, depending upon their unique strengths and limitations.

The advantages and disadvantages of testing and sampling are many for both procedures. Brydon (2018) noted that standardized tests provide a snapshot of an examinee's linguistic abilities. Testing and sampling might both be one-shot assessments, but sampling is a more naturalistic approach to gathering an impression of language and communicative performance. Examiners' and examinees' testing interactions are in some ways artificial and lack the context, social cues, and linguistic demands that are a part of everyday life and that may be a part of sampling interactions (Brydon, 2018). Testing has the advantage of efficiently identifying specific instances of weaknesses in grammar and syntax that might not arise when speakers produce self-generated language. But, as a disadvantage, a specific linguistic form might be assessed as infrequently as one time per test (Finestack et al., 2017), threatening whether the test can reliably identify deficits across instances. Tests might not include a representative array of the grammatical and syntactic constructions that students use in their spontaneous language (Dunn et al., 1996). Test questions might not reveal deficits in functional language skills for daily living or in functional grammar (Scott & Stokes, 1995). Brydon (2018) remarked that standardized assessments are on-demand behavioral performances and might be difficult for youngsters with attention and behavioral difficulties and might not be representative of their true linguistic knowledge and abilities. These highly structured, operant conditioning procedures (Werfel & Douglas, 2017) might confound students' abilities to perform in these structured conditions with their demonstration of language abilities. In addition, although the authors of standardized tests attempt to account for student diversity, in terms of ethnic, cultural-linguistic, socioeconomic, regional or geographic, and any other examinee characteristics, it is not possible for test norms to account for all characteristics of all populations and subpopulations.

Werfel and Douglas (2017) summarized the limitation of using psychometric test results as the predominant method for determining school-age and adolescents' language abilities and their eligibility for speech-language services. Werfel and Douglas (2017) cited several authors (e.g., Dunn et al., 1996; Spaulding, 2012; Spaulding et al., 2006) who asserted that examiners' sole reliance on commercially available instruments may jeopardize accomplishing reliable and/or valid educational assessments. Conceptually, in terms of *construct validity* (i.e., that the test is actually measuring its intended behaviors, achievements, characteristics, traits

attributes, abilities, and/or skills), standardized tests may have a narrow view of the behaviors that demonstrate language capabilities. Instruments may focus on restricted aspects of language, for example, semantics as demonstrated by vocabulary knowledge, limiting *content validity* (i.e., that a test measures a representative sampling of the appropriate knowledge, skills, behaviors, and/or performances that need to be demonstrated to meet the test's purposes). Further, it may be psychometrically problematic to compare language test scores with tests of other learning and performance abilities that are given during an assessment battery (Dunn et al., 1996) and may lend a false sense of reliability across tests that actually assess different capabilities. Werfel and Douglas (2017) reported that IDEA (2004) legislated that educational teams should use formal, standardized tests as well as informal, nonstandardized assessments, which by implication would include qualitative assessments such as language sampling analyses, to interpret students' performance (Peña et al., 2006). State guidelines may stipulate that nonstandardized testing procedures would be used as supplemental verification of norm-referenced scores. Observational measures would contribute to an assessment of whether language difficulties negatively affect educational performance only for those students who score below cutoff scores on norm-referenced measures. This would limit the ability of educational assessment teams to consider language sampling data for all students and sends the message that the norm-referenced tests are more conclusive evidence about language abilities. These restrictions obviate opportunities for documenting reliability of performance across testing and sampling. Or, conversely, the opportunity to look for inconsistencies across convergent language testing and spontaneous language performance is missing. Finally, students who experience repeated testing may become test-wise, which is a threat to test validity (Werfel & Douglas, 2017).

Some studies have explicitly compared language sampling and standardized test results. For instance, Nippold et al. (2009), in a study of 426 adolescents, found that both the mean length of T-unit scores and the *clausal density* scores significantly correlated with scores on the *Concepts and Directions and Recalling Sentences subtests of the Clinical Evaluation of Language Fundamentals, Third Edition* (Semel et al., 1995).

The Utility of Information From Achievement Testing, Abilities Testing, and Diagnostic Testing

School-age and adolescent learners undergo many types of achievement testing at school. Achievement tests that have written response questions might offer an opportunity for SLPs to have a sample of students' written grammatical and syntactic skills. Types of achievement tests include:

- Teacher-designed tests of classroom learning.
- Published tests that accompany curricular and instructional materials, usually representing grade-level expectations.
- Standardized or criterion referenced assessments adopted by the school districts or the other education agencies that oversee the schools or learning environments; testing is for purposes of documenting student achievement and demonstrating accountability in meeting instructional standards; assessments might also be to permit students to advance across grades or to help determine classroom placement or the eligibility to take certain courses or enroll in certain programs, among other reasons for identification of students' characteristics and verification of their learning and performance.
- State-mandated achievement testing that monitors schools' and districts' outcomes.

Commonly, achievement tests are administered in a written format to a whole class or a group of students. Students read the tests independently, or the teacher reads the test to the class or plays a recording of the instructions, and students complete the tests either on paper or on a computer or other electronic device. If any of these tests are administered orally and individually, this might be to accommodate a learner's needs or to modify performance expectations in accordance with a student's Individualized Education Program (IEP). *In the course of most school testing regimens, students would infrequently experience oral testing of their grammar and syntax unless an educational team member, particularly an SLP, has initiated an examination of a student's developmental progress, learning abilities, and/or academic achievement.* As a part of language diagnostic testing, grammatical and syntactic testing would likely be an integral part of the team's overall efforts to investigate whether a younger child is on track developmentally but might be a modest part of how a team determines why an older student is not succeeding in school. As Lundine (2020) noted (as summarized by Scott, p. 133), there is a gap "between the language skills required to succeed in school, where learning depends on the comprehension and production of information encoded in expository discourse, and the availability of tools to assess such skills." This is fundamentally a question of the *ecological validity* of oral grammar and syntax tests and other diagnostic measures, meaning, it is not readily apparent whether *there is congruence between the results of grammar and syntax abilities tests and real-life academic achievement concerns*. Does performance on tests of syntax and grammar generalize to school performance, and/or, conversely, can difficulties with school performance be traced back to capabilities in grammar and syntax (cf. Balthazar & Scott, 2015)? Do diagnostic tests really identify an inherent grammatical and syntactic difficulty and how it affects academic success?

Considerations for Choosing Commercially Available Tests of Grammar and Syntax

For the most part, the test items found on standardized language tests are designed to provoke examinees to converge upon a specific answer or to respond to the divergent, open-ended questions with responses that resemble the range of responses that was produced by the standardization sample (i.e., the people who were tested to obtain the standardized responses). The examiners' manuals for most published tests provide a key to the responses that are scored as being acceptable.

Standardized instruments available commercially offer a variety of items that yield demonstrations of achievements in grammar and syntax. Correct responses show demonstration of the achievements that the questions probe for, and incorrect responses show that the examinee did not demonstrate the expected achievements during the examination context. By extension, *developmental norms for ages and/or grade levels show whether an examinee's performance is similar to peers' performances, and in this way, the examinee would meet the expectations for age and/or grade*. The examinee's performance is either within the peer group's performance range or not. Test creators bear the responsibility of assembling a diverse and inclusive pool of peers that would generate responses that would represent what the greater population of examinees would be likely to demonstrate.

When an examinee's performance, in this case meaning achievement in grammar and syntax, is not within the expected range, achievement can be said to have not been attained. At the moment of testing, the examinee does not yet show this achievement. *From an educational perspective, the learner needs additional learning opportunities in order to potentially achieve the target behaviors*. However, SLPs work from a diagnostic perspective, which is both similar to and different from an achievement perspective. For SLPs, terminology about achievement of performance is recast using diagnostic terminology. If, on the day of testing, an examinee does not demonstrate the achievement of the quantity of behaviors or quality of performance that the standardization sample of peers demonstrated, the SLP uses the examinee's lack of demonstration to support the designation of a diagnostic label. The SLP might diagnose a grammar and/or syntax delay or disorder, which is applied in contrast to the peers whose responses are held to be more developmentally appropriate. *The absence of the achievement behaviors is consequential enough to warrant the application of a diagnostic label*. The SLP might ascribe the performance deficit to the presence of an underlying language and/or learning disability, delay, or disorder. The SLP is in the powerful position of superimposing diagnostic labels onto behavioral achievements. Terminology such as *disability, delay,* or *disorder* recharacterizes the absence of behaviors on a given day that show achievement or knowledge into diagnostic labels that suggest an inherent language and/or learning difficulty. Diagnostic labels may connote the presence of a physiological basis, often characterized as neurodevelopmental (McGregor, 2020; Pennington et al., 2019), for the absence of achievement behaviors. Diagnostic labels place learners into a group of people who share these demonstrations of deficits and/or other diagnostic criteria.

SLPs would take exceptional care to explain to parents and other consumers and stakeholders that sometimes weaker performance is simply a demonstration of an examinee's lack of ability to answer the questions asked, whether due to unfamiliarity with the test items' content, lack of educational background knowledge or life experiences, cultural differences, and/ or other factors that are not intrinsic to the learner's ability to achieve the target behaviors. Other times, weaker performance is the hallmark of a disability, delay, or disorder that is substantiated by how closely the examinee meets the norms for behaviors that are below age and grade expectations. The examinee is performing in ways that younger learners would typically behave, showing achievement that is not commensurate with the examinee's chronological age or grade expectations. The creators of the standardized instruments may supply scoring terminology that would impute this age- or grade-discrepant performance with a diagnostic label, such as mild, moderate, or severe language disorder. *In summary, equating lack of performance on grammatical and syntactic items with the presence of a diagnostic condition needs to be approached cautiously.* The important part of a diagnosis is to convey how learning opportunities and/ or supported interventions could help bring about the expected achievements.

Commercially Available Tests of Grammar and Syntax

SLPs can discover the marketplace of standardized language tests by visiting test publishers' websites. Test review sources, such as Buros Mental Measurements Yearbook and Test Reviews Online, both published by the Buros Center for Testing at the University of Nebraska–Lincoln and affiliated with the University of Nebraska Press, offer experts' scrutiny of a test's purposes, psychometric properties, appropriateness for target populations, methods of construction and standardization, format, administration and scoring procedures, validity, and reliability. The Buros website (https://buros.org) shares a variety of resources to help examiners become better informed about how to evaluate the quality of published tests.

Another way to locate tests of grammar and syntax is to consider research reports about formal tests' properties and usage. For example, Finestack and Satterlund (2018) used a national survey to explore SLPs' use of published tests to identify grammatical and syntactic deficits. Standardized testing was the method of identification reported as "frequently" or "sometimes" used by 84% of respondents who served the elementary school population. The commercial tests most frequently used were, in alphabetical order by title, the Clinical Evaluation of Language Fundamentals (CELF; Wiig et al., 2013), the Comprehensive Assessment of Spoken Language (CASL; Carrow-Woolfolk, 2017), the Oral and Written Language Scales (OWLS; Carrow-Woolfolk, 1995), and the Test of Language Development–Primary (TOLD-P; Hammill & Newcomer, 2008). Spaulding et al. (2006) identified tests that were sensitive and specific to identifying morphosyntactic deficits, including the CELF-4 (Semel et al., 2003), and noted that some tests are more effective than others for differentiating typical versus atypical performance.

A perusal of the marketplace shows the following tests (in alphabetical order by title) have subtests or questions that pertain to school-age and adolescent learners' skills in grammar and syntax as assessed in listening, speaking, reading, and/or writing (Chapter 5 considers the role of grammar and syntax in reading and Chapter 6 addresses written syntax):

- Clinical Evaluation of Language Fundamentals–Fifth Edition (CELF-5; Wiig et al., 2013)
  Comprehensive Assessment of Spoken Language–Second Edition (CASL-2; Carrow-Woolfolk, 2017)
  Detroit Test of Learning Aptitude-Primary: Third Edition (DTLA-P:3; Hammill & Bryant, 2005)
  Illinois Test of Psycholinguistic Abilities–Third Edition (ITPA-3; Hammill et al., 2001)
  Kaufman Test of Educational Achievement, Third Edition (KTEA-3; Kaufman & Kaufman, 2014)
  Oral and Written Language Scales–Second Edition (OWLS-II; Carrow-Woolfolk, 2012)
  Oral Passage Understanding Scale (OPUS; Carrow-Woolfolk & Klein, 2017)

- Reading and Language Inventory, 7th Edition (Bader & Pearce, 2012)
- Test for Auditory Comprehension of Language–Fourth Edition (TACL-4; Carrow-Woolfolk, 2014)
- Test of Adolescent and Adult Language–Fourth Edition (TOAL-4; Hammill et al., 2007)
- Test of Expressive Language (TEXL; Carrow-Woolfolk & Allen, 2014)
- Test of Integrated Language and Literacy Skills (TILLS; Nelson et al., 2016)
- Test of Language Development–Intermediate: Fifth Edition (TOLD-I:5; Hammill & Newcomer, 2020)
- Test of Reading Comprehension–Fourth Edition (TORC-4; Brown et al., 2009)
- Test of Silent Contextual Reading Fluency–Second Edition (TOSCRF-2; Hammill et al., 2014)
- Test of Silent Reading Efficiency and Comprehension (TOSREC; Wagner et al., 2010)
- Test of Written Language–Fourth Edition (TOWL-4; Hammill & Larsen, 2009)

The Properties of Tests of Grammar and Syntax

Some pertinent questions surround the utility and objectives of the standardized or criterion referenced oral tests of grammar and syntax that SLPs administer to school-age and adolescent learners. Generally, these are questions of the *concurrent validity* and *predictive validity* of the tests of grammar and syntax. In various ways, these questions probe the potential for grammar and syntax test scores to concurrently represent the difficulties the student is having in school and to predict a course of action that would improve the student's learning and success. The questions center on *whether grammar and syntax have any part in the student's difficulties in school and if the tests can reveal the characteristics of these difficulties.* Among these questions, specifically, would be these considerations:

(1) Is testing of grammar and syntax able to offer a window onto students' difficulties with developmental progress, learning abilities, and/or academic achievement? Is grammar and syntax testing revelatory or "diagnostic" of an underlying condition? If so, what is this condition, and why does it matter in an academic environment?

(2) In what ways does oral grammar and syntax test performance resemble other demonstrations of school achievement (cf. Balthazar & Scott, 2015)? What kinds of information about language form and its relationship to school learning and achievement can be obtained from the oral tests of grammar and syntax that SLPs administer? Do the tests probe for the kinds of knowledge and skills that have an impact on school success? This is known as psychological realism (N. & Pam, 2013), meaning, establishing how the thinking that is needed to answer test questions is also needed in the real-life circumstances that the test purports to represent.

(3) What features of performance on SLPs' tests of grammar and syntax would be indicators that remediation is necessary and, specifically, that remediation would address the performance problems that hamper school learning and success? *Will targeting grammar and syntax improve school success? What connections need to be made between the grammar and syntax prob-lems that testing can reveal and how school learning is experienced by the student? What connections are there between grammar and syntax problems and how the student performs on accountability measures, from classroom assignments to mandated testing?*

(4) If it is difficult to empirically bridge the gap between language test scores and their bearing on school success, is it simply sufficient to say that grammatical and syntactic weaknesses could potentially have some bearing on school performance deficits, so that students whose grammar and syntax test scores are insufficient should receive remediation on the basis of their test scores? Are test scores a sufficient proxy for detecting a deficit that has some bearing on daily living, which can be revealed if test performance is nonnormative (cf. Gordon Pershey, 2003)? *Does the test score alone have meaning, or does there need to be some other kind of corroborating information that associates the grammar and syntax test performance with the examinee's school difficulties?*

A first step toward addressing these multiple questions is to examine the properties of some tests of oral language to view the aspects of grammar and syntax that they address. Second, it would be relevant to discuss the kinds of language test questions that can probe for grammatical and syntactic skills that are found on published tests or that would be assessments that SLPs can construct informally (e.g., see Finestack et al., 2017). These processes could help establish whether the grammar and syntax test items found on some common diagnostic measures could provide the empirical and corroborating information that fills the gap between language test scores and their bearing on school success. At issue are the structural aspects of the test stimuli, the processing requirements of the tasks, and the relatedness of the test items to naturalistic language behaviors (Scott & Stokes, 1995).

Items That Test Receptive and Expressive Syntax

Testing reveals receptive and expressive syntactic performances. To test receptive syntactic knowledge, test items may focus on grammatical understanding in context. The examiner might ask a student to point to one of three or four pictures that is identified by a sentence spoken by the examiner. Sentence comprehension would be revealed by the learner making an accurate picture selection. When the sentence involves grammatical judgments, such as differentiating a past event that is pictured as opposed to a picture of an ongoing event, some element of receptive knowledge of tense is revealed. For example, if the test pictures are of a boy wearing a wet bathing suit getting out of a swimming pool, and of a boy wearing jeans and a shirt walking toward a swimming pool, and of a boy wearing pajamas and sitting in his bedroom, and the stimulus item is "He was swimming," it is logical to select the boy in the wet bathing suit, but also syntactically accurate, since the wording, "was swimming," shows the tense needed for a recently completed event. Other types of receptive syntax questions might have some elements of sequencing, as when an examinee is asked to consider three sentences presented out of sequential order and place them in sequential order. Explaining the timing or sequence of events requires syntactic skills. An example of three sentences that when correctly arranged in sequential order

would be, "The family bought a birthday cake at a bakery. The family went to grandmother's house. Grandmother blew out the candles on her cake." The correct response is based around ordering the irregular past tense verbs *bought*, *went*, and *blew*. For testing to be accurate, in these examples and in all cases, word meaning, experiential knowledge, and cultural familiarity are needed, but given those preconditions, the items would test receptive syntax, with the examinee being able to logically consider how past events would have occurred and then choose the correct verbs, revealing a component of grammatical knowledge.

Demonstrations of expressive syntax and sentence grammar are obtained by asking examinees to provide sentence-length responses to test probes, but these responses are not spontaneous productions of syntactic constructions, such as what language sampling in a naturalistic setting would reveal; rather, the target responses are elicited productions that have to meet the linguistic structures expected by the task. Expressive syntax might be tested by asking an examinee to use a stimulus word in a sentence and then scoring whether the word is used meaningfully and grammatically. If the stimulus word were *fell*, then a past action involving falling would be needed for a correct response, such as "The leaves fell from the trees." A response like, "The baby will fell on the stairs" would be a syntactic error, but "My basket is fell" would be a semantic error of meaningful use, with *fell* being substituted for *full*. Other test items might ask an examinee to build a sentence from a set of given words, such as "Make a sentence using these words: *fell, leaves, trees*." The response would require the spontaneous use of additional grammatical elements to form a sentence. Both types of sentence construction tasks reveal grammatical usage and sentence building and require the ability to converge upon a correct linguistic response, rather than to just evidence naturally occurring syntax and grammar when speaking spontaneously.

Item Analyses of Tests of Grammar and Syntax

Examiners can review published tests in their entirety or selectively review the subtests or items that contribute to an assessment of learners' grammar and syntax (Scott & Stokes, 1995). It may be telling to determine the syntactic properties of an entire test, as well as *to explore how each item's sentence structure could affect the way that the test content is delivered to the examinees. This is fundamentally an analysis of the structural complexity of the test items.* In short, do the sentences used in the test make the questions hard to understand?

Or, by reviewing only the subset of questions that probe grammar and syntax, examiners could have a greater degree of certainty that these items meet a range of criteria for examining language form as a specific domain of language. This examination raises questions of the constructs behind the test items. In short, are the test questions really about grammar and syntax?

Scott and Stokes (1995, p. 313) suggested that SLPs consider the following six criteria (paraphrased and expanded upon here) to examine published tests to determine whether and how these tests assess grammar and syntax:

(1) What is the level of syntactic complexity addressed by the test questions in general? Does the test appear to have the level of complexity needed for the age or grade level of the examinee?

(2) What syntactic structures are found among the test items? This would entail a syntactic content analysis of the test questions to determine the receptive language load for examinees, such as:

- The length, in words, of the sentences used in the test items.
- The clausal density of the sentences used in test items.
- Frequency and variety of subordinate clause types found in the sentences used in the test items.
- The variety of sentence types used in the test items, such as active voice, passive voice, negatives, questions, and so on.
- Morphological elements, such as words with grammatical affixes, derivational words, and so on used in the sentences in the test items.

(3) Are the syntactic structures tested representative of what is known about syntactic development within the age range of the standardization sample?

(4) What are the processing requirements of the test format? (This would entail a task analysis of the test questions for cognitive and receptive language processing demands. For example, do items require processing a sequence of events that is out of temporal order, as in, *Before you do X, do Y.*)

(5) Are the processing requirements of the test similar to or different from language processing in more naturalistic contexts?

(6) Would test performance predict naturalistic language ability?

Five additional questions for examining published tests would follow, to provide a thorough evaluation of the quality of the test:

(7) How appropriate are the items for assessing grammar or syntax? Does answering each item require grammatical or syntactic skills?

(8) Are the test items really assessing syntax, as opposed to some other skill, such as prior knowledge of the content or topic on which the test questions are based?

(9) Are the processing requirements similar to the kinds of thinking and reasoning that are common to school learning tasks?

(10) Would test performance predict school language abilities and academic success?

(11) What are the metalinguistic demands of the test items? To what extent does the examinee have to think consciously about language as a code and a system, or think about linguistic structure, to answer the questions?

The results of SLPs' analyses of test content would vary depending upon the commercial tests that they choose to examine. For instance, Scott and Stokes (1995) conducted an analysis of three commercial tests that were the current editions of the tests at the time of the publication of their article and found considerable variations across the eight subtests that elicited oral grammatical and syntactic responses, the one subtest of reading that probed grammatical understanding, and the one subtest of written grammar. Their analysis identified the variations in the sentence lengths, clausal density, and syntactic structures used in the test items, meaning, they identified the structures that examinees would need to comprehend to respond accurately. These considerable syntactic variations were true even for subtests of the same format and that were standardized for the same age ranges. For example, sentence repetition tasks across published tests varied as to the lengths of the stimulus sentences and the number of subordinate clauses per sentence. The sentence types that examinees were to imitate were questions, passives, and negatives.

Test Questions That Probe Grammatical and Syntactic Skills: Performance Demands

Relatedly, *a published test can be examined for the syntactic demands inherent in answering the test questions. What grammatical and syntactic skills does the examinee need to possess to formulate an acceptable response?* To an extent, this is an analysis of the content of the test items. Using the response scoring key as a guide, *the items can be examined for the language that they elicit.* To elaborate on Scott and Stokes (1995, p. 313), an item analysis of performance demands can include:

- The length, in words, of the sentences that would be scored as correct.
- The clausal density of the expected responses.
- Frequency and variety of subordinate clause types found in the expected responses.
- The variety of sentence types that are needed to respond, such as active voice, passive voice, negatives, questions, and so on, and the word-ordering skills inherent in formulating these sentences.
- The morphological elements that are expected in the responses, such as words with grammatical affixes, derivational words, and so on.

The following examples are given to describe the process of exploring the performance demands of test questions, rather than to review the content of any specific commercially available tests. The published tests used in the studies reviewed here as procedural examples may be out of date. No comparison to the current editions of these tests is offered, and any interpretations of the current editions based on these past examples would be unwarranted. It is sufficient to state that past and present editions of tests used to measure the syntactic and grammatical capabilities of school-age learners and adolescents generally allow for *two aspects of syntactic competence to be revealed. The first aspect is naturalistic competence in understanding and using syntax and grammar. The second aspect of competence is overt demonstrations of metalinguistic knowledge of syntax and grammar*. Test item analyses would take both aspects into consideration.

As an example of a test item analysis of the grammatical and syntactic skills examinees need to formulate acceptable responses, Finestack et al. (2017) reviewed five commercial language diagnostic subtests normed for preschool and school-age learners that were the current editions of the tests at the time of their study. This review established that, across the five subtests, examinees had 201 elicited opportunities to produce grammatical and syntactic responses. The acceptable responses included:

- Grammatical morphemes (bound morphemes):
  - Nouns: Plurals, derivations of nouns by adding -er (as in *farmer*), possessives
- Verbs:
  - Infinitives
  - Tenses: Copulas in present and past tenses (forms of *to be* as the main verb in the sentence), verbs in the regular and irregular

past, participles (a *smiling* baby), present perfect (*have* or *has* + past participle, e.g., *have tried, has become, have known*), past subjunctive (used in a subordinate clause, connotes unreal or improbable events, e.g., *if I were you, I wish you were here*), future perfect (an action that will be completed in the future, e.g., *next year, they will have been married for 10 years*), past perfect subjunctive (had + past participle, e.g., *I wish I had started earlier*)
- Verb phrases: Future modal *will*, auxiliary *be* and *do*
- Sentence structure: Direct and indirect objects, passive voice, conjunction *and*
- Verb transformations: Contracted and uncontracted copulas in present and past tenses
- Negation: Contractions
- Derivation of adjectives by adding -y (e.g., *mess* to *messy*)
- Obligatory pronouns
- Questions: Yes-no interrogatives, wh-questions
- Prepositional phrases
- Clauses: Embedded clause, prepositional clause, wh-clause, relative clause, *because* clause

These elicitations represent, for the most part, earlier developing grammatical morphemes and clausal structures and would be appropriate for assessing preschool and early elementary school children's language. However, test items that feature only these opportunities are not sensitive to the difficulties with clausal constructions that would need to be identified in older learners. Some of these tests were normed for use through adolescence. *The clausal construction responses totaled nine elicitation opportunities within the 201 test items across the five different published subtests.* This might be an insufficient sampling of the clause structure competence that would be necessary for older learners to succeed in academic contexts. As such, this testing might not reveal if a syntactic weakness is contributing to academic difficulties in children at the upper end of the age norms for the tests.

To explore test items' performance demands, Scott and Stokes (1995) reviewed three commercial tests and found eight subtests designed to measure oral grammar and syntax, one subtest of reading that probed grammatical understanding, and one subtest of written grammar. (See Chapters 5 and 6 for consideration of the reading and writing items, respectively.) Taken together, Table 4–5 reports what can be said about the subtests' items' performance demands. (Table 4–5 is an expansion and reinterpretation of Scott & Stokes, 1995, pp. 313, 318–319.) Of note is that the average clausal density for all items across all subtests was less than 2.0, meaning that the stimuli contained one to two clauses on average, that being a main clause and a subordinate clause, or just a main clause. Performance on any of the subtests could be confounded by regional or social dialects and/or by the cognitive-linguistic abilities taxed, notably vocabulary and lexical knowledge, world knowledge that allows for familiarity with the messages' topics and content, comprehension of the meaning of the stimuli, discourse comprehension, message formulation, verbal reasoning, logical relations, sufficient auditory memory to hold the verbal stimuli in mind, sufficient working memory to perform the linguistic tasks, and general attention, endurance, and task focus. Also potentially confounding is the unpredictable extent to which these linguistic tasks resemble naturalistic daily language use or school language tasks. Some of the tasks may resemble language games that youngsters play or word study games that teachers employ.

Scott and Stokes (1995) assessed that some subtests are not conducive to testing syntax extensively. For example, on the scrambled sentences tasks, the maximum number of words that could be unscrambled is limited by the number of words that an examinee could hold in working memory. This limit is usually about seven words (Miller, 1956) or a series of words that would span a duration of about 20 to 30 seconds (Cherry, 2020). Instead of focusing on stimulus length and complexity, subtests ideally would offer stimulus variety. Scott and Stokes (1995) asserted that, "what makes the older child's language different is new arrangements and increasingly complex combinations of basic forms" (p. 315). Considering Scott and Stokes's (1995, p. 312) reflections, it may be said that *establishing whether the grammar and syntax test items provide the empirical and corroborating information to link language test scores to school success would be a matter of interpretation of what linguistic factors exacerbate school performance problems and whether tests can reveal these factors. Observing that a student has limited syntactic performance on testing or through language sampling is not necessarily explicatory. The nature of how syntax subserves school language demands may not resemble how standardized tests measure syntactic abilities or diagnose syntactic deficits.* Consider that "later-developing structures do not occur (even in adult samples) as frequently as earlier-developing structures. It is difficult to specify what constitutes an appropriate frequency of occurrence. The use of many later-developing forms is a matter of syntactic choice, taking into consideration the

Table 4–5. Grammar and Syntax Subtest Items' Performance Demands

Language Mode	Type of Test Item	Item Administration Procedure	Number of Items Reviewed	Approximate Skill Level	Performance Demands
Listening	Grammaticality judgement	Listen to examiner read a sentence; respond whether the item is said correctly or not	40	Ages 8 to 13	Verbing, pronouns, comparative morphemes -er and -est negation
Listening	Syntactic paraphrase	Listen to examiner read three sentences; state which two have similar meaning	35	Ages 11 to 18	Stimuli had as many as three clauses
Speaking	Sentence combining	Listen to examiner read two to four sentences; combine the input into one sentence	25	Ages 8 to 13	Form a main clause and add one or more subordinate clause; also, adverbial clause, attributive adjective, phrasal coordination, adverbial element, clausal coordination, series construction, relative clause

Speaking	Word ordering, assembling sentences	Listen to the examiner read a scrambled sentence of three to seven words; restate the sentence with the words in order; or restate two versions of a well-ordered sentence	25 + 22 (two subtests on two tests)	Ages 8 to 13	20 trials are simple sentences; 5 trials require forming a complex sentence; constructing noun phrases
Speaking	Sentence repetition	Listen to an examiner read a sentence; repeat the sentence	30 + 26 (two subtests on two tests)	Ages 8 and older	Adverbial, nominal, and relative clauses; questions, passives, negatives
Speaking	Formulating sentences	Examiner provides one or two words, with or without an associated picture; examinee states a full sentence using the stimulus word(s)	20	Ages 8 and older	Stimuli are nouns, verbs, adjectives, used to form adverbial phrases, and, predominately, subordinate or coordinate conjunctions

Note: For the original data that contributed to this expanded interpretation, see Scott, C. M., & Stokes, S. L. (1995). Measures of syntax in school-age children and adolescents. Language, Speech, and Hearing Services in Schools, 26, 309–319.

surrounding discourse context (e.g., previous and anticipated sentences, genre, audience, modality). The structures are not obligatory. This factor, like the previous one, makes it difficult to specify a normative standard of use" (Scott & Stokes, 1995, p. 312). Scott and Stokes added that a factor that could be important to assess is where any particular speaking or writing context would fall on a continuum of unplanned to planned discourse (Danielewicz, 1984). When academic performance involves planning, there are cognitive, linguistic, and contextual requirements that SLPs can help learners become aware of and that SLPs can help learners master. Interventions might focus on helping learners use their grammar and syntax planfully and purposefully in school when listening, speaking, reading, and writing.

It is important for examiners to observe how examinees behave during syntax testing, as a corollary to whether their answers are correct or incorrect. Test-taking behaviors such as attentiveness, speed of response, restating stimuli aloud, using self-talk to process, or seeking visual or tactile supports to aid their auditory processing, such as counting or tapping words onto their fingertips, may help reveal their syntactic processing concerns. Examiners particularly need to observe processing speed and also observe how response accuracy and processing speed interrelate. Accuracy may diminish when stimuli are more complex, but older students should be able to manage more complex syntactic processing than younger children can achieve. Dick et al. (2004) observed that children with language impairments ages 5 to 17 evidenced slower processing speeds but that older examinees showed faster and more accurate processing, even when the syntactic stimuli given to older students were more com-

plex. Dick et al. observed that accuracy and processing speeds varied with syntactic complexity and were influenced by whether sentence forms are regular and familiar (i.e., used frequently in common language).

Test Questions That Probe Grammatical and Syntactic Skills: Metalinguistic Awareness

It is necessary to keep in mind that students' language test performances are not simply their spontaneous demonstrations of the linguistic behaviors probed by the content and constructs tested by the standardized instrument. Depending on the questions, examinees' behaviors and responses may include demonstrations of metalinguistic awareness. Some degree of metalinguistic self-monitoring, or overt examination of the properties of language, or reflection on the use of language, is inherent in students' testing performances (e.g., as observed by Deevy & Leonard, 2018). This is an advantage of testing, because conscious thinking about language (Britton, 1984; Van Dongen, 1986) is not necessarily elicited during sampling of spontaneous language.

Some forms of testing reveal metalinguistic knowledge about syntax and grammar. Mason (2013) noted that students with syntactic difficulties often demonstrate metalinguistic deficits in grammatical awareness. Examinees complete tasks that require an element of thinking about the language used in the test questions, rather than just thinking about the content of the questions. An SLP might predict that an examinee with lower performance on receptive and expressive syntactic test items would have lesser metalinguistic knowledge about syntax. Natural language performance might not be strong enough to support learning about the complexities of language and viewing language as a system to be explored. It's important to consider that an examinee might perform very well on the receptive and expressive syntax tests but not perform as well on the metalinguistic tasks. For school-age children and adolescents, their metalinguistic syntactic knowledge is an important indicator of having acquired mature language skills and having the competence to master grade-level curriculum requirements. Metalinguistic deficits have the potential to have an impact on academic performance, reading comprehension, and written composition abilities. This performance differential between language reception and production tasks versus metalinguistic tasks would suggest that language for daily communication is not at issue, but the cognitive, reflective, metalinguistic understanding of how language is structured and used is problematic. School curriculum, especially English language arts, includes metalinguistic demands for word study, for examining and possibly diagramming sentences, for learning grammatical rules, and for using knowledge of a native language to learn foreign languages.

Scott and Stokes (1995) wrote that there was not a true body of research on the aspects of language processing that are brought to bear to complete the subtests of standardized tests that assess syntactic ability, and, relatedly, there was not enough information on how school-age and adolescent students would describe the thinking strategies they use when taking syntax tests. Nor were there studies of error responses, to show flaws in processing or misunderstanding of test questions. Scott and Stokes (1995) averred that syntax subtests require examinees to manifest more than just naturalistic language abilities. To

some degree, structural awareness of language, meaning metalinguistic awareness, is necessary for satisfactory test performance. To that end, it appears necessary to describe the aspects of metalinguistic awareness that each of the types of subtest items shown in Table 4–5 would require.

Grammaticality judgments are overtly metalinguistic, because the subtest directs examinees to judge whether a grammatical construction is "right or wrong" or "correct or incorrect." Scoring is not fluid or inclusive of dialect differences. This subtest might reveal what it is designed to, that being whether the speaker knows how to analyze the grammar of a given utterance for correctness relative to a mainstream standard. This task presumes that examinees have in mind a standard for comparison, presumably derived from some conscious or unconscious knowledge of how the speakers they come into contact with say these sentences. This task presupposes that they have some notion that there are "correct or right" ways of speaking, as opposed to "incorrect or wrong" ways. This, in turn, presupposes that someone has instructed them about preferred grammars. This begs the question of why anyone would have instructed them. Students whose grammar and syntax reflect General American English may never have been corrected by a teacher or other adult, because the occasion for correction hasn't presented itself. Students may speak "correctly" but not know that this is "correct." Their subtest responses show they are just recognizing which of the verbal choices sounds most like themselves. For students who do not speak a mainstream dialect, the same truth holds for them. They speak in the ways they know how because this is how they have heard those around them speak, and they may never have been expected to change their dialect or been "corrected." They might choose the stimulus forms that sound like themselves or may try to second-guess what other models might say, such as their teachers or speakers that they hear on television. In effect, the metalinguistics of this subtest assess whether examinees have been taught about "correctness." For students to judge grammaticality consciously means that for some reason, they have experienced being corrected or have been taught about correct and incorrect forms, probably in school. Tests of grammaticality may resemble some of the metalinguistic tasks that are found in grade-level curriculum, such as completing worksheets to practice how to correct the form of a written sentence. It might be cautious for SLPs to administer these subtests to students who have experienced this curriculum, but to consider whether grammaticality judgments could mean anything at all to youngsters who have not yet been exposed to this knowledge in school. In all, if a student's language sample reveals mainstream grammar, grammaticality judgments do not reveal anything more about the speaker's productive grammar; it just shows the students can recognize their own grammar. If a student's language sample reveals grammar deficits that cannot be attributed to dialect, some intervention targets are apparent without this testing. This subtest might be used to attempt to uncover additional forms to target and/ or to probe a receptive awareness of mainstream forms. If a student's language sample reveals a grammatical system that reflects the rules of a dialect, it is important to consider whether the subtest is valid for this student at all, since the student's metalinguistic conceptualizations of language forms are dialect dependent, and to consider whether elective code-switching instruction is an appropriate

means for helping the student achieve school success. Educational teams would consider whether this instruction would be conducted as a regular education initiative by SLPs and/or by teachers (ASHA, 1991, 2003, 2010, 2016, 2017, 2018b, n.d.-a), rather than as a special education service.

Syntactic paraphrasing, where students judge the similarity of meaning of sentences that are constructed or worded differently, is a test that taxes processing the semantic-syntactic interface. Sentence-level language comprehension is assessed. Students who do not score well here would need further testing of their knowledge of the meanings of the words, concepts, and sentences where they erred. Their message comprehension would need to be separated from probes of syntactic knowledge. It would not be fair to judge that errors here signal deficiencies in grammar and syntax alone. For example, consider these stimuli:

Quentin was given a gift by his friend.

Quentin received a gift from his friend.

Quentin gave a gift to his friend.

The syntactically paraphrased meanings depend on the passive voice constructions *by his friend* and *from his friend*. But each sentence requires interpreting the meanings of the prepositional phrases *by his friend*, *from his friend*, and *to his friend*. The meanings of *was given* and *received* have to be interpreted as being similar, as opposed to interpreting *given* and *gave* as similar in meaning. Whether these receptive tasks can be processed automatically or would require overt metalinguistic reasoning would vary for each test taker, for each test item.

Sentence combining requires conscious manipulation of syntactic segments. Some examinees may appear to be combining sentences intuitively and effortlessly, while others may reveal their conscious metalinguistic efforts. The sentence stimuli are not simply combined additively. It is more exact to say that the sentences need to be rearranged. Words need to be added, deleted, and rearranged. Most sentence-combining tasks require phrasal coordination or clausal subordination, and the level of difficulty of these tasks varies (cf. Scott & Nelson, 2009). Scott and Stokes (1995) noted that subordinate clauses can be left-branching or right-branching. Left-branching subordinate clauses occur before the main clause verb (in the "left" portion of the written sentence), for example:

- Adverbial clauses (*While she had the chance*, she snuck past her sleeping father.).
- Relative clauses that modify sentence subjects (Her father, *who was sleeping deeply*, did not awaken.).
- Nominal clauses that serve as sentence subjects (*He agreed* he was not the best cook in the family.).

Combining, for example, *Her father was sleeping deeply* and *Her father did not awaken*, results in a sentence with a left-branching subordinate clause: *Her father, who was sleeping deeply, did not awaken*. This syntactic manipulation is more difficult and later developing (Scott & Stokes, 1995). Sentences with left-branching subordination are common to written language and academic writing and cause the listener or reader to have a fair amount of processing load. Right-branching clauses occur in sentence predicates, on the "right" side of the written sentence, and may be somewhat less complex than the left-branching subordinate clauses. Examples include:

- Adverbial clauses that follow the main clause (Tell dad where you are going *before you go out*.).
- Relative clauses that modify object nouns (complement nouns): "Patty realized she didn't have her wallet *in her purse*." The complement is *she didn't have her wallet* and the relative clause *in her purse* modifies the complement.
- Nominal clauses that function as sentence objects or complements (The car is too expensive, *he decided*.).

These right-branching examples combine simpler segments, for example, *The car is too expensive* and *He decided*. As such, sentence branching patterns is one condition that allows examiners to explore the relative productive difficulty of the targeted combined sentences. SLPs can compare these targets to the utterances that examinees produced in their spontaneous language samples, so the differential can be considered. Constructions that students do not produce spontaneously might be difficult for them to manipulate in metalinguistic contexts.

Word ordering or building sentences from a bank of words presented in random order is a metalinguistic task in the sense that on a daily basis, people seldom have to unscramble words to communicate. The examinee is working with words for analytical purposes. The aim of this task is for the test taker to examine the language given and make a conscious choice about how to create a typically worded sentence. For example, *Dollars paid he for lunch his five* can be consciously assembled into *He paid five dollars for his lunch*. This task cannot be completed entirely intuitively or automatically, but it can be completed using a tacit or unwitting understanding of how sentences are spoken, that is, a rather implicit frame for what "sounds" best. In this regard, this subtest can provide some insight into whether test takers have some kind of sentence frame in mind. Conversely, for examinees with a knowledge of parts of speech or other grammar terminology, word ordering can be conducted by overtly searching for a subject, verb, and so on. In any event, for examinees who speak in spontaneous sentences and who perform this task well, this task reveals some of the underpinnings of how their grammatical awareness allows them to speak in sentences and analyze sentence elements. Uneven performance might show the structures that would be harder for them to use, so the subtest may tap whether they have knowledge of certain sentence arrangements that they did not produce spontaneously. Subtest results might suggest sentence forms to build during interventions, although those forms would be addressed using methods other than word ordering, specifically, by using functional tasks for sentence construction and sentence expansion that complement academic expectations. Chapter 5 discusses sentence analysis, as related to reading comprehension, and Chapter 6 describes written sentence construction tasks.

Sentence repetition subtests might show the array of forms that a speaker could spontaneously produce if the speaker were in contexts that would stimulate the opportunity to use any of these forms. It would be reasonable to assume that a speaker cannot repeat a sentence construction that is not part of the speaker's natural repertoire, but this might not be true. Especially for shorter sentences, examinees might just reproduce a string of words from short-term memory and would not

really be uttering a constructed sentence. Sentence repetition subtests provide the opportunity for the examiner to score a variety of repetition error responses. As Leclercq et al. (2014) suggested, if the target is a verbatim repetition, possible errors include not repeating the right number of words, with words added or omitted; not accurately repeating morphological and/or phonological elements; and stating words in an incorrect order. Examiners would assess whether the examinee preserved the semantic and/or pragmatic meaning of the sentence even if errors were produced. Differential interpretations would follow based on speakers' accuracy for lexical (high content) words, *form words* (prepositions, articles, conjunctions, etc.), bound morphemes, and morphological transformations. Leclercq et al. (2014) used principal component analyses to determine that there is a morphosyntactic factor and a lexical factor in sentence repetition skills, meaning, that errors can represent weaknesses in language form and/or content. SLPs would consider the types of errors that examinees produced in sentence repetition tasks and compare these to any similar constructions, accurately or inaccurately produced, in spontaneous language samples. Interventions could target learning to use the forms that examinees did not correctly repeat, as these might be considered less stable, even if the forms were spoken spontaneously. Interventions would work with sentence models, although direct repetitions of models would not resemble how sentence models are used functionally in academic tasks. Instead, students might use sentence models to inspire discussing academic concepts, to talk about stories they have read or other school learning experiences, or to perform other purposeful language tasks. Chapter 6 discusses helping learners work with model written sentences.

Formulating sentences, meaning, making up a sentence around a key word or a few of words, is a common school task. Teachers often ask students to say or write their spelling words or vocabulary words in a sentence. Examinees may have some familiarity with this subtest of a standardized language test. The task complexity will vary according to the part of speech of the key word(s). If the word is a form word (e.g., a preposition, article, conjunction) rather than a content word (e.g., a noun or verb), the task would be more complex (Scott & Stokes, 1995). The stimulus *Make up a sentence with the word "for"* would require a linguistic processing load that outweighs *Make up a sentence with the word "girl."* Chapter 6 describes suggestions for sentence formulation tasks.

Testing may reveal that older students with language impairments might display the skill levels of typically developing younger students (Dick et al., 2004) or may reveal individualized deficit profiles that may or may not reflect developmental progressions in attainment of skills. Syntactic testing is not simply about attainment of developmental expectations. All syntax testing items are not created equally, and examiners need to make interpretations about the importance of performing well or poorly on different types of tasks. It's important for SLPs to analyze the kinds of syntactic tasks that yield better or worse performance for examinees. For example, Dick et al. (2004, p. 363) posited that the psycholinguistic "cues" needed to detect an error in word order within a sentence are highly salient. Children are likely to be sensitive to word order and can process word order errors quickly and accurately. A change in sentence meaning is readily apparent when words are not produced in the correct order. On the other hand, the "cues" for finding errors of morphological selection, such as when examinees are asked to choose between alternate grammatical forms ("there *is* three dollars on the table" versus "there *are* three dollars on the table"), could be less salient, less obvious in the context of a full sentence, and could less predictably result in changing the meaning of the sentence. It is syntactically more difficult to find an error of morphological selection than to find an error of word order in a sentence. Therefore, poor performance on the well-cued tasks, such as word order arrangement, would reveal a greater deficit because the salient and predictable syntactic elements are being missed. Simply put, the examinee has difficulty completing the simpler syntactic tasks.

Clinician-Constructed Probes of Grammatical and Syntactic Skills

SLPs might construct probes to expand upon the kinds of items used in norm-referenced tests. Finestack and Satterlund (2018) conducted a national survey to explore SLPs' use of methods to identify grammatical and syntactic deficits. Among the respondents, 64% reported using informal probes to monitor progress and outcomes. Clinician-constructed probes would serve any purposes that clinicians identify empirically based on their test item analyses. Although these probes are not standardized and, with that, there is not an exact developmental criterion for the ages or grade levels when these probes should be answered correctly, creating informal instrumentation may address some assessment needs and provide a few practical advantages. *SLPs can design probes for demonstration, practice, and/or informal assessments.* Clinicians would establish their purposes for creating their probe targets and then design banks of probes to meet these purposes. For example, these purposes may include:

(1) Additional probes may provide some confidence in the results of a subtest. Having a greater number of performances can enhance the reliability of results, although it is clear that the clinician-constructed probes are not a parallel form of the published test. As Finestack et al. (2017) indicated, standardized tests may probe some grammatical or syntactic constructions only one time or just a few times. SLPs can perform test item analyses and determine the syntactic forms that are missing from the test or that are underrepresented. Huang (2017), a member of the Finestack et al. (2017) team, created a bank of probes that expand the number of opportunities to test certain forms that is available online for SLPs to administer or use as models for constructing their own probes. The items in this bank resemble published subtest items in terms of complexity, format, and types of responses obtained and would bring about a degree of reliability and validity between the published tests and the clinician-constructed probes. Huang (2017; see also Finestack et al., 2017) designed 10 to 12 probes for each target listed below, with one demonstration item and two practice items per target:

Wh-questions

Relative clauses

Reflexive pronouns

Propositional complement clauses

Past tense copula *be*

Passive voice

Irregular past tense

Copula plus preposition

Auxiliary plus verb

Auxiliary plus infinitive

Conjugation to third person -s (notated as 3s)

Conjugation to third person -s (notated as 3s) plus infinitive

SLPs can compare examinees' performance on the probes with subtest performance. The added probes can provide more performance opportunities than the subtest allowed for, so examiners can observe similarities or differences in performance on these additional questions. Administering additional probes after the standardized test is completed would guard against the probes providing any practice effects that might invalidate the test. But it is necessary to keep in mind that the test becomes a practice effort that occurs before the probes, so the probes are subject to practice effects.

(2) **Dynamic assessment** uses practice effects as information that can contribute to the diagnostic process (or, perhaps more accurately, practice opportunities become a part of the test administration paradigm). In dynamic assessment, after a test is administered, either during the same testing session or on another occasion, an examiner provides input or assistance that might influence how an examinee would respond to the test items upon readministration. This input can take the form of expanding the test instructions to include more specific directions, discussing test items, coaching,

demonstrating how to reason through a task or how to respond, modeling correct responses, sharing examples of possible responses, cuing the examinee by offering a partial response that the examinee can expand upon, offering multiple choice responses, or, in this case, offering clinician-constructed test items as practice probes to familiarize the examinee with the task and to teach how to perform the task. Dynamic assessment is similar to a test-teach-retest paradigm, or to a repeated-measures assessment. SLPs may call this approach *stimulability*, meaning, an examinee is able to perform a task after some input or instruction is given. Stimulability shows that a learner is approaching being able to perform a behavior but needs to be taught how to do so. The additional probes can show whether a learner is responsive to teaching attempts. Moreover, examinees can explain why they answered questions in the ways that they did, revealing their metalinguistic awareness. With that, probes can provide an opportunity for the examiner and examinee to reason together metalinguistically as they discuss the cognitive-linguistic properties of how to answer the probes. Examiners cannot score the behaviors that occur during or after dynamic assessment interchanges to compute a standardized test score but would, instead, use the information qualitatively to report on performance and/or to set targets for interventions.

(3) An item analysis can show which test items would potentially be answered incorrectly due to a culture's or community's dialect variations. This analysis would identify the number of questions that are confounded by dia-

lect variations that students might not have a fair chance of answering correctly. If an SLP's item analysis reveals that standardized test items conflict with local dialect norms, SLPs can construct additional probes that would not be affected by dialect variations and use these items as unscored supplements to the published tests. Having a bank of alternative probes on hand would help resolve how the examinee's score was negatively affected by the dialect variations and may establish that an examinee can answer a greater number of questions correctly than the test itself afforded. One option is for the probes to feature General American English constructions that the dialect does not alter, so that there are a sufficient number of items that are dialect neutral.

(4) Clinician-constructed probes can be used on occasions outside of formal testing environments. For example, when students are referred to meet with an SLP for an interview or screening to determine whether testing will be necessary, SLPs can administer a few probes during these informal meetings with students to gauge the student's level of performance. While these items are not a parallel form of a published test, they preview the nature of the test without disclosing any test items.

(5) Clinician-constructed items can be used for practice during interventions, to teach students how to perform the grammatical and syntactic operations that the tests value and that have some practical utility. For instance, sentence combining adds sophistication to speaking and can benefit students who are learning to give speeches or presentations in class and

is a useful editing tool for writers (see Chapter 6).

(6) Clinician-constructed items can be used for progress monitoring. Rather than readministering standardized measures at progress monitoring intervals, which potentially could cause testing effects due to repeated exposure to the same stimuli, SLPs can document how students perform on a task that reflects grade-level content, concepts, and vocabulary, along with the syntactic skills under examination. These probes could reveal how the student uses syntax in the context of working with grade-level information.

Metalinguistic probes might include asking the examinee to make some form of grammaticality judgment about syntactic constructions. Examiners would ask examinees to determine which of two or more grammatical or syntactic forms is correct. This task is akin to asking the examinee to judge when a speaker has made an error of morphological selection (Dick et al., 2004). Taking into consideration that dialect users might have differing morphological systems and therefore differing responses, probes would attempt to be dialect neutral to the extent that is possible given the cultural-linguistic diversity of English speakers. SLPs would need to research the dialect forms used in their practice settings and eschew the dialect variations and instead rely on examples of General American English forms used in their communities.

A question might probe, for example, a comparative suffix, as in, "Which is the better way to say this sentence? *I have three big brothers. The one who was born first is the oldest of them all.* or *I have three big brothers. The one who was born first is the older of them all.*" A follow-up probe would be,

"Why did you choose your answer? What makes this the better way to say this sentence?" The target response would be an overt comparison of the -est and -er morphemes. Or, a yes/no response might be elicited, as in, "Is this sentence said correctly? *I went to see my grandfather. He is oldest than my father.*" The follow-up probe would similarly ask examinees to discuss the morphological choice. Probes might ask the examinee to identify the actor or agent in sentences with varied syntactic arrangements, such as in the active and passive voices (Dick et al., 2004), as in, *The cake batter was ruined by the baker adding spoiled milk. What was ruined? What caused it to be ruined? Who ruined it?*

Another sort of comparison task might ask examinees to determine which sentences have similar syntactic forms or might ask examinees simply to say what is similar about sentences within a group. If the stimuli were, *I had a spelling test, I lost my homework,* and *I am sitting in a chair,* a probe could be "Which two of these sentences are in the past tense (or which tell about the past)?" or "Which sentence is not in the past tense (or does not tell us about the past)?" or, more generally, "Which two of these sentences go together to tell us about the past?" or "Which two sentences are somehow similar in time, and how do you know that?"

Another metalinguistic task might be to ask an examinee to make up a sentence that talks about the present, the past, or the future. Moving beyond this spontaneous expression, the examiner could ask the examinee to explain how the words in the sentence make the sentence be about the present, the past, or the future.

The above examples are somewhat simplistic and only illustrate some simpler components of grammar and syntax, but these examples show that metalinguistic testing is different from testing of receptive understanding and expressive usage of natural language. A more comprehensive description of the construct of how meta-awareness can be infused in testing can be found in the examiner's manual for the *Clinical Evaluation of Language Fundamentals–Fifth Edition Metalinguistics* (CELF-5 Metalinguistics; Wiig & Secord, 2014) and the review of the CELF-5 by Gordon Pershey (2016b).

In all, it would be useful for SLPs to compile a bank of various probes that they can use for different reasons. The targets that need probes and the probes themselves may change over time, and the reasons for needing probes could evolve. SLPs would consider having an evidence base for the probes they construct, for example, that a certain form is documented as being expected for an age or grade level, or that research has used certain forms within studies of certain ages or grade levels. SLPs can take their cues from tests that are on the market for constructing probes that are clear and concise. Grade-level material can inspire the content of probes; for example, if an SLP is testing a third grader, knowing that second graders learned about living in cities versus living in the country might inspire a probe such as, "Use the words *city* and *walk* in a sentence."

Enhancing Metalinguistic Capabilities

Metalinguistic performance in inherent in oral language testing, but these tasks are potentially unfamiliar to school-age and adolescent learners. Metalinguistic test questions may not seem like "schoolwork"

and may lead examinees to question the purposes of these tasks and to doubt their own abilities to answer these kinds of unfamiliar questions. The challenge for SLPs is to design grammar and syntax interventions that can be characterized as explicit (cf. Ebbels, 2014; Eisenberg, 2013; Finestack, 2018; Finestack et al., 2020; Motsch & Riehemann, 2008) or deductive (cf. Finestack & Fey, 2009). These opportunities for overt metalinguistic learning can strengthen the connection between standardized testing and therapy progress monitoring. Sometimes readministration of standardized tests would not be a valid assessment of the content of the interventions that the student has experienced. Interventions necessarily may have been designed to enhance curriculum content or improve functional abilities. The point is that if examinees approach each readministration of standardized tests with only naturalistic language abilities brought to bear, they may not engage with the tests' metalinguistic tasks. It is by teaching examinees to improve their metalinguistic abilities that a change in metalinguistic test performance would be obtained.

A variety of tasks can be infused into classroom language arts lessons and/or speech-language therapy sessions to help familiarize students with common metalinguistic processes for analyzing grammar and syntax. As *students practice metalinguistic awareness during speech-language interventions in ways that are functional for school success*, they recursively become familiar with how standardized tests might expect them to perform. This is not an effort to "teach toward the test"; rather, it is an effort to *validate the cognitive-linguistic processes that allow students to externalize their thinking about language and, in so doing, become better able to respond with conscious thinking processes when test questions ask them to think about language.* Ultimately, *postintervention testing would reveal whether interventions have taught students how to think about language forms.*

Metalinguistic Strategies for School-Age and Adolescent Learners

Several authors suggested strategies to focus on metalinguistic enhancements of students' oral language. As with intervention protocols for naturalistic language growth, SLPs discover the grammatical and syntactic forms already used by the learner and present the new language structures that the learner is developmentally ready to acquire. Porter and Steffin (2006) mentioned that teachers would design lessons to cover the learning prescribed by the academic content standards, but SLPs would design lessons to address language weaknesses that were revealed by diagnostic testing and that can affect how students attain the learning prescribed by the content standards. Both entry points for lesson development provide the opportunity to focus on learning how to think about academic language (cf. Bathazar & Scott, 2017, 2018).

Kamhi (2014) recommended that interventions to improve complex syntax would address "the meaning and/or functions conveyed by the syntactic structure rather than the structure itself" (p. 94). This would suggest that form follows function, with meaning and purposes being the driving forces behind helping learners use syntactic forms. By extension, *metalanguage would be involved as students discuss strategically conveying their meanings and purposes.*

This chapter provides Loban's (1976) recommendations for how teachers and SLPs can guide metalinguistic explorations of language. Loban (1976) provided perhaps the most extensive catalog of forms within the literature, so SLPs have a broad array of forms to use within lesson content, with the initial focus being on forms produced in error and then probing for knowledge of other forms that the student did not evidence during sampling and/or testing. Considering the importance of clausal density for developing mature syntax, Kamhi (2014) proposed that interventions help students formulate dependent clauses by learning subordinating conjunctions (e.g., *because, if, so, so that, before, when*). For example, SLPs would ask students to discuss a meaningful topic and then discuss the sentences they would form to convey that meaning to other people. Their discussion would be about sentence formation choices, such as sentence length or types, word order arrangement, and other sentence properties. In so doing, they would overtly discuss clausal constructions. Moving from saying, "I'm going to join the school chorus. I want to go on trips with the chorus. My best friend is in chorus," to "I'm going to join the school chorus so that I can go on their trips and be with my best friend" would mean that *so that* is overtly discussed as a subordinating conjunction and that the subject "I" can be removed through ellipsis. Identifying the syntactic strategies is the aim here, so students would keep lists of strategies and examples, or make charts, cue cards, reference notebooks, or computer-based tools to reinforce the use of these syntactic strategies. *Objectives and performance data collection account for the metalinguistic descriptions in addition to forming the target responses.* Stimuli would be useful for academic learning. For example, SLPs would guide students in how to examine their school texts for examples of target sentence forms and how to explain the sentence construction strategies that the writers used. (Chapters 5 and 6 describe more reading and writing strategies, respectively.)

Nippold et al. (2009) suggested a general principle for interventions to address deficits in complex syntax. Students would be apt to use lengthy and complex utterances when SLPs focus on content and topics that will inspire detailed messages. Communication contexts need to motivate a need for complex syntax in order to convey more complex thoughts.

Authors have offered suggestions for how to help older learners enhance the use of the syntactic system of language in order to become better at comprehending messages heard in academic settings (e.g., Cirrin & Gillam, 2008; Cirrin et al., 2010). Some of the strategies are general and would be used to comprehend better during classroom instruction, for example, comprehending "teacher talk" (Heath, 1978) in the classroom. The pragmatics of classroom discourse include many types of messages, including directives for students' behaviors and procedures along with feedback on performance, explanations, knowledge-telling, anecdotes, modeling, and social interactions that bring about bonding, trust, team building, and camaraderie.

Teachers of older students are going to speak to their students much like they speak to adults. They would not expect to use the child-directed speech (Ringler, 1981) used by teachers of young children. Teachers are going to speak in long, complex sentences, and there might be ellipses in their utterances, often in the form of pronoun references for nouns. Teachers

expect that much of what they say will become routine for their students (Heath, 1978). Teachers do not expect to have to break down their utterances into simpler constructions or to continually repeat the same procedural or explanatory messages. They expect their indirect messages to be understood ("You might want to recheck your work" means "Recheck your work!"). Heath (1978) pioneered the idea that teachers should be aware of their message functions and know how best to structure these messages. Their sentence form should be crafted to let students know if they are asking, telling, implying, or sharing their own points of view, and they should self-monitor to determine whether they are actually conveying their expectations when their messages are indirect. The burden for comprehension shouldn't be entirely on the students.

Students with language weaknesses might have difficulty making pragmatic judgments about their teachers' intents. SLPs, parents, and educators can help students learn how to listen for *syntactic signal words that can be used to convey pragmatic intents*. These signal words within sentences may include:

- Fill in what speakers mean by their *pronoun references*: for example, they, their, anyone
- Listen for *time-related words*: before, after, until, when, since, always, never
- Listen for *modeling cues*: If a teacher says, "I wonder _____," "I'm trying to figure out _____," "I never really knew that _____." These types of sentences are cues to follow the teacher's lead in thinking about information.

■ Listen for *motivational messages*: "The best way to complete this job is _____," "Students who do well in this subject often _____."

Numerous SLPs, school districts, education agencies, and other entities have posted their objectives for grammar and syntax interventions online. This wealth of online contributions is continuously changing. One document that provides a comprehensive list of standards-based interventions offers metalinguistic objectives for more mature grammatical and syntactic forms, for example, "identify and correctly use prepositional phrases, appositives, and independent and dependent clauses; use transitions and conjunctions to connect ideas" (Porter & Steffin, 2006, p. 9).

Therapy Should Have SPICE

With the acronyms SALT (SALT, 2020b) and SUGAR (Owens & Pavelko, 2020) well known as the names of SLPs' assessment tools for grammar and syntax, it seems fitting to add a little SPICE to the available interventions for grammar and syntax in school-age and adolescent learners. SPICE is the acronym for *Syntactic and Pragmatic Interventions for Clausal Expansions*. The focus of SPICE would be to help learners become metalinguistically aware of the components of clausal expansions. SLPs can use this acronym as a reminder as they construct their interventions.

Scott and Stokes (1995) offered an array of metalinguistic enhancements that are appropriate for students from upper elementary through high school. Students would learn the names of these forms and how to use and describe these forms. *Tasks include not just knowing how to speak using certain forms; the metalinguistic task is to analyze sentences and identify where the target forms are used*. Their array is adapted and expanded here and lends itself well to SPICE.

■ Word structure, specifically, derivational morphology (*electric* becomes *electricity, electrified, electronic*).
■ Prefixes and suffixes (prefixes *anti-, re- dis*, etc.; suffixes *-tion, -ist, ism*, etc.).
■ Nominalization, when verbs become nouns (*transport* becomes *transportation*).
■ Adjectives created when verbs become adjectives (if the verbs *frozen, broken, filtered, bleeding* precede nouns, they become adjectives; also consider verbs of various tenses such as *open and shut case, done deal,* and *fallen snow*).
■ Premodification of noun phrases, as in determiner + noun (*each person, some people*) or determiner + adjective + noun (*each elderly person, some elderly people*).
■ Postmodification of nouns using relative clauses (*people who are elderly*) or prepositional phrases (*some people of an advanced age*).
■ Complex verb phrase structure, e.g., modal auxiliaries (*would have been allowed*) perfect have + en (*having driven so far, we decided to stay*).
■ Adjective phrase expansion (*a sleek and elegant ship*).
■ Adverb phrase expansion (*very beautifully dressed*).
■ Clause structure expansions by increasing numbers of adverbial elements (*the race, which I won although it was my first time and which was run by much better athletes*).

- Complex sentences (subordination) (My dog is fluffy *so, he is not scruffy*).
- Left-branching (preposed adverbial clauses, as in, *While she had the chance*, she snuck past her sleeping father).
- Center embedded relative clauses (Her father, *who was sleeping deeply*, did not awaken).
- Nominal clauses as subjects (*He agreed* he was not the best cook in the family).
- Later-developing adverbial subordinating conjunctions (*unless, even though, whereas, as long as*).
- Appositives (*My teacher, a perfectionist*, expects our papers to have no spelling or punctuation errors).
- Combinations of clause types in one sentence (Her father, *who was sleeping deeply*, did not awaken, *although she stomped her feet right in front of him*).
- Discourse structure (for example, having **pragmatic coherence** across multiple sentences to build the content of a topic).
- Adverbial sentence connectives, conjuncts, and disjuncts (*therefore, however, in addition, furthermore, for example*).
- Ellipsis patterns (*I like math and I like science* becomes *I like math and science*).
- Word order variation for theme and focus (e.g., cleft constructions, often begin with *It* + "be" verb + subject or object + relative clause, as in, It was *last week* that I went on a trip with the school chorus. Expands information about a person, place, thing, time, or reason) (Really Learn English, 2010–2021).

CHAPTER 5

Reading Comprehension: Processing Sentence-Level Grammar and Syntax to Understand the Meaning of Text

This chapter describes how sentence processing is a component of reading comprehension. Sentence processing is predicated upon the understanding of a sentence's use of grammatical elements and its syntactic construction. Deficits in reading comprehension may be connected to underlying deficits in grammar and syntax. This chapter describes strategies to help learners examine sentences found in written texts so that they can better comprehend sentence meaning. This chapter emphasizes how to provide academically relevant speech-language services to school-age children and adolescents. The academic learning needs of higher functioning children and adolescents with language difficulties and specific learning disabilities who may struggle with the structure of language at the sentence level are addressed.

Anticipation Guide

After reading this chapter, readers will be able to answer the following questions:

- How is sentence-level processing a component of reading comprehension?
- How do learners' grammatical understanding and cognitive-linguistic processing of multiword syntax contribute to reading comprehension?

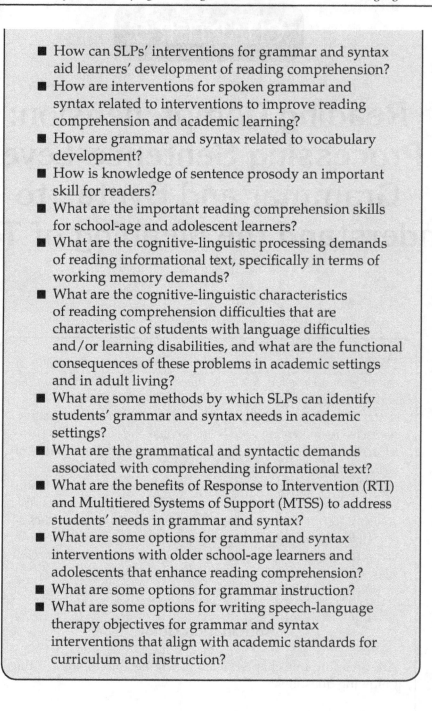

- How can SLPs' interventions for grammar and syntax aid learners' development of reading comprehension?
- How are interventions for spoken grammar and syntax related to interventions to improve reading comprehension and academic learning?
- How are grammar and syntax related to vocabulary development?
- How is knowledge of sentence prosody an important skill for readers?
- What are the important reading comprehension skills for school-age and adolescent learners?
- What are the cognitive-linguistic processing demands of reading informational text, specifically in terms of working memory demands?
- What are the cognitive-linguistic characteristics of reading comprehension difficulties that are characteristic of students with language difficulties and/or learning disabilities, and what are the functional consequences of these problems in academic settings and in adult living?
- What are some methods by which SLPs can identify students' grammar and syntax needs in academic settings?
- What are the grammatical and syntactic demands associated with comprehending informational text?
- What are the benefits of Response to Intervention (RTI) and Multitiered Systems of Support (MTSS) to address students' needs in grammar and syntax?
- What are some options for grammar and syntax interventions with older school-age learners and adolescents that enhance reading comprehension?
- What are some options for grammar instruction?
- What are some options for writing speech-language therapy objectives for grammar and syntax interventions that align with academic standards for curriculum and instruction?

It is important to consider how sentence processing and grammatical understanding affect a learner's ability to learn to read and to then progress as a comprehending reader throughout the learner's years in K–12 education. A learner's knowledge of language form contributes to developing reading abilities that advance beyond simply reading single words (Fang, 2012; Selkirk, 1986). Of importance is how a learner's knowledge of morpho-grammatical constructions and multi-word syntax underlies the sentence-level comprehension necessary for reading (cf. Shanahan, 2021). The primary focus in this chapter is on how the act of reading necessitates comprehending the syntactic arrangement of words in phrases, clauses, sentences, and longer passages. Comprehension of language form contributes to reading abilities primarily in terms of how readers process how words are used in sentences, what sentences mean, and how multiple sentences join together to provide the meaning of a passage. Therefore, developing students' skills for interpreting and using advanced syntactic and semantic forms while reading and writing appears to be essential (Caccamise, 2011). This competence is increasingly critical as students advance through their school years (Ehren et al., 2012; Fang, 2012). The texts they are expected to comprehend and the passages they are expected to write become more grammatically complex, and the occurrence of unfamiliar words and sentence structures increases (Caccamise, 2011; Fisher & Frey, 2015; Sáenz & Fuchs, 2002). SLPs' interventions would provide students with solid skills for understanding and using the grammar and syntax of written language.

Language Form and Reading Comprehension

The elements of language form that allow for learning to read are *phonology* (described as the phonemic structure of language that governs how sounds are used to build words; knowledge of this phonological structure allows learners to correspond spoken sounds to orthographic symbols such as letters or diacritical marks; Adams, 1990; Fraser et al., 2010; Moats, 2000), *morphology* (i.e., the structure of word parts and whole words, and the study of how words are formed; Carlisle, 2000; Carlisle & Stone, 2005; Comrie, 1989; Nagy et al., 2006), and syntax (i.e., the arrangement of words into multi-word messages, in accordance with rules for word order and grammatical usage; Scarborough, 2001). Many authors have addressed the importance of the phonological system of language in learning to read (notably Adams, 1990; Moats, 2000), however, exploration of the phonological basis for developing the ability to read is beyond the scope of this book. Other researchers (e.g., Apel, 2017; Foorman et al., 2012; Nagy et al., 2006; Shaywitz, 2003; Wolter & Collins, 2017) have addressed the morphological basis for learning to read and for developing the word-level skills for becoming an automatic, fluent reader of words. Considerations for the morphological capabilities that contribute to rapid word recognition and comprehension relate to a learner's knowledge of grammatical principles, and, therefore, morphological development relates to the word study skills that allow for grammatical and syntactic processing (Eberhardt, 2013; Nelson, 2013; Scott, 2009; Shanahan, 2021).

Grammatical understanding underlies how readers process how words are arranged in sentences and underlies sentence comprehension. Reading comprehension is dependent upon a reader being able to consider how *word order* in phrases and sentences is a component of meaning. Readers need to understand how *grammatical markers,* such as verb tenses, signal meaning. Some grammatical markers are morphological elements, such as the past tense -ed affix; these are known as grammatical morphemes. Clay (2015, 2106) observed that readers use structural cues, that is, they apply their knowledge of the grammar and structure of the English language to make the text they are reading "sounds right" (*How to Take Running Records*, 2002). Even when a reader errs, or *miscues,* by reading a word or group of words incorrectly, if the attempt "sounds right" relative to the structure and syntax of the English language, the reader has used structural cues to provide an alternate word that is grammatically and/or syntactically appropriate in context even if a reading accuracy error remains. For instance, a text might say, *A pine tree likes lots of rain*, but a reader might say, *A pine tree loves lots of rain*. The third person verbing is preserved in the miscue. In this case, sentence meaning is preserved. If the reader said, *A pine tree lives lots of rain*, an error in sentence meaning would also occur. Readers need to understand how words are used meaningfully in multiword messages, which are generally phrases or sentences. Readers are not reading for word meaning alone, but, rather, are reading for sentence meaning (Adams, 1998; Clay, 2015, 2016; Foorman et al., 2016; Scott, 2009; Shanahan, 2021; Williams, 2019). For example, Carlisle and Stone (2005) reported that skilled readers used syntactic and semantic cues to decode and understand unfamiliar words when reading text. Catts et al. (1999) found that students who performed well on measures of vocabulary diversity and syntax read words more quickly than students whose performance was not as strong on these measures. Presumably, the students' more stable sense of meaning and structure allowed them to read more rapidly.

Beyond comprehension of single sentences, readers need to have a meaningful understanding of how words are used in multisentence messages. The sentences found in written passages need to be comprehended one at a time and as a series of sentences that are arranged to form a paragraph or another type of text passage. Similar to how a listener processes oral language at the sentence level and employs *pragmatic coherence* to processes and link together the meaning of a series of sentences within a spoken discourse (Roth & Spekman, 1984), comprehending readers read not just a sentence at a time, but, rather, they read groups of sentences together, in a series, as components of longer written discourses. Reading comprehension is dependent upon the cognitive-linguistic ability to assemble a series of sentences together to gather their combined meaning (cf. Catts, 2009; Eberhardt, 2013; Fang, 2012; Schleppegrell, 2013; Scott, 2009; Shanahan, 2021).

In summary, some of the sentence processing competencies that contribute to reading comprehension are:

- Readers process words in sentences and determine word meaning in the sentence context.
- Readers process words in sentences by considering how each word contributes to a multiword message, meaning, how the words should be taken together and how each word contributes meaning.
- Readers process the *morphosyntactic* properties of words in sentences to understand, at least implicitly, the basic structural elements of who or what is represented in the sentences (nouns), the actions described (verbs), grammatical number (such

as the number of people referred to in a sentence, as in *teacher* or *teachers*), and possession (signaled by 's).

- Readers process the *morphosyntactic* properties of words in sentences to understand, at least implicitly, sentence tenses as referring to events as marked by verbs in the past, present, or future tenses, and do so by looking for bound morphemes or free morphemes, such as past tense verbs or future modals such as "will."

- Readers process word order to comprehend sentence forms, such as statements and questions, and thus can identify the pragmatic purposes of these sentences.

- Readers process how sentence structure conveys pragmatic meaning, by, for example, the use of imperative forms, exclamations, and phrasal elaborations that allow meanings to be phrased to convey the speaker's or writer's intended effect.

- Readers process the meaning of sentences (e.g., to ask themselves, "Does this make sense to me?") and process the structure of sentence grammar (e.g., to ask "Does this sound right to me?" as in, for example, when a reader says, "*The cup it empty. Oh, that doesn't sound right; this must say, The cup is empty.*" (cf. *How to Take Running Records*, 2002).

- Readers process the overall meaning of any series of sentences; reciprocally, readers process how any specific sentence(s) contributes to the meaning of the overall series of sentences.

SLPs' Services to Aid Language Form and Reading Comprehension

Considering the interrelatedness of grammar and syntax with reading competencies, SLPs can provide services that meaningfully enhance classroom learning for students of any age. Addressing interventions for grammatical and syntactic processing demands can coincide and ally with interventions for vocabulary and concept development, written language composition, narrative language conventions, reading comprehension, and memory skills (e.g., working memory, short-term memory, and long-term memory). Multipurpose intervention strategies would relate to students whose needs in grammar and syntax have a negative effect on their academic learning, completion of classroom assignments, and performance on achievement testing (cf. Kamil et al., 2008). SLPs would have the option to use some of their time with students to adapt the grammar and syntax of mainstream curriculum and assignments to be accessible to students, and/or to differentiate, that is, to simplify, classroom instruction that is grammatically and syntactically complex, and/or to design classroom accommodations and modifications that teachers can implement (cf. Nelson, 2010, 2013; Norris & Hoffman, 1993). As such, the rationale for SLPs' involvement in a comprehensive approach to language and literacy interventions, with a focus on grammar and syntax, is multifaceted and would be individualized to meet learners' needs. Saddler and Graham (2005) remarked that students' understanding and use of syntactic structures would be targeted by implementing focused instruction and interventions and would be embedded throughout the study of the syntax of classroom reading materials and of students' own writing.

Spoken Grammar as Preparation for Reading Comprehension

Some learners may need help with verbal syntax before they can progress to applying syntax to reading comprehension. One tactic is to ask the learner to verbally imitate various target sentence types spoken by the SLP, for example, a compound sentence, or sentences with subordinate clauses, and then discuss the sentence elements with the learner. This initial method of exposure simply allows the speaker to experience producing utterance types that he or she might not regularly speak but that can be found in the types of texts that students read. These imitations should take place within meaningful communication contexts (Eisenberg, 2006; Paul, 2007), as when engaging in a fun activity that pertains to an enjoyable text where the interesting sentences are found. These sentences would be captured and, perhaps, written on posterboard and then illustrated. Memory aids, such as visuals and manipulatives, would help students manipulate the sentence components. For example, sentence strips (cardboard or paper strips with sentences written on them, which can be cut up and rearranged to show clausal structures) could help students learn about clauses, parts of speech, and other grammatical and syntactic forms. Using larger print or highlights can help learners visualize the target sentence elements. The intention of an imitative and manipulative approach would be to help students develop a repertoire of complex utterances. Students would be developing the very basics of sentence awareness skills.

Research on SLPs' Interventions Related to Syntax and Literacy

Several authors have reported suggestions for SLPs' practices for addressing older students' language and literacy needs (ASHA, 2001; Beitchman et al., 1996; Ehren, 2009; Larson & McKinley, 2003; Nelson, 1998, 2010, 2013; Nippold, 2007; Nippold et al., 2009; Paul, 2002, 2007; Scott & Bathazar, 2013). However, there is limited research evidence to document how SLPs' interventions have improved school-age learners' grammar and syntax, and even less evidence to connect SLPs' grammar and syntax interventions to reading success. Finestack and Satterlund (2018) used a national survey to explore SLPs' use of interventions to target grammatical and syntactic interventions. The findings established that 73% of the 224 SLPs who served elementary school students reported that they "sometimes" or "frequently" engaged in some form interventions relevant to academic coursework, 84% addressed narrative language, 92% involved book reading, 71% addressed writing, and 70% used some form of worksheets. It would appear that the grammar and syntax interventions were supported by print, and/or were contextualized within print, and/or were made reinforcing or engaging by the use of print. ASHA (2021) reported that 90% of school SLPs surveyed in 2020 provided services for students' language needs and 36% addressed literacy difficulties, but the survey did not probe the interrelatedness of language and literacy services. In a systematic review of studies of speech-language interventions, Cirrin and Gillam (2008) attributed research-based credibility to methods of syntactic interventions with younger children that included modeling, imitation, and evoked production of syntactic forms. However, "Unfortunately, clinicians who work on syntax and grammatical morphology with school-age children have very little evidence available to draw on when selecting an intervention approach" (Cirrin & Gillam, 2008, p. S126). Cirrin and Gillam continued, "A major gap in the evidence is the lack of research on interventions for 'complex syntax' (e.g., complex sentences, elaborated noun phrases, elaborated verb phrases, interrogatives, etc.) necessary for students with language impairments to function in school settings" (p. S131). Cirrin and Gillam (2008, p. 132) presented further description of the limited research evidence upon which SLPs can base their practices, noting the limited data that exist on service delivery models, such as the effectiveness of classroom-based and collaborative language interventions. Nor was there substantial evidence on the efficacy of collaborative consultation with teachers and other service providers; nor on classroom-based versus non-classroom, individual treatment; nor on group therapy versus individual therapy. There appeared to be a perceived lack of evidence in controlled studies for the use of curriculum-relevant materials and general education standards in language interventions (i.e., ecologically relevant therapy), and for the effects of language therapy on students' progress in the general education curriculum, reading, and writing. Gillam and Cirrin (2008) noted this is "especially problematic for SLPs who work in schools. IDEA requires that special education services must relate to students' progress in the general education curriculum, yet the positive effects of language intervention on students' classroom language performance remain an untested hypothesis" (p. 132).

This perceived lack of evidence could be considered a negative that can be turned into a positive, since it suggests that this area is fertile ground for future research. Potentially, SLPs can implement and document the success of their creative and innovative syntax and literacy interventions in a "practice to research" paradigm, where real-life practices can then be put to the test of controlled studies. Indeed, in the years subsequent to the Gillam and Cirrin (2008) review, several authors have documented successful collaborative language and literacy practices among SLPs and teachers (e.g., Angel et al., 2009; Kumin & Mason, 2011; Loeb & Daniels, 2009; Ritter, 2009), but more explicit research on outcomes for grammar and syntax is needed. SLPs can focus their services to explore how grammar and syntax can aid the development of reading comprehension.

The Cognitive-Linguistic Elements of Reading Comprehension

Numerous cognitive-linguistic capabilities contribute to reading comprehension. Within this array of capabilities, syntactic processing plays a role as a discrete skill. Researchers have explored how school-age children's and adolescents' difficulties with syntax contribute to reading difficulties (Scott, 2004, 2009). Catts and Kamhi (2005) and Nation (2005) documented that language delays or disorders that affect spoken language usage and comprehension similarly affect reading comprehension. Nelson et al. (2004) observed that students with limited syntactic abilities may demonstrate poor reading comprehension at the sentence level and may write using fewer morphemes and with lesser complexity of syntactic structures. Snow et al. (1999) identified that students with deficits in oral language abilities have a similar hinderance in using reading as a means for learning academic information. Eisenberg (2006) observed that when complex syntactic forms are insufficient, learners might not have the language competence needed to support reading to learn information.

The array of cognitive-linguistic processes needed for reading comprehension makes use of sentence-level processing of information, so, in this regard, syntactic processing is a skill that is embedded within the array of cognitive-linguistic skills and that is essential for carrying out these cognitive-linguistic processes. Reading comprehension is a cognitive-linguistic process of *learning through language* to acquire information (Van Dongen, 1986). The *ideational purpose* of language is enacted (i.e., the mental functions that process human experiences and govern logic) (Bloom & Lahey, 1978; Teich, 1999). The *textual purpose* (i.e., the internal organization and communicative nature of a verbal text, be that a conversation or a written passage) (Teich, 1999) is enacted as the reader considers the meaning and structure of the sentences within a text. Reading adds to a reader's fund of verbal information on each reading occasion, to a greater or lesser extent, depending upon the content of the reading material.

Some students may show a breakdown in learning through language (cf. Brinton et al., 2010). They struggle with the oral and written discourse that is necessary for learning, with the result that they may have difficulties understanding concepts, comprehending stories, and acquiring a fund of verbal information.

Conceivably, the information they hear or read is not stored in a learner's *semantic memory* as meaningful sentences and discourses (Tulving, 1972). This difficulty may occur in an individual's comprehension of oral language and, in turn, underlie reading comprehension difficulties (Catts, 1993, 2009). Co-creation of meaningful discourse is an important learning strategy in classrooms and in online learning (Kamil et al., 2008). Students share their learning in centers, peer learning groups, and literature circles. They create group projects such as displays, illustrated books, webpages, and blogs, and participate in online learning communities. A deficit in participation in these tasks could represent that the sentence processing and production involved is cognitive-linguistically taxing for a student.

To achieve literacy, a learner becomes familiar with the elements of language form. The elements of form are symbolized by the written code of language. Reading, spelling, and writing entail cognitively and linguistically manipulating the physical components of language form, which, in print, are represented as letters, punctuation marks, and other symbols. Written language involves intellectually separating the symbolic components of written language form from the meaning of language used for communication. School-age children who experience difficulty with spoken language grammar and syntax and/or with a restricted metalinguistic ability to analyze spoken and/or written language form (as described in Chapter 4) may struggle with reading comprehension. Comprehension beyond a superficial, naturalistic level entails a variety of tasks that are based upon *learning about language* (Van Dongen, 1986), which means analyzing language as a written code and applying metalanguage to study the structure of syllables and words, the system of grammar, and the production of written sentence forms and mechanics according to a set of rules for sentence construction, punctuation, and capitalization. Codebreaking is the fundamental cognitive-linguistic task of learning to be literate. Readers process the elements of the code as they represent the components of meaning. Sentence grammar and written punctuation are arranged together to convey meaning, as in, for instance, wh-question words that begin sentences and the question marks that end the sentences.

Many cognitive-linguistic capabilities are required for manipulation of language form. In particular, capable use of language form is heavily reliant on sequencing of linguistic elements so that the parts achieve a coherent whole. Sequencing the components of language is involved in:

- Speaking (i.e., phoneme sequencing and morpheme sequencing as comprising the elements of spoken syntax).
- Oral sentence formation (i.e., word sequencing to form sentence syntax).
- Spelling (i.e., sequencing of letters and their corresponding sounds).
- Reading decoding (i.e., sounding out words using sequences of letter-sound correspondences).
- Learning syllable patterns (i.e., sequencing letters to represent the syllable chunks of words, so that readers who recall commonly occurring syllable patterns do not need to decode every syllable they read, for example, -ite, -or, am-, ir-).
- Knowledge of the sequential order of morphosyntactic applications, for example, the sequential affixation

of bound morphemes to free morphemes as prefixes (before words), suffixes (after words), or in word transformations (i.e., sequential letter rearrangements that occur within words, such as when forming contractions).
- Writing sentences (i.e., sequencing words and punctuation).

Learners who struggle with any of these aspects of the sequencing of the elemental forms of language may struggle with the processing and comprehension of written text. Arranging these components into coherent wholes, be those syllables, words, or sentences, can be challenging for these learners (cf. Caccamise, 2011).

Language Form Is Essential to Learning the Meanings of Words

Semantics skills include vocabulary knowledge, in terms of breadth, depth, and diversity of vocabulary (Nagy, 1988). Nagy contended that *the most important vocabulary skill is to be able to work with groups of words and make connections between words and their meanings.* This is a cognitive-linguistic process that requires sentence-level usage of words to compare and contrast the variations in word meanings. Nagy described that concepts are learned by comprehending the many words it takes to encompass the concepts at hand and by discovering how the words function together to develop the concepts. Without the support of meaningful sentences, isolated word learning is considered to be much more difficult. Word learning is aided by the verbal reasoning that accompanies processing the meaning of sentences.

Given the well-developed and complex language of older children and teens, Berninger and Abbott (2010) and Paul (2007) proposed that word meaning, grammatical structure, and sentence meaning are interrelated aspects of their comprehension abilities and form an essential language core that is needed for oracy and literacy. Because many new words are encountered in the context of oral and written sentences, competent use of form is associated with improving vocabulary and concept development. *Learning a new word brings about the development of the concepts and ideas that are related to the word. Reciprocally, learning a new concept is linked to learning the words that are used to think about and talk about the concept.* The chances for learning a new word are enhanced if a sentence provides contextual meaning and relevance for the new word (Nagy, 1988). In terms of receptive language enhancement, students may struggle to learn new words when they do not understand the form of the sentences where they have encountered the words (Catts et al., 1999). This means that strong language form skills might aid word learning and concept development, but weak form skills might detract from word learning and concept development. Sentence processing requires the operations of *working memory*. Working memory involves the temporary span of attention, focus, and memory that is used for information processing. The contents of working memory at any given moment include the "information that is in an active or accessible state and is used to complete some form of mental activity" (Boudreau & Costanza-Smith, 2011, p. 153). Learning words in the context of supportive sentence meanings is considered to be a much less effortful task for active working memory (i.e., the demands

for "on-screen memory" for the information that a reader is processing during the moment of reading can be supported by sentence contexts; these include the demands on memory for recall, storage, and linguistic processing that simultaneously occur at the moment of reading and reasoning about text; see Berninger, 2008). Sentence processing can be less taxing on working memory than trying to memorize the meaning of a list of isolated words (Berninger, 2008; Tulving, 1972). Sentences provide the relevant contextual information that helps learners organize the meanings of new words and integrate this information into their storehouses of long-term knowledge (Eberhardt, 2013; Schleppegrell, 2013). With that said, it is important to note that the contrary may be true as well. Comprehension requires short-term storage for the time that is needed to process incoming messages and to interpret the meaning of the messages, which taxes the capacity limits of working memory (Kibby et al., 2004; Montgomery et al., 2016). Working memory must simultaneously store and process the verbal information that is heard or read and prime the individual's response. Processing of sematic-syntactic relationships is essential to comprehension of sentence-length information (Boudreau & Costanza-Smith, 2011; Montgomery & Evans, 2009), but this could consist of a lot of information at one time. For some learners, the complexity of sentences is a burden and word learning may be more efficient if shorter phrases are used to contextualize the meaning of the word, rather than longer sentences.

In an attempt to characterize the relationship between working memory and sentence comprehension in school-age children with language concerns, Montgomery et al. (2021) presented a model that considers the influences of fluid intelligence, controlled attention, working memory, and long-term memory on sentence comprehension. In this model, "working memory serves as a conduit through which syntactic knowledge in long term memory, controlled attention, and general pattern recognition indirectly influence sentence comprehension" (p. 449). Montgomery et al. (2021) determined that for children with language concerns, controlled attention plays a greater role. Working memory influences children's ability to apply their syntactic knowledge when comprehending sentences. Assessment of sentence comprehension and treatment of sentence comprehension deficits would need to take attention, working memory, and long-term memory abilities into consideration.

In terms of expressive language demands, academic tasks require students to use new words and concepts within well-formed, grammatically appropriate sentences. In this context, *vocabulary growth can be conceived of as occurring within the growth of language form. Expansion of linguistic form supports vocabulary growth, and, reciprocally, vocabulary growth supports expansion of linguistic form.* Here, too, working memory may be taxed, and supportive strategies to aid word learning would include the use of multisensory learning, such as visuals (e.g., written information, tables or graphic organizers, pictures, multimedia, and videos); repetition, review, rehearsal, and practice to develop automaticity and fluid recall (in the form of preteaching and previewing, and reteaching and reviewing); breaking down learning tasks into steps (i.e., task analysis); and organizational skills, study skills, and metacognitive instruction so that learners can analyze the processes that they need to apply to learn about the words

and sentences under study (cf. Boudreau & Costanza-Smith, 2011). As an example of a cognitive-linguistically supported word learning strategy, Henry (2018) proposed that teaching English word origins (primarily Anglo-Saxon, Latin, and Greek) provides an organizational framework for learning and remembering words and aids in the study of morphology.

Prosody and Sentence Reading

Gross et al. (2013) explained how skilled oral and silent reading incorporates the *prosody* of spoken language as another aspect of reading comprehension. Speech prosody is a universal feature of all languages (Endress & Hauser, 2010). Prosody is an acoustical feature of speech by which a speaker controls how to connect the speech segments, which are composed of phonemes and syllables, and the suprasegmental features of speech, such as rate of speech, tempo, rhythm, and melody. Prosody includes pitch and cadence variations, from singsong to monotone, as well as the varying amplitude (loudness) or force of production of speech sounds, syllables, and words (Selkirk, 1986). Prosody allows speakers to use suprasegmental variations to emphasize or deemphasize the units of speech production, from phonemes to syllables, words, and sentences. Within a flow of connected speech, prosodic contours are controlled varyingly at the sound, word, sentence, and discourse levels of spoken language output, with speakers making prosodic choices numerous times within every utterance.

Prosody is learned at a young age as a conventional aspect of communicative competence. Prosody signals the function and form of an utterance, such as whether a sentence is a declarative statement or a question and may offer meaning beyond that expressed by word choices or sentence construction (Gross et al., 2013). Speakers are expected to follow social norms for using prosody to convey emotional states and behavioral intentions (Gross et al., 2013). Speakers use prosodic characteristics to convey the aspects of their personalities that they want to put on view, use the prosodic conventions of groups they'd like to show membership in, and use prosody as an interpersonal currency to negotiate social bids for attention, power, or other values or goals.

Comprehension of prosodic variations is an important aspect of receptive language competence. Listeners can ascribe various characteristics to speakers based on the assumptions they make about the speaker's prosody, such as social status, friendliness, attitudes, age, mood, state of health, and other psychological and interpersonal assumptions.

Considering how much information is conveyed by spoken language prosody, it's important to consider whether comprehending readers imbue the messages they read with prosodic contours, based on their past perceptions of how speakers have said similar utterances. Gross et al. (2013) stated, "As a testament to its central role in speech comprehension, prosody is inextricably part of remembered speech" (p. 189). Unlike speech, written language offers no prosodic cues, with the exception of how some readers may take prosodic cues from punctuation, or from the tone of the opening or final sentences of paragraphs, or from dialogue and other conventions of written expression. "Punctuation and syntax assist but underspecify a prosodic rendering of connected text" (Gross et al., 2013, p. 190). Prosody may offer meaning "that may not be captured by word selection, sentence construction, or punctuation" (Gross et al., 2013, p. 189).

Therefore, these multiple elements of phonology, morphology, semantics, and prosody influence the comprehension of language form and function and must be activated whenever an individual reads a text. Specific syntactic demands for reading comprehension are primarily activated at the sentence level. *A reader needs a mental expectation that the words being read will appear in a fairly specific and predictable order within a sentence, along with a knowledge of how the conventions of grammar signal meaning, and the expectation that sentences that appear visually together will have some kind of linked meaning and structure. Readers need to have sentence prosodic contours in mind.* When these syntactic elements work together, a reader is prepared to read fluently and comprehendingly.

The Importance of Reading Comprehension for Older Students

Sentence-level reading comprehension is one of many capabilities that competent readers need to acquire and refine (Biancarosa & Snow, 2006). Scammacca et al. (2007, pp. 1, 12–17), in a U.S. Department of Education–sponsored meta-analysis of the effect sizes of the findings of 31 studies of reading instruction and interventions for students with learning disabilities or who struggle with reading, identified multiple implications for practice with older students. A partial list of these implication includes:

■ Adolescence is not too late to intervene; interventions benefit older students.

- Older students with reading difficulties benefit from interventions focused at both the word and the text level.
- Older students with reading difficulties benefit from improved knowledge of word meanings and concepts.
- Word study interventions are appropriate for older students struggling at the word level.
- Teaching comprehension strategies to older students with reading difficulties is beneficial.

Among the instructional and intervention tasks that contributed to these findings were sentence-level processing and production demands, such as finding sentences that convey main ideas and details, using text vocabulary in sentences, passage comprehension as demonstrated by *cloze sentences* (i.e., fill-in-the-blank questions where the word or words omitted help learners think about the meaning, grammar, and syntax of the sentences), and text passage retelling. *There is a language basis for reading comprehension difficulties, and the remediation of these difficulties is rooted in improving the learner's language processing at the word, sentence, and discourse levels* (Berninger & Abbott, 2010; Catts, 2009; Ehren, 2009; Nation et al., 2004).

The Comprehension Demands of Informational Text

Ehren (2014) recounted that the *Common Core State Standards* (National Governors Association Center for Best Practices, Council of Chief State School Officers, 2010) entail learning expectations related to expository text (i.e., nonfiction,

informational text). Although expository text may be nonlinear or atemporal, texts are crafted so that readers can find information, for example, by visually highlighting key points with bold or italicized text or using organizational features such as a table of contents, a glossary or list of definitions, an index, captions and other labels, and graphs and charts. Realistic illustrations or photos may aid comprehension, along with ancillary online media. Expository text often uses specialized or technical vocabulary, formal grammar and syntax, and longer, more complex sentences. Four types of informational text are prevalent in school curricula (Ehren, 2014; see also Lundine, 2020):

- Literary nonfiction (also known as creative nonfiction), which employs the literary techniques usually associated with fiction or poetry; this genre reports on persons, places, and events in the real world; includes travel writing, nature writing, science writing, sports writing, biography, autobiography, memoir, interviews, and personal essays; readers may need to comprehend flashbacks, foreshadowing, alternative narrators within a text, and nonlinear, atemporal, or nonsequential presentations of events.
- Expository text (also known as exposition), whose purpose is to inform readers about the natural or social world; exposition often does not use characters or characterization, but there may be persons whose experiences are mentioned, or specific persons' cases may be explained; specialized vocabulary is often used.

■ Argument or persuasion.
■ Procedural texts.

Argument, persuasion, and procedural texts are actually forms of expository text. Expository texts include texts that are organized as factual descriptions, enumerations, listings, and sequential reports, and can be structured to present a comparison and contrast, a cause and effect, or a problem and solution pattern. School reading can entail many expository resources in print and digital formats, such as technical texts, how-to books or articles, procedural books, textbooks, encyclopedias, scientific books, journals, atlases, sets of directions, guides, newspapers, and magazine articles. As such, the cognitive-linguistic processing demands for readers of expository texts differ from the demands for comprehending narratives and stories, and expository text may be more challenging for some learners, especially those with language and learning difficulties (Sáenz & Fuchs, 2002).

Reading Difficulties in School-Age and Adolescent Learners

For some learners, deficits in spoken language and literacy may co-occur (ASHA, 2001; Catts et al., 1999; Catts & Kamhi, 2005; Scarborough, 2001; Seiger-Gardner, 2009; Snowling et al., 2000). A spoken language disorder may be diagnosed in a young child before a child is of an age to develop literacy, then the problem may persist and advance from a preschool language impairment to code-based and/or meaning-based literacy deficits during their school years. The symptoms of the language disorder may change over time, such that academic weaknesses in reading and written language arise in learners who

as young children experienced spoken language difficulties (Aram et al., 1984; Beitchman et al., 1996; Catts et al., 2001; Conti-Ramsden & Durkin, 2008; Johnson et al., 1999; King et al., 1982; Snow, 1991; Snowling et al., 2000; Stothard et al., 1998). There are other learners who, as young children, demonstrate overt oral language form that appears undisturbed but whose covert deficits in language form (i.e., in phonology, morphology, syntax, and/or lexical elements) are revealed when they embark upon literacy learning (Adlof, 2020a, 2020b; Moats, 2000; Nelson, 2010; Scarborough, 2001; Soifer, 2018). Note that while language impairments can coexist with dyslexia and related learning disorders that affect reading decoding and comprehension (Catts, 1991), language impairments are considered to be distinct diagnostic entities from dyslexia, reading disorders, and learning disabilities (Adlof, 2020a, 2020b; Berninger, 2008; Bishop & Snowling, 2004; Catts et al., 1999; Catts et al., 2005; Fraser et al., 2010; Soifer, 2018).

However, students who were diagnosed with spoken language disorders at a young age may be diagnosed in their academic years as having a specific learning disability (ASHA, n.d.-a, n.d.-b). Schoenbrodt et al. (1997) stated that communication disorders and learning disabilities can co-occur within the same individual, which can affect how professionals conduct their assessments, classify the nature of the individual's impairments, and subsequently intervene to improve academic and social performance. Students with learning disabilities might be more prone to have difficulties with speech and language than students who do not have learning disabilities (Wiig & Semel, 1984). The change in diagnostic labels, or the addition of another diagnostic label, may signify that learning abilities have become the student's current concern, taking precedence over the original communication difficulties experienced by a younger child learning language (Berninger & Abbott, 2010). In the presence of a language disorder and/or a learning disability, school-age learners may be diagnosed with a written language disorder, which involves impairment in reading decoding, sight word recognition, reading comprehension, written spelling, and/or written expression (ASHA, n.d.-b). Written language disorders can involve any or all of the five language domains (phonology, morphology, syntax, semantics, and pragmatics), as can spoken language disorders (Berninger & Abbott, 2010). Deficits can affect language awareness, reading comprehension, and written language production at the sound-letter, syllable, word, sentence, and discourse levels (Adlof, 2020a, 2020b; ASHA, n.d.-b). The primary criterion for the diagnosis of a specific learning disability is that there is an impairment of one or more of the basic processes involved in understanding or producing spoken and/or written language that affects listening, speaking, reading, writing, spelling, and mathematical calculations (IDEA, 2004). There is considerable symptom overlap across the diagnostic labels of language disorder (spoken and/or written) and specific learning disability, and the functional consequences related to academic difficulties are similar. In common might be the load and effort that is placed on working memory during language-based learning tasks (Berninger, 2008), as well as the demands on attentional skills, such as allocating attention across multiple stimuli, focusing attention to process and reason through tasks, and sustaining the attentional vigilance needed to stay engaged until tasks

are completed (National Research Center on Learning Disabilities, 2017).

Regardless of the diagnostic terminology, these learners experience a condition where their academic growth is impeded because of deficient comprehension and/or use of language, which affects, most notably, language form (Catts et al., 2005; Snow et al., 2999; Soifer, 2018). During the school years, competent receptive language depends upon comprehension of advanced syntactic and morphological constructions. Students are required to gather meaning from multisentence oral messages and written passages (Scott & Balthazar, 2013). Learners are required to listen to teachers speak at length in class (Heath, 1978) and to read texts that use literate language forms (e.g., elaborated noun phrases and verb phrases, anaphora, passive voice, subordinate clauses, etc.; see Chapter 4; Nelson, 2013; Scott & Balthazar, 2013). *Metalinguistic awareness* is a language user's ability to explore language itself, that is, to consider language as an object for exploration and manipulation (Britton, 1984). Metalinguistic awareness is foundational to literacy because printed words must be consciously manipulated. Moving from using language as a form of communication to engaging in schoolwork that requires an intellectual, metalinguistic exploration of language can be quite effortful. Learners may have difficulty learning the meaning-based skills needed for auditory comprehension, reading comprehension, and oral and written expression. They may toil with language-based academic tasks, such as vocabulary, word study, and grammar (Catts et al., 2008; Conti-Ramsden & Durkin, 2008), and may need to exert much effort to achieve language-based organizational skills, such as using various elements of form, including punctuation, paragraph arrangement, titles and section headers, indexes, tables, graphs, and charts (for additional information, see Gordon Pershey, 2018a).

Achieving Adult Literacy

The end goal of literacy education during the school years is to cultivate literate adults. The National Center for Education Statistics, a section of the Institute of Education Sciences of the United States Department of Education, conducted the 2003 National Assessment of Adult Literacy (NAAL) (National Center for Education Statistics, n.d.-c.). Over 19,000 Americans ages 16 and older participated in a comprehensive measure of literacy performance. Data were reported for various subpopulations, such as racial groups, regional groups, age groups, and incarcerated persons.

The NAAL was an assessment of functional English literacy, designed to measure how adults use written language at home, at work, and in their communities (National Center for Education Statistics, n.d.-c). The NAAL characterized the broad range of printed materials that adults use frequently as requiring three types of literacy: prose literacy, document literacy, and quantitative literacy. Different types of literacy tasks and skills are associated with these types of literacy. The assessment questions for prose literacy asked participants to search, comprehend, and use continuous texts, as would be found in editorials, news stories, brochures, and instructional materials. The document literacy skills questions addressed the knowledge and skills needed to search, comprehend, and use noncontinuous texts, as found in job applications, payroll forms, transportation schedules, maps, information tables,

and drug or food labels. The quantitative assessment required applied mathematics skills. Questions asked examinees to identify and perform computations and use numbers embedded in printed materials, as would be needed to balance a checkbook, figure out a tip for a restaurant server, or complete an order form (National Center for Education Statistics, n.d.-b.).

The study data were arrayed into three performance levels (National Center for Education Statistics, n.d.-a.): below basic (the most simple and concrete literacy skills), basic (simple, everyday literacy skills), intermediate (moderately challenging literacy tasks), and proficient (more complex and challenging literacy activities). These levels were applied to the three types of literacy (prose, document, and quantitative). A searchable database of questions is available at https://nces .ed.gov/naal/sample.asp. The following lists are examples of the tasks required to achieve these performance levels (Hauser et al., 2005; National Center for Education Statistics, n.d.-a.; White & Dillow, 2005). Note that many of these tasks are sentence reading and sentence comprehension skills.

Prose Literacy: Continuous Text

Below basic: Locating easily identifiable information in short, commonplace prose texts
Example question: Searching a short, simple text to find out what a patient is allowed to drink before a medical test

Basic: Reading and understanding information in short, commonplace prose texts
Example question: In a pamphlet for prospective jurors, finding an explanation of how people are selected for the jury pool

Intermediate: Reading and understanding moderately dense, less commonplace prose texts, as well as summarizing, making simple inferences, determining cause and effect, and recognizing the author's purpose
Example question: Consulting reference materials to determine which foods contain a particular vitamin

Proficient: Reading lengthy, complex, abstract prose texts as well as synthesizing information and making complex inferences
Example question: Comparing viewpoints in two editorials

Document Literacy: Noncontinuous Text

Below basic: Locating easily identifiable information and following written instructions in simple documents (e.g., charts or forms)
Example question: Reading and signing a form

Basic: Reading and understanding information in simple documents
Example question: Using a television guide to find out what programs are on at a specific time

Intermediate: Locating information in dense, complex documents and making simple inferences about the information
Example question: Identifying a specific location on a map

Proficient: Integrating, synthesizing, and analyzing multiple pieces of information located in complex documents
Example question: Interpreting a table about blood pressure, age, and physical activity

Quantitative Literacy: Numerical Skills

Below basic: Locating numbers and using them to perform simple quantitative operations (primarily addition) when the mathematical information is very concrete and familiar
Example question: Adding the amounts on a bank deposit slip

Basic: Locating easily identifiable quantitative information and using it to solve simple, one-step problems when the arithmetic operation is specified or easily inferred
Example question: Comparing the ticket prices for two events

Intermediate: Locating less familiar quantitative information and using it to solve problems when the arithmetic operation is not specified or easily inferred
Example question: Calculating the total cost of ordering specific office supplies from a catalog

Proficient: Locating more abstract quantitative information and using it to solve multistep problems when the arithmetic operations are not easily inferred and the problems are more complex
Example question: Computing and comparing the cost per ounce of food items

As Secord (2014) noted, the NAAL expectations make it apparent that SLPs are preparing students to function as members of families and households, as workers, and as of citizens of our society. Literacy was operationalized by the NAAL as specific kinds of knowledge and skills that are used for practical purposes and in varying contexts. Secord (2014) summarized that literacy abilities specifically serve the needs for people to be able to classify, reason, and remember. Being literate can amplify how people think, and literate thought is abstract, analytical, logical, reflective, decontextualized, and complex.

Sentence-Level Grammar and Syntax: Identifying Students' Needs

To ascertain how learners' difficulties with grammar and syntax may have a negative impact on their reading comprehension, SLPs would identify students' areas of need by evaluating how well students achieve the operative learning standards (for guidance, see Power-deFur, n.d.; Power-deFur & Flynn, 2012; Rudebusch, 2012; Schraeder, 2012). *It may be possible to connect students' struggles in attaining the reading and language arts curriculum standards to difficulty comprehending the grammatical elements and syntax of instructional materials, such that students are missing the learning opportunities that the materials can provide.* Students who have not accessed curriculum content cannot learn the information (cf. Brozo, 2010; Ehren et al., 2010). SLPs would observe how students perform in class and/or would obtain teachers' reports of students' performance.

SLPs and educators may have a variety of starting points for identifying the teaching and learning opportunities that can serve school-age and adolescent learners' needs related to grammar and syntax. The mandates for school learning and/or the justifications for providing students with supplemental interventions may indicate the contexts in which students have the need to learn more about grammar and syntax. There are a variety

of resources to consult that provide guidance on identifying how to improve literacy outcomes across all students, specifically concerning those students who are at risk or struggling but who do not have marked special needs. For example, the National Research Center on Learning Disabilities (n.d.) offers suggestions for how to establish team efforts and how to determine language and literacy priorities; their website offers materials and resources to address academic outcomes for students, especially as related to literacy for struggling readers.

Starting points for SLPs may include planning and structuring literacy lessons and interventions with these contexts and considerations in mind:

- To encompass the rudiments of literacy, a starting point is to address grammar and syntax as they relate to attaining three of the five "essential areas" of literacy as identified by the National Reading Panel (2000), which include:
  - Reading fluency, reading comprehension, and reading vocabulary, all of which require sentence-level processing and production skills.
- To encompass the expectations for higher-level literacy, a starting point is to consider the vision for preschool to Grade 12 student learning that guided the International Literacy Association and the National Council of Teachers of English during the first decade of the 21st century (see the *Read Write Think* webpage; International Literacy Association and the National Council of Teachers of English, 2021), which contributed to the creation of

the *Common Core State Standards* (National Governors Association Center for Best Practices, Council of Chief State School Officers, 2010). The vision entailed that all students have the opportunities and resources to develop the language and literacy skills needed for full participation in society. These learning experiences include wide reading for learning and enjoyment; structured language study, including phonics, morphology, spelling, grammar, and syntax; strategies for learning vocabulary and comprehending text; instruction in critical thinking; learning technologies and resources, such as computers, Internet access, and school libraries; and policies within educational agencies and systems that respect learners' diverse backgrounds and the cultures and languages of their homes and communities.

■ Another starting point may be to address the specifics of the *Common Core State Standards* (National Governors Association Center for Best Practices, Council of Chief State School Officers, 2010), the school and/or district curriculum, and/or grade-level performance demands:

■ Teachers may report that they have observed students struggle with certain learning and performance demands (e.g., on tests or within classwork) that can be traced to their ability to navigate the grammar and syntax of academic readings; SLPs and other team members may join together to problem solve how to design teaching

and learning approaches to make text more accessible for readers (for example, by using illustrated texts, substituting alternate forms of texts that are more accessible to readers, and viewing related media to establish prior knowledge before reading).

■ SLPs may prefer to start with deficits identified by tests of achievement and abilities, some of which may be standardized and yield diagnostic labels (cf. Porter & Steffin, 2006; some states may require SLPs to use the assessment results that qualified students for services as their intervention objectives):

■ Some test results could indicate that certain specific grammatical and syntactic skills require remediation (for example, a subtest that requires using a key word in a sentence could show this is an area of need; using important words from current class lessons may be an intervention to target sentence formation weaknesses and to reinforce classroom vocabulary); see Chapter 4 for a discussion of test items that reveal syntactic processing deficits; of the tests listed in Chapter 4, those with reading subtests that are relevant to how learners process written syntax are, in alphabetical order by title:

■ Detroit Test of Learning Aptitude–Primary: Third Edition (DTLA-P:3, Hammill & Bryant, 2005)

■ Kaufman Test of Educational Achievement, Third Edition (KTEA-3; Kaufman & Kaufman, 2014)

- Oral and Written Language Scales–Second Edition (OWLS-II; Carrow-Woolfolk, 2012)
- Test of Integrated Language and Literacy Skills (TILLS; Nelson et al., 2016)
- Test of Reading Comprehension–Fourth Edition (TORC-4; Brown et al., 2009)
- Test of Silent Contextual Reading Fluency–Second Edition (TOSCRF-2; Hammill et al., 2014)
- Test of Silent Reading Efficiency and Comprehension (TOSREC; Wagner et al., 2010)

■ Another starting point may be for SLPs and/or teachers to conduct observations of students' verbal participation in classroom discourse, particularly during literate discourse about academic readings (cf. Scott, 1995b), and/or literate discourses may take place during language sampling (see Chapter 4 for information on stimulating higher-level language during language sampling):

- Observations would document how students would benefit from improvement in comprehension of the grammar and syntax of text; this would influence intervention planning, projecting how with better understanding of language form, students could comprehend more enriched discourse.
- SLPs and teachers may note that students are not expressing the quantity and quality of grammatical and syntactic constructions that would be expected for age or grade level; students may not show an actual

measurable grammatical or syntactic impairment or deficit, but they may evidence a lack of facility and a need for enrichment (Nelson, 2013; Scott & Balthazar, 2013).

Response to Intervention (RTI) and Multitiered Systems of Support (MTSS) Frameworks

In some schools and districts, *Response to Intervention* (RTI) frameworks establish some of the strategies for how educational teams identify students' language and literacy needs (Center on Multi-Tiered System of Support at the American Institutes for Research, n.d.; Ehren et al., 2009; Ehren & Whitmire, 2009; Jimerson et al., 2007; National Center on Intensive Intervention at the American Institutes for Research, n.d.; National Research Center on Learning Disabilities, n.d.; National Center on Response to Intervention, 2010). As the RTI Action Network (n.d.) stated, RTI is a multitiered approach to identifying and supporting students with learning needs. RTI has evolved into being referred to as a *Multitiered Systems of Supports* (MTSS), described as "an evidence-based framework that uses data-based problem-solving to integrate instruction, assessment, and intervention designed to meet the academic, behavioral, and social emotional needs of all students" (McKenna et al., 2021, p. 597) that spans from screening students for learning needs through progress monitoring while supports are implemented.

The essential components of RTI/MTSS include high-quality instruction by qualified personnel, research-based curriculum content and instructional methods, and ongoing student assessment and progress monitoring. The RTI/MTSS process begins in general education classrooms (known as Tier I instruction, or universal supports), where teachers, special educators, and/or other specialists, including SLPs, provide struggling learners with learning interventions, often based on principles of *differentiated instruction*, to modify the complexity of the learning content or the materials used for teaching (Ehren et al., 2010; Roth & Troia, 2009), or to lessen performance expectations but still attain the necessary academic gains. Based on how learners respond to these Tier I interventions, whether by making progress or not, the school team makes educational decisions about the types, intensity, and duration of subsequent interventions. Progress is measured in terms of an individual learner's own gains as well as by observing progress in comparison with the learner's peer group.

When Tier I interventions within the general education classroom do not achieve sufficient growth for learners, the multitiered approach provides Tier II interventions, known as targeted interventions, which generally are individualized or small group learning opportunities that supplement classroom instruction and further differentiate the curriculum, lesson content, learning materials, and performance demands to meet learners' needs (cf. Anderson et al., 2013; Bridges, 2011; Ehren et al., 2010). If Tier II interventions do not result in academic progress, Tier III interventions include individualized, intensive interventions that target the students' skills deficits. Students who do not progress in response to Tier III interventions are then referred for a comprehensive educational abilities and psychometric evaluation and are considered for eligibility for special

education services under IDEA (2004). The data collected during Tiers I, II, and III are included and used to make the eligibility decision. It should be noted that RTI/MTSS is not a so-called wait-to-fail approach; on the contrary, parents and educators have the right at any point during the RTI/MTSS process to request a formal educational evaluation to determine eligibility for special education. An RTI/MTSS process cannot be used to deny or delay a formal evaluation for special education (RTI Action Network, n.d.).

Sentence-Level Grammar and Syntax: Suggestions for Interventions

Interventions for reading comprehension deficits can take on two basic approaches. One approach would be to address the language and learning deficits that have been diagnosed based on language and learning abilities testing (see Chapter 4 for a discussion of language abilities testing) and/or by observation of students' work samples and classroom performance, with an ensuing attempt to remediate those specific weaknesses. *The intention is to try to look back at the basic skills that learners should have acquired, identify what they have not acquired, and fill in these gaps.* An approach centered on remediation of basic skills may be more applicable when specific code-based reading skills are absent, for example, when students' weaker word decoding skills lead to a lack of comprehension of words that are read or result in a weaker understanding of words' morphological components. An approach to remediation of weaknesses in basic skills may be less applicable to meaning-based reading deficits, as is the case when reading comprehension deficits that are based on reduced sentence comprehension are present. *The intention would be to teach foundational sentence construction skills that students would generalize to examine sentences in future reading contexts, and thus students would learn how to work with sentences in a more efficient way.* Sentence study, as described in various ways throughout this chapter, can help students examine sentences for their meaning and construction. Ostensibly, the weaker sentence processing abilities that were revealed by testing would be improved, and future testing would yield better performance scores. Presumably, readers who process sentences comprehendingly either unconsciously or consciously process sentences in ways that are similar to what the struggling students would be taught to do, and as struggling students internalize these basic skills, they would be processing sentences in ways that are similar to how facile readers process sentence meaning and structures.

A second approach is to help students learn the tools to use when reading sentences and passages that would allow them to keep up with classroom instruction. It may not be possible to identify the exact nature of a learner's underlying grammatical and syntactic deficits, whether these are more global or are predicated on certain basic knowledge and skills being missing. The intention is not to try to remediate some past lack of development or accomplishment, but to move forward to achieve functional performance in future and to try to help learners keep up with grade-level academics. Students might be taught general approaches to sentence-level reading comprehension, which then become their basic tools, as are described in this chapter. This comprehension toolbox may help students develop a foundation for

processing sentence meaning, but every written passage has its unique structure and wording and needs to be approached as a new comprehension challenge. General reading comprehension strategies are powerful tools for students to use, but, inevitably, there will be passages that challenge the effectiveness of common strategies and will require unique comprehension approaches.

Potentially, SLPs may identify that *some learners need a hybrid approach of remediation of basic skills plus developing new skills that will help them take on future learning challenges.* Either or both approaches would ultimately justify educators' and SLPs' choices for grammar and syntax instruction and interventions.

Interventions for Grammar and Syntax in the Context of the Multiple Cognitive-Linguistic Skills Needed for Reading

A basic tenet of helping readers comprehend the syntax of text is to emphasize that students need to comprehend the form of the text's sentences in order to comprehend the meaning of the sentences (Eberhardt, 2013; Nelson, 2013; Scott & Balthazar, 2013; Schleppegrell, 2013). Sentence study interventions help readers examine the properties of written text. Deep comprehension requires that readers have the ***metalinguistic*** ability to look beyond the text's apparent meanings and explore *how* the text conveys its meanings; specifically, how a sentence imparts its unique meaning. Sophisticated readers actively consider their own processes of comprehension; this means that they consider how they themselves interpret text meanings (Rosenblatt, 1978).

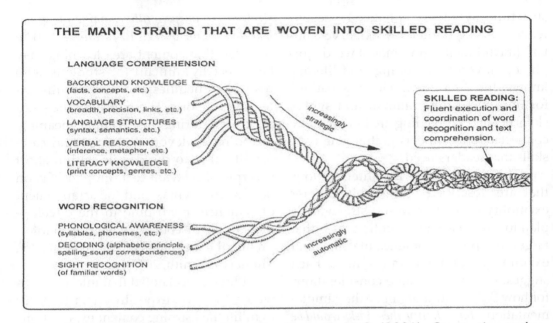

Figure 5–1. The Reading Rope. From Scarborough, H. S. (2001). *Connecting early language and literacy to later reading (dis)abilities: Theory and practice.* In S. Neuman & D. Dickinson (Eds.), *Handbook of research in early literacy* (pp. 97–110). Guilford Press. © Guilford Press. Reprinted with permission of Guilford Press.

The multiple components of the cognitive-linguistic skills that readers need to use to comprehend text are illustrated on the infographic shown in Figure 5–1, titled *The Reading Rope* (Scarborough, 2001). The strands of the rope stand for the multiple cognitive-linguistic skills needed for reading. *The Reading Rope* depicts a set of word recognition skills and a set of language comprehension skills, illustrated as strands of a rope. The word-recognition strands (phonological awareness, decoding, and sight recognition of familiar words) become increasingly automatic and unconscious as readers gain expertise. Concurrently, readers' awareness of the language comprehension strands becomes more overt, conscious, and strategic. Advanced readers use the language comprehension strands to process and comprehend more complex tests. When advanced readers read, they apply their background knowledge, vocabulary, language structures (including grammar and syntax), verbal reasoning, and literacy knowledge (e.g., genres, conventions of print, etc.) to process and comprehend text. Skill development and refinement require instruction and repeated practice and are elements of lifelong learning because, in a sense, everyone is always learning to read better than they have read before.

The strands of *The Reading Rope* allow for identification of the target areas of instruction and intervention, but the tight interwovenness of the strands suggests that one strand of skills cannot be separated from the other strands. Although suggestions for interventions would focus on syntax as a component of language structure, syntax is enhanced because readers' background knowledge, vocabulary (including the grammar of word morphology), verbal reasoning, and literacy knowledge also grow. The suggestions for improving the grammar and syntax skills needed for reading are intentionally connected to the other cognitive-linguistic skills that readers need.

The suggestions for interventions that are described within this chapter exemplify how SLPs would strategically plan to emphasize intervention tasks that target interpreting sentence meaning and examining grammar and syntax. Each suggestion presents some considerations for how SLPs would organize their implementations. *Importantly, these tasks would be situated within the context of overall text comprehension activities and cognitive-linguistic enhancements* (Eberhardt, 2013; Nelson, 2013; Schleppegrell, 2013; Scott & Balthazar, 2013). In a synthesis of the research on comprehension strategies for expository text used with students with learning disabilities, Gajria et al. (2007) categorized *interventions as content enhancements* (e.g., advance organizers, graphic organizers, visual displays, mnemonic illustrations, and computer-assisted instruction) or *cognitive strategy instruction* (e.g., learning about text structure, identifying main ideas, cognitive mapping, and using reciprocal teaching, where students teach one another in small groups to promote text comprehension based on summarizing text, question generating, clarifying understanding, and predicting how texts will develop their content [Palincsar, 1986; Palincsar & Brown, 1984, 1985]). These content and cognitive foci would contribute to planning SLPs' interventions, in that enhancing content can make the language of text more accessible to learners, and *learners need to learn explicit cognitive*

strategies to purposefully examine the grammar and syntax of text. Bryant et al. (2000) reported that content area learning may be especially difficult for students with reading difficulties and may require extensive supports. These include the strategies used during *close reading*, meaning, rereading to devote sustained and careful attention to the details within short excerpts of relevant text. Emphasis is on how words, syntax, and the arrangement of sentences contribute to the development of the discourse, as well as on interpreting the meanings of key passages (cf. Minnery & Smith, 2019).

Ehren (2014) noted that interventions would focus on expository text in order to fulfill the learning content expectations stipulated by the *Common Core State Standards* (National Governors Association Center for Best Practices, Council of Chief State School Officers, 2010). Ehren (2014) expressed that the expectations for the quantity of informational text read, as a proportion of all school reading, would be:

- Grades K–4: 50%
- Grades 5–8: 45%
- Grades 9–12: 70%

Adult independent reading is estimated to be about 80% expository for most readers (Ehren, 2014). Reading informational text requires careful study of the language of informational text, including its grammar and syntax, to gain the depth of knowledge that the text conveys. Informational text may address complex ideas, which would suggest that its sentences would be constructed to be information rich. Clausal structures, tense, and other components of language form would contribute to the meaning of these sentences, which could yield lengthy sentence constructions. Not all sentences that convey information are long, however, and readers need to deduce meaning from the short phrases used in website headings and directories, photo captions, and explanations of graphical tools. Interactive websites, computer settings, phone and tablet menus, and so on use short messages to convey their instructions and choices. Learning about the abbreviated syntax of online informational sources is an important skill, too.

Plan for Activities for Before, During, and After Reading

The first suggestion has to do with *the points in time within a lesson sequence when SLPs would implement content enhancements and/ or cognitive strategy interventions*. Among the many intervention strategies that SLPs can employ, a basic consideration is whether the study of sentence meaning, grammar, and syntax would occur before, during, and/or after reading a text (cf. Allen & Petersen, 2011; Marzola, 2018). The main concerns are whether readers will need comprehension support before, during, or after they read, along with when during an intervention sequence SLPs will look for students' demonstrations of performance.

Before reading activities allow readers to prepare for what they are about to read and, ideally, make the text seem less foreign and intimidating. A text preview is one way to introduce the text. Or, relevant before reading activities would activate a reader's prior knowledge and serve as warm-up exercises before reading. A longer text can be previewed in chunks so it is not so daunting, so a preview might mean going through the text only a section at a time, using multiple preview sessions over time, perhaps on different days.

To acquaint readers with the overall gist of a text before they actually read the passage, chapter, book, website, or other extended text, one common preview practice is to skim and scan the text to look at chapter titles, section headers, page or screen layout, tables or graphs, or other text organizational elements. This is a way to become acquainted with the structure of the text. Previewing illustrations can help readers set some expectations for what the text might be about. Working with words and sentences excerpted from the text before reading can introduce the meanings of selected key words or sentences that will help propel the plot of the narration or the gist of the exposition and can alert readers to tune into these words and sentences during reading. Previewing key sentences can alert readers before reading, so they can tune into the passages where these key sentences occur. Selective previews of text content can pique readers' interest and prepare them to engage with and enjoy the reading.

During reading activities stop the flow of reading, so these interruptions would be designed to make it easier to keep on reading. For example, after reading a page of print, readers could stop and go back and mark sentences that were important or interesting. The flow is suspended, but the lookback reinforces which information to keep in mind as the reading continues. This practice can help SLPs monitor a reader's comprehension, since the opportunity for the learner to choose the important or interesting sentences is a window onto what the student is processing at the sentence level (cf. Marzola, 2018; Shanahan, 2021). If the student selects passages that are not a key to the gist meaning or somehow are not important, SLPs can model marking the sentences that are more important. Marking can be achieved by note writing, underlining, highlighting, or circling within books or on printouts of texts, or by using on-screen markup tools, or by making external notes on paper or index cards or within computer files. It's a simple task to copy key sentences onto index cards and tape them to a wall, thumbtack them onto a bulletin board, or clothespin them onto a clothesline, all of which create a visual and tactile timeline of the important events in the text.

When a longer text is going to be read over the course of several days, SLPs will have to manage the disruptions in the continuity of reading, so planned stopping points are necessary for time management. These session closure points provide opportunities for during reading activities that enhance comprehension. These activities provide a place to pick up where the SLP and students left off when they meet again for their next session. SLPs and students would review the last during reading activity briefly and then move on with reading the next section of text.

After reading activities are a staple of reading comprehension instruction and interventions. Readers review what they have read to demonstrate recall and learning. Or readers participate in text extension activities that inspire meaningful learning and that can be personally relevant and fun. *The critical importance of looking back in text and rereading text can be emphasized here.* Text lookback is an important study skill and is a memory enhancer. Being able to look back in a passage to find important information is a skill that is needed on standardized tests of reading comprehension and state-mandated achievement tests. Test directions often instruct test takers to go back and examine a specific line or paragraph in order to answer a given question.

Comprehension activities that SLPs and teachers commonly use can be adapted for use before, during, and after reading. For example, students can fill in graphic organizers, charts, or concept maps at any or all of these stages of the reading process (cf. Marzola, 2018; Proly et al., 2009). Parts of these organizers can identify grammatical and syntactic properties of texts. If one part of the organizer is used to copy a sentence from the text that talks about a main character, for example, learners can go back and analyze the construction of that sentence for its clauses, adjectives, adverbs, or other elements. Or an organizer can have a section for logging certain sentence constructions in the text, as in, *Find a sentence with a dependent clause* or *Find a sentence with an infinitive verb*.

Ellis and Graves (1990) discussed the after reading phase as entailing comprehension of the meaning of paragraphs and passages. Ellis and Graves (1990) proposed two strategic steps that they called "RAP": *R*ead a paragraph, then (1) *A*sk yourself to find the sentence in the paragraph that tells the main idea of the paragraph, and then (2) *P*ut the main idea into your own words. Summarization of the main idea changes the syntax from the author's own to that of the learner. Brown and Cambourne (1990) referred to this occurrence as "linguistic spillover" and stated that comprehension benefits from rephrasing the text into one's own language. This process allows for syntactic examination of the language of the text and of the oral summary. After reading a series of paragraphs, passages, or any other lengthier text, learners can retell the series of main ideas, again employing their own spoken syntax in contrast to the written syntax of the text. Going beyond a spoken retelling to putting the main ideas down in writing is another strategy to reinforce reading comprehension. As Caccamise (2011) described, producing written summaries of texts may help students improve their reading comprehension.

Ehren (2014) identified some general principles of reading comprehension interventions, based on the consideration that it is challenging to support learners in their comprehension of informational text. SLPs would examine academic texts to predict the syntactic structures that could be difficult for their learners who struggle with language. Intervention strategies can include helping students learn how to review academic texts to identify complex syntactic structures, and then to use metalinguistic skills to examine sentences with complex syntax.

To paraphrase and expand upon Ehren (2014), SLPs who work with school-age and adolescent learners would consider the following elements that enhance reading comprehension. SLPs would describe, model, and help students practice these comprehension strategies:

- Teach students that to "unpack" text is a metalinguistic process; readers have to examine how a text is crafted as well as what it means.
- Explore narrative and expository text structures.
- Study different expository text structures, such as enumeration, problem-solution, compare-contrast, description, cause and effect, sequence or procedure, argumentation or persuasion, and so on.
- Use story grammar elements to comprehend narrative (characters, plot, setting, etc.).
- Identify how punctuation marks signal meaning.

- Recognize phrase and clause boundaries.
- Look at how the author uses word strings, whether sentences, phrases, captions, and so on; ask learners to explain the meaning of the string of words.
- Keep the entirety of the text in mind; integrate information across different parts of the text.
- Explore how texts differ in different school subjects; note that texts differ based on subject matter, as well as by whether they are school texts or general reading material.
- Discuss the special features of texts of different genres, on different subjects, for different audiences, and so on.

Mini-Lessons

SLPs' mini-lessons would include a judicious choice of small amounts of grammatical and/or syntactic information that would not overwhelm or confuse students. As in the example above, *Find a sentence with a dependent clause* or *Find a sentence with an infinitive verb*, this knowledge would have to have been taught at some point prior to the use of the graphic organizer that refers to these sentence constructions. Mini-lessons, an instructional term that Atwell (1987) coined, would consist of structured, brief, to the point, and verbally interactive lesson frameworks delivered before, during, or after reading. Or the mini-lessons could be independent of any reading and simply cover some necessary information and/ or skills. Mini-lessons can be offered as part of a speech-language session, perhaps as a smaller lesson within a longer therapy session, or as a part of a larger classroom lesson. The mini-lesson would help students learn complex grammar and syntax a little bit at a time. For example, if the larger speech-language lesson were to read and discuss the meaning of a portion of a textbook currently being used in social studies class, the mini-lesson would identify some key sentences that exemplify metalinguistic knowledge of a grammatical or syntactic form, for example, the order of descriptive words used in a series, or infinitive verbs, or parallel independent clauses (see Chapter 4). The SLP would take the time to help the students metalinguistically explore the grammar and syntax of the excerpted sentences and would document their understanding using a brief worksheet, activity, learning journal, card sort, or some other active learning device. SLPs would collect data on this performance, having previously set metalinguistic knowledge of sentence grammar and syntax as a therapy objective. SLPs would collect other separate data on the students' understanding of the content of the passages read and could therefore describe any connections between performance on the metalinguistic grammar and syntax activity and the general comprehension activity.

Atwell's (1987) strategies for grammar mini-lessons include:

- Selecting a form to explore.
- Providing models and demonstrations of the adult using and explaining the form.
- Showing examples of how the form is used in student-friendly oral and/or written language contexts.
- Allowing students time for structured practice using the form in speech and/or in writing.
- Sharing ideas and insights about the form.

Other elements of participatory learning, including cultivating a sense of ownership and buy-in, are valuable components of mini-lessons.

Linguistic Microstructures and Macrostructures

Readers' comprehension is aided by learning about linguistic microstructures and macrostructures. Linguistic *microstructures* are the linguistic details within sentences and words. These include word choices, including their morphology and grammatical elements; sentence formation choices; and the minutiae of details that arrange words and sentences into paragraphs or passages. In Figure 5–1, *The Reading Rope* (Scarborough, 2001), microstructures would be represented as elements of language structure and vocabulary. Linguistic *macrostructures* are the broader elements of discourse that readers need to be mindful of, such as differentiating the conventions of genres, for example, the narrative conventions that differ from the conventions of exposition; identifying author's purpose; identifying the intended audiences for a text; elements of overall text organization, structure, style, and presentation; and gleaning the gist meanings of texts. Macrostructures would be identified on *The Reading Rope* by background knowledge, verbal reasoning, and literacy knowledge.

Some text elements are pertinent to both microstructural and macrostructural concerns, for example, how the wording of a sentence (its microstructure) allows it to stand as the topic sentence in a paragraph (which would be its contribution to the macrostructure). Sentence form is a component of how authors impart the meaning, purpose, and function of their sentences (note that *function* is described in Chapter 2 of this text as, for example, using language pragmatically to direct, explain, share personal thoughts, be imaginative, etc.). Fang and Schleppegrell (2010) suggested a combined pedagogical emphasis on language form and message function (which is based on Halliday [1973, 1975] and represents the school of linguistics known as **systemic functional linguistics**). Fang and Schleppegrell (2010) described their approach as *Functional Language Analysis* (FLA). FLA emphasizes how readers need to make the same kinds of pragmatic judgements as listeners, for example, comprehending microstructurally whether they are reading directives, procedures, explanations, knowledge-telling, anecdotes, persuasive or "influencer" messages, and so on. Syntactic-pragmatic judgments can help readers identify the authors' intentions. FLA alerts readers to how a speaker's or writer's meaning is constructed by particular language choices, including syntactic arrangements (Ehren, 2014). Fang and Schleppegrell (2010) advocated that the English grammar system is a resource for meaning making. Listeners and readers can become attuned to the meanings behind syntactic choices. Studying the microstructural and macrostructural language of the text is an effective strategy for text comprehension. Ehren (2014) stated that FLA (Fang & Schleppegrell, 2010) focuses on meaning as presented in three general modes:

- Experiential meanings: Authors structure texts to say something about the world (and how they have experienced it).
- Interpersonal meanings: Within texts are embedded interactions, interpretations, attitudes, and judgments; texts enact social relationships of some kind.
- Textual meanings: How a text is organized to impart a coherent message.

Some ideas for the study of microstructural concerns include:

- Considering that **signal words** can be useful for the study of the microstructures of texts, it would be worthwhile to examine sentences for signal words as a prereading or during reading strategy. Signal words might include *since, before, therefore, most, main, important*, and so on. Learners can discuss the parts of speech of these words, the types of clauses they are found in, or other grammatical and syntactic considerations (as described in Chapter 4). Learners can collect these words and record them in their notebooks, create computer document files for future reference, produce wall charts or posters that serve to remind them of these words, and use other memory-enhancing strategies.
- Does a passage have a main idea statement and/or a topic sentence? What words signal the importance of this sentence? Collect a list of these signal words, such as *main, key, important, chief*, and *essential*, for future reference, using a computer document file, wall poster, notebook, index card file, and so on.
- Does a passage have an identifiable text structure that is evident sentence by sentence, such as enumeration, comparison, problem-solution, and so on? What words, numbers, or lettered outlines signal

these structures? Collect a list of these words and other features for future reference.

- Do text features and/or graphical elements aid comprehension (such as bullets or numbered lists to present details; or is visual salience given to the kernels of information stated in captions, chapter titles, or section headers)? Make a list of these features and "be on the lookout" for them in future reading (cf. Marzola, 2018).

- Use grammar and syntax to improve reading comprehension: Formal microstructural lessons or mini-lessons about some of the grammatical elements and clausal structures (e.g., as those that are described in Chapter 4); SLPs can identify just a few features at a time and these can be addressed until students become well versed on, for example, finding a sentence's main clause and subordinate clause, finding sentences that use the active and the passive voice, and so on.

  - Strategies may include *unpacking sentences* (Ehren, 2014): Within selected passages of school texts, adults and students choose a few sentences of interest to examine for their grammar and syntax, such as their main clauses and dependent clauses.

  - Students keep notes on the unpacking strategies that readers would use often, for example, *find the subject word in the sentence first; look for the kernel of the sentence by striking out unnecessary words that are not part of the kernel.*

- Use *oral interpretation* of text: Read text aloud to identify the meaningful microstructural sentence elements, prosodic contours, and other text features; an expressive reading can help readers read the passage with better comprehension; oral interpretation uses an expressive and interpretive voice; repetitive reading aids reading fluency; text is dramatized to help readers understand its meaning.

- Look for repetitive refrains or repetitive phrasing in texts. Authors who use a certain word arrangement over and again are doing so in order to make a point. Students may relate to the refrains used in songs and poems and would be motivated to examine the grammar and syntax of these lines.

Instruction and interventions that target the use of cohesive devices, such as conjunctions, are often included in reading comprehension and writing interventions. More specifically, students are taught that compound sentences may be marked by coordinating conjunctions such as *and, but,* and *so,* and complex sentences may be marked by subordinating conjunctions such as *before, because,* and *although* (Nippold, 1998). In order for students to succeed in using higher-level language, they must be able to comprehend and formulate complex structures and infer semantic relationships within and across sentences.

A macrostructural focus would encompass a reader's broader literacy knowledge. Literacy knowledge is attained by wide and varied reading of diverse sources. SLPs can acquaint students with different genres of texts, and with texts written for different audiences and purposes, and by engaging with texts that are shared in various ways. Sources abound for bringing literacy diversity to school-age readers (e.g., Rasinski, 2016, whose website features vocabulary, morphology, word study, oral reading fluency, and other literacy learning materials). An emphasis on macrostructure also applies to an appreciation of entire texts. Students can engage in sustained silent reading, shared oral reading, or reading adaptations of text designed for oral performance. Students can practice characters' lines during Reader's Theater, which is a dramatic reading of a script based upon a book (see, for example, *Reader's Theater Scripts and Plays for the Classroom*, 2008, and numerous other online sources that have transformed well-known books into play script format). Other options include a staged reading of a play, that is, reading a play instead of memorizing the lines, or even when memorizing the lines of a play or of a story or poem.

Microstructural and macrostructural analyses can overlap. Some of the strategies are general for exploring microstructures and macrostructures and can be used in similar ways to comprehend written text and/or the oral language used during classroom instruction. Ehren (2009, 2014) proposed that readers engage in tactics for meaning-based analyses of text. Analyses are meant to explore:

- Meaning at the sentence level.
- Meaning based on a series of sentences or longer passages.
- How some sentence meanings may be understood based on a more general understanding of the gist of the text.
- Meaning that relates to an understanding of how texts are organized and to the types of text features an author uses, such as section headers, dialogue, or tables of information.

A paraphrase and expansion of Ehren's (2014) proposals for exploring microstructures and macrostructures would include the following:

- The author's voice.
  - Readers would reflect on what an author's own life experiences might have been. Studying the biographical background of the author might explain why he or she has certain ideas, uses certain words or phrases, or promotes certain viewpoints.
  - What is the author saying about the world? What are the author's interpretations?
  - Which sentences reveal this information?
- The author's craft.
  - How has the author organized the text? What text features can a reader rely on, such as chapter titles, section headers, lists, bold print, and so on?
  - How does the author put words together to create meaningful sentences?
  - Does the author use clear verbal signals, such as identifying which sentences state main ideas and details, or do readers have to "read between the lines" and determine this information for themselves?
- Take-away messages from the text.
  - What questions does the text answer?
  - Which sentences offer important ideas, summaries of information, or other useful content?

When readers are aware of these form-plus-function considerations, they can improve their sentence analysis skills in order to better comprehend the kinds of text-based information that is used within academic assignments. McKeown et al. (1993) and Beck and McKeown (2006) promoted a reading comprehension technique called "Questioning the Author" where students explore what an author is trying to say and how an author uses language to convey these ideas. Teachers may expect this level of understanding of text meaning and of how language is used to impart meaning. In class, that task might be to converge on correct answers to comprehension questions or to take a test on the specific information provided in a text. Or the task might be to write a reflective response to a text (that is, produce a divergent "thinking" response or a personal response). Standardized tests or state-mandated tests may include these types of convergent questions as multiple choice or fill-ins or as divergent analyses in open-ended essay responses. SLPs' interventions can help students learn what to expect on assignments and on tests and can prepare them with strategies and skills to meet these expectations (Kumin & Mason, 2011).

Ehren (2014) further described how SLPs can help students better understand how English grammar functions as a system and is a resource for meaning making. Ehren explained that "unpacking" the system can help students understand sentence grammar. A paraphrase and expansion of Ehren's (2014) "unpacking" would include the following:

- Parts of speech.
  - Find the nouns and the words that describe them (which are adjectives, as in, a *strong* wind)

(these groups of words are noun phrases).
- Find the relative pronouns: pronouns that introduce phrases that describe nouns (as in, the student *who* has the highest test score; the essay *that* is the longest; final exams, *which* are worth more points than other assignments).
- Find the verbs and the words that describe them (adverbs, as in, the wind blew *fiercely*).
- Find the two-word verbs (a verb that needs a preposition following it in order to convey its meaning, for example, *turn on, turn off, turn to; hang on, hang up, hang out*).
- Find the prepositions that begin a prepositional phrase (as in, a flock *of birds*; the mother *of the bride*; a form *for you* to fill out; give the gift *to your sister*).
- Find the "tricky" phrases that have two-word verbs that might look like prepositional phrases (as in, turn *to* your mother, cut *off* the stem); it's a two-word verb if the preposition is needed for this specific meaning of the verb (and, by contrast, go to sleep *at night* has a prepositional phrase, not a two-word verb, because *sleep* stands alone in meaning without *at*).
- Find the infinitive verbs (*to cut, to fill* out) (and do not confuse them with two-word verbs or prepositional phrases).
- Find the question words (*who, what, when, where, why, how, how much, how come, how would*, etc.).
- Find the conjunctions (words that join ideas together [*and, but, so*, etc.]); when these words

introduce a subordinate clause, they are called **subordinating conjunctions** (*Some people like snow, but I don't*), but if they join two sentence elements with equal grammatical value, they are coordinating conjunctions (Last night there was wind and rain. *Wind* and *rain* are equal as nouns).

- Word meanings.
  - Find signal words and phrases (for time, as in *next* or *before*; for importance, as in *most, least, best, necessary, major*; for enhancements of phrases, as in *and wouldn't you know; the funny part was*).
  - Find morphological inflections: How do bound morphemes influence a word's part of speech and word meanings? *Transport* is a verb, but *transportation* is a noun.
- Word strings (clausal structure).
  - Find complete thoughts: These are probably independent clauses (The wind blew fiercely.).
  - Find incomplete thoughts that need more information: These are probably subordinate clauses (The wind blew fiercely, *coming from the north.*).
  - Find the sentence subject: All of the words before the main verb in the sentence (*The wind* blew fiercely).
  - Find the sentence predicate: the main verb and the words that come after this verb in the sentence (The wind *blew fiercely.*). The predicate tells what the subject does, or simply, the predicate is every part of the sentence that is not the subject (*What the predicate of a sentence?* n.d.).

- The meaning of punctuation marks.
  - End of sentence marks: These follow statements of complete thoughts: periods, question marks (The wind blew fiercely!).
  - Mid-sentence semicolon: Used to connect two complete thoughts that are closely related in meaning to form one sentence (The wind blew fiercely; the worst part was how the trees swayed so closely to our windows.).
  - Mid-sentence colon: Used to introduce an explanation or a list (The wind sent them flying: the empty flowerpots, chair cushions, and lightweight decorations on our deck.).
  - Commas: Separate a series of items or ideas (flowerpots, chair cushions, and decorations); separate and set off phrases (not exactly a tornado, but a strong wind, and enough to cause damage); mark a subordinate clause (*Before the storm*, we were complacent about weather.); introduce quotations (My neighbor said, "I will never again take a storm warning lightly.").
  - Quotation marks: Enclose the exact words someone said or wrote ("I will never again take a storm warning lightly.").
- Break down units of meaning.
  - Recognize phrase boundaries and clause boundaries: Break down longer sentences by separating out their clauses and phrases, subjects and predicates, prepositional phrases, signal words, and punctuation cues.

Examining the elements of sentences will help reveal their meanings. Longer sentences can become easier to manage when they are broken down and their construction patterns are discussed by students and SLPs.

- Clauses have subjects and predicates, too, known as clausal subjects and clausal predicates. The clausal subjects identify the noun phrases in the clauses. (*Late last summer*, a strong wind blew, coming from the north. *Late last summer* is a subordinate clause, and its subject is *summer*. The noun phrase is the clause's noun and the words that describe the noun, *Late last*.) The clausal predicate identifies the verb phrases in the clauses. (In late last summer, a strong wind blew, *coming from the north*, this clausal predicate is the verb and the words that follow it within the subordinate clause.)
- Sensory information.
  - Find the components of sentences that can be felt: words about actions or states of being and who or what are "doing, saying, sensing, being" and receiving actions, feelings, states, and so on (Ehren, 2014, p. 7).
- Sentence explorations.
  - If a sentence is hard to understand, look for additional information outside the sentence. Don't get stuck within a difficult sentence.
  - Is a sentence hard to understand because the author left something out? Fill in those gaps.
  - Mark out parts that are confusing. Rewrite them in your own words. Use synonyms for difficult words.
  - Find any mistakes in the sentences that could be hindering its meaning and clarity. Mark these out and rewrite the sentence correctly.
  - Reword information to make it easier to understand.
  - Combine "ideas in different ways that make sense" (Ehren, 2014, p. 8).

The above explanations may be familiar to SLPs who target sentence expansion goals for older speakers. The important components here are that SLPs are aware that (1) reading comprehension goals have similarities to receptive and expressive sentence expansion goals, but sentence expansion is a craft, not just the inclusion of more words per utterance, and (2) reading comprehension goals need to go beyond identifying the meaning of words in text passages and focuses on the meaning of multiword syntax.

Prosodic Interventions

Reading without incorporating sentence prosody may be a factor in reduced reading comprehension (National Research Council, 1999). Learning to apply sentence prosody to improve text comprehension is a skill that might be ongoing for struggling readers. Part of their difficulty might arise simply because cues for the prosodic reading of text are seldom found in written language systems. "This lack of prosodic transparency in written English means few cues for expressive reading. Struggling readers produce oral readings that are prosodically ill formed (Levy et al., 1992). Repeated readings foster prosody development in good readers but not necessarily in poor readers (Levy et al., 1993)" (as cited by Gross et al., 2013, p. 190).

Prosodic interventions would guide readers to apply their knowledge of the natural prosody that they experience in daily spoken language to their *oral interpretation* of the texts they read (cf. Rasinski, 2016) SLPs may need to make school-age readers explicitly aware of spoken language prosody and explain to them how to impart prosody into written text during expressive oral readings. Gross et al. (2013) itemized the many benefits of prosody instruction:

■ Prosody training during oral reading can be internalized "as an expressive inner voice" (Gross et al., 2013, p. 190).

■ Prosodic reading helps readers focus on the high-content, meaningful words in sentences and passages; "skilled, silent readers behave as though they are guided by an inner voice that flags newsworthy content" (Gross et al., 2013, p. 198).

■ Sentences become organized in memory, which increases text recall (Koriat et al., 2002).

■ Cognitive processing of text is facilitated and cognitive load can be more manageable.

■ Prosodic reading is a hallmark of fluent, automatic reading.

Grammar Instruction

Chapter 4 describes how to inventory and assess students' spoken language grammatical and syntactic skills. Establishing students' spoken language status can aid

SLPs in planning how to approach the learners' explorations of the grammar and syntax of text for academic purposes. For example, a document on the Systematic Analysis of Language Transcripts (SALT 20; 2020b) software website titled *Using SALT to Assess the Common Core Grades K–12* (n.d.) compares the SALT elicitation protocols, the language measures that can be obtained using SALT, and the SALT score summary reports to selected *Common Core State Standards* for English Language Arts in the Speaking and Listening strand (National Governors Association Center for Best Practices, Council of Chief State School Officers, 2010). The intention of the SALT document is to offer a reliable and valid comparison of the SALT assessment results to the language skills necessary to achieve the *Common Core State Standards*. This comparison document can help SALT users determine whether the examinees' grammatical and syntactic performance as described on the score summary reports suggest that the learner has developed the language skills necessary to achieve the *Common Core State Standards*, including the skills necessary to participate in the formal instruction in grammar that is likely to be covered within English Language Arts curricula.

From an academic standpoint, grammar is usually meant to encompass the study of the formal patterns of a language. The applicability of these patterns to communicative needs, meaning, their usefulness for reading comprehension and written expression, is not always made explicit to students, and the utility of grammar instruction remains controversial. Hillocks and Smith (1991) wrote that the explicit teaching of grammar has been a part of school curricula since ancient times, but educational research spanning about 90 years established that traditional school grammar instruction tends to have little effect on students' reading, writing, and academic competencies. This criticism tends to be directed at instructional approaches that emphasize memorizing grammar rules. The prevailing instructional paradigm that receives criticism is known as *structural grammar*, which involves learning about grammar by studying its structural features in a decontextualized fashion, with less emphasis on how grammar conveys meaning. Some approaches are based on grammar drills, diagramming sentences, or other tasks taught without functional comprehension contexts. In contrast, *generative grammar* studies the linguistic patterns that speakers and writers authentically and contextually use in order to convey meaning, and this functional approach has met with greater acceptance among educators. However, even when semantics and meaning are a focus of grammar instruction, tormented students and educators may not be able to resist the inevitable pairing of learning "grammar" as involving the use of a "hammer" (e.g., Cazort, 1997, and many others), or they would quip that "grammar" and "glamour" don't easily mix (e.g., Clark, 2011, along with others) and would declare the possibility of "grammar" evoking "tears" (Ormiston-Smith, 2013) and "road rage and panic attacks" (Gilbert, 2012). Humorous and gimmicky grammar books abound, each striving to keep the user's attention (e.g., Gordon, 1993, employed gothic and paranormal themes to illustrate grammatical structures).

Hillocks and Smith (1991) noted that there are essentially three good reasons for teaching grammar:

■ Grammar can provide insight into the way that a language works; grammatical terms can provide a common vocabulary for describing the elements of language and aid in reading comprehension.

■ Grammar can help learners master standard forms of English (that are useful in reading texts that use formal written communication and for expressing information formally when needed).

■ Knowledge of grammar can influence composition skills by improving usage and mechanics and reducing grammatical errors.

Regarding Hillocks and Smith's (1991) first two reasons, having insight into the way that a language works can aid reading comprehension when the overt study of grammatical forms helps readers break down complicated sentences and rephrase them to be more comprehensible. Relatedly, mastering the standard forms of English can help readers comprehend difficult or unfamiliar structures, such as inverted declarative sentences (e.g., *Once there lived a frog and a toad* or *Never have I ever*). Strategies used to find the subject or agent in the sentence, and the verbs, the modifiers, and so on, can be of use. In all, grammar can provide a cognitive framework for the content that readers are trying to understand. (See Chapter 6 for a discussion of how improving usage and mechanics can help writers self-edit based on grammatical rules.)

Similarly, Shaughnessy (1977), in the context of teaching basic writing, stated that grammar instruction can be reduced to four necessities:

■ How to identify and form basic sentence patterns (simple, compound, complex); how to break apart longer sentences and expand shorter sentences.

■ Inflection (the conjugation of verbs and the marking of nouns with plural -s and possessive -'s; adding -self to pronouns; adding -er and -est to adjectives).

- Tense (the 12 tenses: past, present, and future, with four grammatical aspects: progressive, perfect, perfect progressive, and simple. The progressive aspect marks actions that are ongoing, as in *walking*; the perfect marks completed actions, as in *walked*; the perfect progressive marks the completed part of a continuous action, as in *had been walking*; the simple aspect is neither continuous nor completed, as in *walk*).
- Agreement, such as subject-verb agreement or noun-pronoun agreement (grammatical number).

Knowledge of these basic sentence elements can allow readers to comprehend the temporal or sequential concepts written about in texts and to locate the meaningful use of common bound morphemes.

Cloze Procedures Designed to Generate Grammatical Elements

Cloze sentences procedures allow readers to demonstrate linguistic reasoning by filling in a blank inserted into a sentence. Cloze sentence worksheets omit a certain word or words purposefully to help learners think about the meaning, grammar, and syntax of the sentences. Cloze sentences can be used to demonstrate text passage comprehension or to review concepts that have been learned by other kinds of experiences. While some contexts might require learners to supply an exact word recalled from a text or other learning experience, sometimes the fill-in response needs to be one of the many possible words

that completes the sentence grammatically and syntactically. When the learner has to mentally sort through possible words and choose a grammatically and syntactically appropriate construction, the learner demonstrates unconscious or conscious awareness of the linguistic properties that are needed to complete the sentence (Fuchs et al., 1988). The possible responses may be self-generated, that is, spontaneously drawn from the learner's own memory, or the SLP can supply a list of choices. Lists may contain only the possible choices for finishing the worksheet correctly or may contain some additional choices as "foils," or items that would not be used. There can be the same number of choices as there are questions, or there can be more choices than there are questions, thus increasing the difficulty of the choice making task. The choices can offer a range of correct grammatical choices, with one response being the best among the choices, or can offer as "foils" some incorrect grammatical choices. Cloze targets can be grammatical forms that show comprehension of sentence grammar and syntax, for example, maintaining a past tense sentence construction (*Luci watched a movie and _____ a video game*; the fill-in would preserve the past tense, as in *played*) or using a plausible conjunction (*Luci didn't watch a movie _____ she had time after she finished her homework; although* or *when* would be a reasonable conjunction).

> ### Language Objectives for Grammar and Syntax Based on Academic Standards

Porter and Steffin (2006) offered examples of how to transform instructional standards into the performance-based terminology of IEP objectives. In light of the

Table 5–1. Objectives for Grammar and Syntax

Academic Standards	IEP Objectives
Single standard: Identify and use noun-verb agreement	By (date), (Name) will identify noun-verb agreement during structured spoken language tasks (e.g., stimuli derived from pictures, questions, classroom texts, etc.) with _____% accuracy (in ___ out of ____ trials) as measured by oral sentences produced. By (date), (Name) will use noun-verb agreement during structured spoken language tasks (e.g., discussion of classroom subject matter) with _____% accuracy (in ___ out of ____ trials) as measured by oral sentences produced.
Single standard: Combine clauses using coordinating conjunctions	By (date), (Name) will combine clauses using coordinating conjunctions during structured academic tasks (e.g., stimuli derived from pictures, questions, classroom assignments, etc.) with _____% accuracy (in ___ out of ____ trials) as measured by written sentences produced.
Multiple standards: Correct word order; clear and coherent sentences; use of adjectives; formulate sentence subjects and predicates	Objectives to approach multiple standards: Noun phrase expansion in sentence subjects and predicates By (date), (Name) will expand subject nouns into subject noun phrases using adjectives placed in correct word order during structured academic tasks (e.g., stimuli derived from pictures, questions, stories, etc.) with _____% accuracy (in ___ out of ____ trials) as measured by written sentences produced. By (date), (Name) will expand predicate nouns into predicate noun phrases using adjectives placed in correct word order during structured academic tasks (e.g., stimuli derived from pictures, questions, stories, etc.) with _____% accuracy (in ___ out of ____ trials) as measured by written sentences produced.

Source: Expansion of Porter, J., & Steffin, B. (2006). *Speech-language pathology goals and objectives written to the California Standards.*

Porter and Steffin models, Table 5–1 offers some wording for grammar and syntax objectives that complement academic standards and combine listening, speaking, reading, and writing as the means for students to integrate the language systems during their functional performances of tasks. The standards given in Table 5–1 are hypothesized grammar and syntax standards that would be similar to those likely to be found in Reading/Language Arts strands (rather than quoting the actual *Common Core State Standards* [National Governors Association Center for Best Practices, Council of Chief State School Officers, 2010], in that national standards may change and/or the state standards may adapt the Common Core to conform to the requirements of certain states' departments of education). Objectives include aspects of the intervention approaches designed, the materials used, and the students' performance of tasks.

In summary, language form is foundational for oral and written language comprehension and expression. SLPs work with some school-age children and adolescents who are still acquiring language form and with others who are learning about more advanced language forms as they become comprehending readers and competent writers. The goals, objectives, and interventions used for language form are cumulative (Ehren et al., 2009). Academic success is inextricably connected to literacy (Ehren & Whitmire, 2009; Lee & Spratley, 2009), and literacy requires explicit knowledge of language form. It is important that an SLP who is familiar with the elements of language form is part of the school's literacy intervention team (ASHA, 2001; Cunningham & Zibulsky, 2009; Ehren & Ehren, 2007; Ehren et al., 2012).

CHAPTER 6

Improving Grammar and Syntax in Written Language

This chapter describes how learners can improve their written grammar and syntax skills. School success is dependent upon how well students use written language to express their knowledge of and reasoning about academic information. This chapter discusses how the academic tasks that are typical of language arts and literacy curricula make demands on students' knowledge of grammar and syntax, and how accomplishing these tasks requires aspects of metalinguistic awareness. In-school writing entails using sentences competently to complete a variety of assignments, answer questions, communicate with others, perform on mandated achievement testing, and craft a variety of types of expository and narrative texts. Older school-age children and adolescents can develop the metalinguistic awareness to explore the grammar and syntax of sentences written by others and by themselves. This chapter offers strategies for improving learners' written form and expression, with a focus on improving sentence construction and sentence analysis skills. It also discusses supports for learners who are learning about parts of speech, sentence construction, and other rules of language.

Anticipation Guide

After reading this chapter, readers will be able to answer the following questions:

■ What are the in-school and out-of-school writing demands for older school-age learners and adolescents?

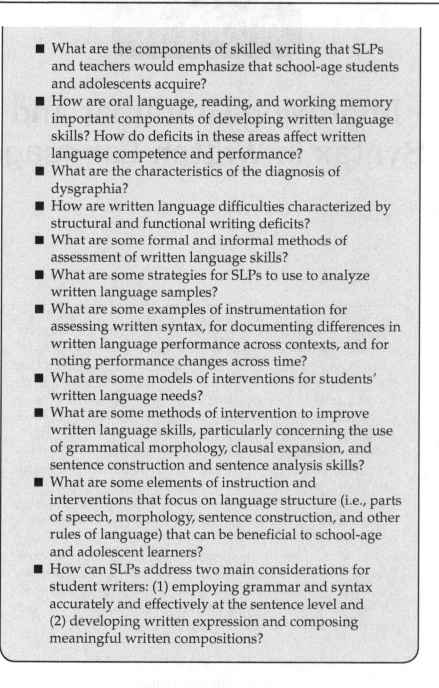

- What are the components of skilled writing that SLPs and teachers would emphasize that school-age students and adolescents acquire?
- How are oral language, reading, and working memory important components of developing written language skills? How do deficits in these areas affect written language competence and performance?
- What are the characteristics of the diagnosis of dysgraphia?
- How are written language difficulties characterized by structural and functional writing deficits?
- What are some formal and informal methods of assessment of written language skills?
- What are some strategies for SLPs to use to analyze written language samples?
- What are some examples of instrumentation for assessing written syntax, for documenting differences in written language performance across contexts, and for noting performance changes across time?
- What are some models of interventions for students' written language needs?
- What are some methods of intervention to improve written language skills, particularly concerning the use of grammatical morphology, clausal expansion, and sentence construction and sentence analysis skills?
- What are some elements of instruction and interventions that focus on language structure (i.e., parts of speech, morphology, sentence construction, and other rules of language) that can be beneficial to school-age and adolescent learners?
- How can SLPs address two main considerations for student writers: (1) employing grammar and syntax accurately and effectively at the sentence level and (2) developing written expression and composing meaningful written compositions?

Written language has become an integral aspect of daily living in the 21st century. This is true even in the lives of school-age children and is especially important for adolescents. Text messages, email, social media, shared calendars and documents, interactive menus and forms, and an ever-growing number of other computerized technologies require users to communicate in writing. Speech-to-text applications can lessen some written language demands to some extent, but there is less control, flexibility, and efficacy for users who are unable or less able to compose a written text. The societal reality that schooling might often or intermittently take place using online learning further increases the demands on students for written communication. Remote learning opportunities and hybrid learning models that combine remote learning plus in-person schooling, instituted either by societal necessity or by personal choice, as is the case with homeschooling, make the use of written communication tools all the more essential.

Linguistic meaning is conveyed by a message's grammatical and syntactic form as well as by its semantic content. School-age learners and adolescents need a sophisticated level of linguistic form that will allow them to comprehend and produce a variety of oral and written sentences (Westby, 2020). Twenty-first century writers of all ages are responsible for producing messages of varying lengths and structures. Even if the necessary written message is only a few words in length, the syntactic structure of the message imparts a portion of its meaning. Syntactic skills for school-age and adolescent writers include crafting brief but clear messages, as well as producing the elaborated syntax that is required for them to demonstrate school learning and to perform well on mandated achievement testing. The two distinct areas of linguistic skill development for student writers are:

(1) Employing vocabulary, morphology, grammar, and syntax accurately and effectively at the sentence level (i.e., *microstructural* skills).
(2) Developing written expression and composing meaningful written compositions (i.e., *macrostructural* skills).

Written language production is, in many ways, a more complex cognitive-linguistic task than are aural language comprehension, oral language production, and reading comprehension (cf. Brinton et al., 2010; Graham & Perin, 2007b; Ehren, 2009; Nelson et al., 2004; Nelson, 2013; Nippold, 1998, 2007; Spencer & Petersen, 2018). Written language development and growth are predicated upon the cognitive-linguistic skills that contribute to receptive and expressive oral language competence and reading decoding and comprehension (Dockrell & Connelly, 2009). Of the four language processes—listening, speaking, reading, and writing—producing written language is arguably the most advanced skill. Written expression entails demands for a coordination of abilities that exceed the abilities needed to listen or read with comprehension and to produce spoken language (Graham & Hebert, 2010). As with spoken language, written language requires cognitive-linguistic and motor skills. Spoken language cognitive-linguistic, auditory-perceptual, and speech motor skills develop earlier and are less varied and complex than the advanced set of cognitive-linguistic, visual-perceptual, and motor skills needed for the manual manipulation of written symbols to create linguistic meaning.

In some learners, early language deficits persist and underlie written language difficulties during the school-age and adolescent periods of development (Bishop & Snowling, 2004). Dockrell and Connelly (2009), in their review of numerous studies, identified multiple properties of the oral to written language continuum of difficulties. They reviewed studies that described both longitudinal and concurrent manifestations of deficits. Learners who exhibit a lack of oral language fluency and/or have deficiencies in oral narration, vocabulary, and/or forming clausal constructions may have weaker written composition skills (see also Fey et al., 2004; Spencer & Petersen, 2018). Learners who have spoken language deficits have a slower rate of written language development, may produce more errors when they write, and may compose shorter texts than typically developing peers. Speed, automaticity, and fluency in reading, handwriting, and spelling appear to contribute positively to written composition skills. Phonological errors may affect spelling.

Regarding text *macrostructure* and the communicative competence of writers with oral language concerns, the integrity of their oral language and verbal reasoning contribute to their compositional skills, which can be negatively affected if oral language and verbal reasoning are impaired. Oral and written language both require elaboration of content and form (cf. Fey et al., 2004; Westby, 2020), but written language requires that writers use the grammar and syntax of written language along with explicit textual *cohesion* strategies. Writing entails knowledge transformation, in that a writer's knowledge has to be reworked and expressed as written text that will be accessible to readers. In older learners with mild to moderate oral language concerns, expository writing may be more markedly affected than written narration, given the information processing demands that are simultaneously required to compose expository text (see Hochman, 2009).

Accordingly, then, deficits in oral language performance may predict that written language performance would be problematic as well, but an absence of oral language difficulty does not guarantee that written language will also be unaffected. *Written language would be regarded as a separate skill set and would be assessed with measures or observational tools that are sensitive to and specific to written language performance.* In the same way that spoken language competence is not regarded as

standing in for skills in phonics, decoding, spelling, reading fluency, or reading comprehension, spoken language performance would not be regarded as depicting written language capabilities.

Regarding Dockrell and Connelly's (2009) summary of semantic considerations, learners with language difficulties generally would have reduced lexical experience, and their texts may not exhibit the word diversity and the use of the quantity and variety of adjectives, adverbs, and adverbial phrases that typical peers would use. Morphological, grammatic, and syntactic deficits would potentially mirror a student's oral language profile and yield the construction of immature and simple sentences rather than complex sentences, along with grammatical errors and the omission of prepositions, articles, and verbs. Verb errors are noteworthy and are evidence of an inherent deficit in language form. Inflectional morphemes that mark tense and agreement may be absent or incorrect. Text *coherence*, expressivity, and meaning may be affected by the writer's morphological (Northey et al., 2016), grammatical, and syntactic limitations. As a general trend, students' written language performance for form, content, and use is worse than their auditory-oral receptive and expressive language and their reading decoding and comprehension abilities.

Producing written language is a demanding task for *working memory*, the temporary span of memory that is used for information processing and concentration that is a central component of executive functioning (Gordon-Pershey, 2018a). Composing a written message, either using paper and pencil or an electronic device, requires holding the message in working memory long enough to manually produce the message. Writers must craft the entirety of their messages sentence by sentence, so working memory for sentence processing is employed and is continually refreshed as sentences are added to the text composition. Added to these working memory demands, the motor skills needed for handwriting or keyboarding would require that attention and cognitive effort be allocated to regulating simultaneous linguistic and motor outputs. Writers must activate stored linguistic and motor memories concurrently. The strength of the storage of both forms of memory is at issue, as is the strength of retrieval of both forms of memory (cf. Nippold, 2007), causing multiple memory storage and retrieval operations to be concurrent. As such, written language performance is inherently a demonstration of working memory operations (cf. Drijbooms et al., 2017).

Learning to formulate written communication is an outgrowth of spoken language development and entails the *metacognitive* and *metalinguistic* examinations of written messages that readers perform, consciously and/or unconsciously (Smith, 1977). The grammar and syntax capabilities that have supported receptive and expressive oral language and reading comprehension that have been presented throughout the other chapters of this book are applicable to how learners develop the grammar and syntax of written language. Learners embark upon the act of writing endowed with a substantial repertoire of oral language grammatical and syntactic forms and need to develop the skills to transition from oral expression to written expression (e.g., see Calkins, 1994, on using spoken language as a scaffold for facilitating writing). To use written grammar is to use printed symbols to systematically represent the sounds, structures, and meaning systems of a language (Chin, n.d.). Written communication overlays the

demands for producing printed symbols onto the foundational language skills of listening, speaking, and reading. Learners who can examine the grammar and syntax of sentences that they have heard, spoken, or read are better prepared to become able to compose written sentences (cf. Gillis & Eberhardt, 2018).

Sharing ideas in writing is both similar to and different from sharing ideas in spoken language, in terms of the use of language form and function. Written language involves selecting appropriate words and grammatical forms, along with using the necessary sentence structural elements, such as clauses and verb tenses, and expressing the writer's intents within the context of the discourse in progress (Christie & Derewianka, 2008; Scott, 1995b; Smith, 1977). The intersection of form, content, and use depicted in Chapter 1, Figure 1–1, and in Chapter 3, Figure 3–1, is paramount for writers. Attaining literacy is dependent upon pragmatic language competence because the motivation to access print or to produce print requires pragmatic purpose or intent. People read and write in order to be part of an interchange. Reading comprehension relies upon a pragmatic understanding of an author's purpose; to read with understanding is to participate in an interaction with the writer of the text (cf. Graham & Hebert, 2010; Rosenblatt, 1978; Ward-Lonergan, 2010). Written language allows writers to put their thoughts on paper (or in digital form) and communicate their purposes and intents to others (or sometimes only to oneself).

Written language interventions are likely to be provided to address higher-order language impairments in learners who are quite capable in many other aspects of life. For some learners, written language may be a single area of deficit amid many learning and performance strengths. In some cases, written language abilities can be discrepant from other learning and performance abilities, which might signal the presence of relative weaknesses in cognition, language, and/or learning that are particular to written language skills. Some learners are semantically, syntactically, and pragmatically strong in spoken language, only to find themselves unable to express their ideas and intentions in writing, and their wording and sentence structure become convoluted and ineffective. The disconnect between their oral communication skills and their written communication skills can be baffling and frustrating. The question becomes why an otherwise "bright" student is unable to convey ideas in writing, and interventions would be directed at enhancing the use of written language form and structure as the conduit for the student's spoken meanings. These conditions may precipitate the diagnosis of a variety of conditions (see Bishop & Snowling, 2004; Dockrell & Connelly, 2009; Silliman & Berninger, 2011; Spanoudis, 2018; Sun & Wallach, 2014), such as specific learning disability, or reading disability, written language difficulties, *dyslexia* (i.e., difficulties learning to read that are not related to lesser cognitive skills), or *dysgraphia* (i.e., difficulties with written language that are either linguistically based, motor based, or based in both language and motor deficits).

Language competence for younger children involves their mastery of the expected developmental vocabulary, grammatical and syntactic forms, and pragmatic purposes that are necessary for communication and learning. In some ways, earlier language development is a process of conformity to language standards and expectations. Nippold (2007, p. 12) commented that language competence for stu-

dents ages 8 or 10 and older, in contrast, is more of a process of "linguistic individualism." Older children and teens become increasingly individualistic in their language development. They learn the words and the grammatical and syntactic forms that suit their own purposes and that advance their own interests in and out of school. Their development is more sophisticated. Their ability to engage in abstract thought increases, their sense of humor evolves, their *metalinguistic* skills make them more aware of the nuances of language, and they engage in a greater degree of social perspective-taking (Nippold, 2007). They code-switch across social groups (cf. Knestrict & Schoensteadt, 2005) and develop a variety of conversational skills and written language formats based on their participation in friendship circles, curricular and extracurricular activities, part-time jobs, and community experiences. Interventions to improve written language would help older school learners actualize their individualistic potentials.

School Writing Expectations

Various studies have explored school writing expectations, including Applebee et al. (2013), Applebee and Langer (2006, 2009, 2011a, 2011b), and Christie and Derewianka (2008). Expectations have varied somewhat over time, but commonalities remain; specifically, that educators' attention to the conventions of grammar and to multiword syntax remains constant (cf. Beers & Nagy, 2009; Graham & Perin, 2007a; Mosenthal, 1983). These studies emphasized that curriculum and instruction that are meaningful to students provide the foundation for learning functional and relevant written communication skills. It has become increasingly valued in educational settings that skills for the use of language form would be taught in the service of conveying students' original and personal thoughts and to facilitate the creative expression of students' ideas and knowledge (cf. Atwell, 1987; Calkins, 1994; Graham at al., 2019; Harris et al., 2008).

Educators expect school learners to express their understanding of academic concepts by producing multisentence oral responses (Hadley, 1998; Silliman & Scott, 2009) and by completing written work using different sentence types. These practices would constitute academic language instruction and would be evidenced as "writing across the curriculum" (Fulwiler & Young, 1982; WAC Clearinghouse, n.d.), signifying that written language expectations are interwoven into all academic subjects. Students would "write to learn" (Applebee, 1984; Emig, 1977; WAC Clearinghouse, n.d.), which means that the act of composing written text becomes an expression of students' individual thinking and reasoning about academic material. Teachers' writing assignments would provoke intellectual discovery and meaningful insights into the concepts under study. Students' vocabularies would be expected to include morphologically complex words that are subject specific (Apel & Werfel, 2014). Teachers would assess how well students arrange words in phrases and sentences that convey meaning, how proficiently students use oral and written grammar, and how competently students use morphologically complex vocabulary (Naremore et al., 1995). Students who have competent narrative language tend to meet teacher expectations and are more likely to have academic success (Christie & Derewianka, 2008; Greenhalgh & Strong,

2001; Peterson & Stoddard, 2018; Silliman & Scott, 2009; Snow, 1991). However, students with a history of language delays or later attainment of language developmental milestones may have a residual delay in the development of narrative competence that persists into their school years (Domsch et al., 2012) and could hinder the transition from oral to written language competence.

The *Common Core State Standards* (National Governors Association Center for Best Practices, Council of Chief State School Officers, 2010) for the Writing strand provide kindergarten to Grade 12 expectations for school writing. The Common Core standards address the content of students' writing (for example, developing a topic by using facts, definitions, and details; conveying ideas and information clearly) and the genres or formats of students' writing (as in, for instance, writing explanations). The Common Core sets the expectations that students would consult references and other sources to bring accuracy to their writings. Emphasis is on skills for making meaning, such as writing topic sentences and concluding sentences, and carefully choosing words, using quotations, and using figurative language. The Common Core includes expectations for creating ancillaries to written sentences and paragraphs, such as drawings, tables, and charts. Use of the conventions of grammar and of varied and increasingly sophisticated sentence syntax as the grade levels advance is explicitly stated in the Common Core standards. Many resources for educators and SLPs are available that explicitly link language and literacy learning tasks and reading and writing activities to the Common Core standards in English/language arts and in the academic content areas (e.g., Applebee et al., 2013; Duffy, 2014; Eberhardt, 2013;

Ehren et al., 2010; Gillis & Eberhardt, 2018; Jennings & Haynes, 2018; Power-deFur, n.d.; Power-deFur & Flynn, 2012; Rudebusch, 2012; Schleppegrell, 2013; Schraeder, 2012). *The intention would be that learning explicitly about the structural features of language would enhance students' use of language in all academic subjects. Better understanding and use of language would help students learn academic content and concepts effectively* (Silliman & Scott, 2009).

Another way to become familiar with school writing expectations is to explore the website for the National Assessment of Educational Progress (NAEP; Institute of Education Sciences, National Center for Education Statistics, n.d.). The NAEP, known as "the Nation's Report Card," is a large-scale national assessment of student achievement that, since 1969, has provided data on the performance of districts, cities, states, and other educational jurisdictions. The assessment sample size varies annually, but the 2021 NAEP report will be based on surveys of about 3,500 schools per month (NAEP, n.d.). Essay writing questions tend to require expository descriptions, persuasion or debate, or narrative creative writing. Examples of the NAEP writing questions for Grades 4, 8, and 12 include the following (NAEP, n.d.):

- Grade 4
  - Describe a favorite object.
  - Describe lunchtime.
  - Persuade a school librarian to acquire certain library items.
  - Write a story about a castle.
- Grade 8
  - Debate lengthening the school year.
  - Design an educational TV show.
  - Persuade the principal to require or not require students to perform community service.

- Grade 12
  - Discuss important inventions or technologies.
  - Debate the importance of voting.
  - Describe the heroes of today.

It is apparent that the essay content becomes increasingly abstract, that is, less self-referential and more related to societal concerns, as the grade levels advance. Information learned at school, and/or from independent reading or viewing of media, and/or in life circumstances would influence how students compose the content of their Grade 8 and 12 writings. The NAEP demands for performance are far more advanced than mere demonstrations of splinter skills for the use of grammar and syntax. However, the rudiments of grammar and syntax are necessary to build students' composition skills and are the components of skilled writing (cf. Gillis & Eberhardt, 2018).

The Components of Skilled Writing

Sedita (2019, 2020; see also International Dyslexia Association, 2020a) developed a visual model of the components of skilled writing and called this model *The Writing Rope* (shown in Figure 6–1), in recognition of Scarborough's (2001) *The Reading Rope* (see Figure 5–1). Sedita (2019) stated that the model provides educators and interventionists with a framework for how to "(1) identify the components of skilled writing, (2) explain how levels of language contribute to skilled writing, (3) identify a set of writing assessments, or (4) suggest a comprehensive curriculum for teaching writing" (p. 1). The metaphorical strands

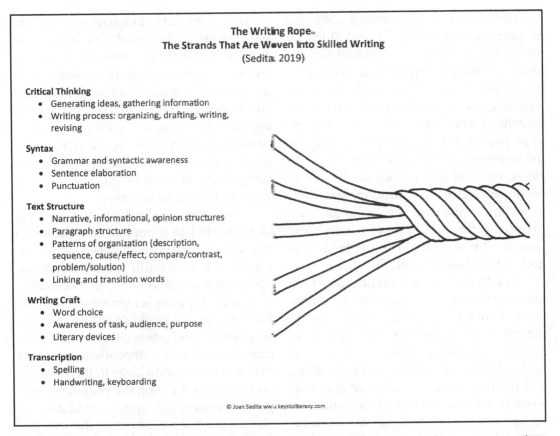

The Writing Rope™
The Strands That Are Woven Into Skilled Writing
(Sedita 2019)

Critical Thinking
- Generating ideas, gathering information
- Writing process: organizing, drafting, writing, revising

Syntax
- Grammar and syntactic awareness
- Sentence elaboration
- Punctuation

Text Structure
- Narrative, informational, opinion structures
- Paragraph structure
- Patterns of organization (description, sequence, cause/effect, compare/contrast, problem/solution)
- Linking and transition words

Writing Craft
- Word choice
- Awareness of task, audience, purpose
- Literary devices

Transcription
- Spelling
- Handwriting, keyboarding

© Joan Sedita www.keystoliteracy.com

Figure 6–1. The Writing Rope. From Sedita, J. (2019). *The strands that are woven into skilled writing* and Sedita, J. (2020). *We need a "Writing Rope!"* © 2019 Joan Sedita www.keystoliteracy.com

of *The Writing Rope* are tightly interwoven, to illustrate that the various subskills of writing intertwine to yield written language competence. Instruction and interventions may focus on specific skills, but the overall goal would be the competent functional use of the interrelated skills.

Sedita's (2019) model identifies the multiple components that are necessary for skilled writing. The Critical Thinking Strand involves the cognitive capabilities needed for crafting text. Executive functions (i.e., abilities in cognitive flexibility that allow for self-organization and planning, as well as self-reflection about learning; working memory; inhibitory control

etc.; see Gordon-Pershey, 2018a) and background knowledge about a topic would allow writers to plan, prepare, and work through the creation of texts. Sedita (2019) included in this strand the writer's conscious awareness of the steps of the writing process (i.e., prewriting, drafting, revising, editing, and proofreading [Murray, 2004]). Among the writer's prewriting plans are establishing the functional pragmatic purposes of their writing (e.g., be that informing, persuading, entertaining, etc.) and envisioning the intended audiences of who would read their writings. Students engage in prewriting brainstorming, gathering information from written and media sources, and creating notes and graphic organizers. The Critical Thinking Strand emphasizes how student writers would be *metacognitive* and purposeful and would benefit from explicit how-to instruction about all of the necessary skills. Sentence-level skills would allow writers to prepare clear notes and plans, compose the sentences within their drafts and revisions, and edit and proofread their texts accurately. Critical thinking and self-reflection allow learners to keep their pragmatic purposes in mind as they write sentence by sentence (Fang & Schleppegrell, 2010; Wallach et al., 2010).

The Syntax Strand emphasizes how individual sentences communicate meaning and are taken together to form the entire message of the text. This strand requires application of the grammar and syntax learned during listening, speaking, and reading. Innate *generative grammar* would contribute to written sentence formation, but then *metacognitive* and *metalinguistic* instruction in sentence structure (i.e., using words, phrases, and clauses grammatically and meaningfully) would help learners consciously communicate information and ideas in writing. Students would benefit from sentence formation skills, such as sentence elaboration and sentence combining (Scott & Nelson, 2009; Weaver, 1998). Reciprocal instruction that examines the syntax of the texts that students read, coupled with generating the syntax needed for the texts that students write, would be a practical approach to enhancing sentence-level skills (Caccamise, 2011; Gillis & Eberhardt, 2018; Graham & Hebert, 2010; Eberhardt, 2013; Nelson, 2013).

Sentence formation skills contribute to writing well-structured texts. The Text Structure Strand teaches students about transition words used within sentences to connect ideas and to link sentences to form paragraphs. This strand recognizes that explicit instruction is needed to develop students' paragraph writing skills, such as the use of main idea sentences and concluding sentences, and to help writers fashion text structure patterns, such as cause and effect. This strand would emphasize multisentence paragraphs as the compilation of accurately and effectively written individual sentences.

The Writing Craft Strand explores skills related to grammar and syntax in the sense that writers choose words purposefully. School writing may include the application of subject-specific vocabulary within the types of sentences that convey identifiable academic concepts. Semantics, syntax, and pragmatics intersect, because word choice is dependent upon how to best communicate ideas to the intended audiences, along with the pragmatic purposes for writing a specific text and the choices needed for achieving the tone and style of writing. Students would learn to write sentences that use dialogue, captions, and other text elements, and to create the language of literary techniques, such as imagery, personification, figurative language, alliteration, and so on. The development of linguistic features is a component of writing communicatively, and overt instruction and demonstration are beneficial experiences for learners (e.g., see Apel & Hall-Mills, 2015).

The Transcription Strand promotes the explicit instruction in phonics, spelling, handwriting, and keyboarding that contributes to writing skills. Language and motor skills are integrated so that students develop automatic and fluent coordination of expressive language together with manual skills. *Dysgraphia* is a specific learning disability that affects the motor abilities needed to learn to write and keyboard. Dysgraphia is the diagnosis that may be used to describe some of the difficulties that some learners have with the cognitive-linguistic components of learning to use written language to express thoughts, ideas, and concepts (International Dyslexia Association, 2020b). Visual-motor and/or fine motor difficulties may impair the learner's ability to visually process, memorize, and reproduce orthography, that is, the letters and other communicative symbols, by hand. Impairments of handwriting and keyboarding can interfere with learning to spell and to write words that learners can understand, speak, and, possibly, read. For some learners, dysgraphia is their only impairment, but for others, dysgraphia coexists with language and/or reading impairments, and/or deficits of attention and/or memory.

According to the International Dyslexia Association (2020b), *orthographic coding* in *working memory* is potentially an area of impairment in dysgraphia. Orthographic coding involves storing print in working memory in order to analyze the letters during reading and/or writing. The letters and words would be learned and stored in long-term memory and linked to the words' meanings and pronunciation for later retrieval. In dysgraphia, the storage and/or retrieval of letters and words, as well as how to physically produce them by writing or keyboarding, is impaired. Berninger and Wolf (2009a, 2009b) suggested that specific interventions for dysgraphia would include phonological awareness and phonics instruction, vocabulary and word study, morphological awareness, orthographic awareness, handwriting skills, and repeated practice to achieve automatic and fluent reading and handwriting. Word-level automaticity would allow learners to proceed to

building automaticity in writing constructions with multiword syntax. During scaffolded instruction and interventions, students might engage in shared writing with SLPs, where they co-create words and sentences, using sharing strategies such as demonstrations and modeling, fill-in-the-blank sentences, paragraph writing templates, and so on, so that students write within a supportive framework (see Van Cleave, 2020). A critical feature of SLPs' interventions is to provide models for students of how to incorporate more advanced vocabulary and complex sentence structure into their writing. Learning school vocabulary and developing more elaborated and sophisticated written syntax are interrelated skills (National Reading Panel, 2000).

As Scarborough (2001) observed is the case in skilled reading, Sedita (2019) observed that, as students develop writing competency, they become increasingly conscious, *metacognitive*, purposeful, and strategic in their application of the components of *The Writing Rope*. Learners also become more unconsciously automatic, fluent, and natural in their use of these capabilities. Writing, as with reading, becomes a cognitive-linguistic process that is an automatic skill in some informal circumstances, for example, when writing notes or a list for oneself, but is a skill that requires conscious self-monitoring much of the time when writers generate any kind of text that is going to be shared with others. The components of writing have to be used in a manner that is conventional enough to impart meaning. Certain "informal" codes, such as the slang words and abbreviated spellings used in text messaging, are actually learned by users consciously, as aspects of the conventions of the linguistic communities that write their texts by using this code. It's paradoxical that the learned spellings and abbreviations of text messaging are passed off in popular culture as being individualistic and spontaneously generated, when it actually may require a specific examination of a word to transform it from conventional spelling to "textese," as in changing "before" to "b4" or "later" to "L8r."

Diagnosing Written Language Difficulties

SLPs' assessments of older students' written language difficulties may entail the use of standardized measures of writing skills, as well as nonstandardized measures that probe for the use of certain writing competencies that meet prescribed criteria, and written language sampling in individual or group contexts, as when conducting classroom-based sampling (Nippold & Sun, 2010), which might afford a view of the performance trends among peers. SLPs can obtain an accumulation of writing samples produced in and out of school, to show students' different forms of written language usage. A writer's use of syntax may vary across text genres, so the accumulation of various genres of writing would yield a more representative assessment of the quality and complexity of written grammar and syntax (Beers & Nagy, 2009).

Written Language Difficulties: Structural and Functional Deficits

As described throughout this text, when an SLP assesses whether a school-age or adolescent student manifests language deficits that are related to weaknesses in

language form, the purpose is to uncover how an examinee may not sufficiently use the structural forms of written language as a code that is shared across speakers and that achieves the purpose of being a means of communication (cf. Christie & Derewianka, 2008). *The language assessment would determine how well an examinee uses the properties of language, which entails using language as a code, as a system, as a means of representing ideas, as a convention of shared meanings, and/or as a means of communication.* Using language as a *system* is revealed by an examinee's understanding of the linguistic structural "parts" that interface to create intelligible written communication and that manifest functionally as a convention of shared meanings. The assessment would also reveal if the examinee used written language intellectually as a means of *representing ideas*. As such, an assessment must ascertain the extent to which the writer's knowledge and application of the codes and systems of written language are not operating properly for functional use. This functional consequence is readily observed during written language sampling and testing, and/or by exchanging written communications with the examinee, and/or by employing an *ecologically valid* approach to assessment that includes ascertaining the examinee's strength of use of written language in various communicative and learning contexts, environments, and settings where written language is needed. The extent to which the structural written language disorder disrupts the examinee's functional written language performance, communicative competence, and/or communicative independence (Hymes, 1971) would be noted as the functional consequences of the written language impairment.

A second assessment consideration is how the presence of structural written language deficits corresponds to the manifestation of a functional deficit in written communication. Minimal, mild, or moderate structural written language difficulties may correspond to a functional deficit in written communication of the same respective degree. But this equivalent level of deficit is not always the case. When there is a certain magnitude of impairment in one or more of the properties of language, what is the corresponding disruption in functional language performance, communicative competence, and/or communicative independence? Primarily, two possibilities ensue.

On the one hand, a learner might have a documented impairment in using language as a code, as a system, as a means of representing ideas, as a convention of shared meanings, and/or as a means of communication, but *may experience less difficulty with the functional use of language than the magnitude of difficulties with structural written language might predict.* Indeed, the separateness of the properties of language would factor into this scenario. *A level of structural language impairment that is worse than the level of functional deficit* would probably suggest that using language as a code, a system, a means of representing ideas, and/or a convention of shared meanings is focal to the impairment, but that using language as a means of communication is less affected. It is possible to imagine several circumstances where a language impairment corresponds to a lesser degree of functional language disorder, as the following two cases exemplify: (1) a learner with a primarily structural deficit, who uses some instances of incorrect, unsophisticated sentence grammar (i.e., in syntax and morphology; the difficulty lies within the code and system properties) but whose written communication is communicatively competent and independent, meaning, the ideas written about are clear enough that the form deficits can be overlooked, and (2) a learner who struggles with language as a means of representing ideas, that being characterized as a learner who struggles to convey the more sophisticated representations of ideas that are part of learning through language in school, and struggles to employ the accompanying language structures in written texts, but who has good communication skills in informal written language contexts; this functional written language deficit matters in contexts where language is used to discuss abstractions but is less apparent in situations where concrete, daily events are discussed. Language structure supports competence and independence in informal written language tasks but not in the more formal language tasks.

On the other hand, *the magnitude of the structural written language difficulties might be less than the corresponding level of functional difficulties. Functional written language can be poorer than would be predicted by the magnitude of the difficulties manifested in written language use.* In some cases, an SLP cannot readily uncover how an examinee's language is not intact as a code, as a system, as a means of representing ideas, as a convention of shared meanings, and/or as a means of communication, but the student is experiencing difficulty with the functional use of written language. A disruption in language performance, communicative competence, and/or communicative independence is evident. It is possible, for instance, for an examinee to perform well enough on a formal test of written language (e.g., spelling, affixation, and sentence formation) but to have poor meaning making in open-ended written language expression tasks, such as would be scored in the context of sentence meaning, paragraph writing, story generation, or other written expression testing tasks. An examinee might perform these expressive tasks well enough as spoken language test items, so it is documented that the examinee knows how to use language as a means of communication, but there is a disconnect when the learner needs to generate functional written language. Because of reduced written language communicative competence, this student has a functional language deficit, but it is as yet uncertain whether or not there is an accompanying structural deficit. Careful analysis of written language phonology, morphology, semantics, grammar, and syntax must be documented, and the interplay between lack of functional communication and structural deficits would be observed.

Quoting the anthropologist and linguist Edward Sapir (1921), Bloom and Lahey (1978) emphasized that a word is "a convenient capsule of thought that embraces thousands of distinct experiences and that is ready to take in thousands more" (p. 6). Sapir maintained that this is not a unidirectional experience, where thought provokes language. He is most famous for the Sapir-Whorf hypothesis (see Harley, 2008), which suggested that the form and characteristics of language influence thought. Being able to speak, write, and/or use other symbol systems influences how individuals think. While the Sapir-Whorf hypothesis has received extensive testing, criticism, and debate, Harley (2008) suggested that there is evidence that linguistic factors can shape cognitive processes. For instance, if certain concepts can be expressed readily in one language but not as easily in another, this would influence how users of certain languages think about those concepts. Similarly, numerical systems associated with some languages influence how numbers, quantities, and calculations are conceptualized and remembered by users of those languages. Therefore, language not only represents ideas about the world; language shapes ideas about the world. Written language, with its possibility for permanence, is a force that continually shapes the world (Smith, 1977). Learners of all levels of abilities deserve the opportunity to generate written messages that can shape the world, if only "their own world," those spaces and environments in which they participate.

Syntactic Knowledge and Syntactic Processing

Part of the diagnostic process might be to try to determine *whether a learner has a deficit primarily in syntactic knowledge or in syntactic processing*. A *deficit in syntactic knowledge* would involve a lack of knowledge of linguistic forms, presumably related to a lack of acquisition of the forms being probed. This is potentially coupled with a lack of sentence analysis skills. As an example, a learner might not know that two sentences have synonymous meanings if the learner is unfamiliar with the syntax used in one or both sentences, as in identifying the equivalence of *When the meal was finished, he left the table* and *He finished the meal and left the table*. The learner could not, then, complete the written language task of writing a third sentence that is similar (e.g., *He left the table when he finished the meal*). Or a learner might not use a target verb in a sentence formation task if this verb is not familiar vocabulary. A learner who is asked to write a sentence using the word *receive* cannot do so if this is an unfamiliar word.

Syntactic processing deficits may have more to do with general cognitive mechanisms, including auditory attention, working memory, or executive control of syntactic reasoning (Drijbooms et al., 2017). Providing the learner with the sentences, *When the meal was finished, he left the table* and *He finished the meal and left the table*, and then asking the learner to write down the two action words in each sentence, or, if the examiner uses grammatical terminology and says, "the two verbs," the response of *finished* and *left* would mean that the learner can process these components and store them in working memory. The task requires the learner to integrate these sentence components and provide a written response that extracts grammatical meaning from the sentence.

Formal Assessment

Farrall (2013, pp. 33–34) reported that formal assessments of written language typically include the following types of subtests:

- Sentence dictation: Examinees transcribe a sentence read aloud by the examiner. Students with grammar and syntax difficulties may have difficulty transcribing sentences with accuracy due to a lack of mental representations of the grammatical and syntactic forms needed.
- Sentence copying: Response may be analyzed for syntactic and mechanical accuracy, including completeness, grammar, spacing between words, handwriting, capitalization, punctuation, and spelling.
- Sentence formulation: Examinees write a sentence based on a scenario or picture and/or write a sentence using a target word or words.

When students are required to read the target first, the task becomes one of both reading (accuracy and vocabulary) and written syntax.

- Fill-in-the-blank sentence completion: Examinees fill in a missing word or add a beginning or ending to a sentence. This task may tap into difficulties with word retrieval and/or with word structure and grammar. Missing verbs measure the skill to employ noun-verb agreement.
- Sentence combining: Examinees combine shorter sentences into one well-formed longer sentence. The task provides information about the examinees' ability to write sentences that make logical connections between ideas, such as causal relationships, and that are dense in their content.
- Sentence elaboration: Examinees expand simple sentences into sentences that are more descriptive and informative.
- Logical sentences: Examinees edit sentences for errors such as incorrect subordination and pronoun referents, or omissions of needed content, or mixed metaphors. This subtest measures reading comprehension as well as alertness to written errors that affect meaning.
- Writing fluency: Examinees write sentences that include target words, often under timed conditions.
- Contextualized sentence writing: Examinees produce writing samples that examiners score based on the presence of different sentence types, vocabulary usage, semantics, and mechanics.

An important consideration is that any formal assessment measures need to be specific enough to show the usage of sophisticated syntactic structures and should examine the complex use of multiple structures together within and/or across sentences (Beers & Nagy, 2009; Nelson & Van Meter, 2007). The instrument would account for and contrast examinees' skills in writing single sentences versus multi-sentence texts (Berninger et al., 2011), as the demands for multisentence meaning-making may have an impact on sentence writing capabilities.

Some of the standardized language tests used by SLPs, educators, and psychologists include subtests that have normative scores for written language. The following tests (in alphabetical order by title; cf. Farrall, 2012, 2013) have subtests or questions that ask school-age and adolescent learners to demonstrate skills in written grammar and syntax:

- Detroit Test of Learning Aptitude–Primary: Third Edition (DTLA-P:3; Hammill & Bryant, 2005)
- Kaufman Test of Educational Achievement, Third Edition (KTEA-3; Kaufman & Kaufman, 2014)
- Oral and Written Language Scales–Second Edition (OWLS-II; Carrow-Woolfolk, 2012)
- Test of Integrated Language and Literacy Skills (TILLS; Nelson et al., 2016)
- Test of Written Language–Fourth Edition (TOWL-4; Hammill & Larsen, 2009)
- Test of Adolescent and Adult Language–Fourth Edition (TOAL-4; Hammill et al., 2007)
- Wechsler Individual Achievement Test–Third Edition (WIAT-III; Wechsler, 2009)

- Woodcock-Johnson III Tests of Achievement (WJ III ACH; Woodcock et al., 2001)

Some of these tests may allow for examinees' discrepancies in grammar and syntax skills to be observed across listening, speaking, reading, and writing performances. Measures must not be biased against written language that is influenced by oral language dialect features.

Some standardized tests rely on a sentence combining subtest as an indicator of written language competence, based on the premise that competence is revealed by the use of clausal structures, phrasal coordination, and other elements that constitute overall sentence complexity. Scoring is based on whether the examinee converges upon a limited array of appropriate syntactic choices, so their spontaneous, naturalistic syntactic abilities are not being measured (Scott & Nelson, 2009). Investing this subtest with the power to determine writing competence requires careful consideration and warrants critique. Sentence combining skill is essentially predicated upon sentence analysis skills. Some students may never have had the opportunity to analyze and combine sentences prior to the testing encounter, so the task may not be meaningful. Students may not have been taught to create the information-packed sentences that result when shorter sentences are combined. The resulting sentences may not resemble the structures used in the examinee's natural oral or written language. If sentence combining is used in the absence of a naturalistic writing sample, the opportunity to observe how the examinee actually writes sentences may be lost. Moreover, the decontextualized sentence stimuli prevent examinees from applying any genre-specific writing knowledge that they may typically use to aid self-expression. Despite these criticisms, Farrall (2013) suggested that sentence combining yields an impression of an examinee's "ability to balance the demands of content and syntax . . . sentence combining represents, at a most crucial level, the intersection between language and thought" (p. 34).

Informal Assessment

As with formal assessments, informal assessment measures would be designed to include tasks that would reveal the use of sophisticated syntactic structures. The written products obtained would demonstrate the examinee's use of multiple grammatical and syntactic structures within and/or across sentences (Beers & Nagy, 2009; Espin et al., 2000; Hall-Mills & Apel, 2015; Nelson & Van Meter, 2007). The informal tasks would demand written examples of multiword syntax and multisentence meaning-making.

Written language assessment would consider (cf. Hall-Mills, 2018):

- The demands of the written mode of communication to produce words and sentence constructions.
- The discourse types assessed (i.e., narrative or expository).
- The degree of independence or the need for assistance that the examinee revealed.
- Evidence of any use of the examinee's use of the writing process approach (Murray, 2004; prewriting, drafting, revising, editing, and proofreading).
- Clinician-constructed criterion-referenced measures that would compare an examinee's performance against predetermined

criteria based on expectations for age or grade (cf. Christie & Derewianka, 2008; Loban, 1976).

- The overall quality of the examinee's performance.
- The ultimate contents of the inventory of skills.

If SLPs are using informal testing as pre-post intervention measurements, the measurement tasks must be specific enough to show changes in syntactic complexity (Catts, 2009; Mason, 2013).

Farrall (2013) provided a comprehensive review of assessment measures, including using descriptive measures (e.g., computing T-units within a writing sample, finding a ratio of correct to incorrect use of words in a sample, or comparing the skills demonstrated or not demonstrated in the sample to what is known about the curriculum that the student has been exposed to in the present and past grades at school). Drawing on Farrall (2012), Farrall (2013, p. 32) proposed the following informal assessment procedures and descriptive checklist:

"1. Describe the handwriting.

2. Type the writing sample word for word (and error for error) into your word processor. Be sure to disable the autocorrect feature. This file will serve as your working draft; it will not be part of your report.

3. Describe the use of mechanics. Mechanics (capitalization and punctuation) are more than just sentence markers. They provide additional information about how to interpret words in phrases, clauses, and sentences.

4. Create a chart with a column for sentences, sentence types, and additional comments or notes. It helps to focus on each sentence individually.

5. Label each sentence type (simple, compound, complex, compound-complex, run-on, or fragment).
6. Ask the following questions: a. Are there different sentence types? b. Are there adjectives, adverbs, or descriptive phrases? c. Is there noun/verb agreement? Are there grammatical errors? d. Is the language repetitive? e. Are the verb tenses correct? f. Describe the vocabulary. g. Do the sentences make sense? h. Do transition words facilitate the sequence and the flow of content?
7. Make additional notes regarding vocabulary and spelling."

Sampling and/or Inventorying Written Language Performance

As described in Chapter 4, language sampling takes place with the aim that the sampling encounter provides an accurate snapshot of the learner's oral and/or written language abilities. As Loban (1976) noted, the learner's use of grammatical and syntactic forms potentially would be spontaneous and productive, and SLPs would have a representative sample of the writer's skills. However, older learners have such vast language repertoires that one sampling encounter may not reveal the true extent of a learner's abilities. This is especially pertinent for written language sampling. One sample might not show the extent of a learner's capabilities or difficulties. The constraints to self-expression brought about by the topic that the SLP assigns or that the student chooses for the written sample, along with the target length of the sample, the motor response required (handwriting or keyboarding), and time pressures during the sampling session, can influence students' performances. For many reasons, a skewed sample might be obtained. Some students might limit themselves to writing the words and sentences they have practiced before and are inclined to think are correct. Other students might not be able to concentrate and focus on demand and are thus unable to show their true abilities. Given all of the happenstances that can interfere with a single sample providing an accurate representation of written language competence, it might be necessary to collect multiple samples and assemble an inventory of written language products that would potentially represent a learner's capabilities across various contexts.

Given the extent to which producing written language taxes working memory, *dynamic assessment* during written language sampling might employ working memory cues to help students marshal their memory resources and thus produce writing samples that would more accurately reflect their written language abilities, without the confounding influence of working memory restrictions. *Memory retrieval can be enhanced a few different ways: by cueing; by aiming for memories that an examinee would access frequently; by aiming for memories that have been acquired, renewed, or refreshed recently; and by aiming for memories that are not in competition with other items in memory* (for more information on memory storage, capacity, and retrieval factors, see Nippold, 2007). For example, if, during a written language sampling session, an examinee selects a topic or is given a topic to write about that is based on familiar, recurring, recently revived information that comes easily to working memory, the written language sample would be less likely to have been confounded by working memory weaknesses and potentially would be a more representative display of actual written language abilities. If, on the other hand, an examinee in some way discloses that the written language sample topic is unfamiliar, is seldom thought about, has not been recently recalled, and is being conflated with other competing concepts, aspects of the lack of fluency in writing about this topic could be related to not being able to bring pertinent information into working memory, rather than being a true exposure of deficits in written language production. Dynamic assessment cues, such as, for prewriting brainstorming, "Tell me what you know about this topic," can help reveal if working memory has brought the topic into conscious scrutiny well enough for the examinee to write about it. Cues like, "Can you tell me any more about it?" would reveal when examinees have exhausted their stored memories related to this topic and would be redirected to a different topic.

Syntax is one of the important *microstructural* elements of writing, and SLPs can analyze written syntax as a discrete skill. However, it is difficult to separate form from meaning. Catts (2009) suggested that examiners should assess written language for its content, meaning, vocabulary, and syntax. To attempt to obtain spontaneous writing samples but to also impose some structure and control, SLPs may want to design structured sampling and inventorying stimuli and multistep protocols that will meet their assessment needs. Considerations would include:

- Does the sampling need to reveal the ability to communicate in writing about certain topics or in certain genres? Is it more meaningful and relevant to school success, for example, to ask a learner to write out an expository description, an explanation, or a set of directions, or to provide a short personal narrative about something that the student likes to do, rather than to request a fictional story narrative? In establishing these pragmatic purposes for writing, sampling might capture school writing skills.

- What linguistic forms should the sample reveal? Chapter 4 presented the Loban (1976) data on the linguistic forms that school-age and adolescent learners would, in many cases, have mastered in spoken and written language, among other information on grammar and syntax development. SLPs can choose a few targets to look for, such as the use of sentences with a main clause and at least one dependent clause.

- Does the learner need the SLP to provide any introduction or explanations in order to establish a working vocabulary for language sampling and inventorying? Does the learner know the terms that are going to be used in the assessment context, such as *sentence, action word, verb*? Can this be known based on past academic performance or inferred from grade-level placement? Would sampling and inventorying be fairer if certain terminology were reviewed at the start of the process?

- What instructions do SLPs give to students for producing writing samples? A general directive, such as, "Please write a description of something that you like to do," is different from, "Please write a description of something that you like to do. Tell me as much as you can. I really want to know all about what you like to do. Explain your ideas using the right words. Remember that this is school writing, so write your sentences as correctly as you can." Or "Please write a description of something that you like to do. Tell me as much as you can. I really want to know all about what you like to do. Use good describing words and action words. Remember that this is school writing, so check your work for correct spelling and punctuation." These kinds of elaborated directions might be necessary to limit the "false positives" of students who appear to have writing deficits when, in actuality, their writing style was just too casual and they did not self-monitor for corrections that they would be able to make if they were directed to be attentive to this consideration.

■ How many samples, from how many writing contexts, would be obtained? Written language samples would be able to show how well a student writes in different contexts, so samples can be obtained from multiple sources and encounters, from either within the context of an SLP's assessment battery or as selected samples presented by students' teachers. In this way, students' production of various genres and levels of formality might be observed for how grammar and syntax are used.

Samples can be analyzed by using any of the strategies for oral language samples, as described in Chapter 4. As with spoken language, there are a number of manual and computerized methods for analyzing the complexity of written language samples produced by school-age

children and adolescents. The information given in Chapter 4 about scoring speakers' productions of clausal constructions can be adapted for scoring written language samples. The subordination index (SI) has been used by prior researchers in studies of written syntax (Nippold, 2010; Nippold et al., 2005; Scott, 1995a). The guidelines for determining the use of independent and subordinate clauses given in Chapter 4 apply to analyses of written syntax (see also *Features of Academic Writing*, n.d.). The primary difference is that instead of using C-units (communication units, i.e., measures of independent clauses plus their modifiers) to analyze spoken language, the written language measurements would be based on T-units (i.e., minimal terminal units, which are measures of each independent clause and all of its subordinate and embedded clauses). The SI is determined by counting the total number of independent and dependent clauses divided by the number of T-units (Nippold, 2010). Computerized analyses of written language samples may be useful tools for SLPs. As described in Chapter 4, the language sample analysis software program, the *Systematic Analysis of Language Transcripts* (SALT; Leadholm & Miller, 1994; Miller & Chapman, 2003; SALT, 2020b) can be used to analyze written language samples, as can the *Coh-Metrix* (Graesser & McNamara, 2011; Graesser et al., 2004), *Analyze My Writing* (n.d.), the *Text Analyzer* (Online-utility.org, n.d.), *The Multidimensional Analysis Tagger* (MAT; Nini, 2019), and the *Tool for the Automatic Analysis of Lexical Sophistication* (TAALES; Kyle & Crossley, 2015; Kyle et al., 2018).

Another option (Mason, 2013) would be to consult the array of spoken syntactic structures proposed by Loban (1963, 1970, 1976), detailed in Chapter 4, and score for the occurrence of these structures in written language samples. Loban's Elaboration Index (Loban, 1976) can be used to compute written sentence complexity and provide a metric to compare an individual's performance across time or to compare performance across individuals. The Elaboration Index accounts for the coordinated use of multiple syntactic elements and gives greater weight to the sophisticated use of multiple syntactic markers.

A written language sample allows SLPs to assess the aspects of written language described on *The Writing Rope* (see Figure 6–1). Taking together the significant characteristics of oral language described in Chapter 4 and combining them with the skills noted on *The Writing Rope* would allow for a checklist of items for assessment that might include:

- Semantics (i.e., the amount and quality of the writer's stored lexical knowledge [Nippold, 2007] that is revealed by this sample)
- Grammatical morphology
- Elements of narration and exposition included in the sample
- Written mechanics, such as spelling, punctuation, and capitalization

Written language sampling can reveal the artifacts of language difficulties that can be observed during spoken language sampling. As an example, (Nippold, 2007) suggested that anomia or word-finding concerns may be evidenced, meaning, the writer's ability to retrieve vocabulary in context. Word-finding might be suspected if the writer leaves sentences or phrases unfinished, appears to circumlocute (e.g., offers longer descriptions instead of using a target word), uses lexical substitutions (e.g., *seat* for *sofa*), uses indefinite pronouns (e.g., *something*), uses empty expressions or filler words (e.g., *all that*

stuff), or demonstrates observable behaviors, such as pausing to find words while writing.

Informally Assessing Grammar and Syntax Using Probes

As discussed in Chapter 4, probes are tasks that the examiner designs in order to uncover certain abilities or performances. Probes might extend the items that are on standardized tests or might represent the written language expectations at various grade levels and thus may yield a general sense of a student's grade-level achievements. Probes might be drawn from a review of a written language sample that a student writes and would function as a form of *dynamic assessment*. For example, an examiner might review a student's paper, then ask the student to write a little bit more about the topic but to use longer sentences, or to add some descriptive words, or to look for some sentences that could be written better. SLPs might point out specific sentences and ask the student to "say this part better" (cf. Eisenberg, 2006). Probes allow for a reexamination of the student's apparent ability as initially depicted, to confirm or refute the initial score or impression.

Considerations when developing probes might include:

- Were the stimuli that were originally used in testing or sampling provided as explicit sentences, or is the examinee expected to perform any inferential thinking to process the sentences and respond? Could probes reduce the need for inferencing and make the stimuli simpler to process but yield a similar written language performance?

- If the original stimuli were open ended (e.g., "Write a story"), probes might be more close-ended or convergent (e.g., "Write about what you have done so far today"; "Write about your favorite school subject"). The pragmatic and narrative demands are reduced, allowing the examinee to generate sentences related to a narrower topic.
- If the original stimuli were convergent, they might not have tapped the examinee's knowledge base. For example, if a picture stimulus is used and the examinee is asked to write a paragraph or story about the picture, there is a risk that the people, settings, and/ or actions shown in the picture are unfamiliar or otherwise not congruent with the examinee's experiential base. Examiners would probe using alternative pictures, photographs, videos, or other visuals that have a high probability of being pertinent to the examinee.
- Students who are constrained by a convergent topic prescribed by a test (e.g., who state, "I would have written more but I didn't really get the test question") can be given open-ended probes ("Okay, then write about something you know about").
- Probes may target writing sentences around a key word or require paragraphs based on a word bank. This focuses the examinee's task semantically and topically.
- Probes can assess how a writer imparts meaning and manipulates sentence elements. For example, the examiner can provide a sentence and ask the examinee to write a synonymous sentence or a variation of the same sentence.
- Probes can ask an examinee to finish a paragraph that the examiner has started writing. In this task, the examiner would start out a paragraph by writing two or three sentences, and the examinee would finish writing the paragraph (e.g., the paragraph would start with, "When new students are starting at our school, there are a few things that they should know. This is what I would tell our new students.").

A Written Language Assessment Tool

Table 6–1 provides a comprehensive, multipurpose written language assessment tool (adapted from Gordon Pershey, 2010). The areas of writing that this inventory accounts for are mechanics, syntax, pragmatics (including narration and exposition), and semantics. Definitions and examples of the grammatical and syntactic elements included in this tool can be found in Chapter 4, and descriptions of the semantic and the pragmatic, narrative, and exposition elements are found throughout this book. Users can adapt this assessment form to meet their needs, by adding or removing items from this checklist.

This assessment inventory allows for analysis of written language samples of any type or length and is useful for writers of any age or level of development. Examiners would simply not consider any of the items that are developmentally too complex for an examinee but rather would inventory only the behaviors that the writer demonstrates. Scoring is entirely observational, with the examiner's qualitative remarks and/or quantitative tal-

Table 6–1. Written Language Assessment Tool

Mechanics

Penmanship of sample:

_____ Cursive _____ Printed _____ Mixed

_____ Neat _____ Adequate _____ Hard to read

Keyboarding:

_____ Few errors _____ Notable errors _____ Many errors, hard to read

---

List all spelling errors:

Word produced   Presumed target word

Reasons for spelling errors:

_____ Phonological _____ Orthographic _____ Mistakes, typos

_____ Grammatical morphology/derivational morphology

Punctuation:

List all punctuation used:

List all:

Errors of omission _____

Errors of substitution _____

Errors of addition _____

_____ Punctuation reflects rhetorical features, sentence boundaries

_____ Capitalization

_____ Paper is titled (if applicable)

_____ Evidence of editing (cross out, erasures, insertions, etc.)

Syntax

Grammar:

Inflectional endings (morphology):

_____ Past tense marking

_____ Third person singular present tense verbing (note dialect influences, especially on third person verbing)

_____ Third person plural present tense verbing (note dialect influences, especially on third person verbing)

_____ Casualness or slang

continues

Table 6–1. *continued*

_____ Plurals

_____ Subject-verb agreement

_____ Possessive forms

_____ Verb consistency (parallel form)

List all:

Errors of omission _____

Errors of substitution _____

Errors of addition _____

Other grammatical errors:

_____

Sentence structure:

_____ Number of words in shortest complete sentence (not counting title, by line, "the end," etc.)

_____ Number of words in longest complete sentence (not counting title, by line, "the end," etc.)

_____ Mean length of complete sentence (not counting title, by line, "the end," etc.)

_____ Variety of sentence types (statement, exclamation, questions of many types, negation, passive voice, etc.)

Person paper is written in (note all):

_____ First _____ Second _____ Third

Sentence types:

_____ Simple (noun + verb + object)   _____ Complex (clauses)

_____ Incomplete   _____ Present tense verbs

_____ Sentence appears complete but a word/words is/are omitted

_____ Coordinate structures

_____ Subordinate structures

_____ Coordinate in place of subordinate

_____ Conjoined clauses without markers (neither lexical, clausal, or punctuation)

_____ Combined sentences (could be parsed to component sentences)

Table 6–1. *continued*

_____	# of T-units (each independent clause + its subordinate and embedded clause)
_____	# of T-units without clauses
_____	# of T-units with clauses
_____	Range of # of words per T-unit

_____	# of high-content words (same word may be counted repeatedly)

Prepositional phrases:

Note how many are used in mid-sentence

_____

Note how many are used to end a sentence

_____

That/who/whose complement

_____

Adverbials (when, if, while, as, like, since, before, after, once, every, etc.)

_____

Postmodification of nouns

_____

Appositives

_____

Complex verb phrase expansions

_____

Pragmatics, Narration, and Exposition

Narrative devices:

_____ Formulaic expressions (one day, once upon a time, the end, happily ever after, etc.)

_____ Genre markers or frames ("this is a story about space aliens; this is an email to a friend")

_____ Formulated objective: (I want to tell about X)

_____ Dialogue: _____ correct use of "" _____ mixed/ incorrect use of ""

Tells what character thinks or feels and describes the emotions character has (mental state words)

_____

_____ Mentions abstractions (e.g., truth)

continues

Table 6–1. *continued*

Rhapsodic features:

_____ Cliches, figures of speech, sayings, lyrics, etc.

_____ Repetitive refrains

_____ Shared situational knowledge (so you see . . .)

_____ Advice for the reader (if this happens to you . . .)

_____ Oral signaling devices (well, I already told you that)

_____ Clarifications (explains by clarifying a point)

_____ Author talks with character or interacts with character

_____ Author or narrator has emotions for the character

Text features:

_____ Constructs a reality or scenario

_____ Relates introductory info to the later portions of the text

_____ Problem posed and/or solved in this scenario

_____ "Diary" tone

_____ Recounts conversations

_____ # of episodes

Paragraph formation:

_____ Intentional and effective _____ Ineffective

Evaluative: Relates something about the writer's attitude or events of significance to the writer

_____

Topicalization:

_____ Written response fits the picture and/or directions

_____ Coheres on a lexical level (keeps talking about related objects, events)

_____ Coheres because of support for premises or elaboration of topic (details)

_____ Predominantly topic-centered (single character or event is elaborated on)

_____ Predominantly topic-associative (episodes are linked thematically; characters and settings may shift, personal perspective may be given along with facts)

_____ Derivative of a well-known story: characters, plot, etc.

_____ Disruptions, digressions mar focus

_____ Overt connections between main ideas are made

_____ A theme or moral is overtly stated

Table 6–1. *continued*

Organization:	
Coherence:	
_____ Unfocused, unrelated, or nonlinear events	
_____ Structure to the discourse content—marks information flow or progression of a plot	
_____ Referential cohesion: Links for organizing content (*next, later, meanwhile*, etc.)	

_____ Author tells how
_____ Author tells that
_____ Author enumerates
_____ Author defines
_____ Author describes
_____ Author classifies
_____ Author compares
_____ Author gives examples
_____ Author makes a final conclusion

_____ Knowledge-telling: Tells, identifies, memory-dumps, with low structure
_____ Knowledge-transforming: Reworks information to create a new whole; analysis

_____Connective statements (*and then*; adverbials, e.g., *later*, temporal terms)	
_____ Intersentential	_____ Within sentences
_____ Causal statements (cause and effect)	
_____ Comparative statements	

Problem pattern:
_____ Reasonable problem
_____ Ambiguous problem
_____ Solution pattern

Progression of events:
_____ Explanatory statements
_____ Alternative structure: Comparison and contrast
_____ Instigation, escalation, capping
_____ Little story within a big story
_____ Use of subtopic (related, coherent change)

continues

Table 6–1. *continued*

Sequence or series of events:

_____ Additive (and then, and then)

_____ Causal

_____ Temporal

_____ Adversative (everything is going one way, then a switch in the action changes how things are going)

_____ Continuative (e.g., You need X; it will give you Y)

_____ Parallel action

_____ Use of evidence

Is the written language sample confusing to read?

_____ Mazes of repetition (same thing is repeated without adding to content, purpose)

_____ Mazes of revision (a revision of a prior statement but this revision adds nothing in terms of clarification, elaboration, detail, enhancement)

_____ Word-finding maze

_____ Incomplete ties between propositions (ideas skip around)

_____ A what happens unit: Who did what to whom?

_____ A where unit

_____ A when unit

_____ A how unit

_____ A why unit

_____ A proposal or goal unit, a lead up to a culminating point

---

Style:

_____ Expressive writing (personal writing: author is in the piece)

_____ Poetic writing (true creative writing, storytelling)

_____ Transactional writing (true expository writing—writer is detached, report is given)

Story grammar:

_____ Characters _____ Main character

_____ Plot: _____ Beginning, middle, end _____ Multiple plots

_____ Setting:_____ Time _____ Place _____ Context

Table 6–1. *continued*

_____ Theme, moral, or purpose	_____ Multiple themes

_____ Affect (tone or internal responses of narrator or character)

_____ Point of view or narrative voice

_____ Omniscient narrator

_____ Character's role is described

_____ Character is described physically

_____ Character(s) has a goal, makes attempts to reach goal

_____ Episodes (initiating event [instantiation], reaction, outcome)

_____ Actions by characters

_____ Complications

_____ Aftermath of the complication is described

Audience:

_____ Audience is teacher/evaluator

_____ Other named audience

_____ No real audience

_____ Audience is self

_____ Writer is an expert to the audience

Semantics

List all conjunctions used:

_____

Word choice:

_____ Use of word meanings (correct, incorrect)

_____ Use of terms is varied, colorful, descriptive

_____ Word substitution errors

_____ Number of words (not counting title, by line, "the end," etc.)

_____ Number of different words

_____ # of different words divided by # of total (type-token ratio)

_____ # of descriptive words, usually adjectives or adverbs

_____ Invented words, neologisms

_____ Indefinite, vague words

continues

Table 6–1. *continued*

_____ Errors in word order
_____ Anaphora
_____ Cataphora
_____ Pronominalization
_____ Ellipsis
_____ Synonyms or near synonyms

Source: Adapted from Gordon Pershey, M. (2010, May). *Structural and discourse features of narrative writings by grade four and six African American students*. Poster presented at the annual conference of the American Educational Research Association, Denver. Available: *American Educational Research Association Online Paper Repository*: http://www.aera.net/Publications /OnlinePaperRepository/AERAOnlinePaperRepository/tabid/12720/Owner/70852/Default.aspx

lies recorded in the scoring blanks and thus providing the data for the examiner's assessment report. The written language productions that are not present in the sample or that are scored as in error or insufficient can contribute to setting intervention objectives. Note that a particular sentence can be scored in different ways. The objective of this inventory is to account for all elements used and for the many ways that sentence elements are used, not to ascertain exactly how a specific feature was used to the exclusion of other ways it could be used.

The tool can account for differences in a student's performance across different genres of writing or across assignments of different types. The examiner would inventory each genre of writing separately and then compare the results. Repeated assessments of students' performance over time are possible. The tool can be shared with teachers and other evaluators, in its entirety or in part. Small, selected portions of the inventory can be used by students for self-assessments and peer assessments.

Interventions to Develop the Grammatical and Syntactic Components of Skilled Writing

SLPs and teachers might find it challenging to effect improvement in their students' written syntax. Catts (2009) observed that research participants improved their performance on measures of reading comprehension, writing quality, and vocabulary but did not improve written syntactic performance. Improvements in syntax need to be targeted specifically, not taken for granted as co-occurring with generalized improvements in written language, such as are evidenced by vocabulary usage or the expression of ideas (cf. Feng & Powers, 2007).

A widely used learning paradigm is the *guided practice model*, where skills acquisition is likely to entail that the learners experience teachers' or SLPs' models and demonstrations of how to perform the skills, then engage in teacher-directed or SLP-directed practice that is supported by the teachers' or SLPs' logical progression of learning tasks. Learners engage in independent practice as a final step toward competence. This is a *gradual release model of learning*, sometimes described, from the teacher's or SLP's standpoint, as "I do, we do, you do" (as explained by Drew, 2019). The development of written language has a somewhat different overall trajectory, in that even very young children experiment with writing independently and gain a certain amount of writing competence intuitively or inductively (Calkins, 1994). Expressing themselves independently in writing is a teacher's or SLP's goal for young children even though they may not employ correctness of grammatical and sentence forms. For older learners, importantly, there is a parallel effort to encourage free expression while they learn more about standard written forms. In this regard, the teachers' and SLPs' models and directed practice opportunities occur contemporaneously with the learners' independent practice, which means that independent, expressive writing in and out of school continues while learners are refining their knowledge of grammar and sentence forms.

SLPs may approach writing interventions in the way that oral language therapy is typically delivered. Learners would be given opportunities to demonstrate written language independence and then SLPs would provide models, cues, prompts, or therapeutic questioning to help learners realize how to improve upon their errors or to minimize where the SLP's assistance is needed. This approach is not always feasible or possible. There is no amount of therapeutic questioning or performance testing that can improve how individuals employ written language forms that they have never previously heard, spoken, read, or written. It's not possible to offer cues to

bring about the use of written forms that are as yet unlearned. SLPs' approaches would by necessity introduce the written language forms that students do not have in their repertoires and/or strengthen the use of the forms that are present but not well ingrained. Rather than attempting to impart too many grammatical concepts to students who are already struggling with written grammar and syntax, SLPs would prioritize presenting the grammatical elements that most affect their students' ability to write effectively (Chin, n.d.), such as nouns and elaborated sentence subjects, verbs and verb phrases, and clauses and phrases that allow for sentence expansions (Jennings & Haynes, 2018; Weaver, 1998).

A Model for a Continuum of Interventions

As an overarching framework, SLPs' interventions to develop the grammar and syntax of written language would exist on a continuum of instructional practices that includes explicit, direct instruction and move gradually to more informal learning (cf. as proposed by Nippold, 2007), as shown in Figure 6–2. At the one end of the continuum is *direct instruction*, sometimes in the form of isolated grammar drills and grammar and syntax practice tasks. The content and meaning of the grammatical morphemes and sentences used as stimuli would be secondary in importance to the forms under study; any content or material could be used as stimuli. Students would learn the names and characteristics of the grammatical forms and then use these forms in practice tasks. Sentence analysis and sentence production are the focal points of the lessons. Working with the intrasentiential elements of subjects, predicates, clauses, and so on would be essential. For example, given the focus on, for example, subordinating conjunctions, students would write sentences that include the target conjunctions, such as *although, since, unless*, and *until*. Or students could fill in sentences where the subordinating conjunctions are missing, either by consulting a word bank for choices or independently thinking of the needed words. SLPs might design games or other participation opportunities to practice these isolated skills. Students might create charts or other reference materials that guide their use of the grammatical forms, such as listing their definitions, rules, and examples that will assist in future sentence analysis and sentence generation tasks. They might create a PowerPoint talk to explain the grammatical forms to other students, to be delivered either live or remotely, and viewed by their peers either synchronously or asynchronously. Using the planned scope and sequence of published grammar curricula would also be included within a direct teaching approach (e.g., see Datchuk, 2017, on the benefits of "precision teaching" of sentence components). The comprehensive and linear nature of these curricula, and the typically short lessons contained within these curricula that can be accommodated within traditional therapy sessions (e.g., perhaps 30 minutes twice per week), make them a viable language therapy option. Media options, such as grammar practice videos and songs, might be supplemental materials. Repetition and frequent practice impress upon the learner a more stable long-term memory storage of these grammatical and syntactic elements, and frequent opportunities for recall and rehearsal would help working memory retrieve these items on demand, because frequently retrieved information is more likely to be easily retrievable (see Nippold, 2007; see also Van Cleave, 2020). The question remains, however, of whether students will implement this grammar knowledge on other occasions when they write for academic and communicative purposes.

Moving along on the continuum of instructional practices shown in Figure 6–2, diverging from a drill and practice approach, interventions would include *planned contextual opportunities*, meaning that SLPs would use academically relevant reading and writing (or students' independent reading, if appropriate) as the context for creating lessons about certain grammatical and syntactic forms (Silliman & Scott, 2009). Sentence analysis and sentence generation, which are tasks that involve working with intrasentiential elements, are the linguistic foci of the lessons, but the allied purpose of exploring academic content is important, too. For example, when skimming the headers within a social studies textbook chapter, the student and SLP would copy out the head-

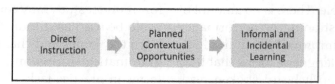

Figure 6–2. Interventions to develop the grammatical and syntactic components of skilled writing.

ers onto the left column of a two-column chart, then, in the right column, expand the terse headers into complete sentences. The SLP could explain that the words added are, for example, prepositions, articles, and conjunctions, as are italicized in the following example: The chapter section header "War in the Pacific" would be written out as "*In* 1941, *the* United States armed forces entered *into* war *with the* Japanese military, *with* battles taking place *throughout the* Pacific region, *on* land *and* sea *and in the* air." Students would continue to discover the use of the *form words* that structure sentence syntax, including prepositions, articles, and conjunctions, as the headers are expanded into sentences. (Form words stand in contrast to **content words,** i.e., the nouns, verbs, and adjectives that convey the majority of the semantic content in sentences. The grammar and syntax lessons would not preclude comprehending the content of the chapter, as obtained by reading and discussing its content. Form and meaning would be interrelated.) The planned contextual opportunities allow for grammar and syntax to be integrated into meaningful writing for purposes of authentic learning, as the example of the sentence expansion task would promote. Much of the discussion throughout this chapter that proposes options for interventions in some way makes use of planned contextual opportunities for learning about intrasentential grammar and syntax and expanding these contextual opportunities by using the target forms in self-generated writing contexts. The quantity and quality of the stimuli for learning are within the SLPs' control and the options for creativity in lesson content are extensive. These speech-language therapy approaches support and reinforce teachers' academic language instruction by encouraging students to apply this language to their writings (Silliman & Scott, 2009; Truckenmiller & Petscher, 2019).

Another benefit of designing sessions around planned contextual opportunities is that it emphasizes *reading to improve writing* and *writing to improve reading*. The reciprocal nature of the receptive and expressive literacy skills is inherent here (Ward-Lonergan, 2010). In older learners, learning new words has been attributed to regularly engaging in wide reading (Anderson et al., 1938; Nagy, 1988; National Reading Panel, 2000; Nippold, 2007). School-age learners can be expected to learn 2,000 to 3,000 new words each year, acquired by the cumulative effects of reading, direct instruction, and general exposure to words during daily living (Nippold, 2007). The better the student's spoken language vocabulary, the more words the student has available to use in writing. Moreover, the multiple exposures to the text passages that are used as stimuli for writing enhance memory and recall of the text information. The information is reviewed in working memory on multiple occasions, with this rehearsal and repetition building long-term storage of the information and, ideally, more accessible and automatic retrieval of strong impressions on demand.

On the right side of Figure 6–2 is the option for interventions to be based on *informal and incidental learning of grammatical and syntactic forms*. In this approach, a beneficial way of helping students improve their command of grammar and syntax in writing is to use students' own writing as the basis for discussing grammatical and syntactic concepts. Rather than using artificially constructed sentences found on skills worksheets, SLPs can use students' writing to help them work toward better grammatical usage, punctuation, and sentence variety (Weaver, 1998). Students' own writings provide the sentences for analysis. SLPs can help learners label the components of their own writing, so that learners can become aware that, for example, they actually use sentence subjects even though they do not yet know this syntactic terminology. Grammatical and syntactic concepts would not seem like unfamiliar abstractions if students can identify them in their own writing and can give these elements a name (Chin, n.d.; Weaver, 1998). This approach can add to the cumulative diagnostic inventory of students' known skills, and thus would help SLPs provide interventions that target students' areas of need and that reinforce their strengths. In a sense, this approach generates a series of language samples that are used for interventions and affords a repeated-measures or a multiple baseline approach to data collection. However, this approach is entirely inductive and not prescriptive. The material that SLPs have to work with to stimulate written language growth is limited to the examples of written language content, form, and usages that the learner brings to the session or creates within the session. Whether the student's writing has enough substance to lend itself to grammatical and syntactic examination and instruction, and whether the student's samples across sessions will have enough variety to provide for a range of meaningful learning experiences, cannot be foreseen. In this approach, SLPs' language interventions are provided using strategies that are similar to a writing workshop approach (Atwell, 1987), where students write freely and learn more about writing by examining, critiquing, and expanding their own work (and possibly that of their peers), and thereby develop self-regulated learning strategies (see Harris & Graham, 1999; Harris et al., 2011; and, notably, Harris et al., 2003, who studied

self-regulation to improve writing in students with disabilities). The approach would work well for learners who can supply rich and developmentally appropriate writing samples each session, but the approach would not offer enough skill-building instruction for students who do not generate the quantity or quality of material needed for workshopping. The serendipitous discovery of grammatical and syntactic elements to explore might not occasion the process of repetitive review of specific elements, which has been shown to build the long-term storage and working memory retrieval networks necessary to use these elements with ease on future occasions (Nippold, 2007).

This continuum offered in Figure 6–2 might suggest possible sequences for interventions. One consideration is that it might be necessary for some intervention plans to begin with direct instruction in grammar and syntax and move, in time, in a linear fashion, to planned contextual opportunities for working with the elements of sentence form, using academic readings as model texts. Then, the more familiar that learners become with grammar and syntax, the more they can examine their own writing and learn skills for revising and editing within the informal and incidental learning contexts that their own writings afford. In this sequence, each strategy for instruction gives way to the next, less structured strategy over time. Alternatively, another possible consideration is to aim for the use of a certain grammatical or syntactic form in directed instruction, planned contextual opportunities, and informal and incidental learning, contemporaneously. The focus is on the selected form, for example, the dependent clause, and this form is explored during exercises, while writing about readings, and when the student needs to produce written texts to accomplish some communicative or academic purposes (Weaver, 1998). Deductive and inductive learning co-occur.

With these two possible instructional sequences in mind, sequential and contemporaneous, it would seem less advantageous for SLPs to begin with informal and incidental learning as the starting point for interventions. The diagnostic elements become increasingly less important over time, and the need for structured introduction of new grammatical and syntactic targets takes on time value. Students might not understand enough about grammatical and syntactic elements to evaluate their own writing and to workshop their way to new learnings. If the SLP models how to identify elements of the student's writing to work with, the student might feel "caught out" or corrected rather than feel supported for growth. Although these caveats are worthy of consideration, a determination of the most beneficial intervention sequence would depend upon each learner's unique capabilities, and SLPs would assess the nature of each learner's strengths and needs and intervene accordingly.

Content, Process, and Product: Three Considerations for Interventions

SLPs' interventions require careful planning of the content and processes that are targeted and the products that learners create. These concurrent considerations are true for most interventions across the SLPs' scope of practice, but they are imperative for written language interventions. In simple terms, *the content of an intervention plan and of the lessons within*

this plan has to do with the knowledge that SLPs would like learners to gain. For example, grammatical content might include learning a sufficient number of the parts of speech to make practical use of this knowledge when writing sentences. Syntactic content might include labeling sentence elements such as subject, predicate, main clause, subordinate clause, and so on, again to be able to use this knowledge for sentence analysis and sentence generation (see, for example, Jennings & Haynes, 2018; Van Cleave, 2020).

The processes of an intervention plan and of the lessons within this plan would entail many of the procedural choices for helping learners succeed. These choices would be made within the paradigms of direct instruction and practice, or structured opportunities for practice, or working with students' spontaneous writings to learn about grammar and syntax. The processes would include locating, identifying, labeling, manipulating, analyzing, and generating the elements of a sentence. Process skills would include word choices within sentences; word ordering in sentences of different types; reviewing, revising, and editing sentences; comparing grammatical and agrammatical sentences; expanding or shortening sentences; and other sentence analysis, generation, and manipulation tasks. Structured tasks that involve working with grammatical elements would be included here, for example, changing a sentence subject from singular to plural and editing the sentence for noun-verb agreement. It may be that the acquisition of process skills is the most extensive aspect of written language interventions.

Products are the tangible components created during interventions. Sometimes SLPs' interventions do not generate tangible products. Speech-language therapy may be conversation based or centered on verbal practice tasks. The verbal exchanges are the actual products, but they are only tangible if they are recorded for review or if careful documentation could re-create the interchanges. *Written language interventions necessitate the creation of written products. One of the foremost considerations for intervention planning and session objectives is determining what the learner will write during the session and possibly before and/or after the session, too. The products are the written outcomes of the interventions and embody the actualization of the content and the processes of the interventions.* The products provide the demonstrations of the learner's written language skills. Products might include, for example, a grammatically standard written sentence with a main clause and a dependent clause, a sentence with two independent clauses joined by a coordinating conjunction, a correctly worded and punctuated wh-question sentence, or a five-sentence paragraph that includes a topic sentence, three sentences that provide paragraph details, and a concluding sentence. The products could take the form of their genre and/or communicative intent, for example, a get well soon email to a teacher, a five-slide PowerPoint for history class, or a half-page entry in a learning journal in math class.

Products do not necessarily have to be finished, edited pieces of writing. Students' prewriting planning would constitute products (Atwell, 1987; Fulwiler & Young, 1982; Murray, 2004), including their free writing, quick writing, or 5-minute writings that they use to get started on a composition; their personal journaling; and their "notes to self" where they record ideas that they will later write about. Murray (2004) wrote extensively about keeping a writer's notebook or a "day-book" that includes diary entries, notes,

and memos but also clippings, mementoes, and other artifacts that can inspire composition.

Grammar and Syntax Instruction and the Teaching of Writing

Hillocks and Smith (1991) reported that students do not necessarily transfer isolated grammar instruction that is separated from writing instruction to improving their own writing. However, this does not necessarily mean that systematic and explicit instruction and interventions would be futile; in fact, quite the contrary (De La Paz & Graham, 2002; Eberhardt, 2013; Feng & Powers, 2005; Gillis & Eberhardt, 2018; Gregory, 2003; International Dyslexia Association, 2010; Kieffer & Lesaux, 2012; Kuehner, 2016; Saddler, 2012). Skills and strategy instruction and interventions would provide a foundation for students' ultimate automatic use of grammatical and syntactic knowledge (Graham & Perin, 2007b; National Reading Panel, 2000).

Learner-friendly grammar instruction and interventions would not seem to the student to be a barrage of continuous drill and testing. Writing is produced for communication, so sentence writing work among students in groups would be a beneficial way to share the grammatical and syntactic constructions being learned and practiced. Shared work among students would entail generating sentences, working on sentence-building tasks, and revising sentences to produce written products (Weaver, 1998) that other people would actually see and enjoy via electronic and/or print formats. Grammar and syntax instruction and interventions would become a natural part of the mini-lessons that begin speech-language sessions and would be carried through during the drafting, revising, editing, and proofreading phases of the writing process (Chin, n.d.).

The important consideration is the amount of transfer of grammatical and syntactic information that SLPs would expect learners to be responsible for independently. Shaughnessy (1977) cautioned not to overemphasize grammatical terminology and overwhelm students' ability to understand and apply the concepts (see Chin, n.d.). As Weaver (1998) suggested, the concepts covered during structured and systematic grammar and syntax lessons would be most relevant to what students need to be able to write about and would be immediately applied to writing contexts. For example, after a mini-lesson (i.e., a short, practical lesson; see Atwell, 1987) on using a series of modifiers (adjectives) in a sentence, SLPs would provide students with the opportunity to write descriptive passages (cf. Datchuk, 2016; Datchuk & Kubina, 2017). Keeping the examples of the NAEP questions in mind (NAEP, n.d.), students could write a few descriptive paragraphs about a favorite class or teacher, using descriptive modifiers in correct series order to explain the positive features of this class or teacher.

Grammatical and Syntactic Necessities

As noted in Chapter 4, Shaughnessy (1977) identified four areas of essential grammar, which could yield emphasis during instruction and interventions: sentence formation, morphological inflection, verb tense, and noun-verb and noun-pronoun agreement. Weaver (1998) suggested that the most essential skills for

writing are based upon the ability to manipulate the syntactic elements of sentences. Competence here would include generating sentences with appropriate subjects, verbs, clauses, and phrases (see *Features of Academic Writing*, n.d.); using sentence-combining skills to build longer sentences and more elaborated syntax; and using punctuation and the mechanics of writing for convention, clarity, and style (Chin, n.d.; Weaver, 1998).

Working toward students' mastery of these essentials of grammar and syntax would include some working definitional knowledge of grammatical and syntactic terms. As Nippold (2007) elaborated, definitions are of practical value for clarity and conciseness of communication, and there are different types of definitions. Definitions tell what something is (as in, *a noun is a person, place, or thing, including an animal, quality, or idea*). Some definitions differentiate one thing from other things, perhaps by negation (as in, a *noun is a quality, such as "a softness," but is not a describing word, like "soft"*). Definitions can employ comparisons (as in, *nouns name things, but adjectives describe things*), or examples (as in, *nouns are persons and places, for example, the president of the United States lives in Washington, D.C.*). Some definitions are operational or situational and tell how something is experienced, as in, *a noun can be perceived by the senses or as an idea within the mind*; people may call this a "working definition." Students would become familiar with mechanisms for defining grammatical and syntactic concepts for purposes of making linguistic elements more accessible, vivid, and usable, so that definitions do not become rote, superfluous, and meaningless verbiage. Students and SLPs could explore online sources of definitions of grammatical and syntactic terms and then refer back to the sites they prefer (for example, *Features of Academic Writing*, n.d.).

To systematically define grammatical and syntactic terms, learners might employ explanatory strategies (cf. Nippold, 2007):

- Tell what something is by explaining how it is used.
- Tell what something is by describing it.
- Tell what something is by explaining its characteristic properties.
- Tell what something is by providing a synonym for it (SLPs would encourage students who use simpler, earlier developing adjectives and adverbs to provide more mature synonyms; similarly, slang and more formal terms would be interchanged depending upon pragmatic contexts; note that word choices can affect sentence grammar).
- Tell what something is by associating it with similar things (an analogy to something similar).
- Tell what something is by telling how it is used, what it does, or how it functions.
- Tell what something is by explaining if it is a part of something else.
- Tell what something is by explaining any aspects of degree that modify it (e.g., sometimes, mostly, lightly).
- Tell what something is by explaining the category of things, actions, or concepts it belongs within (or explain a superordinate categorical terms as having certain subordinates within this category).
- Tell what something is by explaining its characteristic properties by

contrasting it to things that are different.
- Tell what something is by explaining any syllogistic reasoning associated with it (to be X, it must be Y and cannot be Z).

Chin (n.d.) and Van Cleave (2020) recommended the practice of integrating grammar instruction and interventions within tasks where students are composing texts, such as writing paragraphs or stories. SLPs would use the grammar terms that make sense to the students as they are crafting their sentences. By incorporating grammar terms naturally into the processes of drafting, revising, editing, and proofreading, SLPs would help students understand and apply grammar purposefully to their own writing. Strategies such as writing conferences, partner writing, grammar mini-lessons, and peer response groups may facilitate a natural dialogue about grammar and syntax (Chin, n.d.; Graham & Perin, 2007a, 2007b). *Writing conferences* (Atwell, 1987) involve a teaching strategy that educators use that bears a resemblance to an individual or small group speech-language therapy session. The student writer(s) and the teacher engage in a conference about the content and form of the student's academic paper or other type of written product (for example, a letter, a blog post, a petition, or an invitation to a school event, regardless of whether these are a physical or an electronic composition). The writing conference involves the educator helping the student become aware of the strengths and needs of the draft. SLPs would be important writing conference partners for students, within the students' classrooms or in pull-out therapy settings. Therapy objectives can include enhancing the quantity and quality of the students' written language self-analysis, the students' accuracy of responses to the SLP's suggestions and input related to grammatical and syntactic conventions, and progress toward carrying over the written language improvements to future assignments.

Nippold (2007) offered suggestions for *inflectional morphology* (i.e., adding bound morphemes to form grammatical variants, such as changing present tense to past tense, where the resulting words retain the same part of speech) and *derivational morphology* (i.e., where bound morphemes may or may not change a word's part of speech; a root form can yield multiple derivations). Inflectional morphemes and derivational morphemes influence the syntactic roles of words. Inflectional morphemes in English are not complex, involving only verb tense, grammatical person (first, second, and third), and number (singular and plural), and would typically be mastered in spoken language by age 6 or 7 (Nippold, 2007). Derivational morphology continues to develop as learners gain conceptual knowledge in and out of school. Common but complex affixes (prefixes and suffixes) are added to nouns, verbs, adjectives, and adverbs to extend students' vocabularies, as in these examples (for a longer list, refer to Nippold, 2007, pp. 50–52):

- Noun derivations: -ness (happy-happiness); -ster (young-youngster); -ure (close-closure)
- Verb derivations: -ate (active-activate); -ize (colony-colonize)
- Adjective derivations: -ible (reverse-reversible); -most (upper-uppermost); -ward (after-afterward)
- Adverb derivations: -ly (quiet-quietly); -fully (careful-carefully)

More than one affix can be added to a base word, as in the adverb derivations.

Interventions would explore the use of *free morphemes* that can take on derivational affixation (e.g., *enjoy-enjoyment*) along with the derivations built from roots that do not stand alone as words (e.g., *-struct* in *construct-construction*). Nippold (2007) observed that some derivations have greater semantic transparency than others, meaning, the root and affix relationship are more apparent and occur naturally in common linguistic usage. Other words are more semantically opaque, where knowledge of the root and affix may be more obscure and require some level of analysis (e.g., the root *-struct* in *construct-construction*).

Oral Language Usage to Guide Written Language Targets

Chin (n.d.) proposed that grammar and syntax instruction and interventions would begin with students' baseline demonstrations of their knowledge of grammar and syntax, as demonstrated by oral language usage, and would then help students incorporate this knowledge as they write. Connecting students' knowledge of oral language structures to creating written language constructions would be an initial step. SLPs would document oral language usage via sampling (see Chapter 4) and during other opportunities for observation of students' oral language use. Interventions can be directed toward (1) enhancing the use of the forms that students produced, by offering opportunities to use their productive forms in a variety of different contexts, and (2) introducing the use of forms that were not evidenced during sampling. It may be that the students have these forms in their repertoires but simply did not have occasion to display them during sampling, or these may be new forms. Systematic and explicit review of the forms that they use well in oral language, as well as of the forms that they use inconsistently well, would help solidify their oral language skills in preparation for transfer of these skills to written language. Transfer tasks might include creating an audio or video recording using a spoken language version of what students are planning to write and then transcribing it to print, followed by careful revising and editing to transition to a written "voice," with emphasis on word choice, syntax, tone, and other written language conventions. Alternatively, a language experience approach (Stauffer, 1970) might be used. Students, usually in small groups, would dictate a draft of a text for the SLP to transcribe, which eliminates the manual component of writing and frees up the students' cognitive-linguistic resources for composing the wording, syntactic arrangements, and meanings of their composition. Students then revise and edit the transcription of their dictation to achieve a finished product cowritten by the students and adults involved.

Regardless of the intervention approaches used, SLPs would then gradually introduce new oral language forms that would be useful in oral and written contexts. Students may be able to express whether they are familiar with the new forms that the SLP introduces.

Concerns for students' working memory capacity are relevant during oral-to-written language tasks. Just because the multiword syntax under study is written down doesn't mean that the content would not tax a learner's working memory. SLPs would be careful not to tax a learner's auditory working memory. Aural sentence targets cannot be so long as

to make it difficult for the learner to process all of the elements in a sentence when they use their working memory capacity for syntactic arrangements.

Oral language baselines may ensure that students can use an array of developmentally appropriate grammatical and syntactic subskills, for example:

- Integrating word meanings into sentence meanings: Use words in the contexts of sentence grammar and syntax, whether those meanings are consistent whenever they are used in sentences or change across sentences.
- Sentence arrangement skills, such as reversible and nonreversible clause structures; arrangements may be based on whether the *active or passive voice* is used.
  - Reversible: The information can be extracted from either clause, since the nouns can be subjects or objects, as in, *The big dog chased the little dog; the little dog chased the big dog; the little dog was chased by the big dog; the big dog was chased by the little dog.*
  - Nonreversible: The information that completes the sentence meaning is subject-extracted (as in, *The patient took the medicine*, not that the medicine took the patient) or object-extracted (as in, *The patient was helped by the medicine*, which can only mean that the medicine helped the patient, not that the patient helped the medicine).
- Sentence arrangement skills, such as *cleft sentences* that may change the place in the sentence where information is extracted, as in, *It was Caleb who fixed the broken toy*,

with the actor or subject, Caleb, being placed after the verb *fixed*, in the sentence predicate; the sentence subject is found in the predicate position; *It* is considered a null subject, because, although it appears in the subject position, it is not the actual subject of the sentence.

Written Sentence Skills

Instruction and interventions that focus on improving students' sentence writing would address the skills and strategies needed to accomplish sentence generation and sentence analysis (Jennings & Haynes, 2018; Saddler, 2012; Van Cleave, 2020; Weaver, 1998). Sentence generation may include explicit lessons on the elements of sentences and how to use these words, clauses, and phrases to form sentences. Sentence expansion, often accomplished by practicing sentence combining, is an important aspect of explicit instruction and interventions for sentence generation. Sentence analysis skills teach the metacognitive and metalinguistic awareness of how sentences are composed and allow learners to consider how to determine whether sentences are too long, too short, complete, grammatical, and meaningful. Sentence analysis skills would be integrated with revising and editing of meaningful sentences, composed by their teachers and SLPs, or drawn from their in- and out-of-school readings, or composed by themselves and their peers. Breaking down sentences that are too long can be as important as expanding sentences that are too short. Learners would have models of well-composed sentences and would refer to editing rules or strategies that are available online or in their language arts instructional materials. Learning simple

rules, such as "use the active voice whenever possible," can help build a consciousness of how sentences "sound" and "look" when they are well constructed.

Regarding the expansion of language form, Chapter 4 presented the acronym SPICE: *Syntactic and Pragmatic Interventions for Clausal Expansions* as a suggestion for oral language grammar and syntax enhancement. The focus of SPICE for written language would be to help learners become metalinguistically aware of the components of clausal expansions. SLPs can use this acronym as a reminder to emphasize clausal structures as they construct written language interventions.

Sentence Expansions

Loban (1976, p. 35) provided information on the lengths of spoken and written sentences in school-age and adolescent learners, which reflects intrasentential growth, that is, an increased length of sentence that occurs as their sentence forms become more complex (Nippold, 2007). Intrasentential expansion is usually the result of an increase in *clausal density*, notably by increasing the number of times that the speaker or writer uses clausal subordination. These data on the mean number of words per *C-unit* (i.e., independent clauses plus their modifiers) provide parameters for the lengths of sentences that could be targeted by sentence expansion interventions. Loban's (1976) data (see also Nippold, 2007), indicated the length of C-unit was typically:

- Grade 1, ages 6 to 7, spoken sentences with a mean length of 6.88 C-units (Loban had no measures for written sentences).
- Grade 3, ages 8 to 9, spoken sentences with a mean length of

7.62 and written sentence with a mean length of 7.60 C-units.

- Grade 6, ages 11 to 12, spoken sentences with a mean length of 9.82 and written sentence with a mean length of 9.04 C-units.
- Grade 9, ages 14 to 15, spoken sentences with a mean length of 10.96 and written sentence with a mean length of 10.05 C-units.
- Grade 12, ages 17 to 18, spoken sentences with a mean length of 11.70 and written sentence with a mean length of 13.27 C-units.

Students in Loban's (1976) sample younger than Grade 12 produced fairly equivalent oral and written sentence lengths. Older students in Grade 12 demonstrated *greater sentence complexity in writing than in speaking*. These data show fine point distinctions that may not be replicable on a daily basis in communicative or educational contexts. Perhaps a sufficient summary might be to suggest that written sentence expansions might target about 7- or 8-word constructions in mid-elementary school and increase to 9- or 10-word sentences in middle school and 13-word sentences in high school. Scott and Stokes (1995) similarly reported that written sentence length increased from approximately 7 words for students in the third grade to 14 words for students in Grade 12. Other studies provided an array of data on the lengths of written sentences produced by school-age and adolescent writers. Christie and Derewianka (2008) provided written language scores and a trajectory of writing development from ages 6 through 18 for a sample of 400 students, documenting changes in the structural components and functional uses of writing. Maxwell-Reid and Kartika-Ningsih (2020) documented age- and grade-related skills in nominal expansions in adolescent writing. Rose (2021) developed a writing assessment that scores writing samples in relation to Australian grade-level standards, along 14 criteria for genre, register, discourse, grammar, and graphic features. These various tools and banks of data are useful for establishing students' performance, progress monitoring, and creating comparisons of individuals' performance to national standards.

Sentence combining involves joining together short sentences to form longer, more complex sentences. Hillocks (1986, p. 150) noted that teaching sentence combining teaches "systematic knowledge of sentence possibilities." Sentence-combining strategies teach students to vary sentence structure in order to change meaning and to vary their writing style (Chin, n.d.). Sentence combining can teach new ways to begin sentences and to create alternative sentence structures. Complex syntactic structures would tend to include a more varied array of vocabulary terms, and the combination of sentence variety and word variety would enhance the content, clarity, and coherence of students' writing.

Chin (n.d.) suggested that structured sentence-combining exercises provide models and guidance for how to combine sentences, perhaps by filling sentence frames or striking out a predetermined number of words. For example, if two sentences are provided, as in *Mom took her three kids to buy new sneakers. On their way, they stopped to pick up Grandma to bring her along*, the combined sentence could be *On their way to buy new sneakers, Mom and her three kids stopped to pick up Grandma to bring her along*. The cue could be that 22 words become 20, so a frame with 20 blanks is provided. Unstructured sentence-combining exercises allow for a range of responses and more opportunities for fluency and variety (Chin, n.d.). For example, if three sentences are provided: *Mom took her three kids to buy new sneakers. Grandma went along. They had a good time.*, the combined sentence could have many outcomes, for instance, *They had a good time when Grandma went along with Mom and her three kids to buy new sneakers. When Grandma went along with Mom and her three kids to buy new sneakers, they had a good time. Mom and her three kids had a good time when they went to buy new sneakers and Grandma went along.* The meaning of each variation is slightly different.

Nippold (2007) suggested that the use of conjunctions is one important syntactic element in sentence expansion and reported that prior studies identified that throughout elementary, middle, and high school, learners increase their frequency and accuracy of use of subordinating (e.g., *after, although, as, until, when, since, unless,* etc.), coordinating (e.g., *and, but, or,* etc.), and correlative conjunctions (e.g., *either . . . or; neither . . . nor,* etc.). Importantly, Loban (1976) noted that a longer utterance is not always the most sophisticated syntactic form, and phrasal constructions that provide economy of form may entail greater syntactic maturity (as described in Chapter 4).

In general, learning about sentence expansions necessitates knowledge of the *obligatory grammatical transformations* in sentence structures and the *optional grammatical transformations in sentence structures.* SLPs would consider the types of sentences that writers create by employing the obligatory and the optional grammatical transformations and that students would have a functional need to master. Learners may find greater transparency in the rules for obligatory grammatical transformations and may be more comfortable

addressing these contexts first in a learning sequence. For example, the simple rule of coordinating two independent clauses using a coordinating conjunction is fairly simple: *I went to Elise's birthday party. I brought a gift.* becomes *I went to Elise's birthday party and I brought a gift.* The optional grammatical transformation is whether the writer repeats the sentence subject or opts for ellipsis of the subject in the second independent clause: *I went to Elise's birthday party and brought a gift.* The optional grammatical transformation may require discussion about not only the grammatical options but the expressive nuances of the choices, which may relate to pragmatic considerations such as the function of the sentence within the discourse (Christie & Derewianka, 2008), the relative importance of this sentence to overall passage meaning, the social register that the writer would adopt or the relative social positions of the writer and prospective readers, the writer's degree of necessity for being clear and exact in meaning and whether a certain grammatical transformation would be more effective, the purpose of the text and the intended audience, and so on. The overall array of grammatical and syntactic considerations for students' learning about forms that arrange clauses into elaborated sentences would entail learning about:

- Clauses.
- Forms within clauses: Noun phrase expansions.
- Forms within clauses: Verb phrase expansions.
- Forms within clauses: Prepositional phrases, object complements, and so on.
- Clausal transformations: Sentence combining by using dependent clauses, descriptive embedded

clauses, or connecting or conjoining sentences to form a single complex sentence.

- Arranging clauses into elaborated sentences: Obligatory grammatical transformations in sentence structures.
- Arranging clauses into elaborated sentences: Optional grammatical transformations in sentence structures and the options for sentence expansions.

Sentence expansion interventions would be orderly and systematic and would concentrate on discrete skills using a small number of sentence types at a time; for novices or struggling learners, perhaps focusing on just one sentence type at a time would be an efficient and effective process (cf. Saddler, 2012). Students would use grammatical terminology to describe the sentence components. Authentic contexts for expansions might stimulate and motivate their use, for instance, when elaborating on concepts by writing about examples and nonexamples of the concepts, places, people, and so on under discussion (Ortlieb, 2014).

SLPs would construct sentence frames based on relevant stimuli, such as students' academic textbooks or the fiction that students are reading as part of their class curricula (Weaver, 1998). A systematic approach to sentence expansions would have students move through a series of sentence study tasks, including:

- Identify sentence elements that are offered by SLPs (i.e., a receptive demonstration of recognition and knowledge of sentence elements).
- Label sentence elements (i.e., an expressive task that is achieved independently or with cues).

- Define and describe sentence types (i.e., an expansion of expressive labeling, where more detail is expressed; for example, students demonstrate that they know the meanings of various words that are subordinating conjunctions and that they can define and describe clausal subordination).
- Imitate SLPs' writing of sentence types (e.g., the SLP writes a compound or a complex sentence and then the student writes a different, self-generated compound or complex sentence) (a helpful practice is to guide students to think about why writers need compound or complex sentences; for example, to provide a summary or a concluding sentence, a writer may need to use connecting words, such as *because*: *The final reason for people to take their pets to the vet is because it is the best way to keep their pets safe and happy.*).
- Practice (i.e., working with sentence elements in various ways: for example, physically arranging sentence strips or sentence cards where sentence parts can be manipulated, strung together, and rearranged (Weaver, 1998).

Practice opportunities would include using sentence frames to create the following types of sentences, as well as explicitly labeling and defining the sentence elements in the following types of sentence forms (cf. Nippold, 2007) (see Chapter 4 for an expanded description of these sentence elements):

Increase in Length and Variety of Sentence Forms

Simple sentence: One independent clause (I went outside)

Compound sentence: Two independent clauses joined by a coordinating conjunction (and, but, so; I went outside *and* walked onto the grass)

Complex sentence: One independent clause and at least one dependent clause joined by a subordinating conjunction (if, when) (I went outside *when* it was raining), or

An independent clause and a nonfinite verb phrase, such as an infinitive phrase (I went outside *to check the weather*, or

An independent clause and a participle (*Stepping outside*, I checked the weather), or

An independent clause and a gerund (*Walking outside is a seasonal pleasure*)

Compound-complex sentence: At least two independent clauses and at least one dependent clause (*I went outside but it was raining and I cancelled* my daily walk)

Increase in the Use of Clausal Expansion Types (see Chapter 4 for more options):

Example of kernel sentences to expand by using clausal expansion: *Diana was annoyed. Diana missed the bus.*

Nominal expansion: *Diana* was annoyed that *she* missed the bus.

Adverbial expansion: *When* Diana missed the bus, she was annoyed (*when* is a subordinating conjunction that introduces a dependent clause).

Relative clause expansion: Diana, *who missed the bus*, was annoyed.

Nippold (2007), remarking upon Scott and Stokes (1995), noted that nominatives tend to be the most common expansions

in spoken language but are used in written language as well, and that adverbials often represent the expansions that occur in the subjects of written sentences.

Improving Clausal Sophistication

Some sentence expansions do not function to increase sentence length but do function to improve sentence complexity. As Loban (1976) and Nippold (2007) noted, expansions add linguistic sophistication via the judicious use of economy of form. Examples include:

Participial phrases: *Waiting for the light to change*, Diana missed the bus.

Gerund phrases: *Missing the bus* annoyed Diana.

Infinitive phrases: Diana was unhappy *to miss the bus.*

Increasing Sentence Length and the Meaningfulness of Sentence Content

Nippold (2007) described strategies for how writers can increase the complexity of how nouns, verbs, adjectives, and adverbs are used in sentences and contribute to sentence expansions. Some examples include:

Elaborated subjects: *Weather events, such as rain and snow*, can cause Diana to miss the bus.

Postmodification of nouns (i.e., the words that follow a noun modify the noun) using prepositional phrases: The weather *in the morning* caused Diana to miss the bus.

Postmodification of nouns using nonfinite verbs: Diana will catch the next bus *to arrive.*

Appositives to expand nouns: Diana, *a late riser*, missed the bus.

Verb phrase expansions using modal auxiliaries: Diana *should have* gotten up earlier.

Verb phrase expansions using the perfect aspect: Diana *had been sleeping* too late all week.

Passive voice: The bus schedule on Diana's route *was changed* recently.

Coordination of nouns: *Diana and Rocco* missed the bus.

Correlative conjunctions (both, either, neither) to coordinate nouns: *Both* Diana and Rocco are late risers.

Coordination of verbs: Diana *drinks coffee and watches TV* in the morning.

Coordination of adjectives: The bus is *crowded and slow.*

Coordination of adverbs: Diana grumbled *quietly and bitterly.*

Increasing Sentence Length by Using Sentence Combining

Nippold et al. (2009) suggested traditional sentence-building tasks, such as sentence combining, where students combine simple sentences to form compound or complex sentences. Sentence combining is a widely used instructional approach to help writers gain sentence composition skills (e.g., Datchuk & Kubina, 2013; Saddler et al., 2008; Saddler et al., 2018; Scott & Nelson, 2009). Saddler and Graham (2005) reported that sentence combining was found to be superior to grammar instruction in a study of the sentence writing skills of Grade 4 students. Part of the reason for this finding might be that students can see the effects of sentence-combining interventions immediately, within the present instructional or therapeutic context; students have composed new sentences and can reflect on the sentences' structure,

meaning, and functions. Grammar instruction, to be effective, would require students to remember the content of the grammar instruction and apply it spontaneously in a context subsequent to and remote from the instructional or therapeutic context. Moreover, sentence combining is an equalizer among students of varying levels of ability, in the sense that all writers, be they more skilled or struggling, refine their compositions by using sentence combining. Sentence combining can be a linguistically intuitive process that lends itself to peer-to-peer tutoring more readily than would peer-to-peer grammar instruction, which might require some expert knowledge.

An example of the sequence of instruction or interventions that would facilitate sentence combining would be, *Upon completion of explicit instruction about some examples of words that introduce subordinate clauses, students would be asked to combine two or three short sentences by using a word that introduces a subordinate clause.*

An example of how sentence combining can increase *clausal density* would be:

Example of kernel sentences to expand by using sentence combining: I went to school. I went to soccer practice after school.

Responses using clausal subordination: Before I went to soccer practice, I went to school.

After school, I went to soccer practice.

I went to school, then to soccer practice.

Sentence Expansions as Demonstrated by Using Sentence Completion Tasks

A suggestion from Nippold et al. (2009) is to employ sentence completion tasks. SLPs can locate or construct sentences, then remove some content and place blanks within these sentences (filling in the blank is also known as a *cloze* sentence task). Each blank can require phrase-length responses. Sentence completions can be used for narrative or expository oral language. For example, a cloze task for a personal narrative might include:

> I enjoyed the reader's theater activity because _____. I was happy that I was able to _____. I learned that _____. Next time we do reader's theater, I'd like to _____.

Or,

> Before we had reader's theater, I thought that being in a play would be _____. It's called reader's theater because _____. I think reader's theater is best when _____.

Sentence completions for expository language might address phrase length factual messages, rather than single words, for example:

> Three types of clouds are _____.
> When we are trying to predict whether it is going to rain, we consider how the clouds _____.

Drafting and revising allow students to see sentence formation as a series of choices. Students would become comfortable with the drafts of their ideas, then would employ "grammatical concepts as language choices" (Chin, n.d.) as they edit their sentences to convey their thoughts and purposes more exactly.

Intersentential Syntactic Skills

Nippold (2007) noted that syntactic abilities include linguistic devices to link sentences together and build **cohesion** across sentences. These intersentential words are used "between" sentences to link sentence ideas, generally as the first word of a sentence that serves as a link from one sentence to another. Sometimes these are the same *adverbial conjuncts* that are used to show logical relationships as *intrasentential* expansions, such as *therefore, namely, notably, finally,* and *apparently*, as in, *Henry was tired and, apparently, he forgot to turn on the security system*. If the sentences were, *Henry was tired. Apparently, he forgot to turn on the security system.*, "apparently" serves an intersentential function. Intersentential words signal various meanings, including topic transitions (e.g., *meanwhile*), conclusions (e.g., *hence*), differences of opinion (e.g., *conversely*), contrasts (e.g., *ironically*), continuations (e.g., *therefore*), qualifying concepts (e.g., *typically*), or mental states (e.g., *regretfully*).

Chin noted that it is important to help students see grammatical concepts as language choices that can enhance how they convey the meaning and the purpose of their messages (Scott, 1995a). SLPs can set explicit goals for students to use and self-monitor specific aspects of written syntax (cf. Feng & Powers, 2007; Harris et al., 2011; Kieffer & Lesaux, 2012; Mason, 2013). It is possible that SLPs would use the strategy of *imitative writing*, where students imitate the SLP's written models of form and style, to help students explicitly identify the grammatical concepts under study. For example, if the SLP models how to use a subordinate clause in the sentence predicate, the students' sentences would use a subordinate clause in the sentence predicate. Gradually, the model could include some omitted details that the students would generate spontaneously based upon their emerging knowledge of written grammar and syntax and their developing sentence "sense" (Weaver, 1998).

Teachers may emphasize sentence variety as an important writing skill (Killgallon, 1977; Killgallon & Killgallon, 2000; Saddler, 2012; Van Cleave, 2020). Nippold (2007) explained that sentence variety can be taught by helping students use synonyms or near-synonyms to expand sentences or to extend meaning across sentences. Lexical cohesion devices refer to choosing the most appropriate words to continue a discussion of previously mentioned items. In some forms of writing, such as fictional narratives or literary journalism, synonyms or near-synonyms reduce redundancy and increase semantic and syntactic variety, which can improve the aesthetics and creativity of the text. In other forms of writing, the same words must be used repeatedly to keep concepts specific. This might be true in technical writing, reports of scientific data, clinical reports, and news writing. Sentences that build upon one another to enhance meaning may do so based more on their patterns for expansion of ideas rather than by simply varying the word choices. Sentence-to-sentence *coherence*, and thus the development of paragraphs and passages, can employ patterns that are built across sentences to explain associations, contrasts, sequences, conceptual relationships, accumulated evidence, and instances of the general to the specific or the specific to the general. These patterns would influence the intrasentential word choices needed to impart the accrued meaning. Teaching these skills would be worthwhile, as research has indicated that textual coherence devices (e.g., words that signal causal cohesion, connective words, and multiword syntactic complexity) were found to be predictors of written language abilities (Graesser et al., 2004; Louwerse & Cai, 2004). These findings would suggest that effective writers employ an array of cohesion strategies.

Revising and Editing

Chin (n.d.) suggested that once students have a sense of the structures they use in their own writing, they can begin to revise and edit their writing. SLPs can guide students to identify and correct their grammatical usage and sentence structure, as Shaughnessy (1977) and Weaver (1998) recommended. Applying grammar and syntax instruction into the revising and editing process helps students see the relevance of prescriptive grammar and syntax to their own writing. Being able to "say it better" (Eisenberg, 2006) is an important skill for improving form, meaning, and communicative intent. SLPs would choose grammatical and syntactic concepts that are essential for the clear communication of meaning (Chin, n.d.; *Features of Academic Writing*, n.d.; Wallach et al., 2010). A few keys to sentence editing would be:

- Sentence parallelism, often in the form of tense inconsistency (cf. Loban, 1976) (as in, *I finished my yoga class at the park then I was walking home* should be *I finished my yoga class at the park then I walked home*, with simple past tense verbs in each clause).
- Short and clear but not choppy (*I went to a yoga class. It was at the park. I walked to the park. I walked home.* would become *I walked to and from the park for a yoga class* or *I walked to the park for a yoga class and walked home.*).
- Recognize and edit sentences where subordinate clauses are incorrectly formed and interfere with sentence clarity and precision (e.g., Lisa is prone to catching colds, *which she has had from when she was a child*

[cf. Loban, 1976]; edited to be *Since she was a child,* Lisa has been prone to catching colds).

Commercial sources abound for sentence editing practice materials. Model sentences provide practice navigating a variety of editing concerns such as using clauses and phrases, editing for grammatical person and number, optimizing sentence length and complexity, using the active voice, ordering adjectives in a standard way, and so on. Sentences would allow for editing of the mechanics of writing to create meaning. Punctuation, capitalization, use of quotation marks, and so forth would be learned and edited in the service of semantic, syntactic, and pragmatic meanings. The strength of some of the published resources is that the sentence edits are accompanied by explanations of the grammatical rules that govern the edits. Students who intuitively edit can learn the metalinguistic content that will allow for consistent use of this grammatical form, and students who are learning a new grammatical form are transitioning not just to the production of the form but to the metalinguistic awareness of why and how to use this form. In the same way that teachers may include a "daily edit" as a quick task to make good use of time before the morning bell rings or at transition times during the school day, SLPs would have to option to include a "daily edit" within speech-language therapy sessions, where students have the SLP's guidance to edit a small number of model sentences each day, providing cumulative practice and working toward mastery of specific sentence forms. This brief task can have the feeling of being low intensity and low effort, but its impact would be ascertained over time. As for examples of the marketplace of online materials, IXL

Learning (2021) offers a comprehensive website of *Common Core State Standards*–based learning targets and lesson strategies, including banks of sentences for editing. Along with being used to edit students' written sentences, sentence editing software (for instance, *Ginger Grammar,* 2021b) can provide models of correctly edited sentences. These models lend themselves to imitative writing tasks, where students generate their own sentences using the grammar, syntax, and mechanics of the model sentences.

When students are working in groups, SLPs can assign different proofreading tasks to specific individuals in each group (Chin, n.d.). For example, one student might proofread for spelling and punctuation errors, while another would search for noun-verb agreement errors. Ortlieb (2014) referred to one aspect of the revising and editing phase as "feedback and final touches" where writers make sure that their text achieves its desired effect by soliciting the opinions of readers. Sharing, revising, and editing would be incorporated into a socially mediated, rewarding interpersonal experience that reinforces students for the hard work of prewriting and drafting text.

Interventions to Develop Skills in Written Composition

As described by Scardamalia and Bereiter (1985) and Newcomer and Barenbaum (1991), composition entails generating ideas, usually based upon the writer's background knowledge. Ideas for compositions reflect writers' semantic storehouses of meaning and call upon writers' pragmatic past experiences in real-life contexts. Writers recall sets of related information that can be used in their compositions. Beyond idea generation, composition involves planning how to express these ideas. All of this necessitates sustained thinking about a topic, which means that student writers need time to think, to plan, and then to compose their drafts. Newcomer and Barenbaum (1991) noted that students who have difficulty writing try to just "pour out whatever information comes to mind, without organizing their ideas in relationship to the major premise" (p. 579) of their intended composition. SLPs would attend to how students can organize their semantic and pragmatic knowledge bases to approach writing in mindful and planful ways.

Semantic Content: Language Choices When Writing

Students can be taught to structure their writing around information units (Trabasso et al., 1984, as reported by Mason, 2013). An information unit is composed of the phrases or sentences that capture one idea or piece of information. Students can learn to structure their texts around identifying information units and to employ the vocabulary and sentences that convey the information. Sometimes an information unit has a one-to-one correspondence with a sentence, but at other times, an information unit requires multiple sentences. This planning can impose needed restrictions on sentence meaning and keep sentences from veering off topic. Sentences that are determined to be relevant can be refined and edited. This is a meaning-based approach to improving sentence form.

Nippold (2007 p. 35) proposed a "literate lexicon," meaning, an inventory of the types of more sophisticated words that

school-age and adolescent learners would incorporate into their vocabularies. Learners would acquire these more complex words and incorporate their usage in accordance with their appropriate grammatical forms within multiword sentence syntax. These words would be learned by means of direct instruction, which might include teachers' or SLPs' guidance in the morphological analysis and the metalinguistic study of words, their meanings, and their usage in purposeful communications. Learning would also arise from "contextual abstractions" (Nippold, 2007, p. 35), meaning, learning words and phrases in context or via incidental learning, as would occur during a conversation, or when reading, or when viewing media. The word or phrase meaning is abstracted, that is, it is realized, surmised, deduced, or inferred based on contextual semantic, syntactic, and pragmatic information and the meaning of the surrounding messages and circumstances. This process of abstraction can be assisted by sharing ideas with others, or learners can accomplish their realization by thinking independently.

Consideration of the "literate lexicon" would allow SLPs to design grammar and syntax facilitations that use words of sufficient complexity to generate complex sentence structures. A lexicon that is appropriately complex for school-age and adolescent learners (see Nippold, 2007, pp. 35–46, for more detailed explanations) would include:

- Polysemous words (i.e., multiple meaning words), some of which may be abstract, meaning, representational of ideas rather than concrete objects; or words' alternative meanings may be metaphorical or nonliteral; words that change their meanings to become technical terms or terms of art for various disciplines, as in, *run* meaning production: "The factory completed its run of faucet handles"; *run* meaning duration: "The play had a pretty good *run* during summer stock, being performed in six states for an average of four shows per venue"; also prepositions that are employed in numerous semantic and syntactic ways in two-word verbs or other phrasal constructions as in, "she went *up* against another candidate," "count *up* the proceeds," "we ran *up* against an obstacle to meeting our deadline," "it's *up* to you," "that issue is not *up* for discussion").

- One type of polysemy is double-function terms, meaning words that have a physical meaning and a psychological meaning, as in *hard, sweet, cold, deep, crooked, bright*; the primary or more common meaning may be the physical term, or the secondary or less common meaning may be the physical term, depending on the word and the sentence-level context: *He was a cold person* is probably a psychological judgment rather than an observation of a person's temperature.

- Abstract nouns (i.e., words that represent conditions, circumstances, ideas, or states of being, as in, *freedom, endurance, culture, opinion*).

- Adverbs of likelihood (i.e., possibility or probability expressed by subjective meanings or states of gradualness or continuity, e.g., *possibly, likely, probably, definitely, for sure, positively*).

- Adverbs of magnitude (i.e., degrees of meaning that might refer to measurable or perceivable conditions,

e.g., *slight, somewhat, rather, very, extremely*).

- Metacognitive verbs, which are words that refer to thinking (see younger children's development of epistemic words as described in Chapter 2); complex metacognitive terms might include *suggest, imply, predict, interpret, assume, confirm*; verbs may describe veracity (e.g., *telling the truth, kidding, pretending, teasing*), certainty (e.g., *know, expect, be sure, guess*), and cognitive processes (*remember, forget, figure out*).

- Factive verbs assert the truth or certainty of the information that follows the factive verb, as in, "I *know* that you like sports cars."

- Nonfactive verbs convey uncertainty about the information that follows the nonfactive verb, as in "I *think* I have my mom's permission to stay out late tonight."

- Metalinguistic verbs, which are words that refer to how language is formed and used, such as *subject and predicate, title, caption, message, politeness words, independent clause*.

- Mental state words, which are words that go beyond descriptions of simple feeling states like *happy* or *sad* to express more complex mental states, such as *regret, impassioned, conflicted*; mental state words would be applied to one's own mental states and those of others, signaling the ability to empathize with how others think and feel.

Pragmatic Consideration for Composition Skills

Considerations for interventions to improve sentence writing would address how syntactic form is developed in the service of functional pragmatic development and how grammar and syntax help students learn information in academic settings and in daily living (cf. Silliman & Scott, 2009). Chapter 5 discussed the need for students to engage in reading comprehension activities that facilitate becoming familiar with the components and intentions of expository text and narrative text, and that teach the similarities and differences across these text genres. Strong readers have the foundation for becoming strong writers, although the transition from comprehending reading to competent writing is not automatic within or across genres (Purcell-Gates et al., 2007). Students who understand that expository texts primarily serve the purposes of providing information and storing information on record (Smith, 1977) would have learned that the authors of expository text prepare readers to take an *efferent reading* stance (McGee, 1992), meaning, the authors write in ways that allow readers to gain knowledge, perform actions, solve problems, make decisions, analyze concepts, test out propositions, and draw conclusions. Student writers would be guided to use the wording, syntax, and text structures that guide their readers to gather information from texts. The efferent stance is a *macrostructural* concern that is played out at the *microstructural* level, exemplified by word choice, syntactic arrangement, the use of text features such as dialogue or quotations, paragraph development, and other compositional factors. However, not all text is informational, and not all reading is efferent. In contrast, students who understand the purposes of narrative texts would know that narratives primarily serve the purpose of providing an aesthetic experience (Fitzgerald & Teasley, 1986). The *aesthetic*

reading stance (McGee, 1992), whether on the part of readers or writers, is guided by the purpose that texts bring enjoyment to readers and provoke emotional responses. Aesthetic reading brings pleasure and insight to readers, so the writers of narratives, be those nonfiction narratives or fictional narratives, write in "poetic" ways that entice readers to feel emotions while reading; to visualize settings, characters, and events; to react with their hearts as well as their minds; to escape from reality and imagine places, people, and events they have never experienced; to identify with characters and their experiences and, perhaps, gain self-understanding; and to discover deep and personalized meanings when they read. Again, this macrostructural purpose is realized by the microstructural concerns at the word, sentence, paragraph, and chapter levels that writers of narrative attend to carefully (see Justice et al., 2006, for a discussion of microstructural concerns in school-age learners' narratives).

School-age and adolescent learners develop the ability to write narratives, often by being given specific instruction and interventions that address the features of narrative text (Fitzgerald & Teasley, 1986), but some kinds of narratives are easier to fabricate than others. Personal narratives tend to be among the easier narratives to produce, mainly owing to the fact that writers are recalling and describing events that were experienced firsthand. However, within the genre of personal narrative is an array of complexity. Moving from the simple to the complex, types of personal narratives include:

- Recounts: Writings about one's own past experience (that being a lived-through experience or something that was read or learned about).

- The reader would have been present for this event or would have had a similar experience; to an extent, there may be shared situational knowledge; writers do not need to provide as many details, examples, explanations, and so on.
- Accounts: Writings about one's own past experience (a lived-through experience or something that was read or learned about) for an audience that was not present for this experience; there is no presumption of shared situational knowledge, so there is a greater demand on the writers to present the circumstances in a comprehensible fashion to naïve readers.
- Event casts: Writings to portray real or imaginary future events.
  - Some event casts are narratives that predict what will happen in a scenario or acquaint readers with possibilities that are potentially new or yet to be experienced; an example might be asking students to write about how they picture themselves being in a year from the present time.
- Stories: The writer interprets factual or fictitious scenarios and events using story structures, story grammar elements, and the conventions of storytelling.
  - Stories are generally imaginary or fictionalized, even if based on true events.
  - Some stories are told from the point of view of another person, which requires the writer to take on the narrator's point of view.

Based on this progression in complexity, it might not be easy for students to produce a writing sample if given only the instructions, "I want you to write a story." This could well be the most difficult writing task that examiners could request. Consider the writing demands that adults typically have in their daily lives. Adults post recounts and accounts on social media and in correspondences with friends and family with great frequency; in some cases, adults post event casts, such as predicting which candidate will win an election and why this will occur. But it's rare that adults write a story, and it may be impractical to ask students to invest a lot of time in learning how to write stories. Students' future needs would be better served by practicing how to write recounts, accounts, and event casts.

In terms of the complexity of expository writing tasks, a general progression from simpler to more complex writing assignments might include the following:

- Describing processes (for example, writing about changes in the weather).
- Describing meta-processes (for example, writing about how people study changes in the weather).
- Writing about how to make a choice.
- Writing about how to create a product.
- Writing about similarities and/or dissimilarities (among things, events, and circumstances).
- Writing about general categories of things, occurrences, and events and describing specific examples of these general groupings.

Embedded within this task progression are the genres of exposition, for example, descriptive writing, persuasive writing, explanatory writing, and so on. This progression allows for writing about personal observations and experiences, which is a task that might be more accessible and attainable for student writers.

Developmental considerations would be important when SLPs design writing prompts with macrostructural purposes in mind. Nippold (2007) offered that writing prompts would reflect the pragmatic capabilities of school-age and adolescent learners. The topics would need to be relevant to learners' academic preparation in writing and would of an appropriate level of developmental and academic complexity to stimulate writing sophisticated sentences. Some suggestions might include:

- Write dialogue between people and characters; imagine a conversation between yourself and a favorite story character, actor, athlete, musician, and so on.
- Factual comments. Write sentences to tell facts about an item of interest, whether that is a sport, a game, a school subject, a movie or TV show, or the student's family, or neighborhood, or a place where the student likes to go.
- Attend to passage coherence concerns; write sentences to signal topic shifts, for example, "Another thing for us to think about is ____," "Something else that interests me is ____," "Moving on, there is ____."
- Rewrite the same information but for different readers. For example, compose alternative email messages to wish a happy birthday to friends, to a teacher, and to a grandmother. Write sentences that would be appropriate for a class book report to explain why you liked a book, versus writing sentences that you'd

post on social media to share that you like a book.
- Expand the outlines, notes, and semantic webs that are used in class or to study to create full sentences for a school assignment.
- Write sentences to retell a chapter or passage of a fictional book.
- Write sentences to explain how to do something (i.e., procedural writing, for example, how to take care of a pet).
- Write sentences to persuade or influence someone (for example, to ask other students to give a small amount of money to a school fundraiser by purchasing a snack or a special T-shirt) (cf. Brimo & Hall-Mills, 2019).
- Write sentences to give directions to complete a task, for example, packing lunch for school.
- Write descriptive paragraphs (Datchuk, 2016; Datchuk & Kubina, 2017).
- Write about something that happened to you (a personal anecdote), then write about something that happened to someone else (a vicarious anecdote; see Nippold, 2007).

Students' pragmatic awareness helps them differentiate the specific purposes that sentences may have within passages. For example, a topic sentence, a main idea sentence, sentences that supply paragraph details, and concluding sentences would use syntactic elements that are appropriate to the paragraph structure. Chin (n.d.) offered the suggestion that teachers and SLPs would help students revise their sentences to craft the effective word choices for enacting the sentence's role in a passage. Students can read aloud the sentences they write using an interpretive voice (as described in Chapter 5) to help them determine whether their sentences are serving their needed roles within passages.

Mason (2013) described the PLANS writing strategy. PLANS provides a framework for setting writing goals and offers a series of steps for creating written products. These goals bring together the syntactic and pragmatic elements of compositional processes: (1) *P*ick goals for an essay, (2) *L*ist ways to meet goals, (3) *A*nd make *N*otes (creating outlines and notes that have important words and phrases), and (4) *S*equence notes to compose a text. The PLANS process can incorporate as many elements of effective writing strategies as educators and SLPs need to target, for instance, making organizational notes to plan out main ideas and their supporting details. Students can plan how to be more expressive by trying out effective opening and concluding sentences. Students can set goals to choose appropriate vocabulary and check their sources of information so that the material they convey is accurate. Editing goals may remind students to use editorial procedures, such as to combine short sentences into compound or complex sentences or to separate run-on ideas into individual sentences. Proofreading goals can remind students to choose the necessary connector words and to use writing mechanics correctly and to convey meaning. SLPs can set objectives for increasing competence in the use of online sentence construction and punctuation tools, such as *Grammarly* (2021), *Ginger Grammar* (2021b), or the editing functions built into word processing software.

Another consideration that underscores the interrelationship of written language pragmatics and syntax is the relative difficulty of adopting different writing stances, which take into account the communicative perspectives of the authors and the readers of texts. Narrative and expository writing each employ many communicative perspectives, some of which are easier to impart and some of which are more difficult. SLPs would be mindful of the difficulty of the communicative stance that the student writer would be asked to adopt, as this might influence how difficult it might be for students to complete the pragmatic demands of the writing task while bringing to bear their grammatical and syntactic abilities. One important aspect of how writers take on communicative perspectives arises from the extent of the writers' awareness of their audiences' perspectives. Writers would design their communications based on whether they believe that they and their audiences share knowledge or do not share knowledge about the topics or events that will be discussed in the text. There are essentially four communicative perspectives from which writers choose and which influence their syntactic choices when writing:

- Topics and/or events in the writer's and reader's shared present.
- Topics and/or events in the writer's and reader's shared past.
- Topics and/or events presumed to be generally shared or common knowledge.
- Topics and/or events presumed not to be shared or common knowledge and for which the writer provides explanation.

In all, written language competence involves the development of skills as well as the refinement of a craft. As Hansen et al. (1985) and Dyson (1989) discussed, an optimal way to improve students' writing is to create successful writing experiences. A favorable climate for developing competence and confidence features adults who affirm their learners' attempts at writing and provide their own examples of skillful writing, and who model that writing is an enjoyable communicative activity.

Conclusion

The purpose of this text has been to provide readers with an in-depth understanding of the grammatical and syntactic properties of language. The information provided may aid SLPs in becoming better prepared to diagnose grammatical and syntactic difficulties and to appropriately intervene to improve language learning. The intention of this text has been to focus on describing the skills of competent users of grammar and syntax, to explore assessment strategies that can identify deficits in grammar and syntax, and to provide

interventions to improve grammar and syntax. This text has offered suggestions for applying grammar and syntax assessment results to help explain why students may be struggling with school curricular demands.

Each chapter has emphasized explicit and direct teaching of the structure of language. The information provided has identified the importance of uniting grammatical and syntactic interventions with the pragmatic purposes of listening, speaking, reading, and writing, especially within academic learning contexts. As Prutting and Kirchner (1987) noted, pragmatic language capabilities are foundational for developing school-age learners' and adolescents' grammatical and syntactic capabilities. Learners build their knowledge of the structures of language when they are engaged in using language in various contexts and for a variety of learning and communicative purposes. Improving learners' use of the structural properties of language is dependent upon engaging learners in opportunities for functional, purposeful use of these structures.

aesthetic reading stance Whether on the part of readers or writers, being guided by the purpose that texts bring readers enjoyment and provoke emotional responses.

backchannel feedback Remarks that are made to keep the flow of a conversation going. "Uh-huh," "Right," "Yeah," "Mmmm," are commonly used. These messages have intent, but they are also cohesive devices.

bidialectal Using two dialects. Having the features of two dialects.

bootstrapping A phenomenon of learning that applies when a learner has to learn new categories of meaning, organization, or form when she has no prior learning to build upon. The learner must infer the relevant categories, concepts, and rules and create her own generalizations.

bound morphemes Affixes that have no word meaning by themselves (such as "-ed" and "pre-").

C-unit A method for analysis of syntax. Abbreviation for a "minimal communication unit." C-units measure independent clauses plus their modifiers.

case grammar A semantic grammar that looks at a speaker's selection and ordering of semantic elements. Speakers fill a semantic frame for expressing meaning.

catenatives A catenative verb is similar to an auxiliary verb, as both are referred to as helping verbs or linking verbs, but a catenative is called a chain verb, because it can link with other verbs to form a chain or series of events. Examples are verbs such as "keep" ("keep

working") and "promise" ("promise you will go"). In children's language and in adults' informal language, catenatives "wanna" and "gonna" plus a verb are used.

child-directed speech Adult language that is modified and simplified and spoken directly to young children.

clausal density Measured by reporting the average number of clauses produced per C-unit within a language sample.

clause Clauses can be independent, meaning they have a main verb and the syntactic structure to stand alone as a sentence, or subordinate (also known as dependent clauses or clause modifiers), meaning that they do not stand alone as a complete sentence.

close reading Sustained and careful study of the details of relevant texts, with emphasis on how words, syntax, and the arrangement of sentences contribute to the development of the discourse.

cloze sentences Fill-in-the blank sentences. The word or words omitted help learners think about the meaning, grammar, and syntax of sentences.

code-switching A speaker consciously changes linguistic patterns to adopt the linguistic usage or standards of certain communities.

cognition The various mental processes that include perception, awareness, attention, memory, comprehension, reasoning, organization, problem-solving, judgment, planning, self-regulation, imagination, and intuition.

cognitive connectionism A theory that suggests that language arises from cognitive processes, including attention, perception, memory, information processing, and pattern recognition.

cohesion, coherence Connections of ideas across linguistic units, such as across the shorter units of spoken utterances or written sentences, or across longer units that may contain several ideas, such as across conversational topics or paragraph contents.

complement Complements follow a copula and provide description of the subject: "George is *highly skilled*" or to tell what the subject is: "George is *a technician*."

concurrent validity A test's results would agree with other tests or measures administered to an examinee at the same time period.

construct validity Ascertaining that a test is actually measuring its intended behaviors, achievements, characteristics, traits, attributes, abilities, and/or skills.

content validity A test includes a sufficient and representative number of items that test the appropriate knowledge, skills, behaviors, and/or performances to meet the test's purposes.

content words The nouns, verbs, and adjectives that convey semantic content in sentences. In contrast to form words that structure sentence syntax, including prepositions, articles, conjunctions.

conversational speech acts Young children's language intents that follow the use of primitive speech acts, such as statements, descriptions, and acknowledgments.

copula, copular verb Any form of "to be" that is used as a main verb, rather than as an auxiliary verb.

deep structure Regardless of how a message is phrased, the deep structure conveys the real meaning of a message.

deictic terms, deixis Words that change their contextual meanings depending upon the frame of reference of who is speaking (e.g., here/there, this/that, I/you, mine/yours).

derivational morphemes, derivational morphology Bound morphemes that, when added, may or may not change a word's part of speech. Adding the bound morpheme "-er" to "teach" to form "teacher" changes a verb to a noun, but adding "un" to "tie" to create "untie" does not change the part of speech (both are verbs).

descriptive grammar The grammatical patterns and rules that speakers use. No judgment of grammatical correctness or appropriateness is made; the grammar is simply described.

dialects Speech or language variation that arises from the regional and/or social backgrounds of speakers.

differentiated instruction An approach to teaching where teachers provide learners with different abilities with a variety of approaches to learning instructional content and multiple and varied opportunities to demonstrate their learning.

discourse(s) The entirety of any communicative interaction. Also, the genres of communicative interactions, such as conversation, narration, classroom instruction, and so on.

dynamic assessment If a learner does not respond independently to test stimuli but there is reason to believe that the tasks are within the learner's zone of proximal development, dynamic assessment involves coaching a learner on these competencies and then retesting to determine the learner's stimulability for learning.

dysgraphia Difficulties with written language that are either linguistically based, motor based, or based in both language and motor deficits. Related to specific learning disability, or to a primary impairment, or not related to a primary impairment.

dyslexia Difficulties learning to read that are not related to lesser cognitive skills or other primary impairments.

ecological validity, ecologically valid How well test performance represents behaviors in real-life circumstances; how well test scores generalize to predict performance in real-world contexts.

efferent reading stance Whether on the part of readers or writers, being guided by the purpose that texts share information.

explicit memory Conscious, declarative knowledge that is stored in long-term memory.

expository language, exposition Using language to describe factual information.

form words Words that structure sentence syntax, including prepositions, articles, and conjunctions. In contrast to content words, the nouns, verbs, and adjectives that convey semantic content in sentences.

free morphemes True words that have no affixation.

functional Useful, practical, necessary, positive, or meaningful behaviors, events, outcomes, or consequences. Often used to explain providing functional goals and interventions in school learning contexts that benefit learners in practical ways that are relevant to school success. The meaning of "functional" goals, in contrast to academic goals, can connote that some learners are more appropriately served by stressing nonacademic skills for daily living.

fund of information The semantic system is the repository of verbal information. The semantic terms that a child can understand and use reveal the verbal portion of the child's overall knowledge base.

General American English (GAE)/Standard American English (SAE)/Mainstream American English (MAE) The prescriptive grammar used in the United States.

generative grammar The use of words in patterned and rule-governed ways to generate syntactic constructions. The patterns and rules are the generative grammar of language.

grammar A grammar encompasses the totality of the language's phonological, semantic, morphological, and syntactic patterns.

grammatical categories The grammatical categories of English provide sets of rules for combining words to form phrases, clauses, and sentences. The grammatical categories are grammatical person, grammatical number, grammatical tense, grammatical aspect, grammatical mood, grammatical voice, and grammatical gender.

grammatical morphemes Morphemes that convey grammatical elements, such as affixes that mark verb tenses.

grammaticality A speaker's instinctive, unconscious acquisition of rules governing grammar. Speakers acquire the grammatical patterns that they hear in their linguistic communities.

heuristic Using language to find out what other people know and learn from others.

hierarchical syntactic structures Use of the subject + predicate pattern. Generalized use of many sentence forms. Underlying deep structures take on different surface structures.

holophrastic phrase Use of a single word to convey the meaning that a phrase or sentence might hold.

ideational purpose The mental functions that process human experiences and govern logic.

illocutionary act A speaker or writer's intended meaning of a message.

implicit memory Learning that seems to occur mostly unconsciously.

inflectional morphemes, inflectional morphology Bound morphemes form grammatical variants, such as changing present tense to past tense. The resulting words retain the same part of speech (e.g., "look" and "looked" are both verbs).

intransitive verb A verb that does not require an object ("Jane cried").

kinesics Physical movements that convey meaning.

language-based learning disability (LBLD) Language weakness that affects literacy and school learning. Not related to lesser cognitive skills or other primary impairments.

language delay Progress in language development follows a generally typical pattern but is delayed, meaning that progress occurs at a slower rate and takes more time to be achieved.

language difference Speakers (or communities) who use linguistic patterns that differ from standard or mainstream usage have a language difference.

language disorder or *developmental language disorder* In conceptual terms, the extent to which language, as a system, is not operating properly for functional use. In practical terms, language development is disrupted. There is a problem in language skill, developmental sequence, and pace of development. Limitations may include a restricted language repertoire and gaps in skills, such that a child has only some of the language skills that children need.

language impairment A term that conveys that language, as a structured system, is not intact. Language, as a functional system, is compromised. The structure and/or the function of language are not optimal.

language learning disability (LLD) Language weakness that affects literacy and school learning. Not related to lesser cognitive skills or other primary impairments.

learning disability (LD) Deficit(s) in one or more learning modality. Not related to lesser cognitive skills or other primary impairments.

learning modalities Skills and processes required for learning: attentional skills, auditory skills (auditory perception, auditory processing, and auditory memory), visual skills (visual perception, visual processing, and visual memory), visual-spatial skills, visual-motor skills, language, perceptual-motor skills and sensorimotor skills, reasoning skills, memory storage and retrieval, and self-regulation of learning behaviors (such as organization and perseverance).

lexical density An indicator of syntactic maturity based on the proportionately greater use of main parts of speech (i.e., the high-content nouns, verbs, adjectives, etc.) found in any text, as compared to form words such as articles and conjunctions.

lexical diversity A measure of how many different words and different types of words are used within a language sample.

linear syntactic relationships Words said in succession with the intent to bring together the meanings of the words to create meaningful phrases and short sentences. The result is the cumulative meaning of the words said together.

linguistic pragmatics How a communicator structures the linguistic content of a spoken or written message, including its grammar and syntax.

locutionary act Words and sentences that are spoken or written (in print, this includes punctuation and other print devices).

macrostructures, macrostructural skills The linguistic elements that relate to the overall conventions of genre (narration and exposition) and mode (oral or written), along with the broader elements of text organization, style, and presentation.

mean length of utterance (MLU) A method for analysis of syntax. Using a language sample of 50 to 100 spontaneous utterances, tally the total number of morphemes used in each sentence, divide by the number of utterances spoken, and compute a mean length of utterance.

mediation Guiding a learner to self-examine or reflect upon how to perform a behavior.

memory for communication The ability to retain and recall the substance of a discourse.

message formulation The confluence of semantic and syntactic skill with linguistic pragmatics; using words and sentence structure to impart meaning.

message function(s) Analysis of how messages convey meaningful purpose and intent. Based on the study of speech act theory.

metacognition, metacognitive Examining thought processes; often "thinking about one's own thinking."

metalanguage The language used to talk about language. Used to describe the concepts needed to study language. For example, terms such as "suffix," "noun." Language used to learn about language and acquire literacy.

metalinguistic (skills, awareness, analysis, insight) Conscious awareness of language as an object that can be scrutinized and manipulated. The language and conceptual skills that are needed to analyze language form. For example, detecting syntax patterns, parts of speech, bound morphemes.

metasyntactic awareness The language skills needed to analyze language form.

microstructure, microstructural skills Linguistic details within sentences and words: word choices, sentence formation choices, and the arrangement of words and sentences into messages and passages.

miscue, miscues As a verb, to miscue is to misread a word or words. As a noun, a miscue is the mistake that is made in reading when a word or words is misread.

modal auxiliary verbs In the grammatical category of grammatical mood, modal auxiliaries include "may," "can," "must," "ought," "will," "shall," "need," "dare," "might," "could," "would," and "should." Modals precede an unconjugated form of a verb ("might be," "may have," "can deliver").

morphosyntax, morphosyntactic Linguistic elements are definable by both morphological and syntactic criteria and have both morphological and syntactic properties. For example, "snowball" is defined syntactically as a noun and morphologically as a compound word.

Multitiered Systems of Supports (MTSS) Similar to Response to Intervention (RTI), using data-based problem-solving to integrate instruction, assessment, and intervention for students with learning needs.

narrate, narration, narrative Using language to recount events and circumstances that a speaker or writer has experienced, based on real-life experiences or conjectured, fictional, or imaginary scenarios.

nonsentential utterances Spoken language may contain utterances that are not complete sentences but that feature complex syntax. These utterances are sometimes comparable to the dependent clause of a sentence.

oral interpretation Reading a text aloud expressively; dramatize the meaningful sentence elements and prosodic contours to aid reading fluency and comprehension.

orthographic coding Storing print in working memory in order to analyze the letters during reading and/or writing. The letters and words are stored in long-term memory and linked to the words' meanings and pronunciations for later retrieval.

overregularization To use a morphological or syntactic pattern or a lexical meaning in more ways or in more contexts than an adult would use this pattern.

paralanguage, paralinguistic behaviors Physical actions that accompany or replace verbal messages, such as gestures and facial expressions.

perlocutionary act What a listener or reader interprets a message to mean.

postmodification The words that follow a particular word modify that word.

pragmatic cohesion, pragmatic coherence, pragmatic contingency How speakers or writers manage the transitions between utterances or messages.

predictive validity Performance on a test would predict performance during another circumstance, such as in a grade level or class, or when studying a certain subject matter.

prescriptive grammar Teaching and using the grammar that conforms to a language's standard rules and patterns.

presuppose, presuppositional skills To be able to think about what another person might be thinking or intending to communicate. Or, for a speaker to assume about what another person knows, believes, feels, or has experienced, in order to structure a message that is in relation to the needs of the listener.

primitive speech acts Earlier language intents, such as labeling, repeating, and requesting.

productivity (productive language, productively use language) Children can produce utterances that they have not heard said by others.

prosody An acoustical feature of speech that connects the speech segments of phonemes and syllables, plus the suprasegmental features of speech, such as rate, tempo, rhythm, melody, pitch, cadence, and amplitude.

proxemics How spatially close communication partners can comfortably be—from barely an inch to many feet apart.

psycholinguistics A domain of study within two fields, psychology and linguistics, that investigates the interface of thought and language.

readability A measure of the difficulty of a text passage computed based on various factors, such as sentence length, word length, and other morphological, grammatical, and syntactic features of the text.

relational meaning The meaning of a phrase is determined by the placement of the words in a linear structure.

Response to Intervention (RTI) Similar to Multitiered Systems of Supports (MTSS). An instructional model where assessment data and progress monitoring identify the students who need learning supports and inform decisions about instructional supports and interventions.

scaffolding Supports for learning, so that a child can demonstrate the competencies that he can perform with help.

semantic memory As part of the brain's information processing system, the semantic system symbolizes sensory, experiential, and cognitive information as words and stores these relevant words in semantic memory. Speakers have a fund of semantic information—concepts, ideas, experiences, names of objects, and so on—that they refer to by using words.

semantic mitigators Also called semantic softeners. Words speakers use to appear less demanding and more polite. Used with imperatives (as well as in other contexts), examples are "please," "would you kindly," and so on.

semantic relations Meaning making beyond the use of single words. Words joined together have enhanced or alternate meanings. Talking in phrases is more effective than using one word at a time. Words become multipurpose when used in a variety of constructions.

semanticize, semanticity To use a word to stand for something else. When a speaker uses words, he semanticizes. When a child uses words as intellectual symbols, he has attained semanticity.

semiotics The study of the signs and symbols that occur in communication contexts. The study of how symbols become communicative phenomena; how people interpret signs and symbols.

Words, sentences, and nonverbal messages can be analyzed for their symbolic content.

social cognition(s) The thoughts about social circumstances and the social judgments that guide language behavior; the thought processes that allow a speaker to meet the needs of a communication partner.

social constructivism The premise that groups construct knowledge.

social pragmatics A speaker or listener's interactional skills meet situational expectations for appropriate communicative behavior.

social register The level of formality and politeness of an interchange.

social validity The success of a message is dependent upon the appraisals made by listeners.

specific language impairment (SLI) Difficulties in language form and content, with or without impaired pragmatics and/or phonology, not attributable to other primary cognitive or developmental impairments.

specific learning disability (SLD) Deficits in spoken language, and/or in learning to read and/or write, and/or in learning mathematics that are not related to lesser cognitive skills or other primary impairments.

stimulability The ability to demonstrate performance of a task after being given a demonstration of the performance or help performing the task.

structural grammar Learning about grammar by studying its structural features with less emphasis on how grammar conveys meaning.

subordinating conjunctions Conjunctions that introduce a subordinate clause.

subordination index An index of syntactic complexity based on the measurement of a speaker's use of clauses. Determined by counting the total number of clauses produced in a language sample divided by the number of C-units.

successive single-word utterances Words said in succession without a true attempt to slot the words into a syntactic pattern.

surface structure How a message is phrased by its grammatical structures. Surface structure manipulates syntactic form and semantic content to achieve the semantic and pragmatic meaning of the deep structure. Surface structures can be paraphrased but still retain a deep structure.

systemic functional linguistics A functional approach to the study of language. Language develops and is used for purposes of making meaning and communicating. Language form serves the purpose of conveying meaning.

T-unit A method for analysis of syntax. An abbreviation for "minimal terminable unit." T-units measure each main clause (independent clause) and all of its subordinate and embedded clauses (dependent clauses).

textual purpose The internal organization and communicative nature of a verbal text, be that a conversation or a written passage.

theory of mind A child's development of the awareness that other people have different thoughts, perspectives, and frames of reference than the child has himself or herself.

transitive verb A verb that requires an object. "He fixed" is incomplete without an object. If the verb suggests the question "What?" (He fixed what?), it is transitive and requires an object, such as "He fixed the faucet."

type-token ratio (TTR) A measure of semantic diversity that shows the number of different words (the "types") within a total number of words in a language sample (the "tokens) to reveal the breadth of words that a speaker used. As with lexical density, type-token ratio shows how much information is contained within a sample.

underregularization To use a morphological or syntactic pattern or a lexical meaning in fewer ways or in fewer contexts than an adult would use this pattern.

verb density The proportion of verbs as compared to the total number of words within a language sample may show syntactic maturity.

verb phrase constituents The forms needed to create basic sentences and to code contractions, negation, and question forms. Includes modal verbs and morphemic markers for present progressive tense, third person singular present, and past tense (as used by dialect variations).

word order relations Words arranged grammatically into phrases and sentences. Use of longer and more varied sentence forms. The arrangement of words conveys meaning.

working memory The temporary span of memory that is used for information processing; information that is in working memory is an active or accessible state, such that attention and processing are focused on this information.

zone of proximal development (ZPD) The level of competence that a child exhibits when given some assistance.

REFERENCES

Abbeduto, L., Benson, G., Short, K., & Dolish, J. (1995). Effects of sampling context on the expressive language of children and adolescents with mental retardation. *Mental Retardation, 33*(5), 279–288. https://doi.org/10.1044/1092-4388(2011/11-0075)

Adams, M. J. (1990). *Beginning to read: Thinking and learning about print.* Massachusetts Institute of Technology.

Adams, M. J. (1998). The three-cueing system. In J. Osborn & F. Lehr (Eds.), *Literacy for all: Issues in teaching and learning* (pp. 73–99). Guilford Press.

Adlof, S. M. (2020a). *2019 ASHA Research Symposium: Suzanne M. Adlof, reading development and reading difficulties in children with specific language impairment.* Media. https://doi.org/10.23641/asha.13063793.v2

Adlof, S. M. (2020b). Promoting reading achievement in children with developmental language disorders: What can we learn from research on specific language impairment and dyslexia? *Journal of Speech, Language, and Hearing Research, 63*(10), 3277–3292. https://doi.org/10.1044/2020_JSLHR-20-00118

Aikhenvald, A. Y. (2004). *Evidentiality.* Oxford University Press.

Allen, M. M., & Petersen, D. B. (2011). Reading comprehension: A proposal for a hybrid approach. *Perspectives on Language Learning and Education, 18*(1), 13–19. https://doi.org/10.1044/lle18.1.13

Altenberg, E. P., Roberts, J. A., & Scarborough, H. S. (2018). Young children's structure production: A revision of the Index of Productive Syntax. *Language, Speech, and Hearing Services in Schools,* 49(4), 995–1008. https://doi.org/10.1044/2018_LSHSS-17-0092

Amen, D. G. (1998). *Change your brain, change your life: The breakthrough program for conquering anxiety, depression, obsessiveness, anger, and impulsiveness.* Three Rivers Press.

American Psychiatric Association. (2013). *Diagnostic and statistical manual of mental disorders* (5th ed.). American Psychiatric Association.

American Speech-Language-Hearing Association. (1991). *A model for collaborative service delivery for students with language-learning disorders in the public schools* [Paper]. https://doi:10.1044/policy.RP1991-00123 https://www.asha.org/policy/RP1991-00123/

American Speech-Language-Hearing Association. (1993). *Definitions of communication disorders and variations* [Relevant paper]. https://doi:10.1044/policy.RP1993-00208 https://www.asha.org/policy/RP1993-00208/

American Speech-Language-Hearing Association. (2001). *Roles and responsibilities of speech-language pathologists with respect to reading and writing in children and adolescents* [Technical report]. https://doi:10.1044/policy.PS2001-00104 https://www.asha.org/policy/PS2001-00104/

American Speech-Language-Hearing Association. (2003). *American English dialects* [Technical report]. https://doi:10.1044/policy.TR2003-00044 https://www.asha.org/policy/TR2003-00044/

American Speech-Language-Hearing Association. (2004). *Preferred practice patterns for the profession of speech-language pathology* [Preferred practice patterns]. https://doi:10.1044/policy.PP2004-00191 https://www.asha.org/policy/PP2004-00191/

American Speech-Language-Hearing Association. (2010). *Roles and responsibilities of speech-language pathologists in schools* [Professional issues statement]. https://doi:10.1044/policy.PI2010-00317 https://www.asha.org/policy/PI2010-00317/

American Speech-Language-Hearing Association. (2016). *Scope of practice in speech-language pathology* [Scope of practice]. https://doi:10.1044/policy.SP2016-00343 https://www.asha.org/policy/SP2016-00343/

American Speech-Language-Hearing Association. (2017). *Issues in ethics: Cultural and linguistic competence.* https://www.asha.org/Practice/ethics/Cultural-and-Linguistic-Competence/

American Speech-Language-Hearing Association. (2018a). *Assessment tools, techniques, and data sources.* https://www.asha.org/practice-portal/clinical-topics/late-language-emergence/assessment-tools-techniques-and-data-sources/

American Speech-Language-Hearing Association. (2018b). *How to work for change in school settings: FAQs.* https://www.asha.org/advocacy/changefaqs/

American Speech-Language-Hearing Association. (2021, April 3). School-based SLPs treat wide-ranging conditions. *The ASHA Leader.* https://leader.pubs.asha.org/do/10.1044/leader.AAG.26042021.24/full/?utm_source=asha&utm_medium=enewsletter&utm_term=featured&utm_content=042021&utm_campaign=ashanow

American Speech-Language-Hearing Association. (n.d.-a). *School-based service delivery in speech-language pathology.* https://www.asha.org/slp/schools/school-based-service-delivery-in-speech-language-pathology/

American Speech-Language-Hearing Association. (n.d.-b). *Specific learning disabilities.* https://www.asha.org/advocacy/federal/idea/04-law-specific-ld/

American Speech-Language-Hearing Association. (n.d.-c). *Spoken language disorders.* https://www.asha.org/practice-portal/clinical-topics/spoken-language-disorders/

American Speech-Language-Hearing Association. (n.d.-d). *Written language disorders.* https://www.asha.org/practice-portal/clinical-topics/written-language-disorders/

Analysis of the English word and sentence structure [Power Point slides]. (2009). *SlideShare.* http://www.slideshare.net/moniozy/morphemes

Analyze My Writing. (n.d.). https://www.analyzemywriting.com/index.html

Anderson, C. M., Turtura, J., & Parry, M. (2013). Addressing instructional avoidance with Tier II supports. *Journal of Applied School Psychology, 29*(2), 167–182. https://doi.org/10.1080/15377903.2013.778772

Anderson, R. C., Wilson, P., & Fielding, L. (1988). Growth in reading and how children spend their time out of school. *Reading Research Quarterly, 23*(3), 285–303. https://doi.org/10.1598/RRQ.23.3.2

Andolina, C. (1980). Syntactic maturity and vocabulary richness of learning disabled children at four age levels. *Journal of Learning Disabilities, 13*(7), 27–32. https://doi.org/10.1177/002221948001300705

Angel, S. E., Butler, Y. G., Cichra, D. L., Moore, C. C., & Simonet, J. (2009). How do I work with the reading teacher without becoming one? *Perspectives on School-Based Issues, 10*(2), 45–50. https://doi.org/10.1044/sbi10.2.45

Angell, C. A. (2009). *Language development and disorders: A case study approach.* Jones and Bartlett.

Apel, K. (2017). Development and assessment: What do we know? *Perspectives on Language and Literacy, 43*(2), 11–16. https://mydigitalpublication.com/publication/?m=13959&i=398575&p=1&ver=html5

Apel, K., & Hall-Mills, S. (2015). Linguistic feature development across grades and genre in elementary writing. *Language, Speech, and Hearing Services in Schools, 46,* 242–255. https://doi.org/10.1044/2015_LSHSS-14-0043

Apel, K., & Werfel, K. (2014). Using morphological awareness instruction to improve written language skills. *Language, Speech & Hearing Services in Schools, 45*(4), 251–260. https://doi.org/10.1044/2014_LSHSS-14-0039

Applebee, A. N. (1978). *The child's concept of story.* University of Chicago Press.

Applebee, A. N. (1984). Writing and reasoning. *Review of Educational Research, 54*(4), 577–596. https://doi.org/10.3102/00346543054004577

Applebee, A. N., & Langer, J. A. (2006). *The state of writing instruction in America's schools: What existing data tell us.* Center on English Learning and Achievement. University at Albany, State University of New York. https://eric.ed.gov/?id=ED494608

Applebee, A. N., & Langer, J. A. (2009). What is happening in the teaching of writing? *English Journal, 98*(5), 18–28. https://archive.nwp.org/cs/public/download/nwp_file/12493/What_is_Happening_in_the_Teaching_of_Writing_Applebee_Langer.pdf?x-r=pcfile_d

Applebee, A. N., & Langer, J. A. (2011a). *The national study of writing instruction: Methods and procedures.* Center on English Learning and Achievement. University at Albany, State University of New York.

Applebee, A. N., & Langer, J. A. (2011b). A snapshot of writing instruction in middle schools and high schools. *English Journal, 100*(6), 14–27. https://www.jstor.org/stable/23047875

Applebee, A. N., Langer, J. A., Wilcox, K. C., Nachowitz, M., Mastroianni, M. P., & Dawson, C. (2013). *Writing instruction that works.* Teachers College Press and the National Writing Project.

Aram, D. M., Ekelman, B. L., & Nation, J. E. (1984). Preschoolers with language dis-

orders: 10 years later. *Journal of Speech and Hearing Research, 27,* 232–244. https://doi.org/10.1044/jshr.2702.244

Atwell, N. (1987). *In the middle: Writing, reading, and learning with adolescents.* Boynton/Cook.

Austin, J. (1962). *How to do things with words.* Oxford University Press.

Bader, L. A., & Pearce, D. (2012). *Reading and language inventory* (7th ed.). Pearson.

Balason, D. V., & Dollaghan, C. A. (2002). Grammatical morpheme production in 4-year-old children. *Journal of Speech, Language, and Hearing Research, 45*(5), 961–969. https://doi.org/10.1044/1092-4388(2002/078)

Balthazar, C. H., & Scott, C. M. (2015). The place of syntax in school age language assessment and intervention. In T. A. Ukrainetz (Ed.), *School-age language intervention: Evidence-based practices* (pp. 279–334). Pro-Ed.

Balthazar, C. H., & Scott, C. M. (2017). Complex sentence intervention. In R. J. McCauley, M. E. Fey, & R. B. Gillam (Eds.), *Treatment of language disorders in children* (2nd ed.). Brookes.

Balthazar, C. H., & Scott, C. M. (2018). Targeting complex sentences in older school children with specific language impairment: Results from an early-phase treatment study. *Journal of Speech, Language, and Hearing Research, 61*(3), 713–728. https://doi.org/10.1044/2017_JSLHR-L-17-0105

Barako Arndt, K. B., & Schuele, C. M. (2013). Multiclausal utterances aren't just for big kids. *Topics in Language Disorders, 33*(2), 125–139. https://doi.org/10.1097/TLD.0b013e31828f9ee8

Baron-Cohen, S., Leslie, A. M., & Frith, U. (1985). Does the autistic child have a "theory of mind"? *Cognition, 21*(1), 37–46. https://doi.org/10.1016/0010-0277(85)90022-8

Bates, E., Devescovi, A., & Wulfeck, B. (2001). Psycholinguistics: A cross-language perspective. *Annual Review of Psychology, 52,*

369–398. https://doi.org/10.1146.annurev .psych.52.1.369

Bates, E., & MacWhinney, B. (1982). Functionalist approaches to grammar. In E. Wanner & L. Gleitman (Eds.), *Language acquisition: The state of the art* (pp. 173–218). Cambridge University Press.

Bates, E., & MacWhinney, B. (1987). Competition, variation and language learning. In B. MacWhinney (Ed.), *Mechanisms of language acquisition* (pp. 157–193). Erlbaum.

Bates, E., Thal, D., & MacWhinney, B. (1991). A functionalist approach to language and its implications for assessment and intervention. In T. M. Gallagher (Ed.), *Pragmatics of language: Clinical practice issues* (pp. 133–161). Singular Publishing.

Battle, D. E. (2009). Assessment and intervention for culturally and linguistically diverse children. In D. K. Bernstein & E. Tiegerman-Farber (Eds.), *Language and communication disorders in children* (6th ed., pp. 536–576). Pearson Education.

Battle, D. E. (2011). *Communication disorders in multicultural populations* (4th ed.). Elsevier.

Beck, I. L., & McKeown, M. G. (2006). *Improving comprehension with Questioning the Author: A fresh and expanded view of a powerful approach*. Scholastic.

Bedore, L. M., & Leonard, L. B. (1998). Specific language impairment and grammatical morphology: A discriminant function analysis. *Journal of Speech, Language, and Hearing Research, 41*(5), 1185–1192. https://doi.org/10.1044/jslhr.4105.1185

Bedore, L. M., & Peña, E. D. (2008). Assessment of bilingual children for identification of language impairment: Current findings and implications for practice. *The International Journal of Bilingual Education and Bilingualism, 11*(1), 1–29. https:// doi.org/10.2167/beb392.0

Beers, S., & Nagy, W. (2009). Syntactic complexity as a predictor of adolescent writing quality: Which measures? Which genre? *Reading & Writing, 22*(2), 185–200. https://doi.org/10.1007/s11145-007 -9107-5

Beilinson, J. S., & Olswang, L. B. (2003). Facilitating peer-group entry in kindergarteners with impairments in social communication. *Language, Speech, and Hearing Services in Schools, 34*(2), 154–166. https://doi.org/10.1044/0161-1461(2003 /013)

Beitchman, J. H., Wilson, B., Brownlie, E. B., Walters, H., & Lancee, W. (1996). Longterm consistency in speech/language profiles: I. Developmental and academic outcomes. *Journal of the American Academy of Child and Adolescent Psychiatry, 35*, 804–814. https://doi.org/10.1097/00004583 -199606000-00021

Belanger, J. F. (1978). Calculating the Syntactic Density Score: A mathematical problem. *Research in the Teaching of English, 12*(2), 149–153. https://www.jstor.org/sta ble/40170692

Bergmann, A., Hall, K. C., & Ross, S. M. (2007). *Language files: Materials for an introduction to language and linguistics* (10th ed.). The Ohio State University Press.

Berko Gleason, J., & Bernstein Ratner, N. (Eds.). (1997). *Psycholinguistics*. Wadsworth.

Berko Gleason, J., & Bernstein Ratner, N. (Eds.). (2009). *The development of language* (7th ed.). Allyn & Bacon.

Berninger, V. W. (2008). Defining and differentiating dysgraphia, dyslexia, and language learning disability within a working memory model. In M. Mody & E. R. Silliman (Eds.), *Brain, behavior, and learning in language and reading disorders* (pp. 103–134). Guilford Press.

Berninger, V. W., & Abbott, R. D. (2010). Listening comprehension, oral expression, reading comprehension, and written expression: Related yet unique language systems in Grades 1, 3, 5, and 7. *Journal of Educational Psychology, 102*(3), 635–651. https://doi.org/10.1037/a0019319

Berninger, V. W., Nagy, W., & Beers, S. (2011). Child writers' construction and reconstruction of single sentences and construction of multi-sentence texts: Contributions of syntax and transcription to translation. *Reading & Writing, 24*(2), 151–

182. https://doi.org/10.1007/s11145-010-9262-y

Berninger, V. W., & Wolf, B. (2009a). *Helping students with dyslexia and dysgraphia make connections: Differentiated instruction lesson plans in reading and writing.* Brookes.

Berninger, V. W., & Wolf, B. (2009b). *Teaching students with dyslexia and dysgraphia: Lessons from teaching and science.* Brookes.

Bernstein, D. K., & Levey, S. (2009). Language development: A review. In D. K. Bernstein & E. Tiegerman-Farber (Eds.), *Language and communication disorders in children* (6th ed., pp. 28–100). Pearson Education.

Bernstein Ratner, N., Brundage, S. B., & Fromm, D. (2020). A clinician's complete guide to CLAN and PRAAT. *TalkBank.* https://talkbank.org/manuals/Clin-CLAN.pdf

Bernstein Ratner, N., & MacWhinney B. (2016). Your laptop to the rescue: Using the Child Language Data Exchange System Archive and CLAN utilities to improve child language sample analysis. *Seminars in Speech and Language, 37*(2), 74–84. https://doi.org/10.1055/s-0036-1580742

Beverly, B. L., & Williams, C. C. (2004). Present tense *be* use in young children with specific language impairment: Less is more. *Journal of Speech and Hearing Research, 47,* 944–956. https://doi.org/10.1044/1092-4388(2004/070)

Biancarosa, G., & Snow, C. (2006). Reading next—A vision for action and research in middle and high school literacy. *Alliance for Excellent Education.* https://all4ed.org/reports-factsheets/reading-next-a-vision-for-action-and-research-in-middle-and-high-school-literacy/

Biber, D. (1988). *Variation across speech and writing.* Cambridge University Press.

Biber, D. (1992). On the complexity of discourse complexity: A multidimensional analysis. *Discourse Processes, 15*(2), 133–163. https://doi.org/10.1080/01638539209544806

Biber, D., Johansson, S., Leech, G., Conrad, S., & Finegan, E. (1999). *Longman grammar of spoken and written English.* Longman.

Bishop, D. V. M., & Adams, C. (1990). A prospective study of the relationship between specific language impairment, phonological disorders and reading retardation. *Journal of Child Psychology and Psychiatry, 31,* 1027–1050. https://doi.org/10.1111/j.1469-7610.1990.tb00844.x

Bishop, D. V. M., Bright, P., James, C., Bishop, S. J., & Van Der Lely, H. K. J. (2000). Grammatical SLI: A distinct subtype of developmental language impairment? *Applied Psycholinguistics, 21,* 159–181. https://doi.org/10.1017/S0142716400002010

Bishop, D. V. M., & Donlan, C. (2005). The role of syntax in encoding and recall of pictorial narratives: Evidence from specific language impairment. *British Journal of Developmental Psychology, 23,* 25–46. https://doi.org/10.1348/026151004X20685

Bishop, D. V. M., & Snowling, M. J. (2004). Developmental dyslexia and specific language impairment: Same or different? *Psychological Bulletin, 130*(6), 858–886. https://doi.org/10.1037/0033-2909.130.6.858

Blake, J., Quartaro, G., & Onorati, S. (1993). Evaluating quantitative measures of grammatical complexity in spontaneous speech samples. *Journal of Child Language, 20,* 139–152. https://doi.org/10.1017/S0305000900009168

Blank, A., Holt, R. F., & Wagner, L. (2020). Inhibitory control and receptive vocabulary influence aspect comprehension in children. *Applied Psycholinguistics, 41,* 133–151. https://doi.org/10.1017/S0142716419000432

Bloom, L. (1991). *Language development from two to three.* Cambridge University Press.

Bloom, L., & Lahey, M. (1978). *Language development and language disorders.* John Wiley.

Bloom, L., Lifter, K., & Hafitz, J. (1980). Semantics of verbs and the development of verb inflection in child language. *Language, 56*, 386–412. https://doi.org/10.2307/413762

Bock, J. K. (1986). Syntactic persistence in language production. *Cognitive Psychology, 18*(3), 355–387. https://doi.org/10.1016/0010-0285(86)90004-6.

Boersma, P., & Weenink, D. (n.d.). *PRAAT: Doing phonetics by computer.* https://www.fon.hum.uva.nl/praat/

Boudreau, D., & Costanza-Smith, A. (2011). Assessment and treatment of working memory deficits in school-age children: The role of the speech-language pathologist. *Language, Speech, and Hearing Services in Schools, 42*, 152–166. https://doi.org/10.1044/0161-1461(2010/09-0088)

Braginsky, M., Yurovsky, D., Marchman, V., & Frank, M. (2015). *Developmental changes in the relationship between grammar and the lexicon.* dyurovsky.github.io/cdi-grammar/

Branigan, H., & Pickering, M. (2017). An experimental approach to linguistic representation. *Behavioral and Brain Sciences, 40*, e282. https://doi.org/10.1017/S0140525X16002028

Bridges, M. S. (2011). Identifying and addressing reading comprehension within a Response to Intervention framework. *Perspectives on Language Learning and Education, 18*(1), 20–26. https://doi.org/10.1044/lle18.1.20

Brimo, D., & Hall-Mills, S. (2019). Adolescents' production of complex syntax in spoken and written expository and persuasive genres. *Clinical Linguistics & Phonetics, 33*, 237–255. https://doi.org/10.1080/02699206.2018.1504987

Brinton, B., Fujiki, M., & Baldridge, M. (2010). The trajectory of language impairment into adolescence: What four young women can teach us. *Seminars in Speech and Language, 31*, 122–134. https://doi.org/10.1055/s-0030-1252113

Britton, J. N. (1984). Viewpoints: The distinction between participant and spectator role language in research and practice. *Research in the Teaching of English, 18*(3), 320–330.

Brown, H., & Cambourne, B. (1990). *Read and retell.* Heinemann.

Brown, R. (1973). *A first language: The early stages.* Harvard University Press.

Brown, V. L., Wiederholt, J. L., & Hammill, D. D. (2009). *Test of Reading Comprehension–Fourth Edition (TORC-4).* Pro-Ed.

Brozo, V. G. (2010), Response to Intervention or responsive instruction? Challenges and possibilities of Response to Intervention for adolescent literacy. *Journal of Adolescent and Adult Literacy, 53*(4), 277–281. https://doi.org/10.1598/JAAL.53.4.1

Bruner, J. (1978). Learning the mother tongue. *Human Nature, 1*, 42–49.

Bryant, D. P., Vaughn, S., Linan-Thompson, S., Ugel, N., Hamff, A., & Hougen, M. (2000). Reading outcomes for students with and without reading disabilities in general education middle-school content area classes. *Learning Disability Quarterly, 23*(4), 238–252. https://doi.org/10.2307/1511347

Brydon, M. (2018). Why standardized tests might not be enough. *The Informed SLP.* https://www.theinformedslp.com/qa_lsa.html

Caccamise, D. (2011). Improved reading comprehension by writing. *Perspectives on Language Learning and Education, 18*(1), 27–31. https://doi.org/10.1044/lle18.1.27

Calkins, L. (1994). *The art of teaching writing.* Heinemann.

Campbell, L. R. (1993). Maintaining the integrity of home linguistic varieties: Black English Vernacular. *American Journal of Speech-Language Pathology, 2*, 85–86. https://doi.org/10.1044/1058-0360.0201.11

Carlisle, J. (2000). Awareness of the structure and meaning of morphologically complex words: Impact on reading. *Reading and Writing, 12*, 169–190. https://doi.org/10.1023/A:1008131926604

Carlisle, J. F., & Stone, C. A. (2005). Exploring the role of morphemes in word reading. *Reading Research Quarterly, 40*, 428–449. https://doi.org/10.1598/RRQ.40.4.3

Carrow-Woolfolk, E. (1995). *Oral and Written Language Scales (OWLS)*. American Guidance Service, Inc.

Carrow-Woolfolk, E. (2012). *Oral and Written Language Scales–Second Edition (OWLS-II)*. Pro-Ed.

Carrow-Woolfolk, E. (2014). *Test for Auditory Comprehension of Language–Fourth Edition (TACL-4)*. Pro-Ed.

Carrow-Woolfolk, E. (2017). *Comprehensive Assessment of Spoken Language–Second Edition (CASL-II)*. Western Psychological Services.

Carrow-Woolfolk, E., & Allen, E. A. (2014). *Test of Expressive Language (TEXL)*. Pro-Ed.

Carrow-Woolfolk, E., & Klein, A. M. (2017). *Oral Passage Understanding Scale (OPUS)*. Pro-Ed.

Catts, H. W. (1991). Early identification of dyslexia: Evidence from a follow-up study of speech-language impaired children. *Annals of Dyslexia, 41*, 163–177. https://doi.org/10.1007/BF02648084

Catts, H. W. (1993). The relationship between speech-language impairments and reading disabilities. *Journal of Speech and Hearing Research, 36*, 948–958. https://doi.org/10.1044/jshr.3605.948

Catts, H. W. (2009). The narrow view of reading promotes a broad view of comprehension. *Language, Speech, & Hearing Services in Schools, 40*, 178–183. https://doi.org/10.1044/0161-1461(2008/08-0035)

Catts, H. W., Adlof, S. M., Hogan, T. P., & Weismer, S. E. (2005). Are specific language impairment and dyslexia distinct disorders? *Journal of Speech, Language, & Hearing Research, 48*(6), 1378–1396. 10.1044/1092-4388(2005/096)

Catts, H. W., Bridges, M. S., Little, T. D., & Tomblin, J. B. (2008). Reading achievement growth in children with language impairments. *Journal of Speech, Language, and Hearing Research, 51*, 1569–1579. https://doi.org/10.1044/1092-4388(2008/07-0259)

Catts, H. W., Fey, M. E., Zhang, X., & Tomblin, J. B. (1999). Language basis of reading and reading disabilities: Evidence from a longitudinal investigation. *Scientific Studies of Reading, 3*, 331–361. https://doi.org/10.1044/1092-4388(2002/093)

Catts, H. W., Fey, M. E., Zhang, X., & Tomblin, J. B. (2001). Estimating the risk of future reading difficulties in kindergarten children: A research-based model and its clinical implementation. *Language, Speech, and Hearing Services in Schools, 32*, 38–50.

Catts, H. W., & Kamhi, A. G. (2005). *Language and reading disabilities*. Pearson Education.

Cazort, D. (1997). *Under the grammar hammer*. McGraw-Hill Education.

Center for Parent Information Resources. (2017). *Disabilities*. http://nichcy.org/disability/specific/dd

Center on Multi-Tiered System of Support at the American Institutes for Research. (n.d.). *Welcome to the MTSS Center*. Retrieved January 23, 2021, from https://mtss4success.org.

Chall, J. S., & Dale, E. (1995.) *Readability revisited: The new Dale–Chall readability formula*. Brookline Books.

Chamberlain, L. L. (2016). Mean length of utterance and Developmental Sentence Scoring in the analysis of children's language samples. *All Theses and Dissertations. 5966*. https://scholarsarchive.byu.edu/etd/5966

Cherry, K. (2020). *Short-term memory duration and capacity*. https://www.verywellmind.com/what-is-short-term-memory-2795348#:~:text=Short-term%20memory%20is%20limited.%20It%20is%20commonly%20suggested,or%20active%20maintenance%20of%20the%20information%20is%20prevented

Chin, B. (n.d.). *The role of grammar in improving student's writing*. https://abspd.appstate.edu/sites/abspd.appstate.edu/files/inst_pics/Grammar%20in%20Context.pdf

Chomsky, N. (1965). *Aspects of the theory of syntax*. MIT Press.

Chomsky, N. (1968). *Language and mind*. Harcourt, Brace and World.

Christie, F., & Derewianka, B. (2008). *School discourse*. Continuum International Publishing Corp.

Cirrin, F. M., & Gillam, R. B. (2008). Language intervention practices for school-age children with spoken language disorders: A systematic review. *Language, Speech, and Hearing Services in Schools, 39*, S110–S137. https://doi.org/10.1044/0161-1461(2008/012)

Cirrin, F. M., Schooling, T. L., Nelson, N. W., Diehl, S. F., Flynn, P. F., Staskowski, M., . . . Adamczyk, D. F. (2010). Evidence-based systematic review: Effects of different service delivery models on communication outcomes for elementary school-age children. *Language, Speech, and Hearing Services in Schools, 41*, 233–264. https://doi.org/10.1044/0161-1461(2009/08-0128)

Clahsen, H., & Felser, C. (2006). Grammatical processing in language learners. *Applied Psycholinguistics, 27*, 3–42. doi:10.1017/S0142716406060024

Clancy, B., & Finlay, B. (2001). Neural correlates of early language learning. In M. Tomasello & E. Bates (Eds.), *Language development: The essential readings* (pp. 307–330). Blackwell Publishing Ltd.

Clark, M. A. (August 27, 2019). *Using employees' preferred gender pronouns: It's more than common courtesy. It's their civil right.* https://www.shrm.org/hr-today/news/hr-magazine/fall2019/Pages/using-employees-preferred-gender-pronouns.aspx

Clark, R. P. (2011). *The glamour of grammar: A guide to the magic and mystery of practical English*. Little, Brown and Company.

Clay, M. M. (2015). *Change over time in children's literacy development*. Heinemann.

Clay, M. M. (2016). *Literacy lessons designed for individuals* (2nd ed.). Heinemann.

Coh-Metrix Quick Reference Guide. (n.d.). Retrieved March 3, 2021, from csal.gsu.edu/content/coh-metrix-quick-reference-guide.

Coh-Metrix Version 3.0 Indices. (n.d.). Retrieved March 3, 2021, from cohmetrix.memphis.edu/cohmetrixhome/documentation_indices.html.

Comrie, B. (1976). *Aspect*. Cambridge University Press.

Comrie, B. (1985). *Tense*. Cambridge University Press.

Comrie, B. (1989). *Language universals and linguistic typology: Syntax and morphology* (2nd ed.). University of Chicago Press.

Conti-Ramsden, G., & Durkin, K. (2008). Language and independence in adolescents with and without a history of specific language impairment (SLI). *Journal of Speech, Language, and Hearing Research, 51*, 70–83.

Cook, W. A. (1989) *Case grammar theory*. Georgetown University Press.

Costanza-Smith, A. (2010). The clinical utility of language samples. *Perspectives on Language Learning and Education, 17*(1), 9–15.

Craig, H. K., Thompson, C. A., Washington, J., & Potter, S. L. (2003a). Performance of elementary-grade African American students on the Gray Oral Reading Test. *American Journal of Speech-Language Pathology, 13*, 141–154.

Craig, H. K., Thompson, C. A., Washington, J., & Potter, S. L. (2003b). Phonological features of child African American English. *Journal of Speech, Language, and Hearing Research, 46*(3), 623–635.

Craig, H. K., & Washington, J. (2004a). Grade-related changes in the production of African American English. *Journal of Speech, Language, and Hearing Research, 47*, 450–463.

Craig, H. K., & Washington, J. (2004b). Language variation and literacy learning. In C. A. Stone, E. R. Silliman, B. J. Ehren, & K. Apel (Eds.), *Handbook of language and literacy: Development and disorders* (pp. 228–243). Guilford Press.

Craig, H. K., Washington, J., & Thompson-Porter, C. (1998). Average C-unit length in the discourse of African American children from low-income urban homes. *Journal of Speech, Language, and Hearing Research, 41*, 433–444.

Crais, E. (2006). Gesture development from an interactionist perspective. In R. Paul

(Ed.), *Language disorders from a developmental perspective: Essays honoring Robin S. Chapman* (pp. 141–162). Brookes.

Crews, F. C. (1984). *The Random House handbook* (4th ed.). Random House.

Crowley, C. J. (2003). *Diagnosing communication disorders in culturally and linguistically diverse students. ERIC Digest E650.* ERIC Clearinghouse on Disabilities and Gifted Education.

Cruz-Ferreira, M. (Ed.). (2010). *Multilingual norms: Language norming in multilingual context.* Mouton de Gruyter.

Crystal, D., Fletcher, P., & Garman, M. (1976). *The grammatical analysis of language disability.* Arnold.

Crystal, D., Garman, M., & Fletcher, P. (1989). *The grammatical analysis of language disability: A procedure for assessment and remediation* (2nd ed.). Cole and Whurr.

Cunningham, A., & Zibulsky, J. (2009). Introduction to the special issue about perspectives on teachers' disciplinary knowledge of reading processes, development, and pedagogy. *Reading and Writing, 22*(4), 375–378. https://doi.org/10.1007/s11145-009-9161-2

Dahl, O. (1985). *Tense and aspect systems.* Blackwell.

Danielewicz, J. M. (1984). The interaction between text and context: A study of how adults and children use spoken and written language in four contexts. In A. D. Pellegrini & T. D. Yawkey (Eds.), *The development of oral and written language in social contexts* (pp. 243–260). Ablex.

Datchuk, S. (2016). Writing simple sentences and descriptive paragraphs: Effects of an intervention on adolescents with writing difficulties. *Journal of Behavioral Education, 25*(2), 166–188.

Datchuk, S. M. (2017). A direct instruction and precision teaching intervention to improve the sentence construction of middle school students with writing difficulties. *Journal of Special Education, 51*(2), 62–71.

Datchuk, S. M., & Kubina, R. M. (2013). Effects of sentence-combining instruction and frequency building to a performance criterion on adolescents with difficulty constructing sentences. *Journal of Evidence-Based Practices for Schools, 14*(2), 160–185.

Datchuk, S. M., & Kubina, R. M. (2017). A writing intervention to teach simple sentences and descriptive paragraphs to adolescents with writing difficulties. *Education & Treatment of Children, 40*(3), 303–326.

Davis, W. (2010). Implicature. In E. N. Zalta (Ed.), *The Stanford encyclopedia of philosophy* (Winter 2010 ed.). http://plato.stanford.edu/archives/win2010/entries/implicature/

Deevy, P., & Leonard, L. B. (2018). Sensitivity to morphosyntactic information in preschool children with and without developmental language disorder: A follow-up study. *Journal of Speech, Language, and Hearing Research, 61*, 3064–3074. https://doi.org/10.1044/2018_JSLHR-L-18-0038.

De La Paz, S., & Graham, S. (2002). Explicitly teaching strategies, skills, and knowledge: Writing instruction in middle school classrooms. *Journal of Educational Psychology, 94*(4), 687–698.

Denes, P. B., & Pinson, E. N. (2007). *The speech chain: The physics and biology of spoken language* (2nd ed.). W. H. Freeman.

Deno, S. L. (1993). *Curriculum-based measurements.* Digital Commons University of Nebraska–Lincoln. https://digitalcommons.unl.edu/buroscurriculum/3/

Deno, S. L. (2003). Developments in curriculum-based measurement. *Journal of Special Education, 37*(3), 184–192.

Derivational morphemes in English. (2010, September 20). http://my-uad-courses.blogspot.com/2010/09/derivational-morphemes-in-english.html

DeThorne, L. S., Johnson, B. W., & Loeb, J. W. (2005). A closer look at MLU: What does it really measure? *Clinical Linguistics & Phonetics, 19*, 635–648. doi:10.1080/02699200410001716165.

Developmental Disabilities Assistance and Bill of Rights Act of 2000, Pub. L.

No. 106-402, 106th Congress, 114 Stat. 1677. https://www.congress.gov/bill/106th-congress/house-bill/4920

Dick, F., Wulfeck, B., Krupa-Kwiatkowski, M., & Bates, E. (2004). The development of complex sentence interpretation in typically developing children compared with children with specific language impairments or early unilateral focal lesions. *Developmental Science 7*(3), 360–377.

Diessel, H. (2004). *The acquisition of complex sentences.* Cambridge University Press.

The Diversity Center of Northeast Ohio. (2016). *Pronouns: A how-to.* https://www.diversitycenterneo.org/about-us/pronouns/

Dockrell, J. E., & Connelly, V. (2009). The impact of oral language skills on the production of written text. *Teaching and Learning Writing, BJEP Monograph Series II*(6), 45–62. doi:10.1348/000709909X421919

Domsch, C., Richels, C., Saldana, M., Coleman, C., Wimberly, C., & Maxwell, L. (2012). Narrative skill and syntactic complexity in school-age children with and without late language emergence. International *Journal of Language & Communication Disorders, 47*(2), 197–207.

Donahue, M. (1987). Interactions between linguistic and pragmatic development in learning-disabled children: Three views from the state of the union. In S. Rosenberg (Ed.), *Advances in applied psycholinguistics: Volume 1. Disorders of first language development* (pp. 126–179). Cambridge University Press.

Dore, J. (1974). A pragmatic description of early language development. *Journal of Psycholinguistic Research, 3,* 343–350.

Dore, J. (1975). Holophrases, speech acts and language universals. *Journal of Child Language, 2,* 21–40.

Dore, J. (1977a). Children's illocutionary acts. In R. Freedle (Ed.), *Discourse production and comprehension.* Lawrence Erlbaum Associates.

Dore, J. (1977b). "Oh them sheriff": A pragmatic analysis of children's responses to questions. In S. Ervin-Tripp & C. Mitchell-Kernan (Eds.), *Child discourse.* Academic Press.

Dore, J., Gearhart, M., & Newman, D. (1978). The structure of nursery school conversation. In K. E. Nelson (Ed.), *Children's language* (Vol. 1). Gardner Press.

Drew, C. (2019). *Guided practice (I do we do you do): Examples & definition.* https://helpfulprofessor.com/guided-practice/

Dreyfus, H., & Dreyfus, S. (1980). *A five-stage model of the mental activities involved in direct skill acquisition.* University of California, Berkeley Operations Research Center Report. https://www.semanticscholar.org/paper/A-Five-Stage-Model-of-the-Mental-Activities-in-Dreyfus-Dreyfus/efa296060526e40fb81b7498786aba72d546e555

Dreyfus, H. L., & Dreyfus, S. E. (1986). *Mind over machine: The power of human intuition and expertise in the age of the computer.* Basil Blackwell.

Drijbooms, E., Groen, M. A., & Verhoeven, L. (2017). How executive functions predict development in syntactic complexity of narrative writing in the upper elementary grades. *Reading and Writing, 30,* 209–231. doi:10.1007/s11145-016-9670-8

Duchan, J. F., Hewitt, L. E., & Sonnenmeier, R. M. (1994). *Pragmatics: From theory to practice.* Prentice Hall.

Duffy, G. G. (2014). *Explaining reading: A resource for explicit teaching of the Common Core standards* (3rd ed). Guilford Press.

Dunn, M., Flax, J., Sliwinski, M., & Aram, D. (1996). The use of spontaneous language measures as criteria for identifying children with specific language impairment: An attempt to reconcile clinical and research incongruence. *Journal of Speech, Language, and Hearing Research, 39,* 643–654.

Dyson, A. H. (1989). *Collaboration through writing and reading: Exploring possibilities.* National Council of Teachers of English.

Ebbels, S. H. (2014). Effectiveness of intervention for grammar in school-aged children with primary language impairments:

A review of the evidence. *Child Language Teaching and Therapy, 30*(1), 7–40.

Eberhardt, N. C. (2013). Syntax: Somewhere between words and text. *Perspectives on Language and Literacy, 39*(3), 43–49. https://app.box.com/s/6rn9i3zl6blle2qhasudaj84zb9gkvhs

Ebert, K. D., & Scott, C. M. (2014). Relationships between narrative language samples and norm-referenced test scores in language assessments of school-age children. *Language, Speech, and Hearing Services in Schools, 45*(4), 337–350. https://doi.org/10.1044/2014_LSHSS-14-0034

Education for All Handicapped Children Act of 1975, Public Law 94-142. 89 STAT. 773, November 28, 1975. https://www.govinfo.gov/content/pkg/STATUTE-89/pdf/STATUTE-89-Pg773.pdf

Ehren, B. J. (2009) Reading comprehension and expository text structure: Direction for intervention with adolescents. In M. Nippold & C. Scott (Eds.), *Expository discourse in children, adolescents, and adults: Development and disorders* (pp. 217–242). Psychology Press.

Ehren, B. J. (2014, October). *Helping secondary students manipulate the syntax of informational text.* Paper presented at the Ohio Speech Pathology and Educational Audiology Coalition Conference, Columbus, OH.

Ehren, B. J., Deshler, D. D., & Graner, P. S. (2010). Using the content literacy continuum as a framework for implementing RTI in secondary schools. *Theory Into Practice, 49,* 315–322. doi:10.1080/00405841.2010.510760

Ehren, B. J., Ehren. T. C., & Proly, J. L. (2009). *Response to Intervention: An action guide for school leaders.* Educational Research Service.

Ehren, B. J., Murza, K. A., & Malani, M. D. (2012). Disciplinary literacy from a speech–language pathologist's perspective. *Topics in Language Disorders, 32*(1), 85–98.

Ehren, B. J., & Whitmire, K. (2009). Speech-language pathologists as primary contributors to Response to Intervention at the secondary level. *Seminars in Speech and Language, 30*(2), 90–104.

Ehren, T. C., & Ehren, B. J. (2007). Legal mandates: Impetus for improving assessment, diagnosis, and treatment of school-age children and adolescents with developmental language disorders. In A. G. Kamhi, J. J. Masterson, & K. Apel (Eds.), *Clinical decision making in developmental language disorders* (pp. 337–359). Brookes.

Eisenberg, S. L. (2006). Grammar: How can I say it better? In T. A. Ukrainetz (Ed.), *Contextualized language intervention: Scaffolding PreK–12 literacy achievement* (pp. 145–194). Thinking Publications.

Eisenberg, S. L. (2013). Grammar intervention: Content and procedures for facilitating children's language development. *Topics in Language Disorders, 33*(2), 165–178.

Eisenberg, S. L. (2020). Using general language performance measures to assess grammar learning. *Topics in Language Disorders, 40*(2), 135–148. doi:10.1097/TLD.0000000000000215

Eisenberg, S. L., Fersko, T. M., & Lundgren, C. (2001). The use of MLU for identifying language impairment in preschool children: A review. *American Journal of Speech-Language Pathology, 10*(4), 323–342.

Eisenberg, S., & Guo, L. (2016). Using language sample analysis in clinical practice: Measures of grammatical accuracy for identifying language impairment in preschool and school-age children. *Seminars in Speech and Language, 37*(2), 106–116.

Eisenberg, S. L., Guo, L.-Y., & Mucchetti, E. (2018). Eliciting the language sample for Developmental Sentence Scoring: A comparison of play with toys and elicited picture description. *American Journal of Speech-Language Pathology, 27*(2), 633–646. https://doi.org/10.1044/2017_AJSLP-16-0161

Eisenberg, S. L., Ukrainetz, T. A., Hsu, J. R., Kaderavek, J. N., Justice, L. M., & Gillam, R. B. (2008). Noun phrase elaboration in children's spoken stories. *Language,*

Speech, and Hearing Services in Schools, 39(2), 145–157.

Ellis, E. S., & Graves, A. W. (1990). Teaching rural students with learning disabilities: A paraphrasing strategy to increase comprehension of main ideas. *Rural Special Education Quarterly, 10*(2), 2–10.

Emig, J. (1977). Writing as a mode of learning. *College Composition and Communication, 28*, 122–128.

Endress, A. D., & Hauser, M. D. (2010). Word segmentation with universal prosodic cues. *Cognitive Psychology, 61*(2), 177–199. doi:10.1016/j.cogpsych.2010.05.001

The English Club. (1997–2021a). *The 12 basic English tenses.* http://www.englishclub.com/grammar/verb-tenses.htm

The English Club. (1997–2021b). *Future perfect continuous.* https://www.englishclub.com/grammar/verb-tenses_future-perfect-continuous.htm

Englishpage.com. (1997–2021). *Subjunctive.* http://www.englishpage.com/minitutorials/subjunctive.html

English Plus. (1997–2001). *The subjunctive mood.* http://englishplus.com/grammar/00000031.htm

Ervin-Tripp, S. (1970). Discourse agreement: How children answer questions. In J. R. Hayes (Ed.), *Cognition and the development of language* (pp. 79–107). Wiley.

Espin, C., Shin, J., Deno, S., Skare, S., Robinson, S., & Benner, B. (2000). Identifying indicators of written expression proficiency for middle school students. *Journal of Special Education, 34*(3), 140–153.

Every Student Succeeds Act of 2015, Pub. L. No. 114-95 § 114 Stat. 1177 (2015–2016).

Eyer, J., & Leonard, L. (1995). Functional categories and specific language impairment: A case study. *Language Acquisition, 4*, 177–203.

Fang, Z. (2012). Language correlates of disciplinary literacy. *Topics in Language Disorders, 32*(1), 19–34.

Fang, Z., & Schleppegrell, M. J. (2010). Disciplinary literacies across content areas: Supporting secondary reading through functional language analysis. *Journal of*

Adolescent and Adult Literacy, 53(7), 587–597. doi:10.1598/JAAL.53.7.6

Farrall, M. L. (2012). *Reading assessment: Linking language, literacy, and cognition.* John Wiley.

Farrall, M. L. (2013). The assessment of written syntax. *Perspectives on Language and Literacy, 39*(3), 31–36. https://app.box.com/s/6rn9i3zl6blle2qhasudaj84zb9gkvhs

Features of Academic Writing. (n.d.). www.uefap.com/writing/feature/complex.htm

Feeney, C. (2008, January 22). SLPs as reading specialists? [Electronic version] *The ASHA Leader Online. 13*(1) https://leader.pubs.asha.org/toc/leader/13/1

Feng, S., & Powers, K. (2005). The short- and long-term effect of explicit grammar instruction on fifth graders' writing. *Reading Improvement, 42*(2), 67–72.

Ferreira, F., & Patson, N. D. (2007). The "good enough" approach to language comprehension. *Language and Linguistics Compass, 1*, 71–83. doi:10.1111/j.1749-818X.2007.00007.x

Fey, M. E., Catts, H. W., Proctor-Williams, K., Tomblin, J. B., & Zhang, X. (2004). Oral and written story composition skills of children with language impairment. *Journal of Speech, Language & Hearing Research, 47*, 1301–1318. doi:1092-4388/04/4706-1301

Fey, M. E., Long, S. H., & Finestack, L. H. (2003). Ten principles of grammar facilitation for children with specific language impairment. *American Journal of Speech-Language Pathology, 12*, 3–15.

Field, J. (2003). *Psycholinguistics: A resource book for students.* Routledge.

Fillmore, C. (1968). The case for case. In E. W. Bach & R. T. Harms (Eds.), *Universals in linguistic theory* (pp. 1–88). Holt, Rinehart, and Winston.

Finch, S., & Chater, N. (1992). Bootstrapping syntactic categories using statistical methods. In *Proceedings of the 1st SHOE Workshop on Statistical Methods in Natural Language* (pp. 229–235). ITK Proceedings 92/1, Institute for Language Technology and Artificial Intelligence, Tilburg University, The Netherlands. https://www.researchgate.net/publication/313060473_Bootstrapping_syntactic_categories_using_statistical_methods_Background_and_experiments_in_machine_learning_of_natural_language_Proceedings_of_the_1st_SHOE_workshop_on_statistical_methods_in_natural_l

Finestack, L. H. (2018). Evaluation of an explicit intervention to teach novel grammatical forms to children with developmental language disorder. *Journal of Speech, Language, and Hearing Research, 61*(8), 2062–2075.

Finestack, L. H., Bangert, K., & Huang, T. (2017, November). *Using language samples to develop grammatical intervention goals.* Paper presented at the Annual Convention of the American Speech-Language-Hearing Association, Los Angeles, CA. http://www.finestackclil.com/presentations/

Finestack, L. H., Engman, J., Huang, T., Bangert, K. J., & Bader, K. (2020). Evaluation of a combined explicit-implicit approach to teach grammatical forms to children with grammatical weaknesses. *American Journal of Speech-Language Pathology, 29*(1), 1–17.

Finestack, L. H., & Fey, M. E. (2009). Evaluation of a deductive approach to teach grammatical inflections to children with language impairment. *American Journal of Speech-Language Pathology, 18*, 1–14.

Finestack, L. H., & Satterlund, K. E. (2018). Current practice of child grammar intervention: A survey of speech-language pathologists. *American Journal of Speech-Language Pathology, 27*(4), 1329–1351. https://doi.org/10.1044/2018_AJSLP-17-0168

Fisher, C., Gertner, Y., Scott, R. M., & Yuan, S. (2010). Syntactic bootstrapping. *Wiley Interdisciplinary Reviews: Cognitive Science, 1*(2), 143–149. http://onlinelibrary.wiley.com/doi/10.1002/wcs.17/abstract

Fisher, C., Hall, D. G., Rakowitz, S., & Gleitman, L. (1994). When it is better to receive than to give: Syntactic and conceptual constraints on vocabulary growth. *Lingua, 92*, 333–375. http://dingo.sbs.arizona.edu/~hharley/courses/PDF/FisherHallRakowiczGleitman.pdf

Fisher, D., & Frey, N. (2015). Teacher modeling using complex informational texts. *The Reading Teacher, 69*, 63–69. doi:10.1002/trtr.1372

Fiske, S., & Taylor, S. (1991). *Social cognition: From brains to culture.* McGraw-Hill.

Fitzgerald, J., & Teasley, A. (1986). Effects of instruction in narrative structure on children's writing. *Journal of Educational Psychology, 78*(6), 424–432.

Flowerdew, J. (1990). Problems of speech act theory from an applied perspective. *Language Learning, 40*(1), 79–105.

Fogel, H., & Ehri, L. C. (2006). Teaching African American English forms to Standard American English-speaking teachers: Effects on acquisition, attitudes, and responses to student use. *Journal of Teacher Education, 57*(5), 464–480.

Foorman, B., Beyler, N., Borradaile, K., Coyne, M., Denton, C. A., Dimino, J., . . . Wissel, S. (2016). *Foundational skills to support reading for understanding in kindergarten through 3rd grade* (NCEE 2016-4008). National Center for Education Evaluation and Regional Assistance (NCEE), Institute of Education Sciences, U.S. Department of Education. http://whatworks.ed.gov

Foorman, B. R., Petscher, Y., & Bishop, M. D. (2012). The incremental variance of morphological knowledge to reading comprehension in Grades 3–10 beyond prior reading comprehension, spelling, and text reading efficiency. *Learning & Individual Differences, 22*(6), 792–798.

Foster, P., Tonkyn, A., & Wigglesworth, G. (2000). Measuring spoken language: A unit for all reasons. *Applied Linguistics, 21*(3), 354–375.

Frank, M. C., Braginsky, M., Yurovsky, D., Marchman, V., & Kellier, D. (n.d.). *Wordbank.* http://wordbank.stanford.edu

Fraser, J., Goswami, U., & Conti-Ramsden, G. (2010). Dyslexia and specific language impairment: The role of phonology and auditory processing. *Scientific Studies of Reading, 14*(1), 8–29.

Fristoe, M. (1979). Developmental sentence analysis. In F. L. Darley (Ed.), *Evaluation of appraisal techniques in speech and language pathology* (pp. 15–17). Addison-Wesley.

Fuchs, L., Fuchs, D., & Maxwell, L. (1988). The validity of informal reading comprehension measures. *Remedial and Special Education, 9*(2), 20–28. https://journals.sagepub.com/doi/abs/10.1177/074193258800900206

Fulwiler, T., & Young, A. (1982). Introduction. In T. Fulwiler & A. Young (Eds.), *Language connections: Writing and reading across the curriculum* (pp. ix–xiii). National Council of Teachers of English.

Gajria, M., Jitendra, A. K., Sood, S., & Sacks, G. (2007). Improving comprehension of expository text in students with LD: A research synthesis. *Journal of Learning Disabilities, 40*(3), 210–225. https://doi.org/10.1177/00222194070400030301

Gallagher, T. M., & Prutting, C.A. (1983). *Pragmatic assessment and intervention issues in language.* College Hill Press.

Gallagher, T. M., & Prutting, C.A. (1991). *Pragmatics of language: Clinical practice issues.* Singular Publishing Group.

Garbarino, J., Bernstein Ratner, N., & MacWhinney, B. (2020). Use of computerized language analysis to assess child language. *Language, Speech, and Hearing Services in Schools, 51*(2), 504–506. https://doi.org/10.1044/2020_LSHSS-19-00118

Garrity, A. W., & Oetting, J. B. (2010). Auxiliary BE production by African American English-speaking children with and without specific language impairment. *Journal of Speech, Language, and Hearing Research, 53,* 1307–1320.

Garvey, C. (1984). *Children's talk.* Harvard University Press.

Gee, J. P. (1985). The narrativization of experience in the oral style. *Journal of Education, 167,* 9–36.

Gibson, N., & Gordon Pershey, M. (2011, November). *Gesture-speech mismatches:* Considerations for how language is encoded and decoded. Poster presented at the American Speech-Language-Hearing Association Annual Convention, San Diego, CA.

Gilbert, D. G. (2012). *Grammar without road rage & punctuation without panic attacks.* CreateSpace Independent Publishing Platform.

Gillis, M. B., & Eberhardt, N. C. (2018). *Syntax: From knowledge to practice.* Literacy How Professional Learning Series.

Ginger Grammar. (2021). *Sentence rephraser.* https://www.gingersoftware.com/products/sentence-rephraser

Ginsburg, H., & Opper, S. (1979). *Piaget's theory of intellectual development.* Prentice-Hall.

Gleitman, L. (1990). The structural sources of verb meanings. *Language Acquisition, 1,* 135–176.

Gleitman, L. R., Cassidy, K., Nappa, R., Papafragou, A., & Trueswell, J. (2005). Hard words. *Language Learning and Development, 1*(1), 23–64.

Goldin-Meadow, S. (2009). How gesture promotes learning throughout childhood. *Child Development Perspectives, 3,* 106–111.

Goldstein, B. (2000). *Cultural and linguistic diversity resource guide for speech-language pathologists.* Singular Publishing.

Goldstein, B. (2006). Clinical implications of research on language development and disorders in bilingual children. *Topics in Language Disorders, 26,* 318–334.

Goldstein, B. (2011). *Bilingual language development and disorders in Spanish-English speakers* (2nd ed.). Brookes.

Golub, L. S. (1969). Linguistic structures in students' oral and written discourse. *Research in the Teaching of English, 3,* 70–85.

Golub, L. S. (1973). *Syntactic Density Score (SDS) with some aids for tabulating.* https://files.eric.ed.gov/fulltext/ED091741.pdf

Golub, L. S., & Frederick, W. E. (1971). *Linguistic structures in the discourse of fourth and sixth graders.* The University of Wisconsin Research and Development Cen-

ter for Cognitive Learning. https://eric
.ed.gov/?id=ED058322

Golub, L. S., & Kidder, C. L. (1974). Syntactic density and the computer. *Elementary English. 51*(8), 1128–1131.

Goodman, K., Shannon, P., Freeman, Y., & Murphy, S. (1988). *Report card on basal readers*. Richard C. Owens.

Gordon, K. E. (1984). *The transitive vampire: The ultimate handbook of grammar for the innocent, the eager, and the doomed*. Pantheon.

Gordon Pershey, M. (1998). Collaboration models and projected outcomes for school-based language therapy: Sampling the buffet. *Hearsay, Journal of the Ohio Speech-Language-Hearing Association,* 12(1), 32–38.

Gordon Pershey, M. (2000). Children's elicited use of pragmatic language functions: How six- and seven-year-old children adapt to the interactional environments of story scenarios. *Language Awareness,* 9(4), 218–235.

Gordon Pershey, M. (2003). High-stakes testing: The background behind testing-based educational reforms and implications for speech-language pathologists. *Contemporary Issues in Communication Sciences and Disorders, 30,* 47–58.

Gordon Pershey, M. (2010, May). *Structural and discourse features of narrative writings by grade four and six African American students.* Poster presented at the annual conference of the American Educational Research Association, Denver, CO. http://www.aera.net/Publications/OnlinePaper Repository/AERAOnlinePaperRepository /tabid/12720/Owner/70852/Default .aspx

Gordon Pershey, M. (2013, April). *Students' developmental competence in understanding and employing the structural and discourse features of narrative writing: Implications for K–8 instruction.* Paper presented at the Annual Conference of the International Reading Association, San Antonio, TX.

Gordon Pershey, M. (2016a, October). *Putting it in writing: Helping elementary school learners with dyslexia and other language-based learning disabilities develop written language skills.* Paper presented at the New Jersey Branch of the International Dyslexia Association Annual Symposium (NJIDA), Somerset, NJ.

Gordon Pershey, M. (2016b). Review of Wiig, E. H., & Secord, W. A. (2014). *Clinical Evaluation of Language Fundamentals–Fifth Edition Metalinguistics (CELF-5 Metalinguistics).* San Antonio, TX: NCS Pearson, Inc. In J. F. Carlson, K. F. Geisinger, & J. L. Jonson (Eds.), *The twentieth mental measurements yearbook.* Buros Center for Testing. (Also published in *Test Reviews,* https://marketplace.unl.edu/buros/clin ical-evaluation-of-language-fundamentals -fifth-edition-metalinguistics.html)

Gordon Pershey, M. (2018a). Executive function, language, and literacy impairments. In J. Birsh & S. Carreker (Eds.), *Multisensory teaching of basic language skills* (4th ed., pp. 294–335). Brookes.

Gordon Pershey, M. (2018b). Review of Miller, J. F., Iglesias, A. Andriacchi, K., & Nockerts, A. (2016). *Systematic Analysis of Language Transcripts 16 (SALT 16).* Madison, WI: SALT Software, LLC. In J. F. Carlson, K. F. Geisinger, & J. L. Jonson (Eds.), *The mental measurements yearbook.* Buros Center for Testing.

Gordon Pershey, M. (2019a). Functional assessment of communication disorders. In M. J. Ball (Ed.), *The SAGE encyclopedia of human communication sciences and disorders* (pp. 788–790). SAGE.

Gordon Pershey, M. (2019b). Functional communication. In M. J. Ball (Ed.), *The SAGE encyclopedia of human communication sciences and disorders* (pp. 791–793). SAGE.

Gordon Pershey, M., & Rapking, C. (2003). A survey of collaborative speech-language service delivery under large caseload conditions in an urban school district in the United States. *Journal of Speech-Language Pathology and Audiology, 27*(4), 211–220.

Gordon Pershey, M., & Richards, R. (2007, August). *Literacy development in children with communication disorders*. Workshop presented at the Northern Ohio Branch of the International Dyslexia Association Annual Summer Professional Development Series, Cleveland, OH.

Graesser, A. C., & McNamara, D. S. (2011). Computational analyses of multilevel discourse comprehension. *Topics in Cognitive Science, 3*(2), 371–398. https://doi.org/10.1111/j.1756-8765.2010.01081.x

Graesser, A. C., McNamara, D. S., Louwerse, M., & Cai, Z. (2004). Coh-Metrix: Analysis of text on cohesion and language. *Behavior Research Methods, Instruments, & Computers, 36*, 193–202.

Graham, S., & Hebert, M. A. (2010). *Writing to read: Evidence for how writing can improve reading*. Alliance for Excellent Education.

Graham, S., MacArthur, C. A., & Hebert, M. (Eds.). (2019). *Best practices in writing instruction*. Guilford.

Graham, S., & Perin, D. (2007a). A meta-analysis of writing instruction for adolescent students. *Journal of Educational Psychology, 99*(3), 445–476. https://doi.org/10.1037/0022-0663. 99.3.445

Graham, S., & Perin, D. (2007b). *Writing next: Effective strategies to improve writing of adolescents in middle and high schools*. Alliance for Excellent Education.

Grammarly. (2021). https://www.grammarly.com

Gregory, G. (2003). They shall not parse! Or shall they? *Changing English, 10*, 3–33. doi:10.1080/1358684032000055109

Green, L. B. (2020). The Specific Language Impairment/Developmental Language Disorders forum: Fostering a discussion of terminology. *Perspectives of the ASHA Special Interest Groups, 5*(1), 3–5. https://doi.org/10.1044/2019_PERSP-19-00184

Greenhalgh, K. S., & Strong, C. J. (2001). Literate language features in spoken narratives of children with typical language and children with language impairments. *Language, Speech, and Hearing Services in Schools, 32*, 114–125.

Grice, H. P. (1975). Logic and conversation. In P. Cole & J. Morgan (Eds.), *Speech acts (syntax and semantics, 3)* (pp. 41–58). Academic Press.

Gross, J., Millett, A. L., Bartek, B., Bredell, K. H., & Winegard, B. (2013). Evidence for prosody in silent reading. *Reading Research Quarterly, 49*(2), 189–208. doi:10.1002/rrq.67

Guo, L., Eisenberg, S., Bernstein Ratner, N., & MacWhinney, B. (2018). Is putting SUGAR (Sampling Utterances for Grammatical Analysis Revisited) into language sample analysis a good idea? A response to Pavelko and Owens (2017). *Language, Speech, and Hearing Services in Schools, 49*(3), 622–627.

Guo, L., Eisenberg, S., Schneider, P., & Spencer, L. (2019). Percent grammatical utterances between age four and age nine for the Edmonton Narrative Norms Instrument: Reference data and psychometric properties. *American Journal of Speech-Language Pathology, 28*, 1448–1462.

Guo, L., Eisenberg, S., Schneider, P., & Spencer, L. (2020). Finite verb morphology composite between age four and age nine for the Edmonton Narrative Norms Instrument: Reference data and psychometric properties. *Language, Speech, and Hearing Services in Schools, 51*, 128–143.

Guo, L., & Schneider, P. (2016). Differentiating school-aged children with and without language impairment using tense and grammaticality measures from a narrative task. *Journal of Speech, Language, and Hearing Research, 59*(2), 317–329.

Guo, L., Schneider, P., & Harrison, W. (2021). Clausal density between age four and age nine for the Edmonton Narrative Norms Instrument: Reference data and psychometric properties. *Language, Speech, and Hearing Services in Schools, 52*, 354–368.

Gutiérrez-Clellen, V., & Peña, E. (2001). Dynamic assessment of diverse children: A tutorial. *Language, Speech, and Hearing Services in Schools, 32*, 212–224.

Hacker, D. (20003). *A writer's reference* (5th ed.). Bedford/St. Martin's.

Hadley, P. (1998). Language sampling protocols for eliciting text-level discourse. *Language, Speech, and Hearing Services in Schools, 29,* 132–147.

Hadley, P. A., & Rice, M. L. (1996). Emergent uses of BE and DO: Evidence from children with specific language impairment. *Language Acquisition, 5,* 209–243.

Hahne, A., Eckstein, K., & Friederici, A. D. (2004.) Brain signatures of syntactic and semantic processes during children's language development. *Journal of Cognitive Neuroscience, 16*(7), 1302–1318.

Hall-Mills, S. (2018). Language progress monitoring for elementary students. *Perspectives of the ASHA Special Interest Groups SIG 1, 3*(Pt. 4), 170–179.

Halliday, M. A. K. (1973). *Explorations in the functions of language.* Edward Arnold.

Halliday, M. A. K. (1975). *Learning how to mean.* Edward Arnold.

Hammill, D. D., Brown, V. L., Larsen, S. C., & Wiederholt, J. L. (2007). *Test of Adolescent and Adult Language–Fourth Edition (TOAL-4).* Pro-Ed.

Hammill, D. D., & Bryant, B. R. (2005). *Detroit Test of Learning Aptitude–Primary, Third Edition (DTLA-P:3).* Pro-Ed.

Hammill, D. D., & Larsen, S. C. (2009). *Test of Written Language–Fourth Edition (TOWL-4).* Pro-Ed.

Hammill, D. D., Mather, N., & Roberts, R. (2001). *Illinois Test of Psycholinguistic Abilities–Third Edition (ITPA-3).* Pro-Ed.

Hammill, D. D., & Newcomer, P. L. (2008). *Test of Language Development–Primary, Fourth Edition (TOLD-P).* Pro-Ed.

Hammill, D. D., & Newcomer, P. L. (2020). *Test of Language Development–Intermediate: Fifth Edition (TOLD-I:5).* Pro-Ed.

Hammill, D. D., Wiederholt, J. L., & Allen, E. A. (2014). *Test of Silent Contextual Reading Fluency–Second Edition (TOSCRF-2).* Pro-Ed.

Hansen, J., Newkirk, T., & Graves, D. (Eds.) (1985). *Breaking ground: Teachers relate reading and writing in the elementary school.* Heinemann.

Harley, T. A. (2008). *The psychology of language: From data to theory* (3rd ed.). Psychology Press.

Harris, K. R., & Graham, S. (1999). Programmatic intervention research: Illustrations from the evolution of self-regulated strategy development. *Learning Disability Quarterly, 22,* 251–262.

Harris, K. R., Graham, S., MacArthur, C., Reid, R., & Mason, L. H. (2017). Self-regulated learning processes and children's writing. In B. Zimmerman & D. Schunk (Eds.), *Handbook of self-regulation of learning and performance* (pp. 138–152). Routledge.

Harris, K. R., Graham, S., & Mason, L. H. (2003). Self-regulated strategy development in the classroom: Part of a balanced approach to writing instruction for students with disabilities. *Focus on Exceptional Children, 35,* 1–16.

Harris, K. R., Graham, S., Mason, L. H., & Friedlander, B. (2008). *Powerful writing strategies for all students.* Brookes.

Hauser, R. M., Edley, C. F., Koenig, J. A., & Elliott, S. W. (Eds.). (2005). *Measuring literacy: Performance levels for adults, interim report.* National Academies Press.

Head, M. H., & Readence, J. E. (1992). Anticipation guides: Using prediction to promote learning from text. In E. K. Dishner, T. W. Bean, J. E. Readence, & D. W. Moore (Eds.), *Reading in the content areas: Improving classroom instruction* (3rd ed., pp. 227–233). Kendall/Hunt.

Heath, S. B. (1978). *Language in education: Theory and practice, No. 9: Teacher talk: Language in the classroom.* Center for Applied Linguistics. https://files.eric.ed.gov/full text/ED158575.pdf

Hebb, D. O. (1949). *The organization of behavior.* Wiley & Sons.

Hegde, M. N., & Maul, C. A. (2006). *Language disorders in children: An evidence-based approach to assessment and treatment.* Pearson Education.

Heilmann, J. J. (2010). Myths and realities of language sample analysis. *Perspectives on Language Learning and Education, 17*(1), 4–8. https://doi.org/10.1044/lle17.1.4

Heilmann, J. J., Miller, J. F., & Nockerts, A. (2010a). Using language sample databases. *Language, Speech, and Hearing Services in Schools, 41*, 84–95. https://doi.org/10.1044/0161-1461 (2009/08-0075)

Heilmann, J., Nockerts, A., & Miller, J. F. (2010b). Language sampling: Does the length of the transcript matter? *Language, Speech, and Hearing Services in Schools, 41*(4), 393–404. https://doi.org/10.1044/0161-1461(2009/09-0023)

Henry, M. (2018). The history and structure of written English. In J. Birsh & S. Carreker (Eds.), *Multisensory teaching of basic language skills* (4th ed., pp. 540–557). Brookes.

Hewitt, L. E., Hammer, C. S., Yonte, K. M., & Tomblin, J. B. (2005). Language sampling for kindergarten children with and without SLI: Mean length of utterance, IPSYN, and NDW. *Journal of Communication Disorders, 38*, 197–213.

Hicks, S. R. C. (2004). *Explaining postmodernism: Skepticism and socialism from Rousseau to Foucault.* Scholargy Press.

Hillocks, G., Jr. (1986). *Research on written composition: New directions for teaching.* ERIC Clearinghouse on Reading and Communication Skills and the National Conference on Research in English.

Hillocks, G., Jr., & Smith, M. W. (1991). Grammar and usage. In J. Flood, J. M. Jensen, D. Lapp, & J. R. Squire (Eds.), *Handbook of research on teaching the English language arts* (pp. 591–603). Macmillan.

Hinkel, E., & Fotos, S. (2002). *New perspectives on grammar teaching in second language classrooms.* Erlbaum.

Hochman, J. C. (2009). *Teaching basic writing skills: Strategies for effective expository writing instruction.* Cambium Learning Group/Sopris.

Holloway, K. F. C. (1986). The effects of basal readers on oral language structures: A description of complexity. *Journal of Psycholinguistic Research, 15*(2), 141–151.

How to take running records. (2002). scholastic.ca/education/movingupwithliter-acyplace/pdfs/grade4/runningrecords.pdf

Hsu, J. R., Cairns, H. S., & Fiengo, R. W. (1985). The development of grammars underlying children's interpretation of complex sentences. *Cognition, 20*, 25–48.

Huang, T. (2017). *Grammatical probes.* https://drive.google.com/drive/folders/1eCfGl8A6KpABW3edNHE37Ybyt1xsy6rA

Hughes, D. L., Fey, M. E., Kertoy, M. K., & Nelson, N. W. (1994). Computer-assisted instruction for learning Developmental Sentence Scoring: An experimental comparison. *American Journal of Speech-Language Pathology, 3*, 89–95. doi:10.1044/1058-0360.0303.89

Hughes, D. L., Fey, M. E., & Long, S. H. (1992). Developmental Sentence Scoring: Still useful after all these years. *Topics in Language Disorders, 12*(2), 1–12. doi.org/10.1097/00011363-199202000-00003

Hunt, K. (1965). *Grammatical structures written at three grade levels* (NCTE Research Report No. 3). National Council of Teachers of English.

Hunt, K. W. (1970). Syntactic maturity in school children and adults. *Monographs of the Society for Research in Child Development, 35*(1, Serial No. 134).

Hunter, M. (1982). *Mastery teaching.* TIP Publications.

Hymes, D. H. (1971). *On communicative competence.* University of Pennsylvania Press.

Individuals With Disabilities Education Act of 2004, 20 U.S.C. § 1400 *et seq.* (2004). https://sites.ed.gov/idea/

Institute of Education Sciences, National Center for Education Statistics. (n.d.). *National Assessment of Educational Progress.* United States Department of Education. https://nces.ed.gov/nationsreportcard/

International Dyslexia Association. (2010). *Knowledge and practice standards for teachers of reading.* https://dyslexiaida.org/kps-for-teachers-of-reading/#:~:text=The%20IDA%20Knowledge%20and%20Prac

tice%20Standards%20for%20Teach
ers,demonstrate%20to%20teach%20read
ing%20successfully%20to%20all%20
students

International Dyslexia Association. (2020a). *Joan Sedita's Writing Rope.* https://dys lexiaida.org/joan-seditas-writing-rope/

International Dyslexia Association. (2020b). *Understanding dysgraphia.* https://dyslex iaida.org/understanding-dysgraphia-2/

International Literacy Association and the National Council of Teachers of English. (2021). *Read write think.* http://www.read writethink.org/about/standards.html

Isaacs, G. J. (1996). Persistence of non-standard dialect in school-age children. *Journal of Speech, Language, and Hearing Research, 39,* 434–441.

Ivy, L. J., & Masterson, J. J. (2011). A comparison of oral and written English styles in African American students at different stages of writing development. *Language, Speech, and Hearing Services in Schools, 42,* 31–40.

IXL Learning. (2021). *Sixth grade language arts.* https://www.ixl.com/ela/grade-6

Jackson, J. E., & Pearson, B. Z. (2010). Variable use of features associated with African American English by typically developing children ages 4 to 12. *Topics in Language Disorders, 30*(2), 135–144.

Jackson, S. C., & Roberts, J. E. (2001). Complex syntax production of African American preschoolers. *Journal of Speech, Language, and Hearing Research, 44,* 1083–1096.

Jalilevand, N., & Ebrahimipour, M. (2014). Three measures often used in language samples analysis. *Journal of Child Language Acquisition and Development, 2*(1), 1–12. www.jclad.science-res.com/Vol%20 2%20issue%201/Vol%202%20issue%201 %20FULL%20ISSUE%20Galley.pdf

Jennings, T. M., & Haynes, C. W. (2018). *From talking to writing: Strategies for supporting narrative and expository writing.* Landmark Outreach.

Jimerson, S. R., Burns, M. K., & VanDerHeyden, A. M. (2007). Response to intervention at school: The science and practice of assessment and intervention. In S. R. Jimerson, M. K. Burns, & A. M. VanDerHeyden (Eds.), *Handbook of response to intervention* (pp. 3–9). Springer.

Johnson, C. J., Beitchman, J. H., Young, A., Escobar, M., Atkinson, L., Wilson, B., . . . Wang, M. (1999). Fourteen-year follow up of children with and without speech-language impairments: Speech/language stability and outcomes. *Journal of Speech, Language, and Hearing Research, 42,* 744–760.

Johnson, V. E. (2005). Comprehension of third person singular /s/ in AAE-speaking children. *Language, Speech, and Hearing Services in Schools, 36,* 116–124.

Johnston, J. R. (1994). Cognitive abilities of children with language impairment. In R. V. Watkins & M. L. Rice (Eds.), *Specific language impairments in children* (pp. 107–121). Brookes.

Johnston, J. R. (2001). An alternative MLU calculation: Magnitude and variability of effects. *Journal of Speech, Language, and Hearing Research, 44,* 156–164.

Jose, P. E. (1988). Sequentiality of speech acts in conversational structure. *Journal of Psycholinguistics Research, 17,* 65–88.

Josephson, L., & Gordon Pershey, M. (2007, October–November). *Language, reading, and spelling: The interplay.* Paper presented at the 58th Annual Conference of the International Dyslexia Association, Dallas, TX.

Joshi, R. M., Binks, E., Hougen, M., Ocker-Dean, E., Graham, L., & Smith, D. (2009). Teachers' knowledge of basic linguistic skills: Where does it come from? In S. Rosenfield & V. Berninger (Eds.), *Handbook on implementing evidence based academic interventions* (pp. 851–877). Oxford University Press.

Justice, L. M. (2010). *Communication sciences and disorders: A contemporary perspective* (2nd ed.). Allyn & Bacon.

Justice, L. M., Bowles, R. P., Kaderavek, J. N., Ukrainetz, T. A., Eisenberg, S. L., &

Gillam, R. B. (2006). The Index of Narrative Microstructure: A clinical tool for analyzing school-age children's narrative performances. *American Journal of Speech-Language Pathology, 15*(2), 177–191.

Justice, L. M., & Ezell, H. K. (1999). Syntax and speech-language pathology graduate students: Performance and perceptions. *Contemporary Issues in Communication Sciences and Disorders, 26,* 119–127.

Justice, L. M., & Ezell, H. K. (2008). *The syntax handbook.* Pro-Ed.

Kaderavek, J. N. (2011). *Language disorders in children: Fundamental concepts of assessment and intervention.* Pearson Education.

Kamhi, A. G. (2014). Improving clinical practices for children with language and learning disorders. *Language, Speech, and Hearing Services in Schools, 45,* 92–103.

Kamhi, A. G., & Nelson, L. (1988). Early syntactic development: Simple clause types and grammatical morphology. *Topics in Language Disorders, 8*(2), 26–43.

Kamil, M. L., Borman, G. D., Dole, J., Kral, C. C., Salinger, T., & Torgesen, J. (2008). *Improving adolescent literacy: Effective classroom and intervention practices: A practice guide* (NCEE #2008-4027). National Center for Education Evaluation and Regional Assistance, Institute of Education Sciences, U.S. Department of Education. https://ies.ed.gov/ncee/wwc/PracticeGuide/8

Kates, C. A. (1980). *Pragmatics and semantics: An empiricist theory.* Cornell University Press.

Kaufman, A. S., & Kaufman, N. L. (2014). *Kaufman Test of Educational Achievement, Third Edition (KTEA-3).* Pearson.

Kent, R. D. (2004). *The MIT encyclopedia of communication disorders.* MIT Press.

Kibby, M. Y., Marks, W., Morgan, S., & Long, C. J. (2004). Specific impairment in developmental reading disabilities: A working memory approach. *Journal of Learning Disabilities, 37,* 349–363. doi:10.1177/00222194040370040601

Kidder, C. L., & Golub, L. S. (1974, April). *Computer application of a syntactic density measure.* Paper presented at the Annual Meeting of the American Educational Research Association, Chicago, IL. https://files.eric.ed.gov/fulltext/ED090304.pdf

Kieffer, M. J., & Lesaux, N. K. (2012). Effects of academic language instruction on relational and syntactic aspects of morphological awareness for sixth graders from linguistically diverse backgrounds. *Elementary School Journal, 112*(3), 519–545. https://proxy.ulib.csuohio.edu:2096/10.1086/663299

Killgallon, D. (1997). *Sentence composing for middle school: A worktest on sentence variety and maturity.* Heinemann.

Killgallon, D., & Killgallon, J. (2000). *Sentence composing for elementary school: A worktest to build better sentences.* Heinemann.

King, R. R., Jones, C., & Lasky, E. (1982). In retrospect: A fifteen-year follow-up report of speech-language-disordered children. *Language, Speech, and Hearing Services in Schools, 13,* 24–32.

Kiparsky, P. (1982). Lexical phonology and morphology. In I. Yang (Ed.), *Linguistics in the morning calm.* Hanshin.

Klee, T. (1992). Developmental and diagnostic characteristics of quantitative measures of children's language production. *Topics in Language Disorders, 12*(2), 28–41.

Klee, T., & Fitzgerald, M. D. (1985). The relation between grammatical development and mean length of utterance in morphemes. *Journal of Child Language, 12,* 251–269. http://journals.cambridge.org/action/displayAbstract?fromPage=online&aid=2186668

Knestrict, T., & Schoensteadt, L. (2005). Teaching social register and code switching in the classroom. *Journal of Children and Poverty, 11*(2), 177–185.

Koriat, A., Greenberg, S. N., & Kreiner, H. (2002). The extraction of structure during reading: Evidence from reading prosody. *Memory & Cognition, 30*(2), 270–280. doi:10.3758/BF03195288

Kozol, J. (1985). *Illiterate America.* Anchor Press/Doubleday.

Kuehner, A. V. (2016). *A positive approach to good grammar. NADE Digest.* https://files .eric.ed.gov/fulltext/EJ1178108.pdf

Kuhl, P. K. (2010, September 9). Brain mechanisms in early language acquisition. *Neuron, 67,* 713–727. http://life-slc.org /docs/Kuhl-brainmechanisms2010.pdf

Kumin, L., & Mason, G. (2011). Collaborative planning to teach strategies for the language of testing. *Perspectives on School-Based Issues, 12*(4), 139–152. https://doi .org/10.1044/sbi12.4.139

Kunda, Z. (1999). *Social cognition: Making sense of people.* MIT Press.

Kyle, K., & Crossley, S. A. (2015). Automatically assessing lexical sophistication: Indices, tools, findings, and application. *TESOL Quarterly, 49*(4), 757–786. doi:10 .1002/tesq.194

Kyle, K., Crossley, S. A., & Berger, C. (2018). The tool for the analysis of lexical sophistication (TAALES): Version 2.0. *Behavior Research Methods, 50*(3), 1030–1046. doi: 10.3758/s13428-017-0924-4

LaBrant, L. (1933). A study of certain language developments of children in Grades 4–12 inclusive. *Genetic Psychology Monographs, 14*(5), 387–491.

LaParo, K. M., Justice, L., Skibbe, L. E., & Pianata, R. C. (2004). Relations among maternal, child, and demographic factors and the persistence of preschool language impairment. *American Journal of Speech-Language Pathology, 13,* 291–303.

Larson, V. L., & McKinley, N. (2003). *Communication solutions for older students: Assessment and intervention strategies.* Thinking Publications.

Leadholm, B., & Miller, J. (1992). *Language Sample Analysis: The Wisconsin guide.* Bureau for Exceptional Children, Wisconsin Department of Public Instruction.

Leadholm, B. J., & Miller, J. F. (1994). *Language Sample Analysis: The Wisconsin Guide. Bulletin 92424.* Wisconsin State Dept. of Public Instruction.

Leclercq, A.-L., Quemart, P., Magis, D., & Maillart, C. (2014). The sentence repetition task: A powerful diagnostic tool for French children with specific language impairment. *Research in Developmental Disabilities, 35*(12), 3423–3430. https://doi.org /10.1016/j.ridd.2014.08.026

Lee, C., & Spratley, A. (2009). *Reading in the disciplines and the challenges of adolescent literacy.* Carnegie Corporation of New York.

Lee, L. L. (1970). *Developmental Sentence Scoring: A method of quantifying the development of syntax and morphology in children's language. Final report.* Office of Education (DHFW) Bureau of Research. https://files .eric.ed.gov/fulltext/ED043864.pdf

Lee, L. L. (1974). *Developmental Sentence Analysis: A grammatical assessment procedure for speech and language clinicians.* Northwestern University Press.

Lee, L. L., & Canter, S. M. (1971). Developmental Sentence Scoring: A clinical procedure for estimating syntactic development in children's spontaneous speech. *Journal of Speech and Hearing Disorders, 36*(3), 315–340. doi.org/10.1044/jshd.3603 .315

LENA. (2021). *Technology.* https://www.lena .org/technology/.

Lenneberg, E. H. (1967). *Biological foundations of language.* John Wiley & Sons.

Leonard, L. B. (1987). Is specific language impairment a useful construct? In S. Rosenberg (Ed.), *Advances in applied psycholinguistics* (pp. 1–39). Cambridge University Press.

Leonard, L. B. (1995). Functional categories in the grammars of children with specific language impairment. *Journal of Speech and Hearing Research, 38,* 1270–1282.

Leonard, L. B. (1998). *Children with specific language impairment.* MIT Press.

Leonard, L. B. (2000). *Children with specific language impairment.* MIT Press.

Leonard, L. B. (2020). A 200-year history of the study of childhood language disorders of unknown origin: Changes in terminology. *Perspectives of the ASHA Special Interest Groups, 5*(1), 6–11. https://doi .org/10.1044/2019_PERS-SIG1-2019-0007

Leonard, L. B., Eyer, J., Bedore, L., & Grela, B. (1997). Three accounts of the grammatical morpheme difficulties of English-speaking children with specific language impairment. *Journal of Speech, Language, and Hearing Research, 40*, 741–753.

Leonard, L. B., & Fey, M. E. (1991). Facilitating grammatical development: The contribution of pragmatics. In T. M. Gallagher (Ed.), *Pragmatics of language: Clinical practice issues* (pp. 333–355). Singular Publishing.

Levy, B. A., di Persio, R., & Hollingshead, A. (1992). Fluent rereading: Repetition, automaticity, and discrepancy. *Journal of Experimental Psychology: Learning, Memory, and Cognition, 18*(5), 957–971. doi:10.10 37/0278-7393.18.5.957

Levy, B. A., Nicholls, A., & Kohen, D. (1993). Repeated readings: Process benefits for good and poor readers. *Journal of Experimental Child Psychology, 56*(3), 303–327.

Liles, B. Z., & Watt, J. H. (1984). On the meaning of "language delay." *Folia Phoniatric, 36*, 40–48. doi:10.1159/000265719

Loban, W. (1963). *The language of elementary school children*. National Council of Teachers of English.

Loban, W. (1970). *Stages, velocity, and prediction of language development: Kindergarten through Grade Twelve. Final Report*. Bureau of Research Office of Education (Department of Health, Education, and Welfare). https://files.eric.ed.gov/fulltext/ED04 0198.pdf

Loban, W. (1976). *Language development: Kindergarten through Grade 12*. National Council of Teachers of English.

Loeb, D. F., & Daniels, D. B. (2009). Administration of a literacy-based curriculum by teacher and SLP teams. *Perspectives on School-Based Issues, 10*(3), 73–77.

Long, S. (1996). Why Johnny (or Joanne) can't parse. *American Journal of Speech-Language Pathology, 5*(2), 35–42.

Louwerse, M., & Cai, Z. (2004). Coh-Metrix: Analysis of text on cohesion and language. *Behavior Research Methods, Instruments, & Computers, 36*, 193–202.

Lu, X. (2008, May). *Automatic measurement of syntactic complexity using the Revised Developmental Level Scale*. Paper presented at the Twenty-First International Florida Artificial Intelligence Research Society Conference, Coconut Grove, FL.

Lundine, J. P. (2020). Assessing expository discourse abilities across elementary, middle, and high school. *Topics in Language Disorders, 40*(2), 149–165. doi:10.1097/TLD .0000000000000215

Lyons, J. (1968). *Introduction to theoretical linguistics*. Cambridge University Press.

MacLachlan, B. G., & Chapman, R. S. (1988). Communication breakdowns in normal and language learning-disabled children's conversation and narration. *Journal of Speech and Hearing Disorders, 53*, 2–7. https://doi.org/10.1044/jshd.5301.02

MacWhinney, B. (1987). The competition model. In B. MacWhinney (Ed.), *Mechanisms of language acquisition* (pp. 249–308). Erlbaum.

MacWhinney, B. (1996). The CHILDES System. *American Journal of Speech-Language Pathology, 5*(1), 5–14. https://doi.org/10 .1044/1058-0360.0501.05

MacWhinney, B. (2000). *The CHILDES project: Tools for analyzing talk* (3rd ed.). Erlbaum.

MacWhinney, B. (2021a). *Tools for analyzing talk Part 1: The CHAT transcription format*. https://doi.org/10.21415/3mhn-0z89

MacWhinney, B. (2021b). *Tools for analyzing talk Part 2: The CLAN program*. https:// doi.org/10.21415/T5G10

MacWhinney, B. (n.d.). *The TalkBank system*. Retrieved March 24, 2021, from https:// talkbank.org.

MacWhinney, B., & Bates, E. (1989). *Cross-linguistic study of sentence processing*. Cambridge University Press.

Marinellie, S. A. (2004). Complex syntax used by school-age children with specific language impairment (SLI) in child-adult conversation. *Journal of Communication Disorders, 37*(6), 517–533. https://doi.org /10.1016/j.jcomdis.2004.03.005

Marzola, E. S. (2018). Strategies to improve comprehension in the multisensory classroom. In J. Birsh & S. Carreker (Eds.), *Multisensory teaching of basic language skills* (4th ed., pp. 600–645). Brookes.

Mason, L. H., Davison, D. M., Hammer, C. S., Miller, C. A., & Glutting, J. J. (2012). Knowledge, writing, and language outcomes for a reading comprehension and writing intervention. *Springer Science+Business Media E.V., 26*, 1133–1158. doi:10.1007/s1 1145-012-9409-0

Masterson, J., & Kamhi, A. (1991). The effects of sampling conditions on sentence production in normal, reading-disabled, and language learning disabled children. *Journal of Speech and Hearing Research, 34*(3), 549–558. https://doi.org/10.1044/jshr.34 03.549

Maxwell-Reid, C., & Kartika-Ningsih, H. (2020). Nominal expansion in L2 adolescent writing: Functions and realizations of clausal embedding in argumentative texts. *Journal of Second Language Writing.* https://doi.org/10.1016/j.jslw.2020.100751

McCluskey, K. M. (1984). Developmental Sentence Scoring: A comparative study conducted in Portland, Oregon. *Dissertations and Theses. Paper 3383.* https://doi .org/10.15760/etd.5250

McGee, L. (1992). Focus on research: Exploring the literature-based reading revolution. *Language Arts, 69*(7), 529–537. http:// www.jstor.org/stable/41482033

McGinty, A., & Justice, L. (2006). Classroom-based versus pullout interventions: A review of the experimental evidence. *EBP Briefs, 1*(1), 3–25.

McGregor, K. K. (2020). How we fail children with developmental language disorder. *Language, Speech, and Hearing Services in Schools, 51*, 981–992. https://pubs.asha .org/doi/pdf/10.1044/2020_LSHSS-20 -00003

McGregor, K. K., Goffman, L., Owen Van Horne, A., Hogan, T. P., & Finestack, L. H. (2020). Developmental language disorder: Applications for advocacy, research and clinical service. *Perspectives of the ASHA Special Interest Groups, 5*(1), 38–46. https:// doi.org/10.1044/2019_PERSP-19-00083

McKenna, M., Castillo, J., Dedrick, R. F., Cheng, K., & Goldstein, H. (2021). Speech-language pathologist involvement in Multi-Tiered System of Supports questionnaire: Advances in interprofessional practice. *Language, Speech, and Hearing Services in Schools, 52*, 597–611. https:// doi.org/10.1044/2020_LSHSS-20-00084

McKeown, M. G., Beck, I. L., & Worthy, M. J. (1993). Grappling with text ideas: Questioning the author. *The Reading Teacher, 46*, 560–566.

McTear, M., & Conti-Ramsden, G. (1992). *Pragmatic disability in children.* Singular Publishing Group.

Meakins, F. (2007). Computerized Language Analysis (CLAN) from The CHILDES Project. *Language Documentation and Conservation, 1*(1), 107–112. https://www.re searchgate.net/publication/29737229 _Review_of_Computerized_Language _Analysis_CLAN

Mentis, M. (1994). Topic management in discourse: Assessment and intervention. *Topics in Language Disorders, 14*, 29–54.

Menyuk, P. (1969). *Sentences children use.* MIT Press.

Michaels, S. (1981). Sharing time: Children's narrative styles and differential access to literacy. *Language and Society, 10*(3), 423–442.

Michaels, S. (1986). Narrative presentations: An oral preparation for literacy with first graders. In J. Cook-Gumperz (Ed.), *The social construction of literacy* (pp. 94–116). Cambridge University Press.

Michaels, S. (1991). The dismantling of narrative. In A. McCabe & C. Peterson (Eds.), *Developing narrative structures* (pp. 303–351). Erlbaum.

Michelon, P. (2008, February 26). *Brain plasticity: How learning changes your brain.* http://www.sharpbrains.com/blog/2008 /02/26/brain-plasticity-how-learning -changes-your-brain/

Miles, S., Chapman, R., & Sindberg, H. (2006). Sampling context affects MLU in the language of adolescents with Down syndrome. *Journal of Speech and Hearing Research, 49*, 325–337.

Miller, C. A., Kail, R., Leonard, L. B., & Tomblin, J. B. (2001). Speed of processing in children with specific language impairment. *Journal of Speech, Language, and Hearing Research, 44*, 416–433.

Miller, D. G. (1993). *Complex verb formation.* John Benjamins.

Miller, G. A. (1956). The magical number seven, plus or minus two: Some limits on our capacity for processing information. *Psychological Review, 63*(2), 81–97. doi:10.1037/h0043158

Miller, J. F. (1981). *Assessing language production in children: Experimental procedures.* University Park Press.

Miller, J. F., Andriacchi, K., & Nockerts, A. (Eds.). (2011). *Assessing language production using SALT software: A clinician's guide to language sample analysis.* SALT Software LLC.

Miller, J. F., Andriacchi, K., & Nockerts, A. (2016). Using language sample analysis to assess spoken language productions in adolescents. *Language, Speech, and Hearing Services in Schools, 47*, 99–112.

Miller, J. F., Andriacchi, K., & Nockerts, A. (2019). *Assessing language production using SALT Software: A clinician's guide to language sample analysis* (3rd ed.). SALT Software, LLC.

Miller, J. F., & Chapman, R. (2003). *SALT: Systematic Analysis of Language Transcripts* [Computer software]. University of Wisconsin–Madison, Waisman Center, Language Analysis Laboratory.

Miller, J. F., Iglesias, A., Andriacchi, K., & Nockerts, A. (2016). *Systematic Analysis of Language Transcripts 16 (SALT 16).* SALT Software, LLC.

Miller, J. F., & Paul, R. (1995). *The clinical assessment of language comprehension.* Brookes.

Mills, D. L., Plunkett, K., Prat, C., & Schafer, G. (2005). Watching the infant brain learn words: Effects of vocabulary size and experience. *Cognitive Development, 20*(1), 19–31.

Minnery, A., & Smith, A. T. (2018). Close sentence reading to foster decoding and comprehension. *Reading Teacher, 71*(6), 743–748. https://proxy.ulib.csuohio.edu:2096/10.1002/trtr.1680

Moats, L. C. (2000). *Speech to print: Language essentials for teachers.* Brookes.

Moats, L. C., & Foorman, B. F. (2003). Measuring teachers' content knowledge of language and reading. *Annals of Dyslexia, 53*, 23–45. doi:10.1007/s11881-003-0003-7

Moffett, J. (1968). *Teaching the universe of discourse.* Houghton Mifflin.

Montgomery, J. W., & Evans, J. L. (2009). Complex sentence comprehension and working memory in children with specific language impairment. *Journal of Speech, Language, and Hearing Research, 52*, 269–288. doi:1092-4388/09/5202-0269

Montgomery, J. W., Gillam, R. B., & Evans, J. L. (2016). Syntactic versus memory accounts of the sentence comprehension deficits of specific language impairment: Looking back, looking ahead. *Journal of Speech, Language, and Hearing Research, 59*, 1491–1504. doi:10.1044/2016_JSLHR-L-15-0325

Montgomery, J. W., Gillam, R. B., & Evans, J. L. (2021). A new memory perspective on the sentence comprehension deficits of school-age children with developmental language disorder: Implications for theory, assessment, and intervention. *Language, Speech, and Hearing Services in Schools, 52*(2), 449–466. https://doi.org/10.1044/2021_LSHSS-20-00128

morphosyntax. (2021). *The American Heritage® dictionary of the English language* (5th ed.). http://www.thefreedictionary.com/morphosyntax

Mosenthal, P. (1983). Defining classroom writing competence: A paradigmatic perspective. *Review of Educational Research, 53*(2), 217–251.

Motsch, H.-J., & Riehemann, S. (2008). Effects of "context optimization" on the acquisition of grammatical case in children with specific language impairment: An experimental evaluation in the classroom. *International Journal of Language & Communication Disorders, 43*(6), 683–698.

Murray, D. (2004). *Writing to learn* (8th ed.). Wadsworth.

Murza, K. A., & Ehren, B. J. (2020). Considering the language disorder label debate from a school speech-language pathology lens. *Perspectives of the ASHA Special Interest Groups, 5*(1), 47–54. https://doi.org/10.1044/2019_PERSP-19-00077

Myers, M., & Gray, J. (1983). *Theory and practice in the teaching of composition: Processing, distancing, modeling.* National Council of Teachers of English.

N., & Pam, M. S. (2013). *Realism.* https://psychologydictionary.org/realism/

Nagy, W. E. (1988). *Teaching vocabulary to improve reading comprehension.* International Reading Association.

Nagy, W., Berninger, V. W., & Abbott, R. D. (2006). Contributions of morphology beyond phonology to literacy outcomes of upper elementary and middle-school students. *Journal of Educational Psychology, 98*(1), 134–147.

Nagy, W. E., Diakidoy, I. N., & Anderson, R. C. (1991). *The development of knowledge of derivational suffixes* (Tech. Rep. No. 536). University of Illinois, Center for the Study of Reading.

Naremore, R., Densmore, A. E., & Harman, D. R. (1995). *Language intervention with school-aged children: Conversation, narrative, and text.* Singular Publishing Group.

Nash, K. (2021). *English Grammar 101.* https://www.englishgrammar101.com/module-10/clauses/lesson-3/restrictive-and-nonrestrictive-adjective-clauses#:~:text=A%20restrictive%20adjective%20clause%20is%20necessary%20to%20the,wearing%20the%20red%20uniforms%20are%20winning%20the%20game

A nation at risk: The imperative for educational reform: A report to the nation and the secretary of education United States Department of Education by The National Commission on Excellence in Education. (1983). https://edreform.com/wp-content/uploads/2013/02/A_Nation_At_Risk_1983.pdf

Nation, K. (2005). Children's reading comprehension difficulties. In M. J. Snowling & C. Hulme (Eds.), *The science of reading: A handbook* (pp. 249–266). Blackwell.

Nation, K., Clarke, P., Marshall, C., & Durand, M. (2004). Hidden language impairments in children: Parallels between poor reading comprehension and specific language impairment? *Journal of Speech, Language, and Hearing Research, 47,* 199–211.

National Association for the Education of Young Children (NAEYC). (2009). *Developmentally appropriate practice in early childhood programs serving children from birth through age 8.* http://www.naeyc.org/files/naeyc/file/positions/PSDAP.pdf

National Center for Education Statistics. (2020). *Children and youth with disabilities.* https://nces.ed.gov/programs/coe/indicator_cgg.asp

National Center for Education Statistics. (n.d.-a). *Performance levels.* https://nces.ed.gov/naal/perf_levels.asp

National Center for Education Statistics. (n.d.-b). *Three types of literacy.* https://nces.ed.gov/naal/literacytypes.asp

National Center for Education Statistics. (n.d.-c). *What is NAAL?* https://nces.ed.gov/naal/index.asp

National Center on Intensive Intervention at the American Institutes for Research. (n.d.). *Essential components of RTI—A closer look at Response to Intervention.* https://intensiveintervention.org/resource/essential-components-rti-closer-look-response-intervention

National Center on Response to Intervention. (2010). *What is Response to Intervention (RTI).* U.S. Department of Education, Office of Special Education Programs. https://files.eric.ed.gov/fulltext/ED526859.pdf

National Governors Association Center for Best Practices, Council of Chief State School Officers. (2010). *Common Core State Standards.* http://corestandards.org/

National Reading Panel. (2000). *Teaching children to read.* National Institute of Child Health and Human Development. https://www.nichd.nih.gov/sites/de

fault/files/publications/pubs/nrp/Doc uments/report.pdf

National Research Center on Learning Disabilities. (2017). *Understanding learning and attention issues.* https://www.ncld .org./news/state-of-learning-disabilities /understanding-learning-and-attention -issues

National Research Center on Learning Disabilities. (n.d.). *RMC research resources.* https://resources.rmcwebapp.com/spe cial_education/national-research-center -on-learning-disabilities/

National Research Council. (1999). Preventing reading difficulties. In M. S. Burns, P. Griffin, & C.E. Snow (Eds.), *Starting out right: A guide to promoting children's reading success* (pp. 127–146). National Academy Press.

Nelson, N. W. (1998). *Childhood language disorders in context: Infancy through adolescence* (2nd ed.). Allyn & Bacon.

Nelson, N. W. (2010). *Language and literacy disorders: Infancy through adolescence.* Allyn & Bacon.

Nelson, N. W. (2013). Syntax development: Implications for assessment and intervention. *Perspectives on Language and Literacy, 39*(3), 9–15. https://app.box.com/s/6rn 9i3zl6blle2qhasudaj84zb9gkvhs

Nelson, N. W., Bahr, C. M., & Van Meter, A. M. (2004). *The writing lab approach to language instruction and intervention.* Brookes.

Nelson, N. W., Plante, E., Helm-Estabrooks, N., & Hotz, G. (2016). *Test of Integrated Language and Literacy Skills (TILLS).* Brookes.

Nelson, N. W., & Van Meter, A. M. (2007). Measuring written language ability in narrative samples. *Reading & Writing Quarterly, 23,* 287–309.

Newcomer, P. L., & Barenbaum, E. M. (1991). The written composing ability of children with learning disabilities: A review of the literature from 1980 to 1990. *Journal of Learning Disabilities, 24*(10), 578–593.

Nini, A. (2019). The Multi-Dimensional Analysis Tagger. In T. Berber Sardinha & M. Veirano Pinto (Eds.), *Multidimensional analysis: Research methods and current issues* (pp. 67–94). Bloomsbury Academic.

Ninio, A. (2006). *Language and the learning curve: A new theory of syntactic development.* Oxford University Press.

Ninio, A., & Snow, C. E. (1996). *Pragmatic development.* Westview Press.

Ninio, A., Snow, C. E., Pan, B. A., & Rollins, P. R. (1994). Classifying communicative acts in children's interactions. *Journal of Communication Disorders, 27*(2), 157–187.

Nippold, M. A. (1993). Developmental markers in adolescent language: Syntax, semantics, and pragmatics. *Language, Speech, and Hearing Services in Schools, 24,* 21–28.

Nippold, M. A. (1998). *Later language development.* Pro-Ed.

Nippold, M. A. (2004). Research on later language development: International perspectives. In R. Berman (Ed.), *Language development across childhood and adolescence* (pp. 1–8). John Benjamins.

Nippold, M. A. (2007). *Later language development: School-age children, adolescents, and young adults* (3rd ed.). Pro-Ed.

Nippold, M. A. (2010). *Language sampling with adolescents.* Plural Publishing.

Nippold, M. A. (2021). *Language sampling with children and adolescents: Implications for intervention* (3rd ed.). Plural Publishing.

Nippold, M. A., Frantz-Kaspar, M., & Vigeland, L. (2017). Spoken language production in young adults: Examining syntactic complexity. *Journal of Speech, Language, and Hearing Research, 60,* 1339–1347.

Nippold, M. A., Hesketh, L. J., Duthie, J. K., & Mansfield, T. C. (2005). Conversational versus expository discourse: A study of syntactic development in children, adolescents, and adults. *Journal of Speech, Language, and Hearing Research, 48,* 1048–1064.

Nippold, M. A., Mansfield, T. C., & Billow, J. L. (2007). Peer conflict explanations in children, adolescents, and adults: Examining the development of complex syntax. *American Journal of Speech-Language Pathology, 16,* 179–188.

Nippold, M. A., Mansfield, T. C., Billow, J. L., & Tomblin, J. B. (2008). Expository discourse in adolescents with language impairments: Examining syntactic development. *American Journal of Speech-Language Pathology, 17,* 356–366.

Nippold, M. A., Mansfield, T. C., Billow, J. L., & Tomblin, J. B. (2009). Syntactic development in adolescents with a history of language impairments: A follow-up investigation. *American Journal of Speech-Language Pathology, 18,* 241–251.

Nippold, M. A., & Schwarz, I. E. (1996). Children with slow expressive language development: What is the forecast for school achievement? *American Journal of Speech-Language Pathology, 5*(2), 22–25.

Nippold, M. A., & Sun, L. (2008). Knowledge of morphologically complex words: A developmental study of older children and young adolescents. *Language, Speech, and Hearing Services in Schools, 39*(3), 365–373. https://doi.org/10.1044/0161-1461 (2008/034)

Nippold, M. A., & Sun, L. (2010). Expository writing in children and adolescents: A classroom assessment tool. *Perspectives on Language Learning and Education, 17*(3), 100–107.

Nippold, M. A., Vigeland, L., Frantz-Kaspar, M., & Ward-Lonergan, J. (2017). Language sampling with adolescents: Building a normative database with fables. *American Journal of Speech-Language Pathology, 26,* 908–920.

Nippold, M. A., Ward-Lonergan, J. M., & Fanning, J. L. (2005). Persuasive writing in children, adolescents, and adults: A study of syntactic, semantic, and pragmatic development. *Language, Speech, and Hearing Services in Schools, 36,* 125–138.

No Child Left Behind Act of 2001, P.L. 107-110, 20 U.S.C. § 6319 (2002). https://www2.ed.gov/policy/elsec/leg/esea02/107-110.pdf

Nordquist, R. (2018, July 19). *What is a catenative verb?* https://www.thoughtco.com/what-is-catenative-verb-1689832

Norris, J., & Hoffman, P. (1993). *Whole language intervention for school-age children.* Singular Publishing.

Northey, M., McCutchen, D., & Sanders, E. (2016). Contributions of morphological skill to children's essay writing. *Reading & Writing, 29*(1), 47–68.

O'Donnell, R. C., Griffin, W. J., & Norris, R. D. (1967). *Syntax of kindergarten and elementary school children: A transformational analysis* (Research Rep. No. 8). National Council of Teachers of English.

Oetting, J. B., & Horohov, J. E. (1997). Past-tense marking by children with and without specific language impairment. *Journal of Speech, Language, and Hearing Research, 40,* 62–74.

Oetting, J. B., & Newkirk, B. L. (2008). Subject relatives by children with and without SLI across different dialects of English. *Clinical Linguistics and Phonetics, 2*(22), 111–125. https://doi.org/10.1080/02699200701731414

Oetting, J. B., Newkirk, B. L., Hartfield, L. R., & Wynn, C. G. (2010). Index of Productive Syntax for children who speak African American English. *Language, Speech, and Hearing Services in Schools, 41,* 328–339.

Ogilvie, M. (1984). Why do children talk? In L. J. Raphael, C. B. Raphael, & M. R. Valdovinos (Eds.), *Language and cognition: Essays in honor of Arthur J. Bronstein* (pp. 241–248). Plenum Press.

Olsen, M. B. (1997). *A semantic and pragmatic model of lexical and grammatical aspect.* Garland.

O'Neal, M. R., McLean, J. E., & McCormick, G. E. (1983, November). *The use of the Syntactic Density Score as an evaluative criterion measure.* Paper presented at the Twelfth Annual Meeting of the Mid-South Educational Research Association, Nashville, TN. https://files.eric.ed.gov/fulltext/ED237558.pdf

Online-utility.org. (n.d.). *Text Analyzer*. https://www.online-utility.org/text/analyzer.jsp

Ormiston-Smith, T. (2013). *Grammar without tears*. Smashwords.

Ortlieb, E. (2014). *Theoretical models of learning and literacy development*. Emerald Group Publishing Limited.

Owen Van Horne, A., Ebbels, S., Redmond, S., & Finestack, L. H. (2018, March). *SLI, PLI, LLD, or DLD? A debate on terminology in child language research programs*. Paper presented at the Annual Convention of the American Speech-Language-Hearing Association, Boston, MA. www.finestackclil.com/presentations/

Owens, R. E., Jr. (2004). *Language disorders: A functional approach to assessment and intervention* (4th ed.). Pearson Education.

Owens, R. E., Jr. (2005). *Language development: An introduction* (6th ed.). Allyn & Bacon.

Owens, R. E., & Pavelko, S. (2020). *SUGAR: Sampling Utterances and Grammatical Analysis Revised*. https://www.sugarlanguage.org

Owens, R. E., Pavelko, S. L., & Bambinelli, D. (2018). Moving beyond mean length of utterance: Analyzing language samples to identify intervention targets. *Perspectives of the ASHA Special Interest Groups (SIG 1), 3*, 5–22.

Palincsar, A. S. (1986). Reciprocal teaching. In *Teaching reading as thinking*. North Central Regional Educational Laboratory.

Palincsar, A. S., & Brown, A. L. (1984). Reciprocal teaching of comprehension-fostering and comprehension-monitoring activities. *Cognition and Instruction, 1*, 117–175.

Palincsar, A. S., & Brown, A. L. (1985). Reciprocal teaching: Activities to promote read(ing) with your mind. In T. L. Harris & E. J. Cooper (Eds.), *Reading, thinking and concept development: Strategies for the classroom* (pp. 147–159). The College Board.

Pan, B. A., & Uccelli, P. (2009). Semantic development. In J. Berko Gleason & N. Bernstein Ratner (Eds.), *The development of language* (7th ed., pp. 105–138). Allyn & Bacon.

Paradis, J., Genesee, F., & Crago, M. B. (2011). *Dual language development and disorders: A handbook on bilingualism and second language learning* (2nd ed.). Brookes.

Parker, M. D., & Brorson, K. (2005). A comparative study between mean length of utterance in morphemes (MLUm) and mean length of utterance in words (MLUw). *First Language, 35*(3), 365–376. https://journals.sagepub.com/doi/abs/10.1177/0142723705059114

Partee, B. H. (1973). Some structural analogies between tenses and pronouns in English. *Journal of Philosophy, 70*(18), 601–609. http://www.jstor.org/stable/2025024. https://doi.org/10.2307/2025024

Paul, R. (1981). Analyzing complex sentence development. In J. F. Miller (Ed.), *Assessing language production in children: Experimental procedures* (pp. 36–40). University Park Press.

Paul, R. (2002). *Language disorders from infancy through adolescence: Assessment and intervention* (3rd ed.). Mosby.

Paul, R. (2007). *Language disorders from infancy through adolescence* (3rd ed.). Mosby.

Paul, R. (2020). Children's language disorders: What's in a name? *Perspectives of the ASHA Special Interest Groups, 5*(1), 30–37. from https://doi.org/10.1044/2019_PERS-SIG1-2019-0012

Pavelko, S. L., & Owens, R. E. (2017). Sampling Utterances and Grammatical Analysis Revised (SUGAR): New normative values for language sample analysis measures. *Language, Speech, and Hearing Services in Schools, 48*(3), 197–215. https://doi.org/10.1044/2017_LSHSS-17-0022

Pavelko, S., & Owens, R. (2018). Diagnostic accuracy of the Sampling Utterances and Grammatical Analysis Revised (SUGAR) measures for identifying children with language impairment. *Language, Speech, and Hearing Services in Schools, 50*(2), 1–13. https://doi.org/10.1044/2018_LSHSS-18-0050

Pavelko, S. L., Owens, R., Ireland, M., & Hahs-Vaughn, D. L. (2016). Use of language sample analysis by school based SLPs: Results of a nationwide survey. *Journal of Language, Speech, and Hearing Services in Schools, 47*(3), 216–258. https://doi.org/ 10.1044/2016_LSHSS-15-0044

Pearson, B. Z. (2009). Children with two languages. In E. Bavin (Ed.), *Handbook of child language* (pp. 379–398). Cambridge University Press.

Peña, E., Spaulding, T., & Plante, E. (2006). The composition of normative groups and diagnostic decision making: Shooting ourselves in the foot. *American Journal of Speech-Language Pathology, 15,* 247–254.

Pennington, B. P., & Bishop, D. V. M. (2009). Relations among speech, language, and reading disorders. *Annual Review of Psychology, 60,* 283–306. https://www.du.edu /ahss/psychology/dm1/media/docu ments/Relationsamongspeechlanguage andreadingdisorders.pdf

Pennington, B. P., McGrath, L. M., & Peterson, R. L. (2019). *Diagnosing learning disorder: From science to practices* (3rd ed.) Guilford.

Pennington, B. F., Willcutt, E., & Rhee, S. H (2005). Analyzing comorbidity. *Advances in Child Development and Behavior, 33,* 263–304. doi:10.1016/s0065-2407(05)80010-2

Peterson, D. B., & Stoddard, A. (2018) Psychometric requirements of oral and written language progress monitoring assessments. *Perspectives of the ASHA Special Interest Groups SIG 1, 3*(Pt. 4), 180–197.

Pezold, M. J., Imgrund, C. M., & Storkel, H. L. (2020). Using computer programs for language sample analysis. *Language, Speech, and Hearing Services in Schools, 51,* 103–114.

Piaget, J. (1952). *The origins of intelligence in children.* International University Press.

Piaget, J. (1954). *The construction of reality in the child.* Basic.

Pinker, S. (1984). *Language learnability and language development.* Harvard University Press.

Pinker, S. (1989). *Learnability and cognition: The acquisition of argument structure.* MIT Press.

Pinker, S. (2007). *The language instinct: How the mind creates language* (3rd ed.). Harper Perennial Modern Classics.

Porter, J., & Steffin, B. (2006). *Speech-language pathology goals and objectives written to the California Standards.* pluk.org/central directory/Common%20Core%20stan dards/SLPGoalsandObjectivesupdate -1.pdf

Power-deFur, L. (n.d.). *Common Core State Standards: Implications for the S.L.P.* http:// www.speechpathology.com/files/event /05600/05668/ccssslideshandout.pdf

Power-deFur, L., & Flynn, P. (2012). Unpacking the standards for intervention. *Perspectives on School-Based Issues, 13*(1), 11–16.

Proly, J. L., Rivers, J., & Schwartz, J. (2009). Text comprehension: Graphic organizers to the rescue. *Perspectives on School-Based Issues, 10*(3), 82–89.

Prutting, C. (1982). Pragmatics as social competence. *Journal of Speech and Hearing Disorders, 47*(2), 123–134.

Prutting, C., & Kirchner, D. M. (1987). A clinical appraisal of the pragmatic aspects of language. *Journal of Speech and Hearing Disorders, 52,* 105–119.

Purcell-Gates, V., Duke, N. K., & Martineau, J. A. (2007). Learning to read and write genre-specific text: Roles of authentic experience and explicit teaching. *Reading Research Quarterly, 42,* 8–45.

Purdue Online Writing Lab (OWL). (n.d.-a). *Active verb tenses.* https://owl.purdue.edu /owl/general_writing/grammar/verb _tenses/active_verb_tenses.html

Purdue Online Writing Lab (OWL). (n.d.-b). *Introduction to verb of tenses.* https://owl .purdue.edu/owl/general_writing/gram mar/verb_tenses/index.html

Quirk, R., & Greenbaum, S. (1973). *A concise grammar of contemporary English.* Harcourt Brace Jovanovich.

Rasinski, T. (2016). *Timothy Rasinski.* www .timrasinski.com

Reader's Theater Scripts and Plays for the Classroom. (2008). www.teachingheart.net/readerstheater.htm

Really Learn English. (2010–2021). *Cleft sentences*. Retrieved April 3, 2021, from https://www.really-learn-english.com/cleft-sentences.html.

Reaser, J., Adger, C. T., Wolfram, W., & Christian, D. (2017). *Dialects at school*. Routledge.

Reed., V. A., Griffith, F. A., & Rasmussen, A. F. (2009). Morphosyntactic structures in the spoken language of older children and adolescents. *Clinical Linguistics & Phonetics, 12*(3), 163–181. doi:10.3109/02699209808985220

Renaissance Learning. (2021). *ATOS for text*. www1.renaissance.com/Products/Accelerated-Reader/ATOS/ATOS-Analyzer-for-Text

Rescorla, L. (1989). The Language Development Survey: A screening tool for delayed language in toddlers. *Journal of Speech and Hearing Disorders, 54*, 587–599.

Rice, M. L. (2007). Children with specific language impairment: Bridging the genetic and developmental perspectives. In E. Hoff & M. Shatz (Eds.), *Blackwell handbook of language development* (pp. 411–431). Blackwell.

Rice, M. L. (2020). Clinical lessons from studies of children with specific language impairment. *Perspectives of the ASHA Special Interest Groups, 5*(1), 12–29. https://doi.org/10.1044/2019_PERSP-19-00011

Rice, M. L., Redmond, S. M., & Hoffman, L. (2006). Mean length of utterance in children with specific language impairment and in younger control children shows concurrent validity, stable and parallel growth trajectories. *Journal of Speech, Language, and Hearing Research, 49*, 793–808.

Rice, M. L., Smolik, F., Perpich, D., Thompson, T., Rytting, N., & Blossom, M. (2012). Mean length of utterance levels in 6-month intervals for children 3 to 9 years with and without language impairments. *Journal of Speech, Language, and Hearing Research, 53*, 333–349. https://doi.org/10.1044/1092-4388(2009/08-0183)

Rice, M. L., & Wexler, K. (1996). Toward tense as a clinical marker of specific language impairment in English-speaking children. *Journal of Speech and Hearing Research, 39*(6), 1239–1257.

Rice, M., Wexler, K., & Cleave, P. (1995). Specific language impairment as a period of extended optional infinitive. *Journal of Speech, Language, and Hearing Research, 38*, 850–863.

Rice, M. L., Wexler, K., & Hershberger, S. (1998). Tense over time: The longitudinal course of tense acquisition in children with specific language impairment. *Journal of Speech, Language, and Hearing Research, 41*, 1412–1431.

Ringler, N. M. (1981) The development of language and how adults talk to children. *Infant Mental Health, 2*, 71–83.

Ritter, M. J. (2009). The speech-language pathologist and reading: Opportunities to extend services for the children we serve. *Perspectives on School-Based Issues, 10*(2), 38–44.

Rivera-Gaxiola, M., Klarman, L., Garcia-Sierra, A., & Kuhl, P. K. (2005). Neural patterns to speech and vocabulary growth in American infants. *NeuroReport, 16*(5), 495–498.

Rose, D. (2021). *Reading to Learn: Accelerating learning and closing the gap*. Reading to Learn. https://nam02.safelinks.protection.outlook.com/?url=http%3A%2F%2Fwww.readingtolearn.com.au%2F&data=04%7C01%7Cm.pershey%40CSUOHIO.EDU%7Cf12adce7507f423f6ab108d92b3506fd%7Cd7f3e79a943d4aceaeab209030807508%7C0%7C0%7C637588329900602038%7CUnknown%7CTWFpbGZsb3d8eyJWIjoiMC4wLjAwMDAiLCJQIjoiV2luMzIiLCJBTiI6Ik1haWwiLCJXVCI6Mn0%3D%7C2000&sdata=7aBh6BstvbZnPp4Y%2FCi3bbF4xlLJyyNQU%2Bskw%2BraAcI%3D&reserved=0

Roseberry-McKibbin, C. (2007). *Language disorders in children: A multicultural and case perspective*. Pearson Education.

Roseberry-McKibbin, C. (2008). *Multicultural students with special language needs: Practical strategies for assessment and intervention* (3rd ed.). Academic Communication Associates.

Rosenblatt, L. (1978). *The reader, the text, the poem: The transactional theory of the literary work.* Southern Illinois University Press.

Roth, F. P., & Spekman, N. J. (1984). Assessing the pragmatic abilities of children: Part 1. Organizational framework and assessment parameters. *Journal of Speech and Hearing Disorders, 49,* 2–11.

Roth, F. P., & Troia, G. A. (2009). Applications of responsiveness to intervention and the speech-language pathologist in elementary school settings. *Seminars in Speech and Language, 30,* 75–89. doi:10.1055/s-0029-1215716

Roth, F. P., & Worthington, C. K. (2005). *Treatment resource manual for speech-language pathology* (3rd ed.). Thomson Delmar Learning.

Rowley, A. T. (2011, November). *Is grammar knowledge important for an SLP?* Poster presented at the Annual Convention of the American Speech-Language-Hearing Association, San Diego, CA.

RTI Action Network. (n.d.). *What is Response to Intervention?* http://www.rtinetwork.org

Rudebusch, J. (2012). From Common Core State Standards to standards-based IEPs: A brief tutorial. *Perspectives on School-Based Issues, 13*(1), 17–24.

Sachs, J. (2009). Communication development in infancy. In J. Berko Gleason & N. Bernstein Ratner (Eds.), *The development of language* (7th ed., pp. 37–57). Allyn & Bacon.

Saddler, B. (2012). *Teacher's guide to effective sentence writing.* Guilford Press.

Saddler, B., Behforooz, B., & Asaro, K. (2008). The effects of sentence-combining instruction on the writing of fourth-grade students with writing difficulties. *Journal of Special Education, 42*(2), 79–90.

Saddler, B., Ellis-Robinson, T., & Asaro-Saddler, K. (2018). Using sentence combining instruction to enhance the writing skills of children with learning disabilities. *Learning Disabilities: A Contemporary Journal, 16*(2), 191–202.

Saddler, B., & Graham, S. (2005). The effects of peer-assisted sentence-combining instruction on the writing performance of more and less skilled young writers. *Journal of Educational Psychology, 97*(1), 43–54.

Sáenz, L. M., & Fuchs, L. S. (2002). Examining the reading difficulty of secondary students with learning disabilities: Expository versus narrative text. *Remedial and Special Education, 23,* 31–41.

Saussure, F. D. (1983). *Course in general linguistics* (R. Harris, Trans., C. Bally & A. Sechehaye, Eds.). Open Court.

Scammacca, N., Roberts, G., Vaughn. S., Edmonds, M., Wexler, J., Reutebuch, C. K., & Torgesen, J. K. (2007). *Interventions for adolescent struggling readers: A meta-analysis with implications for practice.* RMC Research Corporation, Center on Instruction.

Scarborough, H. S. (1990). Index of Productive Syntax. *Applied Psycholinguistics, 11,* 1–22. doi:10.1017/S0142716400008262

Scarborough, H. S. (2001). Connecting early language and literacy to later reading (dis)abilities: Theory and practice. In S. Neuman & D. Dickinson (Eds.), *Handbook of research in early literacy* (pp. 97–110). Guilford Press.

Scarborough, H. S., & Dobrich, W. (1990). Development of children with early language delay. *Journal of Speech, Language, and Hearing Research, 33*(1), 70–83. https://doi.org/10.1044/jshr.3301.70

Scarborough, H., Wyckoff, J., & Davidson, R. A. (1986). Reconsideration of the relation between age and mean utterance length. *Journal of Speech and Hearing Research, 29*(3), 394–399. https://doi.org/10.1044/jshr.2903.394

Scarborough, H. S., Rescorla, L., Tager-Flusberg, H., Fowler, A. E., & Sudhalter, V. (1991). The relation of utterance length to grammatical complexity in normal and language disordered groups. *Applied Psycholinguistics, 12,* 23–45.

Scardamalia, M., & Bereiter, C. (1985). Research on written composition. In M. Wittrock (Ed.), *Handbook of research on teaching* (3rd ed., pp. 778–803). Macmillan.

Schleppegrell, M. J. (1992). Subordination and linguistic complexity. *Discourse Processes, 15*, 117–131.

Schleppegrell, M. J. (2013). Exploring language and meaning in complex texts. *Perspectives on Language and Literacy, 39*(3), 37–40. https://app.box.com/s/6rn9i3zl6blle2qhasudaj84zb9gkvhs

Schoenbrodt, L., Kumin, L., & Sloan, J. M. (1997). Learning disabilities existing concomitantly with communication disorder. *Journal of Learning Disabilities, 30*(2), 264–281.

Schraeder, T. (2012). Literacy, Common Core State Standards and the school-based speech/language pathologist: Making sense of it all. *Perspectives on School-Based Issues, 13*(1), 3–10.

Schuele, C. M. (2009a). *Complex syntax coding manual.* Unpublished coding manual, Vanderbilt University, Nashville, TN. https://download.lww.com/wolterskluwer_vitalstream_com/PermaLink/TLD/A/TLD_33_2_2013_03_16_BARAKOARNDT_1_SDC1.pdf

Schuele, C. M. (2009b). Language and literacy: What's a speech-language pathologist to do? *Perspectives on School-Based Issues, 10*(2), 33–37. https://doi.org/10.1044/sbi10.2.33

Schuele, C. M. (2010). The many things language sample analysis has taught me. *Perspectives on Language Learning and Education, 17*(1), 32–37. doi:10.1044/lle17.1.32

Schuele, C. M. (2017). The speech-language pathologist's role in reading and writing: In theory meets in reality. *Perspectives of the ASHA Special Interest Groups SIG 1, 2*(Pt. 3), 115–116. https://pubs.asha.org/doi/pdf/10.1044/persp2.SIG1.115

Schuele, C. M., & Larrivee, L. S. (2004). What's my job? Differential diagnosis of the speech-language pathologist's role in literacy learning. *Perspectives on Language Learning and Education, 11*(3), 4–8. https://pubs.asha.org/doi/10.1044/lle11.3.4

Schuele, C. M., & Nicholls, L. M. (2000). Relative clauses: Evidence of continued linguistic vulnerability in children with specific language impairment. *Clinical Linguistics and Phonetics, 14*(8), 563–585.

Schuele, C. M., & Tolbert, L. (2001). Omission of obligatory relative markers in children with specific language impairment. *Clinical Linguistics and Phonetics, 15*(4), 257–274. https://doi.org/10.1080/02699200010017805

Schwartz, P. A. (2007). Special education: A service, not a sentence. *Educational Leadership: Journal of the Association for Supervision and Curriculum Development, 64*(5), 39–42. https://eric.ed.gov/?id=EJ766334

Scott, B. (n.d.). *The Dale-Chall 3,000 word list for readability formulas.* https://readabilityformulas.com/articles/dale-chall-readability-word-list.php

Scott, C. (1988). Spoken and written syntax. In M. Nippold (Ed.), *Later language development: Ages 9 through 19* (pp. 49–95). Pro-Ed.

Scott, C. M. (1995a). Measures of syntax in school-age children and adolescents. *Language, Speech, and Hearing Services in Schools, 26*, 309–319.

Scott, C. M. (1995b). Syntax for school-age children: A discourse perspective. In M. E. Fey, J. Windsor, & S. F. Warren (Eds.), *Language intervention: Preschool through the elementary years* (pp. 107–143). Brookes.

Scott, C. M. (2004). Syntactic contributions to literacy learning. In C. A. Stone, E. R. Silliman, B. J. Ehren, & K. Apel (Eds.), *Handbook of language & literacy: Development and disorders.* Guilford Press.

Scott, C. M. (2009). A case for the sentence in reading comprehension. *Language, Speech, and Hearing Services in Schools, 40*, 184–191.

Scott, C. M. (2020). Language sample analysis: New and neglected clinical applications. *Topics in Language Disorders, 40*(2),

132–134. doi:10.1097/TLD.000000000000 0215

Scott, C. M., & Balthazar, C. (2013). Complex sentence knowledge in children with reading and writing difficulties. *Perspectives on Language and Literacy, 39*(3), 18–26. https://app.box.com/s/6rn9i3zl6blle2qh asudaj84zb9gkvhs

Scott, C. M., & Nelson, N. W. (2009). Sentence combining: Assessment and intervention applications. *Perspectives on Language Learning and Education, 16*, 14–20.

Scott, C. M., & Stokes, S. L. (1995). Measures of syntax in school-age children and adolescents. *Language, Speech, and Hearing Services in Schools, 26*, 309–319.

Scott, C. M., & Windsor, J. (2000). General language performance measures in spoken and written narrative and expository discourse of school-age children with language-learning disabilities. *Journal of Speech, Language, and Hearing Research, 43*, 324–339.

Searle, J. R. (1971). What is a speech act? In J. R. Searle (Ed.), *The philosophy of language*. Oxford University Press.

Searle, J. R. (1972, June 29). Chomsky's revolution in linguistics. *New York Review of Books*. http://www.nybooks.com/ar ticles/archives/1972/jun/29/a-special -supplement-chomskys-revolution-in -lingui/

Searle, J. R. (1975). Indirect speech acts. In P. Cole & J. Morgan (Eds.), *Speech acts (syntax and semantics, 3)* (pp. 187–210). Academic Press.

Secord, W. A. (2014, October). *What makes an outstanding school SLP?* Paper presented at the Ohio School Speech Pathology and Educational Audiology Coalition Conference, Columbus, OH.

Sedita, J. (2019). *The strands that are woven into skilled writing*. https://284ivp1abr 6435y6t219n54e-wpengine.netdna-ssl.com /wp-content/uploads/2020/02/The -Strands-That-Are-Woven-Into-Skilled -WritingV2.pdf

Sedita, J. (2020). *We need a "Writing Rope!"* https://keystoliteracy.com/blog/we -need-a-writing-rope/

Seiger-Gardner, L. (2009). Children with language impairment. In B. B. Shulman & N. C. Capone (Eds.), *Language development: Foundations, processes, and clinical applications* (pp. 271–296). Jones and Bartlett.

Selkirk, E. (1986). *Phonology and syntax: The relation between sound and structure*. MIT Press.

Semel, E., Wiig, E. H., & Secord, W. A. (1995). *Clinical Evaluation of Language Fundamentals, Third Edition (CELF-3)*. The Psychological Corporation.

Semel, E., Wiig, E. H., & Secord, W. A. (2003). *Clinical Evaluation of Language Fundamentals–Fourth Edition*. The Psychological Corporation.

"Semiotics." (2021). Merriam-Webster.com Dictionary. https://www.merriam-web ster.com/dictionary/semiotics

Shanahan, T. (2021). *Shanahan on literacy*. 35.162.70.160/search

Shannon, P. (1989). *Broken promises: Reading instruction in 20th century America*. Bergin & Garvey.

Shannon, P. (1990). *A struggle to continue: Progressive reading instruction in America*. Heinemann.

Shannon, P. (Ed.). (1992). *Becoming political: Readings and writings on the politics of literacy education*. Heinemann.

Shannon, P. (1995). *Text, lies and videotape: stories about life, literacy and learning*. Heinemann.

Shannon, P., & Goodman, K. (Eds.). (1994). *Basal readers: A second look*. Richard C. Owens.

Shapiro, L. P. (1997). Tutorial: An introduction to syntax. *Journal of Speech, Language, and Hearing Research, 40*(2), 254–272.

Shaughnessy, M. P. (1977). *Errors and expectations: A guide for the teacher of basic writing*. Oxford University Press.

Shaywitz, S. (2003). *Overcoming dyslexia*. Vintage Books.

SIL International. (2020). *Mood and modality.* https://glossary.sil.org/term/mood-and-modality

Silliman, E., & Berninger, V. (2011). Cross-disciplinary dialogue about the nature of oral and written language problems in the context of developmental, academic, and phenotypic profile. *Topics in Language Disorders, 31*(1), 6–23.

Silliman, E., & Scott, C. M. (2009). Research-based oral language intervention routes to the academic language of literacy: Finding the right road. In S. Rosenfield & V. W. Berninger (Eds.), *Implementing evidence-based academic interventions in school settings* (pp. 1–39). Oxford University Press. doi:10.1093/med:psych/9780195325355.003.0004

Silva, J., Rivera-Gaxiola, M., & Kuhl, P. K. (2005). An event-related brain potential study of sentence comprehension in preschoolers: Semantic and morphosyntactic processing. *Cognitive Brain Research, 23,* 247–285.

Skarakis-Doyle, E., & Mentis, M. (1991). A discourse approach to language disorders: Investigating complex sentence production. In T. M. Gallagher (Ed.), *Pragmatics of language* (pp. 283–306). Springer. https://doi.org/10.1007/978-1-4899-7156-2_10

Skinner, B. F. (1957). *Verbal behavior.* Appleton-Century-Crofts.

Skinner, B. F. (1986). The evolution of verbal behavior. *Journal of the Experimental Analysis of Behavior, 45,* 112–122.

Slobin, D. I. (1966). Grammatical transformations and sentence comprehension in childhood and adulthood. *Journal of Verbal Learning and Verbal Behavior, 5,* 219–227.

Smith, C. (1997). *The parameter of aspect.* Kluwer.

Smith, C. (2003). *Modes of discourse: The local structure of texts.* Cambridge University Press.

Smith, F. (1977). The uses of language. *Language Arts, 54*(6), 638–644.

Smith, F. (1994). *Writing and the writer* (2nd ed.). Erlbaum.

Smith, T. T., Lee, E., & McDade, H. L. (2001). An investigation of T-units in African American English-speaking and Standard American English-speaking fourth-grade children. *Communication Disorders Quarterly, 22*(3), 148–157.

Snow, C. E. (1991). The theoretical basis for relationships between language and literacy development. *Journal of Research in Childhood Education, 6,* 5–15. https://doi.org//10.1080/02568549109594817

Snow, C. E., Scarborough, H. S., & Burns, M. S. (1999). What speech-language pathologists need to know about early reading. *Topics in Language Disorders, 20,* 48–58.

Snowling, M., Bishop, D. V. M., & Stothard, S. E. (2000). Is preschool language impairment a risk factor for dyslexia in adolescence? *Journal of Child Psychology and Psychiatry, 41,* 587–600.

Soifer, L. H. (2018). Oral language development and its relationship to literacy. In J. Birsh & S. Carreker (Eds.), *Multisensory teaching of basic language skills* (4th ed., pp. 82–139). Brookes.

Southwood, F., & Russell, A. F. (2004). Comparison of conversation, freeplay, and story generation as methods of language sample elicitation. *Journal of Speech, Language, and Hearing Research, 47*(2), 366–376. https://doi.org/10.1044/1092-4388(2004/030)

Spache, G. (1953). A new readability formula for primary-grade reading materials. *The Elementary School Journal, 53*(7), 410–413. doi:10.1086/458513

Spanoudis, G. C., Papadopoulos, T. C., & Spyrou, S. (2018). Specific language impairment and reading disability: Categorical distinction or continuum? *Journal of Learning Disabilities, 52*(1), 1–2. doi.org/10.1177/0022219418775111

Spaulding, T. J. (2012). Comparison of severity ratings on norm-referenced tests for children with specific language impairment. *Journal of Communication Disorders, 45,* 59–68.

Spaulding, T. J., Plante, E., & Farinella, K. A. (2006). Eligibility criteria for language impairment: Is the low end of normal always appropriate? *Language, Speech, and Hearing Services in Schools, 37*(1), 61–72.

Spencer, T. D., & Petersen, D. B. (2018). Bridging oral and written language: An oral narrative language intervention study with writing outcomes. *Language, Speech, and Hearing Services in Schools, 49*, 569–581. https://doi.org/10.1044/2018_LSHSS-17-0030

Stauffer, R. K. (1970). *The language experience approach to the teaching of reading*. Harper & Row.

Stewart, S. R. (1987). Language: Creating a literate environment for reading and writing development. *Communication Disorders Quarterly, 11*(1), 91–106.

Stothard, S. E., Snowling, M. J., Bishop, D. V. M., Chipchase, B. B., & Kaplan, C. A. (1998). Language-impaired preschoolers: A follow-up into adolescence. *Journal of Speech, Language, and Hearing Research, 41*, 407–418.

Strawson, P. F. (1971). Intention and convention in speech acts. In J. R. Searle, (Ed.), *The philosophy of language* (pp. 23–38). Oxford University Press.

Sun, L., & Wallach, G. P. (2014). Language disorders are learning disabilities: Challenges on the divergent and diverse paths to language learning disabilities. *Topics in Language Disorders, 34*(1), 25–38.

Systematic Analysis of Language Transcripts (SALT). (2019a). *C-unit segmentation rules*. https://www.saltsoftware.com/media/wysiwyg/tranaids/CunitSummary.pdf

Systematic Analysis of Language Transcripts (SALT). (2019b). *Subordination index*. http://www.saltsoftware.com/media/wysiwyg/codeaids/SI_Scoring_Guide.pdf

Systematic Analysis of Language Transcripts (SALT). (2020a). *Guide to the SALT 20 Variables*. https://www.saltsoftware.com/media/wysiwyg/analaids/SMR20_Guide.pdf

Systematic Analysis of Language Transcripts (SALT). (2020b). *SALT 20*. https://www.saltsoftware.com/products/salt20

Systematic Analysis of Language Transcripts (SALT). (n.d.). *SALT 20 selection of sample reports*. https://www.saltsoftware.com/media/wysiwyg/ordering/samplereports20.pdf

Tallal, P., Curtiss, S., & Kaplan, R. (1989). *The San Diego Longitudinal Study: Evaluating the outcomes of preschool impairment in language development. Final report*. National Institute of Neurological and Communicative Diseases and Stroke.

Teich, E. (1999). *Systemic functional grammar in natural language generation*. Continuum International Publishing Group.

Templin, M. C. (1957). *Certain language skills in children*. University of Minnesota Press.

Thal, D. J., & Tobias, S. (1992). Communicative gestures in children with delayed onset of oral expressive vocabulary. *Journal of Speech, Language, and Hearing Research, 35*, 1281–1289.

Thordardottir, E. T., & Weismer, S. E. (2001). High-frequency verbs and verb diversity in the spontaneous speech of school-age children with specific language impairments. *International Journal of Language and Communication Disorders, 36*(2), 221–244.

Tomasello, M. (2003). Introduction: Some surprises for psychologists. In M. Tomasello (Ed.), *The new psychology of language: Cognitive and functional approaches to language structure* (pp. 1–14). Erlbaum.

Tomasello, M., & Bates, E. (2001). General introduction. In M. Tomasello & E. Bates (Eds.), *Language development: The essential readings* (pp. 1–11). Blackwell.

Tomasello, M., & Slobin, D. I. (Eds.). (2005). *Beyond nature-nurture: Essays in honor of Elizabeth Bates*. Erlbaum.

Tomlinson, C. (2017). *How to differentiate instruction in academically diverse classrooms* (3rd ed.). Association for Supervision and Curriculum Development (ASCD). www.ascd.org/ASCD/pdf/siteASCD/publications/books/HowtoDifferentiateInstructioninAcademicallyDiverseClassrooms-3rdEd.pdf

Torgesen, J. K. (2002). The prevention of reading difficulties. *Journal of School Psychology, 40*(1), 7–26.

Trabasso, T., Secco, T., & van den Broek, P. (1984). Causal cohesion and story coherence. In H. Mandl, N. L. Stein, & T. Trabasso (Eds.), *Learning and comprehension of text* (pp. 83–110). Erlbaum.

Truckenmiller, A. J., & Petscher, Y. (2019). The role of academic language in written composition in elementary and middle school. *Reading and Writing: An Interdisciplinary Journal, 33,* 45–66. https://doi.org/10.1007/s11145-019-09938-7

Tulving, E. (1972). Episodic and semantic memory. In E. Tulving & W. Donaldson (Eds.), *Organization in memory* (pp. 381–403). Academic Press.

Turkstra, L. S. (2000, December). *Assessment of pragmatic communication ability*. Paper presented at the Cleveland Clinic Foundation 5th Annual Symposium: Nonverbal Learning Abilities, Cleveland, OH.

Tyack, D., & Gottsleben, R. (1974). *Language sampling, analysis, and training: A handbook for teachers and clinicians*. Consulting Psychologists Press.

Tyack, D., & Gottsleben, R. (1986). Acquisition of complex sentences. *Language, Speech, and Hearing Services in Schools, 17*(3), 160–174. https://doi.org/10.1044/0161-1461.1703.160

U.S. Department of Education, National Center for Education Statistics. (n.d.). *National Assessment of Educational Progress (NAEP), selected years, 1992–2019 Reading Assessments, NAEP Data Explorer*. https://nces.ed.gov/programs/coe/indicator_cnb.asp

Using SALT to assess the Common Core Grades K–12. (n.d.) https://www.saltsoftware.com/media/wysiwyg/analaids/CCSS20_grid.pdf

Van Cleave, W. (2020). *From the ground up! Building foundational paragraph skills.* https://sw.dyslexiaida.org/wp-content/uploads/sites/39/2020/02/SWIDA-Paragraphs-1.pdf

Van Dongen, R. (1986). "I like the long name": Young children using literate language. *Insights into Open Education, 18*(8), 3–17.

Van Keulen, J. E., Weddington, G. T., & DeBose, C. E. (1998). *Speech, language, learning, and the African American child.* Allyn and Bacon.

Vinson, B. P. (2012). *Language disorders across the lifespan.* Delmar.

Volkers, N. (2018). Diverging views on language disorders. *The ASHA Leader, 23*(12), 44–53. https://doi.org/10.1044/leader.FTR1.23122018.44

WAC Clearinghouse. (n.d.). *What is writing to learn?* https://wac.colostate.edu/resources/wac/intro/wtl/

Wagner, L. (1998). *The semantics and acquisition of time in language.* University of Pennsylvania Institute for Research in Cognitive Science Technical Report No. IRCS-98-14. https://repository.upenn.edu/ircs_reports/59/?utm_source=repository.upenn.edu%2Fircs_reports%2F59&utm_medium=PDF&utm_campaign=PDFCoverPages

Wagner, R. K., Torgesen, J. K., Rashotte, C. A., & Pearson, N. A. (2010). *Test of Silent Reading Efficiency and Comprehension (TOSREC).* Pro-Ed.

Walden, P. R., Gordon-Pershey, M., & Paul, R. (2014). Communication sampling procedures. In R. Paul (Ed.), *Introduction to clinical methods in communication disorders* (3rd ed., pp. 117–174). Brookes.

Wallach, G. P., Charlton, S., & Christie, J. (2010). What do you mean by that? Constructive beginnings when working with adolescents with language learning disabilities. *Perspectives on Language Learning and Education, 17*(3), 77–84.

Ward-Lonergan, J. (2010). Supporting literacy development in adolescent through written language intervention. *Perspectives on Language Learning and Education, 17*(3), 85–92.

Ward-Lonergan, J. M., Liles, B. Z., & Anderson, A. M. (1999). Verbal retelling abilities in adolescents with and without language-learning disabilities for social studies lectures. *Journal of Learning Disabilities, 32*(3), 213–223.

Weaver, C. (1998). *Lessons to share on teaching grammar in context.* Boynton-Cook.

Wechsler, D. (2009). *Wechsler Individual Achievement Test–Third Edition (WIAT-III).* Pearson.

Weiler, B., & Schuele, C. M. (2014). Joining clauses with subordinate conjunctions: One type of complex syntax. *Perspectives on Language Learning and Education, 21*(4), 192–202. doi:10.1044/lle21.4.182

Werfel, K. L., & Douglas, M. (2017). Are we slipping them through the cracks? The insufficiency of norm-referenced assessments for identifying language weaknesses in children with hearing loss. *Perspectives of the ASHA Special Interest Groups, 2*(9), 43–53. https://doi.org/10.1044/persp2.SIG9.43

Werfel, K. L., Reynolds, G., Hudgins, S., Castaldo, M., & Lund, E. A. (2021). The production of complex syntax in spontaneous language by 4-year-old children with hearing loss. *American Journal of Speech-Language Pathology.* Advance online publication. doi.org/10.1044/2020_AJSLP-20-00178

Wertsch, J. V. (1985). *Vygotsky and the social formation of mind.* Harvard University Press.

Westby, C. E. (2000). A scale for assessing development of children's play. In K. Gitlin-Weiner, A. Sandgund, & C. Schaefer (Eds.), *Play diagnosis and assessment* (pp. 15–57). Wiley.

Westby, C. (2020). The role of syntax in older school-age students. *Word of Mouth, 31*(4), 4–8. https://doi.org/10.1177/1048395020902396a

Westerveld, M. (2011). Sampling and analysis of children's spontaneous language: From research to practice. *ACQuiring Knowledge in Speech, Language and Hearing, 13*(2). https://www.marleenwesterveld.com/wp-content/uploads/2017/05/Westerveld_ACQ-2011.pdf

Westerveld, M. F., & Vidler, K. (2016). Spoken language samples of Australian children in conversation, narration and exposition. *International Journal of Speech Pathology, 18*(3), 88–98. doi:10.3109/17549507.2016.1159332

WGBH-TV, Boston. (Producer). (1985). *Baby talk.* [PBS Nova television series]. https://archive.org/details/NOVABabyTalk

What is the predicate of a sentence? (n.d.). https://www.grammar-monster.com/glossary/predicate.htm#:~:text=The%20predicate%20is%20the%20part%20of%20a%20sentence,is%20shaded.%20(The%20subjects%20of%20the%20sentences%20aren't.)

White, S., & Dillow, S. (2005). *Key concepts and features of the 2003 National Assessment of Adult Literacy* (NCES 2006-471). U.S. Department of Education, National Center for Education Statistics.

Wiig, E. H., & Secord, W. A. (2014). *Clinical Evaluation of Language Fundamentals–Fifth Edition Metalinguistics (CELF-5 Metalinguistics).* NCS Pearson, Inc.

Wiig, E. H., & Semel, E. (1984). *Language assessment and intervention for the learning disabled* (2nd ed.). Merrill.

Wiig, E. H., Semel, E., & Secord, W. A. (2013). *Clinical Evaluation of Language Fundamentals–Fifth Edition (CELF-5).* Pearson.

Williams, J. (2019). *The stories we tell ourselves: Reading Recovery and the MSV myth.* https://readingrecovery.org/the-stories-we-tell-ourselves/

Williamson, G. (2009). *Type-token ratio (TTR).* https://www.sltinfo.com/wp-content/uploads/2014/01/type-token-ratio.pdf

Windsor, J., Scott, C., & Street, C. (2000). Verb and noun morphology in the spoken and written language of children with language learning disabilities. *Journal of Speech, Language, and Hearing Research, 43,* 1322–1336.

Winsler, A. (2003). Introduction to the special issue: Vygotskian perspectives in early childhood education. *Early Education and Development, 14*(3), 253–269.

Wolter, J. A., & Collins, G. (2017). Intervention for students who struggle with language and literacy. *Perspectives on Language and Literacy, 43*(2), 23–26.

Wood, K. D., Lapp, D., Flood, J., & Taylor, D. B. (2008). *Guiding readers through text: Strategy guides for new times* (2nd ed.). International Reading Association.

Woodcock, R., McGrew, K., & Mather, N. (2001). *Woodcock-Johnson III Tests of Achievement (WJ III ACH)*. Riverside.

World Health Organization. (2001). *International classification of functioning, disability, and health*. World Health Organization.

World Health Organization. (2014). *International classification of functioning, disability and health*. https://www.who.int/classifications/international-classification-of-functioning-disability-and-health

Index

Note: Page numbers in **bold** reference non-text material.